Springer Proceedings in Mathematics & Statistics

Volume 89

More information about this series at http://www.springer.com/series/10533

Springer Proceedings in Mathematics & Statistics

This book series features volumes composed of select contributions from workshops and conferences in all areas of current research in mathematics and statistics, including OR and optimization. In addition to an overall evaluation of the interest, scientific quality, and timeliness of each proposal at the hands of the publisher, individual contributions are all refereed to the high quality standards of leading journals in the field. Thus, this series provides the research community with well-edited, authoritative reports on developments in the most exciting areas of mathematical and statistical research today.

Roger E. Millsap • Daniel M. Bolt
L. Andries van der Ark • Wen-Chung Wang
Editors

Quantitative Psychology Research

The 78th Annual Meeting of the Psychometric Society

Springer

Editors
Roger E. Millsap
Department of Psychology
Arizona State University
Tempe, AZ, USA

Daniel M. Bolt
Department of Educational Psychology
University of Wisconsin
Madison, USA

L. Andries van der Ark
University of Amsterdam
Amsterdam, The Netherlands

Wen-Chung Wang
Department of Psychological Studies
The Hong Kong Institute
of Education, Hong Kong
Hong Kong SAR

ISSN 2194-1009 ISSN 2194-1017 (electronic)
ISBN 978-3-319-35377-7 ISBN 978-3-319-07503-7 (eBook)
DOI 10.1007/978-3-319-07503-7
Springer Cham Heidelberg New York Dordrecht London

Softcover reprint of the hardcover 1st edition 2015

Printed on acid-free paper

Springer is part of Springer Science+Business Media (www.springer.com)

Preface

This volume represents presentations given at the 78th annual meeting of the Psychometric Society, organized by Cito and held at the Musis Sacrum in Arnhem, the Netherlands, during July 22–26, 2013. The meeting attracted 334 participants from 28 countries, with 242 papers being presented, along with 49 poster presentations, five pre-conference workshops, three keynote presentations, six invited presentations, six state-of-the-art lecturers, and three invited symposia. We thank the local organizer Anton Béguin and his staff and students for hosting this very successful conference.

After the 77th meeting in Lincoln, Nebraska, the idea was presented to publish a proceedings volume from the conference so as to allow presenters to quickly make their ideas available to the wider research community, while still undergoing a thorough review process. Because the first volume was received successfully, it was suggested that we publish proceedings more regularly. Hence, this is the second volume, and a third volume following the 79th meeting in Madison, Wisconsin, is expected.

We asked authors to use their presentation at the meeting as the basis of their chapters, possibly extended with new ideas or additional information. The result is a selection of 29 state-of-the-art chapters addressing a diverse set of topics, including classical test theory, item response theory, factor analysis, measurement invariance, test equating and linking, mediation analysis, cognitive diagnostic models, marginal models, and multi-level models.

The joy of editing these proceedings was overshadowed by the tragic news that Roger E. Millsap had passed away suddenly on May 9, 2014. As editor of Psychometrika and former president, Roger played an important role in the Psychometric Society. He was also the initiator and principal editor of the proceedings. He passed away shortly after finalizing these proceedings. We will always remember him fondly as the driving force of this project, and we will miss the friendly, helpful, and competent advice of this well-seasoned editor. May you rest in peace Roger.

Amsterdam, The Netherlands — L. Andries van der Ark
Madison, WI, USA — Daniel M. Bolt
Hong Kong — Wen-Chung Wang

Contents

Chapter 1
What Do You Mean by a Difficult Item? On the Interpretation of the Difficulty Parameter in a Rasch Model

Ernesto San Martín and Paul De Boeck

Abstract Three versions of the Rasch model are considered: the fixed-effects model, the random-effects model with normal distribution, and the random-effects model with unspecified distribution. For each of the three, we discuss the meaning of the difficulty parameter starting each time from the corresponding likelihood and the resulting identified parameters. Because the likelihood and the identified parameters are different depending on the model, the identification of the parameter of interest is also different, with consequences for the meaning of the item difficulty. Finally, for all the three models, the item difficulties are monotonically related to the marginal probabilities of a correct response.

1.1 Introduction

In the Rasch model, the probability of success in an item is defined on the basis of a contribution from the part of the person (person ability) and a contribution from the part of the item (item difficulty), while the contribution from the part of the persons does not depend on the item and neither does the effect of the items depend on the person. The Rasch model is, therefore, a main-effect model. The basic formula is the following:

$$Y_{pi} \sim \text{Bern}\left[\Psi(\theta_p - \beta_i)\right], \tag{1.1}$$

E. San Martín (✉)
Faculty of Mathematics and Faculty of Education, Pontificia Universidad Católica de Chile, Vicuña Mackenna 4860, Santiago, Chile

Center for Operations Research and Econometrics CORE, 30 Voie du Roman Pays, Louvain-la-Neuve, Belgium
e-mail: esanmart@mat.puc.cl

P. De Boeck
Department of Psychology, The Ohio State University, 1835 Neil Avenue Columbus, Columbus, OH 43210, USA
e-mail: deboeck.2@osu.edu

R.E. Millsap et al. (eds.), *Quantitative Psychology Research*, Springer Proceedings in Mathematics & Statistics 89, DOI 10.1007/978-3-319-07503-7_1

where $\Psi(x) = \exp(x)/(1+\exp(x))$, θ_p is the effect of the person on the probability, also called ability, and β_i is the effect of the item on the probability, also called the difficulty.

Different choices can be made for how the effects of the persons are considered. Either the persons are modeled with fixed-effects (FE) or with random-effects (RE), and for these random-effects one can either specify the distribution, for example, the normal distribution (RE-N), or one can leave the distribution unspecified (RE-U). The three models have led to three different likelihood functions (or sampling probabilities) and, accordingly, to three different ways to estimate the corresponding parameters: joint maximum likelihood (JML) in the case of the FE model, parametric marginal maximum likelihood (MML) in the case of the RE-N model, and semi-parametric MML in the case of the RE-U model.

It is our purpose to infer the consequences these choices have for the meaning of the other parameter of the model, β_i, the item difficulty. We will make this inference from the likelihood for each of the three types of models. This approach is justified by the fact that the likelihood function is supposed to generate the responses patterns and, therefore, it provides the statistical meaning of the parameters indexing it; for details, see Bamber and Van Santen (2000), Cox and Hinkley (1974), Fisher (1922), and McCullagh (2002). Consequently, the inference proceeds in two steps:

1. One step for the *identified parameterization*, which is the parameterization as far as possible on the basis of the likelihood.
2. Another step for the further identification of the *parameter of interest*, which will require to establish an injective relationship (under constraints, if necessary) between the parameter of interest and the identified parameterization.

It will be shown that the β_i parameters have a different meaning in the three Rasch models. The identified parameterization differs and also the identification of the parameter of interest is different. Furthermore, we will also discuss a condition based on marginal probabilities under which the difficulty of an item i is larger than the difficulty of an item j; this empirical condition can also be related to the empirical difficulty of an item (that is, the proportion of persons correctly answering the item).

In order to differentiate between the three models, item difficulty parameters of the three models will be denoted with different symbols: β_i^{FE}, $\beta_i^{\mathrm{RE\text{-}N}}$, and $\beta_i^{\mathrm{RE\text{-}U}}$. It will be shown that the meaning of these three parameters depends on the choice that is made for how to treat the effects from the part of the persons and the assumptions one is making regarding these effects.

1.2 Fixed-Effects Specification

1.2.1 Assumptions

The specification of a Rasch model rests on the following two assumptions:

Assumption 1: $\{Y_{pi} : p = 1,\ldots,N; i = 1,\ldots,I\}$ are mutually independent.

Assumption 2: For each person p and each item i, $Y_{pi} \sim \text{Bern}(\pi_{pi})$, where $\pi_{pi} = \Psi(\theta_p - \beta_i^{\text{FE}})$ and $\Psi(x) = \exp(x)/(1+\exp(x))$.

1.2.2 Likelihood and Identified Parameters

These assumptions induce the following likelihood function:

$$P^{(\theta_{1:N},\beta_{1:I}^{\text{FE}})}(\mathbf{Y}_1 = \mathbf{y}_1 \ldots \mathbf{Y}_N = \mathbf{y}_\mathbf{N}) = \prod_{p=1}^{N}\prod_{i=1}^{I} \pi_{pi}^{y_{pi}} (1-\pi_{pi})^{1-y_{pi}}$$

$$= \prod_{p=1}^{N}\prod_{i=1}^{I} \frac{\exp[y_{pi}(\theta_p - \beta_i)]}{1+\exp(\theta_p - \beta_i)},$$

where $\mathbf{Y}_p = (Y_{p1},\ldots,Y_{pI})^\top \in \{0,1\}^I$, $\theta_{1:N} = (\theta_1,\ldots,\theta_N)$, and similarly for $\beta_{1:I}$.

The parameter of a Bernoulli distribution is identified. This fact, together with Assumption 1, implies that the identified parameters are $\{\pi_{pi} : p = 1,\ldots,P; i = 1,\ldots,I\}$.

1.2.3 Parameters of Interest

The problem now is to identify the parameter of interest $(\theta_{1:N},\beta_{1:I}^{\text{FE}})$, which means to write them as functions of the identified parameters. From Assumption 2, it follows that

$$\theta_p - \beta_i^{\text{FE}} = \ln\left[\frac{\pi_{pi}}{1-\pi_{pi}}\right], \quad p = 1,\ldots,N; i = 1,\ldots,I;$$

$$\beta_i - \beta_j = \ln\left[\frac{1-\pi_{pi}}{\pi_{pi}}\,\frac{\pi_{pj}}{1-\pi_{pj}}\right], \quad \text{for all person } p \text{ and } i \neq j.$$

These relationships show that $\{\theta_p - \beta_i^{\text{FE}} : p = 1,\ldots,N; i = 1,,\ldots,I\}$ as well as $\{\beta_i^{\text{FE}} - \beta_j^{\text{FE}} : i = 1,\ldots,I,\ j = i,\ldots,I\}$ are identified since they are written as functions of identified parameters. Therefore, the parameters of interest $(\theta_{1:N},\beta_{1:I}^{\text{FE}})$ are identified if one identification restriction is imposed. Two possibilities can be considered:

1. To restrict one person parameter, namely $\theta_1 = 0$. Under this restriction, the difficulty parameter becomes

$$\beta_i^{\text{FE}} = \ln\left(\frac{1-\pi_{1i}}{\pi_{1i}}\right),$$

that is, the logarithm of the ratio between the probability that person 1 incorrectly answers item i and the probability that person 1 correctly answers the item.

2. To restrict one item parameter, namely $\beta_1^{\text{FE}} = 0$. Under this restriction, the difficulty parameter becomes

$$\beta_i^{\text{FE}} = \ln\left(\frac{1-\pi_{pi}}{\pi_{pi}}\,\frac{\pi_{p1}}{1-\pi_{p1}}\right), \tag{1.2}$$

that is, the logarithm of the odd ratio between item 1 and item i for each person p.

The first restriction depends on a specific person who is present in one application of the test. Therefore, the second identification restriction is more convenient since we may apply the same test to various sets of persons; see Andersen (1980).

1.2.4 Relationship of Item Difficulty with Empirical Difficulty

Regarding the relationship between item difficulty and empirical difficulty, from (1.2) it follows that

$$\beta_i^{\text{FE}} > \beta_j^{\text{FE}} \iff P^{(\theta_p,\beta_{1:I}^{\text{FE}})}(Y_{pi}=1) < P^{(\theta_p,\beta_{1:I}^{\text{FE}})}(Y_{pj}=1) \quad \text{for all persons } p. \tag{1.3}$$

Thus, item i is more difficult than item j if the probability that the person correctly answers item i is less than the probability that a person correctly answers item j.

1.2.5 Comments

The previous considerations lead to the following comments:

1. The fixed-effects specification of the Rasch model is a rather easy model from the perspective of identification, easier than the other two specifications, and it is therefore often implicitly used to interpret the parameters of the Rasch model, even when one is interesting in is the random-effects specification; for more discussion, see San Martín and Rolin (2013).
2. On the other hand, for an estimation of the model, mostly the assumption of a random-effects model is made, because the maximum likelihood estimator of the difficulty parameters is inconsistent due to the presence of the incidental parameters. For details, see Andersen (1980), Ghosh (1995), and Lancaster (2000).

1.3 Random-Effects Specification

The random-effects assumption for the persons leads to consider the ability parameters as realizations of an iid process. Using the statistical jargon, the person's abilities are now considered as random-effects.

1.3.1 Assumptions

A random-effects specification rests on the following assumptions:

Assumption 1: $\{\mathbf{Y}_p : p = 1,\ldots,N\}$ are mutually independent conditionally on $\theta_{1:N}$.

Assumption 2: For each person p, the conditional distribution of $\mathbf{Y}_p$ given $\theta_{1:N}$ only depends on θ_p and it is parameterized by $\beta_{1:I}^{\text{RE-N}}$.

Assumption 3: For each person p, $\{Y_{pi} : i = 1,\ldots,I\}$ are mutually independent conditionally on θ_p. This is the so-called axiom of local independence.

Assumption 4: For each item i, $(Y_{pi} \mid \theta_p) \sim \text{Bern}\left[\Psi(\theta_p - \beta_i^{\text{RE-N}})\right]$.

Assumption 5: θ_p's are mutually independent and identically distributed, with a common distribution $\mathcal{N}(0,\sigma^2)$.

1.3.2 Likelihood and Identified Parameters

These assumptions imply that the response patterns $\mathbf{Y}_p$'s are mutually independent and identically distributed. To describe the likelihood function, it is enough to describe the probability of each of the 2^I response patterns, namely

$$
\begin{aligned}
q_{12\cdots I} &= P^{(\beta_{1:I}^{\text{RE-N}},\sigma)}(Y_{p1} = 1, Y_{p2} = 1, \ldots, Y_{p,I-1} = 1, Y_{pI} = 1),\\
q_{12\cdots \bar{I}} &= P^{(\beta_{1:I}^{\text{RE-N}},\sigma)}(Y_{p1} = 1, Y_{p2} = 1, \ldots, Y_{pI,} - 1 = 1, Y_{pI} = 0),\\
\vdots\ & \quad \vdots\\
q_{\bar{1}\bar{2}\cdots \bar{I}} &= P^{(\beta_{1:I}^{\text{RE-N}},\sigma)}(Y_{p1} = 0, Y_{p2} = 0, \ldots, Y_{pI,} - 1 = 0, Y_{pI} = 0),
\end{aligned}
\tag{1.4}
$$

and

$$
P^{(\beta_{1:I}^{\text{RE-N}},\sigma)}(\mathbf{Y}_p = \mathbf{y}) = \int_{-\infty}^{\infty} \prod_{i=1}^{I} \frac{\exp[y_i(\sigma\theta - \beta_i^{\text{RE-N}})]}{1 + \exp(\sigma\theta - \beta_i^{\text{RE-N}})}\, \phi(\theta)\, d\theta,
$$

with $\phi(\cdot)$ as the density of a standard normal distribution. Therefore, the likelihood function corresponds to a multinomial distribution Mult $(2^I, \mathbf{q})$, where $\mathbf{q} = (q_{12\cdots I}, q_{12\cdots I-1,\bar{I}}, \cdots, q_{\bar{1}\bar{2}\cdots\bar{I}})$. Consequently, the parameter $\mathbf{q}$ is the identified parameter.

1.3.3 Parameters of Interest

It is possible to prove that $\beta_{1:I}^{RE-N}$ and σ can be written in terms of the identified parameter $\mathbf{q}$ without restrictions on the item parameters. The proof rests on the following arguments:

1. Let

$$\alpha_i \doteq P^{(\beta_{1:I}^{\text{RE-N}},\sigma)}(Y_{pi}=1) = \int_{-\infty}^{\infty} \Psi(\sigma\theta - \beta_i^{\text{RE-N}})\phi(\theta)\,d\theta \doteq p(\sigma, \beta_i^{\text{RE-N}}).$$

   The parameter α_i is an identified parameter because it is a function of $\mathbf{q}$.

2. The function $p(\sigma, \beta_i^{\text{RE-N}})$ is a strictly decreasing continuous function of $\beta_i^{\text{RE-N}}$. Therefore it is invertible and consequently

$$\beta_i^{\text{RE-N}} = p^{-1}(\sigma, \alpha_i). \tag{1.5}$$

3. For $i \neq j$, let

$$\alpha_{ij} \doteq P^{(\beta_{1:I}^{\text{RE-N}},\sigma)}(Y_{pi}=1, Y_{pj}=1) = \int_{-\infty}^{\infty} \Psi(\sigma\theta - \beta_i^{\text{RE-N}})\,\Psi(\sigma\theta - \beta_j^{\text{RE-N}})\,\phi(\theta)d\theta.$$

   The parameter α_{ij} is also an identified parameter because it is a function of $\mathbf{q}$. Using (1.5), it follows that

$$\begin{aligned}\alpha_{ij} &= \int_{-\infty}^{\infty} \Psi(\sigma\theta - p^{-1}(\sigma,\alpha_i))\,\Psi(\sigma\theta - p^{-1}(\sigma,\alpha_j))\,\phi(\theta)\,d\theta.\\ &\doteq r(\sigma, \alpha_i,, \alpha_j).\end{aligned}$$

   It can be shown that $r(\sigma, \alpha_i, \alpha_j)$ is a strictly increasing continuous function of σ; for details, see San Martín and Rolin (2013). It follows that

$$\sigma = r^{-1}(\alpha_{ij}, \alpha_i, \alpha_j). \tag{1.6}$$

1.3.4 Relationship of Item Difficulty with Empirical Difficulty

Regarding the relationship between item difficulty and empirical difficulty, from (1.5) it follows that

$$\beta_i^{\text{RE-N}} > \beta_j^{\text{RE-N}} \iff P^{(\beta_{1:I}^{\text{RE-N}},\sigma)}(Y_{pi}=1) < P^{(\beta_{1:I}^{\text{RE-N}},\sigma)}(Y_{pj}=1) \quad \text{for all person } p. \tag{1.7}$$

Thus, item i is more difficult than item j if probability that a person correctly answers item i is less than the probability that the person correctly answers item j.

1.3.5 Comments

The previous considerations lead to the following comments:

1. For each person p, the responses are positively correlated, that is,

$$cov^{(\beta_{1:I}^{\text{RE-N}},\sigma)}(Y_{pi},Y_{pj}) > 0$$

   for $i \neq j$. This is a marginal correlation and it follows from both Assumption 3 and the strict monotonicity of $\Psi(\theta_p - \beta_i^{\text{RE-N}})$ as a function of θ_p for all $\beta_i^{\text{RE-N}}$.
2. According to equality (1.6), σ represents the dependency between items i and j induced by both the marginal probabilities α_i and α_j and the joint marginal probability α_{ij}. Furthermore, this dependency is the same for all pairs of items since equality (1.6) is valid for all pairs of items i and j.
3. The item difficulty $\beta_i^{\text{RE-N}}$ is not only a function of the marginal probability α_i of correctly answering the item i, but also of terms of the common dependency.
4. The previous identification analysis is valid in the case $\pi_{pi} = \Phi(\theta_p - \beta_i^{\text{RE-N}})$, where Φ is the distribution function of a standard normal distribution; see San Martín and Rolin (2013). In this case, it is possible to show that

$$\alpha_i = \Phi\left(-\frac{\beta_i^{\text{RE-N}}}{\sqrt{1+\sigma^2}}\right).$$

   Therefore, the difficulty parameter $\beta_i^{\text{RE-N}}$ can be written as

$$\beta_i^{\text{RE-N}} = -\sqrt{1+\sigma^2}\,\Phi^{-1}(\alpha_i). \tag{1.8}$$

   It follows that the difficulty parameter $\beta_i^{\text{RE-N}}$ is decreasing with σ. In other words, the larger the individual differences, the more extreme the difficulty parameters become.
5. There is not an explicit function as (1.8) for the logistic model, but approximately the same equation applies with σ^2 premultiplied by $16\sqrt{3}/(15\pi)$; see Molenberghs et al. (2010), Zeger et al. (1988).
6. The distribution of θ_p can be specified as a $\mathcal{N}(\mu,\sigma^2)$. In this case, the identified parameters are $(\widetilde{\beta}_{1:I}^{\text{RE-N}},\sigma)$, where $\widetilde{\beta}_i^{\text{RE-N}} \doteq \beta_i^{\text{RE-N}} - \mu$. In order to identify the difficulty parameters $\beta_{1:I}^{\text{RE-N}}$ and the scale parameter μ, it is enough to introduce a linear restriction on the item parameters $\beta_{1:I}^{\text{RE-N}}$.

1.4 Semiparametric Specification

As pointed out by Woods and Thissen (2006) and Woods (2006), there exist specific fields, such as personality and psychopathology, in which the normality assumption of θ_p is not realistic. For instance, psychopathology and personality latent variables are likely to be positively skewed, because most persons in the general population have low pathology, and fewer persons have severe pathology. However, the distribution G of θ_p is unobservable and, consequently, though a researcher may hypothesize about it, it is not known in advance of an analysis. Therefore, any a priori parametric restriction on the shape of the distribution G could be considered as a mis-specification.

1.4.1 *Assumptions*

These considerations lead to extend parametric Rasch models by considering the distribution G as a parameter of interest, and thus specifying semi-parametric Rasch models. These models rest on the following assumptions:
Assumptions 1–4 as in the random-effects specification.

Assumption 5: θ_p's are mutually independent and identically distributed, with a common unspecified distribution G.

1.4.2 *Likelihood and Identified Parameters*

As in the random-effects specification, these assumptions imply that the response patterns $\mathbf{Y}_p$'s are mutually independent and identically distributed, with a common multinomial distribution Mult$(2^I, \mathbf{q})$, with $\mathbf{q} = (q_{12\cdots I}, q_{12\cdots I-1,\bar{I}}, \cdots, q_{\bar{1}\bar{2}\cdots\bar{I}})$, where

$$\begin{aligned}
q_{12\cdots I} &= P^{(\beta_{1:I}^{\text{RE-U}},G)}(Y_{p1}=1, Y_{p2}=1, \ldots, Y_{p,I-1}=1, Y_{pI}=1),\\
q_{12\cdots \bar{I}} &= P^{(\beta_{1:I}^{\text{RE-U}},G)}(Y_{p1}=1, Y_{p2}=1, \ldots, Y_{pI,}-1=1, Y_{pI}=0),\\
&\vdots \quad \vdots\\
q_{\bar{1}\bar{2}\cdots \bar{I}} &= P^{(\beta_{1:I}^{\text{RE-U}},G)}(Y_{p1}=0, Y_{p2}=0, \ldots, Y_{pI,}-1=0, Y_{pI}=0),
\end{aligned}$$

and

$$P^{(\beta_{1:I}^{\text{RE-U}},G)}(\mathbf{Y}_p = \mathbf{y}) = \int \prod_{i=1}^{I} \frac{\exp[y_i(\theta-\beta_i^{\text{RE-U}})]}{1+\exp(\theta-\beta_i^{\text{RE-U}})}\, G(d\theta). \tag{1.9}$$

Therefore, the likelihood function is parametrized by $\mathbf{q}$, which corresponds to the identified parameter.

Following San Martín et al. (2011), Equation (1.9) can be rewritten as follows: for all $\mathscr{J} \subset \{1,\ldots,I\} \setminus \emptyset$,

$$P^{(\beta_{1:I}^{\text{RE-U}},G)}\left(\bigcap_{j\in\mathscr{J}}\{Y_{pj}=1\}\cap\bigcap_{j\in\mathscr{J}^c}\{Y_{pj}=0\}\right)=$$

$$=\exp\left(-\sum_{j\in\mathscr{J}}\beta_j^{\text{RE-U}}\right)\times\int_{-\infty}^{\infty}\frac{e^{|\mathscr{J}|\theta}}{\prod_{1\leq i\leq I}(1+e^{\theta-\beta_i^{\text{RE-U}}})}G(d\theta). \tag{1.10}$$

By taking (1.10) with $\mathscr{J}=\{1\}$ and after (1.10) with $\mathscr{J}=\{i\}$, we identify $(\beta_2^{\text{RE-U}}-\beta_1^{\text{RE-U}},\ldots,\beta_I^{\text{RE-U}}-\beta_1^{\text{RE-U}})$ because

$$\beta_j^{\text{RE-U}}-\beta_1^{\text{RE-U}}=\ln\left[\frac{P^{(\beta_{1:I}^{\text{RE-U}},G)}\left(\{Y_{p1}=1\}\cap\bigcap_{2\leq i\leq I}\{Y_{pi}=0\}\right)}{P^{(\beta_{1:I}^{\text{RE-U}},G)}\left(\{Y_{pj}=1\}\cap\bigcap_{i\neq j}\{Y_{pi}=0\}\right)}\right]. \tag{1.11}$$

Not only the item differences can be identified, but also some characteristics of the distribution G. As a matter of fact, working with the identified parameters $\beta_j^{\text{RE-U}}-\beta_1^{\text{RE-U}}$ leads to a shift of θ which we express with $u=\theta+\beta_1^{\text{RE-U}}$. Thus, for all $\mathscr{J}\subset\{1,\ldots,I\}$, (1.9) can be rewritten as

$$P^{(\beta_{1:I}^{\text{RE-U}},G)}\left(\bigcap_{i\in\mathscr{J}}\{Y_{pj}=1\}\cap\bigcap_{j\subset J^c}\{Y_{pj}=0\}\right)=$$

$$=e^{\left[-\sum_{j\in\mathscr{J}}(\beta_j^{\text{RE-U}}-\beta_1^{\text{RE-U}})\right]}\int_{-\infty}^{\infty}\frac{e^{|\mathscr{J}|u}}{\prod_{1\leq i\leq I}\left[1+e^{u-(\beta_i^{\text{RE-U}}-\beta_1^{\text{RE-U}})}\right]}G_{\beta_1^{\text{RE-U}}}(du),$$

where $G_{\beta_1^{\text{RE-U}}}((-\infty,x])\doteq G((-\infty,x+\beta_1^{\text{RE-U}}])$. Therefore, the functionals

$$m_{G_{\beta_1^{\text{RE-U}}}}(k)=\int_{-\infty}^{\infty}\frac{e^{ku}}{\prod_{1\leq i\leq I}\left[1+e^{u-(\beta_i^{\text{RE-U}}-\beta_1^{\text{RE-U}})}\right]}G_{\beta_1^{\text{RE-U}}}(du),$$

for $k=0,1,\ldots,I$, are identified. Note that $m_{G_{\beta_1^{\text{RE-U}}}}(0)=m_{G_{\beta_1^{\text{RE-U}}}}(|\emptyset|)$ corresponds to $P^{(\beta_{1:I}^{\text{RE-U}},G)}(Y_{p1}=0,\ldots,Y_{pI}=0)$. Summarizing, the following $I+1$ relationships follow: For all $\mathscr{J}\subset\{1,\ldots,I\}$ such that $|\mathscr{J}|=k$,

$$m_{G_{\beta_1^{\text{RE-U}}}}(k) =$$

$$= P^{(\beta_{1:I}^{\text{RE-U}},G)}\left(\bigcap_{j\in\mathscr{J}}\{Y_{pj}=1\}\cap\bigcap_{j\in J^c}\{Y_{pj}=0\}\right)\times e^{\left[\sum_{j\in\mathscr{J}}(\beta_j^{\text{RE-U}}-\beta_1^{\text{RE-U}})\right]} \quad (1.12)$$

for $k = 0, 1, \ldots, I$. These $I+1$ identified parameters will be used for an alternative way to identify the difficulties and to derive an interesting difficulty ratio.

1.4.3 Parameters of Interest

In order to identify the item parameters $\beta_{1:I}^{\text{RE-U}}$, the previous equalities suggest to introduce an identification restriction, namely $\beta_1^{\text{RE-U}} = 0$. Under this restriction, the difficulty parameters $\beta_i^{\text{RE-U}}$ are given by Eq. (1.11) with $\beta_1^{\text{RE-U}} = 0$. Moreover, using equalities (1.11) and (1.12) with $\beta_1^{\text{RE-U}} = 0$, the following relations follow:

$$\beta_j^{\text{RE-U}} = \ln\left[\frac{P^{(\beta_{1:I}^{\text{RE-U}},G)}(Y_{p1}=1, Y_{pj}=0)}{P^{(\beta_{1:I}^{\text{RE-U}},G)}(Y_{p1}=0, Y_{pj}=1)}\right] \quad \text{for all persons } p; \quad (1.13)$$

$$\frac{\beta_i^{\text{RE-U}}}{\beta_j^{\text{RE-U}}} = \ln\left[\frac{P^{(\beta_{1:I}^{\text{RE-U}},G)}(Y_{pi}=0, Y_{pj}=1)}{P^{(\beta_{1:I}^{\text{RE-U}},G)}(Y_{pi}=1, Y_{pj}=0)}\right] \quad \text{for all persons } p. \quad (1.14)$$

For a proof, see Appendix.

1.4.4 Relationship of Item Difficulty with Empirical Difficulty

Regarding the relationship between item difficulty and empirical difficulty, from (1.14) it is possible to prove that

$$\beta_i^{\text{RE-U}} > \beta_j^{\text{RE-U}} \iff P^{(\beta_{1:I}^{\text{RE-U}},G)}(Y_{pi}=1) < P^{(\beta_{1:I}^{\text{RE-U}},G)}(Y_{pj}=1) \quad \text{for all person } p. \quad (1.15)$$

Thus, item i is more difficult than item j if probability that a person correctly answers item i is less than the probability that the person correctly answers item j.

1.4.5 Comments

The previous considerations lead to the following comments:

1. Equalities (1.13) and (1.14) apply independent of the distribution G.
2. Equality (1.13) shows that the difficulty of an item j essentially corresponds to a ratio of probabilities involving two items: the item j itself and the item 1. This ratio can be interpreted as a *mirror property* between items 1 and j.
3. Equality (1.14) can also be interpreted as a *mirror property* between items i and j.

1.5 Discussion

In the random-effects specification of the Rasch model, it is not possible to make a distinction between a Rasch model with abilities distributed according to a $\mathscr{N}(0,\sigma^2)$ and a 2PL model with equal discriminations and abilities distributed according to a $\mathscr{N}(0,1)$. Both models are identified and, therefore, this is an example of equivalent models: the distribution generating the response patterns is not enough to distinguish between these two equivalent models. Let us remark that for the 2PL model with different discrimination parameters, the situation is different; for details and a first interpretation of the parameters of interest, see San Martín et al. (2013, Appendix B).

Relations (1.3), (1.7), and (1.15) suggest that the comparison between item difficulties can empirically be interpreted in terms of the proportion of persons answering correctly one or other item. This also suggests that the estimations of the difficulty parameters in the three models will be (almost) perfectly correlated. However, the *meaning* of these estimators is quite different. For the fixed-effects specification, *item difficulty* is interpreted in terms of odd ratio [see equality (1.2)]; for the random-effects specification, *item difficulty* is interpreted as a function of both the marginal probability of correctly answering the item and the dependency common to all pairs of items [see equalities (1.5) and (1.6)]; and for the semi-parametric specification, *item difficulty* is interpreted in terms of the mirror property (1.13).

Appendix

Proof of Equality (1.13)

Consider the reparameterization $\eta_i = \exp(\beta_i)$ and let

$$\mathscr{A}_{\mathscr{J}} = \bigcap_{j\in\mathscr{J}} \{Y_{pj}=1\} \cap \bigcap_{j\in\mathscr{J}^c\setminus\{1,i\}} \{Y_{pj}=0\}.$$

Let $\mathscr{J} \subset \{2,\ldots,I\}$ and $i \notin \mathscr{J}$. Using (1.12), it follows that

$$\begin{aligned} m_G(|\mathscr{J}|+1) &= P^{(\beta_{1:I}^{\text{RE-U}},G)}\left(\{Y_{pi}=1\}\cap\bigcap_{j\in\mathscr{J}}\{Y_{pj}=1\}\cap\bigcap_{j\in(\mathscr{J}\cup\{i\})^c}\{Y_{pj}=0\}\right)\times\prod_{j\in\mathscr{J}}\eta_j\times\eta_i \\ &= P^{(\beta_{1:I}^{\text{RE-U}},G)}\left(\{Y_{p1}=1\}\cap\bigcap_{j\in\mathscr{J}}\{Y_{pj}=1\}\cap\bigcap_{j\in\mathscr{J}^c\setminus\{1\}}\{Y_{pj}=0\}\right)\times\prod_{j\in\mathscr{J}}\eta_j. \end{aligned}$$

It follows that

$$\eta_i = \frac{P^{(\beta_{1:I}^{\text{RE-U}},G)}\left(\{Y_{p1}=1,Y_{pi}=0\}\cap\mathscr{A}_{\mathscr{J}}\}\right)}{P^{(\beta_{1:I}^{\text{RE-U}},G)}\left(\{Y_{p1}=0,Y_{pi}=1\}\cap\mathscr{A}_{\mathscr{J}}\}\right)}. \tag{1.16}$$

for all $\mathscr{J}\subset\{2,\ldots,I\}$ and $i\notin\mathscr{J}$. Therefore, using (1.16),

$$\begin{aligned} \frac{P^{(\beta_{1:I}^{\text{RE-U}},G)}(Y_{pi}=0,Y_{pj}=1)}{P^{(\beta_{1:I}^{\text{RE-U}},G)}(Y_{pi}=1,Y_{pj}=0)} &= \frac{\sum_{\{\mathscr{J}\subset\{2,\ldots,I\}:i\notin\mathscr{J}\}} P^{(\beta_{1:I}^{\text{RE-U}},G)}\left(\{Y_{p1}=1,Y_{pi}=0\}\cap\mathscr{A}_{\mathscr{J}}\right)}{\sum_{\{\mathscr{J}\subset\{2,\ldots,I\}:i\notin\mathscr{J}\}} P^{(\beta_{1:I}^{\text{RE-U}},G)}\left(\{Y_{p1}=0,Y_{pi}=1\}\cap\mathscr{A}_{\mathscr{J}}\right)} \\ &= \frac{\sum_{\{\mathscr{J}\subset\{2,\ldots,I\}:i\notin\mathscr{J}\}} \eta_i\, P^{(\beta_{1:I}^{\text{RE-U}},G)}\left(\{Y_{p1}=0,Y_{pi}=1\}\cap\mathscr{A}_{\mathscr{J}}\right)}{\sum_{\{\mathscr{J}\subset\{2,\ldots,I\}:i\notin\mathscr{J}\}} P^{(\beta_{1:I}^{\text{RE-U}},G)}\left(\{Y_{p1}=0,Y_{pi}=1\}\cap\mathscr{A}_{\mathscr{J}}\right)} \\ &= \eta_i. \end{aligned}$$

Proof of Equality (1.14)

Let $\mathscr{J}$ such that $|\mathscr{J}|=I-2$ and denote the label of two items excluded from $\mathscr{J}$ as i and i'. Using (1.12), it follows that

$$\begin{aligned} m_G(|\mathscr{J}\cup\{i\}|) = P^{(\beta_{1:I}^{\text{RE-U}},G)}&\left(\{Y_{pi}=1\}\cap\bigcap_{j\in\mathscr{J}}\{Y_{pj}=1\}\cap\{Y_{pi'}=0\}\cap\bigcap_{j\in\mathscr{J}^c\setminus\{i'\}}\{Y_{pj}=0\}\right)\times \\ &\times\prod_{j\in\mathscr{J}}\eta_j\times\eta_i, \end{aligned}$$

$$\begin{aligned} m_G(|\mathscr{J}\cup\{i'\}|) = P^{(\beta_{1:I}^{\text{RE-U}},G)}&\left(\{Y_{pi'}=1\}\cap\bigcap_{j\in\mathscr{J}}\{Y_{pj}=1\}\cap\{Y_{pi}=0\}\cap\bigcap_{j\in\mathscr{J}^c\setminus\{i\}}\{Y_{pj}=0\}\right)\times \\ &\times\prod_{j\in\mathscr{J}}\eta_j\times\eta_{i'}. \end{aligned}$$

Therefore,

$$\frac{\eta_i}{\eta_{i'}} = \frac{P^{(\beta_{1:I}^{\text{RE-U}},G)}\left(\{Y_{pi}=0,Y_{pi'}=1\}\cap\bigcap_{j\in\mathscr{J}}\{Y_{pj}=1\}\cap\bigcap_{j\in\mathscr{J}^c\setminus\{i\}}\{Y_{pj}=0\}\right)}{P^{(\beta_{1:I}^{\text{RE-U}},G)}\left(\{Y_{pi}=1,Y_{pi'}=0\}\cap\bigcap_{j\in\mathscr{J}}\{Y_{pj}=1\}\cap\bigcap_{j\in\mathscr{J}^c\setminus\{i'\}}\{Y_{pj}=0\}\right)}. \quad (1.17)$$

Let $\mathscr{J}\subset\{1,\ldots,I\}$ such that $|\mathscr{J}|=I-2$ and take $i,i'\notin\mathscr{J}$. Denote

$$\mathscr{A}_{\mathscr{J}} = \bigcap_{j\in\mathscr{J}}\{Y_{pi}=1\} \quad\cap \bigcap_{j\in\mathscr{J}^c\setminus\{i\}}\{Y_{pi}=0\},$$

$$\mathscr{B}_{\mathscr{J}} = \bigcap_{j\in\mathscr{J}}\{Y_{pi}=1\} \quad\cap \bigcap_{j\in\mathscr{J}^c\setminus\{i'\}}\{Y_{pi}=0\}.$$

Then, using (1.17),

$$\begin{aligned}
\frac{P^{(\beta_{1:I}^{\text{RE-U}},G)}(Y_{pi}=0,Y_{pi'}=1)}{P^{(\beta_{1:I}^{\text{RE-U}},G)}(Y_{pi=1},Y_{pi'}=0)} &= \frac{\sum_{\{\mathscr{J}\subset\{1,\ldots,I\}:|\mathscr{J}|=I-2,i,i'\notin\mathscr{J}\}} P^{(\beta_{1:I}^{\text{RE-U}},G)}(\{Y_{pi}=0,Y_{pi'}=1\}\cap\mathscr{A}_{\mathscr{J}})}{\sum_{\{\mathscr{J}\subset\{1,\ldots,I\}:|\mathscr{J}|=I-2,i,i'\notin\mathscr{J}\}} P^{(\beta_{1:I}^{\text{RE-U}},G)}(\{Y_{pi}=1,Y_{pi'}=0\}\cap\mathscr{B}_{\mathscr{J}})}\\
&= \frac{\eta_i}{\eta_{i'}}\frac{\sum_{\{\mathscr{J}\subset\{1,\ldots,I\}:|\mathscr{J}|=I-2,i,i'\notin\mathscr{J}\}} P^{(\beta_{1:I}^{\text{RE-U}},G)}(\{Y_{pi}=1,Y_{pi'}=0\}\cap\mathscr{B}_{\mathscr{J}})}{\sum_{\{\mathscr{J}\subset\{1,\ldots,I\}:|\mathscr{J}|=I-2,i,i'\notin\mathscr{J}\}} P^{(\beta_{1:I}^{\text{RE-U}},G)}(\{Y_{pi}=1,Y_{pi'}=0\}\cap\mathscr{B}_{\mathscr{J}})}\\
&= \frac{\eta_i}{\eta_{i'}}.
\end{aligned}$$

Proof of Relation (1.15)

Using the same notation introduced above and the ratio $\eta_i'/\eta_{i'}$, it follows that

$$\begin{aligned}
\frac{P^{(\beta_{1:I}^{\text{RE-U}},G)}(Y_{pi'}=1)}{P^{(\beta_{1:I}^{\text{RE-U}},G)}(Y_{pi}=1)} &= \frac{\sum_{\{\mathscr{J}:|\mathscr{J}|=I-2,i,i'\notin\mathscr{J}\}} P^{(\beta_{1:I}^{\text{RE-U}},G)}(\{Y_{pi'}=1,Y_{pi}=0\}\cap\mathscr{A}_{\mathscr{J}})}{\sum_{\{\mathscr{J}:|\mathscr{J}|=I-2,i,i'\notin\mathscr{J}\}} P^{(\beta_{1:I}^{\text{RE-U}},G)}(\{Y_{pi'}=0,Y_{pi}=1\}\cap\mathscr{B}_{\mathscr{J}})}\\
&= \frac{\eta_i}{\eta_{i'}}.
\end{aligned}$$

Acknowledgements This research was partially funded by the ANILLO Project SOC1107 *Statistics for Public Policy in Education* from the Chilean Government.

References

Andersen EB (1980) Discrete statistical models with social science applications. North Holland, Amsterdam
Bamber D, Van Santen JPH (2000) How to asses a model's testability and identifiability. J Math Psychol 44:20–40
Cox DR, Hinkley DV (1974) Theoretical statistics. Chapman and Hall, London
Fisher RA (1922) On the mathematical foundations of theoretical statistics. Philos Trans R Soc Lond A 222:309–368
Ghosh M (1995) Inconsistent maximum likelihood estimators for the Rasch model. Stat Probab Lett 23:165–170
Lancaster T (2000) The incidental parameter problem since 1948. J Econom 95:391–413
McCullagh P (2002) What is a statistical model? (with Discussion). Ann Stat 30:1225–1310
Molenberghs G, Verbeke G, Demetrio CGB, Vieira A (2010) A family of generalized linear models for repeated measures with normal and cojugate random effects. Stat Sci 25:325–347
San Martín E, Rolin J-M (2013) Identification of parametric Rasch-type models. J Stat Plan Inference 143:116–130
San Martín E, Jara A, Rolin J-M, Mouchart M (2011) On the Bayesian nonparametric generalization of IRT-types models. Psychometrika 76:385–409
San Martín E, Rolin J-M, Castro M (2013) Identification of the 1PL model with guessing parameter: parametric and semi-parametric results. Psychometrika 78:341–379
Woods CM (2006) Ramsay-curve item response theory (RC-IRT) to detect and correct for nonnormal latent variables. Psychol Methods 11:235–270
Woods CM, Thissen D (2006) Item response theory with estimation of the latent population distribution using spline-based densities. Psychometrika 71:281–301
Zeger SL, Liang K-Y, Albert PS (1988) Models for longitudinal data: a generalized estimating equation approach. Biometrics 44:1049–1060

Chapter 2
Thurstonian Item Response Theory and an Application to Attitude Items

Edward H. Ip

Abstract The assessment of attitudes has a long history dating back at least to the work of Thurstone. The Thurstonian approach had its "golden days," but today it is seldom used, partly because judges are needed to assess the location of an item, but also because of the emergence of contemporary tools such as the IRT. The current work is motivated by a study that assesses medical students' attitudes toward obese patients. During the item-development phase, the study team discovered that there were items on which the team members could not agree with regard to whether they represented positive or negative attitudes. Subsequently, a panel of $n = 201$ judges from the medical profession were recruited to rate the items, and the responses to the items were collected from a sample of $n = 103$ medical students. In the current work, a new methodology is proposed to extend the IRT for scoring student responses, and an affine transformation maps the judges' scale onto the IRT scale. The model also takes into account measurement errors in the judges' ratings. It is demonstrated that the linear logistic test model can be used to implement the proposed Thurstonian IRT approach.

Keywords Item response theory • Likert scaling • Linear logistic test model • Attitudes toward obese persons • Equal-appearing interval scaling

2.1 Introduction

Together with the Guttman scale, Thurstone and Likert scaling are perhaps the most prominently featured and researched scaling techniques in the history of psychological measurement, especially in the assessment of attitudes. Historically, Thurstone was one of the first quantitative psychologists to set his sights on the development of a theory for psychological scaling (Thurstone 1925, 1928). Thurstone's pioneer work on conception of attitude was based on the assessment of subjective attitudinal responses. The covert responses—or a sample of them—are

E.H. Ip (✉)
Department of Biostatistical Sciences, Wake Forest School of Medicine,
Medical Center Blvd., WC23, Winston-Salem, NC 27157, USA
e-mail: eip@wakehealth.edu

R.E. Millsap et al. (eds.), *Quantitative Psychology Research*, Springer Proceedings in Mathematics & Statistics 89, DOI 10.1007/978-3-319-07503-7_2

linguistically represented in the form of opinion statements, which can then be located on a single evaluative dimension (Ostram 1989). Based on the principle of comparative judgment, Thurstone developed several scaling methods, of which the best known is the equal-appearing interval scale (Thurstone and Chave 1929). Given a collection of items, each of which contains a statement concerning the psychological construct of interest, the technique consists of two steps.

First, a panel of judges is recruited to rate the items in terms of their favorability to the construct of interest. Thurstone suggested using integral values of 1–11 for the rating scale. The 11-point scale then becomes the psychological continuum on which the statements have been judged, and the distribution of judgments obtained is used to calculate a typical value, which can then be taken as the scale-value of the statement on the 11-point psychological continuum. The value could be the median or the mean of the judgment distribution, and descriptive statistics such as standard deviations and the interquartile range are then used to eliminate questions that have overly dispersed judgment scores. Ideally, the equal-appearing interval scale is established by a final collection of items with small dispersions so that the scale-value of the statements on the psychological continuum are relatively equally spaced. In the second step, the statements are presented to subjects with instructions to indicate those with which they are willing to agree and those with which they disagree. The attitude score for a subject is based on the mean or the median of the scale-values of the statements agreed with. In other words, if the responses are dichotomously coded as 1 for Agree and 0 for Disagree, then the attitude score is an average of a weighted combination of the response categories, of which the weights are the scale-score.

One of the most fascinating aspects of Thurstone's scaling procedure is that the scale is determined by expert judges on a unidimensional continuum and that the operating characteristic of a Thurstone item may reflect either an underlying dominant-response process or an ideal-point process (Coombs 1964; Roberts and Laughlin 1996). In the most common form of the dominance mechanism, respondents and items are represented by positions on a latent trait, and the responses are determined by a comparison process: if the respondent's trait value is greater than the item-trait value, then the response to the item is positive; otherwise, the response is negative. The item-characteristic curve (ICC) of the item response for a dominant-response process is monotone and can be well captured by existing item response theory (IRT; Lord 1980) models. An example of a monotone ICC for equal-appearing interval scaling is the Sickness-Impact Profile (SIP; Bergner et al. 1981). Judges rated the SIP items on the severity of the dysfunction described in an item on an equal-interval 11-point scale. The end points were labeled "minimally dysfunctional" and "severely dysfunctional" to provide meaningful referents. An item concerning how sickness impacts work is: "I act irritable and impatient with myself—for example, talk badly about myself, swear at myself, blame myself for things that happen." A monotone ICC for this item implies that a respondent with a higher SIP trait value (more dysfunctional) is more likely to endorse this item than someone with a lower SIP trait value (less dysfunctional). For an empirical comparison between IRT scaling and Thurstone scaling in education, see Williams et al. (1998).

The Thurstone scaling procedure could also be used to describe an ideal point-response process, a model commonly used in attitudinal measurement of political and social views. Like the dominant-response process, the ideal-point process postulates that the individual's response also depends on the relative position of the person's trait value and the position of the item on the scale. However, a respondent in an ideal-point process is more likely to endorse statements that have trait values close to the respondent's. Thus, the ICC from an ideal-point process is not monotonic with respect to the trait and typically has a single peak at the location of the item. These models are often referred to as unfolding models in the IRT literature. An example of an unfolding item is a well-known General Social Survey (GSS) item on legalized abortion. The respondent in the GSS is asked when legalized abortion is allowed on a collection of seven conditions such as: "The family has a very low income and cannot afford any more children" and "The woman wants it for any reason." For respondents who hold a more centralist view about legalized abortion, the likelihood of endorsing the former statement would be higher than it would be for those who hold a liberal view about abortion as well as those who are strong anti-abortion.

In this paper, we only focus on Thurstone's equal-appearing scaling methods for items that do not fold—or items that are supposed to follow a dominant-response process so that their ICCs are monotonic. We argue that the equal-appearing scaling method is a way to set scales according to experts' views of the construct of interest and that it could be operationalized through IRT models in which the location parameter of an item can be obtained by careful scaling of the judges' ratings. The extent to which the judges disagree on the location of an item can be incorporated into the IRT model by assuming that the rating scores from the sample of judges are normally distributed with a mean m and a standard deviation σ, both of which could be directly estimated from the judges' data. As such, the proposed model can be viewed as an IRT implementation for equal-appearing scaling, which is distinct from the Thurstonian item response model proposed in Brown and Maydeu-Olivares (2012). We further demonstrate that the uncertainty associated with the judges' ratings would lead to an attenuation of the slope of the ICC, which, in modern IRT language, means that the information contained in the item is less than 1 at the same scale location but has a steeper slope. Also, we show that through a convolution technique the proposed Thurstonian IRT model can be solved using the estimation procedure for the linear logistic test model (LLTM; Fischer 1973).

The remainder of this paper is organized as follows: first, we describe the Thurston IRT model, then we illustrate the proposed model using a data set collected from a study of attitudes. Finally, we conclude with a discussion.

2.2 Thurstonian IRT: Method

We begin with a simple Rasch model:

$$P(Y_{ij} = 1 \big| \theta_j) = \frac{\exp(\theta_j + b_i)}{1 + \exp(\theta_j + b_i)}, \tag{1}$$

where Y_{ij} is the binary response of individual j to item i, with 1 indicating a correct or positive response; θ_j is the latent trait for individual j; and b_i is the intercept parameter for item i or the individual. We further assume that the intercept parameter b_i is a function of item attributes $\underset{-}{w}_i$ and the judge's rating, which has a mean m_i and variance σ_i^2. Specifically, we write:

$$b_i = \eta_1^T \underset{-}{w}_i + \eta_2 (m_i + \varepsilon_i), \quad \varepsilon_i \sim N\left(0, \sigma_i^2\right), \tag{2}$$

where η denotes regression coefficients.

$$P\left(Y_{ij} = 1 \big| \theta_j, \varepsilon_i\right) = \frac{\exp\left[\theta_j + \eta_1^T \underset{-}{w}_i + \eta_2 (m_i + \varepsilon_i)\right]}{1 + \exp\left[\theta_j + \eta_1^T \underset{-}{w}_i + \eta_2 (m_i + \varepsilon_i)\right]}, \tag{3}$$

$$\theta_j \sim N(0,1), \quad \varepsilon_i \sim N\left(0, \sigma_i^2\right).$$

In other words, we have

$$P\left(Y_{ij} = 1 \big| \theta_j, \varepsilon_i\right) = \frac{\exp\left[\theta_j + b_i' + \eta_2 \varepsilon_i\right]}{1 + \exp\left[\theta_j + b_i' + \eta_2 \varepsilon_i\right]}, \tag{4}$$

where $b_i' = \eta_1^T \underset{-}{w}_i + \eta_2 m_i$.

By integrating out the error term $\eta_2 \varepsilon_i$ through a convolution technique (Zeger et al. 1988; Caffo et al. 2007; Ip 2010), we now have

$$P\left(Y_{ij} = 1 \big| \theta_j\right) = \frac{\exp\left[a_i^* \theta_j + b_i^*)\right]}{1 + \exp\left[a_i^* \theta_j + b_i^*)\right]}, \tag{5}$$

where $a_i^* = \lambda_{\text{logit}}(a_{i1} + \frac{\eta_2 \rho \sigma_i}{\sigma_1})$, $b_i^* = \lambda_{\text{logit}} b_i'$, $\lambda_{\text{logit}} = [k^2 \eta_2^2 (1 - \rho^2) \sigma_i^2 + 1]^{-1/2}$, and $k = 16\sqrt{3}/(15\pi) = 0.588$. The factor a_i^* represents an attenuation factor for the slope of θ, which is assumed to be 1.0 in a Rasch model, and ρ represents the correlation between ε and θ, which is set to zero.

Figure 2.1 shows the change in attenuation as a function of the standard deviation of the measurement error. Generally speaking, when the noise level (measurement error) increases, the attenuation factor becomes smaller and varies almost linearly from no attenuation (=1.0) to a value of 0.5. Notably, the graphs show that attenuation is approximately 0.8 when the noise level (SD = 1) reaches the level of the signal (SD = 1). We call the model specified by Eqs. (4) and (5) the Thurstonian LLTM model.

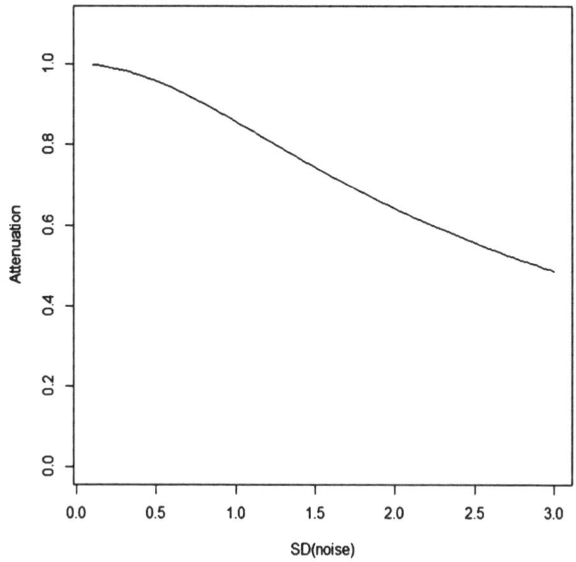

Fig. 2.1 Attenuation factor as a function of the standard deviation of the judges' ratings

2.3 Real Data Example

2.3.1 Data

The data were a subset of data collected from a recent study on the development of a curriculum for medical school students for counseling obese patients. The Nutrition, Exercise, and Weight Management (NEW) study collected attitude data using an instrument—the NEW Attitude Scale (Ip et al. 2013)—which comprises 31 items measuring attitudes across three domains: nutrition, exercise, and weight management. Examples of items include "I do feel a bit disgusted when treating a patient who is obese" (Item 23), and "The person and not the weight is the focus of weight-management counseling" (Item 25). In the item-development process, the study team had a consensus view for some items but divergent views for others. An example of a consensus item was "Overweight individuals tend to be lazy about exercise" (Item 13), which the team agreed represented an unfavorable attitude. An item that solicited divergent views was "Patients are likely to follow an agreed-upon plan to increase their exercise" (Item 10). Some tended to feel that an endorsement of the item suggested a favorable attitude because the physician sounded positive about the outcome, but others argued that the item should be viewed negatively because the physician might not appreciate the challenges that an obese person encountered when prescribed an exercise program. The study team decided to use the Thurstonian approach of soliciting judges' opinions about the positivity/negativity of the items. A total of 201 judges (approximately 50% clinically focused and the remaining research focused) rated the items. A sample of N = 103 medical students completed the instrument. Using the scores that were derived from traditional Thurstone scaling, the test–retest reliability of the instrument was 0.89 (N = 24). Pearson correlations between two other anti-obesity measures were the Anti-Fat Attitudes Questionnaire (AFA; Lewis et al. 1997) and the Beliefs About Obese Persons Scale (BAOP; Allison et al. 1991) were -0.47 and 0.23, respectively. This shows satisfactory convergent validity with existing measures of attitudes toward obese individuals. A full report about the validation of the instrument can be found in Ip et al. (2013).

To illustrate the range of concordance in judges' ratings across items, we used two items as examples. Figures 2.2 and 2.3 show, respectively, the distributions of ratings for Item 23 and Item 25. The former item has a relatively high level of consensus as being indicative of an unfavorable attitude, as demonstrated by the small standard deviation (SD = 0.8). In contrast, Item 25 exhibits high variance in the judges' ratings (SD = 2.2).

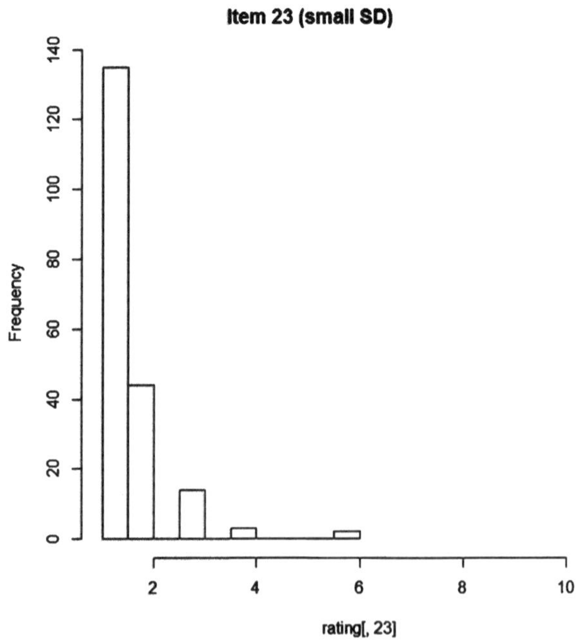

Fig. 2.2 Distribution of judges' ratings for Item 23

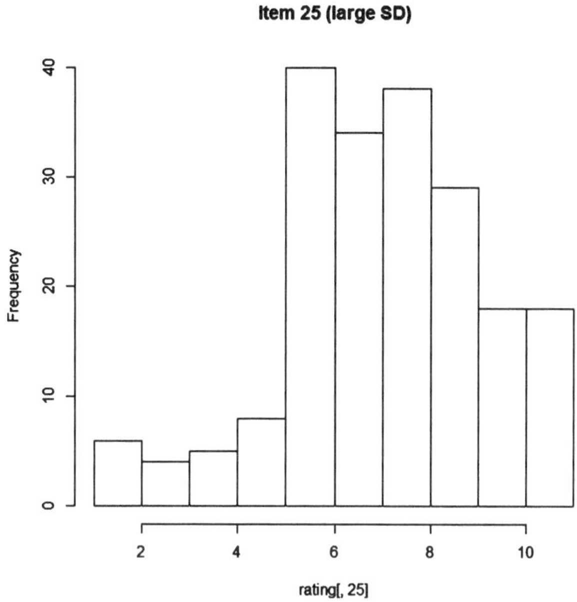

Fig. 2.3 Distribution of judges' ratings for Item 25

Besides the three domains (nutrition, exercise, and weight management) that defined the items, it was expected that some items also carried common characteristics. For example, there were items across the three domains that were related to counseling, and there were also items that were related to motivation of the patient in dieting, exercise, and weight loss. Therefore, we also conducted a factor analysis to extract factors that explained a large proportion of the variance of the items.

We used the Thurstonian LLTM described above to estimate the model parameters, and in addition to the judges' ratings the following two covariates were included: the factor score of the item from factor analysis and the domain to which each item belonged. A standard LLTM program eRm (Mair and Hatzinger 2007) was used to estimate the parameters.

2.3.2 *Results*

The factor analysis resulted in three factors that can be interpreted as (1) a factor for counseling, (2) a factor for motivation of the patient, and (3) a factor for perception about external factors. Table 2.1 summarizes the results from the Thurstonian LLTM and reports the estimates and standard errors (SE). Except for the exercise domain (as compared with weight management), all of the predictors that were entered into the LLTM are significant. Specifically, judges' ratings tend to be highly significant, and each point increase in a judge's rating results in a change of -1.4 in the intercept parameter. Figure 2.4 shows the ICCs for two exemplifying items: the solid line shows that of Item 23 ("Patients tend to be lazy about exercise") and Item 14 ("Patients understand the connection between nutrition and cancer"). The ICC for Item 23 suggests that medical students with higher values on the NEW Attitude Scale are less likely to endorse this item than they are to endorse Item 14. Finally, the effect of measurement error on the attenuation within the LLTM appeared to be small. The attenuation factor for the items in the sample ranged from 0.96 to 0.99.

Table 2.1 Estimates and standard error for Thurstonian LLTM for NEW attitude data

Predictor	Estimate for η	SE
Factor 1	−1.528*	0.115
Factor 2	−0.85*	0.125
Nutrition	0.449*	0.104
Exercise	−0.04	0.102
Judges' ratings	−0.143*	0.02

*$p < 0.01$
Factor 3 is the reference factor

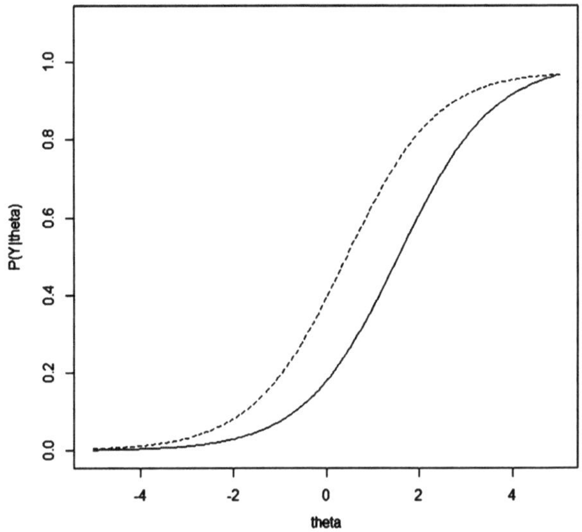

Fig. 2.4 Item-characteristic curves for Item 23 (solid) and Item 14 (dashed)

2.4 Discussion

There is often misunderstanding and confusion in the literature about the use of the Likert scaling method (Likert 1932; Edwards and Kenney 1946). Partly because of the convenience of constructing items and scoring respondents, it is not uncommon to see confusion about the fundamental scaling idea behind the Likert method. In particular, one misconception about the Likert scale that is relevant to this paper is that using the Likert scale does not require a specific scaling procedure—i.e., calibrating the continuum of metric by identifying the locations of the items on the continuum because no judges are required. This is not true. Likert actually suggested more than one way of assigning scale values, and indeed there are at least three groups of persons that are capable to locating items on a continuum: (1) a panel of expert judges, (2) the test developers, and (3) the respondents. Thurstone relied on the first category, and Likert developed methods in using the other two categories of persons. To understand his notion of scaling, we need to briefly describe Likert's assumptions underlying his procedure. Instead of following Thurstone's approach of creating positional statements, Likert used the level of agreement with specific statements to measure attitudes. The "level of agreement" could be codified as Strongly Agree to Strongly Disagree, or as judgmental statements about actions concerning a given situation. In his study about racial attitudes among college students, one of the questions was: "In a community in which the negroes [sic] outnumber the whites, under what circumstances is the lynching of a negro [sic] justifiable?" The possible responses were: "(a) Never. (b) In very exceptional cases where an especially brutal crime against a white person calls for swift punishment. (c) As punishment for any brutal crime against a white person. (d) As punishment for any gross offense [felony or extreme insolence] committed against a white person. (e) As punishment for any act of insolence against a white person." It is difficult not to notice the similarity of these response categories to statements in a Thurstone scaling procedure. The response categories, when expressed in this form could be more appropriately called sub-statements. Indeed, Likert scaling corresponds to a scheme under which the test developers provide the rating for the sub-statements (e.g., see Massof 2002).

The argument that Likert scaling corresponds to a predetermined scale is based on the observation that Likert's "theory" of scaling assumes that attitudes in a population follow a normal distribution and that all items can be positioned on the continuum by assigning them sigma units, or what we call z-scores now. Instead of using continuous values, Likert argued that one could partition the continuum into response categories, each of which signified a level of intensity on the continuum. A critical step that Likert took was to assign ranks (1–5) to these intensity categories.

From the perspective of the Thurstone scaling procedure, Likert scaling is equivalent to assigning transformed z-scores (1–5) as scale values to the sub-statements in an item. If each sub-statement in an attitude instrument is treated as a statement on Thurstone's equal-appearing interval, there would be five distributions at five equally separated positions. In other words, Likert's scaling corresponds to a form of equal-appearing interval scaling in which 5 points are used instead of 11. The test developer assigns the scale value to each item, and it is assumed that the assignment is without error. Alternatively, Likert alluded to the use of the participants as rating "judges"—i.e., the intensity of an item is determined by how frequent high scorers endorse the item (Babbie 2008, p. 188). Thus, although Likert scaling creates the ordinal format in order to avoid the need for external judges when developing scales, the scaling of the items still has to come from somewhere—for example, either from a test developer or from the participants. Some criticized the Thurstone scaling procedure because while it is valid for judges it may not be valid for participants. Yet, this is the whole point of Thurstone—the judges, presumably practitioners and researchers in the field, set the scale for a construct that they have all judged to be measurable using the proposed items. One can even argue that this scaling method would be a more relevant measure for a construct because a construct, after all, is an artifact conceived and created by practitioners and researchers in the field.

In this paper, we attempted to operationalize the Thurstone scaling through an IRT approach by following a two-step procedure: (1) establish a continuous, or at least an approximate, intensity scale by locating each item on this scale through a sample of experts; and (2) map the individual onto this scale by examining the individual's discrete response (e.g., binary agree/disagree to the statement of the item). The proposed Thurstonian LLTM represents a method for this operationalization. As a method grounded in IRT, the LLTM accordingly inherits many of the advantages of the IRT for scaling multiple dichotomous and polytomous responses.

There are some limitations to the current approach. The Rasch model appears to be too restrictive for capturing the diversity in the data, and the ICCs of the 31 items were not as diverse as we expected. A two-parameter logistic LLTM (e.g., Ip et al. 2009) may be more appropriate. Furthermore, in this paper only item attributes were considered, and person attributes such as experience with the professional school were not taken into account. Currently, further work that expands the Rasch model to its two-parameter logistic counterpart and a regression model incorporating person attributes is in progress.

References

Allison DB, Basile VC, Yuker HE (1991) The measurement of attitudes toward and beliefs about obese persons. Int J Eat Disord 10:599–607

Babbie ER (2008) The basics of social research, 4th edn. Thomson Learning, Inc., Belmont, CA

Bergner M, Bobbitt RA, Carter WB, Gilson BS (1981) The sickness impact profile: development and final revision of a health status measure. Med Care 14:787–805

Brown A, Maydeu-Olivares A (2012) Fitting a Thurstonian IRT model to forced-choice data using Mplus. Behav Res Methods 44:1135–1147

Caffo B, An M, Rohde C (2007) Flexible random intercept model for binary outcomes using mixture of normals. Comput Stat Data Anal 51:5220–5235

Coombs CH (1964) A theory of data. Wiley, New York

Edwards AL, Kenney KC (1946) A comparison of the Thurstone and Likert techniques of attitude scale construction. J Appl Psychol 30:72–83

Fischer GA (1973) The linear logistic test model as an instrument in educational research. Acta Psychol 37:359–374

Ip EH (2010) Empirically indistinguishable multidimensional IRT and locally dependent unidimensional item response models. Br J Math Stat Psychol 63:395–415

Ip EH, Smits D, De Boeck P (2009) Locally dependent linear logistic test model with person covariates. Appl Psychol Meas 33:555–569

Ip EH, Marshall S, Crandall SJ, Vitolins M, Davis S, Miller D, Kronner D, Vaden K, Spangler J (2013) Measuring medical student attitudes and beliefs regarding obese patients. Acad Med 88:282–289

Lewis RJ, Cash TF, Jacobi L, Bubb-Lewis C (1997) Prejudice toward fat people: the development and validation of the antifat attitudes test. Obes Res 5:297–307
Likert R (1932) A technique for the measurement of attitudes. Arch Psychol 22(140):1–55
Lord FM (1980) Applications of item response theory to practical testing problems. Erlbaum, Hillsdale, NJ
Mair P, Hatzinger R (2007) Extended Rasch modeling: the eRm package for application of IRT models in R. J Stat Softw 20(9). Last assessed December 11th, 2013. http://www.jstatsoft.org/v20/i09/paper
Massof RW (2002) The measurement of vision disability. Optom Vis Sci 79:516–552
Ostram TM (1989) Interdependence of attitude theory and measurement. In: Pratkanis AR, Breckler SJ, Greenwald AG (eds) Attitude structure and function. Lawrence Erlbaum Associates, Hillsdale, NJ, pp 11–36
Roberts JS, Laughlin JE (1996) A unidimensional item response model for unfolding responses from a graded disagree–agree response scale. Appl Psychol Meas 20:231–255
Thurstone LL (1925) A method of scaling psychological and educational tests. J Educ Psychol 16:433–451
Thurstone LL (1928) Attitudes can be measured. Am Coll Sociol 33:529–554
Thurstone LL, Chave EJ (1929) The measurement of social attitudes. University of Chicago Press, Chicago
Williams VSL, Pommerich M, Thissen D (1998) A comparison of developmental scales based on Thurstone methods and item response theory. J Educ Meas 35:93–107
Zeger SL, Liang KY, Albert P (1988) Models for longitudinal data: a generalized estimating equation approach. Biometrics 44:1049–1060

Chapter 3
Robustness of Mixture IRT Models to Violations of Latent Normality

Sedat Sen, Allan S. Cohen, and Seock-Ho Kim

Abstract Unidimensional item response theory (IRT) models assume that a single model applies to all people in the population. Mixture IRT models can be useful when subpopulations are suspected. The usual mixture IRT model is typically estimated assuming normally distributed latent ability. Research on normal finite mixture models suggests that latent classes potentially can be extracted even in the absence of population heterogeneity if the distribution of the data is nonnormal. Empirical evidence suggests, in fact, that test data may not always be normal. In this study, we examined the sensitivity of mixture IRT models to latent nonnormality. Single-class IRT data sets were generated using different ability distributions and then analyzed with mixture IRT models to determine the impact of these distributions on the extraction of latent classes. Preliminary results suggest that estimation of mixed Rasch models resulted in spurious latent class problems in the data when distributions were bimodal and uniform. Mixture 2PL and mixture 3PL IRT models were found to be more robust to nonnormal latent ability distributions. Two popular information criterion indices, Akaike's information criterion (AIC) and the Bayesian information criterion (BIC), were used to inform model selection. For most conditions, the performance of BIC index was better than the AIC for selection of the correct model.

3.1 Introduction

Item response theory (IRT) models have been designed to describe the relationship between observed item responses and latent variables (Embretson and Reise 2000). The successful applications of standard IRT models depend on several assumptions such as unidimensionality, invariance, local independence, and monotonicity (Reckase 2009). For instance, one set of item characteristic curves (ICCs) can be

S. Sen (✉)
University of Georgia, Athens, GA, USA
e-mail: sedatsen@harran.edu.tr

A.S. Cohen • S.-H. Kim
Harran University, Sanliurfa, Turkey for Sedat Sen and University of Georgia, GA, USA
e-mail: acohen@uga.edu; shkim@uga.edu

R.E. Millsap et al. (eds.), *Quantitative Psychology Research*, Springer Proceedings in Mathematics & Statistics 89, DOI 10.1007/978-3-319-07503-7_3

used to describe the relationship between item responses and the underlying latent trait by assuming that all individuals come from a single homogeneous population. However, other modeling approaches may be more appropriate when there are subgroups of respondents with different response-trait relationships. Several models have been developed to overcome violations of standard IRT models including multidimensional IRT models (Reckase 2009), multiple group IRT models (Bock and Zimowski 1997), and mixture IRT (MixIRT) models (Rost 1990; Mislevy and Verhelst 1990). MixIRT models, for example, may be more useful when the invariance assumption is violated (von Davier et al. 2007).

The popularity of MixIRT models has increased with the applications of these models to many psychometric issues such as detecting test speededness (Bolt et al. 2002; Wollack et al. 2003; Yamamoto and Everson 1997) and differential item functioning (Cohen and Bolt 2005; Cohen et al. 2005; Samuelsen 2005), identifying different personality styles (von Davier and Rost 1997), and identifying solution strategies (Mislevy and Verhelst 1990; Rost and von Davier 1993), as well as classifying response sets (Rost et al. 1997).

The MixIRT model is based on finite mixture models (Titterington et al. 1985). Finite mixture models are used in a number of latent variable models including latent class analysis (LCA; Clogg 1995), structural equation models (Arminger et al. 1999; Jedidi et al. 1997), growth mixture models (GMMs) (Li et al. 2001), and factor mixture analysis (FMA; Lubke and Muthén 2005). Typically, finite mixture models are used to explain the underlying heterogeneity in the data by allocating this heterogeneity to two or more latent classes. One problem with the application of these models is that the extracted classes may not always reflect the heterogeneity in the population (Bauer and Curran 2003). It may be possible to obtain some extraneous classes as an artifact of misspecification. For instance, Bauer and Curran (2003) demonstrated that nonnormality in the data can lead to identification of spurious latent classes even in the absence of population heterogeneity (McLachlan and Peel 2000; Bauer and Curran 2003). Similar situations have been observed in mixture Rasch models when model specific assumptions are violated (Alexeev et al. 2011).

In contrast to application of multiple group IRT models, the number of groups (or classes) may not be known a priori in exploratory applications of mixture models. In a typical exploratory approach to determine the number of latent classes, several models may be fit to the data. The model with the best fit is often selected based on some statistical criteria (e.g., information criterion indices). Since the extracted classes are latent (i.e., unobserved), one can never be sure about the true number of latent classes. Thus, identification of the correct number of latent classes has become a longstanding and unresolved issue in finite mixture models research. This issue has been studied for a number of latent variable models (Alexeev et al. 2011; Bauer 2007; Bauer and Curran 2003) or model selection statistics (Li et al. 2009; Nylund et al. 2007; Tofighi and Enders 2007; Wall et al. 2012).

Bauer and Curran (2003) examined the effect of nonnormality on the detection of the number of latent classes in GMMs. Data were generated for single-class data sets with normal and nonnormal distributions and then analyzed with one- and two-class solutions. Results indicated that a one class solution was a better fit for normal data and a two class solution (i.e., a spurious class) was a better fit for nonnormal data. Results further suggested that data with nonnormal distributions may cause over-extraction of latent classes even in a single homogeneous population.

Tofighi and Enders (2007) investigated the performances of nine different fit indices (information criteria and likelihood based statistics) within the context of GMMs. They showed that the sample-size adjusted BIC (SABIC; Sclove 1987) and the Lo–Mendell–Rubin (LMR; Lo et al. 2001) likelihood ratio test are promising in determining the number of classes. Similarly, Nylund et al. (2007) compared the performances of information criteria and hypothesis tests using the likelihood ratio test with three different mixture models: LCA, factor mixture models (FMMs), and GMMs. Results indicated that the bootstrap likelihood ratio test (BLRT) performed better than LMR or likelihood-ratio tests for determining the correct number of classes in the LCA models with continuous outcomes, the FMM and the GMM models. Results also showed that the Bayesian information criterion (BIC; Schwarz 1978) was superior to Akaike's information criterion (AIC; Akaike 1974) and consistent AIC (CAIC; Bozdogan 1987) for all three types of mixture model analyses. Li et al. (2009) examined the performances of five fit indices for dichotomous mixture Rasch, 2-parameter (2PL), and 3-parameter logistic (3PL) IRT models using an MCMC algorithm. Results of a simulation study showed that in most conditions BIC performed better than the deviance information criterion (Spiegelhalter et al. 1998), AIC, pseudo Bayes factor (PsBF), and posterior predictive model checks (PPMC).

Alexeev et al. (2011) investigated the effects of violation of the Rasch model assumption of equal discriminations on detection of the correct number of latent classes in a mixture Rasch model. Spurious latent classes were observed when data generated with a single-class 2PL IRT model were analyzed with a mixture Rasch model. Results showed further that even a single item with a high discrimination could result in detection of a second class even though the data were generated to be a single class.

Even small departures from model assumptions may have an effect on the number of latent classes detected as well as on model parameter estimates (Alexeev et al. 2011; Bauer 2007; Bauer and Curran 2003). Although latent nonnormality has been investigated in the context of IRT (Bock and Aitkin 1981; Seong 1990; Woods 2004; Zwinderman and Van den Wollenberg 1990), similar work has not been reported with MixIRT models. As was shown for the GMM (Bauer and Curran 2003), it is important to know whether the nonnormality may be responsible for generating additional latent classes in MixIRT models. The purpose of this study, therefore, was to examine the impact of distributional conditions on the extraction of latent classes. We do this in the context of MCMC estimation with dichotomous MixIRT models.

3.2 Method

A Monte Carlo simulation study was conducted to investigate the following research question: Is the accuracy of detection of latent classes affected by using a normal prior on ability parameters when the latent ability distribution is nonnormal?

3.2.1 *Simulation Design*

The following conditions were simulated: Sample size (600 and 2,000 examinees), test length (10 and 28 items), and five ability distributions (bimodal symmetric, normal, platykurtic, skewed, and uniform). Data were simulated for each of the three dichotomous IRT models $\times$ 3 MixIRT models $\times$ 2 latent class models (LCMs; one- and two-classes) $\times$ 2 sample sizes $\times$ 2 test lengths $\times$ 5 ability distributions = 360 conditions. Twenty-five replications were generated for each condition.

Examinee ability parameters were simulated for normal, skewed, platykurtic, bimodal symmetric, and uniform distributions. For the normal distribution condition, ability parameters were randomly sampled from a standard normal distribution with unit variance (i.e., $N(0, 1)$). Skewed and platykurtic data were generated using the power method proposed by Fleishman (1978). Skewness and kurtosis values were 0.75 and 0.0 for skewed data and 0.0 and −0.75 for platykurtic data, respectively. These values were selected to represent typical nonnormality situations as described by Pearson and Please (1975) for skewness less than 0.8 and kurtosis between −0.6 and 0.6. For the uniform condition, ability parameters were randomly drawn from Uniform(−2, 2). The ability parameters for the bimodal symmetric condition were randomly drawn from a combination of two normal distributions: $N(-1.5, 1)$ and $N(1.5, 1)$. All of the conditions were generated using a program written in R (R Development Core Team 2011). Graphical representations of the four nonnormal generating distributions are presented in Fig. 3.1. A standard normal distribution curve is superimposed on each figure for reference. It should be noted that these are actual generating distributions for ability parameters.

Generating item parameters were obtained for the Rasch model, 2PL and 3PL IRT model estimates using data from the Grade 9 mathematics test of the Florida Comprehensive Assessment Test (FCAT; Florida Department of Education 2002) using MULTILOG 7.03 (Thissen 2003). Estimated item parameters for these three models are presented in Tables 3.1 and 3.2 (*a*—slope parameter, *b*—threshold parameter, and *c*—guessing parameter).

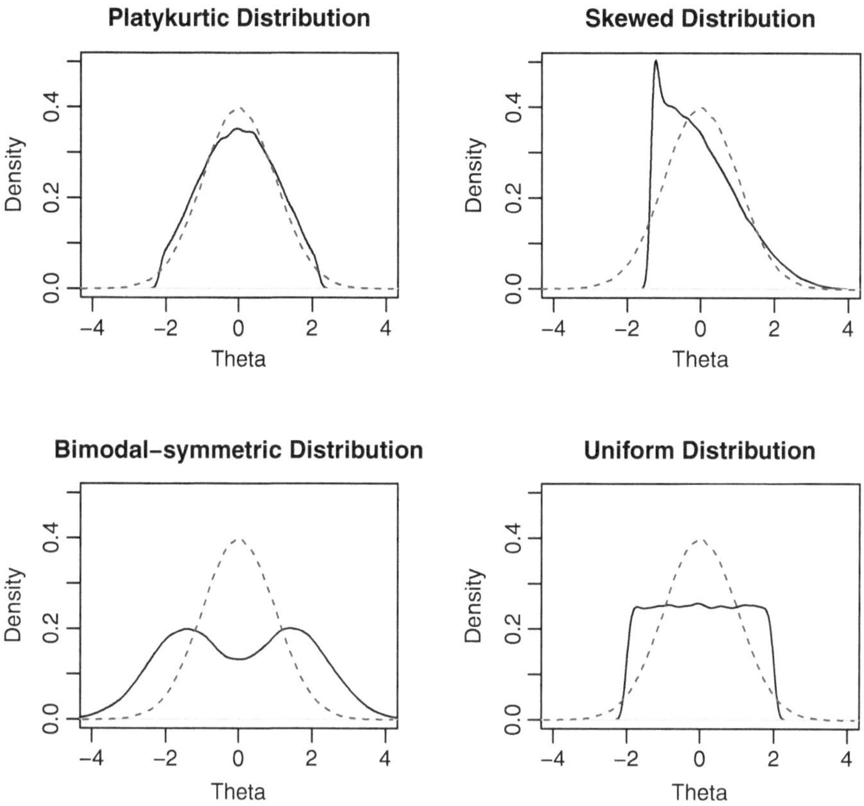

Fig. 3.1 Generating distributions for ability parameters

Table 3.1 Item parameters used for data generation for ten-item condition

	Rasch model	2PL model		3PL model		
Item	*b*	*a*	*b*	*a*	*b*	*c*
1	−1.83	0.91	−1.84	0.91	−0.37	0.53
2	−0.07	0.93	−0.07	1.17	0.69	0.30
3	−0.15	1.21	−0.13	1.23	0.39	0.24
4	0.90	0.84	0.94	0.91	1.23	0.16
5	−0.38	0.94	−0.37	0.66	−0.06	0.12
6	−0.59	1.14	−0.51	0.75	−0.37	0.06
7	0.98	0.76	1.14	0.76	1.38	0.14
8	0.51	1.06	0.45	1.58	0.88	0.22
9	0.99	0.34	2.37	3.87	1.67	0.28
10	0.19	1.27	0.15	1.05	0.46	0.14

Table 3.2 Item parameters used for data generation for 28-item condition

	Rasch model		2PL model		3PL model	
Item	*b*	*a*	*b*	*a*	*b*	*c*
1	−1.72	1.05	−1.66	1.45	−0.45	0.50
2	−0.09	0.88	−0.10	1.96	0.76	0.31
3	−0.16	1.24	−0.16	2.10	0.40	0.24
4	0.81	0.72	1.04	1.62	1.35	0.19
5	−0.37	0.93	−0.39	1.14	0.05	0.16
6	−0.57	1.28	−0.50	1.35	−0.34	0.06
7	0.91	0.72	1.16	1.31	1.40	0.15
8	0.45	1.07	0.42	2.82	0.88	0.22
9	0.91	0.38	2.08	3.97	1.67	0.26
10	0.16	1.27	0.12	1.85	0.48	0.15
11	0.69	0.67	0.95	2.42	1.34	0.25
12	0.42	0.94	0.43	2.26	0.93	0.23
13	0.93	0.69	1.26	3.61	1.35	0.22
14	1.22	0.98	1.24	2.67	1.29	0.14
15	0.31	0.94	0.32	1.66	0.81	0.20
16	1.19	0.92	1.25	2.88	1.30	0.16
17	0.27	1.18	0.23	2.47	0.72	0.22
18	−1.54	1.61	−1.15	1.59	−1.15	0.03
19	−0.39	1.69	−0.32	1.83	−0.15	0.06
20	−0.41	1.46	−0.35	1.77	−0.03	0.14
21	−0.34	1.01	−0.34	1.27	0.12	0.17
22	−0.30	1.22	−0.28	2.84	0.46	0.32
23	0.18	1.87	0.08	2.45	0.30	0.09
24	0.09	0.76	0.13	2.03	0.97	0.32
25	0.10	0.70	0.15	1.01	0.72	0.18
26	−0.31	1.01	−0.31	1.12	−0.09	0.08
27	−0.33	0.91	−0.35	0.93	−0.32	0.00
28	−0.47	1.43	−0.39	1.83	−0.01	0.17

3.2.2 *Model Framework*

The three dichotomous MixIRT models investigated in this study are described below. These models can be viewed as straightforward extensions of traditional Rasch, 2PL and 3PL IRT models, respectively. First, the mixed Rasch model (MRM; Rost 1990) is described below. This model is a combination of two latent variable models: a Rasch model and a LCM. MRMs explain qualitative differences according to the LCM portion of the model and quantitative differences according to the Rasch model portion of the model. The assumption of local independence holds for the MRM as it does for the LCM and Rasch model. In addition, the MRM assumes that the observed item response data come from a heterogeneous population that can be subdivided into mutually exclusive and exhaustive latent classes (Rost 1990; von Davier and Rost 2007). The conditional probability of a correct response in the MRM can be defined as

$$P(x_{ij}=1)=P_{ij}=\sum_{g=1}^{G}\pi_g\frac{\exp(\theta_{jg}-\beta_{ig})}{1+\exp(\theta_{jg}-\beta_{ig})}, \tag{3.1}$$

where x_{ij} is the 0/1 response of examinee j to item i (0 = incorrect response, 1 = correct response), π_g is the proportion of examinees for each class, θ_{jg} is the ability of examinee j within latent class g, and β_{ig} denotes difficulty of item i within latent class g. As proposed in Rost (1990), certain constraints on item difficulty parameters and mixing proportions are made for identification purposes so that $\sum_i \beta_{ig}=0$ and $\sum_g^G \pi_g = 1$ with $0<\pi_g<1$.

The probability of a correct response in a mixture 2PL (Mix2PL) IRT model can be written as

$$P(x_{ij}=1)=P_{ij}=\sum_{g=1}^{G}\pi_g\frac{\exp[\alpha_{ig}(\theta_{jg}-\beta_{ig})]}{1+\exp[\alpha_{ig}(\theta_{jg}-\beta_{ig})]}, \tag{3.2}$$

where α_{ig} denotes the discrimination of item i in class g. In the Mix2PL model, both the item difficulty and item discrimination parameters are permitted to be class-specific. Similarly, the mixture 3PL (Mix3PL) IRT model is assumed to describe unique response propensities for each latent class. This model also allows item guessing parameters to differ in addition to item difficulty and discrimination parameters. As for the MRM and Mix2PL model, each latent class also can have different ability parameters. The probability of a correct response for a Mix3PL model can be described as

$$P(x_{ij}=1)=P_{ij}=\sum_{g=1}^{G}\pi_g\left(\gamma_{ig}+(1-\gamma_{ig})\frac{\exp[\alpha_{ig}(\theta_{jg}-\beta_{ig})]}{1+\exp[\alpha_{ig}(\theta_{jg}-\beta_{ig})]}\right), \tag{3.3}$$

where γ_{ig} is guessing parameter for item i in class g. The MixIRT models have been applied in a number of studies (e.g., Cohen and Bolt 2005; Li et al. 2009).

3.2.3 MCMC Specification

As is the case with traditional IRT models, MixIRT models can also be estimated either using MLE or MCMC methods in the Bayesian context. MLE algorithms are applied in several software packages including Latent GOLD (Vermunt and Magidson 2005), mdltm (von Davier 2005), Mplus (Muthén and Muthén 2011), R (psychomix package; Frick et al. 2012), and Winmira (von Davier 2001). MCMC estimation is possible using the WinBUGS computer software (Spiegelhalter et al. 2003), Mplus and proc MCMC in SAS (v. 9.2; SAS Institute, Cary, NC, USA). MRM estimations can be obtained using any of these software packages. The Mix2PL IRT model can be fit using the Latent GOLD, Mplus and WinBUGS programs, however, only the WinBUGS program has the capability at this time of estimating the Mix3PL IRT model. Thus, the computer software WinBUGS was used in this study for estimating all the models to be studied. In this study, the Rasch model, 2PL and 3PL IRT models were generated to have one class. In order to see whether a two-class solution (i.e., a spurious class situation) will fit where a one-class model was simulated, each MixIRT model was fitted with one- and two-class solutions.

MCMC estimation model specifications are described below including specifications of priors and initial values. In two-group model estimations, 0.5 was used as initial values for the mixing proportions. The starting values for all other parameters were randomly generated using the WinBUGS software. The following prior distributions were used for the MRM:

$$\begin{aligned}
\beta_{ig} &\sim \text{Normal}(0,\, 1),\\
\theta_j &\sim \text{Normal}(\mu(\theta), 1),\\
\mu(\theta)_g &\sim \text{Normal}(0,\, 1),\\
g_j &\sim \text{Bernoulli}(\pi_1, \pi_2),\\
(\pi_1, \pi_2) &\sim \text{Dirichlet}(.5,\, .5),
\end{aligned}$$

where θ_j represents the ability parameter for examinee j, β_{ig} is the difficulty parameter of item i within class g, and $c_j = \{1,2\}$ is a class membership parameter. Estimates of the mean and standard deviation for each latent class, μ_g and σ_g, can also be estimated via MCMC. As in Bolt et al. (2002), σ_g was fixed at 1 for both groups. A Dirichlet distribution with 0.5 for each parameter was used as the prior for π_g for the two-group models. In addition, a prior on item discrimination was used in the Mix2PL and Mix3PL models. A prior on guessing parameter was also used in the Mix3PL. These two priors are defined as follows:

$$\begin{aligned}
\alpha_{ig} &\sim \text{Normal}(0, 1)I(0,),\\
\gamma_{ig} &\sim \text{Beta}(5, 17).
\end{aligned}$$

An appropriate number of burn-in and post burn-in iterations needs to be determined in order to remove the effects of starting values and obtain a stable posterior distribution. Several methods have been proposed to determine the convergence assessment and the number of burn-in iterations. The convergence diagnostics by Gelman and Rubin (1992) and Raftery and Lewis (1992) are currently the most popular methods (Cowles and Carlin 1996). In this study, convergence diagnostics were assessed with these two methods using the R package called convergence diagnosis and output analysis for MCMC (CODA; Plummer et al. 2006). For the MRM conditions, 6,000 burn-in iterations and 6,000 post-burn-in iterations were used based on the diagnostic assessment. For the Mix2PL IRT model conditions,

7,000 burn-in iterations and 7,000 post burn-in iterations were used, and 9,000 burn-in iterations and 9,000 post burn-in iterations were used in all Mix3PL IRT model conditions.

3.2.4 Model Selection

For traditional IRT models, model selection is typically done using likelihood ratio test statistics for nested models and information criterion indices for nonnested models. Since MixIRT models are nonnested models, only information criterion indices can be used to determine the correct number of latent classes. Several information criterion indices have been proposed with different penalization terms on the likelihood function. AIC and BIC indices and their extensions (i.e., SABIC and CAIC) are often used to select the best model from among a set of candidate models based on the smallest value obtained from the same data. In this study, only AIC and BIC indices were used. These two indices are discussed below. AIC can be calculated as

$$\mathrm{AIC} = -2\log L + 2p, \tag{3.4}$$

where L is the likelihood function and p is the number of estimated parameters calculated as follows:

$$p = m * I * j + m * j - 1, \tag{3.5}$$

where m can have values from 1 to 3 for the MRM, Mix2PL, and Mix3PL IRT models, respectively, I denotes the number of items, and j is the number of latent classes. For example, $j = 2$ is used for a two-class MixIRT solution. AIC does not apply any penalty for sample size and tends to select more complex models than BIC (Li et al. 2009). As can be seen below, the BIC index applies a penalty for sample size and for the number of parameters. As a result, BIC selects simpler models than AIC. The BIC has been showed to perform better than AIC for selection of dichotomous MixIRT models (Li et al. 2009; Preinerstorfer and Formann 2011). BIC can be calculated as follows:

$$\mathrm{BIC} = -2\log L + p * \log(N), \tag{3.6}$$

where L is the likelihood of the estimated model with p free parameters and $\log(N)$ is the logarithmic function of the total sample size N. It should be noted that the likelihood values in these equations are based on ML estimation. Since we used MCMC estimation, the likelihood values in these equations were replaced with the posterior mean of the deviance $\overline{D(\xi)}$ as obtained via MCMC estimation (Congdon 2003; Li et al. 2009) where ξ represents all estimated parameters in the model.

3.2.5 Evaluation Criteria

Recovery of item parameters was assessed using root mean square error (RMSE) which is computed as follows:

$$\mathrm{RMSE}_{(\beta_i)} = \sqrt{\frac{\sum_{i=1}^{I}\sum_{r=1}^{R}(\beta_i - \hat{\beta}_{ir})^2}{RI}}, \tag{3.7}$$

where β_i and $\hat{\beta}_i$ are generating and estimated item difficulty parameters for item i, respectively. I is the number of items and R is the number of replications. This formula was also used for calculation of the RMSE for item discrimination and item guessing parameters. In order to make an accurate calculation, the estimated parameters were placed on the scale of the generating parameters using the mean/mean approach (Kolen and Brennan 2004). It should be noted that item parameter estimates from one-class mixture IRT solutions were used to calculate the RMSE between the generated single-class IRT data sets. In addition, a percentage of correct detection of simulated latent classes was calculated based on smallest AIC and BIC indices for each condition. The proportion of correct detections for the single-class condition was used as the percentage of correct identification.

3.3 Results

As mentioned earlier, each data set was generated to have one class. The data generated by the Rasch model were fitted with the MRM and the data generated by 2PL and 3PL IRT models were fitted with Mix2PL and Mix3PL IRT models, respectively. These three models were fit with one-class and two-class models using standard normal priors on ability parameters for each simulation condition. The mean RMSE values of item parameters for each condition were calculated and are given in Tables 3.3, 3.4, and 3.5. The proportion of correct positives for the three MixIRT models was calculated based on minimum AIC and BIC between one-class and two-class solutions. For instance, the number of classes for the given data set was defined as correct when the information index for a one-class solution was smaller than that of two-class solution. These proportions are presented in Tables 3.6, 3.7, and 3.8 for each condition. Condition names given in the first column of Tables 3.3, 3.4, 3.5, 3.6, 3.7, and 3.8 include model name, number of items, and number of examinees. For example, the condition Rasch10600 indicates a data condition generated with the Rasch model for ten items and 600 examinees.

Table 3.3 summarizes the mean RMSE values of item difficulty parameters for three MixIRT models. Mean RMSE values of item difficulty parameter for MRMs were found to be less than 0.10 for most of the conditions. RMSE values were around 0.15 in only three of the bimodal data conditions. As shown in Table 3.3, mean RMSE values of the Mix2PL and Mix3PL IRT models were larger than those

Table 3.3 Mean RMSE values of item difficulty parameters over 25 replications

Condition	Bimodal	Normal	Platykurtic	Skewed	Uniform
Rasch10600	0.164	0.093	0.083	0.087	0.095
Rasch28600	0.146	0.089	0.091	0.093	0.095
Rasch102000	0.149	0.077	0.085	0.074	0.088
Rasch282000	0.097	0.051	0.050	0.050	0.057
2PL10600	0.337	0.187	0.196	0.179	0.199
2PL28600	0.280	0.131	0.135	0.133	0.131
2PL102000	0.364	0.111	0.136	0.109	0.161
2PL282000	0.286	0.072	0.072	0.077	0.107
3PL10600	0.777	0.391	0.371	0.363	0.387
3PL28600	0.675	0.204	0.206	0.214	0.290
3PL102000	0.776	0.333	0.341	0.339	0.426
3PL282000	0.617	0.132	0.137	0.183	0.230

Table 3.4 Mean RMSE values of item discrimination parameters over 25 replications

Condition	Bimodal	Normal	Platykurtic	Skewed	Uniform
2PL10600	1.677	0.148	0.144	0.155	0.298
2PL28600	1.524	0.131	0.129	0.138	0.275
2PL102000	1.778	0.086	0.098	0.088	0.357
2PL282000	1.813	0.071	0.069	0.078	0.368
3PL10600	1.220	0.574	0.538	0.515	0.522
3PL28600	1.125	0.730	0.744	0.470	0.545
3PL102000	1.280	0.448	0.503	0.511	0.471
3PL282000	2.176	0.417	0.440	0.452	0.452

for the MRM. Mean RMSE values appear to increase as the complexity of model increases. RMSEs for the Mix2PL IRT model condition with 28 items and 2,000 examinees, however, were less than 0.11 for all except the bimodal symmetric distribution. For the Mix2PL analyses, mean RMSE values seemed to decrease as the number of examinees increases. The mean RMSE values for the bimodal distribution were relatively higher for the Mix3PL IRT model. Mean RMSE values were around 0.30 for normal, platykurtic, skewed, and uniform distributions. These results are consistent with previous simulation studies with MixIRT models (Li et al. 2009).

Mean RMSE values for item discrimination parameter estimates for the Mix2PL and Mix3PL IRT models are presented in Table 3.4. As expected, RMSE values for the Mix2PL and Mix3PL IRT models for the bimodal symmetric distribution were the largest. Those for the uniform distribution were the second largest. Mean RMSE values appeared to be smaller for all of the Mix2PL conditions for the normal, platykurtic, and skewed distributions. Mean RMSE values for the

Table 3.5 Mean RMSE values of item guessing parameters over 25 replications

Condition	Bimodal	Normal	Platykurtic	Skewed	Uniform
3PL10600	0.096	0.089	0.088	0.092	0.089
3PL28600	0.061	0.063	0.058	0.073	0.653
3PL102000	0.092	0.085	0.086	0.093	0.093
3PL282000	0.039	0.047	0.049	0.074	0.048

Table 3.6 The correct positive rates for MRM analyses over 25 replications

	Bimodal		Normal		Platykurtic		Skewed		Uniform	
Condition	AIC	BIC	AIC	BIC	AIC	BIC	AIC	BIC	AIC	BIC
Rasch10600	0	0	2	25	6	23	0	19	0	2
Rasch102000	1	13	0	19	0	22	0	14	0	0
Rasch28600	0	0	20	25	20	25	15	25	10	25
Rasch282000	3	15	7	25	4	25	1	21	0	0

Mix3PL IRT model condition also decreased as the number of examinees increased, although there was no clear pattern as the number of items increased. Table 3.5 summarizes mean RMSE values for the guessing parameter estimates. For most of the conditions, mean RMSE values appeared to decrease as the number of items and the number of examinees increased. Mean RMSE values for item guessing parameters were relatively lower than those for item difficulty and discrimination parameters. This is because the item guessing parameter estimates are always between zero and one. Thus, the recovery of item guessing parameters is often easier than the recovery of other item parameters, particularly discrimination parameters.

Table 3.6 summarizes the correct positive rates for MRM analyses. As shown in Table 3.6, the BIC index performed well in the MRM analysis under normal, platykurtic, and skewed conditions. However, the proportions of correct positives for the BIC index for the bimodal and uniform conditions were low except in the 28 items and 600 examinees condition. The performance of AIC was lower than BIC for the MRM analyses. AIC did not provide high correct identification rates in the normal distribution conditions. Both AIC and BIC showed good performance in data conditions with 28 items and 600 examinees except for bimodal data. In most of the other simulation conditions, the correct positive rate for AIC index was very low and close to zero.

Table 3.7 presents the correct positive rates for Mix2PL IRT model analyses. For almost all conditions, the correct positive rates of the BIC index were found to be almost perfect except for the skewed data conditions. Although the results of the AIC index in the Mix2PL IRT model analyses provided higher correction rates than that of the MRM analyses, the overall performance of AIC index was worse than BIC results. Correct positive rates for AIC ranged from 0 to 10 in more than half of the conditions. Based on the results from AIC index, latent nonnormality causes spurious latent class in Mix2PL IRT model estimation. However, results based on

Table 3.7 The correct positive rates for Mix2PL analyses over 25 replications

	Bimodal		Normal		Platykurtic		Skewed		Uniform	
Condition	AIC	BIC	AIC	BIC	AIC	BIC	AIC	BIC	AIC	BIC
2PL10600	5	25	9	25	7	25	1	16	7	25
2PL102000	6	24	2	22	6	25	0	2	2	17
2PL28600	25	25	25	25	24	25	10	25	19	25
2PL282000	18	25	12	22	21	25	0	10	2	25

Table 3.8 The correct positive rates for Mix3PL analyses over 25 replications

	Bimodal		Normal		Platykurtic		Skewed		Uniform	
Condition	AIC	BIC	AIC	BIC	AIC	BIC	AIC	BIC	AIC	BIC
3PL10600	15	25	17	25	13	25	14	25	6	25
3PL102000	2	25	3	24	3	22	23	24	2	17
3PL28600	25	25	25	25	25	25	25	25	25	25
3PL282000	17	25	23	25	16	25	21	25	5	25

the BIC index did not show strong evidence for existence of spurious latent class in Mix2PL IRT model estimation with nonnormal latent distributions.

Table 3.7 presents the correct positive rates for Mix3PL IRT model analyses. In all distribution conditions, BIC supported selection of one class in 100 % of the replications at all three sample size × two test length conditions. Only the conditions with ten items and 2,000 examinees yielded lower results in terms of the BIC index. The number of correct selections was higher for AIC for the Mix3PL model compared to the previous models. Consistent with the previous results, however, the number of correct selections by AIC was lower than for BIC. Further, AIC had problems with selecting the correct model in most of the uniform data conditions. AIC failed to detect the correct model for the ten items and 2,000 examinees one-class condition. It appears that the Mix3PL IRT models were more robust to latent nonnormality than either the MRM or Mix2PL IRT models based on results for both the AIC and BIC.

3.4 Discussion

The two-class MixIRT model was consistently judged to be a better representation of the data than the one-class model when the data were analyzed with the MRM under both bimodal and uniform data conditions. As expected, MRM analyses of the data with normal and typical nonnormal ability distributions (i.e., skewed and platykurtic) did not show any over-extraction. Both of the indices provided similar results; however, the overall performance of AIC was worse than the BIC.

The results of the Mix2PL and Mix3PL analyses showed similar patterns. For most of the conditions, nonnormality did not appear to lead to over-extraction with either the Mix2PL or MiX3PL IRT models. These results were not consistent with the results of the MRM analyses. However, the relative performance of fit indices in the Mix2PL and Mix3PL IRT model analyses was consistent with the analyses of MRM in that the AIC selected solutions with two-classes more than BIC. This also was consistent with previous research on model selection that found AIC to select more complex model solutions.

Results suggested that latent nonnormality may be capable of causing extraction of spurious latent classes with the MRM. More complex models, however, such as the Mix2PL and Mix3PL appeared to be more robust to latent nonnormality in that both tended to yield fewer spurious latent class solutions. With respect to the penalty term used in the information indices considered here, the more parameters added to the model, the larger the penalty term. In addition, the performance of the information indices used to determine model fit also may be a function of the underlying distribution of the data. Thus the interpretability of the latent classes in any model selected also needs to be considered in determining model selection. Relying only on statistical criteria may not always yield interpretable solutions. Results in this study suggested that it may be misleading, even under the most ideal conditions, to use the AIC index for identifying number of latent classes. Thus, the solution accepted should be expected to have sufficient support not only from statistical criteria but also from the interpretability of the classes. Further research on the impact of different nonnormal distributions would be helpful, particularly with respect to more extreme skewness and kurtosis conditions that can sometimes arise in highly heterogeneous populations. The skewed and platykurtic data sets in this study were limited to typical nonnormality conditions. It may be useful to investigate the effects of extreme violations of normality on detection of the number of latent classes.

References

Akaike H (1974) A new look at the statistical model identification. IEEE Trans Autom Control 19:716–723. doi:10.1109/TAC.1974.1100705

Alexeev N, Templin J, Cohen AS (2011) Spurious latent classes in the mixture Rasch model. J Educ Meas 48:313–332. doi:10.1111/j.1745-3984.2011.00146.x

Arminger G, Stein P, Wittenberg J (1999) Mixtures of conditional mean- and covariance-structure models. Psychometrika 64:475–494. doi:10.1007/BF02294568

Bauer DJ (2007) Observations on the use of growth mixture models in psychological research. Multivar Behav Res 42:757–786. doi:10.1080/00273170701710338

Bauer DJ, Curran PJ (2003) Distributional assumptions of growth mixture models: implications for over-extraction of latent trajectory classes. Psychol Methods 8:338–363. doi:10.1037/1082-989X.8.3.338

Bock RD, Aitkin M (1981) Marginal maximum likelihood estimation of item parameters: application of an EM algorithm. Psychometrika 46:443–459. doi:10.1007/BF02293801

Bock RD, Zimowski MF (1997) Multiple group IRT. In: van der Linden WJ, Hambleton RK (eds) Handbook of modern item response theory. Springer, New York, pp 433–448

Bolt DM, Cohen AS, Wollack JA (2002) Item parameter estimation under conditions of test speededness: application of a mixture Rasch model with ordinal constraints. J Educ Meas 39:331–348. doi:10.1111/j.1745-3984.2002.tb01146.x
Bozdogan H (1987) Model selection and Akaike's information criterion (AIC): the general theory and its analytical extensions. Psychometrika 52:345–370
Clogg CC (1995) Latent class models. In: Arminger G, Clogg CC, Sobel ME (eds) Handbook of statistical modeling for the social and behavioral sciences. Plenum Press, New York, pp. 311–359
Cohen AS, Bolt DM (2005) A mixture model analysis of differential item functioning. J Educ Meas 42:133–148. doi:10.1111/j.1745-3984.2005.00007
Cohen AS, Gregg N, Deng M (2005) The role of extended time and item content on a high-stakes mathematics test. Learn Disabil Res Pract 20:225–233. doi:10.1111/j.1540-5826.2005.00138.x
Congdon P (2003) Applied Bayesian modelling. Wiley, New York
Cowles MK, Carlin BP (1996) Markov chain Monte Carlo convergence diagnostics: a comparative review. J Am Stat Assoc 91:883–904. doi:10.1080/01621459.1996.10476956
Embretson SE, Reise SP (2000) Item response theory for psychologists. Erlbaum, Mahwah
Fleishman AI (1978) A method for simulating non-normal distributions. Psychometrika 43:521–532. doi:10.1007/BF02293811
Florida Department of Education (2002) Florida Comprehensive Assessment Test. Tallahassee, FL: Author
Frick H, Strobl C, Leisch F, Zeileis A (2012) Flexible Rasch mixture models with package psychomix. J Stat Softw 48(7):1–25. Retrieved from http://www.jstatsoft.org/v48/i07/
Gelman A, Rubin DB (1992) Inference from iterative simulation using multiple sequences. Stat Sci 7:457–472. Retrieved from http://www.jstor.org/stable/2246093
Jedidi K, Jagpal HS, DeSarbo WS (1997) Finite mixture structural equation models for response-based segmentation and unobserved heterogeneity. Mark Sci 16:39–59. doi:10.1287/mksc.16.1.39
Kolen MJ, Brennan RL (2004) Test equating: methods and practices, 2nd edn. Springer, New York
Li F, Duncan TE, Duncan SC (2001) Latent growth modeling of longitudinal data: a finite growth mixture modeling approach. Struct Equ Model 8:493–530. doi:10.1207/S15328007SEM0804_01
Li F, Cohen AS, Kim S-H, Cho S-J (2009) Model selection methods for mixture dichotomous IRT models. Appl Psychol Meas 33:353–373. doi:10.1177/0146621608326422
Lo Y, Mendell NR, Rubin DB (2001) Testing the number of components in a normal mixture. Biometrika 88:767–778. doi:10.1093/biomet/88.3.767
Lubke GH, Muthén BO (2005) Investigating population heterogeneity with factor mixture models. Psychol Methods 10:21–39. doi:10.1037/1082-989X.10.1.21
McLachlan G, Peel D (2000) Finite mixture models. Wiley, New York
Mislevy RJ, Verhelst N (1990) Modeling item responses when different subjects employ different solution strategies. Psychometrika 55:195–215. doi:10.1007/BF02295283
Muthén LK, Muthén BO (2011) Mplus user's guide, 6th edn. Author, Los Angeles
Nylund KL, Asparouhov T, Muthén BO (2007) Deciding on the number of classes in latent class analysis and growth mixture modeling: a Monte Carlo simulation study. Struct Equ Model 14:535–569. doi:10.1080/10705510701575396
Pearson ES, Please NW (1975) Relation between the shape of population distribution and the robustness of four simple test statistics. Biometrika 62:223–241. doi:10.1093/biomet/62.2.223
Plummer M, Best N, Cowles K, Vines K (2006) CODA: convergence diagnosis and output analysis for MCMC. R News 6:7–11. Retrieved from http://cran.r-project.org/doc/Rnews/Rnews_2006-1.pdf#page=7
Preinerstorfer D, Formann AK (2011) Parameter recovery and model selection in mixed Rasch models. Br J Math Stat Psychol 65:251–262. doi:10.1111/j.2044-8317.2011.02020.x
R Development Core Team (2011) R: a language and environment for statistical computing. R Foundation for Statistical Computing, Vienna. Retrieved from http://www.R-project.org/
Raftery AE, Lewis S (1992) How many iterations in the Gibbs sampler. Bayesian Stat 4:763–773

Reckase MD (2009) Multidimensional item response theory. Springer, New York
Rost J (1990) Rasch models in latent classes: an integration of two approaches to item analysis. Appl Psychol Meas 14:271–282. doi:10.1177/014662169001400305
Rost J, von Davier M (1993) Measuring different traits in different populations with the same items. In: Steyer R, Wender KF, Widaman KF (eds) Psychometric methodology. Proceedings of the 7th European meeting of the psychometric society in Trier. Gustav Fischer, Stuttgart, pp 446–450
Rost J, Carstensen CH, von Davier M (1997) Applying the mixed-Rasch model to personality questionaires. In: Rost R, Langeheine R (eds) Applications of latent trait and latent class models in the social sciences. Waxmann, New York, pp 324–332
Samuelsen KM (2005) Examining differential item functioning from a latent class perspective. Doctoral dissertation, University of Maryland
SAS Institute (2008) SAS/STAT 9.2 user's guide. SAS Institute, Cary
Schwarz G (1978) Estimating the dimension of a model. Ann Stat 6:461–464. doi:10.1214/aos/1176344136
Sclove LS (1987) Application of model-selection criteria to some problems in multivariate analysis. Psychometrika 52:333–343. doi:10.1007/BF02294360
Seong TJ (1990). Sensitivity of marginal maximum likelihood estimation of item and ability parameters to the characteristics of the prior ability distributions. Appl Psychol Meas 14:299–311. doi:10.1177/014662169001400307
Spiegelhalter DJ, Best NG, Carlin BP (1998) Bayesian deviance, the effective number of parameters, and the comparison of arbitrarily complex models. Research Report No. 98-009. MRC Biostatistics Unit, Cambridge
Spiegelhalter D, Thomas A, Best N (2003) WinBUGS (version 1.4) [Computer software]. Biostatistics Unit, Institute of Public Health, Cambridge
Thissen D (2003) MULTILOG: multiple, categorical item analysis and test scoring using item response theory (Version 7.03) [Computer software]. Scientific Software International, Chicago
Titterington DM, Smith AFM, Makov UE (1985) Statical analysis of finite mixture distributions. Wiley, Chichester
Tofighi D, Enders CK (2007) Identifying the correct number of classes in a growth mixture model. In: Hancock GR, Samuelsen KM (eds) Mixture models in latent variable research. Information Age, Greenwich, pp 317–341
Vermunt JK, Magidson J (2005) Latent GOLD (Version 4.0) [Computer software]. Statistical Innovations, Inc., Belmont
von Davier M (2001) WINMIRA 2001 [Computer software]. Assessment Systems Corporation, St. Paul
von Davier M (2005) mdltm: software for the general diagnostic model and for estimating mixtures of multidimensional discrete latent traits models [Computer software]. ETS, Princeton
von Davier M, Rost J (1997) Self monitoring-A class variable? In: Rost J, Langeheime R (eds) Applications of latent trait and latent class models in the social sciences. Waxmann, Muenster, pp 296–305
von Davier M, Rost J (2007) Mixture distribution item response models. In: Rao CR, Sinharay S (eds) Handbook of statistics. Psychometrics, vol 26. Elsevier, Amsterdam, pp 643–661
von Davier M, Rost J, Carstensen CH (2007) Introduction: extending the Rasch model. In: von Davier M, Carstensen CH (eds) Multivariate and mixture distribution Rasch models: extensions and applications. Springer, New York, pp 1–12
Wall MM, Guo J, Amemiya Y (2012) Mixture factor analysis for approximating a nonnormally distributed continuous latent factor with continuous and dichotomous observed variables. Multivar Behav Res 47:276–313. doi:10.1080/00273171.2012.658339
Wollack JA, Cohen AS, Wells CS (2003) A method for maintaining scale stability in the presence of test speededness. J Educ Meas 40:307–330. doi:10.1111/j.1745-3984.2003.tb01149.x
Woods CM (2004) Item response theory with estimation of the latent population distribution using spline-based densities. Unpublished doctoral dissertation, University of North Carolina at Chapel Hill

Yamamoto KY, Everson HT (1997) Modeling the effects of test length and test time on parameter estimation using the HYBRID model. In: Rost J, Langeheine R (eds) Applications of latent trait and latent class models in the social sciences. Waxmann, Munster, pp 89–98

Zwinderman AH, Van den Wollenberg AL (1990) Robustness of marginal maximum likelihood estimation in the Rasch model. Appl Psychol Meas 14:73–81. doi:10.1177/014662169001400107

Chapter 4
An Option-Based Partial Credit Item Response Model

Yuanchao (Emily) Bo, Charles Lewis, and David V. Budescu

Abstract Multiple-choice (MC) tests have been criticized for allowing guessing and the failure to credit partial knowledge, and alternative scoring methods and response formats (Ben-Simon et al., Appl Psychol Meas 21:65–88, 1997) have been proposed to address this problem. Modern test theory addresses these issues by using binary item response models (e.g., 3PL) with guessing parameters, or with polytomous IRT models. We propose an option-based partial credit IRT model and a new scoring rule based on a weighted Hamming distance between the option key and the option response vector. The test taker (TT)'s estimated ability is based on information from both correct options and distracters. These modifications reduce the TT's ability to guess and credit the TT's partial knowledge. The new model can be tailored to different formats, and some popular IRT models, such as the 2PL and Bock's nominal model, are special cases of the proposed model. Markov Chain Monte Carlo (MCMC) analysis was used to estimate the model parameters and it provides satisfactory estimates of the model parameters. Simulation studies show that the weighted Hamming distance scores have the highest correlation with TTs' true abilities, and their distribution is also less skewed than those of the other scores considered.

Keywords Item Response Theory • MCMC • Partial credit • Partial knowledge • Hamming distance • Multiple Choice • Scoring rule

4.1 A New Scoring Rule for Multiple-Choice Items

Multiple-Choice (MC) tests are widely used as an evaluation tool in aptitude and achievement testing. The main reasons for their popularity are their efficiency (they require less time per item to administer than tests requiring open-ended responses), standardization in format, timing and administration, and the accuracy

Y. Bo (✉) • C. Lewis • D.V. Budescu
Department of Psychology, Fordham University, Rose Hill Campus,
441 East Fordham Road, Bronx, NY, USA
e-mail: ybo@fordham.edu

R.E. Millsap et al. (eds.), *Quantitative Psychology Research*, Springer Proceedings in Mathematics & Statistics 89, DOI 10.1007/978-3-319-07503-7_4

and objectivity of their scoring. However, MC tests have serious disadvantages. Because of the binary scoring (correct or incorrect) typically used, they cannot capture the test takers' (TTs') various levels of partial knowledge (e.g., Budescu and Bar-Hillel 1993; Ben-Simon et al. 1997). Another potential drawback is that the MC format may encourage "guessing." The "guessing problem" and the tests' inability to measure partial knowledge have motivated psychometricians to develop alternative measurement methods to improve the measurement of the TTs' "true" state of knowledge.

Attempts to improve MC tests rely on reduction of the scope of guessing and avoidance of dichotomous scoring. These approaches are consistent with the common view that a TT's true knowledge is continuous, thus any attempt to score his/her responses dichotomously would result in some loss of information (e.g., Hutchinson 1982; Ben-Simon et al. 1997). The methods developed include alternative scoring rules for MC items, changing the items' structure, changing the response method, and differential item/option weighting.

The well-known "correction for guessing" formula (Holzinger 1924; Thurstone 1919) counts the number of correct answers, but it penalizes incorrect answers. This approach replaces binary scoring with trinary scoring for every item. The expected scores for omitting an item or "wild" guessing are equal, so this formula reduces the incentive for "wild" guessing, especially for risk averse TTs who may choose to leave items unanswered.

Budescu and Bar-Hillel (1993) explain that the "correction for guessing" scoring rule has been justified on moral/ethical grounds as well as psychometric grounds, such as improvement in the reliability of the test (e.g., Ben-Simon et al. 1997; Ruch and Stoddard 1925). Budescu and Bar-Hillel (1993) have criticized the cognitive and decision theoretical foundations of this approach. Recently, Budescu and Bo (2014, in press) proposed a model that combines elements from Item Response Theory (IRT) to describe the tests and Behavioral Decision Theory to describe the TTs' behavior. Their analysis shows that penalties for incorrect answers have detrimental effects for both TTs and test makers. TTs who are risk averse, loss averse, and overly conservative are penalized disproportionately, and the distributions of estimated scores are biased, display higher variance, and are more skewed as a function of the severity of the penalty.

Elimination testing (ET) was proposed by Coombs et al. (1956) to measure partial knowledge. It allows TTs to eliminate as many incorrect response options as they can possibly identify and TTs are scored based on the number of correct and incorrect eliminations. Subset selection testing (SST), proposed by Dressel and Schmidt (1953), uses a complementary approach. It requires TTs to select those options that are likely to be correct and scores on the basis of the number of correct and incorrect selections. Both ET and SST measure partial knowledge and they both penalize incorrect identification of one or more options. Various studies have shown that ET and SST discourage wild guessing, discriminate among different levels of knowledge and, in most cases, tend to improve the psychometric quality of a test (e.g., Jaradat and Tollefson 1988; Gibbons et al. 1977). One disadvantage of these response/scoring formats is that they require longer administration times than the standard MC response format. Also, as predicted by Prospect Theory (PT) (Kahneman and Tversky 1979; Tversky and Kahneman 1992), several studies have found that the selected set of options identified as correct was smaller under the SST than under the ET rule, indicating that respondents were more willing to take risks under the SST. Thus the two scoring rules, although mathematically equivalent, seem to induce different response strategies on the part of TTs (Bereby-Meyer et al. 2003; Yaniv and Schul 1997, 2000).

Ben-Simon et al. (1997) developed a classification system of the alternative response formats and scoring methods that have been proposed to improve MC tests. The classification system includes (1) Differential item weighting based on objective criteria; (2) Differential option weighting; (3) Changes to the item structure; (4) Changes to the response method.

(1) *Differential item weighting based on objective criteria.* The basic principle of these methods is to assign different weights to different items. The weights could be related to item difficulty, validity, diagnostic ability, or be based on regression or factor-analytical models. Empirical studies have yielded mixed results (Gulliksen 1950; Stanley and Wang 1970; Wang and Stanley 1970; Sykes and Hou 2003).
(2) *Differential option weighting.* The underlying principle of these methods is to differentiate the severity of errors by assigning different weights to incorrect answers. The weights can be based on experts' judgment, a theory of the structure of knowledge (Smith 1987), or a prior knowledge of the weightings (Ben-Simon et al. 1997). Studies and reviews (for example, Frary 1989; Haladyna 1988; Echternacht 1976) show that there might be advantages to these methods in terms of improved internal consistency reliability. However, these methods are not very popular (Frary 1989) because of the high cost of developing weighting schemes, the complicated methods of calculating scores, and the difficulties associated with explaining the scoring procedures to the TTs.
(3) *Changes to the item structure.* Various unusual item structures abandon the convention of the MC items of choosing one response option. An example is MC items with multiple correct options, where TTs are instructed to choose more than one correct option. The final score is the number of correct options identified and, in some versions, incorrect answers may be penalized. The chance of guessing correctly the response pattern for these items is reduced greatly, compared to a standard MC item. Imagine an MC item with five options, and with two of the options being correct. If the instructions ask the TTs to choose two options, the chance of selecting the correct pair by chance is the reciprocal of the total number of possible pairs, $1/(5*4/2) = 1/10$. If the TTs are instructed to choose all that apply, the chance of selecting the correct pattern by chance is the reciprocal of the total number of possible response patterns $=1/31$. The major disadvantages of these methods are the difficulty in constructing these unusual items and longer administration time.
(4) *Changes to the response method.* The methods in this group use weights given by TTs, which involve self-assessment of knowledge, including internal

> calibration of their true knowledge and their confidence in their responses. Studies have shown that tests with these response methods have better psychometric properties (Michael 1968; Pugh and Brunza 1975; Hambleton et al. 1970; Rippey 1970) than traditional MC tests. However, the studies of Jacobs (1971), Hansen (1971) and Swineford (1938, 1941) lead one to conclude that there is a non-cognitive factor of "miscalibration" operating in the confidence testing procedure that contaminates the results, yielding an increase in error. In addition, these response methods involve longer administration time and require more complex scoring procedures than simple binary (e.g., number correct scoring) or trinary scoring (e.g., formula scoring) rules.

Modern test theory attempts to address this issue in different ways. For example, the 3-parameter logistic (3PL) IRT model (Birnbaum 1968) has a "guessing" parameter. Formally, it is a lower-asymptote parameter, allowing a nonzero probability of answering correctly by TTs at the lowest level of the trait. The 3PL IRT model doesn't assume "random/wild" guessing, and the lower-asymptote parameter is not fixed (as it in formula scoring). The model addresses the TTs' guessing behavior through an item parameter, rather than a person parameter, which doesn't consider the fact that different TTs could have different strategies. The Rasch model (1PL) and 2PL model do not consider guessing and also do not provide credit for partial knowledge. The sufficient statistics for the 1PL and 2PL models are (weighted) number correct scores.

Categorical response IRT models seek to extract the maximum information regarding the TTs' true state of knowledge for each item. Bock's (1972) nominal response model is an unordered polytomous response IRT model. The graded response model (Samejima 1969), partial credit model (Masters 1982), and generalized partial credit model (Muraki 1992) are IRT models for categorical responses with a predetermined order. Samejima (1979) and Thissen and Steinberg (1984) extended Bock's nominal response model to allow for the effects of guessing. Samejima added a "don't know" latent response category for MC items. She assumed that the proportion of those who tend to guess any of the options, given that they are in the "don't know" category, should be fixed across observed response categories (and should equal the reciprocal of the number of response options for each item). Thissen and Steinberg's model allows the position or labeling of the alternatives to affect the distribution of these guessed responses. Bechger et al. (2005) developed a model with a guessing component for the multiple-category response MC tests. Their model assumes a two-stage process: 1) the TT eliminates the distracters he/she recognizes to be wrong; 2) the TT guesses randomly among the remaining answers. San Martin et al. (2006) developed a 1PL model that includes a guessing probability that depends on the ability of the TTs.

It is difficult to solve the guessing problem by invoking a simple mathematical model because the TTs' responses to an item may be based on various levels and types of partial knowledge, and the strategy of responding in such cases can vary from person to person. As an alternative, we suggest to focus on the TTs' behavior and improve the estimation of their abilities, including their partial knowledge.

We focus here on MC items with multiple correct options. Such items are used currently in large-scale assessments such as the GRE and TOEFL. Currently, ETS, who administers the GRE[1] and TOEFL tests, uses a binary scoring rule that can be called grouped number correct/right: TTs have to choose *all the correct answers* to get full credit; otherwise, they receive no credit, even if they endorse some of the correct options.[2]

This scoring rule only focuses on TTs' choices of the correct options and ignores the distracters. This is perfectly sensible for "regular" MC items, but not for the alternative, and more complex items with multiple correct options. Grouped number correct scores don't differentiate among TTs who choose distracters only and those who choose some correct options and some distracters. TTs of the latter type should presumably receive some credit because they endorsed some of the correct responses, so their choices actually reflect the fact that they have the knowledge to exclude wrong options.

We propose a new scoring rule in which items are scored based on (a) the identification of the correct options as well as (b) the correct rejection of distracters, thus giving TTs partial credit for any correct decision. Additionally, we propose an option-based partial credit model to provide a statistical foundation for estimation of the TTs' scores under the new rule.

4.2 The Weighted Hamming Distance Scoring Rule

Item scores. To motivate the new proposed scoring rule, we first describe a different way of looking at the "standard" binary scoring procedure. Imagine an item with one correct response option. Let the "key" response vector for item j with K_j options, $\rho_j = \left(\rho_{j1}, .., \rho_{jk}, \ldots, \rho_{jK_j}\right)$, consist of a "1" for the correct answer and "0" elsewhere, and let the response of TT_i be represented by a vector $\boldsymbol{r_{ij}}$, that has a "1" for the answer selected by the TT as the correct one and "0" elsewhere. Now imagine comparing the two vectors in an element-wise fashion and counting the number of agreements and disagreements. The score of TT_i for item j is defined as the number of agreements between the vectors and can be calculated by:

$$S_{ij} = K_j - \sum_{k=1}^{K_j} \left| r_{ijk} - \rho_{jk} \right| . \tag{1}$$

[1]Based on the items from "Practice Book for the Paper-based GRE revised General Test," 26 % of the verbal items and 10 % of the quantitative items are of this type.

[2]In the text completion items, it is probably more justified to use grouped number correct scoring than it is for MC items with multiple correct options, since the choice for each blank depends on the other choices.

The sum of mismatches $\sum_{k=1}^{K_j} \left| r_{ijk} - \rho_{jk} \right|$ is the Hamming distance between the two vectors (Hamming 1950). The scoring rule is based on the Hamming distance, but is maximized when the distance is zero (perfect matching). In the case being considered (items with a single correct response option), there will always be either perfect matching or two mismatches, so the only two possible scores are K_j and $K_j - 2$.

We propose two extensions to this rule. First assume that not all mismatches are considered equally important or severe, so one can define a version of the scoring rule that weights options differentially, according to a predetermined vector of (positive) weights, $\boldsymbol{w_j}$:

$$SW_{ij} = \sum_{k=1}^{K_j} w_{jk} - \sum_{k=1}^{K_j} w_{jk} \left| r_{ijk} - \rho_{jk} \right| . \tag{2}$$

The weighted sum of mismatches $\sum_{k=1}^{K_j} w_{jk} \left| r_{ijk} - \rho_{jk} \right|$ is the weighted Hamming distance between the two vectors. Evidently, this differential weighting provides a way of assessing partial knowledge.

To address the issue of guessing, we make a more radical suggestion, namely, to allow items to have *multiple correct answers*. Suppose that a MC test consists of n items, and there are K_j response options for item j. The number of correct options may vary across items (e.g., there could be two correct options for some items and one correct option for the other items[3]). In general, say item j has Q_j correct answers ($Q_j < K_j$). The key vector consists of Q_j ones and ($K_j - Q_j$) zeros. The response vector may have the same cardinality, but it is also possible to imagine cases where TTs are not informed of the number of correct answers and they may end up over-, or under-estimating, the number of correct answers (Q_j). The original scoring rule, as well as the weighted scoring rule, could be used for these items.

Test scores. A test may include items with various numbers of options, thus the maximal scores of the items are different because of different numbers of distracters. To eliminate the item score scale indeterminacy, the raw item scores could be "normalized" by dividing the item scores by the corresponding sum of option weights. The test scores would then be given by the sum of the normalized item scores.

$$SW_i = \sum\nolimits_{j=1}^{J} \frac{\sum\nolimits_{k=1}^{K_j} w_{jk} - \sum\nolimits_{k=1}^{K_j} w_{jk} \left| r_{ijk} - \rho_{jk} \right|}{\sum\nolimits_{k=1}^{K_j} w_{jk}} \tag{3}$$

[3]The GRE revised General Test has such items for which TTs are asked to choose all the options that apply.

Assume that the TTs are told that item j, which has $K_j = 5$ options (A, B, C, D, E), could have $Q_j = 2$ correct options. Suppose the response options A and B are correct, while options C, D, and E are incorrect, so the key response vector for the item is $\rho_j = (1, 1, 0, 0, 0)$. Table 4.1 shows the ten possible response patterns ($\boldsymbol{r}$) that identify exactly two options as correct. Each of the response patterns is scored by four different scoring rules: the regular Hamming distance (equal weights) scoring rule, the standardized weighted Hamming distance scoring rule, the grouped number right scoring, and the standardized weighted number right scoring. The weighted number correct score does not use distracter information and is based only on the two correct options. Group number correct scores only credit the correct response pattern and give no credit to any other response pattern. The four scores are listed in order of the discrimination they allow between the TTs.

Table 4.1 Possible response patterns for items with 5 options with 2 correct answers

A	B	C	D	E	Score based on group number right	Standardized score based on weighted number correct with weights w_j	Score based on Hamming distance	Standardized score based on weighted Hamming distance with weights w_j
1	1	0	0	0	1	1	5	1
1	0	1	0	0	0	$\frac{w_1}{TW2}$	3	$\frac{w_1+w_4+w_5}{TW1}$
1	0	0	1	0	0	$\frac{w_1}{TW2}$	3	$\frac{w_1+w_3+w_5}{TW1}$
1	0	0	0	1	0	$\frac{w_1}{TW2}$	3	$\frac{w_1+w_3+w_4}{TW1}$
0	1	1	0	0	0	$\frac{w_2}{TW2}$	3	$\frac{w_2+w_4+w_5}{TW1}$
0	1	0	1	0	0	$\frac{w_2}{TW2}$	3	$\frac{w_2+w_3+w_5}{TW1}$
0	1	0	0	1	0	$\frac{w_2}{TW2}$	3	$\frac{w_2+w_3+w_4}{TW1}$
0	0	1	1	0	0	0	1	$\frac{w_5}{TW1}$
0	0	1	0	1	0	0	1	$\frac{w_4}{TW1}$
0	0	0	1	1	0	0	1	$\frac{w_3}{TW1}$

Notes: $TW1 = w_1 + w_2 + w_3 + w_4 + w_5$, $TW2 = w_1 + w_2$

If a TT chooses two answers (i.e., a response pattern) randomly, the chance of answering correctly and getting full credit is 1/10. Thus the new format and scoring rule reduces the chance to guess correctly by a factor of 2, compared to a regular MC item with $K = 5$ options with only $Q = 1$ correct option.

Neither the standard binary IRT models (Rasch; 2PL; 3PL) nor any of the various polytomous IRT models, including the partial credit model by Masters (1982), Samejima's graded response model (1969, 1972), Bock's nominal categories model (1972), Thissen and Steinberg's (1984) multiple-choice model or Andersen's rating scale model (1977) can estimate the TTs' ability in a way that fully captures the richness of this new scoring rule. Next, we propose a new option-based partial credit IRT model associated with the scoring rule, so that the estimation of the TTs' ability is based on information both from correct options and from distracters.

4.3 An Option-Based Partial Credit Model

The model assumptions. The model belongs to the large family of IRT models. So this model is built upon the assumption of item local independence. In addition, the model is formulated using an option local independence assumption. The option local independence assumption is similar to the item local independence assumption in that the former assumes that the choices of the options are independent from each other after the effect of the underlying trait is conditioned out, while the latter assumes that the responses to the items are independent from each other after partialling out the effect of the underlying trait. The item local independence assumption is often thought of as capturing and describing the actual process used by the TT. We do not make similar claims about the option local independence assumption which is, simply, a convenient mathematical way of modeling the test responses. The key feature of the option local independence assumption is to reduce the number of parameters associated with an item and mathematically combine them in the service of a simpler model.

The model. Let $P_{jk}(\theta_i)$, the "true" probability that the ith TT correctly responds to option k for item j, be represented by:

$$P_{jk}(\theta_i) = \frac{x_{ijk}}{1 + x_{ijk}}, \tag{4}$$

in which

$$x_{ijk} = \exp\left[a_{jk}\left(\theta_i - b_{jk}\right)\right], \quad \text{for } k = 1, \ldots, K_j. \tag{5}$$

Here a_{jk} is the (positive) option discrimination parameter and b_{jk} is the option difficulty parameter of the kth option for the jth item. Let $r_{ijk} = 1$ if test taker i selects option k for item j, and $r_{ijk} = 0$ otherwise. To facilitate readability, we discuss a model for MC items in which the first Q_j options are correct, and the remaining (K_j - Q_j) are incorrect. If, for example, $Q_j = 2$, the probability of $r_{ijk} = 1$ for the two correct options is

$$\Pr\left(r_{ijk} = 1 \,|\, \theta_i\right) = P_{jk}(\theta_i) \quad \text{for } k = 1, 2.$$

and the probability of $r_{ijk} = 1$ for the incorrect options is

$$\Pr\left(r_{ijk} = 1 \,|\, \theta_i\right) = 1 - P_{jk}(\theta_i) \quad \text{for } k = 3, \cdots, K_j.$$

Test takers (TTs). There is a population of TTs who differ in their abilities (θ_i).

The test. The test is a collection of n MC items, and there are a total of $\sum_{j=1}^{n} K_j$ pairs of option parameters (a_{jk}, b_{jk}), where a_{jk} is the option discrimination and b_{jk} is the option difficulty parameter of the kth option for the jth item.

If there are no restrictions on the number of options that may be selected and TTs don't know the number of correct options within an item, we assume conditional independence among the responses to the options of each item. So the probability of a response pattern is the product of probabilities of the corresponding option responses. Thus the likelihood of a response pattern for item j for a given TT is, simply, the product of the probability of the responses for the 2 correct options and the $(K_j - 2)$ incorrect options:

$$p\left(r_{ij1},\cdots,r_{ijK_j}\left|\theta_i\right.\right)$$
$$=\prod_{k=1}^{2}\left[P_{jk}\left(\theta_i\right)\right]^{r_{ijk}}\left[1-P_{jk}\left(\theta_i\right)\right]^{1-r_{ijk}}\prod_{k=3}^{K_j}\left[P_{jk}\left(\theta_i\right)\right]^{1-r_{ijk}}\left[1-P_{jk}\left(\theta_i\right)\right]^{r_{ijk}} \tag{6}$$

Following the same logic, if a test taker is told there are two correct options and is required to select *exactly two options* for an item, so $\sum_{k=1}^{K_j} r_{ijk} = 2$, the conditional probability of any permissible response pattern is the unconditional probability of the response pattern divided by the sum of all permissible response patterns:

$$p\left(r_{ij1},\cdots,r_{ijK_j}\left|\theta_i,\Sigma r_{ijk}=2\right.\right)=\frac{p\left(r_{ij1},\cdots,r_{ijK_j}\left|\theta_i\right.\right)}{\sum_{\Sigma r_{ijk}=2}p\left(r_{ij1},\cdots,r_{ijK_j}\left|\theta_i\right.\right)}. \tag{7}$$

Note that, with any such restriction on the permissible response patterns, the option responses are no longer independent in the model. The unconditional likelihood of a response pattern for item j for a given TT can be written as:

$$p\left(r_{ij1},\cdots,r_{ijK_j}\left|\theta_i\right.\right)=\frac{\prod_{k=1}^{2}\left(x_{ijk}^{r_{ijk}}\right)\prod_{k=3}^{K_j}\left(x_{ijk}^{1-r_{ijk}}\right)}{\prod_{k=1}^{K_j}\left(1+x_{ijk}\right)} \tag{8}$$

Similarly, the probability of a response pattern, divided by the sum of the probabilities for all the permissible response patterns, that is the likelihood of a response pattern when TTs are instructed to choose exactly two options, can be written as:

$$p\left(r_{ij1},\cdots,r_{ijK_j}\left|\theta_i,\Sigma r_{ijk}=2\right.\right)=\frac{\prod_{k=1}^{2}\left(x_{ijk}^{r_{ijk}}\right)\prod_{k=3}^{K_j}\left(x_{ijk}^{1-r_{ijk}}\right)}{\sum_{\Sigma r_{ijk}=2}\left[\prod_{k=1}^{2}\left(x_{ijk}^{r_{ijk}}\right)\prod_{k=3}^{K_j}\left(x_{ijk}^{1-r_{ijk}}\right)\right]}. \tag{9}$$

4.4 A General Version of the Model

The option-based partial credit model is very general and flexible and can be applied to different test settings and it can be tailored to different item types and levels of information (as conveyed through instructions) about the structure of the item. Table 4.2 gives a partial list of different item types and instructions to which the model can be adapted.[4]

Table 4.2 Examples of different item types and instructions

	Number of correct options	Number of options that a TT is told to choose
Case 1	1	1
Case 2	2	No restriction (all that apply)
Case 3	3	3
Case 4	2	≤2
Case 5	1	≤3

4.5 Relationship with 2PL IRT Model

It is easy to re-express the 2PL IRT model as a special case of the option-based partial credit model. In this case all the items have only one correct option, and the sufficient statistic of the 2PL IRT model is the weighted number correct score. Thus, the information from the distracters does not contribute to the estimation of the TTs' ability. To make the option-based partial credit model imitate the 2PL model, the first option should be coded as correct with the other (K - 1) options coded as incorrect, and their option discrimination parameters set to 0. To be more specific, Eq. (5) can be rewritten as $x_{ij1} = \exp[a_{j1}(\theta_i - b_{j1})]$ and $a_{jk} = 0$ so $x_{ijk} = 1$ for $k = 2, \ldots, K$. Then the model probability for the "correct" response pattern (1,0,…,0) can be written as

$$p\left(1,0,\ldots,0\middle|\theta_i,\sum r_{ijk}=1\right)=\frac{x_{ij1}}{x_{ij1}+(K-1)}=\frac{\exp\left[a_{j1}\left(\theta_i-b_{j1}\right)-\ln\left(\mathrm{K}-1\right)\right]}{\exp\left[a_{j1}\left(\theta_i-b_{j1}\right)-\ln\left(\mathrm{K}-1\right)\right]+1}$$
$$=\frac{\exp\left[a_j\left(\theta_i-b_j\right)\right]}{\exp\left[a_j\left(\theta_i-b_j\right)\right]+1} \tag{10}$$

[4]Please note that the model is by no means restricted only to the scoring rules listed in the table.

in which $b_j = b_{j1} + \frac{\ln(K-1)}{a_{j1}}$ is the adjusted item difficulty parameter, and $a_j = a_{j1}$ is the item discrimination parameter.

4.6 Relationship with Bock's Nominal Model

Bock's nominal response model is another special case. Bock's nominal IRT model gives the probability of choosing option h, for $h = 1,.., K$, given θ, as

$$p\left(h\middle|\theta\right) = \frac{\exp\left(z_h\right)}{\sum_{k=1}^{K} \exp\left(z_k\right)}, \tag{11}$$

in which $z_k = a_k(\theta - b_k)$. If we define $x_k = \exp(z_k)$, Bock's model can be rewritten as

$$p\left(h\middle|\theta\right) = \frac{x_h}{\sum_{k=1}^{K} x_k}. \tag{12}$$

In our model, we consider a more general response format than Bock's, namely that more than one option may be chosen. For this purpose, we use a vector $\boldsymbol{r}$, of zeros and ones, with $r_h = 1$ indicating that option h has been chosen and $r_h = 0$ indicating that it has not been chosen. Using this notation, we may rewrite Bock's model once again as

$$p\left(r\middle|\theta, \sum r_k = 1\right) = \frac{\prod_{k=1}^{K} x_k^{r_k}}{\sum_{k=1}^{K} x_k}, \tag{13}$$

with the condition $\sum r_k = 1$ used to indicate that only one option is chosen in Bock's model. Now consider the version of our model where there is only one correct option (the first) and the TT must choose exactly one option:

$$p(\mathbf{r}|\theta, \Sigma r_k = 1) = \frac{x_1^{r_1} \prod_{k=2}^{K} x_k^{1-r_k}}{\sum_{\Sigma r_k = 1} \left[x_1^{r_1} \prod_{k=2}^{K} x_k^{1-r_k} \right]}. \tag{14}$$

Divide the numerator and denominator of this expression by $\prod_{k=2}^{K} x_k$:

$$p(\mathbf{r}|\theta, \Sigma r_k = 1) = \frac{x_1^{r_1} \prod_{k=2}^{K} x_k^{-r_k}}{\sum_{\Sigma r_k = 1} \left[x_1^{r_1} \prod_{k=2}^{K} x_k^{-r_k} \right]}. \tag{15}$$

Next, rewrite the denominator of this expression as

$$\sum_{\Sigma r_k=1}\left[x_1^{r_1}\prod_{k=2}^{K}x_k^{-r_k}\right]=x_1+\sum_{k=2}^{K}x_k^{-1}, \tag{16}$$

so the response probability becomes

$$p\left(\mathbf{r}\,|\,\theta,\Sigma r_k=1\right)=\frac{x_1^{r_1}\prod_{k=2}^{K}x_k^{-r_k}}{x_1+\sum_{k=2}^{K}x_k^{-1}}. \tag{17}$$

If we define $y_1=x_1$ and $y_k=x_k^{-1}$ for $k=2,\cdots,K$, we may rewrite Eq. (17) as

$$p\left(\mathbf{r}\,|\,\theta,\Sigma r_k=1\right)=\frac{\prod_{k=1}^{K}y_k^{r_k}}{\sum_{k=1}^{K}y_k}, \tag{18}$$

in which, for $k=2,\cdots,K$, we have $y_k=x_k^{-1}=\{\exp[a_k(\theta-b_k)]\}^{-1}=\exp[-a_k(\theta-b_k)]$. This has the same form as Bock's nominal model.

For identifiability, Bock's model requires a linear constraint for the discrimination parameters (for instance, that they sum to zero), as well as one for the intercept parameters. Thus, using Bock's framework, and setting the first discrimination parameter to be positive implies that the discrimination parameters for options 2 through K are all negative!

4.7 Sufficient Statistics

In Eq. (9), we use $x_{ijk}=exp[\alpha_{jk}(\theta_i-b_{jk})]$, for $k=1,\ \ldots,\ K_j$ to replace x_{ijk} in the numerator. The numerator can be rewritten as

$$\prod_{k=1}^{2}\left(x_{ijk}^{r_{ijk}}\right)\prod_{k=3}^{K_j}\left(x_{ijk}^{1-r_{ijk}}\right)=exp\left\{\theta_i\left[\sum_{k=1}^{2}r_{ijk}a_{jk}+\sum_{k=3}^{K_j}\left(1-r_{ijk}\right)a_{jk}\right]\right.$$
$$\left.-\left[\sum_{k=1}^{2}r_{ijk}a_{jk}b_{jk}+\sum_{k=3}^{K_j}\left(1-r_{ijk}\right)a_{jk}b_{jk}\right]\right\} \tag{19}$$

The option responses are related to θ_i only through the weighted sum:

$$\sum_{k=1}^{2} r_{ijk}a_{jk} + \sum_{k=3}^{K_j} \left(1 - r_{ijk}\right) a_{jk}.$$

In other words, this weighted sum—which is the weighted Hamming distance score—is a sufficient statistic for estimating θ_i:

$$\sum\nolimits_{k=1}^{2} r_{ijk}a_{jk} + \sum_{k=3}^{K_j} \left(1 - r_{ijk}\right) a_{jk} = \sum_{k=1}^{K_j} a_{jk} - \sum_{k=1}^{2} a_{jk} \left(1 - r_{ijk}\right) - \sum_{k=3}^{K_j} r_{ijk}a_{jk}.$$

Note that the right-hand side of the equation matches the definition of the weighted Hamming distance score (Eq. (2)) by replacing the actual key response vector ρ_j, in which the first two options are correct, and using the option discrimination parameters as the weights.

4.8 Item Information Statistics

To simplify notation, in addition to dropping subscripts for items and TTs, consider using negative discrimination parameters for the response functions corresponding to incorrect options. Formally, for an incorrect option, k, and positive discrimination parameter, a_k, we may write the probability of $r_k = 1$ for option k is as follows:

$$Pr\left(r_k = 1 \middle| \theta\right) = 1 - \frac{exp\left[a_k\left(\theta - b_k\right)\right]}{1 + exp\left[a_k\left(\theta - b_k\right)\right]} = \frac{1}{1 + exp\left[a_k\left(\theta - b_k\right)\right]} \\ - \frac{exp\left[-a_k\left(\theta - b_k\right)\right]}{1 + exp\left[-a_k\left(\theta - b_k\right)\right]}. \quad (20)$$

Thus the unconditional probability of a response pattern can be written as:

$$p\left(r_1, \ldots, r_K \middle| \theta\right) = \frac{\prod_{k=1}^{K} x_k^{r_k}}{\prod_{k=1}^{K}\left(1 + x_k\right)}, \quad (21)$$

in which $x_k = \exp[a_k(\theta - b_k)]$, and the discrimination parameters for incorrect options are negative. Equation (21) applies regardless of the number, or location, of the correct options.

Now let R denote the set of all permissible response vectors $\boldsymbol{r}' = (r_1, \ldots, r_K)$. For instance, R might refer to the set of all those response vectors for which $\sum_{k=1}^{K} r_k = 2$. Then using Eq. (21), the model can be written as:

$$p\left(r \middle| \theta, r \in R\right) = \frac{\prod_{k=1}^{K} x_k^{r_k}}{\sum_{r \in R}\left(\prod_{k=1}^{K} x_k^{r_k}\right)}. \tag{22}$$

The derivative of the log likelihood for an item with respect to the ability θ is

$$\frac{\partial}{\partial\theta}\left\{log\left[p\left(r \middle| \theta, r \in R\right)\right]\right\} = \sum_{k=1}^{K} r_k a_k - \left[\sum_{r \in R}\left(\prod_{k=1}^{K} x_k^{r_k}\right)\right]^{-1} \sum_{r \in R}\left\{\prod_{k=1}^{K} x_k^{r_k}\left[\sum_{h=1}^{K}\left(r_h a_h\right)\right]\right\}. \tag{23}$$

(The detailed derivation can be found in Appendix 1.) After substituting the expressions (22) and (23) into the expression (24),

$$I(\theta) = \sum_{r \in R}\left[p\left(r \middle| \theta, r \in R\right)\left(\frac{\partial}{\partial\theta}\left\{\log\left[p\left(r \middle| \theta, r \in R\right)\right]\right\}\right)^2\right], \tag{24}$$

we can obtain the Fisher information function for an item following the model.

4.9 Response Pattern Curves and Option Response Curves

To illustrate the model we explore the response pattern curves, option response curves, and marginal response curves for a single, hypothetical, item with $K = 5$ options (A, B, C, D, E). The first $Q = 2$ options, A and B, are correct and the TTs are explicitly instructed to only choose $Q = 2$ options. The option parameters for the item are listed in Table 4.3. We consider a synthetic population with 61 groups of TTs with abilities ranging from -3 to 3 in increments of 0.1 (i.e. -3.0, -2.9,..., 2.9, 3.0).

Table 4.3 Option parameters for the item

	Option parameters for item j				
	Option 1	Option 2	Option 3	Option 4	Option 5
Discrimination	2.0	1.5	1.0	0.5	0.3
Difficulty	−0.7	1.2	0.0	−1.0	1.5

Figure 4.1 shows the response pattern curves for the model. The ten curves with different line symbols represent the ten possible response patterns. They can be categorized into three groups. The monotonically increasing curve is the correct response pattern, representing a TT who obtains a score of 5 using the unweighted Hamming distance. The non-monotonic curves represent the response patterns in which a TT chooses only one of the correct options. These are the cases where the TT obtains a score of 3 using (unweighted) Hamming distance scoring. The monotonically decreasing curves represent the response patterns in which a TT

chooses neither of the correct options, and obtains a score of 1 using the unweighted Hamming distance. It is clear from an examination of the curves that there is an ordinal correspondence between ability (θ) and the Hamming distance score. The relationship among the three groups of response patterns (the key response pattern, the response patterns with only one correct option, the response patterns without any correct options) is more pronounced in Fig. 4.2, which plots the marginal response pattern curves and uses the same symbols. Clearly, as the proficiency increases, so does the probability of answering the item correctly.

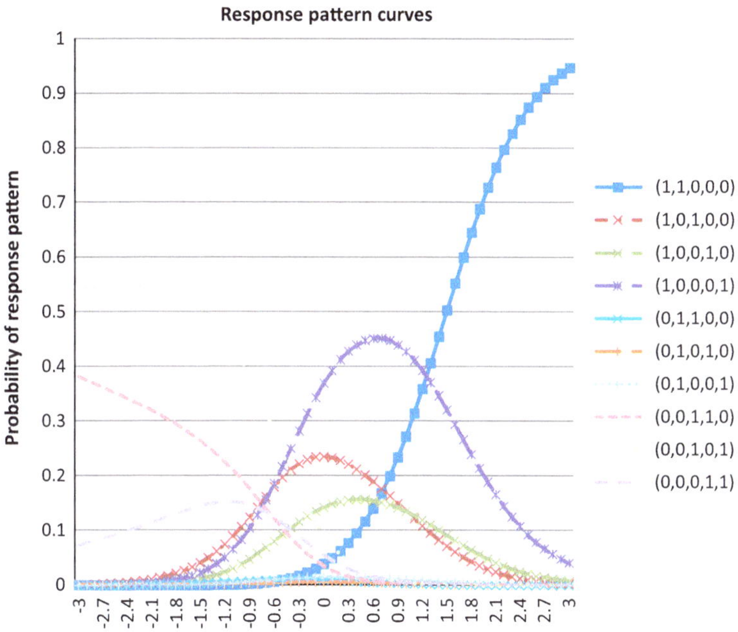

Fig. 4.1 Response pattern curves for the hypothetical item (see parameters in Table 4.3)

Figure 4.3 shows the option response curves for the model. The curves are based on the sum of all the corresponding response patterns. For example, the curve for option A is the sum of the curves for all the response patterns in which option A was selected. The marginal probabilities of selecting the two correct options (option A and option B) increase as the TTs' proficiencies increase. The marginal probabilities of selecting the three incorrect options decrease as the TTs' proficiencies increase.

4.10 Simulation Studies

In the following, we will present two simulation studies to assess the weighted Hamming distance scoring rule and to test the ability of an MCMC algorithm to recover the model's parameters.

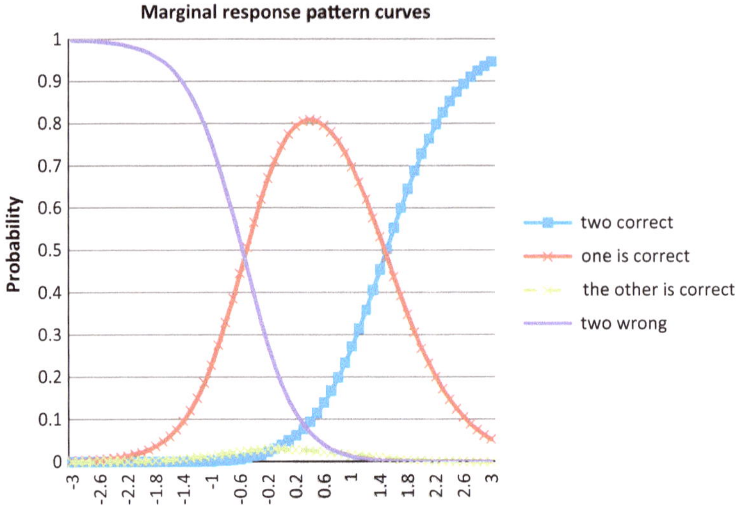

Fig. 4.2 Marginal response pattern curves for the hypothetical item (see parameters in Table 4.3)

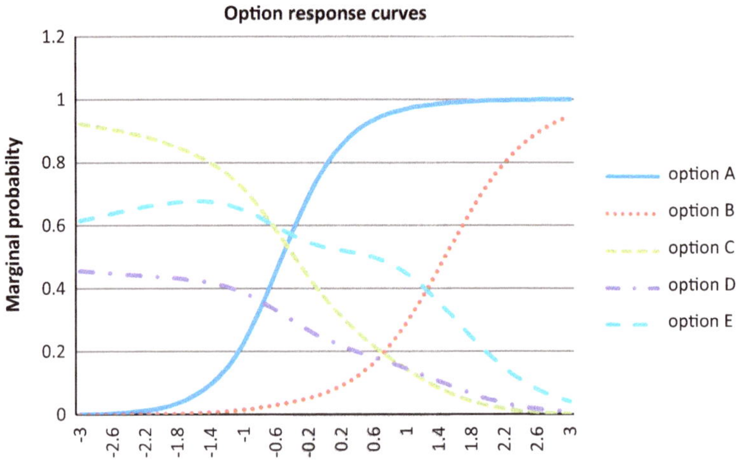

Fig. 4.3 Option response curves for the hypothetical item (see parameters in Table 4.3)

Simulation study 1. We simulated item responses to examine the model's ability to estimate TTs' true abilities, and compare these estimates to alternative scoring rules. A total of $N = 10{,}000$ TTs' proficiencies sampled from a standard normal distribution were used to simulate item responses for three tests of length 10. For all three tests, there are $K = 5$ options per item and the first $Q = 2$ options are correct. The simulated TTs choose exactly two options (there is no ommision). The probabilities of all $N = 10{,}000$ TTs' responses to each option in all items within a test were calculated using the 2PL IRT model with the corresponding option parameters in each of the three tests. Each of the probabilities was compared against a random uniform number between 0 and 1. If the former is greater than the latter, the simulated TT considers the option to be correct; otherwise not. To make the simulated response patterns match the underlying item instruction (choosing only two options), only response patterns that consisted of exactly two endorsements ("1") and three rejections ("0") were included. Response patterns with more, or fewer, than two correct answers were discarded, and the procedure was repeated until the generated response pattern was one of the permissible patterns under the item instruction.

All the items have identical option discrimination and option difficulty parameters in each of the three tests. The different tests represent three different spacings of the option discrimination parameters, a crucial factor in determining the correlations between the scores and the ability. We used four different scoring rules: weighted Hamming distance, simple (equally weighted) Hamming distance, weighted number correct scores, and grouped number correct scores. (Please refer to Table 4.1.)

In the first test, the option difficulty parameters are (1.0, 1.0, 0.0, 0.0, 0.0), and the option discrimination parameters are (1.2, 2.0, 0.3, 0.4, 0.8) for all 10 items. Figure 4.4 is the scatter plot matrix (splom) in which the diagonal cells show five frequency distributions: true ability, weighted Hamming distance, unweighted Hamming distance, weighted number correct, and grouped number correct scores, respectively. The two distributions based on the number correct scores are much more skewed than the two distributions related to Hamming distance scores. The product moment correlations between the four different scores and the true abilities can be found in the first row of the splom. The correlation between the true abilities and the weighted Hamming distance scores is 0.86—higher than for all the other scores. The correlation between the grouped number correct scores (the ones currently employed for the GRE) and the abilities, 0.64, is much lower than the other three correlations.

Table 4.4 summarizes the descriptive statistics—mean, standard deviation (SD), median and skewness—for all the scores. In addition, to measure the deviations of the scores from the true ability parameters, we include Root Mean Squared Difference (RMSD) and the Mean Absolute Difference (MAD) between the standardized scores and the ability parameters. Means and the SDs of the measures are reported in the table. In this case, the weighted Hamming distance scores are superior to the other scores. The advantage over unweighted Hamming distance and weighted number correct scores is trivial (around 0.02), but is more pronounced (more than 0.2) when compared to the grouped number correct scores.

Figure 4.5 gives results for a test in which there are 10 items with identical option parameters: the option discrimination parameters are (1.5, 0.6, 0.9, 0.7, 1.0) and the option difficulty parameters are (1.0, 1.0, 0.0, 0.0, 0.0). The distributions of all four scores are positively skewed, but the weighted number correct scores and the grouped number correct scores are much more skewed than the other two. The corresponding descriptive statistics of the distributions can be found in Table 4.5. The correlation between the weighted Hamming distance scores and the distribution of ability is slightly higher (by 0.01) than the correlations of the simple Hamming

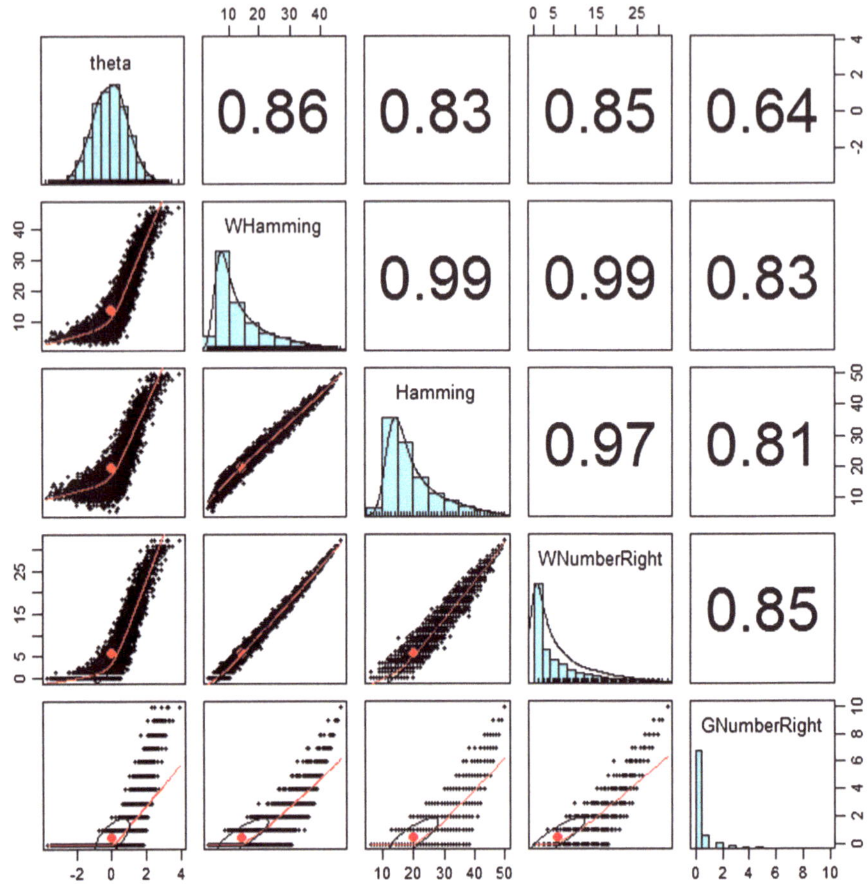

Fig. 4.4 SPLOM of estimates for a test with ten identical items [option difficulty parameters (1,1,0,0,0), and option discrimination parameters (1.2,2,0.3,0.4,0.8)]

distance and the weighted number correct scores. The correlation for the grouped number correct scores is much lower than the other three. The deviation statistics in Table 4.5 show that the weighted Hamming behaves slightly better (by 0.01) than the Hamming and the weighted number correct scores and is much better (by 0.22 in MAD and by 0.29 in RMSD) than the grouped number correct scores.

The splom in Fig. 4.6 represents a test in which there are 10 items with identical option discrimination parameters (0.3, 1.5, 0.6, 0.1, 0.9) and option difficulty parameters (1.0, 1.0, 0.0, 0.0, 0.0). The weighted Hamming distance scores have a higher correlation with the true abilities than do the other three scores. Replicating the results from Figs. 4.4 and 4.5, the grouped number correct scores have the lowest correlation with the actual abilities, and the weighted number correct scores have a higher correlation than the unweighted Hamming distance scores. The descriptive statistics are shown in Table 4.6. The differences between the deviations of the

Table 4.4 Summary statistics of scores for a test with 10 identical items (option difficulty parameters (1.0,1.0,0.0,0.0,0.0), and option discrimination parameter (1.2, 2, 0.3, 0.4, 0.8))

Variable	Statistic Mean	SD	Median	Skew	MAD	SD(AD)	RMSD
True θ	0	1	0	0	–	–	–
Weighted Hamming	13.64	8.87	10.50	0.35	0.43	0.33	0.54
Standardized weighted Hamming	0	1	−0.35				
Simple Hamming	19.80	8.18	17.00	0.34	0.46	0.36	0.58
Standardized simple Hamming	0	1	−0.34				
Weighted NR	5.58	6.63	3.20	0.36	0.44	0.34	0.56
Standardized weighted NR	0	1	−0.36				
Grouped NR	0.54	1.35	0	0.40	0.66	0.53	0.85
Standardized grouped NR	0	1	−0.40				

Note: *Absolute Deviation(AD)* = $|\theta_i - \text{standardized score}_i|$; *Skew* = *(Mean − Median)/SD*

Table 4.5 Summary statistics of scores for a test with ten identical items (option difficulty parameters (1.0,1.0,0.0,0.0,0.0), and option discrimination parameters (1.5,0.6,0.9,0.7,1.0))

Variable	Statistic Mean	SD	Median	Skew	MAD	SD(AD)	RMSD
True θ	0	1	0	0	–	–	–
Weighted Hamming	18.75	7.95	16.60	0.27	0.42	0.33	0.53
Standardized weighted Hamming	0	1	−0.27				
Simple Hamming	21.06	8.01	19.00	0.26	0.43	0.33	0.54
Standardized simple Hamming	0	1	−0.26				
Weighted NR	4.22	4.27	2.70	0.36	0.43	0.33	0.54
Standardized weighted NR	0	1	−0.36				
Grouped NR	0.59	1.25	0	0.47	0.64	0.51	0.82
Standardized grouped NR	0	1	−0.47				

Note: *Absolute Deviation* = $|\theta_i - \text{score}_i|$; *Skew* = *(Mean − Median)/SD*

weighted Hamming and the other scores are more pronounced in this case than in the other two cases. The mean of absolute deviations of the weighted Hamming is at least 0.06 lower than those of the other scores and the RMSD of the weighted Hamming is at least 0.08 lower than those of the other scores.

From the above simulations with tests with varying option discrimination parameters, we conclude that the weighted Hamming distance scores are consistently the most highly correlated with the true abilities and that the group number correct scores consistently have the lowest correlations. The other descriptive statistics presented support this pattern.

Simulation study 2. The purpose of this simulation is to address the issue of recovery of the option-based partial credit model's parameters. We simulated responses of 500 TTs (with proficiencies sampled from a standard normal distribution) to a test of 15 items with identical parameters using the option-based

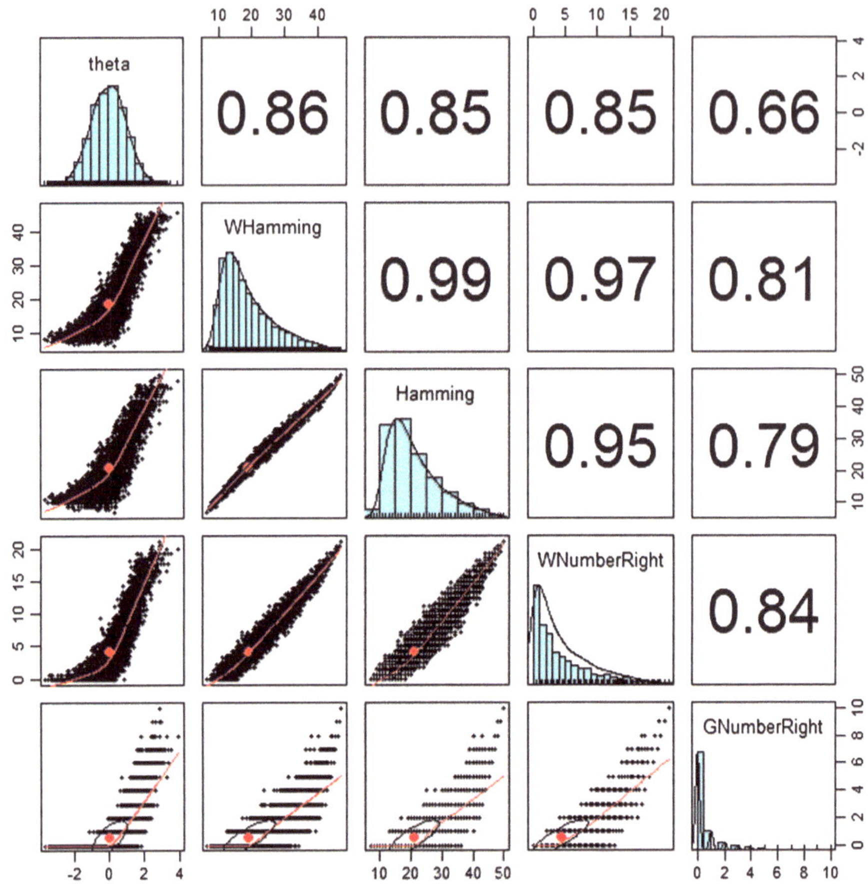

Fig. 4.5 SPLOM of estimates for a test with ten identical items [option difficulty parameters (1.0,1.0,0.0,0.0,0.0), and option discrimination parameters (1.5,0.6,0.9,0.7,1.0)]

partial credit model. There are $K = 5$ options per item and the first $Q = 2$ options are correct. All the option difficulty parameters are set to 0. The option discrimination parameter vector is (0.3, 1.5, 0.6, 0.1, 0.9). The TTs' responses were simulated to choose two options only.

We used a Markov Chain Monte Carlo (MCMC) algorithm to estimate the model parameters. We ran 3 MCMC chains, each with 10,000 iterations. The first 5,000 for each chain were discarded. The priors used for each of the option discrimination parameters and the option difficulty parameters were $N(0,5)$. All the code[5] was written in R (R Core Development Team 2013) and used WinBugs (Lunn et al.

[5]Interested readers may email Yuanchao Emily Bo (ybo@fordham.edu) for the R and WinBugs code.

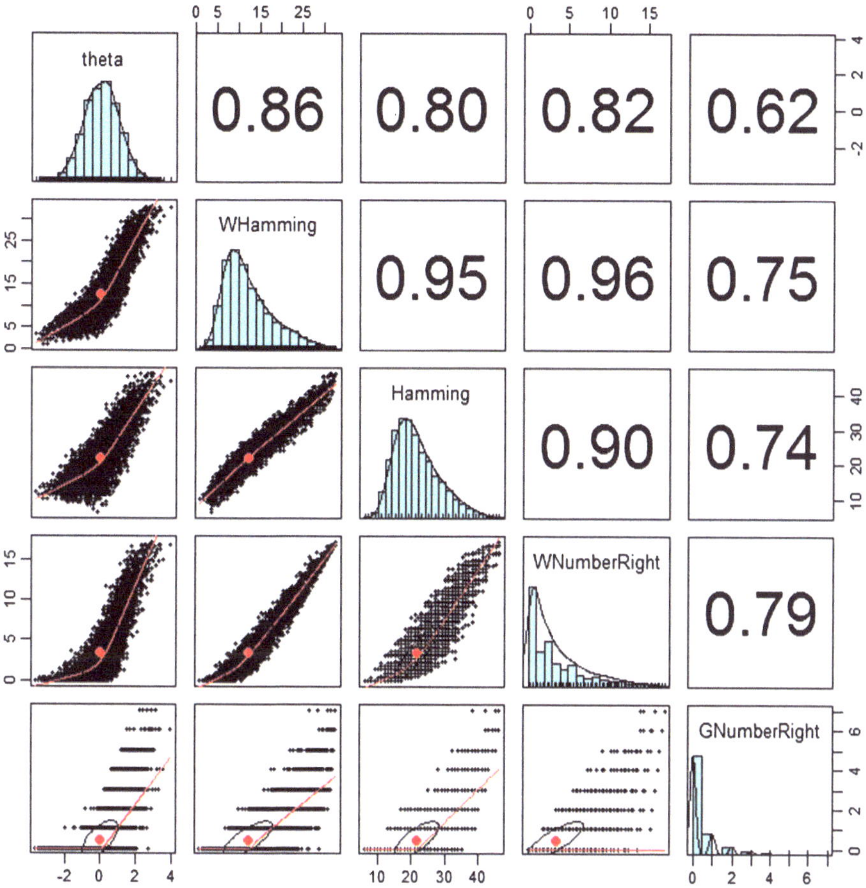

Fig. 4.6 SPLOM of estimates for a test with ten identical items [option difficulty parameters (1.0,1.0,0.0,0.0,0.0), and option discrimination parameters (0.3,1.5,0.6,0.1,0.9)]

2000). Table 4.7 shows the results for the recovery of the option discrimination parameters. The standard deviations of the posterior means for the parameters vary across items from 0.04 for option D to 0.20 for option B. The discrepancies ("bias") between the mean of the posterior means and the parameter values vary across items between 0.03 for options A and C, and 0.13 for option E. The (RMSD) across items for the posterior means are within the range of 0.09–0.20. The overall RMSD for the estimated option discrimination parameters is 0.15. The range of the posterior standard deviations is from 0.1 to 0.3.

Table 4.8 shows the results for the option difficulty parameters. The true values are all 0 and the mean of the posterior means across items and options is 0.03. The standard deviation across items and options of the posterior means is 0.28.

Table 4.6 Summary statistics of scores for a test with 10 identical items [option difficulty parameters (1.0,1.0,0.0,0.0,0.0), and option discrimination parameters (0.3,1.5,0.6,0.1,0.9)]

	Statistic						
Variable	Mean	SD	Median	Skew	MAD	SD(AD)	RMSD
True θ	0	1	0	0	–	–	–
Weighted Hamming	12.45	5.91	11.00	0.25	0.42	0.32	0.52
Standardized weighted Hamming	0	1	−0.25				
Simple Hamming	21.64	6.66	20.00	0.25	0.50	0.38	0.63
Standardized simple Hamming	0	1	−0.25				
Weighted NR	3.45	3.52	2.10	0.38	0.48	0.36	0.60
Standardized weighted NR	0	1	−0.38				
Grouped NR	0.45	0.93	0	0.49	0.68	0.54	0.87
Standardized grouped NR	0	1	−0.49				

Note: Absolute Deviation = $|\theta_i - \text{score}_i|$; Skew = (Mean − Median)/SD

The bias across options and items for the posterior means is 0.03. The overall RMSD across options and items for the posterior means of the option difficulty parameters is 0.28.

We also used the MCMC algorithm to estimate the ability parameters of the 500 TTs, the true values having been sampled from a $N(0,1)$ distribution. The mean across test takers of the posterior mean ability parameters is -0.005, and the standard deviation is 0.94. The overall RMSD for the posterior means of the ability parameters is 0.31.

4.11 Discussion

The first stimulation study confirms the superiority of the weighted Hamming distance over grouped number correct scores in estimating TTs' abilities when the proposed model is used to generate the item responses. The weighted Hamming distance scoring improves estimation of TTs' abilities by assigning partial credit and extracting information from distracters. The second simulation study demonstrates that one can implement a parameter estimation procedure for the proposed model using WinBugs and R. In this example the MCMC algorithm provides satisfactory estimates of the model parameters when the model is used to generate the item responses.

The weighted Hamming distance scoring can be considered as a combination of elimination scoring (Coombs et al. 1956) and the subset selection method (Dressel and Schmidt 1953). Each of these rules is asymmetric and focuses its attention on the potentially correct or incorrect options. The new method highlights both aspects and TTs have the opportunity to express their partial knowledge by either eliminating a subset of the options or endorsing some of them. A potential problem of the scoring rule is that full misinformation cannot always be identified when a TT chooses to respond. Take an example of an item for which TTs are instructed to

Table 4.7 Option discrimination parameter posterior means obtained by MCMC

est_alpha	Option A	Option B	Option C	Option D	Option E
Item 1	0.2	1.6	0.7	0.1	1.3
Item 2	0.2	1.6	0.7	0.2	1.1
Item 3	0.3	1.6	0.7	0.2	1.0
Item 4	0.2	1.5	0.6	0.2	1.1
Item 5	0.2	1.4	0.5	0.2	1.2
Item 6	0.4	1.3	0.6	0.3	0.9
Item 7	0.3	1.6	0.6	0.2	1.1
Item 8	0.3	1.7	0.6	0.2	0.8
Item 9	0.4	1.3	0.3	0.2	0.8
Item 10	0.1	0.9	0.8	0.1	1.2
Item 11	0.3	1.6	0.5	0.2	0.9
Item 12	0.3	1.5	0.8	0.2	1.1
Item 13	0.2	1.5	0.6	0.2	1.0
Item 14	0.3	1.6	0.7	0.2	1.0
Item 15	0.3	1.2	0.8	0.2	1.0
Mean	0.27	1.46	0.63	0.19	1.03
Std Dev	0.08	0.20	0.13	0.04	0.14
True value	0.30	1.50	0.60	0.10	0.90
Bias	−0.03	−0.04	0.03	0.09	0.13
RMSE	0.09	0.20	0.13	0.10	0.19

Note: The output results from WinBugs and R are rounded by default to the first decimal place

choose only 2 out of 5 options. In all 10 possible response patterns TTs gain credit for correct endorsement(s). The problem could be solved by allowing omission and assuming full misinformation when a TT chooses to omit. Another solution is to specify the scoring rule in a way that the sum of the possible number of choices that a TT can choose is the total number of options in the item. For example, in a 3-option MC item, TTs are instructed to choose 1 or 2 options; in a 5-option item, TTs are instructed to choose 2 or 3 options.

The item information function of the model is the variance of the weighted Hamming distance (see proof in Appendix 2). Optimal test design seeks items that minimize the sampling variance of the (ML) estimates of the ability parameters by maximizing the test information. So items with the largest conditional variance at the target ability of their "scores" (as defined by the weighted Hamming distance) should be chosen to construct the test. In other words, the ideal items are those with the largest standard error of measurement for the item score. This is a "paradox" for the model that also occurs with the Rasch model (Andrich 1988).

The option-based partial credit model and its underlying scoring mechanism-weighted Hamming distance scores are the very first attempt in the Psychometric

Table 4.8 Option difficulty parameter posterior means obtained by MCMC

est_beta	Option A	Option B	Option C	Option D	Option E	Mean
Item 1	−0.6	0.0	0.1	0.0	0.1	−0.08
Item 2	−0.4	−0.1	−0.2	0.6	0.1	0.00
Item 3	0.6	0.1	−0.2	−0.3	0.0	0.04
Item 4	−0.3	0.1	0.2	0.1	0.2	0.06
Item 5	0.0	0.1	0.1	0.5	0.1	0.16
Item 6	−0.3	0.0	0.2	0.4	0.0	0.06
Item 7	−0.5	0.1	0.3	−0.5	0.0	−0.12
Item 8	−0.1	0.1	0.1	0.1	0.1	0.06
Item 9	0.0	−0.1	0.2	0.0	0.2	0.06
Item 10	−0.1	0.2	0.0	−0.1	−0.1	−0.02
Item 11	−0.2	0.2	0.0	0.2	−0.2	0.00
Item 12	0.3	0.0	−0.1	−0.1	−0.2	−0.02
Item 13	0.3	0.1	0.0	−0.2	−0.1	0.02
Item 14	1.0	0.2	−0.3	−0.1	0.0	0.16
Item 15	1.0	0.1	−0.3	−0.2	−0.2	0.08
Mean	0.05	0.07	0.01	0.03	0.00	0.03
Std Dev	0.48	0.09	0.18	0.29	0.13	0.28
True value	0.00	0.00	0.00	0.00	0.00	0.00
Bias	0.05	0.07	0.01	0.03	0.00	0.03
RMSE	0.50	0.12	0.19	0.30	0.14	0.28

Note: The output results from WinBugs and R are rounded by default to the first decimal place

literature to provide both a feasible and simple scoring procedure for multiple selection MC items and partial credit to TTs by using the information in the distracters. The results from the simulation studies confirm the unique contribution of the weighted Hamming distance scores in manifesting TTs' latent traits and the feasibility of using the MCMC algorithm to recover the model parameters.

Appendix 1

We can use the following form to derive the Fisher information for an item

$$I(\theta) = E\left[\left(\frac{\partial}{\partial\theta}\log p(X;\theta)\right)^2 \middle| \theta\right].$$

The logarithm of the likelihood for the model given in Eq. (22) is

$$log\left[p\left(r\middle|\theta,r\in R\right)\right]=\sum_{k=1}^{K}r_k log(x_k)-log\left[\sum_{r\in R}\left(\prod_{k=1}^{K}x_k^{r_k}\right)\right].$$

Note that

$$\frac{\partial}{\partial\theta}\log\left(x_k\right)=a_k,\ \frac{\partial x_k^{r_k}}{\partial\theta}=r_k a_k x_k^{r_k}.$$

So

$$\frac{\partial}{\partial\theta}\left\{log\left[p\left(r\middle|\theta,r\in R\right)\right]\right\}=\sum_{k=1}^{K}r_k a_k-\left[\sum_{r\in R}\left(\prod_{k=1}^{K}x_k^{r_k}\right)\right]^{-1}\sum_{r\in R}\left[\frac{\partial}{\partial\theta}\left(\prod_{k=1}^{K}x_k^{r_k}\right)\right].$$

The derivative in the last term may be simplified as follows:

$$\frac{\partial}{\partial\theta}\left(\prod_{k=1}^{K}x_k^{r_k}\right)=\sum_{h=1}^{K}\left[\left(\frac{\partial x_h^{r_h}}{\partial\theta}\right)\prod_{k\neq h}^{K}x_k^{r_k}\right]=\sum_{h=1}^{K}\left[\left(r_h a_h x_h^{r_h}\right)\prod_{k\neq h}^{K}x_k^{r_k}\right]=\prod_{k=1}^{K}x_k^{r_k}\left[\sum_{h=1}^{K}\left(r_h a_h\right)\right].$$

Thus, we may write the derivative of the log likelihood for an item as

$$\begin{aligned}&\frac{\partial}{\partial\theta}\left\{log\left[p\left(r\middle|\theta,r\in R\right)\right]\right\}\\&=\sum_{k=1}^{K}r_k a_k-\left[\sum_{r\in R}\left(\prod_{k=1}^{K}x_k^{r_k}\right)\right]^{-1}\sum_{r\in R}\left\{\prod_{k=1}^{K}x_k^{r_k}\left[\sum_{h=1}^{K}\left(r_h a_h\right)\right]\right\}.\end{aligned}$$

Appendix 2

Start with the expression for the derivative of the log likelihood,

$$\begin{aligned}&\frac{\partial}{\partial\theta}\left\{log\left[p\left(r\middle|\theta,r\in R\right)\right]\right\}\\&=\sum_{k=1}^{K}r_k a_k-\left[\sum_{r\in R}\left(\prod_{k=1}^{K}x_k^{r_k}\right)\right]^{-1}\sum_{r\in R}\left\{\prod_{k=1}^{K}x_k^{r_k}\left[\sum_{h=1}^{K}\left(r_h a_h\right)\right]\right\}\end{aligned}$$

and notice that the second term is actually the expected value of the quantity $\sum_{h=1}^{K}(r_h a_h)$. Specially, if we define

$$s(r) = \sum_{h=1}^{K}(r_h a_h),$$

we may write

$$E\left[s(r)\middle|\theta,\ r\in R\right]$$
$$=\sum_{r\in R}\left[p\left(r\middle|\theta, r\in R\right)s(r)\right]=\sum_{r\in R}\left\{\left[\frac{\prod_{k=1}^{K}x_k^{r_k}}{\sum_{r\in R}\left(\prod_{k=1}^{K}x_k^{r_k}\right)}\right]\left[\sum_{h=1}^{K}(r_h a_h)\right]\right\}.$$

This allows us to rewrite the derivative of the log likelihood as

$$\frac{\partial}{\partial\theta}\left\{log\left[p\left(r\middle|\theta, r\in R\right)\right]\right\}=\sum_{k=1}^{K}r_k a_k - E\left[s(r)\middle|\theta,\ r\in R\right]$$
$$=s(r)-E\left[s(r)\middle|\theta,\ r\in R\right].$$

The item information function then becomes

$$I(\theta)=\sum_{r\in R}\left[p\left(r\middle|\theta, r\in R\right)\left(\frac{\partial}{\partial\theta}\left\{\log\left[p\left(r\middle|\theta, r\in R\right)\right]\right\}\right)^2\right]$$
$$=\sum_{r\in R}\left[p\left(r\middle|\theta, r\in R\right)\left(s(r)-E\left[s(r)\middle|\theta,\ r\in R\right]\right)^2\right].$$

Since the right-hand side of this expression is the conditional variance of $s(\boldsymbol{r})$, we may write

$$I(\theta)=var\left[s(r)\middle|\theta, r\in R\right].$$

References

Andersen EB (1977) Sufficient statistics and latent trait models. Psychometrika 42:69–81
Andrich D (1988) Rasch models for measurement. Sage Publications, Beverly Hills
Bechger TM, Maris G, Verstralen HHFM, Verhelst ND (2005) The Nedelsky model for multiple choice items. In: van der Ark LA, Croon MA, Sijtsma K (eds) New developments in categorical data analysis for the social and behavioral sciences. Erlbaum, Mahwah, pp 187–206

Ben-Simon A, Budescu DV, Nevo B (1997) A comparative study of measures of partial knowledge in multiple-choice tests. Appl Psychol Meas 21:65–88

Bereby-Meyer Y, Meyer J, Budescu DV (2003) Decision making under internal uncertainty: the case of multiple-choice tests with different scoring rules. Acta Psychol 112:207–220

Birnbaum A (1968) Some latent trait models and their use in inferring an examinee's ability. In: Lord FM, Novick MR (eds) Statistical theories of mental test scores. Addison-Wesley, Reading

Bock RD (1972) Estimating item parameters and latent ability when responses are scored in two or more nominal categories. Psychometrika 37:29–51

Budescu DV, Bar-Hillel M (1993) To guess or not to guess: a decision theoretic view of formula scoring. J Educ Meas 30:227–291

Budescu DV, Bo Y (in press) Analyzing test-taking behavior: decision theory meets psychometric theory. Psychometrika

Coombs CH, Milholland JE, Womer FB (1956) The assessment of partial knowledge. Educ Psychol Meas 16:13–37

R Development Core Team (2013) R: a language and environment for statistical computing [computer software]. R Foundation for Statistical Computing, Vienna. Retrieved from http://www.R-project.org/

Dressel PL, Schmidt J (1953) Some modifications of the multiple choice item. Educ Psychol Meas 13:574–595

Echternacht GJ (1976) Reliability and validity of option weighting schemes. Educ Psychol Meas 36:301–309

Frary RB (1989) Partial-credit scoring methods for multiple-choice tests. Appl Meas Educ 2:79–96

Gibbons JD, Olkin I, Sobel M (1977) Selecting and ordering populations: a new statistical methodology. Wiley, New York

Gulliksen H (1950) Theory of mental tests. Wiley, New York

Haladyna TM (1988) Empirically based polychromous scoring of multiple choice test items: A review. Paper presented at the annual meeting of the American Educational Research Association, New Orleans

Hambleton RK, Roberts DM, Traub RE (1970) A comparison of the reliability and validity of two methods for assessing partial knowledge on a multiple-choice test. J Educ Meas 7:75–82

Hamming RW (1950) Error detecting and error correcting codes. Bell Syst Tech J 29:147–160

Hansen R (1971) The influence of variables other than knowledge on probabilistic tests. J Educ Meas 8:9–14

Holzinger KJ (1924) On scoring multiple response tests. J Educ Psychol 15:445–447

Hutchinson TP (1982) Some theories of performance in multiple-choice tests, and their implications for variants of the task. Br J Math Stat Psychol 35:71–89

Jacobs SS (1971) Correlates of unwarranted confidence in responses to objective test items. J Educ Meas 8:15–19

Jaradat D, Tollefson N (1988) The impact of alternative scoring procedures for multiple-choice items on test reliability, validity and grading. Educ Psychol Meas 48:627–635

Kahneman D, Tversky A (1979) Prospect theory: an analysis of decisions under risk. Econometrica 47:313–327

Lunn DJ, Thomas A, Best N, Spiegelhalter D (2000) WinBUGS – a Bayesian modeling framework: concepts, structure, and extensibility. Stat Comput 10:325–337

Masters GN (1982) A Rasch model for partial credit scoring. Psychometrika 47:149–174

Michael JC (1968) The reliability of a multiple choice examination under various test-taking instructions. J Educ Meas 5:307–314

Muraki E (1992) A generalized partial credit model: application of an EM algorithm. Appl Psychol Meas 16:159–176

Pugh RC, Brunza JJ (1975) Effects of a confidence weighted scoring system on measures of test reliability and validity. Educ Psychol Meas 35:73–78

Rippey RM (1970) A comparison of five different scoring functions for confidence tests. J Educ Meas 7:165–170

Ruch GM, Stoddard GD (1925) Comparative reliabilities of objective examinations. J Educ Psychol 16:89–103

Samejima F (1969) Estimation of ability using a response pattern of graded scores. Psychometrika Monograph, No. 18

Samejima F (1972) A general model for free-response data. Psychometrika Monograph, No, 18.

Samejima F (1979) A new family of models for the multiple choice item (Research Report No. 79-4). University of Tennessee, Department of Psychology, Knoxville

San Martin E, del Pino G, de Boeck P (2006) IRT models for ability-based guessing. Appl Psychol Meas 30:183–203

Smith RM (1987) Assessing partial knowledge in vocabulary. J Educ Meas 24:217–231

Stanley JC, Wang MD (1970) Weighting test items and test item options, an overview of the analytical and empirical literature. Educ Psychol Meas 30:21–35

Swineford F (1938) Measurement of a personality trait. J Educ Psychol 29:295–300

Swineford F (1941) Analysis of a personality trait. J Educ Psychol 32:348–444

Sykes RC, Hou L (2003) Weighting constructed-response items in IRT-based exams. Appl Meas Educ 16:257–275

Thissen D, Steinberg L (1984) A response model for multiple choice items. Psychometrika 49:501–519

Thurstone LL (1919) A method for scoring tests. Psychol Bull 16:235–240

Tversky A, Kahneman D (1992) Advances in prospect theory: cumulative representation of uncertainty. J Risk Uncertainty 5:297–323

Wang MW, Stanley JC (1970) Differential weighting: a review of methods and empirical studies. Rev Educ Res 40:663–705

Yaniv I, Schul Y (1997) Elimination and inclusion procedures in judgment. J Behav Decis Mak 10:211–220

Yaniv I, Schul Y (2000) Acceptance and elimination procedure in choice: noncomplementarity and the role of implied status quo. Organ Behav Hum Decis Process 82:293–313

Chapter 5
A General Saltus LLTM-R for Cognitive Assessments

Minjeong Jeon, Karen Draney, and Mark Wilson

Abstract The purpose of this paper is to propose a general saltus LLTM-R for cognitive assessments. The proposed model is an extension of the Rasch model that combines a linear logistic latent trait with an error term (LLTM-R), a multidimensional Rasch model, and the saltus model, a parsimonious, structured mixture Rasch model. The general saltus LLTM-R can be used to (1) estimate parameters that describe test items by substantive theories, (2) evaluate the latent constructs that are associated with the knowledge structures of the test items, and (3) test hypotheses on qualitative differences between the sub-populations of subjects with different problem solving strategies, cognitive processes, or developmental stages. Bayesian estimation of the proposed model is described with an application to a test of deductive reasoning in children.

Keywords Saltus model • Mixture IRT • LLTM • LLTM-R • Multidimensional IRT • Deductive reasoning

5.1 Introduction

In psychometrics, it is an important research topic to identify the response processes, strategies, and knowledge structures that are involved in solving test items (Embretson 1984). Several item response theory (IRT) models have been developed to study theoretical or practical construct representation, task decomposition, and information processing of test items. For example, the linear logistic test model

M. Jeon (✉)
The Ohio State University, 228 Lazenby Hall 1827, Neil Avenue Columbus, Columbus, OH 43210, USA
e-mail: jeon.117@osu.edu

K. Draney
University of California, Berkeley, Tolman Hall, Berkeley, CA 94720, USA
e-mail: kdraney@berkeley.edu

M. Wilson
University of California, Berkeley, 4415 Tolman Hall, Berkeley, CA 94720, USA
e-mail: markw@berkeley.edu

R.E. Millsap et al. (eds.), *Quantitative Psychology Research*, Springer Proceedings in Mathematics & Statistics 89, DOI 10.1007/978-3-319-07503-7_5

(LLTM; Fischer 1973) models task decomposition of test items that underlie the knowledge structure. In multidimensional IRT models, item features are used to form sub-tests that represent different theoretical constructs (e.g., Embretson 1984; Kelderman and Rijkes 1994). Mixture IRT models are developed to investigate qualitatively different sub-populations of subjects with different problem solving strategies, cognitive processes, or developmental stages (e.g., Wilson 1989; Mislevy and Verhelst 1990; Bolt et al. 2001)

The purpose of the study is to present an extension of the Rasch model that includes LLTM, multidimensionality, and mixture components. For the LLTM component, we use an extended version of the LLTM that allows for a random deviation term for items (LLTM-R; Janssen et al. 2004). For multidimensionality, a between-item multidimensional Rasch model is adopted as a special case of the general multidimensional random coefficients multinomial logit model (MRCML; Adams et al. 1997). For the mixture component, we use an extension of the saltus model (Wilson 1989) that is a confirmatory mixture Rasch model (Rost 1990). The elegance of the saltus model is its parsimony and theory-based structure which is well suited for building a complex mathematical model to evaluate an underlying substantive theory.

The following section gives a general description of the proposed model, which is referred to as a general saltus LLTM-R. Estimation of the model is illustrated with an example of children's deductive reasoning. Further uses of the proposed model are discussed at the end.

5.2 Model

This section lays out the basic structures of the proposed model: (1) LLTM, (2) multidimensionality, and (3) mixture components. The final model will be expressed as a combination of these basic building blocks. Discussion will be limited to dichotomous items for convenience, but extensions to polytomous items are straightforward.

5.2.1 *Linear Logistic Test Models*

We begin by briefly describing a regular one parameter logistic (1PL) IRT or Rasch model. For a dichotomous response y_{ij} (1 if correct, 0 if not) to item i ($i = 1,\ldots,I$) for person j ($j = 1,\ldots,N$), the conditional probability for a correct response can be expressed as

$$\Pr(y_{ij} = 1|\theta_j) = \frac{\exp[\theta_j - \beta_i]}{1+\exp[\theta_j - \beta_i]}, \tag{5.1}$$

where θ_j is a latent variable, representing ability, trait, scale, or proficiency for person j. θ_j can be considered as a fixed parameter but is more often viewed as a random variable with a distributional assumption defined over the population of people. For convenience, we specify a normal distribution $\theta_j \sim N(\mu, \sigma^2)$ although other distributions can be considered. To identify the model, we constrain $\mu = 0$. Otherwise, $\sum_i \beta_i = 0$ could be imposed, where β_i represents the position of item i on the latent scale and is usually called the item difficulty parameter for item i.

Suppose a cognitive theory suggests that the effects of items can be decomposed into relevant stimulus features. The item parameter β_i can then be expressed as a linear function of the stimulus features. An important example of this type is the LLTM (Fischer 1973). Under the LLTM, a model for item parameters can be written as

$$\beta_i = \sum_{q=0}^{Q} \beta_q X_{iq}, \tag{5.2}$$

where β_q is the regression coefficient or the effect of the item feature X_{iq} ($q = 1, \ldots, Q$, typically, $Q < I$) on the item difficulty β_i, with β_0 as the intercept. The $I \times (Q+1)$ matrix $\mathbf{X}$ is called an item design matrix, and its vector $\mathbf{X}_i$ indicates the extent to which item i exhibits each item characteristic.

The LLTM is based on the strong assumption that item difficulty is perfectly predicted by the item characteristics. That is, items in the same "item groups" that have the same combination of values on the item properties are assumed to have equal difficulties. We can relax this assumption by allowing for a random deviation of each item, resulting in a random effects LLTM (LLTM-R; Janssen et al. 2004)

$$\Pr(y_{ij} = 1|\theta_j) = \frac{\exp\left[\theta_j - \Sigma_{q=0}^{Q} \beta_q X_{iq} + \varepsilon_i\right]}{1 + \exp\left[\theta_j - \Sigma_{q=0}^{Q} \beta'_q X_{iq} + \varepsilon_i\right]}, \tag{5.3}$$

where $\varepsilon_i \sim N(0, \sigma_\varepsilon^2)$. Here the variance σ_ε^2 can be interpreted as the residual variance of the regression model for β_i or a within-population variance of β_i across items belonging to the same item group (Janssen et al. 2004). By adding the error term ε_i, items in the same "item groups" can be modeled to have unequal difficulties which may arise from item-specific features, such as wording or content of the items (Rijmen and De Boeck 2002).

5.2.2 *Multidimensional Rasch Models*

The Rasch model (5.1) and LLTM-R (5.3) all assume a single underlying latent trait θ_j, implying all items are located on the same scale that the test measures. In practice, however, the trait to be measured may be more complex than what is assumed by the model. For example, a complex performance can be understood by taking into account knowledge structures, cognitive processes, or interactions between multiple component behaviors.

In the LLTM, the item properties have a quantitative effect on the items. On the other hand, the item task properties may lead to sub-tests that require qualitatively different types of problem solving behaviors, locating subjects on different sub-scales on a multidimensional latent space (Kelderman and Rijkes 1994).

Assuming that a test consists of K sub-scales of items, model (5.1) can be extended for dimension k

$$\Pr(y_{i(k)j} = 1|\theta_j) = \frac{\exp\left[\theta_{jk} - \beta_i\right]}{1 + \exp\left[\theta_{jk} - \beta_i\right]}, \tag{5.4}$$

where $y_{i(k)j}$ is the response to item i in dimension k for person j, θ_{jk} is the kth latent trait for person j, and β_i is difficulty for item i. For all K sub-scales, the model can be expressed as

$$\Pr(y_{ij} = 1|\theta_j) = \frac{\exp\left[\sum_{k=1}^{K} r_{ik}\theta_{jk} - \beta_i\right]}{1 + \exp\left[\sum_{k=1}^{K} r_{ik}\theta_{jk} - \beta_i\right]}, \tag{5.5}$$

where θ_j is a K-dimensional vector representing the positions on K continuous latent variables and $\theta_j = (\theta_{j1}, \ldots, \theta_{jK})'$, and r_{ik} is the ith row and kth column element of $I \times K$ score matrix R whose vector $\mathbf{r}_i$ contains only one non-zero element (equal to 1), indicating which sub-scale item i belongs to. θ_j is assumed to have a multivariate normal distribution as $\theta_j \sim N(\mu, \Sigma)$, where μ is a K dimensional vector of means and Σ is a $K \times K$ variance–covariance matrix. As in the Rasch model, we constrain $\mu = \mathbf{0}$ to identify the model. Since each item measures only one dimension, the model is called a between-item multidimensional model (Adams et al. 1997). The advantage of using the multidimensional model (instead of analyzing the K scales separately) is threefold: (1) the multi-component test structure is explicitly taken into account, (2) disattenuated correlations between the dimensions are provided (Briggs and Wilson 2003), and (3) more accurate parameter estimates are obtained by relying on the relationship between the dimensions (Adams et al. 1997; Rijmen and De Boeck 2005). Model (5.5) is a special instance of the multidimensional random coefficients multinomial logit model (MRCML; Adams et al. 1997).

Several IRT models have been developed to combine LLTM and multidimensional models. Fischer and Forman (1982) presented the linear logistic model with relaxed assumptions (LLRA) in the context of measuring change. In LLRA, item task components are associated with different latent traits at different time points. In the general multicomponent latent trait model (GLTM) (Embretson 1984), different cognitive components are associated with different latent traits or sub-scales. Rijmen and De Boeck (2002) presented a random weights linear logistic test model (RW-LLTM), which can be seen as a within-item multidimensional model where item properties have both fixed and random effects. The random slope for the constant represents a general dimension that is measured by all items, and the random slopes for item properties represent dimensions or sub-scales of the test.

5.2.3 *Mixture Rasch Models*

The unidimensional and multidimensional Rasch models (5.1) and (5.5) commonly assume that the sub-scale(s) that a test is measuring is the same for all subjects. However, the group of subjects may consist of qualitatively different sub-groups, because of their different cognitive strategies (e.g., Mislevy and Verhelst 1990), developmental stages (e.g., Wilson 1989), or problem-solving processes (e.g., Bolt et al. 2001). Since their group membership is unobserved, the sub-groups are referred to as latent classes. The resulting model becomes a mixture IRT model.

Suppose there are G qualitatively different sub-groups (latent classes). Within each sub-group, the same item response model is assumed to hold. For example, by assuming a Rasch model within a class, the response model of the mixture Rasch model can be written as

$$\Pr(y_{ij}=1|\theta_j)=\sum_{g=1}^{G}\pi_g \Pr(y_{ij}=1|\theta_{jg},g),$$
$$\Pr(y_{ij}=1|\theta_{jg},g)=\frac{\exp\left[\theta_{jg}-\beta_{ig}\right]}{1+\exp\left[\theta_{jg}-\beta_{ig}\right]}, \tag{5.6}$$

where π_g is the probability of belonging to latent class g ($g=1,\ldots,G$), and θ_{jg} is the ability for person j in latent class g. Within a class, we assume $\theta_{jg}\sim N(\mu_g,\sigma_g^2)$, and β_{ig} is the item difficulty of item i specific to latent class g. This implies that items are located on the same scale within a latent class, but across latent classes, the scale might be qualitatively different. To anchor the metric across latent classes and to identify the model, $\mu_g=0$ or $\sum_i \beta_{ig}=0$ should be imposed within each class g. This restriction is important to ensure scale comparability across latent classes. The metric can be anchored relative to the scale of a reference group by fixing the mean of only one group to zero, e.g., $\mu_1=0$ with the first latent class as the reference group. However, in this case anchor items should be chosen, whose parameters are invariant across classes (Cho et al. 2013).

Mislevy and Verhelst (1990) extended the mixture Rasch model (5.6) by combining with LLTM (5.1). The resulting model becomes a mixture LLTM and can be written as

$$\Pr(y_{ij}=1)=\sum_{g=1}^{G}\pi_g\frac{\exp\left[\theta_{jg}-\Sigma_{q=0}^{Q}\beta_{qg}X_{iq}\right]}{1+\exp\left[\theta_{jg}-\Sigma_{q=0}^{Q}\beta'_{qg}X_{iq}\right]}, \tag{5.7}$$

where π_g is the probability of belonging to latent class g, and the ability θ_{jg} is assumed to follow a normal distribution within class g, $\theta_{jg} \sim N(\mu_g, \sigma_g^2)$, with $\mu_g = 0$ for identification and metric anchoring. q $(= 1, .., Q)$ is an index for item predictors and β_{qg} is the class-specific regression coefficient for each item predictor for class g with β_{0g} is the intercept.

5.2.4 *Saltus Models*

Recall that the mixture Rasch model in (5.6) assumes class-specific item difficulties for different latent classes. Suppose a substantive theory suggests that there are a subset of items whose difficulty systematically increases or decreases from one class to another. Using the item groups that are associated with corresponding latent classes, a parsimonious version of the mixture Rasch model can be formulated, which is the saltus model (Wilson 1989).

In the saltus model, the item parameters are posited to be equal across all latent classes. Instead, the qualitative difference from one class to another is captured by a shift parameter, also called a saltus parameter, which is basically the effect of the item groups (representing latent classes) on the latent scale.

Assuming G qualitatively different latent classes and corresponding H item groups, a saltus response model can then be specified as

$$\Pr(y_{ij} = 1|\theta_j) = \sum_{g=1}^{G} \pi_g \Pr(y_{ij} = 1|\theta_{jg}, g),$$

$$\Pr(y_{ij} = 1|\theta_{jg}, g) = \frac{\exp\left[\theta_j - \beta_i + \sum_{h=1}^{H} \tau_{gh} w_{ih}\right]}{1 + \exp\left[\theta_j - \beta_i + \sum_{h=1}^{H} \tau_{gh} w_{ih}\right]}, \tag{5.8}$$

where τ_{gh} is the shift or saltus parameter that represents the effect of item group h in latent class g. It is important to note that item groups have the same number of levels as person latent classes ($G = H$). τ_{gh} is also the regression coefficient for w_{ih}, whose vector $\mathbf{w}_i$ contains only one non-zero element (equal to 1) and indicates the item group that item i belongs to. As in model (5.6), π_g is a probability of belonging to latent class g ($g = 1, \ldots, G$), and θ_{jg} is the ability for person j in latent class g with $\theta_{jg} \sim N(\mu_g, \sigma_g^2)$. To identify the model, we can have a constraint, either $\sum_i \beta_i = 0$ or $\mu_1 = 0$ ($g = 1$ as the reference group). Note that since all items work as anchor items in the saltus model, it is sufficient to fix the mean of only one latent class to 0. In the mixture Rasch model, arbitrary anchor items should be chosen for setting the metric relative to the reference group.

To illustrate the saltus or shift parameters, suppose two latent classes and three item groups ($G = H = 3$). Matrix T of the shift parameters can then be written as

$$\begin{bmatrix} \tau_{11} & \tau_{12} & \tau_{13} \\ \tau_{21} & \tau_{22} & \tau_{23} \\ \tau_{31} & \tau_{32} & \tau_{33} \end{bmatrix},$$

where τ_{gh} represents the effect of item group h in person class g or an advantage or a disadvantage that people in class g have for items in item group h. Therefore, τ_{gh} can be seen as an indication of differential item functioning for item group h between class g and class h. To estimate the saltus parameters, further restrictions should be imposed as follows: the first row τ'_{1h} $(h = 1, \ldots, H)$ and the first column τ_{g1} $(g = 1, \ldots, G)$ are set to zero (Mislevy and Wilson 1996).

The saltus model was originally developed in a developmental context. Different developmental stages are assumed for the population of people and the item groups are based on the substantive developmental theory. However, the model can also be applied to other contexts where test items are constructed in such a way to successfully predict the rates between latent classes (Mislevy and Wilson 1996).

5.2.5 General Saltus LLTM-R

Finally, the proposed model can be formulated as a combination of models (5.3), (5.5), and (5.8). Specifically, the proposed model is based on the following four assumptions: (1) item difficulty is expressed as a regression model of Q item properties with an item-specific random error, (2) a test can be better represented by K dimensional sub-scales of items, (3) the population of people consists of G qualitatively different sub-populations or latent classes, and (4) the qualitative differences between latent classes are well captured by a set of shift parameters in each sub-scale of the test.

The resulting response model in dimension k can be written as

$$\Pr(y_{i(k)j} = 1|\theta_{jk}) = \sum_{g_k=1}^{G} \pi_{g_k} \Pr(y_{i(k)j} = 1|\theta_{jkg}, g_k),$$

$$\Pr(y_{i(k)j} = 1|\theta_{jkg}, g_k) = \frac{\exp\left[\theta_{jkg} - \sum_{q=0}^{Q} \beta_q X_{iq} + \varepsilon_i + \sum_{h=1}^{H} \tau_{kgh} w_{ih}\right]}{1 + \exp\left[\theta_{jkg} - \sum_{q=0}^{Q} \beta_q X_{iq} + \varepsilon_i + \sum_{h=1}^{H} \tau_{kgh} w_{ih}\right]}, \quad (5.9)$$

where π_{g_k} is the probability of belonging to class g_k $(g_k = 1, \ldots, G)$ in sub-scale k $(k = 1, \ldots, K)$, θ_{jkg} is an ability for person j in sub-scale k for class g, and τ_{kgh} is the shift parameter for the effect of item group h in person class g in dimension k. The random error is $\varepsilon_i \sim N(0, \sigma_\varepsilon^2)$, and θ_{jkg} is the kth ability for person j in class g. Within class g, a K dimensional vector of ability $\boldsymbol{\theta}_{jg} = (\theta_{j1g}, \ldots, \theta_{jKg})'$ is assumed to follow a multivariate normal distribution, $\theta_{jg} \sim N(\mu_g, \Sigma_g)$, where μ_g is a K dimensional mean vector and Σ_g is a $K \times K$ covariance matrix. For identification, we set the means of the reference latent class to 1, $\mu_1 = 0$ ($g = 1$ as the reference latent class), implying the test metric is set relative to the reference class across dimensions. In model (5.9), the saltus parameter τ_{kgh} is specific to dimension k, meaning that the effect of item group h (on person latent class g) can be different in each sub-scale (dimension) of the test. When $K = 1$, the model becomes a unidimensional saltus LLTM-R. Therefore, we refer model (5.9) to as a general saltus LLTM-R as it includes both uni- and multi-dimensional saltus LLTM-R.

Various extensions of mixture IRT models have been presented, for example, a mixture LLTM (e.g., Mislevy and Verhelst 1990), a mixture random weights LLTM (e.g., Fieuws et al. 2004), a multidimensional mixture model for longitudinal analysis (e.g., Cho et al. 2010; von Davier et al. 2011), for cross-country large-scale data analysis (e.g., De Jong and Steenkamp 2010), and a mixture bifactor IRT model (e.g., Cho et al. 2014). However, these is no extension of a mixture IRT model including the decomposition of the item (LLTM with an error) and person sides (multidimensionality) simultaneously. Furthermore, the saltus model has not been part of these developments although due to its parsimonious and confirmatory nature, the saltus model has great potential as a mathematical tool to construct and evaluate a complex cognitive theory.

5.3 Estimation

Several maximum likelihood (ML) software packages are available for estimating mixture IRT models, such as LatentGold (Vermunt and Magidson 2005), WIN-MIRA (von Davier 2001), and Mplus (Muthén and Muthén 2008) and for the saltus model, software by Draney (2007). Although a variety of complex mixture IRT models are estimable with these software packages, none appears able to estimate the proposed model.

A major obstacle is due to the inclusion of the random error term in the structural part of the mixture IRT model. With a simultaneous inclusion of random item and person variations, the model involves crossed random effects, for which ML estimation is inhibited for the high-dimensional integrals in the likelihood function. General-purpose software for estimating crossed random effects models (e.g., `xtmelogit` in Stata StataCorp 2009, `lme4` R package Bates and Maechler 2009) is also not available because of the mixture component of the model.

As an alternative to ML, we adopt a Bayesian estimation with a Markov chain Monte Carlo (MCMC) method for estimating the proposed general saltus LLTM-R. MCMC methods have been found particularly useful in estimating mixture distributions (Diebolt and Robert 1994), including mixtures that involve random effects within classes (Lenk and DeSarbo 2000). With MCMC, a class membership parameter is readily sampled for each observation at each stage of the Markov chain (Robert 1996).

To implement an MCMC algorithm, a freely available software, WinBUGS (Lunn et al. 2000) is used in this study. The WinBUGS software adopts Gibbs sampling or adaptive rejection sampling based on its own check to determine the best sampling method for each parameter.

The following prior distributions are assumed for the parameters of model (5.9):

$$
\begin{aligned}
g_k &\sim \text{Multinomial}(1, \pi_{g_k}[1:G]), \\
\pi_k &= (\pi_{1_k}, \ldots, \pi_{G_k}) \sim \text{Dirichlet}(\alpha_1, \ldots, \alpha_G), \\
\beta_q &\sim N(0, 10), \ (q = 0, \ldots, Q), \\
\tau_{kgh} &\sim N(0, 10), \ (g = 1, \ldots, G, h = 1, \ldots, H), \\
\sigma_\varepsilon &\sim \text{Gamma}(1, 1), \\
\theta_{jg} &\sim N(\mu_g, \Sigma_g), \\
\mu_{kg} &\sim N(0, 10), \ (g = 2, \ldots, G), \\
\Sigma_g &\sim \text{Wishart}^{-1}(R, 2),
\end{aligned}
$$

where the hyperparameters $(\alpha_1, \ldots, \alpha_G)$ for the Dirichlet distribution are set to 1, and R for the inverse Wishart is set to a $K \times K$ identity matrix. The means of the first latent class (as the reference group) are fixed to 0 ($\mu_{k1} = 0$) in each dimension k.

Using MCMC for estimation of models with mixture components implies that label switching should be addressed with the posterior samples. Label switching involves permutations of the class labels resulting in the same value of the likelihood, or the log-posterior in the Bayesian context. With MCMC, label switching can occur within- and between-chains. Within-chain label switching can be monitored by examining the marginal posterior distribution. A unique mode means that there is a unique labeling of classes, while multiple modes mean that the labels of latent classes are mixed up within the chain. Between-chain label switching can be monitored by checking out the modality of the marginal posterior distributions for each chain. If different modes are observed between the chains, between-chain label switching exists, implying the latent classes have a different order across chains (Cho et al. 2013).

A common strategy for removing label switching is to impose artificial identifiability constraints on the model parameters (e.g., De Jong and Steenkamp 2010), but this method does not always provide a satisfactory solution (Stephens 2000). In this study, we monitored label switching by examining the modality of the marginal posterior distribution of model parameters within and across chains. If observed, label switching is corrected by matching the labels of latent classes by comparing the estimates of the other parameters between and within chains (e.g., Bolt et al. 2001; Cho and Cohen 2010; Cho et al. 2010, 2013).

Unlike many mixture IRT models where the number of latent classes is found by an exploratory search, the proposed general saltus LLTM-R is a confirmatory approach and therefore the number of latent classes is given as a priori.

5.4 Illustration: Deductive Reasoning

In this section, we illustrate the general saltus LLTM-R in the context of cognitive development of children in deductive reasoning.

5.4.1 Data

We used the data from the Competence Profile Test of Deductive Reasoning—Verbal (DRV; Spiel et al. 2001; Spiel and Gluck 2008) that was developed based on Piaget's cognitive-developmental theory (Piaget 1971), in order to assess the competence profile and competence level of children in deductive reasoning. According to the theory, children move through four developmental stages that qualitatively differ in the cognitive processes: the sensorimotor, the preoperational, the concrete-operational, and the formal-operational stages (Spiel et al. 2001). The DRV focused on the transition from the concrete-operational stage to the formal-operational stage. In the concrete operational stage, children are able to perform logical operations, but only be represented by concrete objects. In the formal operational stage, children are able to perform abstract operations on abstractions as well as concrete objects. The progress from one stage to another involves a major reorganization of the thinking process used by children to solve various sorts of problems (Draney et al. 2007).

The DRV consists of 24 items that systematically vary in three major characteristics in a $4 \times 3 \times 2$ orthogonal design:

1. Type of inference: Modus Ponens (MP), Modus Tollens (MT), Negation of Antecedent (NA), and Affirmation of Consequent (AC)
2. Content of the conditional: Concrete (CO), Abstract (AB), and Counterfatual (CF)
3. Presentation of the antecedent: no negation (NN) and Negation (NE)

To develop the DRV, six premises were first developed for four main different types of syllogistic inference. Specifically, each item consists of a given premise ("if A, then B") and a conclusion. The task is to evaluate a conclusion, assuming the premise as given. The four types of inferences are: Modus Ponens (A, therefore B), Negation of Antecedent (Not A, therefore B or not B), Affirmation of Consequent (B, therefore A or not A), and Modus Tollens (Not B, therefore not A). Modus ponens (MP) and modus tollens (MT) are biconditional conclusions, and therefore the response to the items is either "yes" or "no." For negation of antecedent (NA) and affirmation of consequent (AC), the correct solution is "perhaps" as the premise does not allow for deciding whether these conclusions are correct. NA and AC items are also called logical fallacies because they provoke the choice of a biconditional, but logically incorrect conclusion ("no" for NA, "yes" for AC).

It has been shown that people at the concrete-operational stage treat all four inferences as biconditional (e.g., Evans et al. 1993; Janveau-Brennan and Markovits 1999). The probability of correctly solving the fallacy items increases with progress in cognitive development, but the performance on biconditional items (MT and MP) sometimes decreases because people who have noticed the uncertainty of the fallacies tend to overgeneralize (e.g., Byrnes and Overton 1986; Markovits et al. 1998).

In addition to the major factor (type of inference), two moderator variables were considered to construct the items: (1) content of the conditional (Concrete (CO), Abstract (AB), and Counterfatual (CF) items) and (2) presentation of the antecedent (no negation (NN) and Negation (NE) items). Research has shown that Concrete items are easier to solve than Abstract and Counterfactual items but differences between abstract and counterfactual items are unclear (e.g., Overton 1985). Also it has been shown that when negation was used in the antecedents, items become more difficult to solve (e.g., Roberge and Mason 1978).

Table 5.1 lists example items corresponding to four inference types that have Concrete content (CO) and no negation (NN) features.

Table 5.1 Example DRV items that correspond to four types of inference with Concrete content (CO) and no negation (NN)

Type of inference	Item	Correct solution
Modus ponens (MP)	Tom is ill. Is Tom lying in his bed?	Yes
Modus tollens (MT)	Tom is not lying in his bed. Is Tom ill?	No
Negation of antecedent (NA)	Tom is not ill. Is Tom lying in his bed?	Perhaps
Affirmation of consequent (AC)	Tom is lying in his bed. Is Tom ill?	Perhaps

The premise is "If Klaus is ill, he is lying in his bed"

The DRV data were collected in various secondary schools in Graz, Austria. To cover a broad age range, students in grades 7 through 12 (ages 11 to 18) participated. Altogether, data from 418 participants, 162 females and 256 males, were included in the analyses. Participants were about equally distributed across grades. Questionnaires were administered in classrooms during regular class hours and no time limits were set. To control for order effects, two task versions (A and B) were constructed with different random orders of the items. Half of the participants were presented with each version (Spiel et al. 2001). The item responses were coded dichotomously, with 1 for correct, and 0 for incorrect responses.

5.4.2 Method

There were two previous empirical analyses on this dataset. Spiel et al. (2001) analyzed the data using the mixture Rasch model. They found that a model with three latent classes fit the data best, with class 1 correctly solving only MP and MT items correctly, class 2 starting to solve correctly NA and AC items but making mistakes in MP and MT items, and class 3 performing better in NA and AC item than class 2. Draney et al. (2007) employed a saltus model to analyze the data. In their two-class analysis, they defined two item groups (MP/MT vs. NA/AC) and in a three-class analysis, defined three item groups (MP/MT, NA/AC, and AB/CF). They found that the three-class model fit the data better than the two-class model but could not clearly identify the characteristics of the third latent class.

These previous analyses suggest that (1) there are two clear sub-populations of people that are well represented by MP/MT and NA/AC items, respectively, (2) a third class is likely to exist, but its characteristics are not evident based on these previous research, and (3) it is unclear how the two moderator factors, the content of the conditional and presentation of antecedent play a part in identifying and discriminating different latent classes.

Based on the reasoning, our mathematical modeling stems from the following rationale: First, we investigate the role of the test design factors in understanding the development of deductive reasoning of children. Therefore, we directly model the item design factors as the predictors of item parameters in the model. Six item predictors are considered based on three design factors as follows:

- Type of inference: NA, AC, MT, (MP: reference)
- Content of the conditional: AB, CF (CO: reference)
- Presentation of antecedent: NE (NN: reference).

We also allow for a random deviation of each item in the prediction model for a realistic prediction.

Second, we assume that there are at least two distinct sub-populations of children whose membership is unknown. The sub-populations represent two distinct developmental stages, Concrete-operational stage, and Formal operational stage.

Third, the two sub-populations are well described by the major design factor, type of inference. Hence, the two item groups are used to represent the concrete- and formal-operational stages, respectively

- Concrete operational items: MP, MT
- Formal operational items: NA, AC.

Fourth, the other two design factors, content of the conditional and presentation of antecedent, are assumed to represent qualitatively different cognitive features and therefore, can be used to define the sub-scales of the test as

- Two sub-scales by presentation of antecedent: NN, NE
- Three sub-scales by conditional of the conditional: CO, AB, CF.

By the content of the conditional (CO, AB, and CF), some sub-scales contain only a few items. Hence, we apply the two sub-scales for empirical analysis.

Based on these assumptions, we specify two general saltus LLTM-R models to fit the data: (1) unidimensional saltus LLTM-R with an overall dimension ($K = 1$), and (2) two-dimensional saltus LLTM-R with NN and NE dimensions ($K = 2$). In the two-dimensional model with NN and NE dimensions, the item feature of NE for Presentation of antecedent (NN: reference) is not included in the model since it is used to define the sub-scales. As a comparison with an existing model, we consider a mixture LLTM (Mislevy and Verhelst 1990) that was presented in Eq. (5.7).

The priors are specified as described in Sect. 5.3. Posterior samples were obtained based on 100,000 iterations including 90,000 burn-in with five thinning. Three chains were used with three different starting values. For convergence checking, the Gelman and Rubin (1992) method and the Geweke (1992) method were used in addition to graphical checks.

5.4.3 Results

We first estimated the mixture LLTM in (5.7) with two latent classes and the class-specific feature difficulty parameters. Table 5.2 lists the parameter estimates (posterior means) and standard errors (posterior standard deviations) of the model.

Table 5.2 Parameter estimates (posterior means) and standard errors (posterior standard deviations) for the mixture LLTM

	Class 1			Class 2	
Par	Est	SE	Par	Est	SE
β_{01}	−2.48	0.15	β_{02}	−1.27	0.12
β_{11}(NA)	3.73	0.19	β_{12}(NA)	−0.04	0.13
β_{21}(AC)	3.94	0.22	β_{22}(AC)	0.34	0.13
β_{31}(MT)	0.63	0.12	β_{32}(MT)	1.04	0.10
β_{41}(AB)	0.56	0.10	β_{42}(AB)	0.44	0.08
β_{51}(CF)	0.54	0.10	β_{52}(CF)	0.62	0.08
β_{61}(NE)	0.62	0.08	β_{62}(NE)	0.34	0.08
σ_1	0.44	0.07	σ_2	0.86	0.07
π_1	0.50	0.03	π_2	0.50	0.04

Table 5.2 shows that most differences between class 1 and 2 were found in β_{1g}, β_{2g}, and β_{3g}, which were the difficulty parameters for NA, AC, and MT item features. The NA and AC items were more difficult and the MT/MP items were relatively easier in class 1 than class 2. This means that class 1 and 2 were distinguished from each other in terms of their performance on the NA/AC and MT/MP items; class 1 can be regarded as the concrete-operational stage and class

2 as the formal-operational stage. The estimated proportions of children were 0.50 and 0.50 in class 1 and 2, respectively. The estimated standard deviations of ability were larger in class 2 ($\hat{\sigma}_2$=0.86) than in class 1 ($\hat{\sigma}_2$=0.44).

The result of the mixture LLTM confirms our assumption that the type of inference (NA/AC, MT/MP) can be used to represent the formal and concrete-operational stages. Table 5.3 lists the results of the saltus LLTM-R analyses.

In the unidimensional model, the shift parameter τ_{122} was estimated as −4.3, meaning that the NA and AC items were significantly more difficult in class 2 than in class 1. Since τ_1 indicates the effects of NA/AC items (vs. MT/MP items) on the probability of correctly solving an item, the estimated feature difficulties for NA and AC items are $\hat{\beta}_{12} = \hat{\beta}_1 - \hat{\tau}_{122} = 4.00$ and $\hat{\beta}_{22} = \hat{\beta}_2 - \hat{\tau}_{122} = 4.53$ in class 2 and

Table 5.3 Parameter estimates and standard errors for the uni-dimensional saltus LLTM-R (1D) and two-dimensional saltus LLTM-R (2D)

		LLTM-R(1D)		LLTM-R(2D)	
	Par	Est	SE	Est	SE
Structural part	β_0	−1.24	0.51	−0.99	0.51
	β_1(NA)	−0.30	0.56	−0.40	0.57
	β_2(AC)	0.23	0.55	0.13	0.57
	β_3(MT)	0.85	0.55	0.87	0.56
	β_4(AB)	0.54	0.48	0.56	0.50
	β_5(CF)	0.68	0.47	0.69	0.50
	β_6(NE)	0.44	0.39	–	–
	σ_ε	0.95	0.18	0.98	0.18
$k=1$		Overall		Dim1: NE	
shift$_{22}$	τ_{122}	−4.3	0.17	−4.53	0.22
mean$_2$	μ_{12}	1.54	0.12	1.56	0.16
sd$_1$	σ_{11_1}	0.94	0.07	1.16	0.10
cov$_1$	σ_{12_1}			0.88	0.14
sd$_2$	σ_{22_1}	0.51	0.08	0.82	0.08
prop$_1$	π_{1_1}	0.51	0.03	0.50	0.04
prop$_2$	π_{2_1}	0.49	0.03	0.50	0.04
$k=2$				Dim2: NN	
shift$_{22}$	τ_{222}			−4.53	0.22
mean$_2$	μ_{22}			1.69	0.16
sd$_1$	σ_{11_2}			0.51	0.10
cov$_2$	σ_{12_2}			0.18	0.09
sd$_2$	σ_{22_2}			0.53	0.10
prop$_1$	π_{1_2}			0.51	0.04
prop$_2$	π_{2_2}			0.50	0.04

NN and NE are No Negation and Negation; The shift (saltus) parameter: τ_{kgh}, $k=1,2$ and $G=H=2$; Means: μ_{kg}, $k=1,2$ and $g=2$; Standard deviations and covariances: σ_{kkg}, $k=1,2$ and $g=1,2$; Proportion of belonging to latent class g: π_{g_k}, $k=1,2$ and $g=1,2$. Est is the posterior mean and SE is the posterior standard deviation

$\hat{\beta}_{11} = \hat{\beta}_1 = -0.30$ and $\hat{\beta}_{21} = \hat{\beta}_2 = 0.23$ in class 1. This implies that class 2 can be seen as the concrete-operational stage and class 1 as the formal-operational stage as expected. The proportions of children in class 1 and 2 were estimated as 0.51 and 0.49, respectively, which was similar to the results from the mixture LLTM. Unlike the mixture LLTM, however, the overall mean of ability for each latent class was estimated (except the reference group). The estimated mean of ability (μ_{12}) for class 2 was 1.54; because the estimated item intercept parameter ($\hat{\beta}_0$) contributes to the overall ability, the overall mean ability for class 2 is $\hat{\mu}_{12} + \hat{\beta}_0 = 1.54 - 1.24 = 0.3$ and the overall mean ability for class 1 is $\mu_{11} + \hat{\beta}_0 = 0 - 1.24 = -1.24$ ($\mu_{11} = 0$). That is, μ_{12} represents the difference in the overall mean ability between class 1 and 2 and it was significantly different from zero. This means that the overall proficiency of the formal-operational group was lower than that of the concrete-operational group; it might be because children who noticed the uncertainty of the fallacies in MP/MT items overgeneralized the problems and got those items wrong. This was consistent with findings in Byrnes and Overton (1986) and Markovits et al. (1998). The estimated standard deviations of ability were 0.94 and 0.51 in class 1 and 2, respectively.

In the two-dimensional model, the shift parameter was estimated as -4.53 in the NE dimension and in the NN dimension. This means that the NA/AC items were relatively more difficult in class 2 than in class 1 in both dimensions. In the NE dimension, the estimated mean proficiency for class 2 was 1.56 and in the NN dimension, the estimated mean for class 2 was 1.69, which were significantly different from the zero means of class 1 (reference group) in both dimensions. In the NE dimension, about 50 and 50 % of students were observed in class 1 and 2, and in the NN dimension, 51 and 49 % of students were observed in class 1 and 2. The overall abilities of the formal-operational group were lower in both NE and NN dimensions than those of the concrete-operational group. The standard deviations were estimated as 1.16 and 0.82 in class 1 and 2 in the NE dimension, and 0.59 and 0.53 in class 1 and 2 in the NN dimension. The estimated correlations ($\frac{\hat{\sigma}_{12}}{\hat{\sigma}_{11}\hat{\sigma}_{22}}$) between the NE and NN dimensions were somewhat different between class 1 and class 2, which were 0.92 in class 1 and 0.67 in class 2. This implies that the presentation of antecedent (NE/NN) of items might be related to the performance on different types of inferential items (NA/AC, MT/MP). For instance, the performance of students who can correctly solve NA/AC items (class 1) is not influenced by whether items are presented with negation (NE) or no negation(NN). In contrast, the performance of students who cannot correctly solve NA/AC items (class 2) is influenced by whether items are presented with negation (NE) or no negation (NN). This explains lower correlations between the NE and NN dimensions in class 2 than in class 1.

5.5 Discussion

In this paper, the specification, estimation, and illustration of a general saltus LLTM-R are presented. The general saltus LLTM-R combines three Rasch models: a linear logistic latent trait with an error term (LLTM-R), multidimensional, and mixture Rasch models. The saltus model is chosen to specify the mixture component of the model because of its parsimony and confirmatory nature. Qualitative differences between latent classes are captured by a shift parameter in the saltus model rather than all item parameters as in typical mixture models. In addition, in the saltus model latent classes are posited as a priori based on a theory rather than found by exploratory search.

The proposed model can best be applied to well-designed educational or psychological tests where definite hypotheses of the behavior elicited by the test items are available. Specifically, the model can be used to (1) estimate parameters that describe test items by substantive theories, (2) evaluate the latent constructs that are associated with the knowledge structures of the test items, and (3) test hypotheses on qualitative differences between the sub-populations of subjects with different problem solving strategies, cognitive processes, or developmental stages.

The model is illustrated in a developmental context, but its application should not be limited to that context. First, it can be applied to psychological or educational assessment data where the test items are constructed in such a way to be associated with presumed latent classes. Second, the model can also be useful to analyze longitudinal data where a different latent trait is assumed at a different time point. Significant changes in shift parameters imply there is a "shift" in item difficulty across time for the group of items that represent different latent classes.

Acknowledgements The authors would like to thank Professor Wen-Chung Wang for his helpful comments and suggestions to our manuscript.

References

Adams RJ, Wilson M, Wu M (1997) Multilevel item response models: an approach to errors in variable regression. J Educ Behav Stat 22:47–76

Bates D, Maechler M (2009) lme4: linear mixed-effects models using S4 classes, R package version 0.999375-31. http://cran.rproject.org/package=lme4

Bolt DM, Cohen AS, Wollack JA (2001) A mixture item response for multiple choice data. J Educ Behav Stat 26:381–409

Briggs DC, Wilson C (2003) An introduction to multidimensional measurement using Rasch models. J Appl Meas 4:87–100

Byrnes JP, Overton WF (1986) Reasoning about certainty and uncertainty in concrete, causal, and propositional context. Dev Psychol 22:793–799

Cho S-J, Cohen AS (2010) A multilevel mixture IRT model with an application to DIF. J Educ Behav Stat 35:336–370

Cho S-J, Cohen A, Kim S-H, Bottge B (2010) Latent transition analysis with a mixture IRT measurement model. Appl Psychol Meas 34:583–604

Cho S-J, Cohen AS, Kim S-H (2013) Markov chain Monte Carlo estimation of a mixture item response theory model. J Stat Comput Simul 83:278–306

Cho S-J, Cohen AS, Kim S-H (2014) A mixture group bi-factor model for binary responses. Struct Equ Modeling 21:375–395

De Jong MG, Steenkamp J-BEM (2010) Finite mixture multilevel multidimensional ordinal IRT models for large scale cross-cultural research. Psychometrika 75:3–32

Diebolt J, Robert CP (1994) Estimation of finite distributions through Bayesian sampling. J R Stat Soc Series B 56:363–375

Draney K (2007) The saltus model applied to proportional reasoning data. J Appl Meas 8:438–455

Draney K, Wilson M, Gluck J, Spiel C (2007) Mixture models in a developmental context. In: Hancock R, Samuelson KM (eds) Latent variable mixture models. Information Age, Charlotte, pp 199–216

Embretson SE (1984) A general multicomponent latent trait model for response processes. Psychometrika 49:175–186

Evans JSBT, Newstead SE, Byrne RMJ (1993) Human reasoning: the psychology of deduction. Erlbaum, Mahwah

Fieuws S, Spiessens B, Draney K (2004) Mixture models. In: Boeck D, Wilson M (eds) Explanatory item response models: a generalized linear and nonlinear approach. Springer, New York, pp 317–340

Fischer GH (1973) Linear logistic test model as an instrument in educational research. Acta Psychol 37:359–374

Fischer GH, Forman AK (1982) Some applications of logistic latent trait models with linear constraints on the parameters. Appl Psychol Meas 6:397–416

Gelman A, Rubin DB (1992) Inference from iterative simulation using multiple sequences. Stat Sci 7:457–472

Geweke J (1992) Evaluating the accuracy of sampling-based approaches to calculating posterior moments. In: Bernardo JM, Berger JO, Dawiv AP, Smith AFM (eds) Bayesian statistics. Clarendon Press, Oxford, pp 169–193

Janssen R, Schepers J, Peres D (2004) Models with item and item group predictors. In: Boeck PD, Wilson M (eds) Explanatory item response models. Springer, New York, pp 198–212

Janveau-Brennan G, Markovits H (1999) The development of reasoning with causal conditionals. Dev Psychol 35:904–911

Kelderman H, Rijkes CPM (1994) Loglinear multidimensional IRT models for polytomously scored items. Psychometrika 59:149–176

Lenk PJ, DeSarbo WS (2000) Bayesian inference for finite mixtures of generalized linear models with random effects. Psychometrika 65:93–119

Lunn D, Thomas A, Best N, Spiegelhalter D (2000) WinBUGS - a Bayesian modelling framework: concepts, structure, and extensibility. Stat Comput 10:325–337

Markovits H, Fleury M-L, Quinn S, Venet M (1998) The development of conditional reasoning and the structure of semantic memory. Child Dev 69:742–755

Mislevy RJ, Verhelst N (1990) Modeling item responses when different subjects employ different solution strategies. Psychometrika 55:195–215

Mislevy RJ, Wilson M (1996) Marginal maximum likelihood estimation for a psychometric model of discontinuous development. Psychometrika 41–71:61

Muthén L, Muthén B (2008) Mplus user's guide. Muthen & Muthen, Angeles

Overton WF (1985) Scientific methodologies and the competence- moderator performance issue. In: Neimark ED, de Lisi R, Newman JL (eds) Moderators of competence. Erlbaum, Hillsdale, pp 15–41

Piaget J (1971) Biology and knowledge. University of Chicago Press, Chicago

Rijmen F, De Boeck P (2002) The random weights linear logistic test model. Appl Psychol Meas 26:271–285

Rijmen F, De Boeck P (2005) A relation between a between-item multidimensional IRT model and the mixture Rasch model. Psychometrika 70:481–496

Roberge JJ, Mason EJ (1978) Effects of negation on adolescents' class and conditional reasoning abilities. J Gen Psychol 98:187–195
Robert CP (1996) Mixtures of distributions: inference and estimation. In: Gilks WR, Richardson S, Spiegelhalter DJ (eds) Markov Chain Monte Carlo in practice. Chapman & Hall, Washington, pp 441–464
Rost J (1990) Rasch models in latent classes: an integration of two approaches to item analysis. Appl Psychol Meas/ 14:271–282
Spiel C, Gluck J (2008) A model based test of competence profile and competence level in deductive reasoning. In Hartig J, Klieme E, Leutner D (eds) Assessment of competencies in educational contexts: state of the art and future prospects. Hogrefe, Gottingen, pp 41–60
Spiel C, Gluck J, Gossler H (2001) Stability and change of unidimensionality: the sample case of deductive reasoning. J Adolesc Res 16:150–168
StataCorp (2009) Stata statistical software: release 11. StataCorp LP, College Station
Stephens M (2000) Dealing with label switching in mixture models. J R Stat Soc Series B 62:795–809
Vermunt J, Magidson J (2005) Latent GOLD 4.0 [Computer program]. Statistical Innovations, Belmont
von Davier M (2001) WINMIRA [Computer program]. Assessment Systems Corporation, St. Paul
von Davier M, Xu X, Carstensen CH (2011) Measuring growth in a longitudinal large-scale assessment with a general latent variable model. Psychometrika 76:318–336
Wilson MR (1989) Saltus: a psychometric model of discontinuity in cognitive development. Psychol Bull 105:276–289

Chapter 6
Multidimensional IRT Models to Analyze Learning Outcomes of Italian Students at the End of Lower Secondary School

Mariagiulia Matteucci and Stefania Mignani

Abstract In this paper, different multidimensional IRT models are compared in order to choose the best approach to explain response data on Italian student assessment at the end of lower secondary school. The results show that the additive model with three specific dimensions (reading comprehension, grammar, and mathematics abilities) and an overall ability is able to recover the test structure meaningfully. In this model, the overall ability compensates for the specific ability (or vice versa) in order to determine the probability of a correct response. Given the item characteristics, the overall ability is interpreted as a reasoning and thinking capability. Model estimation is conducted via Gibbs sampler within a Bayesian approach, which allows the use of Bayesian model comparison techniques such as posterior predictive model checking for model comparison and fit.

Keywords Item response theory • Multidimensional models • Gibbs sampling • Student assessment

6.1 Introduction

In the last decades the debate in educational research highlights the importance of analyzing students' performances for supporting educational policies in order to allocate resources, reform formative curricula, train teachers, monitor standards, and promote equal opportunity of access. In this context the study of the educational outcomes defined as the competences acquired has a primary role and recently there has been an increased focus on defining tools to assess the performances. Such points accentuate the growing interest assumed by international standardized tests, such as OECD-PISA, PIRLS, and TIMSS, that guarantee important results on students' achievement determinants (Grek 2009).

M. Matteucci (✉) • S. Mignani
Department of Statistical Sciences, University of Bologna, via Belle Arti 41, 40126 Bologna, Italy
e-mail: m.matteucci@unibo.it; stefania.mignani@unibo.it

R.E. Millsap et al. (eds.), *Quantitative Psychology Research*, Springer Proceedings in Mathematics & Statistics 89, DOI 10.1007/978-3-319-07503-7_6

In educational practice the concept of competence reflects a person's potential to meet cognitive demands in specific areas of learning (domains). Adequate tools for measuring competence need to be based on models that represent the internal structure in terms of specific basic skills and abilities and take into account changes occurring in learning and developmental processes. Furthermore, measurements of competence should build on psychometric models that link the empirical measurement operations with theoretical (cognitive) models of competencies (Koeppen et al. 2008).

In the field of educational measurement, item response theory (IRT) is a popular approach for modeling the probabilistic relationship between responses to test items and individual abilities. IRT models are often used under the assumption of unidimensionality, i.e. the presence of a single or at least one predominant latent ability, while more complex structures incorporating specific abilities could explain the response process. In fact, it often happens that a test consists of different subscales or domains involving explicitly several ability dimensions.

The attention has recently been devoted to models that include more than one latent trait, the so-called multidimensional IRT (MIRT) models (see, e.g., van der Linden and Hambleton 1997; Reckase 2009). These models perform better than separate unidimensional models in fitting the subtests because they are able to describe the data complexity, taking into account correlated abilities and also the hierarchical structure typical of mental abilities.

Within the multidimensional context, different approaches are possible: explorative models where all latent traits are allowed to load on all item response variables or confirmatory models where the relations between the observed and the latent variables are specified in advance. By adopting a confirmatory approach, it is also possible to assume the concurrent presence of general and specific latent traits underlying the response process (Sheng and Wikle 2008).

Different MIRT models can be distinguished on the basis of statistical relations between latent dimensions and test items. The pattern of these relations can be defined by a loading matrix with a simple structure (between-item multidimensionality) or by a complex loading structure (within-item multidimensionality). Another distinction is among noncompensatory and compensatory models, where a lack in one ability naturally compensates for the other (Reckase 2009).

Moreover, the main goal of multidimensional measurement is to assess multiple different abilities that are necessary for performing successfully within a given content domain. In general, the key question is if there is a scale score primarily reflecting variation on a single construct, or due to multiple non-ignorable sources of variability, subscales need to be formed (Reise et al. 2010).

In many assessment cases, content domains show a hierarchical structure with dimensions on different levels that vary in their degree of generality and abstraction. On the highest levels of these hierarchies, dimensions represent overall ability levels while, on lower levels of the hierarchy, dimensions represent more specific abilities. Additive models and higher-order models are two alternative approaches for dealing with items that assess several related domains that are hypothesized to comprise a general structure. Additive models are potentially applicable when there are a general factor and multiple domain specific factors, each of which is hypothesized to account for the unique influence of the specific domain over the general factor (Chen et al. 2006). In addition, researchers may be interested both in the domain specific factors and in the general factor. Higher-order models are potentially applicable when the lower-order factors are substantially correlated with each other and there is a higher-order factor that is hypothesized to account for the relationship among the lower-order factors. In the additive model, we can directly examine the strength of the relationship between the domain specific constructs and their associated items, as the relationship is reflected in the loadings, whereas these relationships cannot be directly tested in the higher-order model as the domain specific factors are represented by the disturbances of the first-order factors (Yung et al. 1999; Chen et al. 2006). However, the differences between the two models become more important when researchers are also interested in the contribution of the one or more specific abilities besides the general/higher-order factor. The choice of a model preferred against another should be made only with regard to the specific research question especially because different models may be equivalent in terms of fitting (Hartig and Hohler 2009; Huang et al. 2013).

In this paper, a MIRT approach is considered to analyze the structure of a large-scale standardized test developed to assess specific abilities. We focus on the data coming from annual surveys conducted by the National Evaluation Institute for the School System (INVALSI) at different school grades. The INVALSI develops tests to assess pupils' Italian language and mathematics competencies, and administers them to the whole population of primary school students (second and fifth grade), lower secondary school students (sixth and eighth grade), and upper secondary school students (tenth grade). The INVALSI test consists of two subtests representing learning specific domains and, consequently, it is appropriate to assume a multidimensional structure. Each subtest contains both items which mainly measure the literacy, i.e. the specific competence intended as the capability of using suitable instruments and procedures to solve a particular task, and items which mainly measure the reasoning and thinking ability. We consider data from the administration of the INVALSI test at the end of lower secondary school (eighth grade). The choice of the eighth grade assessment data is motivated by the fact that students receive a test score based on their performance, which contributes to the definition of the final student score at the end of lower secondary school within a state certification exam with legal validity. In this test, the Italian language test is further divided into two separate sections: reading comprehension and grammar. Within this assessment, it is particularly relevant the need for multidimensional evaluation measures meeting the purposes, which inspired the test development.

Hence, in this work, we propose the use of the additive model with one general and three specific factors, where the specific factors are intended to measure the ability within each domain of the test (reading comprehension, grammar, and mathematics) in terms of literacy, and the general factor measures the reasoning and thinking skills that determine the learning achievement primarily. Considering these definitions for the latent abilities, we believe that the general ability can be correlated with reading comprehension, grammar, and mathematics abilities, because these specific literacy abilities all directly involve reasoning and thinking. The model that we assumed and estimated represents indeed the best solution with respect to the data structure and the INVALSI purposes.

We show that the proposed model fit the data better in comparison with other multidimensional models, it is consistent with the assumed test structure, and it is able to describe the relations among the latent abilities precisely and, most important, meaningfully. The study of dimensionality characteristics is very important to interpret correctly the test structure and to estimate test scores reflecting the presence of different ability dimensions. Our work represents the first attempt to model this complex structure considering different number of dimensions and orders and introducing a correlation between the abilities.

A further innovative and important aspect of our proposal deals with the estimation procedure. In fact, an approach suitable to model the dependencies among parameters and sources of uncertainty for different kinds of IRT models is needed. For years, the standard methodology has been mainly involving marginal maximum likelihood (MML). Unfortunately, this estimation method may be computational heavy due to the approximation of integrals involved in the likelihood function, especially for increasingly complex models. Moreover, the success of MML estimation based on the EM algorithm strongly depends on the choice of starting values.

One possible alternative is offered by Markov chain Monte Carlo (MCMC) methods, in a fully Bayesian framework. This approach has the advantage of estimating item parameters and individual abilities jointly and it is proved to be more accurate and efficient in parameter estimation compared with the usual MML method (Albert 1992). MCMC is powerful for complicated models where the probabilities or expectations are intractable by analytical methods or other numerical approximation. Furthermore, at the end of the analysis, the user has access to the entire posterior distribution of every parameter, not just to a point estimate and standard error.

Another important advantage concerns the model comparison that can be carried out using Bayes factors, Bayesian deviance, and a Bayesian predictive approach, i.e. posterior predictive model checks. These model comparison techniques provide an alternative method of checking model assumptions (Cowles and Carlin 1996; Sahu 2002; Spiegelhalter et al. 2002; Sinharay and Stern 2003), for example unidimensionality versus multidimensionality.

Among the MCMC methods, the Gibbs sampler (Geman and Geman 1984) has been successfully applied to estimation of IRT models (see, e.g., Albert 1992; Béguin and Glas 2001; Fox and Glas 2001; Edwards 2010). The method is straightforward to implement when each full conditional distribution is a known distribution that is easy to sample from.

In this paper we refer to the estimation procedure developed by Sheng and Wikle (2008, 2009) for both additive and hierarchical models. We should provide useful insights to encourage a diffuse use of (a) multidimensional models with complex ability structures, and (b) Bayesian estimation via MCMC, among educational and psychological researchers and practitioners. In fact, MCMC offers the many above mentioned advantages including, from a practical point of view, a relative ease of implementation and the availability of free software. Unfortunately, the method is not largely used, probably due to the computational intensiveness that limited its use in the past.

The paper is organized as follows. In Sect. 6.2, MIRT models are reviewed, in Sect. 6.3 we present the results, while in Sect. 6.4 we address the main issues and conclusions.

6.2 MIRT Models

Within IRT models, we refer here to normal ogive modes for binary data (Lord and Novick 1968), where Y_{ij} denotes the response variable for the respondent i to item j, with $i = 1,\ldots,n$ and $j = 1,\ldots,k$, and $P(Y_{ij} = 1)$ is the probability of a correct response expressed as the standard normal cumulative distribution function of item and person parameters.

In the simplest case, it is possible to assume a single, or at least predominant, latent ability underlying the response process. By considering the class of models with two item parameters, the unidimensional two-parameter normal ogive (2PNO) model (Lord and Novick 1968) can be formulated as follows:

$$P\left(Y_{ij} = 1 \middle| \theta_i, \alpha_j, \delta_j\right) = \Phi\left(\alpha_j\theta_i - \delta_j\right) = \int_{-\infty}^{\alpha_j\theta_i - \delta_j} \frac{1}{\sqrt{2\pi}} e^{-t^2/2} dt, \tag{6.1}$$

where α_j is the discrimination parameter for item j representing the slope of the item characteristic curve (ICC), δ_j is the difficulty or threshold parameter for item j denoting the location of the ICC, and θ_i is the ability for the subject i. Figure 6.1 shows a unidimensional model in the path diagram representation, where circles and squares represent the latent variables and the item response variables, respectively. Parameter estimation of model (6.1) via the Gibbs sampler algorithm within MCMC methods was proposed by Albert (1992).

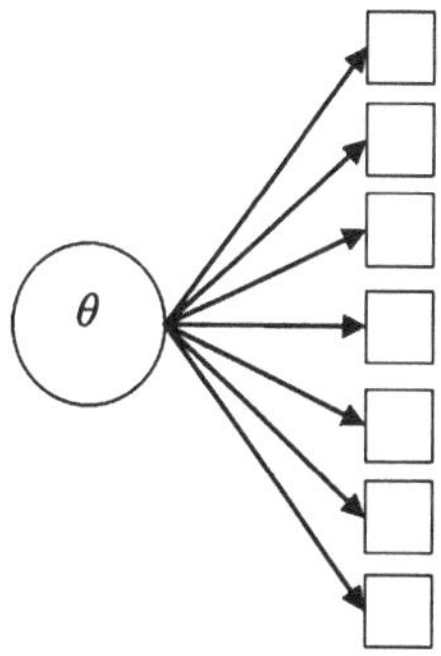

Fig. 6.1 Graphical representation for the unidimensional model

Turning to a multidimensional solution, the choice of an explorative or a confirmatory approach is required. In the former approach, all latent traits are allowed to load on all item response variables, while in the latter approach the existence of relations between the observed and the latent variables is specified in advance. We refer here to a confirmatory approach only. In fact, we assume that a test consisting of k items is specifically designed to assess a set of m domains, i.e. the test is divided into m subtests each containing k_v items, where $v = 1,..m$.

Under this confirmatory approach, the first intuitive solution is to assume that each item is related to a single latent ability only, turning out with m separate unidimensional models. This kind of relationship among observed items and abilities is called between-item multidimensionality (Wang et al. 2004). Within this approach, Sheng and Wikle (2007) introduced the estimation via Gibbs sampler for the so-called 2PNO multi-unidimensional model, expressed as follows:

$$P\left(Y_{vij} = 1 \middle| \theta_{vi}, \alpha_{vj}, \delta_{vj}\right) = \Phi\left(\alpha_{vj}\theta_{vi} - \delta_{vj}\right) = \int_{-\infty}^{\alpha_{vj}\theta_{vi} - \delta_{vj}} \frac{1}{\sqrt{2\pi}} e^{-t^2/2} dt, \quad (6.2)$$

where each parameter is specific for the vth dimension and the abilities may be correlated. The multi-unidimensional model is shown graphically in Fig. 6.2 for the bidimensional case.

An alternative multidimensional approach is based on the assumption of the concurrent presence of general and specific latent traits underlying the response process (Sheng and Wikle 2008). This approach is derived from the corresponding models in the traditional factor analysis for continuous observed variables such as bi-factor or hierarchical models and higher-order factor models (see Holzinger and Swineford 1937; Schmid and Leiman 1957; Yung et al. 1999). A first approach consists in specifying the same measurement model (6.2) adding a linear relation among each latent trait to a general, overall ability. In the IRT literature, these models are called higher-order models (de la Torre and Song 2009) or hierarchical models (Sheng and Wikle 2008). In the following, we will refer to the 2PNO hierarchical model

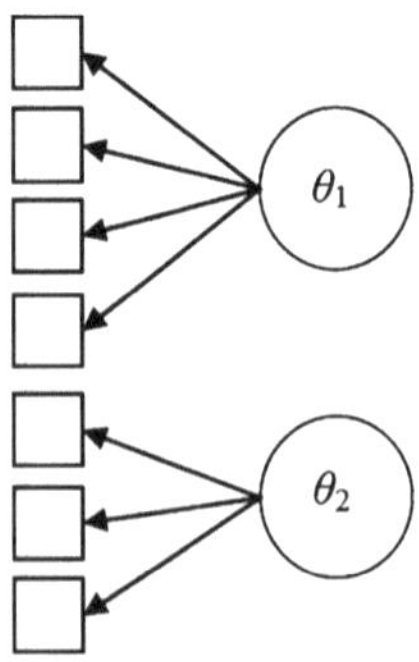

Fig. 6.2 Graphical representation for the multi-unidimensional model. The abilities may be correlated, even not graphically shown

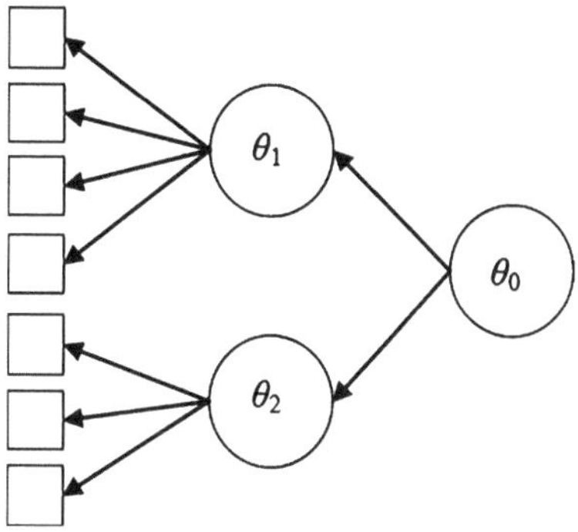

Fig. 6.3 Graphical representation for the hierarchical model

$$P\left(Y_{vij}=1\middle|\theta_{vi},\alpha_{vj},\delta_{vj}\right)=\Phi\left(\alpha_{vj}\theta_{vi}-\delta_{vj}\right)=\int_{-\infty}^{\alpha_{vj}\theta_{vi}-\delta_{vj}}\frac{1}{\sqrt{2\pi}}e^{-t^2/2}dt, \quad (6.3)$$

where $\theta_{vi} \sim N(\beta_v\theta_{0i}, 1)$ and β_v is a measure of association among the general and the vth specific latent trait. A graphical representation of the hierarchical model (6.3) is provided in Fig. 6.3.

An estimation procedure for the hierarchical model via Gibbs sampler was proposed by Sheng and Wikle (2008, 2009) and Sheng (2010).

A second approach consists in assuming that the general ability directly affects the candidate's responses, and that this effect is summed to the effect of specific factors to determine the probability of a correct response to a given test item for the so-called 2PNO additive model (Sheng and Wikle 2009) as follows:

$$\begin{aligned}P\left(Y_{vij}=1\middle|\theta_{0i},\theta_{vi},\alpha_{0j},\alpha_{vj},\delta_{vj}\right)&=\Phi\left(\alpha_{0j}\theta_{0i}+\alpha_{vj}\theta_{vi}-\delta_{vj}\right)=\\=\int_{-\infty}^{\alpha_{0j}\theta_{0vi}+\alpha_{vj}\theta_{vi}-\delta_{vj}}\frac{1}{\sqrt{2\pi}}e^{-t^2/2}dt,\end{aligned} \quad (6.4)$$

The model involves the estimation of a general and a specific discrimination parameter α_{0j} and α_{vj}, respectively, and a threshold parameter δ_{vj} for each item j. Moreover, for each subject i, an overall ability θ_{0i} and m specific abilities θ_{vi} are estimated. The abilities may be correlated and are assumed to be distributed as $\theta_i \sim N_{m+1}(\mathbf{0}, P)$, where $\mathbf{P}$ is the correlation matrix. A graphical representation for model (6.4) is provided in Fig. 6.4. In the literature on traditional factor models, Fig. 6.4 represents the so-called bi-factor model (Holzinger and Swineford 1937) with orthogonal factors. In the IRT literature, this underlying structure was extended to models for categorical response variables (see, e.g., Gibbons and Hedeker 1992). Moreover, Sheng and Wikle (2009) introduced a Gibbs sampler algorithm for the estimation of model parameters, including the case of correlated latent variables.

In the following section, the Gibbs sampler algorithm is briefly reviewed for model (6.4) only. In fact, the additive model represents the most general structure and the estimation procedure can be easily derived for all the models discussed here. Analogously to traditional factor analysis, where the standard second-order

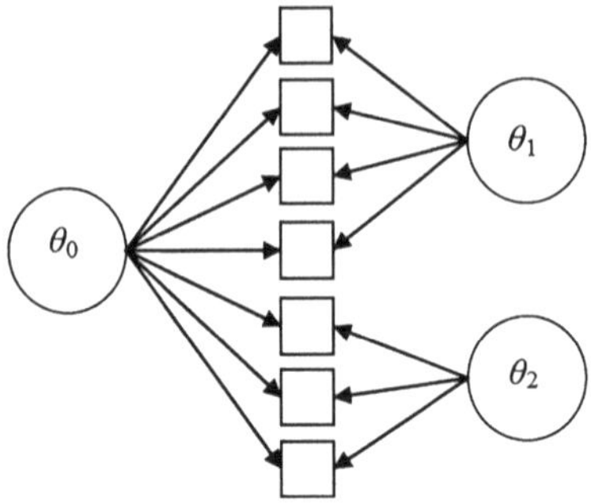

Fig. 6.4 Graphical representation for the additive model. The abilities may be correlated, even not graphically shown

model was demonstrated to be a constrained case of the bi-factor model (Yung et al. 1999; Chen et al. 2006), it can be demonstrated that the hierarchical model (6.3) is a special case of the additive model (6.4). As discussed in Sect. 1, the general ability has the same meaning in both approaches while the specific abilities for the additive model are equivalent to the disturbances of the first-order factors for the hierarchical model.

6.2.1 Estimation of the Additive Model via Gibbs Sampler

The use of the Gibbs sampler in the estimation of the 2PNO additive model (6.4) was proposed by Sheng and Wikle (2009) and implemented in the MATLAB package IRTm2noHA by Sheng (2010). The algorithm involves the specification of the conditional distribution of each variable with respect to all the other variables. Within a Bayesian approach, the item parameters, the abilities, and the correlations among the traits are viewed as random variables with their own prior distribution.

First, independent continuous underlying variables $Z_{vij} \sim N(\alpha_{0j}\theta_{0i} + \alpha_{vj}\theta_{vi} - \delta_{vj}, 1)$ are introduced so that binary response variables $\{Y_{vij}\}$ are viewed as indicators of values of $\{Z_{vij}\}$, as follows:

$$Y_{vij} = \begin{cases} 1 \text{ if } Z_{vij} > 0, \\ 0 \text{ if } Z_{vij} \leq 0. \end{cases} \tag{6.5}$$

Second, we should specify the prior distributions. Normal priors can be assumed for the item parameters $\xi_{vj} = (\alpha_{0j}, \alpha_{vj}, \delta_{vj})'$, i.e. $\xi_{vj} \sim N_{m+2}(\mu_{\xi_v}, \Sigma_{\xi_v})$, with $\mu_{\xi_v} = (\mu_{\alpha_{0v}}, \mu_{\alpha_v}, \mu_{\delta_v})'$ and $\Sigma_{\xi_v} = \text{diag}\left(\sigma^2_{\alpha_{0v}}, \sigma^2_{\alpha_v}, \sigma^2_{\delta_v}\right)$. A multivariate normal prior of dimension $m+1$ is assumed for the abilities: θ_i $N_{m+1}(\mathbf{0},\mathbf{R})$, where $\theta_i = (\theta_{0i}, \theta_{1i}, \ldots, \theta_{mi})'$ is the vector of general and specific abilities for the subject i, with $i = 1, \ldots, n$, $\mathbf{0}$ is a vector of length $m+1$ of zeros and $\mathbf{R}$ is the corresponding variance–covariance matrix. In particular, $\mathbf{R}$ is a constrained covariance matrix with diagonal elements equal to 1 and off-diagonals elements being the ability correlations. Following Sheng and Wikle (2009), an unconstrained covariance matrix Σ_{m+1} is introduced with a noninformative prior $\mathrm{P}(\Sigma) \propto |\Sigma|^{-\frac{m+1}{2}}$ so that **R** can be derived directly from Σ.

Given the prior distributions, the joint posterior distribution of interest is given by

$$\mathrm{P}\left(Z,\theta,\xi,\Sigma\middle|Y\right) \propto f\left(Y\middle|Z\right)\mathrm{P}\left(Z\middle|\theta,\xi\right)\mathrm{P}(\xi)\mathrm{P}\left(\theta\middle|R\right)\mathrm{P}(\Sigma). \tag{6.6}$$

Because distribution (6.6) has an intractable form, it is appropriate to resort to the Gibbs sampler in order to simulate iteratively from the single treatable conditional distributions until convergence. Conditional distributions are:

1. $\mathbf{Z} \mid \theta, \xi, \mathbf{Y}$
2. $\theta \mid \mathbf{Z}, \xi, \mathbf{R}, \mathbf{Y}$
3. $\xi \mid \theta, \mathbf{Z}, \mathbf{Y}$
4. $\Sigma \mid \theta, \xi, \mathbf{Y}$.

Then, the final step consists in transforming the variance–covariance matrix Σ in the correlation matrix **R**.

The first conditional distribution is a truncated normal as follows:

$$Z_{ij}\middle|\theta,\xi,y \sim \begin{cases} N(\eta_{vij};1) \text{ with } Z_{vij} > 0 \text{ if } Y_{vij} = 1 \\ N(\eta_{vij};1) \text{ with } Z_{vij} \leq 0 \text{ if } Y_{vij} = 0 \end{cases} \tag{6.7}$$

where $\eta_{vij} = \alpha_{0j}\theta_{0i} + \alpha_{vj}\theta_{vi} - \delta_{vj}$.

The second conditional distribution is

$$\theta_i\middle|Z,\xi,R,y \sim N_{m+1}\left((A'A+R)^{-1}A'B;(A'A+R)^{-1}\right), \tag{6.8}$$

where **A** is a k by $m+1$ matrix containing in the first column the general discrimination parameters and in the remaining m columns a block diagonal matrix with elements $\alpha_v = (\alpha_{v1}, \ldots, \alpha_{vkv})$, i.e. the specific discrimination parameters, and **B** is a vector of length k with elements $Z_{vi} + \delta_v$.

The third conditional distribution is multivariate normal as follows:

$$\xi_{vj}\middle|\theta,Z,y \sim N_3\left(\left(X_v'X_v+\Sigma_{\xi_v}{}^{-1}\right)^{-1}\left(X_v'Z_{vj}+\Sigma_{\xi_v}{}^{-1}\mu_{\xi_v}\right);\right)\left(X_v'X_v+\Sigma_{\xi_v}{}^{-1}\right)^{-1}, \tag{6.9}$$

where $\mathbf{X}_v = [\theta_v, -\mathbf{1}]$. It is also possible to include in distribution (6.9) an indicator function to ensure positive discrimination parameters (see, e.g., Sheng and Wikle 2009).

The last conditional distribution is an inverse Wishart distribution, as follows:

$$\Sigma\middle|\theta,\xi,y \sim W^{-1}\left(S^{-1},n\right), \tag{6.10}$$

where $S = \sum_{i=1}^{n} (C\theta_i)(C\theta_i)'$ and $C = \text{diag}\left(\left(\prod_{v=1}^{m}\prod_{j=1}^{k_v}\alpha_{0vj}\right)^{1/k}, \left(\prod_{j=1}^{k_1}\alpha_{1j}\right)^{1/k_1}, \ldots, \left(\prod_{j=1}^{k_m}\alpha_{mj}\right)^{1/k_m}\right)$.

Finally, the correlation matrix **R** should be transformed from the variance–covariance matrix Σ. For identification purposes, at each iteration, the ability parameters are rescaled to have mean equal to zero and standard deviation equal to one. For the same reason, the item parameters are rescaled to preserve the likelihood (details can be found in Bafumi et al. 2005). Within this approach, the general ability is allowed to be correlated to the specific abilities. However, it should be noted that high correlations are not supported by the model, because a problem of multicollinearity is posed.

6.2.2 *Model Selection*

One of the most important issues in educational and psychological measurement is the choice of an adequate model. This decision is crucial and should account for (a) the aim of the assessment and the capability of interpretation of the results; (b) the statistical fit of the model to the observed data.

Firstly, if the data clearly show a multidimensional structure in sub-domains, all the multidimensional approaches allow to increase the measurement precision and the reliability of each subscale, especially for high correlated domains and for multiple short subtests (de la Torre and Patz 2005; Wang et al. 2006). The choice of the best multidimensional model primarily depends on the evaluation objectives and on the specific test used to reach them.

In a multi-unidimensional model, a construct domain is broken apart into its separate distinct correlated elements. This model is most reasonable when a scale is composed of multiple items with similar content, but in this model there is no one common overall dimension to be measured or that directly affects item variance.

It is clear that if a researcher intends to both recognize multidimensionality and simultaneously consider the idea of a single important overall construct, the higher-order or additive models are the best choices. In fact the higher-order model places that the factors are correlated because they share a common cause. In other words, this model states that the overall construct is a "second-" or "higher-order" dimension that explains why two or more specific dimensions are correlated. This model doesn't assume there is a direct relationship between the item and the general construct, but rather the relationship between this general trait and each item is mediated through the specific factor, an indirect effect as just said before.

On the other side, the additive model describes a latent structure where each item loads on both a general and a specific factor directly. The general factor reflects what is common among the items and represents the individual differences on the dimension that a researcher is most interested in (e.g., learning achievement). Moreover, two or more specific factors represent common factors measured by the items that potentially explain item response variance not accounted for by the general factor. The additive model is a generalization of the most popular bi-factor model, where all traits (common and specific) are orthogonal. Several papers show the traditional second-order model is nested within the bi-factor model, and thus, the more general bi-factor can be used to evaluate the decrement in fit resulting from placing the restrictions inherent in the correlated traits, second-order, and unidimensional models (Yung et al. 1999; Chen et al. 2006; Reise et al. 2010).

In real data applications, the additive model allows to take into account general and domain specific factors simultaneously, whereas the higher-order model "forces" a primary trait to be a domain specific factor. Moreover, in the additive model the contribution of the group factors to prediction of an external variable can be studied independently of the general factor. This model allows to test measurement invariance and group mean differences at both the general and group factor levels.

Besides the specific goal of the assessment and the possibility of interpreting the results meaningfully, the statistical aspects for model choice should be taken into account. From a statistical point of view, the model choice pertains to the selection of the model that fits the data best. Certainly, one of the strengths of Bayesian methods is represented by model comparison techniques. Within this approach, Bayes factors, Bayesian deviance, and a Bayesian predictive approach, i.e. posterior predictive model checks can be used to test multiple hypotheses and to compare the fit of different models (Sinharay and Stern 2003; Sinharay et al. 2006).

6.3 Case Study

In this application we take into account response data coming from the INVALSI national assessment for the eighth grade in the scholastic year 2008/2009 on a sample of $n = 1{,}548$ students. The Italian language subtest consists of 30 reading comprehension items (R1–R30) and 10 grammar items (G1–G10), while the mathematics subtest consists of 21 items (M1–M21). All items are multiple-choice with one correct answer and can be easily recoded into binary (1 = correct response, 0 = incorrect response) so that 2PNO models could be used.

Given the test specification, a multidimensional ability structure can be clearly assumed. In particular, two different confirmatory structures could be used, by dividing the items into two subgroups (Italian language and mathematics items) or three subgroups (reading comprehension, grammar, and mathematics items).

An explorative analysis was also conducted to verify the existence of different subscales for the mathematics test. Despite the items were classified as belonging to four different domains (numbers, geometry, functions and relationships, and data and predictions), no evidence of multidimensionality was found and the presence of a predominant latent variable is assumed.

Table 6.1 Test reliability for the estimated models

	Test reliability			
Unidimensional	0.88			
Two specific dimensions	*Overall*	*Italian language*		*Mathematics*
Multi-unidimensional	–	0.86		0.82
Hierarchical	0.73	0.86		0.82
Additive	0.74	0.74		0.72
Three specific dimensions	*Overall*	*Reading comprehension*	*Grammar*	*Mathematics*
Multi-unidimensional	–	0.85	0.74	0.82
Hierarchical	0.78	0.84	0.74	0.82
Additive	0.76	0.72	0.56	0.74

A comparison was conducted in order to choose the best model in terms of data fit. First of all, the unidimensional model (6.1) was estimated by using the MATLAB package IRTuno by Sheng (2008a). Then, the multi-unidimensional model (6.2) was taken into account with both two or three specific dimensions. Model estimation was conducted with the MATLAB package IRTmu2no by Sheng (2008b). Finally, the hierarchical model (6.3) and the additive model (6.4) were estimated again with two or three specific dimensions but assuming one overall ability too. Parameter estimation was conducted by using the MATLAB package IRTm2noHA (Sheng 2010). For all models, convergence of the Gibbs sampler was assessed by checking that the Gelman–Rubin statistic was around or close to 1 for each parameter. This required 20,000 total and 10,000 burn-in iterations.

Firstly, test reliability was computed for the different models as reported in Table 6.1. The results show that the reliability is sufficiently large to be useful for most approaches. The weakest subscale is represented by the grammar test where the number of items is probably too low with respect to the complexity of this domain. Moreover, the mathematics test seems to be weaker than the Italian language test in terms of reliability and this may be due to the presence of much more heterogeneous items. Both for the multi-unidimensional and hierarchical models, test reliabilities are rather large for all subscales. In the additive model, the addition of a general ability reduces the reliabilities associated with the specific traits. This effect is not observed for the hierarchical model, as the specific factors are a linear function of the general one.

Table 6.2 reports the results for the deviance information criterion (DIC; Spiegelhalter et al. 2002) for all models.

As can be clearly seen from the results, a multidimensional approach should be preferred in comparison with a unidimensional one, which is associated with the highest DIC = 96272.61. In the comparison of models with two or three specific traits, the highest number of dimensions should be definitely chosen. By comparing different approaches with three specific dimensions, the additive model with DIC = 94381.91 turns out to be the best model. By considering DIC, test reliability, and test structure jointly, we believe that the additive model with three

Table 6.2 DIC for the estimated models

	DIC	
Unidimensional	96272.61	
	Two specific dimensions	Three specific dimensions
Multi-unidimensional	95163.57	94902.07
Hierarchical	95158.37	94900.61
Additive	94587.39	94381.91

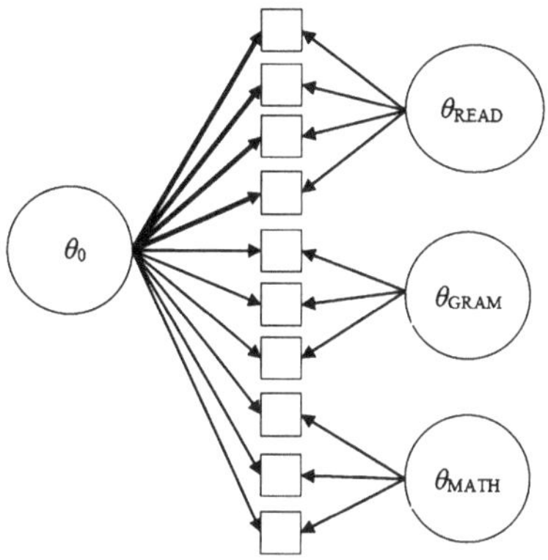

Fig. 6.5 Graphical representation for the chosen additive model with three specific dimensions and one general ability for the INVALSI test data

specific dimensions would be an appropriate choice for the evaluation purposes. Based on these considerations, we assume that the item response probability depends on a general cognitive ability, on a specific literacy on the item topic, and on the joint effect that these abilities have in the problem solving. Therefore, we introduce correlations among all the traits, so that general and specific dimensions are not totally separated, in accordance with the cognitive process we assume to explain the learning achievement.

The latent structure is made of three specific abilities ($\theta_1 =$ reading comprehension ability, $\theta_2 =$ grammar ability, $\theta_3 =$ mathematics ability) and a general, overall ability θ_0 with a compensatory effect in determining the probability of a correct response, as graphically represented in Fig. 6.5.

The INVALSI test was developed in order to assess not only specific literacy but also general ability, i.e. reasoning and thinking capability. For this reason, a latent structure consisting of both specific and general abilities is a good solution. In the comparison among the additive and the hierarchical model, the former should be preferred. This can be proved not only in terms of DIC but also by using posterior predictive models checks (PPMC). In fact, the choice of a Bayesian approach allows the use of PPMC for assessing model fit (Sinharay and Stern 2003) by comparing the observed data to replicated data sampled from the posterior predictive distribution. Within IRT models, Sinharay et al. (2006) evaluated a number of different discrepancy measures and suggested the use of the odds ratio as measure of associations among item pairs in order to detect lack of fit. This approach is implemented in the IRTm2noHA package (Sheng 2010), where the odds ratio and

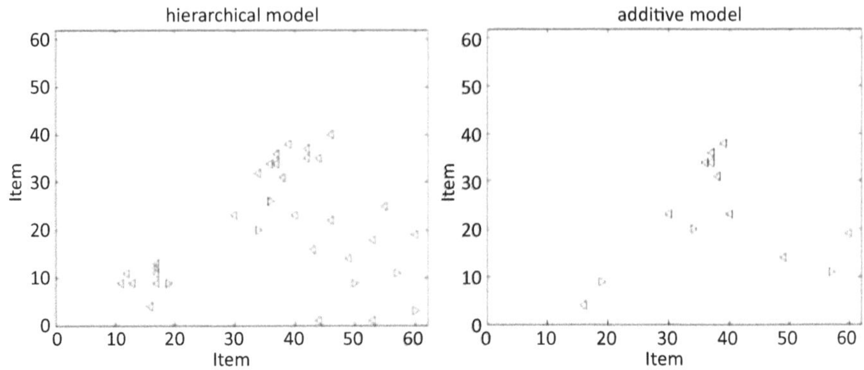

Fig. 6.6 PPMC of the hierarchical and the additive models for the INVALSI test data

the corresponding PPP-values are calculated for each item pair, as shown in Fig. 6.6 for the hierarchical model (on the left) and the additive model (on the right) with three specific abilities. In particular, Fig. 6.6 highlights with a triangle the extreme predicted odds ratios, i.e. tail-area probabilities PPP-values for odds ratios larger than 0.995 or smaller than 0.005. Clearly, the additive model is associated with a smaller number of extreme predicted odds ratios in comparison with the hierarchical model. Henceforth, the results for the additive model will be taken into account.

The estimated item parameters are shown in Table 6.3. The model requires, for each item, the estimation of a general discrimination parameter α_0, a specific discrimination α_v, and a difficulty parameter δ_v, for $v = 1, \ldots, 3$ first-order dimensions. For each parameter, the mean of the posterior distribution of the samples, i.e. the expected a posterior (EAP) estimate, and the corresponding standard deviation (SD) are reported.

The item parameters have been estimated accurately, as proved by the standard deviations describing a low statistical uncertainty. Furthermore, Monte Carlo standard errors (MCSE) computed according to the batching method were all lower than 0.01.

The discrimination parameters are largely positive for most items, suggesting that the assumed structure is consistent and able to give information on the contribution of each dimension. As can be clearly seen from the results, the test items can be divided into three main groups depending on the discrimination parameter estimates and the comparison between the general α_0 and the specific α_v discrimination. In a first group, we can include items with considerably higher estimates for the specific discrimination than for the general discrimination which can be interpreted as items measuring literacy mainly. In a second group, items assumed to measure thinking and reasoning skills, instead of mere literacy, can be included. These items are characterized by a higher general discrimination parameter in comparison with the specific one. Lastly, a third group of items can be identified by both positive and balanced discrimination parameters. In order to endorse these items, both literacy

Table 6.3 Item parameter estimates for the additive model

		α_0		α_v		δ_v	
Domain	Item	EAP	SD	EAP	SD	EAP	SD
Reading	R1	0.18	0.09	0.64	0.09	−0.38	0.04
	R2	0.16	0.08	0.27	0.08	−1.03	0.04
	R3	0.18	0.07	0.27	0.08	−0.69	0.04
	R4	0.15	0.07	0.29	0.07	−0.33	0.03
	R5	0.22	0.09	0.44	0.09	−1.11	0.05
	R6	0.58	0.10	0.37	0.10	−1.23	0.06
	R7	0.30	0.08	0.25	0.08	−0.52	0.04
	R8	0.36	0.08	0.31	0.08	−0.09	0.03
	R9	0.94	0.09	0.09	0.06	−0.75	0.05
	R10	0.14	0.05	0.04	0.03	0.15	0.03
	R11	0.90	0.08	0.05	0.04	−1.02	0.05
	R12	0.76	0.08	0.11	0.07	−0.80	0.04
	R13	0.70	0.08	0.10	0.06	−0.63	0.04
	R14	0.21	0.07	0.27	0.08	−0.68	0.04
	R15	0.51	0.08	0.10	0.07	−1.11	0.05
	R16	0.06	0.05	0.33	0.06	0.18	0.03
	R17	1.29	0.11	0.07	0.06	−0.99	0.06
	R18	0.45	0.08	0.35	0.08	−0.41	0.04
	R19	0.06	0.04	0.18	0.06	0.63	0.03
	R20	0.30	0.08	0.24	0.08	−0.28	0.03
	R21	0.13	0.08	0.46	0.08	−1.05	0.04
	R22	0.32	0.10	0.61	0.10	−0.99	0.05
	R23	0.10	0.07	0.62	0.10	−1.68	0.07
	R24	0.08	0.05	0.27	0.06	−0.07	0.03
	R25	0.21	0.07	0.27	0.08	−0.07	0.03
	R26	0.30	0.08	0.38	0.08	−0.45	0.04
	R27	0.08	0.06	0.53	0.07	−0.73	0.04
	R28	0.16	0.08	0.48	0.08	−0.67	0.04
	R29	0.21	0.09	0.50	0.09	−0.80	0.04
	R30	0.45	0.11	0.42	0.11	−1.58	0.07
Grammar	G1	0.31	0.08	0.39	0.08	−1.35	0.05
	G2	0.29	0.08	0.53	0.07	−0.44	0.04
	G3	0.45	0.08	0.44	0.07	−0.87	0.04
	G4	0.04	0.03	0.40	0.06	0.18	0.03
	G5	0.44	0.10	0.64	0.09	−1.29	0.06
	G6	0.12	0.07	0.52	0.06	−0.16	0.03
	G7	0.23	0.12	0.92	0.10	−0.24	0.04
	G8	0.66	0.10	0.52	0.09	−1.67	0.08
	G9	0.49	0.09	0.27	0.09	1.71	0.07
	G10	0.26	0.05	0.15	0.05	−0.49	0.03
Maths	M1	0.17	0.05	0.17	0.05	−0.93	0.04
	M2	0.25	0.07	0.57	0.06	−0.99	0.05
	M3	0.14	0.05	0.31	0.05	−0.03	0.03
	M4	0.39	0.07	0.53	0.07	−1.20	0.05
	M5	0.14	0.06	0.18	0.07	−1.51	0.05
	M6	0.49	0.08	0.73	0.07	−1.03	0.05
	M7	0.16	0.07	0.76	0.07	−0.70	0.04
	M8	0.11	0.05	0.48	0.05	−0.59	0.04
	M9	0.23	0.06	0.57	0.06	−0.32	0.04
	M10	0.14	0.06	0.64	0.06	−0.61	0.04
	M11	0.22	0.06	0.48	0.06	−0.67	0.04
	M12	0.24	0.07	0.67	0.07	−1.06	0.05
	M13	0.35	0.06	0.42	0.05	−0.70	0.04
	M14	0.41	0.07	0.67	0.06	−0.69	0.04
	M15	0.14	0.06	0.54	0.06	−0.61	0.04
	M16	0.14	0.05	0.47	0.05	−0.49	0.04
	M17	0.06	0.04	0.60	0.06	−0.97	0.04
	M18	0.19	0.08	0.84	0.08	0.87	0.05
	M19	0.12	0.06	0.58	0.06	−0.51	0.04
	M20	0.08	0.05	0.37	0.05	−0.35	0.03
	M21	0.07	0.04	0.40	0.05	−0.67	0.04

and reasoning abilities are needed. In this last group of items, the interaction among the general and specific abilities is more evident.

In the reading comprehension subtest, items R1, R16, R21, R22, R23, R24, R27, R28, R29 can be included in the first group. These items mainly require lexical competence and local or global comprehension of the text to be solved. On the contrary, items R6, R9, R11, R12, R13, R15, R17 are characterized by a higher estimate in the general discrimination parameter with respect to the specific one and require to interpret, identify a meaning, or make an inference from the text. The remaining items are associated with both positive and moderate discrimination parameters. This means that, in order to be solved, the item needs both a specific ability in reading comprehension and a more general capability of reasoning and thinking.

By looking at the results for the grammar subtest, it can be noticed that most items (G2, G4, G5, G6, G7) are related more specifically to grammar literacy. These items require the knowledge of morphology and linguistic syntax. The remaining items are related to both a specific and an overall ability, by requiring to understand the meaning or the communicative use of a word or a sentence.

In the mathematics subtest, most items are associated with high specific discrimination parameters, denoting a stronger relationship with the corresponding literacy instead of the thinking and reasoning ability. In fact, the mathematics items were designed with a special focus on the specific competence especially on numbers and geometry. On the other hand, items with a moderate general discrimination parameter deal with relations and functions (D4, D6), measurement, data and prevision (D13), and space and figures (D14). All these items have a strong reasoning component.

The threshold parameters δ_v can be used to identify the difficulty level of the item. However, for this model, it is not possible to order univocally the items by difficulty level on the basis the parameter estimate. In fact, this order may vary depending on various combination of ability ranges. By fixing the ability scores at their mean value ($\widehat{\theta}_0 = \widehat{\theta}_v = 0$), it is possible to interpret the difficulty of the items for a median student, by evaluating the standard normal cumulative distribution function at minus the threshold parameter. This means that, as the threshold parameter decreases, the probability of a correct response for a median individual increases. As can be easily noticed from Table 6.3, most items are associated with a negative threshold parameter with few exceptions (R10, R16, R19, G4, M18). This means that that the test is unbalanced in favor of "easy" items, where the probability of endorsing the item for a student with an average reasoning ability and specific ability, depending on the item subgroup, is higher than 50 %.

To sum up, the reading comprehension items need a higher reasoning and thinking ability in comparison with grammar and especially mathematics items which are more related to the specific competence (literacy). On average, the grammar items are associated with a relative easiness of solution for a student with mean abilities.

An advantage of using the additive model is the possibility to score students on both the overall and the specific dimensions. In this way, it is possible to

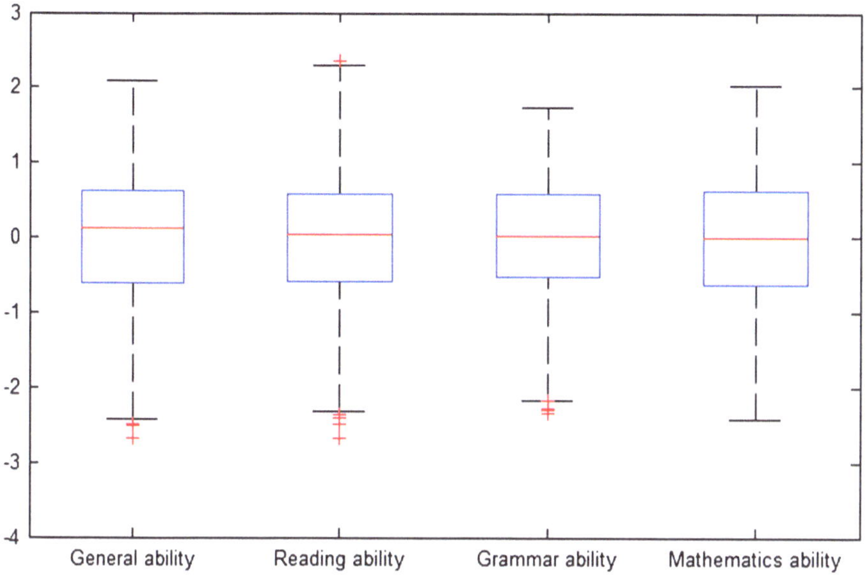

Fig. 6.7 Box-plots of the estimated ability scores for the additive model

Table 6.4 Estimated correlations among the abilities (MCSE in *brackets*)

	θ_0	θ_{READ}	θ_{GRAM}	θ_{MATH}
θ_0	1.00 (0.00)			
θ_{READ}	0.60 (0.08)	1.00 (0.00)		
θ_{GRAM}	0.24 (0.12)	0.62 (0.07)	1.00 (0.00)	
θ_{MATH}	0.35 (0.07)	0.55 (0.05)	0.50 (0.05)	1.00 (0.00)

evaluate students both on reasoning and thinking capability and on specific literacy. In particular, each specific ability score can be interpreted as a residual ability in comparison with the overall ability. The box-plots of the ability estimates in the sample are shown in Fig. 6.7.

The overall and the reading abilities are able to score the subjects on the widest range of values. On the contrary, the grammar test contains only ten items and the estimated ability scores cover the smallest interval. Median values are close to zero for all abilities, while variability is lower for the grammar ability.

In the additive model, the general and specific abilities are assumed to be correlated. Estimates of these correlations are reported in Table 6.4.

The results confirm that the assumption of correlated traits is appropriate. Moreover, the estimated correlations are not so high to cause a multicollinearity problem. As expected, the reasoning and thinking ability θ_0 is fairly correlated to the reading ability, whose items mostly require reasoning capability. On the contrary, θ_0 is slightly correlated to grammar and mathematics abilities, whose items mainly assess specific literacy. Obviously, there is a fair correlation among the reading comprehension and grammar ability and, generally, the specific dimensions are correlated to each other. This empirical evidence suggests that the use of a model with correlated abilities is needed in order to explain deeply the underlying response structure.

Concluding Remarks

In educational studies, the analysis of outcomes has a primary role and, recently, there has been an increased focus on defining tools to assess the competences acquired by students. Adequate tools for measuring competence need to be based on psychometric models that represent the internal structure in terms of specific basic abilities. One of the main approaches is IRT. IRT models are often used under the assumption of a single or at least one predominant latent ability but, in real applications, tests often consist of different subscales or domains involving explicitly several ability dimensions. For this reason, the attention has recently been devoted to MIRT models incorporating multiple abilities taking into account the hierarchical structure typical of mental abilities.

Additive models and higher-order models are two alternative approaches for dealing with items that assess several related domains. Additive models consider a general factor and multiple domain specific factors, each of which is hypothesized to account for the unique influence of the specific domain over the general factor. Higher-order models consider lower-order factors correlated with each other and a higher-order factor that is hypothesized to account for the relationship among the lower-order factors. The model choice should be made with regard to the specific research question especially because different models may be equivalent in terms of fit.

In this paper, a multidimensional additive IRT model is proposed in order to explain response data for the INVALSI test administrated at the end of lower secondary school (eighth grade). We propose the use of the additive model with one general and three specific factors, where the specific factors are intended to measure the abilities within each domain of the test (reading comprehension, grammar, and mathematics) in terms of literacy, and the general factor is interpreted as measuring reasoning and thinking skills. The model includes the correlations among the different traits because the existence of an association among these abilities is well known. To estimate the model we use MCMC methods, in a fully Bayesian framework. This approach has the advantage of estimating item parameters and individual abilities jointly and it is more accurate and efficient compared with the usual MML method. MCMC is powerful for complicated models where the probabilities or expectations are intractable by analytical methods or other numerical approximation. We show that the proposed model fit the data better in comparison with other multidimensional models. The model is consistent

(continued)

with the assumed test structure, it offers evidences on the item measurement characteristics and it is able to describe the relations among the latent abilities meaningfully.

The results clearly show the cognitive test structure. Student performances depend on a general factor, called reasoning and thinking ability, with a more or less pronounced impact on single items, and on three specific literacy factors. According to the results, it was possible to classify each item on the basis of the predominant cognitive characteristics. In particular, within each domain there are items mainly measuring the literacy component, i.e. the capability of applying concepts and procedures, while other items measure a more general component by involving reasoning and thinking abilities. Lastly, for some items, the two components are equivalent. In the reading subtest there is quite a balance among the different item types, while in the grammar and especially in the mathematics subtest there are more items with a greater score for the literacy.

These results probably depend on how these topics are taught at school and how the students are evaluated. In Italy, the mathematics is still a subject which is strongly related to notions and, as a consequence, students are required to merely use instruments while less attention is given to reasoning skills. This may partially justify the low results of Italian students within international student assessments such as OECD PISA or TIMSS, where the number of items requiring not only literacy but especially reasoning capability is quite relevant.

The item classification based on different weights (discrimination parameters) for the abilities may be extremely useful for evaluators in order to better understand the learning outcomes and to use the information provided to modify the test structure and to build new items.

The additive model allowed to score separately students on both overall and specific dimensions. In order to endorse the item, the specific ability is the prevalent component in the grammar and mathematics subtests, while the overall ability has a larger effect for the reading comprehension subtest.

The results give important recommendations to test developers and policy makers on learning contents and processes and on instruments for the evaluation of performances.

This work represents a first attempt of analyzing the results of the INVALSI test from a multidimensional perspective, by offering important causes for reflection and opening the way for in-depth analyses using more sophisticated but more flexible methods in comparison with classical techniques to deal with complex testing situations. The results could also be used by INVALSI in order to assign a final test score and separate subtest scores to students. The Institute is currently working on new tests containing items classified according to both the content domain and the cognitive process needed to

(continued)

solve the item. We expect that new data would allow a multidimensional analysis also for the mathematics subtest. As a consequence, it will be possible to include more than one second-order trait and a third-order general trait (Huang et al. 2013).

Acknowledgments This research has been partially funded by the Italian Ministry of Education with the FIRB ("Futuro in ricerca") 2012 project on "Mixture and latent variable models for causal-inference and analysis of socio-economic data."

References

Albert JH (1992) Bayesian estimation of normal ogive item response curves using Gibbs sampling. J Educ Stat 17:251–269
Bafumi J, Gelman A, Park DK, Kaplan N (2005) Practical issues in implementing and understanding Bayesian ideal point estimation. Polit Anal 13:171–187
Béguin AA, Glas CAW (2001) MCMC estimation and some model-fit analysis of multidimensional IRT models. Psychometrika 66:541–562
Chen FF, West SG, Sousa KH (2006) A comparison of bifactor and second-order models of quality of life. Multivar Behav Res 41(2):189–225
Cowles MK, Carlin BP (1996) Markov chain Monte Carlo convergence diagnostics: a comparative review. J Am Stat Assoc 91:883–904
de la Torre J, Patz RJ (2005) Making the most of what we have: a practical application of multidimensional item response theory in test scoring. J Educ Behav Stat 30(3):295–311
de la Torre J, Song H (2009) Simultaneous estimation of overall and domain abilities: a higher-order IRT model approach. Appl Psychol Meas 33:620–639
Edwards MC (2010) A Markov chain Monte Carlo approach to confirmatory item factor analysis. Psychometrika 75:474–497
Fox JP, Glas CAW (2001) Bayesian estimation of a multilevel IRT model using Gibbs sampling. Psychometrika 66:271–288
Geman S, Geman D (1984) Stochastic relaxation, Gibbs distributions and the Bayesian restoration of images. IEEE Trans Pattern Anal Mach Intell 6:721–741
Gibbons RD, Hedeker DR (1992) Full-information item bi-factor analysis. Psychometrika 57:423–436
Grek S (2009) Governing by numbers: the PISA effect in Europe. J Educ Policy 24(1):23–37
Hartig J, Hohler J (2009) Multidimensional IRT models for the assessment of competencies. Stud Educ Eval 35:57–63
Holzinger KJ, Swineford F (1937) The bi-factor method. Psychometrika 2:41–54
Huang HY, Wang WC, Chen PH, Su CM (2013) Higher-order item response models for hierarchical latent traits. Appl Psychol Meas 37(8):619–637
Koeppen K, Hartig J, Klieme E, Leutner D (2008) Current issues in competence modeling and assessment. J Psychol 216(2):61–73
Lord FM, Novick MR (1968) Statistical theories of mental test scores. Addison-Wesley, Reading
Reckase M (2009) Multidimensional item response theory. Springer, New York
Reise SP, Moore TN, Haviland MG (2010) Bi-factor models and rotations: exploring the extent to which multidimensional data yield univocal scale scores. J Pers Assess 92(6):544–559
Sahu SK (2002) Bayesian estimation and model choice in item response models. J Stat Comput Simulat 72:217–232

Schmid J, Leiman JM (1957) The development of hierarchical factor solutions. Psychometrika 22:53–61
Sheng Y (2008a) Markov chain Monte Carlo estimation of normal ogive IRT models in MATLAB. J Stat Softw 25(8):1–15
Sheng Y (2008b) A MATLAB package for Markov chain Monte Carlo with a multi-unidimensional IRT model. J Stat Soft 28(10):1–20
Sheng Y (2010) Bayesian estimation of MIRT models with general and specific latent traits in MATLAB. J Stat Soft 34(10):1–27
Sheng Y, Wikle C (2007) Comparing multiunidimensional and unidimensional item response theory models. Educ Psychol Meas 67(6):899–919
Sheng Y, Wikle C (2008) Bayesian multidimensional IRT models with an hierarchical structure. Educ Psychol Meas 68(3):413–430
Sheng Y, Wikle C (2009) Bayesian IRT models incorporating general and specific abilities. Behaviormetrika 36(1):27–48
Sinharay S, Stern HS (2003) Posterior predictive model checking in hierarchical models. J Stat Plan Inf 111:209–221
Sinharay S, Johnson MS, Stern HS (2006) Posterior predictive assessment of item response theory models. Appl Psychol Meas 30:298–321
Spiegelhalter D, Best N, Carlin B, van der Linde A (2002) Bayesian measures of model complexity and fit. J R Stat Soc: Ser B 64:583–640
van der Linden WJ, Hambleton RK (1997) Handbook of modern item response theory. Springer, New York
Wang W-C, Chen P-H, Cheng Y-Y (2004) Improving measurement precision of test batteries using multidimensional item response models. Psychol Methods 9:116–136
Wang W-C, Yao G, Tsai Y-J, Wang J-D, Hsieh C-L (2006) Validating, improving reliability, and estimating correlation of the four subscales in the WHOQOL-BREF using multidimensional Rasch analysis. Qual Life Res 15:607–620
Yung YF, Thissen D, McLeod LD (1999) On the relationship between the higher-order factor model and the hierarchical factor model. Psychometrika 64:113–128

Chapter 7
Graphical Representations of Items and Tests That are Measuring Multiple Abilities

Terry A. Ackerman and Robert A. Henson

Abstract This article compares graphical representations of items and tests for four different multidimensional item response theory (MIRT) models: compensatory logistic model, the noncompensatory logistic model, a noncompensatory diagnostic model (DINA), and a compensatory diagnostic model (CRUM/GDM). Graphical representations can provide greater insight for measurement specialists and item/test developers about the validity and reliability of the multidimensional tests. They also can provide a link between quantitative analyses and substantive interpretations of the score scale and inform the test development process.

Over the past several years there has been a growth of interest in multidimensional item response (MIRT) models, especially diagnostic classification models (DCM) (Rupp et al. 2010). These new MIRT models take a different approach in the type of information they provide. Specifically, instead of providing ability estimates along latent continuums the DCM provide information about whether examinees have achieved a pre-designated level of competency on each trait being measured. The purpose of this paper is to examine graphical representation of four particular two-dimensional MIRT models to illustrate how different aspects of each model can be represented. Graphical representations can provide greater insight for measurement specialists and item/test developers about the validity and reliability of the multidimensional tests. They also can provide a link between quantitative analyses and substantive interpretations of the score scale and inform the test development process. The models that will be examined are the compensatory logistic model, the noncompensatory logistic model, a noncompensatory diagnostic model (DINA), and a compensatory diagnostic model (CRUM/GDM). We will exam four particular aspects of each model from a graphical perspective: item representation, information representation, true score estimation, and conditional estimation.

T.A. Ackerman (✉) • R.A. Henson
University of North Carolina at Greensboro, 1300 Spring Garden St., Greensboro, NC 27284, USA
e-mail: taackerm@uncg.edu

R.E. Millsap et al. (eds.), *Quantitative Psychology Research*, Springer Proceedings in Mathematics & Statistics 89, DOI 10.1007/978-3-319-07503-7_7

7.1 The Models

The first model is the compensatory logistic model. This is a direct extension of the 2-PL unidimensional model. The two-dimensional compensatory model can be expressed as

$$P_{ij} = \frac{1.0}{1.0 + e^{-1.7(a_{1i}\theta_{1j} + a_{2i}\theta_{2j} + d_i)}} \tag{7.1}$$

where a_{1i} and a_{2i} represent the discrimination parameters for item i on dimension one and two, respectively; and, θ_{1j} and θ_{2j} denote the latent abilities for subject j. In this model, item difficulty for each dimension is indeterminate, thus we have just one overall difficulty parameter for item i, d_i. This model is described as "compensatory" because the abilities weighted by an item's respective discrimination parameters are additive in the logit. Thus, being "low" on one ability can be compensated by being "high" on the other ability. This aspect will be illustrated later in the article.

The second model is the noncompensatory model given as

$$P_{ij} = \left[\frac{1.0}{1.0 + e^{-1.7(a_{1i}\theta_{1j} - b_{1i})}}\right]\left[\frac{1.0}{1.0 + e^{-1.7(a_{2i}\theta_{2j} - b_{2i})}}\right]. \tag{7.2}$$

In this model for a given item i each dimension has a discrimination parameter, a_{1i} and a_{2i}, as well as a difficulty parameter, b_{1i} and b_{2i}. Also θ_{1j} and θ_{2j} denote the latent abilities on the two dimensions for subject j. Notice also that this model is essentially the product of two 2PL unidimensional IRT models, one for each dimension. The multiplicative nature of this model also implies that being "low" on one dimension cannot be compensated by being "high" on the other dimension. That is, the overall probability of correct response is never greater than the largest probability of the two dimensions. Specifically, if the first dimension (θ_1) component is 0.20 and then even if the second dimensional component (θ_2) was 1.0, the overall probability of correct response would only be 0.20.

The third model is the two-dimensional compensatory diagnostic model (CGUM/GDM). Using the notation presented in Rupp et. al. (2010) this model can be expressed as

$$P_{ij} = \frac{1.0}{1.0 + e^{-1.7(\lambda_{1i}\alpha_{1j} + \lambda_{2i}\alpha_{2j} + \lambda_{0i})}} \tag{7.3}$$

where λ_{1i} and λ_{1i} are the discrimination parameters for item i on the first and second dimensions, α_{1j} and α_{2j} denote the two latent dichotomous abilities for subject j, and λ_{0i} represents the difficulty parameter for item i. Note that this model is very similar to the compensatory model given in Eq. 7.1. The difference between the two is that there are only two values of the latent attributes in α and the overall interpretation of the intercept. As opposed to defining an "average" difficulty of the item, λ_{0i} is related to the probability of a correct response for someone who has not mastered any of the measured attributes.

The final model is the noncompensatory diagnostic model called the DINA (the Deterministic Noisy "and" model, Junker and Sijtsma 2001). In contrast to the compensatory model, the DINA divides examinees into only two groups. The first group has mastered all measured attributes by the item ($\eta_{ij} = 1$) and thus should correctly respond to the item and a second group that has not mastered at least one of the measured items ($\eta_{ij} = 0$) and should miss the item. Given the groups defined by η_{ij}, the probability of correct response to item i for person j can be written as

$$P_{ij} = (1 - s_j)^{\eta_i} g_j^{(1-\eta_i)} \tag{7.4}$$

where s_j is referred to as the "slip" parameter and specifies the probability that an examinee who should answer the item right "slips up" and misses the item. The parameter g_j represents the probability that and examinee correctly "guesses" (i.e., the guessing the parameter) the answer when in fact they are expected to miss the item.

7.2 Item Representation: Compensatory and Noncompensatory Items

For the compensatory and noncompensatory items, because they are based upon a continuous two-dimensional latent space, researchers can graphically represent the probability of correct response for subject j for item i for all θ_{1j}, θ_{2j} combinations as a response surface. This surface is the two-dimensional analog to the unidimensional item characteristic curve (ICC). An example of such a surface for a compensatory item with parameters $a_1 = 0.80$, $a_2 = 1.40$, and $d = -0.30$ from four different perspectives is shown in Fig. 7.1. These figures were created using the software CA-DISSPLA.

An example of a response surface for the noncompensatory model having parameters

$a_1 = 2.0$, $a_2 = 0.9$, $b_1 = 0.6$, and $b_2 = 0.5$ is shown from four different perspectives in Fig. 7.2. The effect of the multiplicative nature of this model can be seen by the curving of the surface.

The response surfaces are not very helpful in that only one can be examined at a time unlike their unidimensional ICC counterparts. A more helpful representation would be to construct the contour plot for each surface. Such plots illustrate the equi-probability contours of the response surface. Representations of such plots are shown in Figs. 7.3, 7.4, and 7.5 for the compensatory model. In Fig. 7.3 the item contours represent an item that only discriminates only among levels of θ_1 with parameters $a_1 = 1.5$, $a_2 = 0.0$, and $d = 0.3$. Notice the examinees A and B, whohave

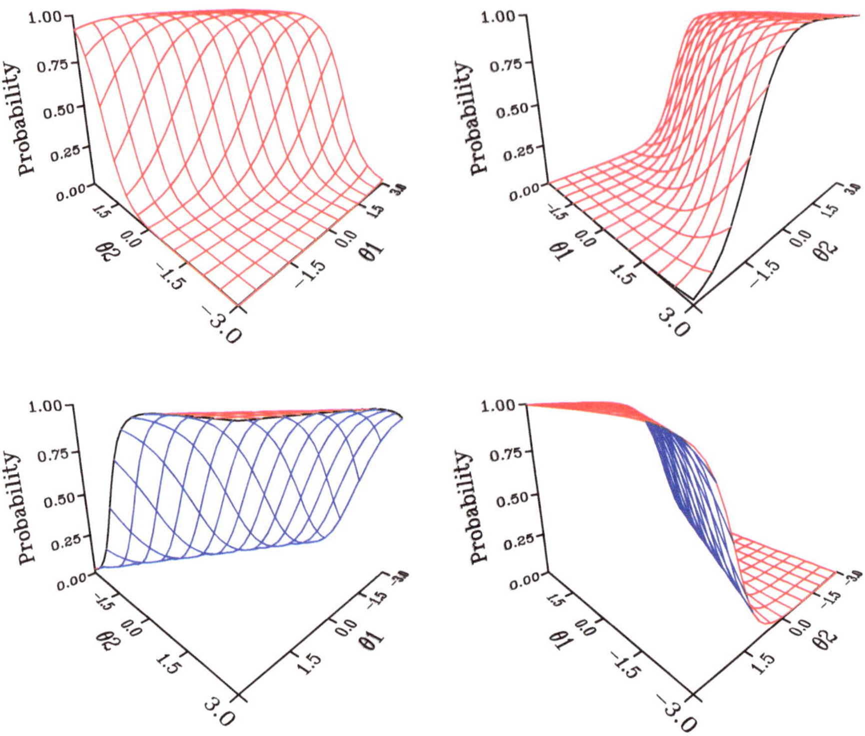

Fig. 7.1 An example item characteristic surface

a θ_1 value of about -1 yet differ greatly on their θ_2 abilities, have exactly the same probability of correct response, 0.2. That is, even though there is a huge discrepancy in their θ_2 values, there is no compensation when an item is distinguishing between levels of proficiency on only one ability. Notice also that examinees B and C, who have the same θ_2 ability but differ greatly on their θ_1 abilities, do have quite different probabilities of correct response, 0.2 for B and 0.8 for C. One should also note that the larger the a-parameters the steeper the response surface and the closer together the equi-probability contours.

In Fig. 7.4 the contour plot for an item that is measuring both θ_1 and θ_2 equally is displayed. That is, $a_1 = a_2 = 1.0$. In this figure note examinees A and B have opposite "profiles." That is, examinee A is low on θ_1 but high on θ_2. Examine B is high on θ_1 and low on θ_2. However, due to the compensatory nature of this model, both examinees have the same probability of correct response, 0.7. Thus, compensation in this model is maximal when both dimensions are being measured equally well. (This also is why some researchers refer to this model as a partially compensatory model, because the degree of compensatory is a function of the discrimination parameters. As seen in Fig. 7.3, when only one latent trait is being measured, there is no compensation.)

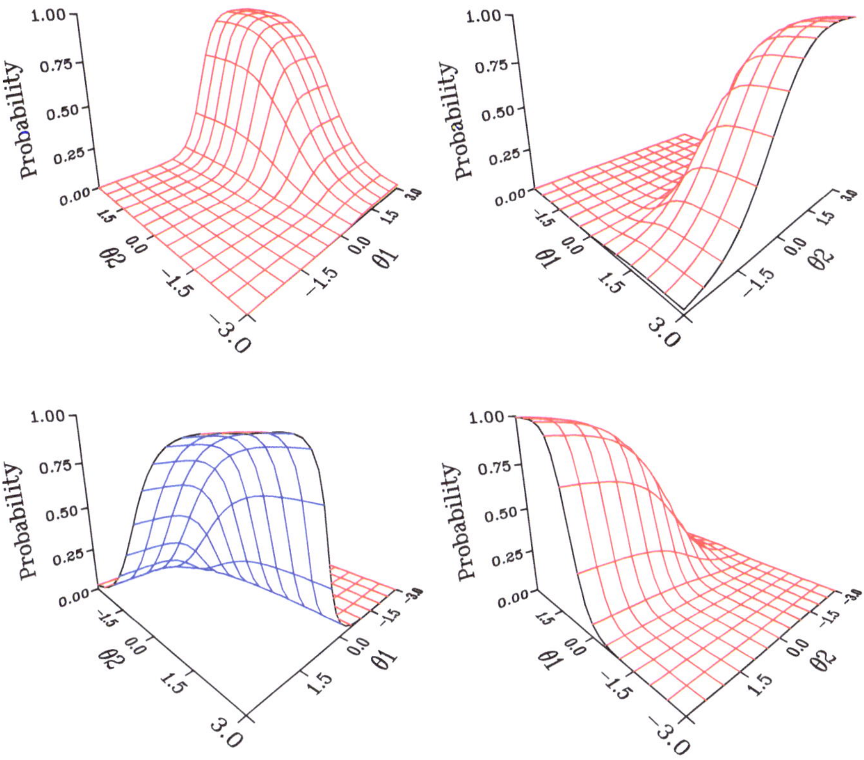

Fig. 7.2 An example of a noncompensatory response surface

The contour plot also helps one to see the difference between the compensatory and noncompensatory models. The curving around of the response surface is much more noticeable when viewed in terms of contours. The contour plot for the noncompensatory model with parameters $a_1 = 1.2$, $a_2 = 1.1$, $b_1 = -0.60$, and $b_2 = 0.50$ is displayed in Fig. 7.5. Notice also in this figure that subjects A, B, and C all have approximately the same probability of correct response, even though their ability profiles are quite distinct. That is, examinee A is high on θ_2 and low on θ_1, examinee B is low on θ_1 and low θ_2, whereas examinee C has the opposite profile of examinee A and is low on θ_2 and high on θ_1. Clearly in this case, there is no compensation, being high on one ability offers no compensation for examinees who are low on the other ability.

Although contours are an improvement over response surfaces, practitioners can only examinee one item at a time with this method. Perhaps the best way to illustrate items for these two models is using vectors. Following the work of Reckase (1985), Reckase and McKinley (1991), Ackerman (1994a, b), Ackerman (1996), and Ackerman et al. (2003) an item can be represented as a vector where the length of the vector, MDISC, is a function of the discrimination of the item,

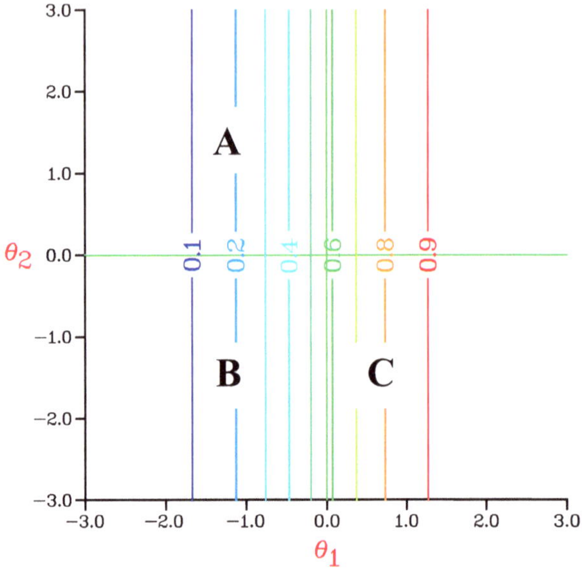

Fig. 7.3 A contour plot for an item measuring only $\theta 1$

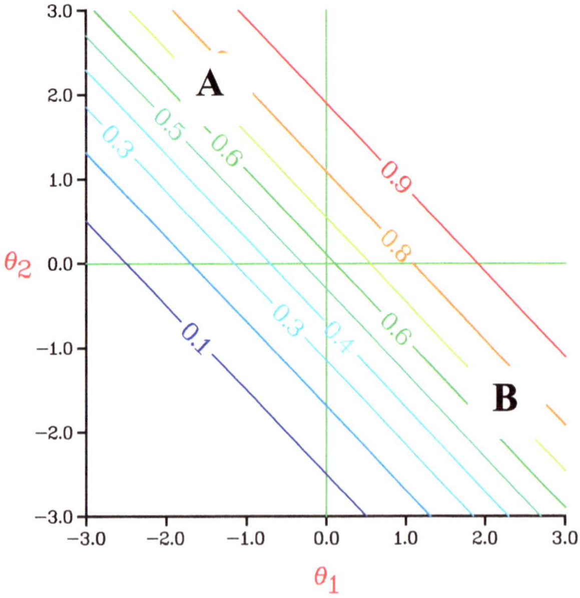

Fig. 7.4 A contour plot for a compensatory item with equal discrimination parameters

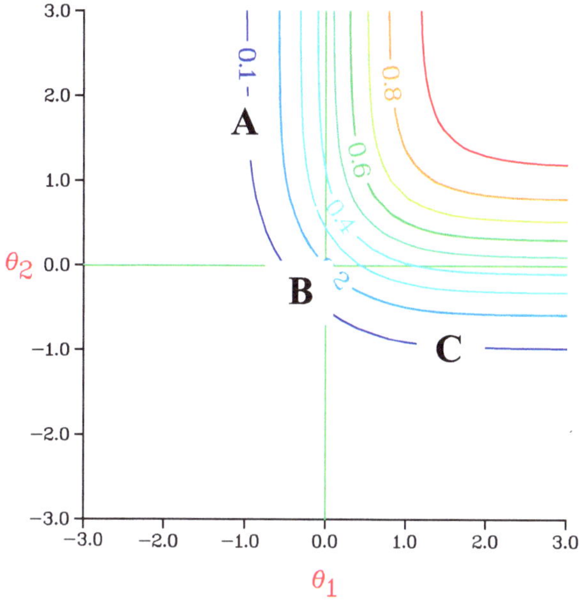

Fig. 7.5 A contour plot for a noncompensatory item

$$\mathrm{MDISC} = \sqrt{\left(a_1^2 + a_2^2\right)}. \tag{7.5}$$

The vector is orthogonal to and lies on the $p = 0.5$ equi-probability contour. All vectors lie on a line that passes through the origin of the $\theta_1 - \theta_2$ coordinate system. Because discrimination parameters are constrained to be positive, vectors can only lie in the first and third quadrants. The distance from the origin to the tail of vector, D, is equal to

$$\mathrm{D} = \frac{-\mathrm{d}}{\mathrm{MDISC}}. \tag{7.6}$$

The angular direction of the vector with the θ_1-axis, α, can be obtained using the formula

$$\alpha = \cos^{-1}\left(\frac{a_1}{\mathrm{MDISC}}\right). \tag{7.7}$$

Note that the angular direction is a function of the ratio of the a_1 parameter with MDISC. If $a_2 = 0$, then the vector will lie along the θ_1-axis. If $a_1 = a_2$, the vector will lie at a 45° angle. An example of an item vector in relationship to a response surface is illustrated in Fig. 7.6.

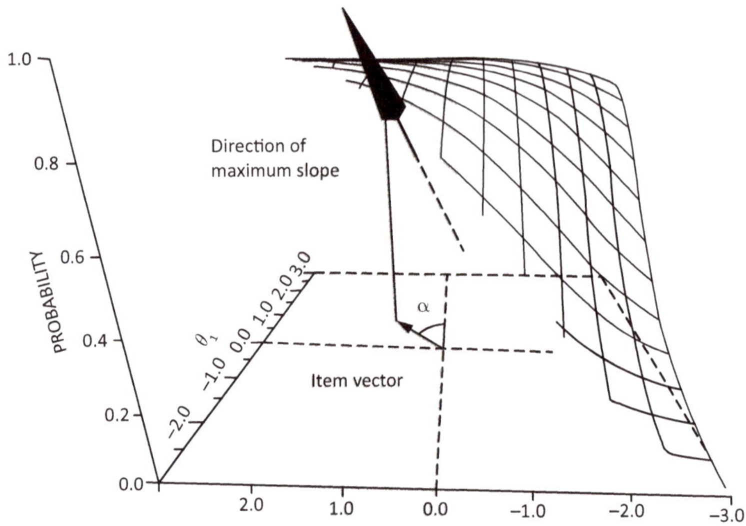

Fig. 7.6 An item vector shown in relationship to its corresponding response surface

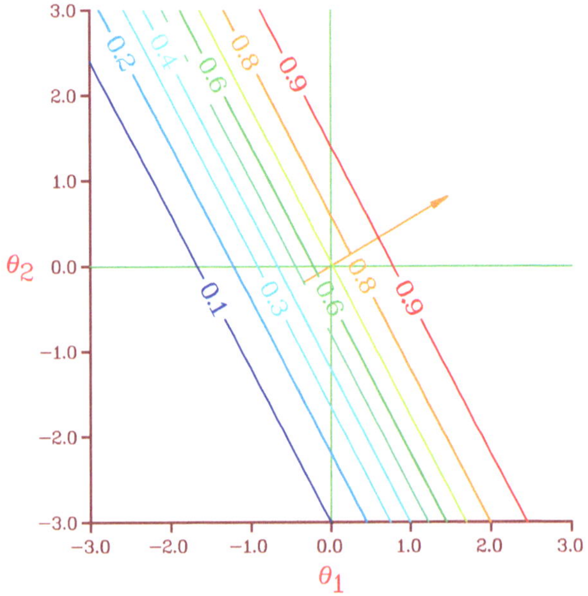

Fig. 7.7 An example of an item vector for a compensatory item

In Fig. 7.7 a vector is imposed upon a contour plot of an item. The parameters for this item are $a_1 = 1.8$, $a_2 = 1$, and $d = 0.8$. Note that the more discriminating an item is, the closer together the equi-probability contours and the longer the vector.

Item vectors can be color coded according to content. When this is done practitioners can answer several different questions. Are items from a certain content area more discriminating or more difficult? Do different items from different content areas measure different ability composites? How similar are the vector profiles for different yet "parallel" forms? An example illustrating what a group of vectors for a particular would look like is illustrated in Fig. 7.8. Note in this 101-item test, there are three main categories of items, each color coded differently. Notice how items for each content tend to lie within a relatively narrow sector.

Vector representation for the noncompensatory model has not been well developed. This is an area that needs to be studied more in the future.

Fig. 7.8 Item vectors for a 101-item test

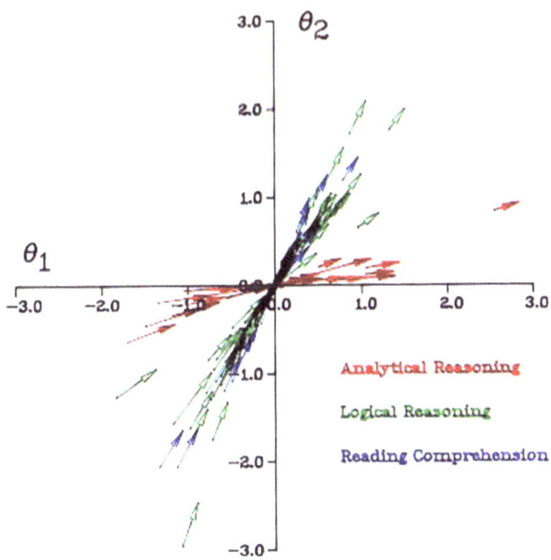

7.3 Item Representation: Compensatory and Noncompensatory Diagnostic Model

For the two diagnostic models the item representation is quite different. Specifically, when using the MIRT models presented first with continuous ability, a smooth surface was plotted to represent the ICC. However, in the case of diagnostic models an examinee's ability is represented as a set of classes, where each class is defined by mastery or nonmastery of a set of skills. Therefore, there will not be a smooth surface in ICC for diagnostic modeling. Instead it is better represented as a bar plot. Figures 7.9 and 7.10 provide examples of such bar plots. In this example, there are only two attributes. The plots on the left in each figure represent plots that are most similar to the surfaces discussed previously. The z-axis represents the probability of

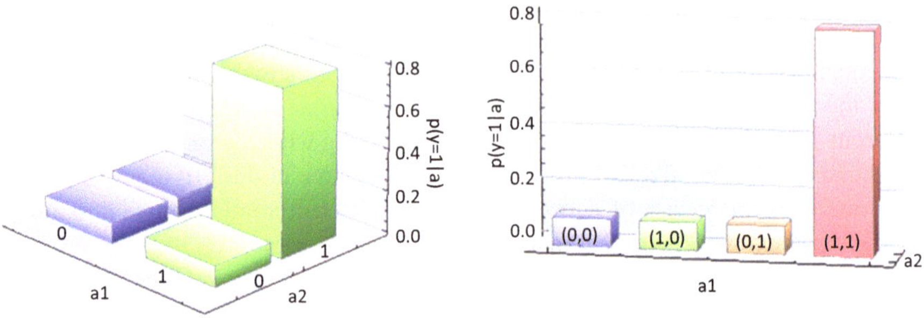

Fig. 7.9 Item representations for the noncompenstory DINA model where s = 0.1 and g = 0.1

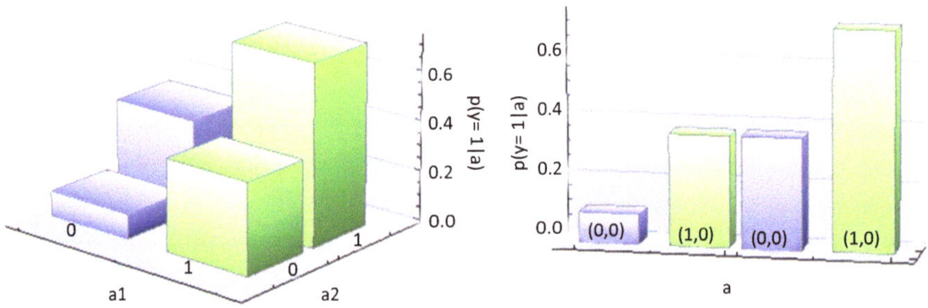

Fig. 7.10 Item representation for a compensatory diagnostic model $\lambda_0 = -2$ $\lambda_1 = 1.5$, and $\lambda_2 = 1.5$

a correct response given an examinee's attribute mastery profile. The *x* and *y* axes represent the values of the first and second attributes. Notice that because diagnostic models assume that individuals can be characterized as either masters or nonmasters then there are only two possible values for each attribute.

While this approach of providing a three-dimensional plot can be useful with two attributes, typical diagnostic models have more than two attributes. The plots on the left of Figs. 7.9 and 7.10 do not easily extend to more typical examples of diagnostic models. The plots on the right provide an alternative design to provide the items ICC. In these two-dimensional plots each bar represents by a specific class (i.e., mastery profile). By plotting each profile as its own class, such a graph could be provided for more than two attributes. The limitation of such a method is that the "shape" of the graph cannot be easily described because the ordering of classes is somewhat arbitrary. However, one recommended ordering is to increase the number of mastered attributes from left to right, as in done in these example plots. In addition, the number of classes increases exponentially with the number of attributes.

Contour plots could also be constructed in simple cases where only two dimensions are being measured. However, in these cases they would not prove to be as useful as was the case when continuous abilities where used. A contour plot for two attributes would create a simple two-by-two grid where each square contains the corresponding probability of a correct response for each combination of mastery/nonmastery. For this reason we do not include additional contour plots for diagnostic models.

Like the models presented first, these graphs do not naturally allow for the presentation of several items on the same plot. Vector plots were used to summarize what is being measured by several items on a single plot. Vector plots are more difficult to conceptualize for diagnostic models. These plots could be reproduced when using a compensatory model. Recall that the CRUM has weights (discrimination parameters) for each attribute. As a result these weights could be plotted as coordinates, which could be used to indicate what is being measured and to what degree. However, the interpretation would be limited to substantive meanings. For example, when using a continuous model the vector's location was related to the ability combinations that resulted in a probability of a correct response equal to 0.50. For diagnostic models, only a finite number of probabilities are possible and so it is unlikely that a probability of 0.50 is ever predicted by the model.

Vector plots for the DINA model could also be determined in this case, but may not be overly informative. The DINA model can either rely on only a single attribute or measure both in the two-attribute example. However, if both attributes are measured, the DINA model assumes that each attribute is measured equally. Thus, for the DINA model, these vectors would only point in one of three directions, only along the x-axis, only along the y-axis, and at a 45° angle (i.e., between these two). Future research should consider alternative vector representations for diagnostic model and explore their usefulness.

7.4 Information Representation for the Compensatory Logistic Model

Unlike the unidimensional IRT model in which the Fischer information function yields a unimodal curve that indicates how accurately each ability along the latent continuum is being assessed by an item or a test, in two dimensions determining the information is more complicated. With both the compensatory and noncompensatory models information is both a function of the discrimination parameters and the direction or composite of skills being measured. That is, for a single location on the latent ability plane, the accuracy of the ability estimation is a function of what $\theta_1 - \theta_2$ composite is being measured.

Representation of test information for these two models is done through a series of vectors (Ackerman 1994a, b). The latent ability plane is broken up into a 49-point grid, i.e. a seven-by-seven grid from $\theta_1, \theta_2 = -3$ to $+3.0$ in increments of 1. At each of the 49 θ_1, θ_2 combinations, the amount of information is estimated from 0° to 90° in 10° increments. The length of each information vector for the compensatory model is given as vector $\mathrm{I}(\theta_1, \theta_2)$ computed using the formula

$$\mathrm{I}(\theta_1,\theta_2) = (\cos\alpha)^2 \mathrm{Var}\left(\widehat{\theta}_1 \middle| \theta_1,\theta_2\right) + (\sin\alpha)^2 \mathrm{Var}\left(\widehat{\theta}_2 \middle| \theta_1,\theta_2\right) + (2\sin 2\alpha)$$
$$\mathrm{Cov}\left(\widehat{\theta}_1,\widehat{\theta}_2 \middle| \theta_1\theta_2\right) \quad (7.8)$$

where α is defined in Eq. 7.7. If the test is measuring different content, how do the information profiles compare across the different contents? Is the information profile similar across "parallel" forms? An example of such a "clamshell plot" is shown in Fig. 7.11. The amount of information is greatest in a diagonal band extending from the upper left (high θ_2 low θ_1 to the lower right (high θ_1, low θ_2). At the origin the information appears to be maximal in the direction composites between 30° and 60°. Notice further that the amount of information drops significantly as one moves away from the origin in the first and third quadrants. Little information accuracy exists at latent ability points (2, 2) and (−2, −2).

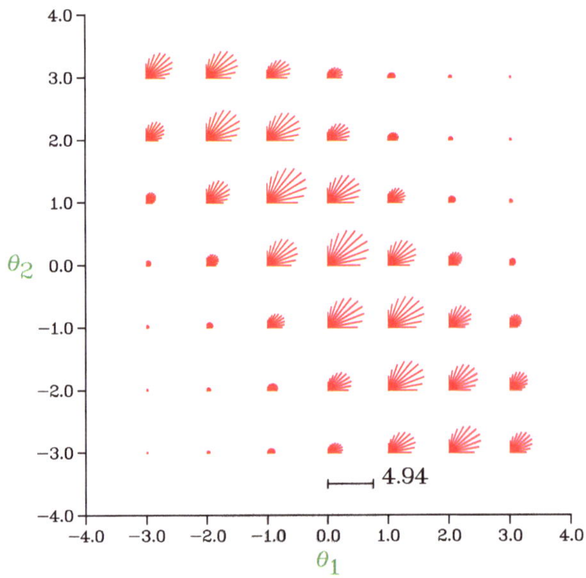

Fig. 7.11 Test Information vectors displayed as "clamshell" plots

Multiple categories can be easily compared in the test information plots by using two different colors, one for each content. At each of the 49 latent ability locations, the color representing the content that provides the most information is used. An example of this is shown in Fig. 7.12. In this plot one can see that at the origin content 1 provides the more accurate estimation of abilities combinations at 40°, whereas Content 2 appears to be measuring θ_1 more accurately.

One final representation of test information is a number plot. In this type of plot at each of the 49 points the information is computed for each composite direction from 0° to 90° in 1° increments. The number representing the direction having the maximum information is indicated. The size of the font used to represent the number

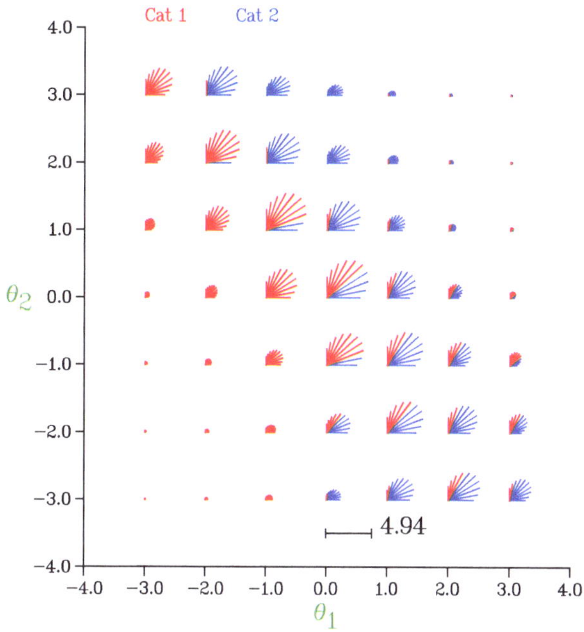

Fig. 7.12 Test information vectors comparison of two different contents

is a function of the amount of information. An example of such a plot is displayed in Fig. 7.13. In this diagram it is clear that the composite that is being best measured throughout the latent ability plane is at $62^\circ - 63^\circ$. This creates a very consistent interpretation of the composite of skills being measured for all examinees.

As was the case for the item vector representation, the formulation of information for the noncompensatory model has not been well developed. This also is an area for future research.

7.5 Information Representation for the Diagnostic Models

Whereas Fisher's information is quite common in IRT models that assume continuous abilities in one or more dimensions, it is not applicable in diagnostic models. For Fisher's information to be computed the ICC must be a continuous and smooth function or surface. DCMs define ability based on the mastery or nonmastery of attributes and thus and define classes. As a result, an alternative to Fisher's information must be used. Chang and Ying (1996) discuss the use of Kullback–Liebler information (KLI) to be used as an alternative to Fisher's information in IRT. KLI was described a global approach to information, whereas Fisher's information is described as a local measure of information. The advantage of KLI is that it is

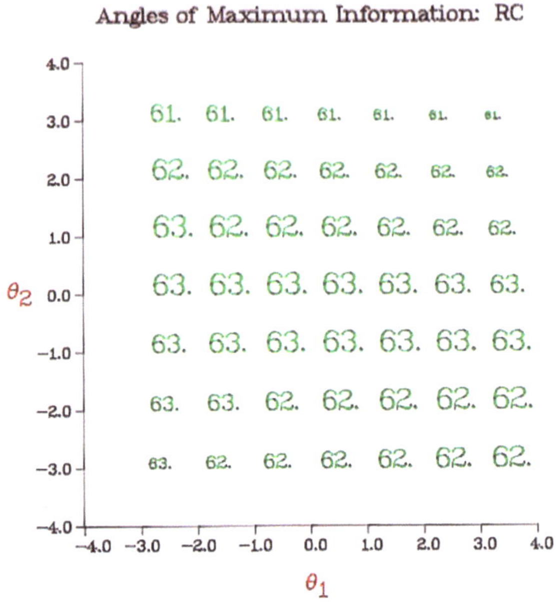

Fig. 7.13 An example of a test information number plot

defined even when the ICC is not a continuous smooth function or surface and so can be used when the underlying model is a DCM (Henson and Douglas 2005).

Specifically, the KLI can be used to measure the "discrimination" (or distance) between two different attribute patterns α_j and α_k as an indication of how different the response is expected to be between the two different attribute patterns. Notice that if the expected responses are different then this item helps differentiate between the two different attribute patterns. The KLI between these two different attribute patterns is:

$$\mathrm{KL_i}\left(\alpha_j, \alpha_k\right) = \sum_{x=0}^{1} \mathrm{P}\left(x \middle| \alpha_j\right) \ln\left(\frac{\mathrm{P}\left(x \middle| \alpha_j\right)}{\mathrm{P}\left(x \middle| \alpha_k\right)}\right) \tag{7.9}$$

where $P(x|\alpha)$ is the probability of a response x given the examinee has the attribute pattern α. However, the KLI only provides the discrimination power (or information) between two attribute patterns and thus, this value must be computed for all possible pairs of attribute patterns. Where this value is large, the item is most informative and where this value is small the item does not discriminate well between those two respective attribute patterns (Henson and Douglas 2005).

Henson and Douglas (2005) suggest storing the information of the KLI for all possible pairwise comparisons in a matrix; however, it can also be plotted (see Fig. 7.14) to provide a visual display of what attribute patterns are discriminated by a given item. In Fig. 7.14 attribute patterns are along the x and y axes. The z axis represents the value of the KLI for that combination. Notice that the values when comparing attribute pattern $\{0, 0\}$ to $\{1, 1\}$ are the largest, indicating that these two attribute patterns are highly discriminated. In contrast, the KLI is 0 when comparing any attribute pattern to itself. Finally, attribute patterns that differ by mastery of only one attribute have mild discrimination. Thus the KLI plot can be interpreted in a similar way as Fisher's information is used in IRT with continuous latent variables.

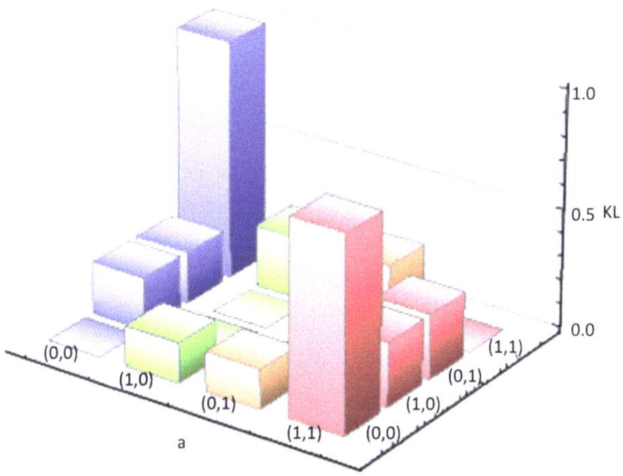

Fig. 7.14 An example of and item's discrimination through all pairwise KLI

7.6 True Score Representation for the Compensatory Logistic Model

In this section only the compensatory model will be discussed, although the noncompensatory extension closely follows. In unidimensional IRT the true score representation allows practitioners to relate the latent ability scale to the expected number correct scale. In the two-dimensional case this translates to relating the latent ability plane to the expected number correct surface. This is achieved by summing the probability of correct response to all of the test items at each point in the latent ability plane and then using this information to create a true score surface. This is illustrated in Fig. 7.13. In this plot the equal-expected score contours are shown on the latent ability plane. Every θ_1, θ_2 combination that lies on the same contour would be expected to achieve the same number correct score. Thus, every subject along the contour corresponding to a true score of 80 would be expected to achieve a score of 80 on the test. Above the latent ability plane is the true score surface.

The contour is important from a practitioner's perspective when cut-scores are set to determine licensure or certification. Such plots indicate the different combinations of $\theta 1$, $\theta 2$ that would be expected to successfully meet the cut score, giving more insight into what combinations of skills would be represented by examinees who passed (Fig. 7.15).

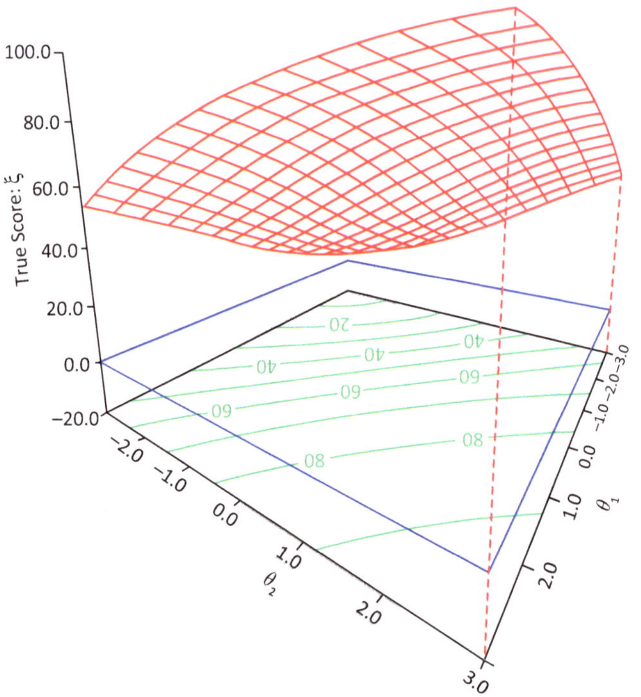

Fig. 7.15 An example of a true score surface and corresponding contours

One interesting comparison that can be created is the difference between two contour surfaces. Such a plot, shown in Fig. 7.16, can aid practitioners to examine the degree of parallelism between two test forms. That is, if two tests were truly parallel, examinees would have the same expected score on each form. In Fig. 7.16, the difference surface and corresponding contours are illustrated for two 40-item math tests. Where the surface lies above the no-difference plane examinees would be expected to achieve a higher score on Form A. Conversely, where the surface dips below the no-difference plane examinees would be expected to score higher on Form B. Thus, examinees near the origin would be expected to score slightly higher on Form A.

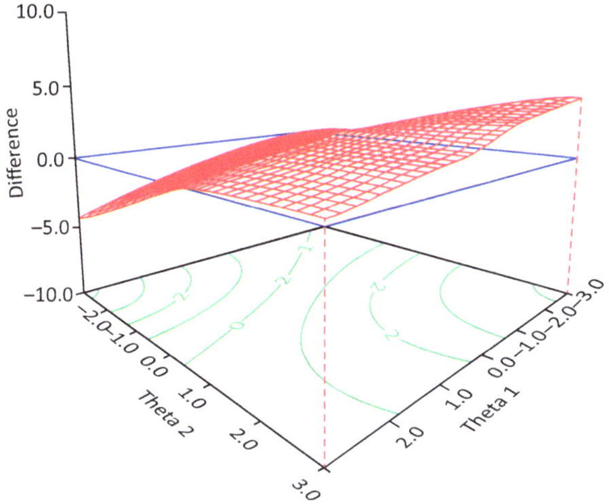

Fig. 7.16 A surface plot indicated the difference between the true score surface of Form A minus the true score surface of Form B

7.7 Conditional Estimation for the Compensatory Logistic Model

One final graphical analysis is one which allows practitioners to visualize the consistency of an observed number correct score scale. In this analysis, the θ_1, θ_2 centroids for each number correct score are plotted on the latent ability plane. This is, where the $(\overline{\theta}_1, \overline{\theta}_2)$ for each raw score is located. An example for a short ten-item test is shown in Fig. 7.17. In this figure the number correct score is located at the position of its corresponding $(\overline{\theta}_1, \overline{\theta}_2)$ centroid. This is an ideal situation because the centroids are linear meaning the composite being measured does not change throughout the observable score scale. Practitioners should be concerned when this plot is not linear, such as when there is a confounding of difficulty and dimensionality. This could occur when easy items are measuring one skill and difficult items are measuring another skill.

Another interesting arrangement is to plot the centroids for different content categories. In Fig. 7.18 centroids plots are shown for a test having three different content areas. In this figure the centroid plot for each content is displayed along with the centroid plot for the overall test. Somewhat amazingly, the three contents are measuring quite different composites, yet when all three are combined the plot becomes linear. The item vectors for this test are displayed in Fig. 7.8. Clearly this situation would have implication for equating. That is, should the test be equated by content, or as a single test? Also displayed in this picture are ellipses about the numbers for each score category. These ellipses are red if $\sigma^2_{\theta 1} > \sigma^2_{\theta 2}$ and green if $\sigma^2_{\theta 1} < \sigma^2_{\theta 2}$, thus indicating which ability is being measured better.

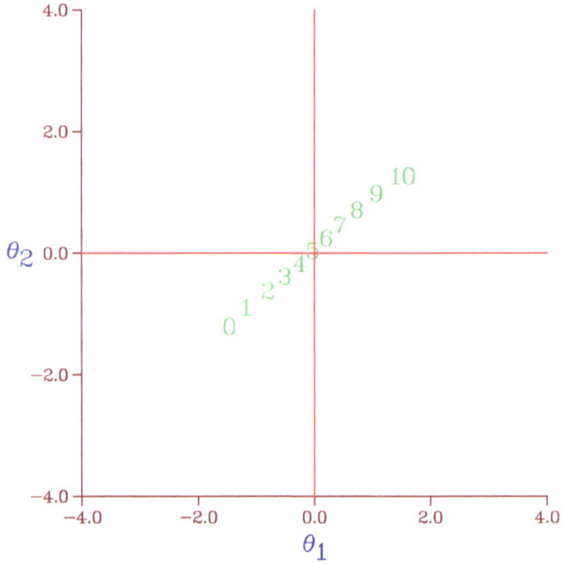

Fig. 7.17 A centroid plot for a 10-item test

7.8 Conditional Analyses from a DCM Perspective

An analogous situation to the centroid plot in a diagnostic model is to create a likelihood graph of each raw score category for each pattern of mastery. Such a graph is shown in Fig. 7.19. For a test that is measuring only two attributes there are actually four possible profiles of mastery (0, 0), (0, 1), (1, 0), (1, 1). A graph indicating the likelihood of each possible score on a 31-item test is displayed for each of the four attribute patterns. As would be expected, the complete mastery case (1, 1) has the largest likelihood for the higher level score categories.

7.9 Discussion

In this paper four different models were illustrated, the compensatory and noncompensatory logistic models and their diagnostic counterparts, the noncompensatory diagnostic model and the compensatory diagnostic model. Graphical illustrations of four different psychometric analyses were examined. These include item representation, test information, true score representation, and conditional representation. By examining these illustrations practitioners should begin to better understand.

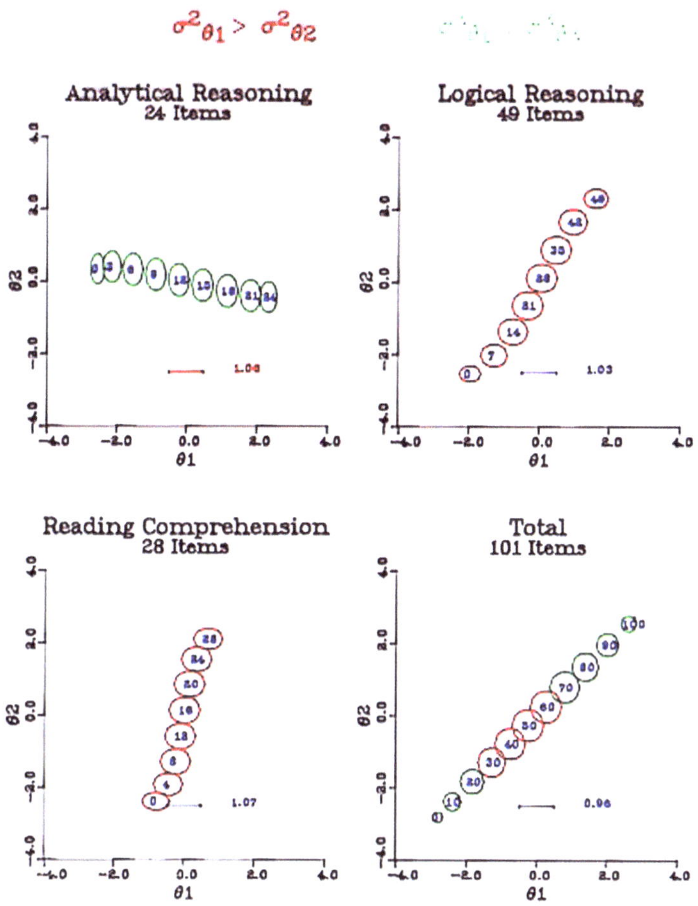

Fig. 7.18 Conditional plots for a 101-item test having three different content areas

Too often researchers and testing practitioners immerse themselves in statistical analyses to understand their assessment results. Hopefully this paper has helped to illustrate how graphical analyses can also provide a great deal of insight into what items and the test as a whole are measuring when the test data are truly multidimensional. This information should cross validate descriptive statistics, statistical analyses, as well as the tables of specification. Equally important one should never overlook the substantive analyses and relate the actual items to what both the graphical and numerical results are indicating.

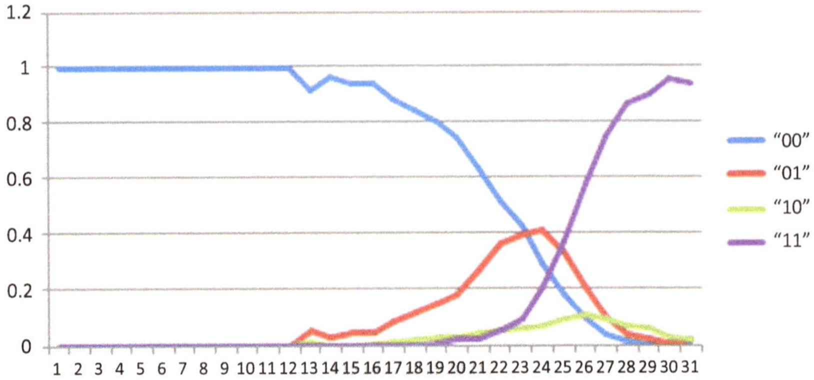

Fig. 7.19 Likelihood curves for each score possibility for each attribute profile is displayed

References

Ackerman TA (1994a) Using multidimensional item response theory to understand what items and tests are measuring. Appl Meas Educ 7:255–278

Ackerman TA (1994b) Creating a test information profile in a two-dimensional latent space. Appl Psychol Meas 18:257–275

Ackerman TA (1996) Graphical representation of multidimensional item response theory analyses. Appl Psychol Meas 20(4):311–330

Ackerman T, Gierl M, Walker C (2003) Using multidimensional item response theory to evaluate educational and psychological tests. Educ Meas Issues Pract 22(Fall):37–53

CA-DISSPLA (Version 11) (1987) [Computer software]. Islandia: Computer Associates International, Inc.

Chang HH, Ying Z (1996) A global information approach to computerized adaptive testing. Appl Psychol Meas 20:213–229

Henson R, Douglas J (2005) Test construction for cognitive diagnosis. Appl Psychol Meas 29(4):262–277

Junker B, Sijtsma K (2001) Cognitive assessment models with few assumptions, and connections with nonparametric item response theory. Appl Psychol Meas 25(3):258–272

Reckase MD (1985) The difficulty of test items that measure more than one ability. Appl Psychol Meas 9:401–412

Reckase MD, McKinley RL (1991) The discrimination power of items that measure more than one dimension. Appl Psychol Meas 14:361–373

Rupp A, Templin J, Henson R (2010) Diagnostic measurement theory: methods and applications. Guilford Press, New York

Chapter 8
New Item-Selection Methods for Balancing Test Efficiency Against Item-Bank Usage Efficiency in CD-CAT

Wenyi Wang, Shuliang Ding, and Lihong Song

Abstract Cognitive diagnostic computerized adaptive testing (CD-CAT) is a popular mode of online testing for cognitive diagnostic assessment (CDA). A key issue in CD-CAT programs is item-selection methods. Existing popular methods can achieve high measurement efficiencies but fail to yield balanced item-bank usage. Diagnostic tests often have low stakes, so item overexposure may not be a major concern. However, item underexposure leads to wasted time and money on item development, and high test overlap leads to intense practice effects, which in turn threaten test validity. The question is how to improve item-bank usage without sacrificing too much measurement precision (i.e., the correct recovery of knowledge states) in CD-CAT, which is the major purpose of this study. We have developed several item-selection methods that successfully meet this goal. In addition, we have investigated the Kullback–Leibler expected discrimination (KL-ED) method that considers only measurement precision except for item-bank usage.

8.1 Introduction

Cognitive diagnosis has received significant attention recently, especially since the No Child Left Behind Act (Representatives 2001) mandated that diagnostic feedback (cognitive strengths and weaknesses) should be provided to students, teachers, and parents. Cognitive diagnostic assessment (CDA), which combines psychometrics and cognitive science, has received increasing attention recently, but it is still in its infancy (Leighton and Gierl 2007). The CDA based on the incidence Q-matrix (Embretson 1984; Tatsuoka 1995) is quite distinct from traditional

W-Y. Wang • S-L. Ding
College of Computer Information Engineering, Jiangxi Normal University, Nanchang 330022, China
e-mail: wenyiwang2009@gmail.com

L-H. Song (✉)
Elementary Educational College, Jiangxi Normal University, Nanchang 330027, China
e-mail: viviansong1981@163.com

R.E. Millsap et al. (eds.), *Quantitative Psychology Research*, Springer Proceedings in Mathematics & Statistics 89, DOI 10.1007/978-3-319-07503-7_8

item-response theory. The entries in each column of the incidence Q-matrix indicate which skills or knowledge are involved in the solution of an item. The Q-matrix plays an important role in establishing the relationship between the latent attributes and the ideal-response patterns in order to provide information about students' cognitive strengths and weaknesses. Conversely, CDA requires the specifications of which latent attributes are measured by which items and how these characteristics are related to one another. Leighton et al. (2004) suggest the attribute hierarchy method (AHM) as follows. First, the hierarchy of attributes must be identified through protocol techniques before item construction. Second, items are developed by specialists using the attribute hierarchy. Finally, the attribute hierarchy and item attributes should be validated. In real situations, it will cost a lot of money to identify attributes through specialists. If the item-attribute specification is incorrect, invalid inferences will be made based on students' performance.

Online testing is available in numerous international, national, and state assessment programs (Quellmalz and Pellegrino 2009). A flourishing research area in psychological and educational measurement is computerized adaptive testing (CAT). One advantage of CAT is the increased measurement efficiency that is associated with items tailored to an individual examinee's ability level. CAT can provide more efficient estimates of continuous or discrete latent traits of interest than nonadaptive testing.

Researchers have attempted to combine the two above mentioned research areas and developed cognitive diagnostic computerized adaptive testing (CD-CAT) algorithms (McGlohen 2004; Tatsuoka 2002; Tatsuoka and Ferguson 2003; Xu et al. 2003). The essential components of fixed-length or variable-length CD-CAT include (a) a cognitive diagnostic model, (b) a calibrated item bank (Q-matrix and item parameters), (c) an entry level (starting point), (d) an item-selection rule, (e) a scoring method, and (f) a termination criterion. Three of the most popular item-selection methods in CD-CAT are based on the Kullback–Leibler (KL) information, Shannon entropy (SHE) (Cheng 2009), and expected discrimination (ED) method (Shang and Ding 2011). These three methods can achieve high efficiency and accuracy; however, they often lead to unbalanced item usage. Cognitive diagnostic tests are often low stakes, so item overexposure may not be a great concern. Because item development usually involves a long and costly process of writing, reviewing, and pretesting, a large number of unused items are undesirable (Veldkamp and Linden 2010). Although the restrictive progressive method and restrictive threshold method have been proposed to balance item exposure and measurement accuracy (Wang et al. 2011), they do not directly control item-exposure rates to a predetermined level.

CAT is attractive to practitioners because it yields a high measurement precision with a short test. Studies have been conducted to investigate the possibility of variable-length CD-CAT (Cheng 2009, 2010; Xu et al. 2003), in which different examinees may receive different test lengths. Variable-length CAT is desirable because each examinee receives a similar degree of measurement precision. A less explored but important issue in variable-length CD-CAT is how to maintain good item-bank usage.

There are solutions to improving item-bank usage, such as a careful item-bank design and a good item-exposure control (Breithaupt et al. 2010; Veldkamp and

Linden 2010). In this chapter, we proposed several new methods based on the randomization strategy and halving algorithms for item-bank usage and a general algorithm for measure efficiency in the context of CD-CAT. The remainder of this chapter is organized as follows. First, a review of common item-selection methods is presented. Second, new item-selection methods for item-bank usage and measurement efficiency are described. Third, the details of the simulation studies are reported. Finally, conclusions and discussions are provided.

8.2 Review of Existing Item-Selection Methods for CD-CAT

To introduce the existing literature, one commonly used cognitive diagnostic model is described here. The "deterministic input; noisy 'and' gate" (DINA) model (de la Torre and Douglas 2004; Haertel 1989; Junker and Sijtsma 2001) is a parsimonious and interpretable model that requires only two parameters for each item (i.e., g_j and s_j) regardless of the number of attributes being considered. The item-response function for the DINA model is as follows:

$$P_j(\boldsymbol{\alpha}_\mathbf{i}) = P\left(X_{ij} = 1 \middle| \boldsymbol{\alpha}_\mathbf{i}\right) = g_j^{1-\eta_{ij}}(1-s_j)^{\eta_{ij}},$$

where the deterministic latent response $\eta_{ij} = \prod_{k=1}^{K} \alpha_{ik}^{q_{kj}}$ indicates whether examinee i possesses all of the attributes required for item j. $\boldsymbol{\alpha}_\mathbf{i}$ denotes a knowledge state from the universal set of knowledge states ($\mathbf{Q_s}$). The entries of a Q-matrix indicate 1 or 0, in which $q_{kj} = 1$ when item j involves attribute k for answering item j correctly; otherwise, $q_{kj} = 0$. The parameter s_j refers to the probability of slipping and incorrectly answering the item when $\eta_{ij} = 1$, and g_j is the probability of correctly guessing the answer when $\eta_{ij} = 0$. X_{ij} refers to the response of examinee i to item j.

After the item bank is calibrated with a cognitive diagnostic model, when applying adaptive testing to the cognitive diagnostic, one must determine how to choose items for examinees. The sequential application of test items can be naturally implemented in the context of computer adaptive testing, in which items can be administered one at a time. Table 8.1 presents a list of the item-selection methods included in this review, along with pertinent references and with the abbreviations that will be used to refer to these methods.

There are two heuristic approaches to solve the problem of the sequential selection of items in the poset model (Tatsuoka 2002; Tatsuoka and Ferguson 2003), which is very similar to the DINA model (Tatsuoka 2009).

Table 8.1 List of reviewed item-selection methods

Method abbreviation	Model(s)	Exposure rates	Reference(s)
SHE	Poset	NA	Tatsuoka (2002)
SHE, HA	Poset		Tatsuoka and Ferguson (2003)
SHE, KL	FM	High	Xu et al. (2003)
SHE, KL, FI	3PL,FM	High	McGlohen and Chang (2008)
SHE, KL, PWKL, HKL	DINA	NA	Cheng (2009)
GDI, MMGDI	DINA	NA	Cheng (2010)
ED	DINA	NA	Shang and Ding (2011)
RP-PWKL; RT-PWKL	RUM	Low	Wang et al. (2011)
KL; MPI	2PL, HO-DINA	High	Wang et al. (2012)
Mutual information	DINA	NA	Wang (2013)
SHE; FI	3PL, DINA	NA	Liu et al. (2013)
KL, PWKL, SHTVOR	DINA,FM	Low	Hsu et al. (2013)

Note: *SHE* Shannon entropy procedure, *HA* halving algorithm, *KL* Kullback–Leibler algorithm, *GDI* global discrimination index, *MMGDI* modified maximum global discrimination index (balancing attribute coverage), *PWKL* posterior-weighted KL, *HKL* hybrid KL, *RP-PWKL* restrictive progressive PWKL, *RT-PWKL* restrictive threshold PWKL, *FI* Fisher information, *MPI* maximum-priority method, *ED* expected discrimination method, *RD* randomized selection, *poset* partially ordered sets model, *2PL* two-parameter logistic, *3PL* three-parameter logistic

The first intuitive method is the halving algorithm (HA), which chooses an item for examinee i randomly from a set of items:

$$\left\{j^{(t+1)}\right\} = \arg\min_{j \in R_i^{(t)}} \left(\left|\pi_j(i,t) - 0.5\right|\right),$$

where $\pi_j(i,t) = \sum_{c:\boldsymbol{\alpha}_c' \mathbf{q_j} \geq \mathbf{q_j}' \mathbf{q_j}} \pi\left(\boldsymbol{\alpha}_\mathbf{c} \middle| i,t\right)$. Supposing that t items are selected, $R_i^{(t)}$ represents the set of available items at stage t. Supposing that the prior is chosen as π_{0l} for each knowledge state from the universal set of knowledge states, the posterior distribution $\pi(\boldsymbol{\alpha}_\mathbf{c}|i,t)$ after t responses observed can then be written as:

$$\pi\left(\boldsymbol{\alpha}_\mathbf{c} \middle| i,t\right) \propto \pi_{0c} L\left(\mathbf{X}_i, \boldsymbol{\alpha}_\mathbf{c}\right),$$

where $L(\mathbf{X}_i, \boldsymbol{\alpha}_\mathbf{c})$ is the likelihood function, and it is simply the product of each item-response function when local independence is assumed. Computationally, this algorithm is very simple. It does not depend on the item parameters of the DINA model except through the posterior distributions $\pi(\boldsymbol{\alpha}_\mathbf{c}|i,t)$ and $\mathbf{q_j}$. At stage t, the posterior distribution of examinee i is divided into two parts by item j. HA selects the items that partition the knowledge states universality into two parts closest to one-half in terms of mass, and then an item is randomly selected for administration from a group of several items near the optimal one-half in terms of mass.

The second item-selection rule is SHE. The basis for SHE comes from information theory. SHE chooses an item $j^{(t+1)}$ for examinee i that satisfies:

$$j^{(t+1)} = \arg\min_{j \in R_i^{(t)}} \left(\sum_{x=0}^{1} H\left(\pi_{t+1} \middle| X_{ij} = x\right) \Pr\left(X_{ij} = x \middle| u_i^{(t)}\right) \right),$$

where

$$H\left(\pi_{t+1} \middle| X_{ij} = x\right) = -\sum_{\boldsymbol{\alpha}_\mathbf{c} \in \mathbf{Q_s}} \pi\left(\boldsymbol{\alpha}_\mathbf{c} \middle| i, t+1\right) \log \pi\left(\boldsymbol{\alpha}_\mathbf{c} \middle| i, t+1\right),$$

$$\Pr\left(X_{ij} = x \middle| \mathbf{u_i^{(t)}}\right) = \sum_{\boldsymbol{\alpha}_\mathbf{c} \in \mathbf{Q_s}} P\left(X_{ij} = x \middle| \boldsymbol{\alpha}_\mathbf{c}\right) \pi\left(\boldsymbol{\alpha}_\mathbf{c} \middle| i, t\right),$$

and $\pi(\boldsymbol{\alpha}_\mathbf{c}|i, t+1)$ denotes the posterior distribution updated at stage $t + 1$ given item j and $X_{ij} = x$.

Another familiar selection rule is the KL algorithm (KL) based on Kullback–Leibler information (Chang and Ying 1996; Xu et al. 2003). KL chooses an item $j^{(t+1)}$ for examinee i that satisfies:

$$j^{(t+1)} = \arg\max_{j \in R_i^{(t)}} \left(KL_{ij}\left(\widehat{\alpha}^t\right)\right),$$

where $KL_{ij}\left(\widehat{\alpha}^{(t)}\right) = \sum_{\boldsymbol{\alpha}_\mathbf{c} \in \mathbf{Q_s}} \sum_{x=0}^{1} \log \left[\frac{P\left(X_{ij} = x \middle| \widehat{\alpha}_i^{(t)}\right)}{P\left(X_{ij} = x \middle| \alpha_c\right)} \right] P\left(X_{ij} = x \middle| \widehat{\alpha}_i^{(t)}\right)$, and $\widehat{\alpha}^t$ is the current knowledge-state estimate.

To quantify the contribution of each knowledge state to the KL index (Wang 2013) or to reflect the updated posterior distribution for each knowledge state, the posterior weighted KL (PWKL) index proposed as a Bayesian version of the KL index (Cheng 2009) can be written as:

$$PWKL_{ij} = \sum_{\boldsymbol{\alpha}_\mathbf{c} \in \mathbf{Q_s}} \left\{ \pi\left(\boldsymbol{\alpha}_\mathbf{c} \middle| i, t\right) \sum_{x=0}^{1} \log \left[\frac{P\left(X_{ij} = x \middle| \widehat{\alpha}_i^{(t)}\right)}{P\left(X_{ij} = x \middle| \alpha_c\right)} \right] P\left(X_{ij} = x \middle| \widehat{\alpha}_i^{(t)}\right) \right\}.$$

Researchers suggest that SHE and KL must control exposure rates (Xu et al. 2003), and alternative exposure-control techniques may be an interesting area of future research (McGlohen and Chang 2008). To create exposure control in adaptive testing, by applying the primary idea of the restrictive progressive method with the PWKL information, Wang et al. (2011) proposed the following modified index (RP-PWKL):

$$RP - PWKL_{ij} = 1 - \exp_j / r[(1 - t/L)Rj + PWKL_{ij} * \beta t/L],$$

where r = the certain maximum exposure rate that will be maintained, $\exp_j$ = the current exposure rate for item j, t = number of items administered, L = test length, $H^* = \max_{j \in R_i^{(t)}} (PWKL_{ij})$, β is a weight, and R_j follows the uniform distribution $U(0, H^*)$. The term "progressive" is reflected by the weight $(1 - t/L)$ of the random component. Specifically, the role the information plays in the item-selection process increases as the exam progresses, whereas the role of the stochastic component decreases. It is reasonable that, at the beginning of the test, when the knowledge-state estimates markedly differ from the final estimates, the information should contribute little to the item selection. However, as the test progresses and the provisional-ability estimates approach the true ability of the examinee, the information component should gain importance.

Additionally, to maintain exposure control in adaptive testing, Wang et al. (2011) propose another modified index (PT-PWKL):

$$\left\{j^{(t+1)}\right\} = \left\{j \middle| H^* - \delta \leq PWKL_{ij} \leq H^*\right\},$$

where $\delta = \left[H^* - \max_{j \in R_i^{(t)}} (PWKL_{ij})\right] f(t)$, and $f(t)$ is a monotonically decreasing function. The function $f(t)$ can take various forms, for example, $f(t) = (1 - t/L)^{\beta}$.

Another new selection rule for the DINA model is the expected discrimination method (ED) (Shang and Ding 2011). It is based on the idea of maximum likelihood estimation and can be written as:

$$j_i^{(t+1)} = \arg\max_{j \in R_i^{(t)}} \left(\sum_{k,l:\alpha_k,\alpha_l \in Q_s} \left(\pi\left(\alpha_k \middle| i,t\right) f\left(\alpha_k, \alpha_l, j\right) \pi\left(\alpha_l \middle| i,t\right) \right) \right),$$

where the discrimination function

$$f\left(\alpha_k, \alpha_l, j\right) = \begin{cases} 1 - s_j & if\ \eta_{kj} = 1\ and\ \eta_{lj} = 0 \\ 1 - g_j & if\ \eta_{kj} = 0\ and\ \eta_{lj} = 1 \\ 0.5 & otherwise \end{cases}.$$

There are other methods based on the Bayesian network (Collins et al. 1993; Millán and Pérez-de-la-Cruz 2002), order theory (Wu et al. 2006), transition diagrams (Lin and Ding 2007), and so on.

8.3 New Item-Selection Methods

Although several item-selection methods focus on maximizing the psychometric efficiency of the test whereas others focus on balancing the item-exposure rate in CD-CAT, we must consider how to balance the test efficiency with the item-bank-usage efficiency in CD-CAT. There are several questions that we would like to answer: (a) How well does the theoretical HA method perform in CD-CAT? (b) How is it possible to extend the HA method to improve the pool utilization? (c) How is it possible to extend RP-PWKL and RT-PWKL to variable length CD-CAT? (d) How is it possible to define the flexible-discrimination function of ED for other cognitive diagnostic models?

8.3.1 Randomization HA Method

For better pool utilization, a random component is added into the HA method as the progressive strategy (Revuelta and Ponsoda 1998); the modified HA method can be written as:

$$\left\{j_i^{(t+1)}\right\} = \left\{j \in R_i^{(t)}, c_j(i,t) \geq r\max\left(c_j(i,t)\right)\right\},$$

where $c_j(i, t) = \pi_j(i, t)(1 - \pi_j(i, t))$, the value of r ranges from 0 to 1 and it plays the role of balancing the measurement accuracy and the exposure control. The randomization halving algorithm (RHA) method differs from HA in that we intentionally embed a constant weight r. For the new method, the weight r is assigned two different values, 0.75 [called RHA(0.75)] and 0.5 [called RHA(0.5)], to illustrate the role of this parameter in increasing the measurement accuracy and exposure control. The contribution of a random component is important at the beginning of the test and decreases in influence as the test progresses.

8.3.2 VRP-PWKL and VPT-PWKL for the Variable-Length CD-CAT

In both RP-PWKL and RT-PWKL, *t*/*L* reflects the relative importance of the random component and the information measure, but it is not suitable for use in variable-length CD-CAT. Supposing a variable-length CD-CAT terminated when the posterior probability that an examinee belongs to a given state exceeds 0.80 (Huebner 2010; Tatsuoka 2002), we extend RP-PWKL and RT-PWKL to the variable-length CD-CAT by using $\frac{\max_l\left(\pi\left(\alpha_l \middle| i,t\right)\right)}{0.8}$ as the alternative of the value of $\frac{t}{L}$ in RP-PWKL and PT-PWKL. VRP-PWKL and VPT-PWKL are used here to distinguish the original methods.

8.3.3 The Kullback–Leibler expected discrimination Method

Because the definition of the discrimination function in the ED method is established in the DINA model, we must establish a more general discrimination function that can be widely used in other cognitive diagnostic models. Because KL information is a commonly used objective function and is not symmetric, we let the discrimination function $f\left(\alpha_{l_1},\alpha_{l_2},q_j\right)$ be $KL_j\left(\alpha_{l_1},\alpha_{l_2}\right)$, and the resulting, new, flexible methods can be written as:

$$j_i^{(t+1)} = \arg\max_{j\in R_i^{(t)}} \left(\sum_{l_1,l_2} \pi\left(\alpha_{l_1}\middle| i,t\right) KL_j\left(\alpha_{l_1},\alpha_{l_2}\right) \pi\left(\alpha_{l_2}\middle| i,t\right)\right).$$

This new method is now generally denoted the Kullback–Leibler expected discrimination (KL-ED) method.

8.3.4 Similarities and Differences Between These Item-Selection Methods

It is important to highlight some of the key similarities and differences between these methods. It is apparent that there are identical distributional dependents for each method but with different criteria. For the RHA method, it selects the item that partitions the knowledge states universality into two parts closest to one-half in terms of the posterior distribution $\pi(\boldsymbol{\alpha}_{\mathbf{c}}|i,t)$. For VRP-PWKL, VPT-PWKL, and the KL-ED methods, the equations all multiply the KL index with the corresponding posterior distributions $\pi(\boldsymbol{\alpha}_{\mathbf{c}}|i,t)$. One difference is that the RHA method does not depend on the item parameters of the DINA model, whereas others do. Another difference is that they have different levels of computational complexity: the RHA method is very simple to compute, whereas the KL-ED method is computationally intensive. Fortunately, under the DINA model, KL-ED can be expressed explicitly as:

$$j_i^{(t+1)} = \arg\max_{j\in R_i^{(t)}} \left(w_j c_j\left(i,t\right)\right),$$

where $w_j = \left(1-s_j-g_j\right)\left(\log\frac{1-s_j}{g_j}+\log\frac{1-g_j}{s_j}\right)$ captures the discrimination power of item j. Then, the KL-ED method can be regarding as a weighted HA method. It also presents a simpler formula designed to make the KL-ED method under the DINA model amenable to real-time CD-CAT.

8.4 Simulation Study

8.4.1 Simulation Design

The performances of the item-selection procedures were evaluated and compared to each other by means of simulation studies. Because the KL-ED method only considers the measurement precision, it is expected that the KL-ED method results in better precision. When the random component becomes large, the RHA method will decrease the precision and provide better overlap control. It is also expected that the performance of the RHA method appears promising in fixed-length and variable-length testing.

Two simulation studies were performed, one using a simulated-item bank, and the other based on items calibrated from real data (Table 8.2). The simulated data are generated with independent structures using six attributes. The following are the details of the first simulation study. Under the simulation item bank, we consider fixed-length and variable-length testing. For fixed-length testing, a stopping rule is used, and the test length L is assumed to be 18. For variable-length testing, two stopping rules are used, with stopping being invoked if one of the rules calls for it. One rule calls for stopping when the largest posterior probability value exceeds 0.80. The other is a fixed-maximum-length stopping rule (18). For the calibrated item bank, we only consider the fixed-length testing for content constraints.

8.4.2 Evaluation Criterion

For each simulation condition, the following evaluation criteria are calculated to evaluate the performances of the item-selection methods, including three measurement-precision criteria and two pool-utilization criteria.

8.4.2.1 Correct Classification Rate of the Attribute Patterns

Letting N be the number of subjects, given the simulated or true attribute patterns α_i and the estimated attribute patterns $\widehat{\alpha}_i$, $i = 1, 2, \ldots, N$, the correct classification rate (CCR) of the attribute patterns is the proportion of the entire attribute patterns identified correctly for all subjects (Chen et al. 2012; Henson 2005). CCR can be written as:

$$CCR = \frac{1}{N}\sum_{i=1}^{N} I\left(\widehat{\alpha}_i, \alpha_i\right),$$

where $I\left(\widehat{\alpha}_i, \alpha_i\right)$ is an indicator function that uses ones if the vector α_i is equal to $\widehat{\alpha}_i$ and zeroes otherwise.

Table 8.2 Design of the simulation

	Simulated-item bank	Item bank calibrated from real data
Attribute structure	Independent structure using six attributes	Independent structure using eight attributes
Item-pool structure	The average number of attributes measured per item is 1.6 Item parameters were generated from U (0.05, 0.25) 200 dichotomously scored items were generated	The average number of attributes measured per item is 1.06 The means of the guessing and slipping parameters are 0.3503 and 0.2575, respectively 352 dichotomously scored English items were generated
Examinee generation	Sample size is 1,920 The attribute mastery patterns were generated to take each of the 2^6 possible patterns with equal probability	Sample size is 1,000 The attribute mastery patterns were generated to take each of the 2^8 possible patterns with equal probability
CD-CAT	The initial $\boldsymbol{\alpha}$ is randomly generated Fixed-length 18 or variable-length Maximum likelihood estimation (MLE) method is used to update $\widehat{\boldsymbol{\alpha}}$	The initial $\boldsymbol{\alpha}$ is randomly generated Fixed-length 40 or variable-length MLE method is used to update $\widehat{\boldsymbol{\alpha}}$
Evaluation criterion	Correct classification rate of attribute patterns Marginal correct classification rate of attributes Equivalent class rate of attribute patterns Pearson's χ^2 statistic The frequency of each item	

8.4.2.2 Marginal Correct Classification Rate of the Attributes

The marginal correct classification rate (MCCR) of the attributes is the proportion of attributes identified correctly for all subjects (Chen et al. 2012; Henson 2005). MCCR can be written as:

$$\mathrm{MCCR} = \frac{1}{NK}\sum_{i=1}^{N}\sum_{k=1}^{K} I\left(\widehat{\alpha}_{ik}, \alpha_{ik}\right),$$

where $I\left(\widehat{\alpha}_i, \alpha_i\right)$ is an indicator function that uses one if the value α_{ik} is equal to $\widehat{\alpha}_{ik}$ and zeroes otherwise, and K is the numbers of attributes.

8.4.2.3 Equivalent Class Rate of Attribute Patterns

The set of the test items have been administered to examinee i adaptively. Let the Q-matrix of these items be the test Q-matrix ($Q_t^{(i)}$). Let $\widehat{\alpha}_i$ be the estimation of the attribute pattern after the test has been completed. Given the universality of the attribute patterns and the test Q-matrix, the ideal-response patterns are determined by the latent response $\eta_{ij} = \prod_{k=1}^{K} \alpha_{ik}^{q_{kj}}$. If $\widehat{\alpha}_i$ belongs to the equivalent class of the attribute patterns in which several different attribute patterns correspond to a single ideal item-response pattern (Tatsuoka 2009), we define the indication function $I\left(\widehat{\alpha}_i, Q_t^{(i)}\right)$ to be one, or otherwise as zero. For all examinees, the equivalent class rate of the attribute patterns is defined as follows:

$$\mathrm{ECR} = \frac{1}{N}\sum_{i=1}^{N} I\left(\widehat{\alpha}_i, Q_t^{(i)}\right).$$

The larger the equivalent class rate or the error rate is, the worse the measurement precision is.

8.4.2.4 Pearson's χ^2 Statistic (Chang and Ying 1999)

Let the observed exposure rate for the jth item be:

$$\mathrm{er}_j = \frac{number\ of\ times\ the\ jth\ item\ is\ used}{N}.$$

Therefore, the desirable uniform rate for all items is:

$$\overline{er}_j = \overline{L}/M = \sum_{i=1}^{N} L_i/NM,$$

where $\overline{L}$ is the average test length across examinees, L_i is the test length for examinee i and M is the size of the item bank. The following scaled χ^2 is designed to measure the similarity of the observed and desired exposure rates:

$$\chi^2 = \sum_{j=1}^{m} (\mathrm{er}_j - \overline{er}_j)^2 / \overline{er}_j,$$

which captures the discrepancy between the observed and the ideal item-exposure rates, and it quantifies the efficiency of the item-bank usage. One of the primary goals of an item exposure-control method is to make the best use of all items in the bank. The smaller the value of the chi square is, the more even the exposure rates become. If a method results in a low chi-square value, then most (if not all) of the items have been fully used.

8.4.2.5 Test Overlap Rate (Chang and Zhang 2002)

Let $\overline{O}$ denote the mean number of the shared items for each of the $C_N^2 = N(N-1)/2$ pairs of examinees. Dividing the mean number of the overlapping items by the average test length, the test overlap becomes:

$$TOR = \frac{\overline{O}}{\overline{L}} = \sum_{m=1}^{\binom{N}{2}} O_m / \binom{N}{2} \overline{L},$$

in which O_m is the number of overlapping items encountered by the mth pair of two examinees.

8.5 Results

The evaluation criteria corresponding to the first simulation study under the simulation item bank are shown in Tables 8.3 and 8.4. Table 8.3 shows the results of fixed-length CD-CAT and Table 8.4 shows the results of variable-length CD-CAT.

For fixed-length CD-CAT, Table 8.3 suggests that KL-ED and PWKL without any exposure control generate the highest precision but also the largest chi-square value and the largest test overlap rate (TOR); For RP-PWKL, HA, RHA(0.75), RHA(0.5), the loss in the measurement precision is even smaller, but the decrease in chi square and the overlap rate is remarkable; the advantage of the RHA(0.75) method is more apparent. Given a precomputation table of the KL index for each item, the CPU times for all algorithms to select an item on a notebook with an Intel Core Duo CPU (T6570 2.1 GHz) are less than 0.043 s.

Table 8.3 Fixed-length CD-CAT under the simulation item bank (test length 18)

Methods	Measurement precision			Pool utilization		Time(s)
	CCR	MCCR	ECR	χ^2	TOR	
KL-ED	0.908	0.982	0.000	96.70	0.607	0.041
PWKL	0.907	0.981	0.000	92.26	0.584	0.041
RT-PWKL	0.850	0.969	0.005	5.99	0.127	0.041
RP-PWKL	0.796	0.954	0.009	0.22	0.096	0.041
HA	0.856	0.970	0.000	4.81	0.120	0.041
RHA(0.75)	0.845	0.969	0.001	0.90	0.100	0.041
RHA(0.5)	0.807	0.960	0.002	1.26	0.102	0.041
Stra_KL-ED	0.854	0.968	0.009	32.25	0.266	0.041
RD	0.504	0.882	0.250	0.09	0.095	0.043

Note: In the Stra_KL-ED approach, the items in the item bank are stratified with different attribute patterns. Stra_KL-ED selects a stratification based on the average of KL-ED, and then one item is randomly selected to be administered.

Table 8.4 Variable-length CD-CAT under the simulation item bank for all examinees

Methods	Measurement precision			Pool utilization		Test length	Number of examinees
	CCR	MCCR	ECR	χ^2	TOR		
KL-ED	0.769	0.954	0	101.79	0.62	10.34	1,920
PWKL	0.789	0.958	0	99.15	0.606	10.39	1,920
VRT-PWKL	0.785	0.955	0.002	4.81	0.096	12.68	1,920
VRP-PWKL	0.734	0.94	0.023	0.14	0.077	13.93	1,920
HA	0.805	0.962	0	4.39	0.095	13.34	1,920
RHA(0.75)	0.785	0.957	0.001	1.07	0.079	13.76	1,920
RHA(0.5)	0.765	0.952	0.001	1.27	0.084	14.47	1,920
Stra_KL-ED	0.776	0.948	0.002	22.55	0.19	12.43	1,920
RD	0.505	0.883	0.244	0.08	0.093	17.45	1,920

For variable length CD-CAT, Table 8.4 suggests that variable-length CD-CAT provides examinees with roughly the same level of measurement precision using few items (13.34 vs. 18) than for HA and RP-PWKL (CCR, 0.7979 vs. 0.796); the performances of the VRT-PWKL method, the RHA(0.75) method, and the RHA(0.5) method are more comparable in both precision and pool utilization; moreover, the performances of the KL-ED method and the PWKL method are also comparable in terms of precision. Tables 8.5 and 8.6 suggest that the RHA (0.5) method works better than the other methods for balancing the test efficiency with the item-bank usage efficiency.

The evaluation criteria corresponding to the second simulation study under the item bank calibrated from real data are shown in Table 8.7. Table 8.7 indicates that (as shown in Table 8.1) KL-ED and PWKL generate the highest precision with the

Table 8.5 Variable-length CD-CAT under the simulation item bank for examinees who finished their CAT without the largest posterior probability being greater than 0.8

	Measurement precision			Pool utilization			
Methods	CCR	MCCR	ECR	χ^2	TOR	Test length	Number of examinees
KL-ED	0.450	0.846	0.000	96.19	0.593	18	40
PWKL	0.436	0.876	0.018	87.87	0.551	18	55
VRT-PWKL	0.527	0.895	0.016	6.20	0.123	18	186
VRP-PWKL	0.515	0.883	0.100	0.41	0.095	18	410
HA	0.565	0.907	0.000	4.42	0.115	18	246
RHA(0.75)	0.519	0.889	0.000	2.73	0.107	18	293
RHA(0.5)	0.598	0.913	0.005	2.70	0.107	18	366
Stra_KL-ED	0.556	0.899	0.039	14.96	0.171	18	232
RD	0.433	0.864	0.303	0.12	0.095	18	1,613

Table 8.6 Variable-length CD-CAT under the simulation item bank for examinees who finished their CAT with the largest posterior probability greater than 0.8

	Measurement precision			Pool utilization			
Methods	CCR	MCCR	ECR	χ^2	TOR	Test length	Number of examinees
KL-ED	0.767	0.953	0.000	103.65	0.631	9.98	1,880
PWKL	0.767	0.953	0.000	101.46	0.619	10.16	1,865
VRT-PWKL	0.820	0.964	0.000	5.02	0.094	12.42	1,734
VRP-PWKL	0.826	0.963	0.000	0.28	0.073	13.29	1,510
HA	0.824	0.967	0.000	4.48	0.093	12.76	1,674
RHA(0.75)	0.833	0.968	0.000	1.01	0.076	13.14	1,627
RHA(0.5)	0.828	0.968	0.000	1.12	0.079	13.63	1,554
Stra_KL-ED	0.818	0.962	0.000	24.82	0.199	11.68	1,688
RD	0.772	0.958	0.000	0.72	0.080	14.87	307

Table 8.7 Fixed-length CD-CAT under the item bank calibrated from real data (test length 40)

	Measurement precision			Pool utilization		
Methods	CCR	MCCR	ECR	χ^2	TOR	Time(s)
KL-ED	0.906	0.987	0.000	197.25	0.691	0.154
PWKL	0.898	0.986	0.000	181.06	0.644	0.155
RT-PWKL	0.756	0.962	0.001	46.45	0.251	0.153
RP-PWKL	0.670	0.949	0.000	4.41	0.129	0.156
HA	0.552	0.923	0.000	14.15	0.157	0.154
RHA(0.75)	0.571	0.927	0.000	6.17	0.134	0.157
RHA(0.5)	0.530	0.922	0.001	4.77	0.130	0.157
Stra_KL-ED	0.572	0.931	0.001	18.44	0.169	0.147
RD	0.273	0.852	0.135	0.31	0.117	0.148

largest chi-square value and the largest TOR; For RP-PWKL, HA, RHA (0.75), RHA (0.5), the MCCRs are quite similar, but the decrease in the CCR is remarkable because the test measures a larger number of attributes.

Table 8.8 presents the item exposure-rate distribution. We can see that RHA(0.75) without the maximum exposure-rate control obtains more similar results than RP-PWKL with the maximum exposure-rate control. In RP-PWKL and RT-PWKL, we limit the maximum exposure rates to 0.15 and 0.3 for the simulation and the calibration item banks, respectively.

Conclusion and Discussion

The chapter proposes two item-selection methods for CD-CAT. First, according to the idea of randomization strategies, in which the selection of the item is always made at random among the most informative items, the RHA is proposed. For the RHA, all items within the specified range are available for selection rather than an arbitrary or only one number. Second, using KL information as a discrimination function of ED, KL-ED is proposed to handle other cognitive diagnostic models, besides the DINA model. Moreover, we show the connections among KL-ED, HA and RHA; KL-ED can be regarded as a weighted HA method, weighted by the corresponding item parameters; and HA can be regarded as RHA without adding a random component between different item attribute vectors in the Q matrix of the item pool.

Then, two simulation studies are performed, one using a simulated-item bank, and the other based on items calibrated from real data. Eight item-selection strategies are taken into consideration in these studies, including random, posterior-weighted KL (PWKL), RP-PWKL, RT-PWKL, ED, halving algorithm (HA), KL-ED, Stra_KL-ED, and RHA. In addition, VRP-PWKL and VRT-PWKL are proposed for variable-length CD-CAT as an extended version of RP-PWKL and RT-PWKL. Simulation studies for fixed- or variable-length CD-CAT are conducted based on these methods, and the results are compared in terms of pattern or attribute classification correct rate, error rate, item-exposure rate, or TOR.

The simulation results show that the KL-ED method generates the highest precision. RHA, HA, and RP-PWKL have more balanced usage of the item bank and slight decrements of the CCR of the attribute pattern, but RP-PWKL and RT-PWKL suppress overexposure by adding a restriction so that the maximum exposure rate will be kept lower than a predetermined value. VRT-PWKL and VRP-PWKL are suitable for both fixed-length and variable-length test situations.

Although the results from the simulation study are encouraging, the application of these new methods to other cognitive diagnostic models should be studied further in CD-CAT. It is a limitation of this study that the experiment is conducted under only two independent attribute structures. The studies should

(continued)

Table 8.8 Proportion of items with different item-exposure rates

Item bank	Length	Methods	[0 0.02]	[0.02 0.05]	[0.05 0.1]	[0.1 0.15]	[0.15 0.2]	[0.2 0.3]	[0.3 1]
Simulation	Fixed	RP-PWKL	0	0	166	34	0	0	0
		RHA(0.75)	0	5	127	68	0	0	0
	Variable	VRP-PWKL	0	0	197	3	0	0	0
		RHA(0.75)	3	23	171	3	0	0	0
Calibration	Fixed	RP-PWKL	0	0	193	100	39	20	0
		RHA(0.75)	0	0	179	89	72	12	0

be conducted on additionally attribute hierarchies, such as linear, convergent, divergent, and unstructured hierarchical structures (Leighton et al. 2004).

Although this method can be effective for limiting the item exposure at the time of administration, it is a short-term solution (Breithaupt et al. 2010). Thus, another method should be targeted for the usage efficiency of raw items and should consider how to implement online item attribute calibration in CD-CAT. Chang and Lu (2010) noted that the online calibration for ordinary CAT may be one of the most cost-effective processes. The great significance of the Q-matrix in CDA has been widely recognized, and the online item attribute calibration method may be important for item replenishing.

Acknowledgments This work is partially supported by the National Natural Science Foundation of China (30860084, 31160203, 31100756,31360237), the Ministry of Education of Humanities and Social Planning Project of China (13YJC880060), the Specialized Research Fund for the Doctoral Program of Higher Education (20103604110001, 20103604110002, 20113604110001), the Jiangxi Provincial Social Science Planning Project (12JY07), the Jiangxi Provincial Education Planning Project (13YB032), the Jiangxi Provincial Department of Education Science and Technology Project (GJJ11385, GJJ10238, GJJ13207, GJJ13226), and the Jiangxi Normal University Youth Growth Fund. All opinions and conclusions are solely those of the authors. The authors are indebted to the editor and reviewers for their constructive suggestions and comments on the earlier manuscript.

References

Breithaupt K, Ariel AA, Hare DR (2010) Assembling an inventory of multistage adaptive testing systems. In: van der Linden WJ, Glas CAW (eds) Elements of adaptive testing. Springer, New York, pp 247–266

Chang H-H, Zhang J (2002) Hypergeometric family and item overlap rates in computerized adaptive testing. Psychometrika 67(3):387–398

Chang H-H, Ying Z-L (1996) A global information approach to computerized adaptive testing. Appl Psychol Meas 20(3):213–229

Chang H-H, Ying Z-L (1999) a-stratified multistage computerized adaptive testing. Appl Psychol Meas 23(3):211–222

Chang Y-CI, Lu H-Y (2010) Online calibration via variable length computerized adaptive testing. Psychometrika 75(1):140–157

Chen P, Xin T, Wang C, Chang H-H (2012) On-line calibration methods for the DINA model with independent attributes in CA-CAT. Psychometrika 77(2):201–222

Cheng Y (2009) When cognitive diagnosis meets computerized adaptive testing: CD-CAT. Psychometrika 74(4):619–632

Cheng Y (2010) Improving cognitive diagnostic computerized adaptive testing by balancing attribute coverage: the modified maximum global discrimination index method. Educ Psychol Meas 70(6):902–913

Collins JA, Greer JE, Huang SX (1993) Adaptive assessment using granularity hierarchies and Bayesian nets. Paper presented at the 3rd international conference intelligent tutoring systems

de la Torre J, Douglas J (2004) Higher-order latent trait models for cognitive diagnosis. Psychometrika 69:333–353

Embretson SE (1984) A general latent trait model for response processes. Psychometrika 49(2):175–186
Haertel EH (1989) Using restricted latent class models to map the skill structure of achievement items. J Educ Meas 26(4):301–321
Henson R (2005) Test construction for cognitive diagnosis. Appl Psychol Meas 29(4):262–277
Hsu CL, Wang WC, Chen SY (2013) Variable-length computerized adaptive testing based on cognitive diagnosis models. Appl Psychol Meas 37(7):563–582
Huebner A (2010) An overview of recent developments in cognitive diagnostic computer adaptive assessments. Pract Assess Res Eval 15(3):1–7. Available online: http://pareonline.net/getvn.asp?v=15&n=13
Junker BW, Sijtsma K (2001) Cognitive assessment models with few assumptions, and connections with nonparametric item response theory. Appl Psychol Meas 25:258–272
Leighton JP, Gierl MJ (2007) Why cognitive diagnostic assessment? In: Leighton JP, Gierl MJ (eds) Cognitive diagnostic assessment for education: theory and applications. Cambridge University Press, New York, pp 3–18
Leighton JP, Gierl MJ, Hunka SM (2004) The attribute hierarchy method for cognitive assessment: a variation on Tatsuoka's rule-space approach. J Educ Meas 41(3):205–237
Lin H-J, Ding S-L (2007) An exploration and realization of computerized adaptive testing with cognitive diagnosis. Acta Psychologica Sinica 39:747–753
Liu H-Y, You X-F, Wang W-Y, Ding S-L, Chang H-H (2013) The development of computerized adaptive testing with cognitive diagnosis for an English achievement test in China. J Clas 30:152–172
McGlohen MK (2004) The application of cognitive diagnosis and computerized adaptive testing to a large-scale assessment. Unpublished Doctorial Dissertation, University of Texas at Austin
McGlohen MK, Chang H-H (2008) Combining computer adaptive testing technology with cognitively diagnostic assessment. Behav Res Methods 40(3):808–821
Millán E, Pérez-de-la-Cruz JL (2002) A Bayesian diagnostic algorithm for student modeling and its evaluation. User Model User-adapt Interact 12:281–330
Quellmalz ES, Pellegrino JW (2009) Technology and testing. Science 323(2):75–79
Representatives, U. S. H. o. (2001) Text of the 'No Child Left Behind Act'. Public Law No. 107–110, 115 Stat. 1425
Revuelta J, Ponsoda V (1998) A comparison of item exposure control methods in computerized adaptive testing. J Educ Meas 35(4):311–327
Shang Z-Y, Ding S-L (2011) The exploration of item selection strategy of computerized adaptive testing for cognitive diagnosis. J Jiangxi Norm Univ (Nat Sci) 35(4):418–421
Tatsuoka C (2002) Data analytic methods for latent partially ordered classification models. J R Stat Soc: Ser C: Appl Stat 51:337–350
Tatsuoka C, Ferguson T (2003) Sequential classification on partially ordered sets. J R Stat Soc Ser B (Stat Methodol) 65(1):143–157
Tatsuoka KK (1995) Architecture of knowledge structures and cognitive diagnosis: a statistical pattern classification approach. In: Nichols PD, Chipman SF, Brennan RL (eds) Cognitively diagnostic assessments. Erlbaum, Hillsdale, pp 327–359
Tatsuoka KK (2009) Cognitive assessment: an introduction to the rule space method. Taylor & Francis Group, New York
Veldkamp BP, van der Linden WJ (2010) Designing item pools for adaptive testing. In: van der Linden WJ, Glas CAW (eds) Elements of adaptive testing. Springer, New York, pp 231–245
Wang C (2013) Mutual information item selection method in cognitive diagnostic computerized adaptive testing with short test length. Educ Psychol Meas 73(6):1017–1035
Wang C, Chang H-H, Douglas J (2012) Combining CAT with cognitive diagnosis: a weighted item selection approach. Behav Res Methods 44:95–109

Wang C, Chang H-H, Huebner A (2011) Restrictive stochastic item selection methods in cognitive diagnostic computerized adaptive testing. J Educ Meas 48(3):255–273

Wu H-M, Kuo B-C, Yang J-M (2006) Evaluating knowledge structure-based adaptive testing algorithms and system development. Educ Technol Soc 15:73–88

Xu XL, Chang HH, Douglas J (2003) A simulation study to compare CAT strategies for cognitive diagnosis. Paper presented at the annual meeting of the American Educational Research Association, Chicago

Chapter 9
Comparison of Linear, Computerized Adaptive and Multi Stage Adaptive Versions of the Mathematics Assessment of Turkish Pupil Monitoring System

Semirhan Gökçe and Giray Berberoğlu

Abstract The purpose of this study is to compare the results of computer based linear Turkish Pupil Monitoring System (TPMS) administrations with Computerized Adaptive Testing (CAT) and Multi Stage Adaptive Testing (MSAT) results in mathematics assessment. On the basis of the real data obtained from TPMS, different CAT scenarios were tested in post-hoc simulations with various starting rules, termination criteria, and different control strategies of CAT using either Maximum Likelihood (ML) or Weighted Maximum Likelihood (WML) estimation procedures. Results of the CAT study indicated that WML with easy initial item difficulty, fixed test reliability termination along with item exposure and content control strategies produced defensible results. Alternatively, a multi stage scenario was designed to compare the efficiency of CAT and MSAT. Examinees were administered a fixed subtest with 15 items followed by two subtests having ten items each. Using MSAT in TPMS seemed to be producing more valid results in terms of content sampling than CAT.

Keywords Pupil monitoring system • Computerized adaptive testing • Multistage adaptive testing • Ability estimation method • Item exposure control and content control

---

S. Gökçe (✉)
Cito Türkiye, ODTU Teknokent Galyum Blok B13, Ankara 06800, Turkey

Nigde University Faculty of Education, Central Campus, Nigde 51240, Turkey
e-mail: semirhan@gmail.com

G. Berberoğlu
Department of Secondary Science and Mathematics Education, Middle East Technical University, Dumlupinar Bulvari, Ankara 06800, Turkey
e-mail: giray@metu.edu.tr

R.E. Millsap et al. (eds.), *Quantitative Psychology Research*, Springer Proceedings in Mathematics & Statistics 89, DOI 10.1007/978-3-319-07503-7_9

9.1 Introduction

9.1.1 Pupil Monitoring System

Today, monitoring students' growth in learning is the major concern of many educational systems. Teachers may develop growth curves for their students' learning based on the scores obtained on teacher-made tests but the main problem here is that the teachers use different assessment methods, which do not allow mapping ability estimations on the same scale. The Pupil Monitoring System (PMS) provides continuous evaluation of pupils over several years to monitor their learning development (Glas and Geerlings 2009; Vlug 1997). The PMS has some unique psychometric properties such as: using incomplete test design, locating each pupil's score in proficiency level descriptions for the purpose of providing criterion-referenced interpretation of the test results. The PMS not only monitors pupils' learning according to national standards but also allows the comparison of individuals within norm groups. For example, National Institute for Educational Measurement in the Netherlands develops one of the well-known PMS in which coherent sets of standardized linear tests are used to assess 4–12 years old pupils in arithmetic, language, and world orientation subjects. Pupils are given different standardized linear tests at different time and analyses based on IRT framework allow the representation of test scores on the same scale so that teachers could make decisions about the progress of students' learning process and could determine the relative position of pupils compared to norm groups. Based on the principles of PMS developed in the Netherlands, Cito Türkiye developed Turkish Pupil Monitoring System (TPMS) for Turkish students. The TPMS focuses on the evaluation of higher order thinking skills, calibrates items by using One Parameter Logistic model (OPLM), uses anchor items and incomplete test design to equate different test forms both vertically and horizontally and it is a linear computer based test (Özgen Tuncer Ç 2008; İş Güzel et al. 2009).

Glas and Geerlings (2009) recommend using computerized adaptive test in the PMS because of two main reasons. One of them is the measurement efficiency since the difficulty of the test items is changing according to the pupils' ability level. It is a well-known fact that pupils from different ability levels have different growth rates but the tests need to be informative at each ability level. Therefore, adapting the test items (test item difficulty) to pupils' abilities has a positive impact on measurement efficiency. The second advantage is the possibility of testing on demand since pupils can take the test on their most suitable time period. It is related to flexibility of testing date and time because using computerized adaptive tests in PMS facilitates examinees to take the test whenever they feel ready. Thus, it is aimed to implement the TPMS as a computer adaptive test (CAT) in Turkey. The major issue in this process is the method through which the test items will be delivered.

In CAT, the items are selected individually according to the responses of the pupils. Different than CAT, there is another approach in which instead of administering an individual item a group of items is administered which is called testlet.

This procedure is known as Multi Stage Adaptive Testing (MSAT). There are studies in the literature indicating the superiority of MSAT over CAT. According to Rotou et al. (2003), MSAT produced slightly higher reliability than CAT. Furthermore, MSAT requires content considerations in developing the testlets which bring the expertise in assembling the items with respect to their content specifications. On the other hand, CAT basically uses an algorithm which selects items with respect to item information functions. Thus, MSAT seems more compatible with the test development process in line with item specifications (Wainer and Kiely 1987; Wainer et al. 1990).

The purpose of this study is to investigate the applicability of computerized adaptive testing (CAT) and multistage adaptive testing (MSAT) to TPMS. For this purpose, pupils' real responses in mathematics assessment of the TPMS were used and compared with respect to the results of post-hoc CAT simulations by two different ability estimation methods such as Maximum Likelihood or Weighted Maximum Likelihood. Through these estimation processes different starting rules, termination criteria, and control strategies were simulated and ability estimations were compared with the ones obtained as a result of real TPMS administration. Three starting rules, such as easy, medium, and difficult initial item difficulties, three termination criteria, such as fixed test length and fixed reliability and four control strategies such as no control, only content control, only exposure control, and both content and exposure control were implemented in the analyses. In the final step, the result of the optimum CAT algorithm was compared with MSAT where a fixed subtest with 15 items as a starting test followed by two subtests having ten items each were used.

9.2 Method

In the present study, real responses of 3,073 pupils to 322 mathematics items between 2010 and 2012 were used. The participants of the real TPMS administration were from sixth grade level. In the analyses, the reported standard scores of the students in the real TPMS administration were used as criterion to evaluate different post-hoc CAT and MSAT simulations.

9.2.1 Item Bank

One of the major issues of CAT studies is the size of the item bank. In the present study, the linear computer based TPMS was used to investigate the comparability of ability estimates with the ones obtained through CAT simulations. The linear nature of the TPMS somehow limits the number of items used in the mathematics sub-dimensions. This would definitely limit the size of the item bank to be used in CAT simulations if study is conducted in the sub-dimension level. In order to increase the number of items in the item bank different sub-dimensions were combined. Since the items in the TPMS were basically designed to assess the understanding of mathematical concepts and principles within the daily life context and problem solving skills regardless of the sub-dimensions, combination of items from different subtests of TPMS seems a defensible approach, as long as they measure a unidimensional trait. In order to meet the unidimensionality requirement, the items for the item bank were selected by the factor analysis. The selected items were all loaded on the first factor even though they come from various subtests of the TPMS. As a result of this analysis, the items from different sub-dimensions of mathematics which were loaded on the same factor are assumed to measuring a general mathematical ability of the students. Finally, 78 items in "geometry," 65 items in "measurement," 114 items in "numbers," and 65 items in "probability and statistics" were selected for the item bank for further CAT analysis. The item bank contained 322 items and the distribution of the item parameters is given in Fig. 9.1.

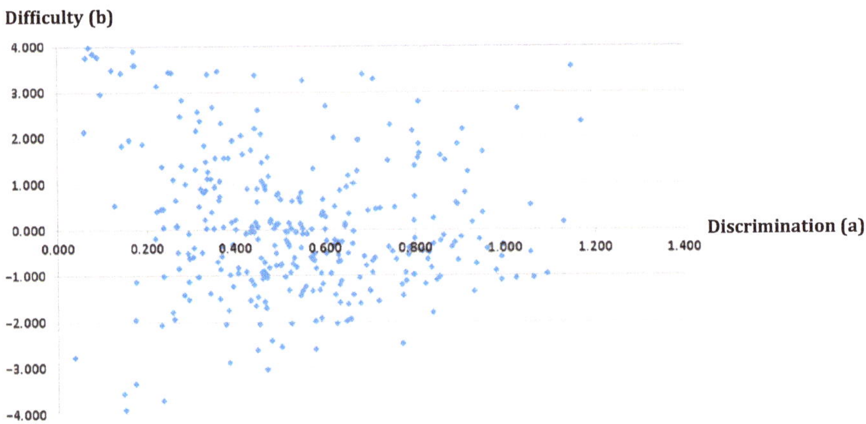

Fig. 9.1 Distribution of item parameters

9.2.2 *Simulations*

The first researcher developed web-based simulation software by using PHP programming language and MySQL database. For each simulation scenario 1,000 examinees were selected randomly from the sample.

9.2.2.1 CAT Phase

In order to find out the optimum CAT algorithm for the TPMS, by the use of different ability estimation procedures different starting rules, test length, and item exposures were used in the simulations. The two estimation procedures such as "maximum likelihood (ML)" versus "weighted maximum likelihood (WML)" were used for each condition to be tested. Three different starting rules were used with different initial item difficulties, such as starting the test with an easy item (b value between −1.5 and −0.5), item with moderate difficulty (b value between −0.5 and 0.5), or with a more difficult item (b value between 0.5 and 1.5). For the fixed-length termination criteria three different test lengths were used, such as 15, 25, and 35 items. For the fixed test reliability three standard error values, such as 0.20, 0.30, and 0.40 were used in the analyses. Item exposure control was carried out by Sympson and Hetter's (1985) strategy, whereas for content control Kingsbury and Zara (1991) control strategy were used. In Sympson and Hetter strategy, the probability of using the same item during CAT administration is controlled by considering the frequency of each item's usage in the process. In Kingsbury and Zara strategy, the content of the items is taken into consideration. In the present study, since the item bank includes items from numbers, geometry, measurement, and probability&statistics, using this strategy actualizes total item delivery in CAT procedure in line with the weights of the sub-dimensions in the item bank. Thus, each individual CAT administration samples out all the sub-dimensions with respect to their weights in the item bank. It is expected that at the end of CAT simulations, the most optimum approach which provides reasonable reliability and test length will be determined. This approach will be further compared with the MSAT.

9.2.2.2 MSAT Phase

In this phase, 322 items in the bank were grouped into 8 intervals according to the highest information they provide. The theta intervals and the number of items within each interval are presented in Table 9.1.

Table 9.1 Distribution of the items to intervals according to the highest information

Interval of theta	Number of items
[−4.00, −3.00)	8
[−3.00, −2.00)	19
[−2.00, −1.00)	50
[−1.00, 0.00)	90
[0.00, 1.00)	77
[1.00, 2.00)	35
[2.00, 3.00)	30
[3.00, 4.00)	13
Total	322

Each MSAT administration contains 35 items. MSAT phase starts with 15 items from average difficulty level (items having item difficulties between −1.00 and 1.00) considering balanced content coverage. After initial ability estimation was calculated based on 15-item testlet, two more testlets containing ten items each were administered. If there is no remaining item to be administered in the interval, MSAT algorithm selected the most informative items from the nearest interval. Finally, a total of 35 items were administered to randomly selected 1,000 examinees.

9.2.3 *Statistical Analyses*

After obtaining all ability estimations from different simulation scenarios, basically the correlation coefficient was used to evaluate the congruence between simulation and real TPMS results. TPMS reports one standard score for each sub-dimension. Each student has four subscale scores for the mathematics assessment which are not on the same metric. Thus, the scores obtained in simulations were correlated with each of the subscale scores of the real TPMS administration. In the correlational analyses given below, the median of correlations obtained between the simulation and each of the subscale scores of TPMS were reported in the tables.

9.3 Results

9.3.1 *Results of Post-hoc Simulations*

9.3.1.1 Determination of Optimum Starting Rule with Fixed Test Reliability Termination Criteria

First post-hoc simulation was implemented by ML and WML ability estimation methods under three different starting rules and three different standard error values as a termination rule. As a starting rule, initial item was selected either from easy items (item difficulty between −1.50 and −0.50), moderate items (item difficulty between 0.50 and 1.50), or difficult items (item difficulty between +0.50 and +1.50). For the termination, fixed test reliability of SE = 0.20, SE = 0.30, and SE = 0.40 constraints. Table 9.2 indicates number of items administered under fixed test reliability termination rule through ML and WML ability estimations. Within the simulations, ability estimations of the participants were calculated after the termination criteria were met for all 1,000 randomly selected participants.

As it is seen from Table 9.2, more items are used to obtain more reliable ability estimations as expected but when the standard error is fixed to 0.30, the number of items in the test seemed to be the most rational choice.

Then, ability estimations of the randomly selected participants were correlated with the real TPMS mathematics assessment scores. The correlations are presented in Table 9.3.

As it is seen in Table 9.3, correlation coefficients under WML estimations seem to be relatively higher. Weighted Maximum Likelihood provides slightly

Table 9.2 Number of items administered under different starting rules and fixed test reliability termination rules in ML and WML

Estimation	Starting rule	Termination rule: fixed test reliability		
		SE < 0.40	SE < 0.30	SE < 0.20
ML	−1.50 < b < −0.50 (Easy)	15.29	34.53	128.78
	−0.50 < b < +0.50 (Moderate)	15.56	34.47	128.84
	+0.50 < b < +1.50 (Difficult)	15.60	34.76	128.47
WML	−1.50 < b < −0.50 (Easy)	15.27	33.34	127.29
	−0.50 < b < +0.50 (Moderate)	15.4	33.28	126.63
	+0.50 < b < +1.50 (Difficult)	15.47	33.64	127.07

Table 9.3 Median of the correlation coefficients between CAT ability estimations and TPMS mathematics assessment scores under different starting rules and fixed test reliability termination rules

Estimation	Starting rule	Termination rule: fixed test reliability		
		SE < 0.40	SE < 0.30	SE < 0.20
ML	−1.50 < b < −0.50 (Easy)	0.792*	0.826*	0.898*
	−0.50 < b < +0.50 (Moderate)	0.790*	0.825*	0.898*
	+0.50 < b < +1.50 (Difficult)	0.788*	0.826*	0.897*
WML	−1.50 < b < −0.50 (Easy)	0.801*	0.837*	0.909*
	−0.50 < b < +0.50 (Moderate)	0.803*	0.836*	0.906*
	+0.50 < b < +1.50 (Difficult)	0.790*	0.831*	0.908*

*All correlations are significant at the 0.01 level

higher correlations especially for the 0.30 and 0.40 standard error criteria than the Maximum Likelihood estimations.

9.3.1.2 Determination of Optimum Starting Rule with Fixed Test Length Termination Criteria

Second post-hoc simulation was designed to compare the results of fixed-length termination rule under 15, 25, and 35 items for different starting rule. Table 9.4 indicates the standard error values in ML and WML ability estimations.

For fixed test length simulations, 35 items provided more reliable ability estimations as expected. Table 9.5 indicates the correlations of real TPMS ability estimates with the estimates obtained under different test length constraints through ML and WML procedures.

As it is seen from Table 9.5, there is a positive relationship between the test length and the correlation coefficients. WML ability estimation method provides slightly higher correlations than ML. Standard error values were directly related to the reliability of the test scores. In fixed-length test administration, standard error of each score is estimated separately and can be different from one estimation to another but the students take the same number of test items. On the other hand,

Table 9.4 Mean standard error estimations under different starting rules and fixed test length termination rules in ML and WML

		Termination rule: fixed test length		
Estimation	Starting rule	N = 15	N = 25	N = 35
ML	−1.50 < b < −0.50 (Easy)	0.397	0.328	0.295
	−0.50 < b < +0.50 (Moderate)	0.399	0.326	0.295
	+0.50 < b < +1.50 (Difficult)	0.397	0.327	0.294
WML	−1.50 < b < −0.50 (Easy)	0.397	0.325	0.293
	−0.50 < b < +0.50 (Moderate)	0.398	0.326	0.292
	+0.50 < b < +1.50 (Difficult)	0.396	0.326	0.292

Table 9.5 Median of the correlation coefficients between CAT ability estimations and TPMS mathematics assessment scores under different starting rules and fixed test length termination rules

		Termination rule: fixed test length		
Estimation	Starting rule	15 items	25 items	35 items
ML	−1.50 < b < −0.50 (Easy)	0.781*	0.816*	0.840*
	−0.50 < b < +0.50 (Moderate)	0.782*	0.815*	0.840*
	+0.50 < b < +1.50 (Difficult)	0.780*	0.812*	0.841*
WML	−1.50 < b < −0.50 (Easy)	0.786*	0.818*	0.846*
	−0.50 < b < +0.50 (Moderate)	0.789*	0.819*	0.848*
	+0.50 < b < +1.50 (Difficult)	0.784*	0.821*	0.849*

*All correlations are significant at the 0.01 level

fixing standard error value in CAT administration guarantees the same reliability for the ability estimations but examinees respond to different number of test items. It is obvious that each method has its own pros and cons with respect to termination rules. On the other hand, different starting rules did not create any difference in the analyses. The results also revealed that almost in all the estimations WML provided slightly better results over ML.

9.3.1.3 Determination of a Need to Content and Item Exposure Control Strategies

Mathematics item bank of TPMS contained items from four different sub-dimensions such as geometry (GE), measurement (ME), numbers (NU), and probability & statistics (PS). In real TPMS administration, students take almost the same number of items in each sub-dimension in the same grade level. Naturally, the real TPMS administration controls item exposure by considering the sub-dimensions of mathematics. As was explained before, for the purpose of increasing the number of items in the item bank, items from different sub-dimensions of the TPMS which were loaded on the same factor were piled up together. This brought the necessity of item content and exposure control in the present study for improving the content validity of the CAT administrations. For this purpose, CAT simulation was carried out by content and exposure controls in order investigate the average number of items to be used in CAT administration and the correlation of ability estimates obtained through content and exposure controls with the ones obtained in real TPMS administration.

Thus, in this particular simulation four different scenarios were tested such as (1) no use of content and exposure control, (2) use of only content control, (3) use of only exposure control, and finally (4) using both content and exposure controls were checked. The stopping rule was set as fixed test reliability with standard error 0.30. The number of items administered and correlation coefficients between ability estimations were indicated in Table 9.6.

Table 9.6 Median of the correlation coefficients between CAT ability estimations and subscales of TPMS mathematics assessment scores under different control strategies

	Average number of items administered	Correlation coefficient
No content and exposure control	33.05	0.830*
Exposure control only	64.48	0.838*
Content control only	34.30	0.842*
Both content and exposure control	74.75	0.887*

*All correlations are significant at the 0.01 level

The TPMS reports standard scores for each sub-dimension of the mathematics domain. However, in the present study for the purpose of increasing the size of the item bank items from different sub-domain are combined together. Thus, in the correlation analysis the standard scores obtained in real TPMS administration for each sub-dimension were averaged.

Using control strategies increased the number of items administered as expected. "CAT with content control" needed one more item in average than "CAT with no control." Moreover, the number of items in the test is almost doubled when Sympson and Hetter (SH) exposure control was used. The maximum item exposure rate was 0.28 in SH strategy.

9.3.2 Comparison of Multi Stage Adaptive Testing Results with TPMS

It is clearly seen that the content and exposure controls are two important concerns, when the content validity of the CAT administration is considered. As it is seen from the previous analysis, using both content and exposure controls increases the number of items tremendously. In fact, in the real TPMS administration almost the same number of items was used in linear test administration. For instance, in the sixth grade, a total of 78 items are used in the linear TPMS. Thus, using CAT with both content and exposure controls does not bring any parsimony in the number of items being used during the testing process. On the other hand, MSAT naturally brings the content and exposure controls in designing the testlets. In the last step of the present study MSAT simulation was carried out for the purpose of predicting the real TPMS standard scores.

The correlation of 0.846 obtained between the ability estimations of MSAT and TPMS. In this comparison, the test is terminated when standard error was lower than 0.30. The mean of the standard errors of ability estimation was obtained as 0.298 in this particular analysis. Additionally, the maximum item exposure rate of MSAT was 0.31.

Conclusion

Current TPMS mathematics assessments use linear computer based tests in which the item responses are analyzed within the framework of OPLM. This study provides a further step to investigate the applicability of adaptive test strategies in the TPMS. A set of simulations based on real responses of examinees indicated that CAT ability estimations provide higher correlation with the real TPMS mathematics assessment scores when the algorithm is set on (1) WML ability estimations rather than ML because of profitable statistical properties (2) fixed reliability estimates with the SE (smaller than 0.30 constraint) rather than fixed test length (Eggen and Straetmans 2000; Eggen and Verschoor 2006; Boyd et al. 2010).

The major concern of the CAT administration is the content validity especially in the subject matters such as mathematics, where there are different sub-dimensions. In this respect using exposure and content control approximates the number of items used in the CAT administration to linear TPMS administration. Considering the importance of content validity MSAT provided a defensible approach with 35 items used in total. This is as half as the CAT simulation with both controls. However, since the content of the testlets is under the control of tester, it seems possible to determine the item exposures and sample out different sub-domains in the preparation of the content of the testlets and as a consequence of this, validity of the test contents could be enhanced. Moreover, MSAT is simple to administer and provides almost the same reliability with the CAT administration. This is not a surprising result when the studies conducted by Macken-Ruiz (2008) and Rotou et al. (2003) are considered. As a result of the analyses, the researchers suggest using MSAT with WML estimation of abilities if the TPMS will be administered in adaptive test format.

References

Boyd AM, Dodd BG, Choi SW (2010) Polytomous models in computerized adaptive testing. In: Nering ML, Ostini R (eds) Handbook of polytomous item response theory models. Routledge, New York, pp 229–255

Eggen TJHM, Straetmans GJJM (2000) Computerized adaptive testing for classifying examinees in three categories. Educ Psychol Measu 60:713–734

Eggen TJHM, Verschoor AJ (2006) Optimal testing with easy or difficult items in computerized adaptive testing. Appl Psychol Meas 30:379–393

Glas CAW, Geerlings H (2009) Psychometric aspects of pupil monitoring systems. Stud Educ Eval 35:83–88

İş Güzel Ç, Berberoğlu G, Demirtaşl*ı* N, Ar*ı*kan S, Özgen Tuncer Ç (2009) Öğretim programlar*ı*n*ı*n öğrenme ç*ı*kt*ı*lar*ı* aç*ıs*ından değerlendirilmesi. Cito Egitim: Kuram ve Uygulama, Say*ı* 6:9–30

Kingsbury GG, Zara AR (1991) A comparison of procedures for content-sensitive item selection in computerized adaptive tests. Appl Meas Educ 4:241–261

Macken-Ruiz CL (2008) A comparison of multi-stage and computerized adaptive tests based on the generalized partial credit model. Dissertation Presented to the Faculty of the Graduate School of the University of Texas at Austin

Özgen Tuncer Ç (2008) Cito Turkiye öğrenci izleme sistemi (ÖIS) ve ÖİS'te soru geliştirme süreci. *Cito Eğitim: Kuram ve Uygulama,* Tan*ı*t*ı*m Say*ıs*ı, pp 22-26

Rotou O, Patsula L, Manfred S, Rizavi S (2003) Comparison of multi-stage tests with computerized adaptive and paper and pencil tests. Paper presented at the annual meeting of the American Educational Research Association (AERA) and the National Council on Measurement in Education (NCME) held between April 21–25, 2003, Chicago, IL

Sympson JB, Hetter RD (1985) Controlling item-exposure rates in computerized adaptive testing. In: Proceedings of the 27th annual meeting of the Military Testing Association, San Diego, CA: Navy Personnel Research and Development Center, pp 973–977

Vlug KMF (1997) Because every pupil counts: the success of the pupil monitoring system in the Netherlands. Educ Inf Technol 2(4):287–306

Wainer H, Kiely GL (1987) Item clusters and computerized adaptive testing: a case for testlets. J Educ Meas 24:185–201

Wainer H, Dorans NJ, Green FB, Steinberg L, Flaugher R, Mislevy RJ, Thissen D (1990) Computerized adaptive testing: a primer. Lawrence Erlbaum Associates Inc., Mahwah

Chapter 10
Optimal Sampling Design for IRT Linking with Bimodal Data

Jiahe Qian and Alina A. von Davier

Abstract Optimal sampling designs for an IRT linking with improved efficiency are often sought in analyzing assessment data. In practice, the skill distribution of an assessment sample may be bimodal, and this warrants special consideration when trying to create these designs. In this study we explore optimal sampling designs for IRT linking of bimodal data. Our design paradigm is modeled to gain the efficiency in linking and equating in analyzing assessment data and presents a formal setup for optimal IRT linking. In an optimal sampling design, the sample structure of bimodal data is treated as being drawn from a stratified population. The optimum search algorithm proposed is used to adjust the stratum weights and form a weighted compound sample that minimizes linking errors. The initial focus of the current study is the robust mean–mean transformation method, though the model of IRT linking under consideration is adaptable to generic methods.

Keywords Optimal sampling design • Stratified population • Complete grouped jackknifing • Optimum search

10.1 Introduction

For a complex standardized assessment with multiple test forms, typically used linking procedures could have large errors and be unstable over time because of heterogeneity of the samples across administrations and of the seasonality in test results. Such variability can adversely affect scale invariance over time and reduce efficiency in linking and equating. In this paper, we use the term linking to describe a transformation of IRT parameters from two or more test forms to establish a common scale, particularly a linear transformation of the IRT parameters from the two test forms. Although the same instrument and test specifications are administered across different regions, equating and linking procedures can still be unstable because of sample heterogeneity. An unstable linking is a major cause of

J. Qian (✉) • A.A. von Davier
Educational Testing Service, Research and Development,
Rosedale Rd, MS 02-T, Princeton, NJ 08541, USA
e-mail: jqian@ets.org; avondavier@ets.org

R.E. Millsap et al. (eds.), *Quantitative Psychology Research*, Springer Proceedings in Mathematics & Statistics 89, DOI 10.1007/978-3-319-07503-7_10

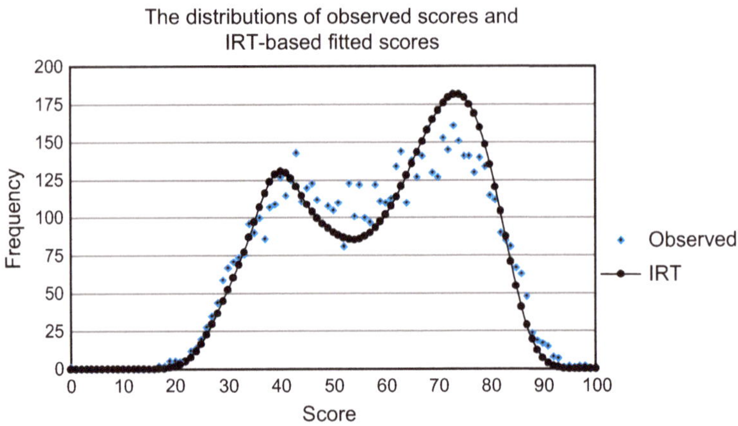

Fig. 10.1 The distributions of observed scores and IRT-based fitted scores

defective analysis and is always a concern to test investigators (Dorans and Holland 2000; Kolen and Brennan 2004; von Davier and Wilson 2008; Zumbo 2007).

In practice, the skill distribution of an assessment sample may be bimodal. Samples with bimodal distributions in test data could also arise during the introductory period of a new assessment instrument and/or when unexpected events prevent certain groups of examinees from participating. The disparity among multiple ability groups in an actual sample can be substantial, possibly yielding test data with bimodal distributions. A typical example of bimodal data (Duong and von Davier 2012), to be discussed later, is exhibited in the plot in Fig. 10.1 in Sect. 10.3.1. In scenarios such as these, making a decision ahead of time to include or exclude specific groups is a demanding task. Optimal, or at least improved, sampling designs for an IRT linking are sought to improve the efficiency in linking and equating in analyzing assessment data (Berger 1991, 1997; Lord and Wingersky 1985; Qian et al. 2013; van der Linden and Luecht 1998). The concept of optimal sampling design for linking and equating has been discussed by many researchers in the equating literature (Berger and van der Linden 1992; Buyske 2005; Stocking 1990). Our design paradigm is modeled after the work of Berger and presents a formal setup of optimal IRT linking (von Davier and von Davier 2011). The formal expression of this IRT linking, expressed as a restriction function on the parameter space as given in von Davier and von Davier, is a constrained optimization problem which can be practically and quickly approximated using the optimum searching approach described in Sect. 10.2.5.

An offshoot of this study is focused on searching for an optimal design to gain efficiency in item calibration by maximizing the determinant of the information matrix on the item parameters of IRT models (Berger et al. 2000; Buyske 2005; Jones and Jin 1994). The optimum searching algorithm (Beveridge and Schechter 1970; Wilde 1964) seeks an optimal solution of a nonlinear programming problem such as IRT linking and, in this study, is applied to bimodal data to form a weighted stratified sample that minimizes linking errors. Samples with bimodal distributions warrant special consideration when trying to create these optimal designs.

In optimal sampling design, the sample structure of bimodal data is treated as being drawn from a stratified population (Cochran 1977). Our linking design will adjust stratum weights to achieve an optimal linking according to a criterion based on a function of the information matrix. When a target population is available, weighting techniques (Cochran 1977) are often used to achieve a stabilized linking (Qian et al. 2013). Duong and von Davier (2012) used weighting techniques to reduce the disparity between a sample and its target population (by aligning the proportions of the demographic groups in the sample to those of the target population). In this way, a weighted sample distribution is made to be consistent with the distribution of the target population (Kish 1965). Rather than achieving stabilized linking, this study aims to reduce linking errors. Note that, although this study is focused on applying optimal sampling design to data with bimodal distributions, this method can be extended and used for optimal design to the assessment samples with a stratified structure (Qian & Spencer 1994).

In this study, the model of IRT linking under consideration is quite general and encompasses many types of linking procedures, including mean–sigma and mean–mean (m–m), concurrent calibration, fixed-parameters calibration, the test characteristic curves approach of Stocking and Lord (1983, S-L TCC), and the test characteristic curves approach of Haebara (1980, as cited in Kolen and Brennan 2004). Although the initial focus of the current study is the robust m–m transformation method (Loyd and Hoover 1980; Mislevy and Bock 1990), the optimal sampling design proposed in this study can be readily extended to other types of linking, such as the S-L TCC approach.

In Sect. 10.2, we introduce the methodology of the study, including study design, optimal sampling designs for IRT linking, complete grouped jackknifing, and the algorithm used to solve our constrained optimization problem. In Sect. 10.3, we document the empirical results of weighting examinee samples in IRT linking. The final section offers a summary and conclusions.

10.2 Methodology

10.2.1 Test Design

In this study, data collection is based on the NEAT design with nonequivalent groups from an anchor test (Angoff 1984; von Davier et al. 2004). There are two forms involved in linking: one operational form that contains the operational items and a set of anchor items, labeled X and U, respectively, and one reference form with the same common anchor U in a calibrated item pool. Moreover, all the items in the pool have already been placed on a base scale through simultaneous linking

(Haberman 2009). The design links the IRT model parameters of the operational form with those of the reference form in the pool through the common anchor.

10.2.2 Structure of Bimodal Data and Stratum Weights

Let $\mathbb{P}$ be a sample drawn from a population $\mathbb{P}$. Assume the sample has a two-stratum structure, $\mathbb{p} = \{\mathbb{p}_1, \mathbb{p}_2\}$, and the strata sample sizes are $\{n_{\mathbb{p}_1}, n_{\mathbb{p}_2}\}$. The stratum weight equals the ratio of stratum size to total size. The stratum weight vector for $\mathbb{P}$ is labeled as $W_{\mathbb{p}} = \{W_{\mathbb{p}_1}, W_{\mathbb{p}_2}\}$. Clearly, both $W_{\mathbb{p}_1}$ and $W_{\mathbb{p}_2}$ are between 0 and 1, and

$$W_{\mathbb{p}_1} + W_{\mathbb{p}_2} = 1. \tag{10.1}$$

Nevertheless, the initial partition of weights in $W_{\mathbb{p}}$ is usually not optimized for linking.

Our goal is to find a set of optimized stratum weights $W_{\mathbb{p}}^* = \{W_{\mathbb{p}_1}^*, W_{\mathbb{p}_2}^*\}$ that minimizes linking error. Let $\omega = W_{\mathbb{p}_1}^*$ and then $W_{\mathbb{p}_2}^* = 1 - \omega$. In the special case when $\omega = 1$, the linking only uses the data from the first stratum and when $\omega = 0$, the linking only uses the data in the second stratum. These extreme cases deviate from the target population substantially, and such a selection of groups in a sample, as expected, will result in lost efficiency in linking, as shown by the results in Sect. 10.3.

10.2.3 A General Model for Linking Errors and Mean–Mean IRT Linking

In general, IRT linking takes place after IRT calibration (except for the case of concurrent calibration). In the calibration, the two-parameter logistic regression (2PL) IRT model is used to fit the dichotomous data (Lord 1980; Muraki and Bock 2002).

For data $\mathbb{P}\cdot$ ($\mathbb{P}_1$ or $\mathbb{P}_2$), let $X_{\mathbb{p}.}$ and $U_{\mathbb{p}.}$ be the subsets of the data X and U, of the operational items and anchor items, respectively. Let vectors $\xi_{\mathbb{p}} = (X_{\mathbb{p}_1}, U_{\mathbb{p}_1}, X_{\mathbb{p}_2}, U_{\mathbb{p}_2})$, $\xi_{\mathbb{Q}} = (X_{\mathbb{Q}}, U_{\mathbb{Q}})$ for the reference data $\mathbb{Q}$, and $\xi = (\xi_{\mathbb{p}}, \xi_{\mathbb{Q}})$. Let $\pi_{\mathbb{P}.}$ be ability distribution for $\mathbb{P}.$. Let $\beta_{X_{\mathbb{P}.}}$ and $\beta_{U_{\mathbb{P}.}}$ be the item parameter vector for $X_{\mathbb{P}.}$ and $U_{\mathbb{P}.}$. Let $\eta_{\mathbb{p}} = \{\eta_{\mathbb{p}_1}, \eta_{\mathbb{p}_2}\}$ be the item parameter vector and ability distribution for $\{\mathbb{p}_1, \mathbb{p}_2\}$, where $\eta_{\mathbb{p}_1} = \left(\beta_{X_{\mathbb{P}_1}}, \beta_{U_{\mathbb{P}_1}}, \pi_{\mathbb{p}_1}, \omega\right)$, and $\eta_{\mathbb{p}_2} = \left(\beta_{X_{\mathbb{P}_2}}, \beta_{U_{\mathbb{P}_2}}, \pi_{\mathbb{p}_2}, 1 - \omega\right)$. Let $L_{\mathbb{P}_1} = L(\eta_{\mathbb{p}_1}; X_{\mathbb{p}_1}, U_{\mathbb{p}_1})$ and $L_{\mathbb{P}_2} = L(\eta_{\mathbb{p}_2}; X_{\mathbb{p}_2}, U_{\mathbb{p}_2})$ be the log-likelihood functions for $\{\mathbb{p}_1, \mathbb{p}_2\}$. For the reference form data $\mathbb{Q}$ in a pool, let $\eta_{\mathbb{Q}} = (\beta_{U_{\mathbb{Q}}}, \pi_{\mathbb{Q}})$ be the item parameter vector and ability distribution and let $L_{\mathbb{Q}} = L(\eta_{\mathbb{Q}}; X_{\mathbb{Q}}, U_{\mathbb{Q}})$ be the log-likelihood function. $\eta = \{\eta_{\mathbb{p}}, \eta_{\mathbb{Q}}\}$. Note that the reference distribution (from $\mathbb{Q}$) is unimodal. Also note that the data sets

$\mathbb{Q}$ and $\mathbb{P}$ are independent and $\mathbb{P}_1$ and $\mathbb{P}_2$, in separate strata in $\mathbb{P}$, are also independent. Then, $L_{joint} = L_{\mathbb{P}_1} + L_{\mathbb{P}_2} + L_{\mathbb{Q}}$ is the joint log-likelihood function for the IRT model applied to data X and anchor U.

10.2.3.1 Mean–Mean IRT Linking

For given ω, let a_{2l} and b_{2l} ($l = 1, 2, \ldots L$) be the slope and difficulty parameter estimates of the items on anchor U, and let $\overline{a}_{2\cdot}$ and $\overline{b}_{2\cdot}$ be means of a_{2l} and b_{2l}, respectively. Let a_{1l} and b_{1l} be the slope and difficulty parameter estimates on the reference form, and let $\overline{a}_{1\cdot}$ and $\overline{b}_{1\cdot}$ be the means of a_{1l} and b_{1l}.

The m–m transformation parameters (Kolen and Brennan 2004; Loyd and Hoover 1980) are

$$A = \frac{\overline{a}_{2\cdot}}{\overline{a}_{1\cdot}}$$

and

$$B = \overline{b}_{1\cdot} - A\,\overline{b}_{2\cdot}.$$

In an improved robust m–m transformation (Haberman 2009), the A parameter estimates are

$$A = \exp\left[\overline{\log}\left(a_{2\cdot}\right) - \overline{\log}\left(a_{1\cdot}\right)\right],$$

where $\overline{\log}\left(a_{2\cdot}\right) = L^{-1}\sum_{l=1}^{L}\log\left(a_{2l}\right)$ and $\overline{\log}\left(a_{1\cdot}\right) = L^{-1}\sum_{l=1}^{L}\log\left(a_{1l}\right)$. Let θ_2 and θ_2^* be the ability scores for the same examinee on the operational and reference forms, respectively. The score transformation between two forms is $\theta_2^* = A\theta_2 + B$.

10.2.3.2 A General Model for Linking

Following von Davier and von Davier (2011) notations, let $\mathbb{R}(\omega, \eta) = \{R_a(\omega, \eta), R_b(\omega, \eta)\}$ be the conditional restrictions on an anchor U for the m–m linking for the 2PL and the symbols a and b stand for the restrictions of slope and difficulty, respectively. Its components are

$$R_a(\omega, \eta) = \left(\sum_{l=1}^{L} a_{2l} - \sum_{l=1}^{L} a_{1l}\right)$$

and

$$R_b(\omega,\eta) = \left(\sum_{l=1}^{L} b_{2l} - \sum_{l=1}^{L} b_{1l}\right).$$

In order to obtain the optimal weighting for this constrained optimization problem by applying the Lagrange multiplier method, the general linking model for IRT linking (von Davier and von Davier 2011) can be expressed as

$$\Lambda\left(\eta, \lambda, \omega, \theta \middle| \xi\right) = L_{joint} + \lambda' \mathbb{R}(\omega,\eta), \tag{10.2}$$

where λ is a vector of Lagrange multipliers and $\mathbb{R}(\omega, \eta)$ is the constraint function for this model. Note that in linking to a pool, the anchor items in the reference form item pool had been calibrated and updated periodically (Haberman 2009). In a linking process, all the parameters in $L_{\mathbb{Q}}$ in L_{joint} are fixed; the term $L_{\mathbb{Q}}$ can be dropped and the model can be simplified to

$$\Lambda(\eta_{\mathbb{P}}, \lambda, \omega, \theta | \xi_{\mathbb{P}},) = \left(L_{\mathbb{P}_1} + L_{\mathbb{P}_2}\right) + \lambda' \mathbb{R}(\omega, \eta_{\mathbb{P}}). \tag{10.3}$$

For some λ, the optimal solution is the maximum of Eq. (10.3). To find the restricted maximum likelihood estimates, the task is to obtain a solution for the following equations

$$\nabla L_{joint} + \lambda' \nabla \mathbb{R}(\omega,\eta) = 0,$$

$$\mathbb{R}(\omega,\eta) = 0,$$

where ∇L_{joint} and $\nabla \mathbb{R}(\omega, \eta)$ denote the gradients of L_{joint} and $\mathbb{R}(\omega, \eta)$, respectively (Nocedal and Wright 2006; Silvey 1970).

10.2.4 Variance Estimation and Optimal Weighting

10.2.4.1 Linking Error

A complete grouped jackknife repeated replication method (CGJRR; Haberman et al. 2009) is used to estimate the standard errors of the whole linking procedure, including IRT calibration, item parameter scaling, and IRT linking. Although CGJRR is effective and powerful, as a resampling method, it can be computationally intensive and, in application, we usually need to adjust the grouping approach based on how data are sampled. Alternatively, other methods of variance estimation can also be used to estimate linking errors, such as balanced repeated replication (BRR), the bootstrap method, and the Taylor series method (Wolter 2007). To conduct CGJRR, first, the examinees in the sample were randomly aggregated into J (*120* in this study) groups of similar sizes. Then the jth jackknife replicate sample was formed by deleting the jth group from the whole sample, and therefore, 120 jackknife replicate samples were formed in total.

Given ω, for the whole sample and each jackknife replicate sample, we conducted the same IRT calibration, scaling, and equating procedure. Then we estimated the jackknifed standard errors of the parameters of interest. Let μ be the parameter estimated from the whole sample and $\mu_{(j)}$ be the estimate from the jth jackknife replicate sample. The jackknifed variance of μ was estimated by

$$V(\mu) = \frac{J-1}{J} \sum_{j=1}^{J} \left[\mu_{(j)} - \mu_{(.)}\right]^2, \tag{10.4}$$

where $\mu_{(.)}$ is the mean of all $\mu_{(j)}$ (Wolter 2007). The variance estimate $V(\mu)$ is just one measure of linking error, which is empirically unimodal.

10.2.4.2 Minimizing the Linking Error

In this paper we are interested in minimizing the linking error. Let $\overline{\theta}$ be the mean of transformed scores of θ_2^*. The linking error of $\overline{\theta}$ can be expressed as $V(\eta_{\mathbb{P}}, \omega, \bar{\theta} | \xi_{\mathbb{P}})$, for example, the $V\left(\overline{\theta}\right)$ mentioned above. The task of optimal weighting is to find a solution of ω that minimizes $V(\eta_{\mathbb{P}}, \omega, \bar{\theta} | \xi_{\mathbb{P}})$. The other statistics of interest include the transformation parameters A and B, and in these cases, the task is then to find an optimal ω that minimizes $V(\eta_{\mathbb{P}}, \omega, A | \xi_{\mathbb{P}})$ and $V(\eta_{\mathbb{P}}, \omega, B | \xi_{\mathbb{P}})$. The symbol $V(\cdot)$ is used to refer to linking error from here on. Thus the new model for linking errors becomes

$$\Lambda^*(\eta_{\mathbb{P}}, \lambda, \omega, \theta | \xi_{\mathbb{P}}) = V(\eta_{\mathbb{P}}, \lambda, \omega, \theta | \xi_{\mathbb{P}}) + \lambda \mathbb{F}(\omega, \eta), \tag{10.5}$$

where λ is the Lagrange multiplier, $\mathbb{F}(\omega, \eta)$ is the constraint function for adjusted ω, and $V(\eta_{\mathbb{P}}, \lambda, \omega, \theta | \xi_{\mathbb{P}})$ is a linking error term. Under this model, the task is to yield an optimal ω that minimizes $\Lambda^*(\eta_{\mathbb{P}}, \lambda, \omega, \theta | \xi_{\mathbb{P}})$.

Kuhn and Tucker (1951) discussed the optimality conditions for a Lagrange problem, such as the models for linking errors in Eqs. (10.3) and (10.5). Because solving the general model involves the whole linking procedure, including IRT calibration, item parameter scaling, and IRT linking, it is a demanding task to obtain the analytical solution for the equation. In this study, instead of solving the Lagrange problem analytically, we used the optimum searching approach, described in Sect. 10.2.4, to find the optimal ω, which minimizes a quantity $V(\eta_{\mathbb{P}}, \omega, \theta | \xi_{\mathbb{P}})$ in Eq. (10.5) iteratively. Before introducing the optimum seeking algorithm, we discuss the existence of an optimal solution ω that minimizes the linking error of a statistic of interest.

10.2.4.3 Existence of Optimal Weighting

The linking errors $\mathrm{V}(\eta_{\mathbb{P}}, \omega, \theta|\xi_{\mathbb{P}})$ in Eq. (10.5) are measured by variances and/or mean squared errors (MSEs) of the statistics of interest. The variance and MSE are quadratic functions. Assume $\widehat{\theta}$ is an estimator of θ. The MSE of $\widehat{\theta}$ is

$$\mathrm{MSE}\left(\widehat{\theta}\right) = V\left(\widehat{\theta}\right) + \left[E\left(\widehat{\theta}\right) - \theta\right]^2.$$

Let $\overline{y}_1^*$ and $\overline{y}_2^*$ be the means of transformed scores for the first and second strata, respectively. For the stratified sample the mean estimate is $\overline{y}^* = \omega\overline{y}_1^* + (1-\omega)\overline{y}_2^*$ and the variance estimator $V(\overline{y}^*) = \omega^2 V(\overline{y}_1^*) + (1-\omega)^2 V(\overline{y}_2^*)$. Let $f_1(\omega) = V(\overline{y}^*)$. For ω, the function of linking error $f_1(\omega)$ is convex on (0, 1). Because

$$\frac{df_1(\omega)}{d\omega} = 2\omega\left[V(\overline{y}_1^*) + V(\overline{y}_2^*)\right] - 2V(\overline{y}_2^*),$$

when

$$\omega = \frac{V(\overline{y}_2^*)}{V(\overline{y}_1^*) + V(\overline{y}_2^*)} \in (0,\ 1),$$

the $f_1(\omega)$ reaches its minimum on (0, 1).

Similarly, there also exists an optimal ω that minimizes the MSE. Define the biases of $\overline{y}^*$, $\overline{y}_1^*$, and $\overline{y}_2^*$: $\Delta = E(\overline{y}^*) - \overline{Y}^*$, $\Delta_1 = E(\overline{y}_1^*) - \overline{Y}_1^*$, and $\Delta_2 = E(\overline{y}_2^*) - \overline{Y}_2^*$,. Assume the bias estimates for the two strata are approximately equal, $\Delta_1 \approx \Delta_2$; then, for a stratified sample, the squared bias of $\overline{y}^*$ can be expressed as $\Delta^2 = \omega\Delta_1^2 + (1-\omega)\Delta_2^2$. Because the MSE of an estimate equals the sum of the variance and the squared bias of the estimate, this implies that $\mathrm{MSE}(\overline{y}^*) = \omega^2\mathrm{MSE}(\overline{y}_1^*) + (1-\omega)^2\mathrm{MSE}(\overline{y}_2^*)$. Let $f_2(\omega) = \mathrm{MSE}(\overline{y}^*)$. Because $\Delta_1 \approx \Delta_2$,

$$\frac{df_2(\omega)}{d\omega} \approx 2\omega\left[V(\overline{y}_1^*) + V(\overline{y}_2^*)\right] - 2V(\overline{y}_2^*).$$

When

$$\omega \approx \frac{V(\overline{y}_2^*)}{V(\overline{y}_1^*) + V(\overline{y}_2^*)} \in (0,\ 1),$$

the $f_2(\omega)$ reaches its minimum on (0, 1). The optimum ω that minimizes the MSE, with the assumption of $\Delta_1 \approx \Delta_2$, approximates the minimizer for variance. So the linking error of variance is used in assessing the weighting effects in Sect. 10.3.2.

Although it is difficult to provide an analytic proof of the existence of an optimal ω that minimizes the linking errors of the linking parameters A and B, the empirical curves of the linking errors of these linking parameters are all approximately quadratic. Section 10.3.2 provides the empirical curves in Fig. 10.3a–d.

10.2.5 An Algorithm to Yield Optimal Weighting for IRT Linking

The optimum searching approach (Beveridge and Schechter 1970; Wilde 1964) is an iterative method. Its algorithm alternates between two steps: the first step is to conduct IRT calibration and m–m linking; the second step, given the linking obtained from the first step, is the use of the optimum seeking approach to narrow the range for ω. Iteration continues until a solution for ω is found, i.e., the range is narrower than a small control length, say ε. The ω yielded by the iterative algorithm converges to the optimal solution for $\Lambda^*(\omega, \eta, \theta|\xi)$ which satisfies the constraint condition in Eq. (10.1). Of note is the fact that the golden ratio, $\frac{\sqrt{5}-1}{2} \approx 0.618$, is often used in fast optimum searching (Wilde 1964) as in the algorithm described below.

We start with four initial values of ω (i.e., the stratum weight for $\mathbb{P}_1$), $(\omega_1^0, \omega_2^0, \omega_3^0, \omega_4^0) = (0, 0.382, 0.618, 1)$, and then we narrow the range for ω until it converges. When the vector for ω is set, the vector of $1-\omega$ (i.e., the stratum weight for $\mathbb{P}_2$) can be determined correspondingly. For example, when ω equals 0.382, which is the second value of the four initial values of ω, then $1-\omega = 0.618$. Note that the two points in the middle, ω_2^0 and ω_3^0, divide the possible range of ω, which is [0, 1] initially, into three subsegments with sequential proportions that satisfy the golden ratio: 0.382 and 0.618. Let $(V_1^0, V_2^0, V_3^0, V_4^0)$ be the vector of the corresponding linking errors with $(\omega_1^0, \omega_2^0, \omega_3^0, \omega_4^0)$, and let $(\eta_1^0, \eta_2^0, \eta_3^0, \eta_4^0)$ be the vector of the corresponding parameters of item calibration. Let ε be a small control constant and let $i=0$. The optimization algorithm we use (Hua et al. 1989; Wilde 1964) consists of three steps after this initial setup:

a. *Narrow the range of* ω:
   If $V_2^i < V_3^i$, then let $\omega^* = \omega_1^i + 0.618 * \omega_2^i$ and vector $(\omega_1^{i+1}, \omega_2^{i+1}, \omega_3^{i+1}, \omega_4^{i+1}) - (\omega_1^i, \omega^*, \omega_2^i, \omega_3^i)$; otherwise let $\omega^* = \omega_2^i + 0.618 * \omega_3^i$ and $(\omega_1^{i+1}, \omega_2^{i+1}, \omega_3^{i+1}, \omega_4^{i+1}) = (\omega_2^i, \omega_3^i, \omega^*, \omega_4^i)$.
b. *Conduct a mean–mean linking*:
   Based on the data set with $(\omega_1^{i+1}, \omega_2^{i+1}, \omega_3^{i+1}, \omega_4^{i+1})$, calibrate the items and let the parameter vector be $(\eta_1^{i+1}, \eta_2^{i+1}, \eta_3^{i+1}, \eta_4^{i+1})$. Note that three out of the four elements in the vector remain the same as in the previous loop iteration and only η_2^{i+1} or η_3^{i+1} need to be estimated.
c. *Judge if a solution of* ω *has been reached*:
   Based on $(\eta_1^{i+1}, \eta_2^{i+1}, \eta_3^{i+1}, \eta_4^{i+1})$, conduct linking and let the vector of linking errors be $(V_1^{i+1}, V_2^{i+1}, V_3^{i+1}, V_4^{i+1})$. If $|V_2^{i+1} - V_3^{i+1}| < \varepsilon$, then stop; otherwise, $i = i+1$, and go to step a).

10.3 Data and Results

10.3.1 Data Resources

10.3.1.1 An Example of Bimodal Data

Figure 10.1 presents a typical example (Duong and von Davier 2012) of the distribution of bimodal data from an English listening assessment that consists of 100 dichotomous items. In addition to the observed scores in the figure, the IRT-based fitted scores were estimated based on Lord and Wingersky's recursion algorithm (Kolen and Brennan 2004; Lord and Wingersky 1985). The data came from 6,852 test takers that are classified into two groups based on level of education. In the first group of 2,808 (41 %) test takers, whose scores are clustered around the left mode, the level of education is lower than a bachelor's degree; the second group of 4,044 (59 %) have a bachelor's degree or higher. In this study we use real but manipulated data that match the shape of the bimodal distribution described in Fig. 10.1.

10.3.1.2 Data Resources Used in Analysis

Because it is difficult to obtain record-based bimodal data as shown in Fig. 10.1, we decided to create the data sets with bimodal distributions from real assessment samples. In the analysis, we employed four administrations of a reading assessment from a large-scale international language test; these tests were administered across different testing seasons. All of the examinees had responses to 42 operational items from two blocks having 14 and 28 items, respectively. The IRT linking was accomplished using both internal and external anchors. The anchor items were used to link the scale of a new test form to the scale of reference forms.

The initial task of the data analysis was to form bimodal data from the original data. We dropped 14–17 % of the cases from the original samples, respectively. Specifically, the percentage of the reduced cases in the score range of [21, 22] is 10 %, the percentage in [23, 25] is 35 %, the percentage in [26, 28] is 55 %, the percentage in [29, 30] is 35 %, and the percentage in [31, 32] is 10 %. Figure 10.2a–d present the four original Reading data sets and the corresponding bimodal data sets formed after 25 % of the cases in the mid-score range were dropped. Then, based on score and demographic variables, we partitioned all cases into two groups that form the two strata of the sample structure of bimodal data. The first group consists of all the cases in the score range of [1, 20], around 65–75 % of the cases in [21, 26] and 28–35 % of the cases, in [27, 32] who plan to apply for college level studies or have other plans, and around 35–45 % of the cases in [21, 32] who plan to apply for graduate level studies. The test takers in the second group are all those with scores of 33 and above, and all those not included in the first group. Specifically, Table 10.1 shows the sample sizes for all four samples, their bimodal subsamples,

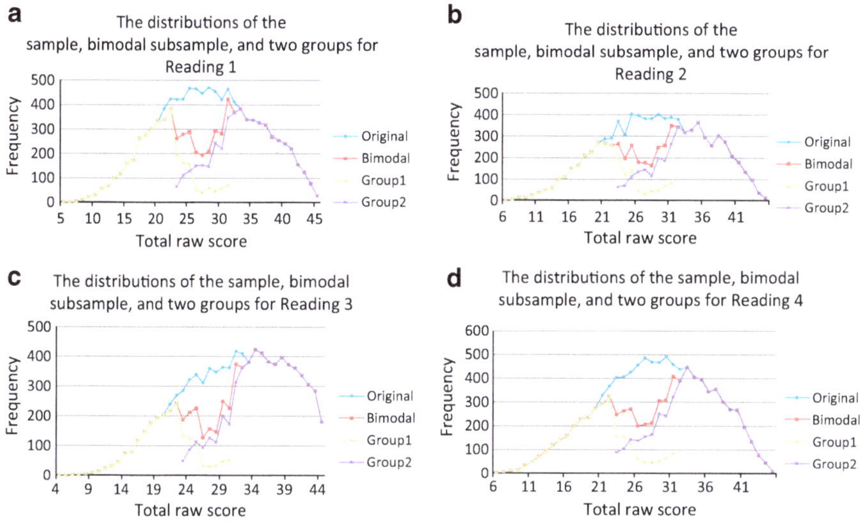

Fig. 10.2 The distributions of the sample, bimodal subsample, and two groups for reading 1 (**a**), reading 2 (**b**), reading 3 (**c**), and reading 4 (**d**)

Table 10.1 Statistics of the Samples, Bimodal Subsamples, and two groups in each data set

Data	Original sample	The size of bimodal subsample	Percentage of cases reduced (%)	Sample size of G1	Sample size of G2
Reading1	10,313	8,585	16.8	3,542	5,043
Reading2	8,628	7,226	16.2	2,771	4,455
Reading3	9,454	8,159	13.7	2,249	5,910
Reading4	10,120	8,359	17.4	3,091	5,268

and the groups in each data set; Fig. 10.2a–d present the distributions for the original samples, bimodal subsamples, and the groups in each data set.

10.3.2 Results

The evaluation of weighting effects is based on the comparisons of the variances of the m–m linking based on an optimally weighted sample against those based on an unweighted sample.

Figure 10.3a–d present the curves of the jackknifed standard errors of m–m linking parameters A and B for the four Reading data sets. The curves of standard errors are approximately quadratic when the stratum weight ω changes on (0, 1); this shows that, on each curve, there exists an optimal ω at which the standard error of A (or B) reaches its minimum. Figure 10.4a–d are the curves of the jackknifed standard errors of mean score estimates for the four Reading data sets. The curves

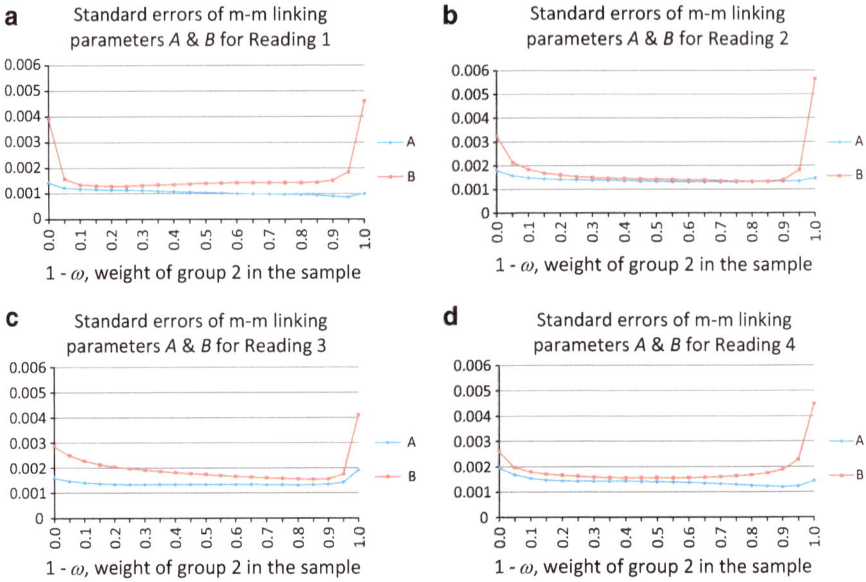

Fig. 10.3 Standard errors of m–m linking parameters A & B for reading 1 (**a**), reading 2 (**b**), reading 3 (**c**), and reading 4 (**d**)

are also approximately quadratic when the stratum weight ω changes on (0, 1). Note that in Sect. 10.2.4 we have shown that the linking errors of the mean estimates, variances, and/or MSEs, are convex on (0, 1).

In Table 10.2, we present the two types of jackknifed SEs for the bimodal subsample, i.e., SE_{opt} for the optimally weighted sample and SE_{un} for the unweighted sample. In the analysis, the convergence criterion for the optimization algorithm was set as $|V_2^{i+1} - V_3^{i+1}| < 0.0001$. The algorithm usually converged within 5–7 iterations. The ratio of SE_{un} to SE_{opt} ranges between 1.01 and 1.23 and the averages of these ratios for the transformation parameters A and B are 1.10 and 1.08, respectively, whereas the average of these ratios for the mean estimates is about 1.11. The efficiency of the m–m linking based on an optimally weighted sample is indeed improved.

10.4 Summary

In this study, we have applied optimal sampling techniques to yield an optimally weighted linking for bimodal data. This is an improvement over the conventional procedure of weighted IRT linking (Qian et al. 2013) that is designed to achieve a stable scale across multiple forms or to obtain an unbiased estimation in statistical inference. In this study, based on the definition of an optimal sampling design

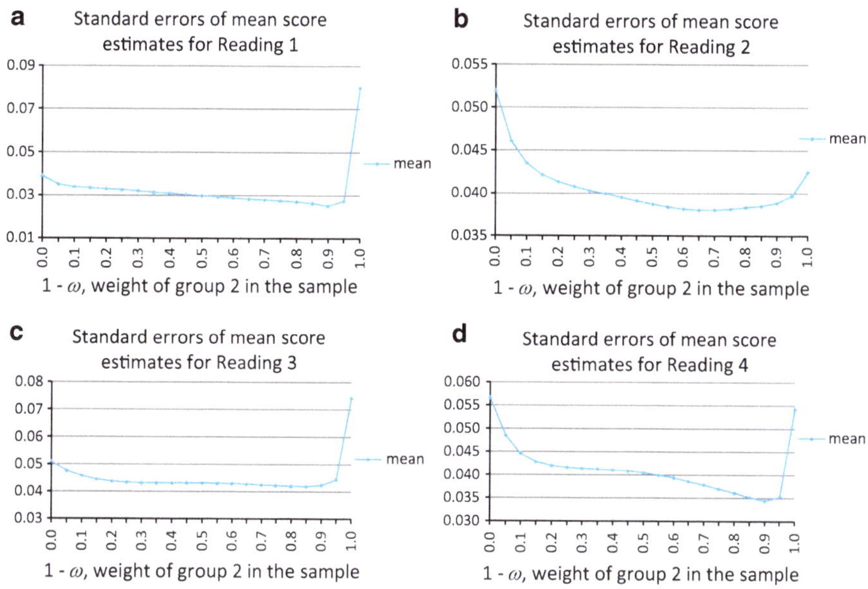

Fig. 10.4 Standard errors of mean score estimates for reading 1 (**a**), reading 2 (**b**), reading 3 (**c**), and READING 4 (**d**)

Table 10.2 The SEs of the estimates of interest for unweighted and optimally weighted samples and the efficiencies of a linking with optimally weighted bimodal sample

Transformation parameter/mean	Data set	SE_{un}	SE_{opt}	Optimal ω	Number of iteration	$\frac{SE_{un}}{SE_{opt}}$
A	Reading 1	0.00106	0.00087	0.93	7	1.21
A	Reading 2	0.00134	0.00132	0.65	6	1.01
A	Reading 3	0.00135	0.00133	0.79	7	1.02
A	Reading 4	0.00141	0.00122	0.89	6	1.16
B	Reading 1	0.00141	0.00130	0.21	7	1.08
B	Reading 2	0.00143	0.00135	0.84	7	1.06
B	Reading 3	0.00173	0.00154	0.85	7	1.12
B	Reading 4	0.00159	0.00151	0.46	5	1.05
Mean	Reading 1	0.02983	0.02418	0.94	6	1.23
Mean	Reading 2	0.03873	0.03804	0.65	6	1.02
Mean	Reading 3	0.04314	0.04199	0.84	7	1.03
Mean	Reading 4	0.04046	0.03451	0.89	6	1.17

(Berger 1991, 1997), we (a) achieved a formal optimal sampling design for IRT linking conducted on tests with bimodal data; (b) improved the efficiency of such linking procedures based on a different optimality criterion, i.e., by minimizing the error of the whole linking procedure; (c) provided a practical quality control method to IRT linking procedures with large-scale testing data collected from a population with heterogeneous subpopulations; and, finally, (d) applied a rapidly convergent, iterative algorithm to find an optimal solution for a general model of IRT linking.

From the empirical data analyzed, the optimal sampling design was shown to reduce the errors, on average, by 10 %. This is a fast and practical approach as the iterative algorithm can usually converge close to an optimal solution in less than seven iterations.

The focus of this study was on optimally weighted bimodal samples for IRT linking. Future research will be aimed at developing a generalized optimal sampling design to attain improved efficiency in obtaining a stable linking. In practice, the skill distribution of an assessment sample is often influenced by some examinee demographics, such as gender, age, region/native country, time studying a foreign language, or grade level. We can recode such demographic variables to their own binary-type responses, and then, based on these variables, we can form a cross-tabulated structure of the sample. On the marginal distribution of each variable, there are two categories (strata), and our task for this multivariate optimization problem is to adjust the category allocation on each margin to yield a solution which minimizes linking errors.

Acknowledgments The authors thank Jim Carlson, Shelby Haberman, Yi-Hsuan Lee, Ying Lu, and Daniel Bolt for their suggestions and comments. The authors also thank Shuhong Li and Jill Carey for their assistance in assembling data and Kim Fryer for editorial help. Any opinions expressed in this paper are solely those of the authors and not necessarily those of ETS.

References

Angoff WH (1984) Scales, norms, and equivalent scores. Educational Testing Service, Princeton

Berger MPF (1991) On the efficiency of IRT models when applied to different sampling designs. Appl Psychol Meas 15:293–306

Berger MPF (1997) Optimal designs for latent variable models: a review. In: Rost J, Langeheine R (eds) Application of latent trait and latent class models in the social sciences. Waxmann, Muenster, pp 71–79

Berger MPF, van der Linden WJ (1992) Optimality of sampling designs in item response theory models. In: Wilson M (ed) Objective measurement: theory into practice, vol 1. Ablex, Norwood, pp 274–288

Berger MPF, King CYJ, Wong WK (2000) Minimax D-optimal designs for item response theory models. Psychometrika 65:377–390

Beveridge GSG, Schechter RS (1970) Optimization: theory and practice. McGraw-Hill, New York

Buyske S (2005) Optimal design in educational testing. In: Berger MPF, Wong WK (eds) Applied optimal designs. Wiley, New York, pp 1–19

Cochran WG (1977) Sampling techniques, 3rd edn. Wiley, New York

Dorans NJ, Holland PW (2000) Population invariance and equitability of tests: basic theory and the linear case. J Educ Meas 37:281–306

Duong M, von Davier AA (2012) Observed-score equating with a heterogeneous target population. Int J Test 12:224–251

Haberman SJ (2009) Linking parameter estimates derived from an item response model through separate calibrations (research report 09–40). Educational Testing Service, Princeton

Haberman SJ, Lee Y, Qian J (2009) Jackknifing techniques for evaluation of equating accuracy (research report 09–39). Educational Testing Service, Princeton

Haebara T (1980) Equating logistic ability scales by a weighted least squares method. Jpn Psychol Res 22(3):144–149
Hua L-K, Wang Y, Heijmans JGC (1989) Optimum seeking methods (single variable). In: Lucas WF, Thompson M (eds) Mathematical modelling, vol 2. Springer, New York, pp 57–78
Jones DH, Jin Z (1994) Optimal sequential designs for on-line item estimation. Psychometrika 59:59–75
Kish L (1965) Survey sampling. Wiley, New York
Kolen MJ, Brennan RL (2004) Test equating, scaling, and linking: methods and practices. Springer, New York
Kuhn HW, Tucker AW (1951) Nonlinear programming. In: Neyman J (ed) Proceedings of the second Berkeley symposium on mathematical statistics and probability, University of California Press, Berkeley, pp 481–492
Lord FM (1980) Applications of item response theory to practical testing problems. Erlbaum, Hillsdale
Lord MF, Wingersky MS (1985) Sampling variances and covariances of parameter estimates in item response theory. In: Weiss DJ (ed) Proceedings of the 1982 IRT/CAT conference, Department of Psychology, CAT Laboratory, University of Minnesota, Minneapolis
Loyd BH, Hoover HD (1980) Vertical equating using the Rasch model. J Educ Meas 17:179–193
Mislevy RJ, Bock RD (1990) BILOG 3, 2nd edn. Scientific Software, Mooresville
Muraki E, Bock RD (2002) PARSCALE (Version 4.1) [Computer software]. Scientific Software, Lincolnwood
Nocedal J, Wright SJ (2006) Numerical optimization. Springer, New York
Qian J, Spencer B (1994). Optimally weighted means in stratified sampling. In: Proceedings of the section on survey research methods, American Statistical Association, pp 863–866
Qian J, von Davier AA, Jiang Y (2013) Achieving a stable scale for an assessment with multiple forms: weighting test samples in IRT linking. In: Millsap RE, van der Ark LA, Bolt DM, Woods CM (eds) Springer proceedings in mathematics & statistics, new developments in quantitative psychology. Springer, New York, pp 171–185
Silvey SD (1970) Statistical inference. Penguin Books, Baltimore
Stocking ML (1990) Specifying optimum examinees for item parameter estimation in item response theory. Psychometrika 55:461–475
Stocking ML, Lord FM (1983) Developing a common metric in item response theory. Appl Psychol Meas 7:201–210
van der Linden WJ, Luecht RM (1998) Observed-score equating as a test assembly problem. Psychometrika 63:401–418
von Davier M, von Davier AA (2011) A general model for IRT scale linking and scale transformation. In: von Davier AA (ed) Statistical models for test equating, scaling, and linking. Springer, New York, pp 225–242
von Davier AA, Wilson C (2008) Investigating the population sensitivity assumption of item response theory true-score equating across two subgroups of examinees and two test formats. Appl Psychol Meas 32:11–26
von Davier AA, Holland PW, Thayer DT (2004) The kernel method of test equating. Springer, New York
Wilde DJ (1964) Optimum seeking methods. Prentice-Hall, Englewood Cliffs
Wolter K (2007) Introduction to variance estimation, 2nd edn. Springer, New York
Zumbo BD (2007) Validity: foundational issues and statistical methodology. In: Rao CR, Sinharay S (eds) Handbook of statistics, vol 26, Psychometrics. Elsevier Science B.V, Amsterdam, pp 45–79

Chapter 11
Selecting a Data Collection Design for Linking in Educational Measurement: Taking Differential Motivation into Account

Marie-Anne Mittelhaëuser, Anton A. Béguin, and Klaas Sijtsma

Abstract In educational measurement, multiple test forms are often constructed to measure the same construct. Linking procedures can be used to disentangle differences in test form difficulty and differences in the proficiency of examinees so that scores for different test forms can be used interchangeably. Multiple data collection designs can be used for collecting data to be used for linking. Differential motivation refers to the difference in test-taking motivation that exists between high-stakes and low-stakes administration conditions. In a high-stakes administration condition, an examinee is expected to work harder and strive for maximum performance, whereas a low-stakes administration condition elicits typical, rather than maximum, performance. Differential motivation can be considered a confounding variable when choosing a data collection design. We discuss the suitability of different data collection designs and the way they are typically implemented in practice with respect to the effect of differential motivation. An example using data from the Eindtoets Basisonderwijs (End of Primary School Test) highlights the need to consider differential motivation.

Keywords Data collection design • Differential motivation • Linking

In educational measurement, multiple test forms are often constructed to measure the same construct to prevent item disclosure and maintain fairness. To make accurate comparisons of results, different test forms are created with as equal content and psychometric properties as possible. However, it is unlikely that the test forms will be perfectly comparable. Therefore, score differences between test forms

M.-A. Mittelhaëuser (✉)
Cito, Postbus 1034, 6801 MG Arnhem, The Netherlands
e-mail: Marie-Anne.Mittelhaeuser@cito.nl

A.A. Béguin
Cito, Postbus 1034, 6801 MG Arnhem, The Netherlands

K. Sijtsma
Tilburg University, Postbus 90153, 5000 LE Tilburg, The Netherlands

R.E. Millsap et al. (eds.), *Quantitative Psychology Research*, Springer Proceedings in Mathematics & Statistics 89, DOI 10.1007/978-3-319-07503-7_11

can be attributed either to differences in difficulty of the test forms or to differences in proficiency of the examinees. Equating and linking[1] procedures can be used to disentangle differences between test form difficulty and differences between the proficiency of examinees (von Davier 2013) so that scores on different test forms can be used interchangeably (see Angoff 1971; Holland and Rubin 1982; Kolen and Brennan 2004). Multiple data collection designs can be considered for collecting data to be used for linking. Choosing one type of data collection design over another depends on practical and statistical limitations. For example, differential student motivation for test taking needs to be considered when choosing a data collection design (Holland and Wightman 1982). Differential motivation refers to the difference with respect to test-taking motivation that exists between high-stakes and low-stakes administration conditions. In a high-stakes administration condition, an examinee is expected to work harder and strive for maximum performance, whereas a low-stakes administration condition elicits typical, rather than maximum, performance. Even though essentially all data collection designs are effective when all examinees are sufficiently motivated, the way in which data collection designs are typically implemented in practice results in some data collection designs being more robust against the effect of differential motivation than others.

In this paper, we first discuss differential motivation, followed by an overview and discussion of the robustness of linking procedures against the effect of differential motivation for five well-known types of data collection designs. Then, an example is used to highlight the need to consider differential motivation when choosing a data collection design for linking.

11.1 Differential Motivation

Researchers often implicitly assume that a test score is a valid indicator of an examinee's best effort (Wolf and Smith 1995). However, accumulated evidence shows that if item performance does not contribute to the test score or if no feedback is provided, examinees may not give their best effort (Kiplinger and Linn 1996; O'Neill et al. 1996; Wise and DeMars 2005). Unusual patterns of item scores or under-performance are common for low-stakes administration conditions. Within the item response theory (IRT) framework, unusual item-score patterns and under-performance threaten the correct estimation of examinee proficiency and item parameters (Béguin and Maan 2007). For example, Mittelhaëuser et al. (2011) found that, compared to using common items administered in a high-stakes condition, using common items administered in a low-stakes condition to link two high-stakes tests yielded different conclusions about the proficiency distributions.

[1]Despite the theoretical difference between linking and equating, the same statistical methods are used in the two procedures. Therefore, the terms equating and linking are used interchangeably for the purpose of this paper.

Many studies have focused on preventing, detecting, or correcting the effect of differential motivation. For example, Wise and Kong (2005) pointed out that the effort an examinee devotes to an item may vary throughout the test. Furthermore, Wolf et al. (1995) found that the effect of the administration condition on test performance differs substantially for different groups of items. In particular, items scoring highly on perceived difficulty or items considered mentally taxing were more affected by a difference in administration condition. Despite the growing knowledge of differential motivation, in practice, the effect differential motivation has on data is hard to detect and correct. Reise and Flannery (1996, p. 12) address this problem by stating, "Typical performance tests are usually not taken as seriously by examinees as are maximum performance measures. ... which is potentially more damaging to the measurement enterprise than any of the other so-called 'response biases.'" Since differential motivation might threaten the correct estimation of examinee proficiency and item parameters, thereby threatening the link between two test forms, differential motivation has to be taken into account when choosing a data collection design for linking.

11.2 Data Collection Designs

This section provides an overview of five well-known types of data collection designs suitable for linking and addresses the robustness of linking procedures and the way data collection designs are typically implemented in practice against the effect of differential motivation. A detailed description of these data collection designs and a discussion of the general advantages and disadvantages can be found in the equating literature (see, e.g., Béguin 2000; Kolen and Brennan 2004; Scheerens et al. 2003; von Davier et al. 2004). A distinction is made between data collection designs in which the tests to be linked are administered to equivalent groups (i.e., single-group design or equivalent-groups design) or to non-equivalent groups (i.e., common-item non-equivalent groups design, pre-test design or linking-groups design). Symbolic representations of the data collection designs are presented in Fig. 11.1 in the form of person-by-item matrices. Rows correspond to examinee data and columns to item data. Shaded areas represent combinations of items and examinees for which data are available. Blank areas represent combinations of items and examinees for which no data are available. The ordering of the items presented in the figures does not necessarily correspond to the ordering of items in the test form. Furthermore, sample sizes are not proportional to the sizes of the shaded and blank areas in the figures.

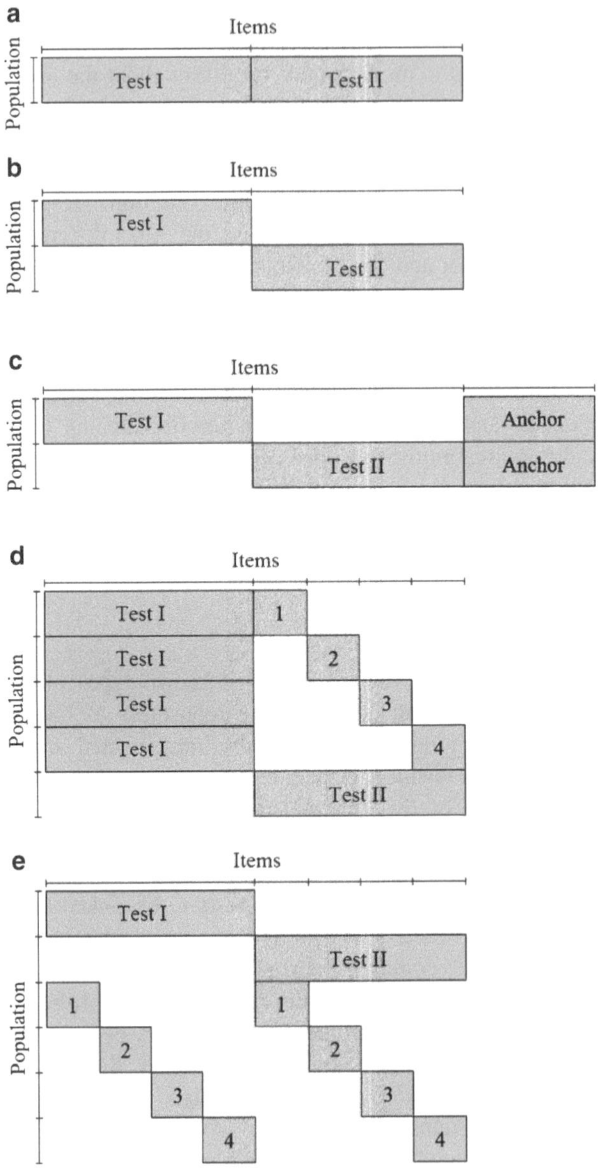

Fig. 11.1 (**a**) Single-group design, (**b**) equivalent-groups design, (**c**) common-item non-equivalent groups design, (**d**) pre-test design, and (**e**) linking-groups design

11.2.1 Single-Group or Equivalent-Groups Designs

The first data collection design is the single-group design (Fig. 11.1a). Both test forms are presented to a single group of examinees. An important assumption is that the proficiency of examinees does not change from one test form to the next. By assuming that the proficiency of examinees does not change, score differences between the two test forms can be attributed to differences in test form difficulty. Differential motivation should not pose a problem when using this data collection design if both test forms are administered under the same (high-stakes) conditions. However, if Test I is administered in a condition where the stakes are higher than in the administration condition of Test II, score differences between the test forms, due to differences in administration conditions, will be attributed to differences in test difficulty, resulting in overestimation of the difficulty of Test II.

The equivalent-groups design (Fig. 11.1b) is a variation on the single-group design in which each test form is administered to separate, non-overlapping groups of examinees. An important assumption is that the groups are randomly equivalent. By assuming that the groups are randomly equivalent, score differences between the two test forms can be attributed to differences in test form difficulty. Similar to the single-group design, differential motivation should not pose a problem if both tests are administered under the same (high-stakes) conditions. However, if Test I is administered in a condition where the stakes are higher than in the administration condition of Test II, overestimation of the difficulty of Test II is likely.

Kolen and Brennan (2004, pp. 17–19) give an empirical example of differential motivation in a (supposedly, counterbalanced) single-group design. They describe how a dataset collected according to a single-group design was used to scale an old test form and a new test form of the Armed Services Vocational Aptitude Battery (ASVAB) (Maier 1993). It appeared that many examinees were able to distinguish the items of the old test form and the new test form. Furthermore, many examinees were aware that only the items of the old test form were used to determine the score that was employed for selection purposes. Therefore, examinees were more motivated to answer the items of the old test form than the items of the new test form. This difference in stakes between the items from the old test form and items from the new test form resulted in high scores on the new test form, resulting in an estimated 350,000 individuals entering the military between January 1, 1976 and September 30, 1980 who should have been judged ineligible (Maier 1993).

11.2.2 Non-equivalent Groups Designs

In non-equivalent groups designs, examinees taking different test forms are assumed to be drawn from different populations. These designs are especially useful when it is unrealistic to assume random equivalence of examinee groups. For example, in educational measurement, the proficiency level of examinee groups may differ.

Data in non-equivalent groups designs are collected from the administration of two non-overlapping test forms to two different groups. The data contain no information to disentangle the differences in test form difficulty and the differences in examinees' proficiency. Therefore, non-equivalent groups designs must be 'linked.' Using the common-item non-equivalent groups design, pre-test design or linking-groups design will establish the link in three different ways.

The common-item non-equivalent groups design (Fig. 11.1c) is the most frequently used data collection design for equating test results across programs and testing organizations (von Davier 2013). In this data collection design, test forms are administered to non-overlapping and non-equivalent groups of examinees. Both groups, or samples of both groups, are administered an additional set of common items, which are often referred to as anchor items. Since the anchor items are the same across different groups of examinees, the difference in difficulty between the two test forms can be identified from the relative performance of both groups on the anchor items. The common-item non-equivalent groups design has two variations, one using an internal anchor and the other using an external anchor (Kolen and Brennan 2004, p. 19). When using an internal anchor, the score on the anchor items counts towards the score on the test form, whereas using an external anchor, the score on the anchor items does not count towards the score on the test form. In an internal-anchor design, the test form and anchor items are administered under the same (high-stakes) administration conditions, and differential motivation should not pose a problem when using this data collection design. Whether differential motivation poses a problem to the external-anchor design depends on the way the design is implemented in practice.

First, differential motivation might be a problem when using an external anchor design if examinees can distinguish which items count towards the score on the test form (i.e., items belonging to the test form) and which items do not (i.e., items belonging to the external anchor). If external anchor items are administered as a separately timed test section, examinees are most likely aware that the scores on these items do not count towards their score on the test form and differential motivation is likely to have an effect. However, if external anchor items are administered at the same time as the test form and examinees are not able to distinguish which items count towards the score on the test form, differential motivation will most likely not pose a problem. Second, differential motivation might be a problem when its effects are unequal between the two populations that are administered the external anchor items. If the effects are equal, differential motivation does not pose a problem and the linking result is unbiased. To see this, one may notice the following. In the common-item non-equivalent groups design the difference in difficulty between the test forms is estimated in two steps. First, the difference in proficiency between the populations is estimated from the relative performance of both populations on the anchor items. Second, the difference in difficulty of the forms is determined based on the relation between the anchor items and the items of the test forms. If the effect of differential motivation is equal among the populations administered the external anchor items, the difficulty of the external anchor items is overestimated, but the relative performance of both populations on the external anchor items represents the true difference between population proficiency; hence, the linking result is unbiased.

In the pre-test design (Fig. 11.1d), different subgroups are administered one of the test forms (Test I), and each subgroup receives a different additional subset of items intended for use in the new test form (Test II). In this way, items can be pre-tested to examine their psychometric properties before including them in a test form, here Test II. The score on the pre-test items usually does not count towards the score on the test form, since their psychometric properties are unknown at the time of administration. The number of items administered together with Test I is often relatively small to maintain the security of items in the new form (Béguin 2000). The pre-test items should be administered in such a way that the examinees cannot distinguish between the pre-test items and the items of the actual test form. In this case, differential motivation should not have an effect on the linking result. However, examinees might be able to distinguish the items of the actual test form and the pre-test items, for example, when the pre-test items are administered as a separately timed test section. In this case, differential motivation results in an overestimation of the differences in proficiency between the two test forms.

An application of the pre-test design can be found in the standard-setting procedure for the Swedish Scholastic Aptitude Test (SweSat; Emons 1998; Scheerens et al. 2003). The additional items do not count towards an examinee's score and examinees are not aware of which items do not belong to the actual examination, thereby guaranteeing the same level of motivation of the examinees on both the SweSat items and the items that are pre-tested.

Using the linking-groups design (Fig. 11.1e), a link can be established between the test forms by means of linking groups (Béguin 2000; Scheerens et al. 2003). Linking groups consists of examinees who do not participate in the actual administration of Test I and Test II, but are administered subsets of items from both test forms. Since these examinees are administered subsets of items from both test forms, the difference in difficulty between the two test forms can be estimated from the relative performance of the linking groups on the subsets of items from Test I to Test II. Differential motivation should not pose a problem if the subsets of items are administered to the linking groups in the same (high-stakes) condition as Test I and Test II. If linking groups are administered the items in a lower-stakes condition than Test I and Test II, differential motivation does not necessarily pose a problem. If the effects of differential motivation within the linking groups are equal among the subset of items from Test I to Test II, the linking result is unbiased. To see this, one may notice that if the effects of differential motivation are equal among the subsets of items, the relative performance of the linking groups on the subsets of items from Test I to Test II remains the same and the linking result is unbiased.

11.3 Example: Linking Mathematics Tests Using Different Data Collection Designs

This section introduces the mathematics scales of the '*Eindtoets Basisonderwijs*' (End of Primary School Test) and the different data collection designs that can be used for linking the mathematics scales of the Eindtoets Basisonderwijs 2011 and the Eindtoets Basisonderwijs 2012. The linking results obtained using different data collection designs are compared.

11.3.1 Eindtoets Basisonderwijs

The Eindtoets Basisonderwijs is administered each year at the end of Dutch primary education to give pupils, their parents, and their school advice about the type of secondary education most appropriate for the pupil. Each year, approximately 80 % of all primary schools in The Netherlands participate in the test. Even though the advice provided by the Eindtoets Basisonderwijs is not binding, almost all pupils consider the test high-stakes. This is caused by social and parental pressure and ample media attention. In addition, some more selective secondary schools use the test scores as part of their admission requirements. Item secrecy is vital; hence, the test form is renewed each year. The test forms of 2011 and 2012 each contained 60 mathematics items.

11.3.2 Method

11.3.2.1 Data

Samples of examinees were used to link the mathematics scales. The samples contained 4,841 examinees for the 2011 test form and 5,150 examinees for the 2012 test form.

Data were available to establish the link between the mathematics scales using either an equivalent-groups design (Fig. 11.1b), a common-item non-equivalent groups design (Fig. 11.1c) with either an internal or external anchor, a pre-test design (Fig. 11.1d) or a linking-groups design (Fig. 11.1e). When using the equivalent-groups design to link the mathematics scales, it was assumed that the samples of 2011 and 2012 were randomly equivalent when estimating the item parameters. Therefore, the differences between the proficiency distributions of the 2011 and 2012 samples did not have to be estimated.

The common-item non-equivalent groups design could be applied to the mathematics scales in two ways, since both an internal anchor and an external anchor were available. When using internal anchor items, samples of examinees were administered a different test form, which in both cases included 20 anchor items and 40 items from the test form. The anchor items count towards the final score on the Eindtoets Basisonderwijs and examinees were not aware that they had been presented an alternative test form. Therefore, differential motivation was not expected to pose a problem. The internal anchor items were administered to 3,027 and 2,708 examinees in 2011 and 2012, respectively. The external anchor items were administered in a low-stakes condition as a separately timed test. Schools often use this setup as an additional measurement of proficiency in preparation for the Eindtoets Basisonderwijs. The external anchor test was administered in the same month as the Eindtoets Basisonderwijs. The external anchor test, consisting of 50 mathematics items, was administered to 1,696 and 1,756 examinees in 2011 and 2012, respectively.

To pre-test the mathematics items intended for use in the Eindtoets Basisonderwijs 2012, 22 pre-test booklets (ranging from 28 to 62 items) were administered in 2011 approximately two to three weeks before the administration of the Eindtoets Basisonderwijs 2011. The number of examinees who were administered the pre-test booklets ranged from 244 to 347. Since the same pre-test items were administered in more than one pre-test booklet, the number of observations per item was larger, ranging from 276 to 976. The pre-test booklets were administered in a low-stakes condition. Similar to the common-item non-equivalent groups design, the link was established for the 2011 and 2012 samples.

Subsets of items intended for use in the Eindtoets Basisonderwijs 2011 or the Eindtoets Basisonderwijs 2012 were pre-tested on different samples of examinees to examine the psychometric properties of the items. These samples of examinees could be used as linking groups in a linking-groups design. Twenty pre-test booklets (ranging from 27 to 63 items) were administered in 2010 approximately two to three weeks before the administration of the Eindtoets Basisonderwijs 2010. The number of examinees who were administered the pre-test booklets ranged from 150 to 349. Since the same pre-test items were administered in more than one pre-test booklet, the number of observations per item was larger and ranged from 194 to 692. The pre-test booklets were administered in a low-stakes condition.

11.3.2.2 Analyses

Marginal maximum likelihood estimates of the proficiency distributions of the examinees who were administered the 2011 or 2012 test forms were obtained using the Rasch model (Rasch 1960). According to the Rasch model, the probability of passing an item i for individual j is a function of proficiency parameter θ_j and can be given by

$$P\left(X_{ij}=1\middle|\theta_j\right)=\frac{\exp(\theta_j-\beta_i)}{1+\exp(\theta_j-\beta_i)},$$

where β_i is the difficulty parameter of item i. OPLM software was used to estimate the Rasch model (Verhelst et al. 1995). The differences in mean proficiency of the 2011 and 2012 samples were compared between the different data collection designs used. Student's t-tests were used to determine whether mean proficiency of the samples of 2011 and 2012 differed significantly. Cohen's d was used to assess the effect size (Cohen 1988).

It may be argued that the Rasch model properties of unidimensionality, nonintersecting response curves, and a zero lower asymptote may not be appropriate for the data sets investigated here. However, Béguin (2000) showed that the procedure involving the Rasch model for equating the examinations in the Netherlands is robust against violations of unidimensionality and guessing. We assumed that this result could be generalized to our data and that the use of the Rasch model was appropriate. To investigate whether this assumption was valid, the data analysis was repeated on item sets from which items that did not fit the Rasch model were removed.

11.3.3 Results

Table 11.1 shows the estimated proficiency means of the mathematics scales of the Eindtoets Basisonderwijs 2011 and 2012. For all data collection designs, the mean proficiency of the population presented with the 2012 test form was higher than the population presented with the 2011 test form. All effects were significant at a 0.01 level, but the effect size is considered to be very small when using the common-item non-equivalent groups designs or the linking-groups design, and medium when using the pre-test design (Cohen 1988). It appears as if differential motivation has a noticeable effect on the resulting link when using a pre-test design with link items administered in a low-stakes condition.

Item misfit was investigated using Infit and Outfit statistics (Wright and Masters 1982) available in the eRm package in R (Mair et al. 2010). In scale construction,

Table 11.1 Proficiency distributions of the end test using different data collection designs

Data collection design	Population	N	M	SD	Cohen's d/Sign. Student's t
Common-item internal	2011	4841	1.232	1.038	0.07/**
	2012	5150	1.306	1.064	
Common-item external	2011	4841	1.133	1.037	0.07/**
	2012	5150	1.208	1.062	
Pre-test design	2011	4841	0.050	1.036	0.47/**
	2012	5150	0.547	1.061	
Linking-groups design	2011	4841	1.176	1.037	0.12/**
	2012	5150	1.303	1.062	

**$p < 0.01$

items having an Infit Mean Square value or Outfit Mean Square value outside the range of 0.5–1.5 (Linacre 2002) are usually not selected. Items of the Eindtoets Basisonderwijs and the internal anchor had Outfit Mean Square and Infit Mean Square statistics between 0.5 and 1.5, indicating that the Rasch model was consistent with these items (Linacre 2002). Among the external anchor items, one item had an Outfit Mean Square statistic of 2.031. From the 467 items, which were pre-tested in 2011 and used to link the test forms according to a pre-test design, 14 items had an Outfit Mean Square statistic higher than 1.5. A total of 516 items were pre-tested in 2010 and used to link the test forms according to a linking-groups design, of which 15 items had an Outfit Mean Square statistic higher than 1.5. Given the total number of items, the small numbers of misfitting items indicate that the Rasch model is consistent with these datasets. Deleting the misfitting items from the different data collection designs led to the same conclusion, which is the overestimation of the difference in proficiency distributions when using a pre-test design.

11.4 Discussion

Empirical data analyses illustrate the potential effect of differential motivation on results of linking using different data collection designs. Since there is no reason to assume that differential motivation affects the linking result when using a common-item non-equivalent groups design with an internal anchor, the different linking results can be compared with the linking result of this data collection design. The results suggest that the equivalent-groups design is not appropriate for linking both test forms of the Eindtoets Basisonderwijs, since there is a small, although significant difference in proficiency distributions between the samples who were presented either the 2011 or the 2012 test forms. Even though examinees were aware that the items of the external anchor test did not count towards the score on the Eindtoets Basisonderwijs, both common-item non-equivalent groups designs provide the same result. The most likely explanation for this result is that the effects of differential motivation are approximately equal for both populations administered the external anchor test, which leads to the unbiased estimation of the difference between the proficiency of both populations. The same explanation is likely for the linking-groups design, on the basis of which the same conclusion has to be drawn as for both common-item non-equivalent groups designs. Even though all types of data collection designs led to the conclusion that the mean proficiency of the population presented with the 2012 test form was significantly higher compared to the population presented with the 2011 test form, the effect size when using the pre-test design was larger compared to the other data collection designs. Using a pre-test design with linking items administered in a low-stakes administration condition produced differential motivation causing an overestimation of the difference in proficiency distributions, which is consistent with expectation.

All data collection designs may be effective provided all examinees are sufficiently motivated. However, the way in which data collection designs are typically implemented in practice results in some data collection designs being more robust against the effect of differential motivation than others. The conclusions with respect to the different data collection designs can therefore only be generalized to the extent that data collection designs are implemented in the same way as they were implemented for the Eindtoets Basisonderwijs. To illustrate this, the link items used in the external anchor design, pre-test design, and linking-groups design are administered as separately timed tests in low-stakes conditions. The differences between the data collection designs with respect to the estimated proficiency distributions will undoubtedly be negligible if the link items are administered in high-stakes conditions. Furthermore, we expect that administering the link items in a low-stakes condition at the same time as the Eindtoets Basisonderwijs with examinees being able to distinguish link items and items from the test form, results in larger differences between the data collection design with respect to the estimated proficiency distributions. To see this, one may notice that under these circumstances the difference in performance on the link items and the items from the test form is expected to be larger, since examinees are likely more inclined to spend effort on answering items correctly from the test form than the link items.

The question that remains is how the effect of differential motivation can be modeled. For example, when items are administered in a low-stakes administration condition, is it possible to classify item-score vectors as either resulting from motivated or unmotivated performance? If this is true, a mixture IRT model with latent classes might be useful for linking high-stakes tests when differential motivation is known to have an effect (Mittelhaëuser et al. in 2013). Alternatively, examinees might be motivated to a certain degree to answer items correctly in which case a multidimensional IRT model (Embretson and Reise 2000; Reckase 2009) might be useful. Furthermore, person-fit methods (e.g., Meijer and Sijtsma 2001) may be used to investigate how differential motivation affects the individual item-score vector. Since the results suggest that differential motivation has an effect on the linking result in different data collection designs, using methods that produce greater insight into the effect differential motivation has on linking tests administered in a high-stakes condition is valuable for measurement practice and measurement research.

References

Angoff WH (1971) Scales, norms, and equivalent scores. In: Thorndike RL (ed) Educational measurement, 2nd edn. American Council of Education, Washington, pp 508–600

Béguin AA (2000) Robustness of equating high-stakes tests. Unpublished doctoral dissertation, Twente University, Enschede, The Netherlands

Béguin AA, Maan A (2007) IRT linking of high-stakes tests with a low-stakes anchor. Paper presented at the 2007 Annual National Council of Measurement in Education (NCME) meeting, April 10–12, Chicago

Cohen J (1988) Statistical power analysis for the behavioural sciences, 2nd edn. Lawrence Erlbaum Associates, Hillsdale

Embretson SE, Reise SP (2000) Item response theory for psychologists. Lawrence Erlbaum, Mahwah
Emons WHM (1998) Nonequivalent groups IRT observed-score equating: its applicability and appropriateness for the Swedish Scholastic Aptitude Test. Twente University (unpublished report)
Holland PW, Rubin DR (eds) (1982) Test equating. Academic, New York
Holland PW, Wightman LE (1982) Section pre-equating: a preliminary investigation. In: Holland PW, Rubin DR (eds) Test equating. Academic, New York, pp 271–297
Kiplinger VL, Linn RL (1996) Raising the stakes of test administration: the impact on student performance on the National Assessment of Educational Progress. Educ Assess 3:111–133
Kolen MJ, Brennan RL (2004) Test equating, scaling, and linking, 2nd edn. Springer Verlag, New York
Linacre JM (2002) What do infit and outfit, mean-square and standardized mean? Rasch Meas 16:878
Maier MH (1993) Military aptitude testing: the past fifty years (DMCM Technical Report 93-700). Defence Manpower Data Center, Montery, CA
Mair P, Hatzinger R, Maier M (2010) eRm: Extended Rasch Modeling. Retrieved from http://CRAN.R-project.org/package=eRm
Meijer RR, Sijtsma K (2001) Methodology review: evaluating person fit. Appl Psychol Meas 25:107–135
Mittelhaëuser M, Béguin AA, Sijtsma K (2011) Comparing the effectiveness of different linking designs: the internal anchor versus the external anchor and pre-test data (Report No. 11-01). Retrieved from Psychometric Research Centre Web site: http://www.cito.nl/~/media/cito_nl/Files/Onderzoek%20en%20wetenschap/cito_mrd_report_2011_01.ashx
Mittelhaëuser M, Béguin AA, Sijtsma K (2013) Modeling differences in test-taking motivation: exploring the usefulness of the mixture Rasch model and person-fit statistics. In: Millsap RE, van der Ark LA, Bolt DM, Woods CM (eds) New developments in quantitative psychology. Springer, New York, pp 357–370
O'Neill HF, Sugrue B, Baker EL (1996) Effects of motivational interventions on the National Assessment of Educational Progress mathematics performance. Educ Assess 3:135–157
Rasch G (1960) Probabilistic models for some intelligence and attainment tests. Danish Institute for Educational Research, Copenhagen
Reckase MD (2009) Multidimensional item response theory models. Springer Verlag, New York
Reise SP, Flannery WP (1996) Assessing person-fit on measures of typical performance. Appl Meas Educ 9:9–26
Scheerens J, Glas C, Thomas SM (2003) Educational evaluation, assessment and monitoring: a systematic approach. Swets & Zeitlinger, Lisse
Verhelst ND, Glas CAW, Verstralen HHFM (1995) One-parameter logistic model (OPLM). Cito, National Institute for Educational Measurement, Arnhem
von Davier AA (2013) Observed-score equating: an overview. Psychometrika 78:605–623
von Davier AA, Holland PW, Thayer DT (2004) The kernel method of test equating. Springer, New York
Wise SL, DeMars CE (2005) Low examinee effort in low-stakes assessment: problems and potential solutions. Educ Assess 10:1–17
Wise SL, Kong X (2005) Response time effort: a new measure of examinee motivation in computer-based tests. Appl Meas Educ 18:163–183
Wolf LF, Smith JK (1995) The consequence of consequence: motivation, anxiety and test performance. Appl Meas Educ 8:227–242
Wolf LF, Smith JK, Birnbaum ME (1995) The consequence of performance, test, motivation, and mentally taxing. Appl Meas Educ 8:341–351
Wright BD, Masters GN (1982) Rating scale analysis. Mesa Press, Chicago

Chapter 12
Vertical Comparison Using Reference Sets

Anton A. Béguin and Saskia Wools

Abstract When tests for different populations are compared, vertical item response theory (IRT) linking procedures can be used. However, the validity of the linking might be compromised when items in the procedure show differential item functioning (DIF), violating the assumption of the procedure that the item parameters are stable in different populations. This article presents a procedure that is robust against DIF but also exploits the advantages of IRT linking. This procedure, called *comparisons using reference sets*, is a variation of the scaling test design. Using reference sets, an anchor test is administered in all populations of interest. Subsequently, different IRT scales are estimated for each population separately. To link an operational test to the reference sets, a sample of the items from the reference set is administered with the operational test. In this article, a simulation study is presented to compare a linking method using reference sets with a linking method using a direct anchor. From the simulation study, we can conclude that the procedure using reference sets has an advantage over other vertical linking procedures.

12.1 Theoretical Framework

In educational measurement, results of different tests or test forms often need to be compared, for example, when comparing examinations from 1 year to the next (Béguin 2000). Since the tests can differ in difficulty and other measurement properties, techniques are developed to make results comparable or to maintain scores across forms. This process is called linking or equating (Holland and Dorans 2006, pp. 193–195). Linking procedures can be divided into two types. The first type assumes that the groups of students taking different operational test forms are sampled from the same population. The second type accommodates groups sampled from different populations; this difference is estimated based on the administration of some common items (Holland and Dorans 2006, pp. 197–201). The common items are referred to as anchors or anchor tests, and the results on these anchors are used to estimate the difference in proficiency between the groups in the design.

A.A. Béguin (✉) • S. Wools
Cito, Institute for Educational Measurement, Postbus 1034, 6801 MG Arnhem, The Netherlands
e-mail: Anton.Beguin@cito.nl; Saskia.Wools@cito.nl

R.E. Millsap et al. (eds.), *Quantitative Psychology Research*, Springer Proceedings in Mathematics & Statistics 89, DOI 10.1007/978-3-319-07503-7_12

A special case of linking occurs when the aim is to assess growth and the results are compared across grades. This type of comparison is called vertical scaling or vertical linking. In contrast to this, linking of operational tests administered in the same grade or in a similar population is also referred to as horizontal linking. Vertical linking procedures (see, e.g., Carlton 2011; Harris 2007; Kolen and Brennan 2004, pp. 372–418; Kolen 2006, pp. 171–180) are largely comparable to the default linking techniques. Similar to regular equating and linking procedures, some forms of linking data (e.g., results on anchor tests) are used to compare two assessments suitable for different age or grade levels. Often an item response theory (IRT) model is applied to construct a common scale for the characteristics of the items from the two assessments. Application of IRT provides additional flexibility in the linking design, but depending on the linking approach, different restrictions on the parameter space are assumed (Von Davier and Von Davier 2004, 2012). These assumptions determine how the item parameters for different test forms are placed on a single scale. In the ideal linking design, item parameters between forms can be scaled to be the same. In vertical linking, the assumptions used to place the forms on a single scale provide an additional challenge, since vertical linking must take into account that some item characteristics differ between groups of students (differential item functioning or DIF). The standard procedures deal with this in a way that is not necessarily robust. As a standard feature of vertical linking, items that are considered to show DIF are removed from the anchor mostly on statistical grounds and sometimes regardless of their content. Obviously, treating DIF in a linking procedure in this way is somewhat arbitrary and could be a threat to the validity of the linking. This is especially a concern when selective removal of items alters the construct that is measured in the anchor, consequently influencing the linking of the test forms for the different groups in the design. Especially in testing situations, where we expect a large proportion of items with differences in the item characteristics, this threat to validity could have serious implications for the inferences made from vertical linking. The same validity threat could occur in horizontal equating if data samples from populations with a largely different educational background are compared. Here, differences in performance on individual items may also be the result of bias or DIF and not a difference in proficiency. In both cases, how the relative performance of the groups of students in the design is evaluated depends on the particular items in the anchor. If more items that are relatively easy for a particular group of students are included in the anchor, the perceived relative performance of this group compared to the other groups will increase.

We developed a procedure that is robust against DIF. The newly developed procedure, called comparison using reference sets, is based on an existing procedure described by Petersen et al. (1989) that uses a scaling test design, which has been applied on the Iowa Test of Basic Skills. In this design, the same anchor test is administered with an operational test in samples of all the populations of interest. In each population, there is a single group linking design (e.g., Holland and Dorans 2006, p. 197; Kolen and Brennan 2004) to link the operational test for this population to the anchor. Two operational tests aimed at different populations are compared based on the predicted scores on the anchor. Petersen et al. (1989) referred to the above procedure as Hieronymus scaling and called the anchor test in the above procedure a scaling test. The scaling test contains test items representative of the content domains from all the tests compared, but the test is designed to be short enough for administration as an anchor next to the operational test. A potential drawback of the design is that in educational assessments it is often not appropriate to test a majority of students with a number of items that are too easy or too difficult and hence provide no relevant information on the performance level of these students (Carlton, 2011, p. 60).

12.2 Technique

The procedure for (vertical) comparison using reference sets draws on the idea of the scaling test but combines it with IRT. The two operational tests that are compared link to a large anchor test called a reference set. A typical design of the data structure for vertical comparison is graphically represented in Fig. 12.1. Items are on the horizontal axis and persons are on the vertical axis. The gray areas in the graph represent the available data in the design, and the white space reflects data missing by design.

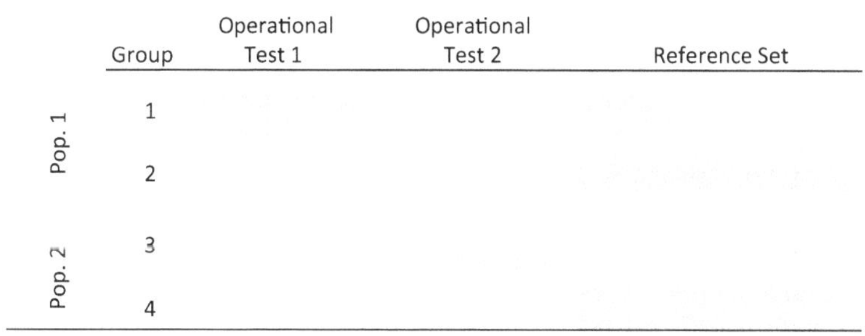

Fig. 12.1 Design linking two operational tests based on a reference set

In this design, four groups of students from two different populations take either a reference set or an operational test together with an anchor to the reference set. Both Groups 1 and 2 are samples from Population 1. Group 1 takes operational test 1 and a part of the reference set, and Group 2 takes all the items on the reference test. A similar pattern occurs for Groups 3 and 4 from Population 2.

Within the procedure for (vertical) comparison using reference sets, five steps are distinguished:

1. Construct a set of items suitable to form a basis of comparison. This is referred to as a reference set;
2. Administer the reference set in all the populations using an incomplete design;

3. Estimate an IRT scale on the reference set for each population separately;
4. Administer the operational tests for each population, together with a sample of the items from the reference set that is most suitable to the population;
5. Link the assessment to the reference set and compare between the different populations.

In Step 1, we constructed the reference set, which is the basis for comparison. This reference set is a relatively large set of items (e.g., 50–80 items) designed to be an optimal measurement of the intended construct for all relevant populations. For this reason, it contains a representative mix of items from the underlying content domains and the relevant assessments that need to be compared. The reference set is composed in such a way that if it is administered in the different populations, none of the groups of students is advantaged. This is mainly a content argument. The total construct operationalized in the reference set should be fair to all populations. Individual items in the reference set could perform relatively differently in the different populations, but the measurement based on all the items should be unbiased. Differences between the populations in results on the reference set should be due to differences in proficiency and not the result of the selection of specific items in the reference set. To use the reference set as a valid basis for comparison, the reference set must be regarded as a high-quality operationalization of the underlying standard (that needs to encompass the different populations and grades).

To support the claim that the reference set is a high-quality operationalization, a rigorous construction process is used. In the construction phase of the reference set, a number of stakeholders—independent content experts and representatives from each grade level—must be involved to achieve concordance on the content of the operationalization of the standard. The reference set can theoretically function similarly to the classical scaling test, but the number of items in the set will be too large for it to practically function as an anchor test next to an operational test. Therefore, in Step 2, data on performance of the students on the reference set is collected separately from the linking of operational tests. For each population of students in the design, the items from the total reference set are administered using an incomplete design. Such an incomplete design entails that not all the items are administered to all the students, but are administered in such a way that the results on all the items can be scaled as if they were administered to a group of students taking the reference sets. From that perspective, the graphical representation in Fig. 12.1 is a simplification of the actual design, since the incomplete nature of the administration in Groups 2 and 4 is ignored. Using the data from the samples, separate IRT scales are estimated for each population (Step 3). In this way, we model the behavior of each specific population on the reference set. Due to the separate scales for each population, we allow for different item characteristics between the populations.

In traditional linking with separate calibration, these scales are linked to a common scale, but here we assume the scales will not necessarily fit a common metric. This is more flexible than the difference between IRT scales that is due to the potential difference in scale identification. The ordering of items within each scale could be different, allowing for DIF between the populations. Finally, operational tests are linked to the reference set using a sample of items from the reference set that fit the intended population (Step 4). As a result, the operational test can be compared to the reference set, but due to the different IRT scales for the different populations, the operational tests are not on a common scale with one another. A comparison between the operational tests can be based on the predicted performance (e.g., number-correct score) on the reference set (Step 5).

The procedure using reference sets deviates from existing linking procedures. It does not directly predict response behavior on the operational tests, as is done in classical linking procedures such as observed score equating (see Kolen and Brennan 2004), and it does not assume a single IRT scale over the operational test, as is done in observed score number-correct equating (Zeng and Kolen 1995). Comparison using reference sets results in a more flexible procedure in comparison with the traditional vertical linking procedures and, as a consequence, this procedure is robust against the effect of DIF in the anchor.

12.3 Methods

To illustrate the procedure using reference sets, a small simulation study was carried out in which the effectiveness of comparison using reference sets was compared with two other linking procedures based on three different designs. In this study, we sampled data for two operational tests that needed to be compared and were suitable for different populations. Next to the data of the operational forms, we sampled data for a reference set administered in the same two populations that also took the operational tests. Furthermore, we sampled data linking the operational tests to the reference set. This design resembled a situation where some of the students who took the operational test were also administered an anchor test consisting of part of the reference set. In a separate test, administration data were collected of the performance of this population on all items from the reference set. The data structure is graphically represented in Fig. 12.2.

In design 1, the reference set consisted of three item subsets (A, B1, and B2). Subset A was unbiased, B1 was biased in favor of population 1, and B2 was biased in favor of population 2. If subset B1 is seen as more suitable to population 1, and B2 as more suitable to population 2, then subset B1 provides unbiased latent trait estimates for subjects from population 1 but not from population 2, whereas B2 provides unbiased latent trait estimates for subjects from population 2 but not from population 1. In design 1, two populations were administered six different test forms in total. Population 1 contained three groups. Group 1 was administered operational test 1, Group 3 was administered the reference set, and Group 2 took operational test 1 and an anchor (A and B1) to the reference set. For population 2, a similar design occurred in which Groups 4 and 5 were administered operational test 2; Group 5 also took an anchor form (A and B2). Group 6 was administered the reference set. In summary, operational test 1 was linked to the reference set by a

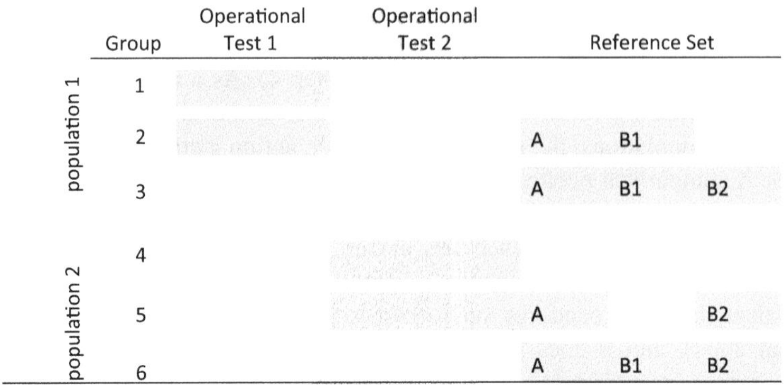

Fig. 12.2 Design with *unbiased* direct linking and comparing based on reference set

common administration of subsets A and B1, while operational test 2 was linked to the reference set using subsets A and B2.

Alternative designs (Figs. 12.3 and 12.4) were simulated in which both operational tests were linked to the reference set using an anchor with an unbiased and biased part (containing A and B1) and a totally biased anchor containing only B1 (design 3), respectively.

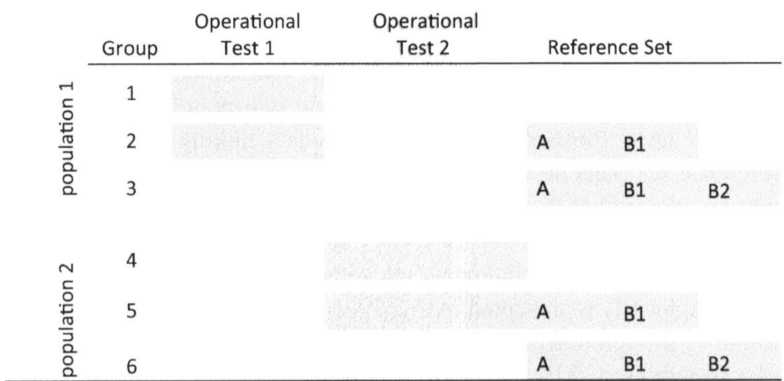

Fig. 12.3 Design with *partly biased* direct linking and comparison based on reference set

Data were simulated based on parameters from operational tests in which a vertical equating problem was present. In this case, the parameters were based on results from a test bank with ten equated versions of a mathematics test administered at the end of secondary education in the Netherlands. In total, 11,320 students in two pre-academic tracks of secondary education in the Netherlands took one of the 10 test versions. Sample size per item was more than 2,100 for each item and at least 500 for each combination of an item and a population. This assessment was designed to provide a valid measurement of the same standard in both populations.

The populations differed in proficiency. In addition, 67 of the 259 items that were administered showed DIF between the populations when using the One Parameter Logistic Model (OPLM; Verhelst et al. 1994). This model is a variation of the 2-Parameter Logistic (2-PL) IRT model in which the discrimination parameters are fixed to discrete values. In practice, the values of the discrimination parameters are often estimated for part of the data and used as fixed values for the remainder of the data. The advantage of the OPLM model is that it combines some favorable properties of the Rasch models, such as the ability to use conditional maximum likelihood estimation and well-developed test statistics, with the flexibility of a two-parameter model (Verhelst et al. 1994; Verhelst and Glas 1995). In the 2-PL model, the probability of a correct response of a person i on an item j, denoted $X_{ij}=1$, is written as

$$P(X_{ij}=1)=\frac{\exp(\alpha_j\theta_i-\beta_j)}{1+\exp(\alpha_j\theta_i-\beta_j)},$$

where α_j is the discrimination parameter of item j, β_j is the difficulty parameter, and θ_i is the proficiency of person i. In the OPLM, α_j is fixed to an integer value prior to model estimation and is therefore denoted as a constant a.

	Group	Operational Test 1	Operational Test 2	Reference Set		
population 1	1					
	2				B1	
	3			A	B1	B2
population 2	4					
	5				B1	
	6			A	B1	B2

Fig. 12.4 Design with '*biased*' direct linking and comparison based on reference set

For the simulation, four sets of items were selected from the available data. One set of 20 biased items that favored students from educational track 1 (B1) and a set of 20 biased items that favored students from educational track 2 (B2) were selected from the 67 biased items. To complete the simulated reference set alongside the biased items, a set of 20 unbiased items were randomly sampled from the 192 items without DIF. To sample the operational tests, parameters of a random sample of 60 unbiased items were used. The crucial aspect of this simulation study was to assess the effect of biased items on the linking of the operational tests. Since the operational tests were only administered in a single population, and the tests aimed at the same standard, we used the same parameter values for both operational tests 1 and 2. The advantage of this approach is that the true relation of the tests is known. In this way, the results of the linking can be easily evaluated since the two tests are simulated to be of equal difficulty. Based on these parameters, estimate data were generated according to designs 1, 2, and 3. The item parameter values a and β that were used in the simulation are given in Tables 12.1 and 12.2. For the items in blocks B1 and B2 of the anchor, a separate set of item parameters is given for both educational tracks (Tables 12.3 and 12.4). Therefore, these items will perform differently in the two different populations. The average difference in difficulty between populations 1 and 2 is -0.144 in Block 1 and 0.158 in Block 2.

In the samples, the operational tests included 3,000 persons, and the anchor and the reference set included 1,000 persons in each population. For each design, 100 samples were drawn. Data were simulated using a 2-PL model with item parameters from the separate analyses for each of the groups in the original data. Two population conditions were used, a non-equivalent and an equivalent group

Table 12.1 Item parameters used to generate data for operational test forms

Item	a	β	Item	a	β	Item	a	β	Item	a	β
1	3	−0.795	16	2	−0.411	31	2	−1.644	46	3	−0.560
2	3	−0.627	17	3	−0.670	32	3	0.040	47	3	−0.873
3	4	−0.827	18	2	−0.510	33	3	0.274	48	3	−0.547
4	2	−1.370	19	3	−0.690	34	2	−0.398	49	2	−0.551
5	2	−0.335	20	3	−0.581	35	3	−0.229	50	2	−0.110
6	3	0.017	21	3	−1.050	36	2	0.084	51	3	−1.005
7	5	0.642	22	3	−0.443	37	1	−0.501	52	2	−1.282
8	2	−0.824	23	2	−0.718	38	3	−1.612	53	3	−1.005
9	1	1.792	24	4	−0.598	39	2	−0.331	54	2	−0.091
10	3	−0.735	25	2	−1.370	40	4	0.012	55	5	0.407
11	3	−0.942	26	3	−0.703	41	2	−0.091	56	3	0.274
12	2	−0.369	27	4	−0.936	42	3	0.405	57	3	0.429
13	2	−0.331	28	4	0.286	43	2	−0.649	58	2	−0.448
14	1	−1.268	29	3	−0.458	44	4	0.026	59	3	−0.884
15	3	−0.154	30	4	0.427	45	4	0.179	60	2	0.631

Table 12.2 Item parameters used to generate data for anchor A

Item	a	β	Item	a	β
1	2	−0.551	11	4	−0.662
2	3	−0.627	12	3	−0.443
3	3	−0.503	13	3	−0.087
4	2	−1.046	14	4	0.011
5	3	−0.581	15	2	−0.552
6	3	0.049	16	3	−1.005
7	2	0.543	17	5	−0.931
8	3	−0.499	18	2	0.170
9	3	−0.193	19	1	−0.232
10	2	0.284	20	3	−0.817

Table 12.3 Item parameters for items in anchor B1 for two different populations

Item	a_1	β_1	a_2	β_2	Item	a_1	β_1	a_2	β_2
1	2	−0.156	3	−0.177	11	3	0.101	3	−0.019
2	3	−0.489	4	−0.521	12	3	0.650	4	0.519
3	2	0.456	3	0.419	13	4	−0.588	3	−0.730
4	3	0.110	3	0.057	14	3	−0.431	1	−0.573
5	4	0.068	6	0.002	15	2	−0.671	2	−0.818
6	4	0.124	4	0.052	16	2	−1.008	2	−1.185
7	4	0.123	4	0.040	17	2	−0.558	1	−0.754
8	3	0.033	3	−0.055	18	2	−0.642	2	−0.852
9	1	0.824	1	0.716	19	3	−0.447	2	−0.727
10	2	−0.120	3	−0.231	20	2	−0.756	1	−1.421

Table 12.4 Item parameters for items in anchor B2 for two different populations

Item	a_1	β_1	a_2	β_2	Item	a_1	β_1	a_2	β_2
1	2	−0.083	1	0.353	11	2	−1.115	3	−0.986
2	2	0.050	2	0.303	12	3	−0.238	4	−0.110
3	3	−0.141	2	0.097	13	4	−0.249	4	−0.144
4	2	−0.378	1	−0.142	14	4	−0.243	2	−0.142
5	2	−0.559	3	−0.332	15	3	−0.712	3	−0.627
6	3	−0.227	4	−0.039	16	5	−0.053	3	0.028
7	2	−1.167	2	−0.981	17	3	−0.890	3	−0.809
8	3	−0.754	3	−0.583	18	2	−0.589	3	−0.510
9	3	−0.028	3	0.133	19	4	−0.528	3	−0.454
10	2	−1.034	2	−0.900	20	5	−0.034	5	0.022

condition. It was assumed that proficiency distributions were normally distributed, so $\theta \sim N(\mu_g, \sigma_g)$, with μ_g and σ_g as the mean and standard deviation for group g. In the equivalent group condition, the proficiency parameters in each of the groups in the design were sampled from $N(0, 0.3)$. In the non-equivalent groups' conditions, the two populations were assumed to differ in proficiency. The proficiency of population 1 was $N(0.3, 0.3)$ distributed, while population 2 had a $N(0, 0.3)$ distribution. This difference was similar to the difference in mean proficiency found in the operational tests on which the parameters of the simulation study were based.

12.4 Analyses

The data sampled in the three designs were analyzed using the 2-PL model and estimated using BILOG-MG (Zimowski et al. 1996). For each of the designs, three procedures for linking the operational tests were compared:

A. *Direct anchor*: Direct linking using concurrent estimation based on the anchor and ignoring the data from the reference set (Groups 1, 2, 4, and 5).
B. *Direct total*: Direct linking using concurrent estimation based on the total design (Groups 1–6).
C. *Comparison through the reference sets*: Operational tests linked with the reference set separately for each population (linking of operational test 1 based on Groups 1, 2, and 3, and of operational test 2 based on Groups 4, 5, and 6).

The direct linking procedure using the anchor and ignoring the data of the reference set is comparable to a standard linking procedure. The direct linking procedure based on the total design occurs less often in practice but uses the same data as the comparison using reference sets. So in the total design, the anchor items are administered more often than in the data used for direct linking based on only the anchor. For evaluating the procedure based on the reference set, direct linking using the total data therefore provides a relevant and potentially fairer comparison.

12.5 Evaluation of Results

To evaluate the quality of the linking procedures, differences in results between direct linking and comparison based on reference sets were assessed. The quality of the linking of operational tests 1 and 2 was evaluated for each of the procedures and designs. For the direct linking procedures, the IRT-observed-score (OS) equating of number-correct (NC) scores (Zeng and Kolen 1995) was used. Here, the estimated score distributions of operational tests 1 and 2 were estimated for population 1. In the comparison based on reference sets, a calibration was carried out for each of the populations separately. Based on the first calibration, operational test 1 and the reference set were linked using OS-NC linking. This provided estimated comparable scores between operational test 1 and the reference set. In the same way, the estimated comparable scores between operational test 2 and the reference set were determined using the data from population 2.

Score distributions were computed using the estimated item and population parameters and integrating over the population distribution of θ; that is

$$f_r(x) = \int \sum_{\{x|r\}} f_r\left(x\middle|\theta\right) g\left(\theta\middle|\mu_g, \sigma_g\right) \partial\theta,$$

where $\{x\ |r\ \}$ stands for the set of all possible response patterns resulting in a scorer. In the case of normally distributed populations, the integrals were computed using Gauss–Hermite quadrature (Abramowitz and Stegun 1972). At each of the quadrature points, a recursion formula by Lord and Wingersky (1984) was used to obtain $f_r(x|\theta)$, the score distribution of respondents of a given proficiency, θ. To obtain accurate results, 180 quadrature points were used.

12.5.1 Criterion

The criterion to evaluate the quality of the linking was based on comparing equivalent score points from the various linking procedures with the true equivalent score points (Hanson & Béguin 2012). Let $s_{true,\, r}$ be the score point on operational test 2 that is equivalent with the score point r on operational test 1 based on the true parameters. Since the item parameters of operational tests 1 and 2 used in generating the samples were identical, $s_{true,\, r} = r$ for all r, let s_{hr} be an equivalent score point on operational form 2 to score r on operational form 1 estimated in replication h. To compare the equivalent score points in different conditions, a mean squared error (MSE) was calculated by summing over score points and samples:

$$MSE = \frac{1}{61 * 100} \sum_{r=0}^{60} \sum_{h=1}^{100} \left(s_{hr} - s_{true,r}\right)^2. \tag{1}$$

The MSE provided a measure of the deviation of the comparison table of the score distributions of the operational tests, and therefore provided a relevant basis for comparison of the different linking procedures. The procedures with a higher MSE were less accurate than procedures with a lower value. Additional information about the performance of the linking procedures was obtained by decomposition of the MSE into terms representing the average of the squared bias of equivalent score points and the average variance of equivalent score points. So,

$$MSE = \frac{1}{61} \left[\sum_{r=0}^{60} \left(\bar{s}_r - s_{true,r}\right)^2 + \frac{1}{100} \sum_{h=1}^{100} \left(s_{hr} - \bar{s}_r\right)^2 \right],$$

where $\bar{s}_r$ is the mean equivalent score of score point r over replications; that is,

$$\bar{s}_r = \frac{1}{100} \sum_{h=1}^{100} s_{hr}.$$

An alternative measure of the deviation of the comparison table of the score distributions of the operational tests is the mean absolute error (MAE). The MAE is obtained if the squared error in (1) is replaced by the absolute value of the error. So,

$$MAE = \frac{1}{61 * 100} \sum_{r=0}^{60} \sum_{h=1}^{100} \left| s_{hr} - s_{true,r} \right|.$$

The scale of the MAE is more easily interpreted than the MSE, since the MAE reports the average deviation in score points. Therefore, a value of 0.6 can be seen as an average deviation of 0.6 score points.

12.6 Results

Comparison using reference sets was contrasted with IRT number-correct observed equating using three different designs, two linking conditions for the IRT calibration and both equivalent and non-equivalent groups. In Table 12.5, the mean absolute error, mean squared error, bias, and variance are given for the different designs and linking conditions.

For comparison using reference sets, the MAE and MSE were mostly comparable over the different designs. Somewhat larger MAE and MSE were found only in design 3, with equivalent groups. This effect is due to a larger mean variance in this condition. For the direct linking procedures, the MAE and MSE were larger in design 2 than in design 1. For these procedures, the error in design 3 increased substantially due to an increase in mean squared bias.

Table 12.5 Results for the different conditions

Design	Group	Method	MAE	MSE	Mean squared bias	Mean variance
1	Equivalent groups	Reference sets	0.64	0.41	0.09	0.32
		Direct anchor	0.28	0.29	0.00	0.29
		Direct total	0.20	0.20	0.01	0.20
1	Non-equivalent groups	Reference sets	0.60	0.37	0.06	0.31
		Direct anchor	0.30	0.32	0.04	0.27
		Direct total	0.25	0.26	0.07	0.19
2	Equivalent groups	Reference sets	0.69	0.45	0.10	0.35
		Direct anchor	0.63	0.67	0.48	0.19
		Direct total	0.63	0.67	0.48	0.19
2	Non-equivalent groups	Reference sets	0.58	0.36	0.06	0.30
		Direct anchor	0.53	0.54	0.35	0.19
		Direct total	0.52	0.53	0.33	0.20
3	Equivalent groups	Reference sets	0.81	0.60	0.07	0.53
		Direct anchor	1.25	2.21	1.91	0.30
		Direct total	1.24	2.16	1.87	0.29
3	Non-equivalent groups	Reference sets	0.67	0.45	0.04	0.41
		Direct anchor	1.10	1.73	1.48	0.26
		Direct total	1.08	1.68	1.43	0.25

Direct linking using calibration with only the anchor or linking using the total data including the reference sets resulted in a smaller MAE, except for design 3, where the MAE was smaller for the comparison with the reference sets. Direct linking using the total data in all designs resulted in a smaller equal MAE and MSE than linking using only the anchor. Comparison using reference sets yielded a smaller MSE for all conditions using designs 2 and 3. This is due to a smaller bias in these conditions, since in all conditions the comparison using reference sets had a larger variance than the direct linking conditions.

The distribution of the contribution to MSE for the equivalent groups condition over score points is given in Figs. 12.5, 12.6, and 12.7. For the non-equivalent groups, the results were similar. In designs 2 and 3, the MSE is larger than 1 for a substantial part of the score distribution, while the MSE for comparison based on the reference sets is smaller than or equal to 1 for all score points in all conditions. This indicates that in design 2, the MAE is smaller for the direct linking procedures compared to the comparison based on reference sets, while this relation is reversed for the MSE.

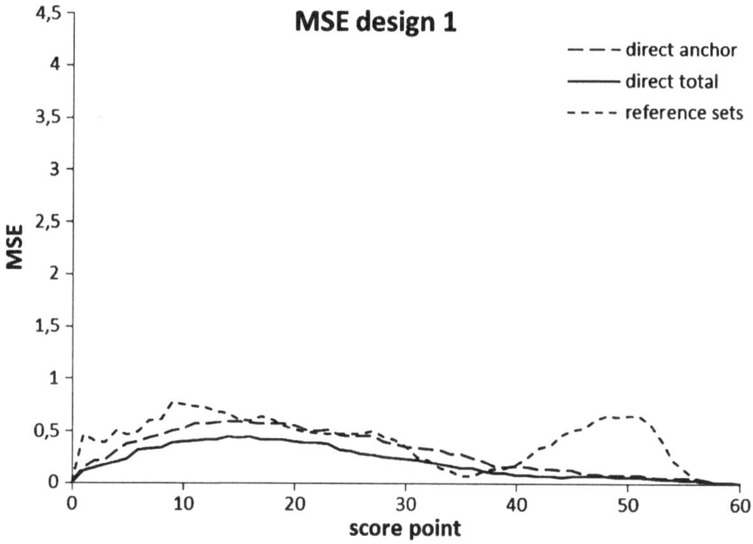

Fig. 12.5 MSE for each score point in design 1 and equivalent groups

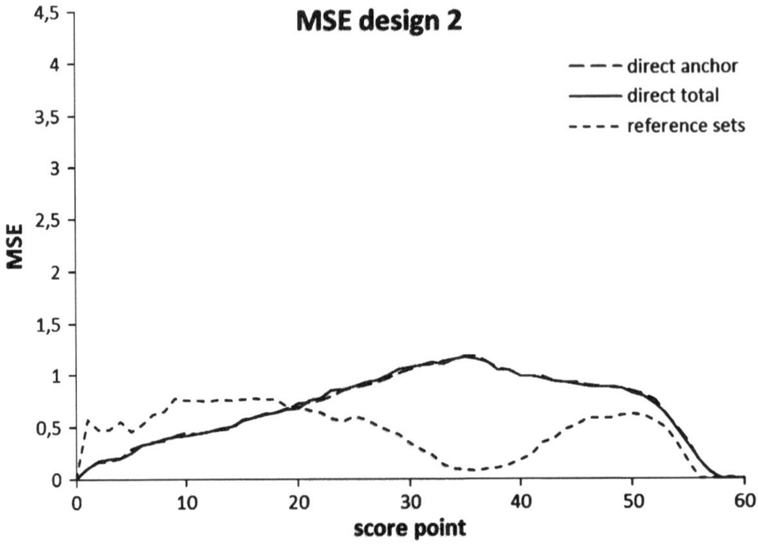

Fig. 12.6 MSE for each score point in design 2 and equivalent groups

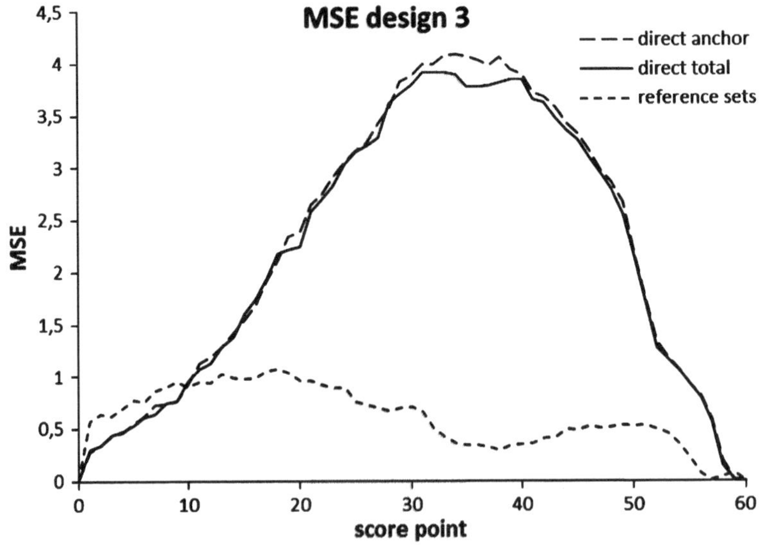

Fig. 12.7 MSE for each score point in design 3 and equivalent groups

12.7 Conclusions and Discussion

The simulation study showed that the results of a comparison based on a reference set were stable across the different simulated conditions. The sum of the variance of the comparison using reference sets was larger than in the direct linking conditions. This can be explained because the comparison involves two separate linking analyses linking operational tests to the reference test. The results of these linking analyses were combined based on discrete score distributions. The two linking analyses both added some variance, while the comparison based on discrete score distributions was vulnerable to variance due to rounding error.

In design 1, the direct linking approach was theoretically unbiased for the linking using only the anchor and not the reference set. In this analysis, the biased items (blocks B1 and B2) were only administered in a single group. The actual linking items were the unbiased items (block A). In the direct linking analysis using the total design (which included the reference set), direct linking led to some misfit due to the bias of blocks B1 and B2 in the two reference set administrations in populations 1 and 2. This did not lead to substantial bias in the outcomes since the anchor for both populations was biased in favor of the population that was administered the anchor. In design 2, direct linking should lead to biased results due to the use of an anchor in which half of the items favored one of the populations. The comparison using the reference sets should not be affected by this biased anchor. In the simulation study, this result was confirmed by the analyses wherein the direct linking clearly showed more biased results than the comparison using reference sets. In the analyses on the data of design 3, results were even more pronounced. The bias of the direct linking approaches was severe, and the results of the comparison using reference sets were comparable to the results for designs 1 and 2. As expected, direct linking using all the available data provided slightly better results than direct linking using only the anchor. This is due to the additional data on the anchor items that is available in the reference set. In the given conditions, with at least 1,000 observations for each item in the design, this effect is relatively small, but it probably would have been larger in conditions with fewer observations of the anchor items. The relative performance of the comparison based on the reference set was also as expected. In designs 2 and 3, the mean squared bias of this procedure did not change compared to design 1. Using direct linking, the mean squared bias in designs 2 and 3 was clearly increased compared to the unbiased design 1.

It can be concluded from this simulation study that the proposed procedure (using a comparison based on reference sets) performed as was expected. It is fair to mention that the simulation study confirmed the theoretical advantage of the proposed procedure using reference sets. However, as with all simulation studies, some restraint should be used in generalizing these results. Although empirical data were used as a starting point, only a limited number of potential aspects of the involved models were studied. In future research, additional validation studies should be done in addition to empirical piloting of the procedure using reference sets.

In conclusion, this study introduced a procedure that could form a basis for vertical comparison that is robust against DIF between populations. Comparison using reference sets is a promising procedure that aims to better suit construct comparability between assessments used in populations that differ substantially in age, relative performance level, or curriculum. This procedure could be helpful for testing students at different grade levels, students who have followed different curricula, or students from different education tracks who need to comply with the same performance standard. Practical examples are the levels in the Key Stage 2 and 3 tests in England and Wales, which must be comparable between students aged 11 and 14 (Ofqual 2011). Another example are the recently introduced standards in the Netherlands (Scheerens et al. 2012). There, test results must be comparable between students aged 12, 16, and 18. The procedure introduced in this present research can also be used in horizontal equating to compare performance of different subgroups or populations whose test-takers are likely to respond to items in a different way. This might occur in international comparison studies such as PISA. This could also occur in the USA if students from different states, using different curricula, are compared on the common core standards.

References

Abramowitz M, Stegun IA (1972) Handbook of mathematical functions. Dover Publications, New York

Béguin AA (2000) Robustness of equating high-stakes tests. Doctoral thesis, University of Twente, Enschede

Carlton JE (2011) Statistical models for vertical linking. In: von Davier AA (ed) Statistical models for test equating, scaling, and linking. Springer, New York, pp 59–70

Hanson BA, Béguin, AA (2002) Obtaining a common scale for item response theory parameters using separate versus concurrent estimation in the common-item equating design. Appl Psychol Meas 26:3–14

Harris DJ (2007) Practical issues in vertical scaling. In: Dorans NJ, Pommerich M, Holland PW (eds) Linking and aligning scores and scales. Springer, New York, pp 233–252

Holland PW, Dorans NJ (2006) Linking and equating. In: Brennan RL (ed) Educational measurement, 4th edn. Praeger, Westport, pp 189–220

Kolen MJ (2006) Scaling and norming. In: Brennan RL (ed) Educational measurement, 4th edn. Praeger, Westport, pp 155–186

Kolen MJ, Brennan RL (2004) Test equating, 2nd edn. Springer, New York

Lord FM, Wingersky MS (1984) Comparison of IRT true-score and equipercentile observed-score "equatings". Appl Psychol Meas 8:453–461

Ofqual (2011) A Review of the Pilot of the Single Level Test Approach (Ofqual/11/4837). Author, Coventry, UK. Retrieved from: http://dera.ioe.ac.uk/2577/1/2011-04-13-review-of-pilot-single-level-test-approach.pdf

Petersen NS, Kolen MJ, Hoover HD (1989) Scaling, norming and equating. In: Linn RL (ed) Educational measurement, 3rd edn. American Council on Education and Macmillan, New York, pp 221–262

Scheerens J, Ehren M, Sleegers P, De Leeuw R (2012) OECD review on evaluation and assessment frameworks for improving school outcomes. Country background report for the Netherlands.

OECD, Brussels. Retrieved from: http://www.oecd.org/edu/school/NLD_CBR_Evaluation_and_Assessment.pdf
Verhelst ND, Glas CAW (1995) The one parameter logistic model. In: Fischer GH, Molenaar IW (eds) Rasch models: foundations, recent developments, and applications. Springer, New York, pp 215–238
Verhelst ND, Glas CAW, Verstralen HHFM (1994) OPLM: computer program and manual. [Computer Program]. Cito, Arnhem
Von Davier M, Von Davier AA (2004) A unified approach to IRT scale linking and scale transformations (ETS Research Reports RR-04-09). ETS, Princeton
Von Davier M, Von Davier AA (2012) A general model for IRT scale linking and scale transformations. In: von Davier AA (ed) Statistical models for test equating, scaling, and linking. Springer, New York, pp 225–242
Zeng L, Kolen MJ (1995) An alternative approach for IRT observed-score equating of number-correct scores. Appl Psychol Meas 19:231–240
Zimowski MF, Muraki E, Mislevy RJ, Bock RD (1996) BILOG-MG: multiple-group IRT analysis and test maintenance for binary items. [Computer Program]. Scientific Software International, Inc., Chicago

Chapter 13
A Dependent Bayesian Nonparametric Model for Test Equating

Jorge González, Andrés F. Barrientos, and Fernando A. Quintana

Abstract Equating methods utilize functions to transform scores on two or more versions of a test, so that they can be compared and used interchangeably. In common practice, traditional methods of equating use parametric models where, apart from the test scores themselves, no additional information is used for the estimation of the equating transformation. We propose a flexible Bayesian nonparametric model for test equating which allows the use of covariates in the estimation of the score distribution functions that lead to the equating transformation. A major feature of this approach is that the complete shape of the score distribution may change as a function of the covariates. As a consequence, the form of the equating transformation can change according to covariate values. We discuss applications of the proposed model to real and simulated data. We conclude that our method has good performance compared to alternative approaches.

13.1 Introduction

Equating is a family of statistical models and methods that are used to make test scores comparable on two or more versions of a test, so that scores on these different test forms, intended to measure the same attribute, may be used interchangeably (see, e.g., Holland and Rubin 1982; Kolen and Brennan 2004; von Davier et al. 2004; Dorans et al. 2007; von Davier 2011). To avoid the confounding of differences in form difficulty with those of test takers' abilities, different equating designs to

J. González (✉)
Faculty of Mathematics, Pontificia Universidad Católica de Chile,
Av. Vicuña Mackenna 4860, Macul, Santiago, Chile

Measurement Center MIDE UC, Pontificia Universidad Católica de Chile,
Av. Vicuña Mackenna 4860, Macul, Santiago, Chile
e-mail: jgonzale@mat.puc.cl

A.F. Barrientos • F.A. Quintana
Faculty of Mathematics, Pontificia Universidad Católica de Chile,
Av. Vicuña Mackenna 4860, Macul, Santiago, Chile
e-mail: anfebar@puc.cl; quintana@mat.uc.cl

R.E. Millsap et al. (eds.), *Quantitative Psychology Research*, Springer Proceedings in Mathematics & Statistics 89, DOI 10.1007/978-3-319-07503-7_13

collect data are used. Once these effects are corrected, the purpose of equating is to obtain comparable scores for both groups, by adjusting for differences in difficulty of the test forms.

Let T_x and T_y be the random variables denoting the scores on tests X and Y which are to be equated, with associated cumulative distributions functions (c.d.f) $S^x = S(t_x)$ and $S^y = S(t_y)$, respectively. In what follows we assume that scores on X are to be equated to the scale of scores on Y, but arguments and formulas for the reverse equating are analogous. Let t_x and t_y be the quantiles in the distributions of tests X and Y for an arbitrary common cumulative proportion p of the population, such that $t_x = S^{x^{-1}}(p)$ and $t_y = S^{y^{-1}}(p)$. It follows that an equivalent score t_y on test Y for a score t_x on X can be obtained as

$$t_y = \varphi(t_x) = S^{y^{-1}}(S^x(t_x)). \tag{13.1}$$

In the equating literature, function $\varphi(t_x)$ is known as the equipercentile transformation. A graphical representation of the equipercentile method of equating is shown in Fig. 13.1. Note that because $\varphi(t_x)$ is built from distribution functions, the equipercentile equating method is nonparametric by nature.

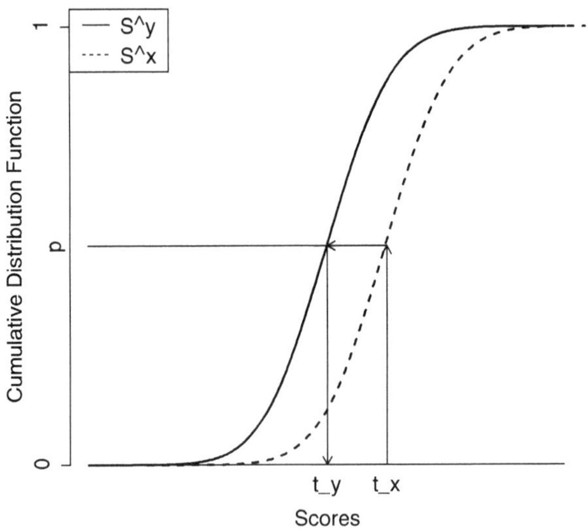

Fig. 13.1 Graphical representation of equipercentile equating. A score t_x in test X is mapped into a score on the scale of test Y using $t_y = \varphi(t_x) = S^{y^{-1}}(S^x(t_x))$

Because sum scores (i.e., total number of correct answers) are typically used in measurement programs, an evident problem with (13.1) is the discreteness of the score distributions, rendering their corresponding inverses unavailable. The common solution given to this problem in the equating literature is to actually "continuize" the discrete score distributions S^x and S^y, so that (13.1) may be properly used for equating.

In many applications, complementary information besides the test scores themselves is available most of the time (e.g., examinee gender, type of school, point in time of the administration, etc.), yet the use of covariates seems to be a rather unexplored topic in the equating literature. It is natural to think that the information provided by covariates could improve the equating task. Additionally, despite the nonparametric nature of the transformation $\varphi(t_x)$, the problem of obtaining a point estimate of it has traditionally relied on either parametric or semi-parametric models (González and von Davier 2013). For instance, in the linear equating transformation (Kolen and Brennan 2004) both S^x and S^y are assumed to be a location-scale family of distributions leading to $\varphi(t_x;\boldsymbol{\pi}) = \mu_y + \frac{\sigma_y}{\sigma_x}[t_x - \mu_x]$ where in this case $\boldsymbol{\pi} = (\mu_X, \mu_Y, \sigma_X, \sigma_Y)$ are the means and standard deviations of the two score distributions. Constraining the inference to a specific parametric form, however, may limit the scope and type of inferences that can be drawn. Indeed, in many practical situations, a parametric model could not describe in a proper way the observed data. Bayesian nonparametric (BNP) generalization of parametric statistical models (see, e.g., Ghosh and Ramamoorthi 2003; Müller and Quintana 2004; Hjort et al. 2010) allow the user to gain model flexibility and robustness against mis-specification of a parametric statistical model. See Müller and Mitra (2013) who give many examples that highlight typical situations where parametric inference might run into limitations, and BNP can offer a way out.

In this paper we propose a flexible Bayesian nonparametric model for test equating which allows the use of covariates in the estimation of the score distribution functions that lead to the equating transformation. A major feature of this approach, compared to other traditional methods, is that not only the location but also the complete shape of the score distribution may change as a function of the covariates.

The rest of this paper is organized as follows. We briefly review the Bayesian nonparametric modeling approach in Sect. 13.2, presenting the dependent BNP model for test equating which allows the use of covariates. Section 13.3 illustrates the uses and applications of the model in both simulated and the real data. The paper finishes in Sect. 13.4 with conclusions and discussions.

13.2 Bayesian Nonparametric Modeling

In this section we present the proposed model, including a brief description of nonparametric models. We develop the material to the extent needed for clarity of presentation.

13.2.1 Nonparametric Models

Statistical models assume that observed data are the realization of random variables following some probability distribution. Let $x_1, \ldots, x_n$ be observed data defined on a sample space $\mathscr{X}$, and distributed according to a probability distribution F_θ, belonging to a known family $\mathscr{F} = \{F_\theta : \theta \in \Theta\}$. This setup is referred to as a *parametric* model whenever Θ is assumed to be a subset of a finite dimensional space. In the parametric Bayesian framework (e.g., Gelman et al. 2003), a prior $p(\theta)$ is defined on Θ. Parametric Bayesian inference is then based on the posterior distribution $p(\theta \mid x)$, which is proportional to the product of the prior $p(\theta)$ and the likelihood $p(x \mid \theta)$.

Although the parametric approach is adequate in many situations, it could not be realistic in many others. For instance, under a normal model, all we can possibly learn about the distribution is determined by its mean and variance. The nonparametric approach starts by focusing on spaces of distribution functions, so that uncertainty is expressed on F itself. Of course, the prior distribution $p(F)$ should now be defined on the space $\mathscr{F}$ of all distribution functions defined on $\mathscr{X}$. If $\mathscr{X}$ is an infinite set, then $\mathscr{F}$ is infinite-dimensional, and the corresponding prior model $p(F)$ on $\mathscr{F}$ is termed *nonparametric*. The prior probability model is also referred to as a *random probability measure* (RPM), and it essentially corresponds to a distribution on the space of all distributions on the set $\mathscr{X}$. Thus Bayesian nonparametric models are probability models defined on a function space (Müller and Quintana 2004). These models are dealt with in the same spirit as the usual parametric Bayesian models, and all inferences are based on the implied posterior distribution. BNP methods have been the subject of intense research over the past few decades. For a detailed account, we refer the reader to Dey et al. (1998), Ghosh and Ramamoorthi (2003), and Hjort et al. (2010).

13.2.2 The Dirichlet Process (DP) and the DP Mixture (DPM) Model

The most popular RPM used in BNP is the DP introduced by Ferguson (1973). We say that F is a DP with parameters m and F^*, denoted as $F \sim DP(m, F^*)$, if for every partition of the sample space $A_1, \ldots, A_p$, $F(A_1), \ldots, F(A_p)$ is jointly distributed as $\text{Dir}(mF^*(A_1), \ldots, mF^*(A_p))$. Here, F^* is a base measure specifying the mean, $E(F) = F^*$, and m is a parameter that helps in determining the uncertainty of F. The DP is a conjugate prior under iid sampling which means that, given the data, the posterior distribution of F is also a DP.

A convenient way to express the DP is via Sethuraman's (1994) representation, which states that $F \sim DP(m, F^*)$ can be constructed as

$$F(\cdot) = \sum_{i=1}^{\infty} \omega_i \delta_{\theta_i}(\cdot), \tag{13.2}$$

where $\delta_{\theta_i}(\cdot)$ denotes a point mass at θ_i, $\theta_i \overset{\text{iid}}{\sim} F^*$, $\omega_i = U_i \prod_{j<i}(1 - U_j)$, and $U_j \overset{\text{iid}}{\sim} Beta(1, M)$. Note that by definition, the resulting random probability functions are discrete. Equation (13.2) is usually called a *stick-breaking representation*. The discrete nature of the DP implies that it cannot be used as a probability model

for densities. A standard approach to deal with this problem is to define a mixture of smooth densities based on the DP, commonly called DPM.

The increase in applications of BNP methods in the statistical literature has been motivated largely by the availability of simple and efficient methods for posterior computation in DPM models (Ferguson 1983; Lo 1984). The DPM models incorporate Dirichlet process (DP) priors (Ferguson 1973, 1974) for components in Bayesian hierarchical models, resulting in an extremely flexible class of models. In particular, a DPM model g is defined as

$$g(\cdot \mid F) = \int_{\Theta} \psi(\cdot, \theta) F(d\theta), \tag{13.3}$$

where for every $\theta \in \Theta$, $\psi(\cdot, \theta)$ is a probability density function, where $\Theta \subseteq \mathbb{R}^q$ and F is a DP defined on Θ. Due to their flexibility and ease in implementation, DPM models are now routinely employed in a wide variety of applications (see, e.g., Hjort et al. 2010). Furthermore, a rich theoretical literature about support, posterior consistency, and rates of convergence (Lo 1984; Ghosal et al. 1999; Lijoi et al. 2005; Ghosal and Van der Vaart 2007) justify the use of DPM models for inference in single density estimation problems.

13.2.3 *Dependent Prior Probability Models*

In many applications, it is desirable to allow for dependence of the data on covariates. For instance, in linear regression models the mean of responses is allowed to change with covariates. Expanding on this idea, under a BNP approach it is desired to define a probability model that features a set of covariate-dependent continuous distributions $\mathscr{F} = \{F_z : z \in \mathscr{X}\}$, where now the entire shape of F changes with z, and not just the mean or some other particular functional of the distribution. The nonparametric model is then changed to $x_1, \ldots, x_n \mid F_z \overset{i.i.d}{\sim} F_z$ with a corresponding prior $p(\mathscr{F})$ on $\mathscr{F} = \{F_z : z \in \mathscr{X}\}$. Such models are known as *dependent nonparametric models*. Here, the main problem, which has received substantial attention over the past few years, is to construct $p(\mathscr{F})$, a probability model for a set of covariate-dependent continuous probability distributions, such that the result has good theoretical properties and can be easily applied.

13.2.3.1 Dependent Dirichlet Processes

MacEachern (1999, 2000) proposed a dependent Dirichlet process (DDP) where dependence is achieved by changing the elements ω and θ in the stick-breaking representation (13.2) of F by independent stochastic processes such that

$$F_z(\cdot) = \sum_{i=1}^{\infty} \omega_i(z) \delta_{\theta_i(z)}(\cdot) \tag{13.4}$$

where $\omega_i(z) = U_i(z)\prod_{j<i}(1-U_j(z))$ and both $\theta_i(z)$ and $U_i(z)$ are independent stochastic processes with $U_j \overset{\text{iid}}{\sim} Beta(1,M)$. Notice that the DDP can be used as a mixing distribution in a mixture model, exactly as in (13.3) so that it is possible to define a predictor-dependent mixture model.

MacEachern (1999, 2000) also considered a version of the process with predictor-independent weights, $F_z(\cdot) = \sum_{i=1}^{\infty} \omega_i \delta_{\theta_i(z)}(\cdot)$. Versions of the predictor-dependent mixture models based on single weights DDP have been successfully applied to ANOVA (De Iorio et al. 2004), survival (De Iorio et al. 2009; Jara et al. 2010), spatial modeling (Gelfand et al. 2005), functional data (Dunson and Herring 2006), time series (Caron et al. 2006), discriminant analysis (De la Cruz et al. 2007), and longitudinal data analysis (Müller et al. 2005).

On the other hand, extensions of the DP for dealing with related probability distributions include the DPM mixture of normals model for the joint distribution of the response and predictors (Müller et al. 1996), the hierarchical mixture of DPM (Müller et al. 2004), the hierarchical DP (Teh et al. 2006), the order-based DDP model (Griffin and Steel 2006), the nested DP (Rodriguez et al. 2008), the kernel-stick breaking process (Dunson and Park 2008), among many others. Based on a different formulation of the conditional density estimation problem, Tokdar et al. (2010) and Jara and Hanson (2011) proposed alternatives to convolutions of dependent stick-breaking approaches, which yield conditional probability measures with density w.r.t. Lebesgue measure without the need of convolutions.

A particular kind of prior for dependent BNP models is the dependent Bernstein–Dirichlet prior which we describe next.

13.2.3.2 Dependent Bernstein Polynomial Priors

As earlier, we begin with the non-dependent version and then extend it to incorporate dependence. Let H be a function on the $[0,1]$ interval. The kth order Bernstein polynomial of H (Lorentz 1986) is defined by

$$B(t;k,H) = \sum_{j=0}^{k} H\left(\frac{j}{k}\right)\binom{k}{j} t^j(1-t)^{k-j}, \tag{13.5}$$

with derivative

$$b(t;k,H) = \sum_{j=1}^{k} w_{jk}\beta(t \mid j, k-j+1), \tag{13.6}$$

where $w_{jk} = H(j/k) - H((j-1)/k)$, and $\beta(\cdot \mid a,b)$ denotes the beta density with parameters a and b. Note that if H is a distribution function whose support is the unit interval, then $B(t;k,H)$ is also a distribution function on $[0,1]$. Moreover, if $H(0)=0$, then $b(t;k,H)$ is the corresponding density function.

Starting from this definition, and additionally assuming both H and k as random quantities, Petrone (1999) proposed the resulting random distribution based on $B(\cdot;k,H)$ as a class of prior distributions on the space $\mathscr{F}$ of distributions on $\mathscr{X} = [0,1]$. Let $p(k)$ represent the probability mass function of a random variable k on the positive integers. We say that a random distribution F follows a Bernstein–Dirichlet prior, denoted as $F \mid F_0 \sim BDP(k, MF_0)$ if F can be represented as $B(\cdot;k,H)$ in (13.5), where $H \mid F_0 \sim DP(M, F_0)$.

The Bernstein–Dirichlet prior defined above can be extended to allow for dependence on covariates. MacEachern (1999) proposed to introduce covariate dependence in the elements of the stick-breaking representation. Borrowing from this idea, Barrientos et al. (2012) used an alternative definition of MacEachern's DDP and defined a dependent Bernstein polynomial process (DBPP). The dependence is introduced by replacing the DP mixing distribution H in (13.5) by a dependent stick-breaking process defined in terms of transformed stochastic processes indexed by predictors $z \in \mathscr{Z}$.

For a detailed definition and a description of good properties related to the association structure, continuity, and support of the DBPP process as well as the asymptotic behavior of the posterior distribution, the reader is referred to Barrientos et al. (2012).

In our application, a simplified version of the general DBPP model will be used. In this version, the dependence on covariates is accounted for by using a dependent stick-breaking process with common weights, and support points given by stochastic processes indexed by predictors $z \in \mathscr{Z}$. This version of the model is called *single weights* DBPP and it is denoted by wDBPP (Barrientos et al. 2012). Consider then $k \sim p(k \mid \lambda)$, where $p(k \mid \lambda)$ is the Poisson(λ) distribution, truncated to $\{1,2,\ldots\}$.

The model then becomes

$$s(z)(\cdot) = \sum_{j=1}^{\infty} w_j \beta\left(\cdot \mid \lceil k\theta_j(z) \rceil, k - \lceil k\theta_j(z) \rceil + 1\right), \tag{13.7}$$

where $\lceil \cdot \rceil$ denotes the ceiling function, $\theta_j(z) = h_Z(r_j(z))$, and

$$w_j = v_j \prod_{i<j} [1 - v_i],$$

and where $r_1, r_2, \ldots$ are independent and identically distributed real-valued stochastic processes with probability measure indexed by the parameter Ψ, h_z is a function defined on a set $\mathscr{H} = \{h_Z : z \in \mathscr{Z}\}$ of known bijective continuous functions, and $v_1, v_2, \ldots$ are independent random variables with common distribution indexed by a parameter α. We denote (13.7) by $\mathscr{S} = \{S_Z \doteq S(z) : z \in \mathscr{Z}\} \sim wDBPP(\alpha, \lambda, \Psi, \mathscr{H})$. We will discuss specific choices for h_Z and the $\{r_i\}$ processes in Sect. 13.3. It should be noted that under equivalent assumptions on the parameters defining the process, the wDBPP retains all the properties shown for the general version of the model.

13.3 Dependent BNP Model for Equating and Illustrations

Let T be the random variable denoting the scores with $S(t)$ the associated probability distribution function. For a vector of covariates z, we are interested in modeling the covariate-dependent score distributions, which will be used to obtain the equating transformation $\varphi(t;z)$. With a slight abuse of notation, we will denote this as $S_z(t) = S(t \mid Z = z)$, stressing the fact that is not meant to be interpreted as stochastic conditioning, but as expressing dependence of the distribution on covariates z.

As noted before, we need to specify a prior probability model for the set $\mathscr{S} = \{S_Z : z \in \mathscr{Z}\}$. We use a DBPP so that

$$\mathscr{S} = \{S_Z : z \in \mathscr{Z}\} \sim wDBPP(\alpha, \lambda, \Psi, \mathscr{H}). \tag{13.8}$$

As an example, assume that a new test form X is to be equated to an old form Y. In this case the covariate values denote the test form administered, that is, $Z \in \{X, Y\}$. The c.d.f. of interest would be $S(t \mid Z = z)$. Thus having score data and assuming $\mathscr{S} = \{S_Z \doteq S(z) : z \in \mathscr{Z}\} \sim wDBPP(\alpha, \lambda, \Psi, \mathscr{H})$ we can express the equating function as

$$\varphi(t;z) = S^{-1}(S(t \mid Z = X) \mid Z = Y)$$

where in this case $\varphi(t;z)$ corresponds to the transformation function which puts scores on version X in the scale of version Y. As the equating function is not available in closed form for the adopted model, in practice we need to compute it as part of an MCMC-type of posterior simulation scheme.

Note that other kind of covariates such as examinee's gender and type of school can also be used. The combination of all these variables will produce different versions of the test score distributions (e.g., the score distribution of females in 2008 coming from municipal schools). This produces a number of possible equatings, which amounts to the number of combinations of levels in the covariates. In the application below, we will focus only on two covariates, the examinee gender and the year of administration, so that a total of 4 score distributions will be available for equating.

13.3.1 *Illustrations*

13.3.1.1 Simulation Study

To illustrate the performance of the dependent BNP model for equating, a total of eighteen simulated data sets were generated. The varying factors are the type of distribution, the combination of covariates considered that lead to different models for score distributions, and the sample size. The covariates are $Z = (Z_1, Z_2)$ where $Z_1 = \{M, F\}$ is gender and $Z_2 = \{Y_1, Y_2\}$ the year of application.

We consider two different general scenarios. The conditional distributions for Scenario I are unimodal with asymmetry induced by the value of the covariates. For instance, we could want to deliberately make the score distribution for males and females differ and have the model capture this feature. For Scenario II, we consider more complex score distributions, for instance, presenting bimodalities. Score distributions of this type emerge when gaps and spikes in the distributions or zero frequencies or other atypical situations are present in the data. The combination of levels of covariates lead to four models: (1) one where the score distributions indexed by both year and gender differ; (2) one where differences occur for gender only in year 2; (3) one where differences arise in years but not in gender; and (4) one where no differences in the score distributions are due to the covariates. For each combination of models and scenarios, three different sample sizes $n = 250$, 500, and 1,000 were considered, leading to a total of eighteen simulated data sets.

The computational implementation of the models is based on MCMC methods. A full description of the MCMC implementation used here is given in Appendix E of the supplementary material of Barrientos et al. (2012). All calculations were done in the R software (R Development Core Team 2013). The BDP is implemented in the general-purpose Bayesian non- and semi- parametric R library DPpackage (Jara et al. 2011). User-friendly functions and wrappers specially written for the dependent BNP models for test equating will be incorporated in the SNSequate R library (González 2014).

For the wDBPP model we assume that $h_z(\cdot) = \exp\{\cdot\}/(1+\exp\{\cdot\})$, $r_j(z) = z^T\gamma_j$ and $\gamma_j \mid \mu, \mathbf{S} \stackrel{iid}{\sim} N_p(\mu, \mathbf{S})$, $j = 1, 2, \ldots$. The model specification was completed by assuming

$$v_j \mid \alpha \stackrel{iid}{\sim} \text{Beta}(1, \alpha), \quad k \mid \lambda \sim \text{Poisson}(\lambda)\mathbb{I}_{\{k>1\}},$$

$$\mu \mid \mathbf{m}_0, \mathbf{S}_0 \sim N_p(\mathbf{m}_0, \mathbf{S}_0), \quad \mathbf{S} \mid \nu, \Psi \sim IW_p(\nu, \Psi),$$

where $IW_p(\nu, \mathbf{A})$ denotes the p-dimensional inverted-Wishart distribution with degrees of freedom ν and scale matrix $\mathbf{A}$. The models were fit by assuming $\lambda = 25$, $\mathbf{m}_0 = \mathbf{0}_p$, $\mathbf{S}_0 = 2.25 \times \mathbf{I}_p$, $\nu = p+2$ and $\alpha = 1$.

For each simulated data set, one Markov chain was generated completing a total number of 110,000 iterations. The full chain was subsampled every ten iterations, after a burn-in period of 10,000 samples, to give a reduced chain of length 10,000. Standard tests (not shown), as implemented in the BOA R library (Smith 2007), suggested convergence of the chains.

The posterior inferences for the conditional densities showed that for each scenario, sample size and version of the proposed model, the corresponding estimates follow closely the true densities. In most cases, the true model was completely covered by 95 % point-wise highest probability density (HPD) bands, and the quality of the estimation improved as the sample size increases. As an example, Fig. 13.2 shows estimated score distributions as well as equating transformations when $n = 1{,}000$ in Scenario II, and where the score distributions of males and females were generated so that they do not differ for year 1, but do so for year 2. It can be seen in Fig. 13.2c that the equating function that maps the scores of males to the scale of females for year 1 is accordingly estimated as an identity line. This is not the case for year 2, where indeed the equating function substantially differs from the identity line.

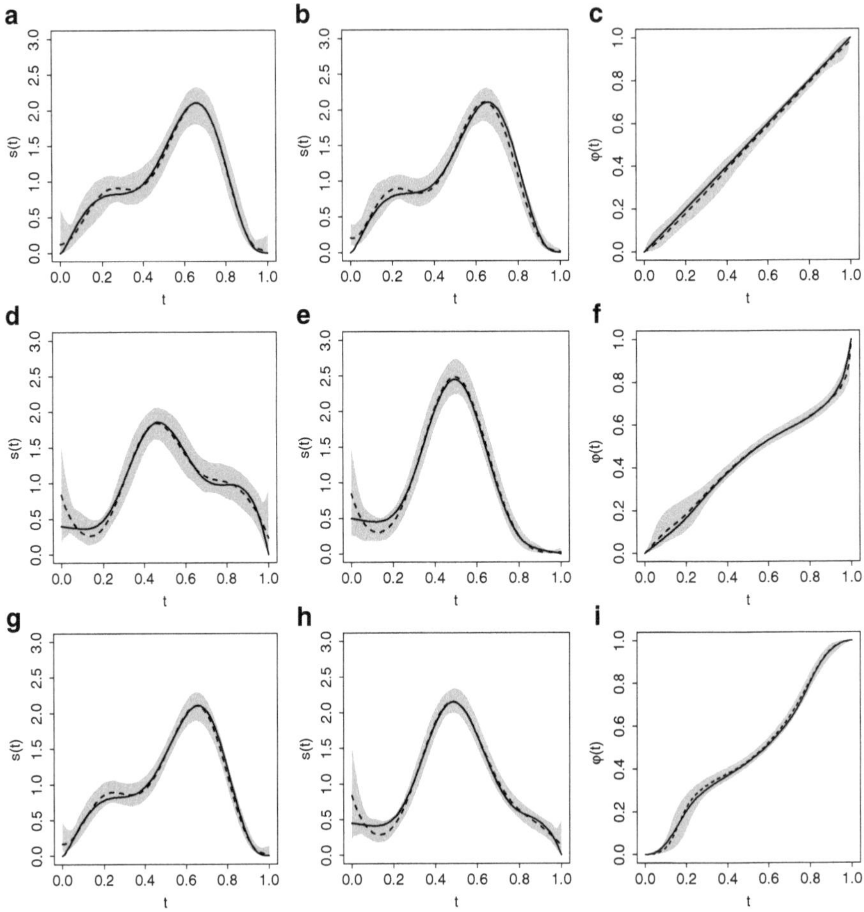

Fig. 13.2 Simulated data—Scenario II ($n = 1{,}000$). True (*continuous line*), posterior mean (*dotted line*), and 95 % point-wise HPD intervals (in *gray*) for conditional densities [panels (**a**), (**b**), (**d**), (**e**), (**g**), (**h**)], and equating functions [panels (**c**), (**f**), and (**i**)]. (**a**) Males (M) in year 1 (Y1). (**b**) Females (M) in year 1 (Y1). (**c**) Males to females in Y1. (**d**) Males (M) in year 2 (Y2). (**e**) Females (M) in year 2 (Y2). (**f**) Males to females in Y2. (**g**) Year 1 (Y1). (**h**) Year 2 (Y2). (**i**) Year 1 to Year 2

13.3.1.2 Real Data Application

We use data from a private national evaluation system in Chile called SEPA (Sistema de Evaluación del Progreso en el Aprendizaje; *System of Assessment Progress in Achievement*) administered by the measurement center MIDE UC. SEPA consists of tests specifically designed to assess achievement in students from first to eleventh grade in the fields of Language and Mathematics. The program started in 2007 and until now, the SEPA tests have been applied in 230 schools, corresponding to about 70,000 students throughout Chile. We consider the SEPA mathematics test applied for eighth degree students in the years 2008 and 2009. Note that because the sum scores we consider are discrete and the DBPP defines continuous distribution functions in the unit interval, we first mapped the scores into the unit interval. After equating calculations are made, the inverse mapping is used to obtain equated scores in the original discrete scale.

Figure 13.3 shows estimated score distributions as well as equating transformations for each of the four combinations of gender and year. We see that for both years, the corresponding score distributions do not differ by much, and the equating transformations are close to linear. See Fig. 13.3a–f. As a comparison, we considered an aggregated model where gender is now ignored. In this case we can clearly see from Fig. 13.3g–i that the score distributions in years 1 and 2 do differ and the equating function that maps the scores from the year 1 scale form to the year 2 scale form is nonlinear. This suggests that ignoring the gender effect creates differences in the estimated score distributions. These differences are softened when incorporating gender into the analysis. In either case, the particular features of such distributions are adequately captured by the proposed model.

13.4 Concluding Remarks

The estimation and statistical inference of equating functions can be approached either under a parametric, semi-parametric, or (fully) nonparametric approach (González and von Davier 2013). In this paper we have introduced a novel dependent Bayesian nonparametric model for test equating, which features the use of covariates for the estimation of score distributions that lead to the equating transformation. In a simulation study, the model was shown to capture very well different types of shapes in the score distributions. An advantage of the dependent BNP model for equating is that it does not need pre-smoothing, selection of bandwidth parameters, or derivation of standard error of equating (SEE), either analytically or asymptotically, as do other equating methods.

The proposed approach can be extended in many different ways, by replacing the random probability measure from Bernstein polynomials with suitable continuous alternatives such as Polya tree processes (Mauldin et al. 1992; Lavine 1992, 1994), and mixtures of polya trees (Hanson and Johnson 2002), to name just a few. The motivation is that all these nonparametric models lead to continuous distributions,

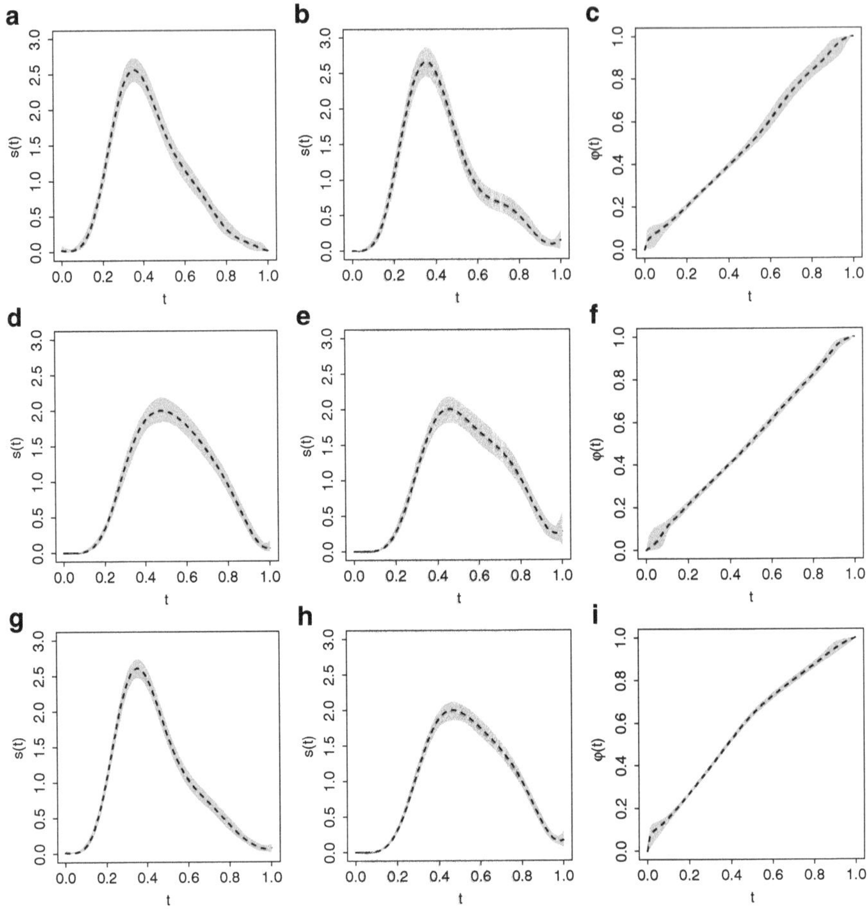

Fig. 13.3 SEPA data—posterior mean (*dotted line*), and 95 % point-wise HPD intervals (in *gray*) for conditional densities [panels (**a**), (**b**), (**d**), (**e**), (**g**), (**h**)], and equating functions [panels (**c**), (**f**), and (**i**)]. (**a**) Males in year 1. (**b**) Females in year 1. (**c**) Males to females in Y1. (**d**) Males in year 2. (**e**) Females in year 2. (**f**) Males to females in Y2. (**g**) Year 1. (**h**) Year 2. (**i**) Year 1 to year 2

so that the general strategy used in this paper to obtain equated scores still applies. The comparison between our proposed dependent BNP model for test equating and other equating methods is a subject of future research.

Acknowledgements The first author acknowledges partial support of Fondecyt 11110044 and Anillo SOC1107 grants. The second author was partially funded by Fondecyt 3130400 grant. The third author was partially funded by Fondecyt grant 1100010.

References

Barrientos AF, Jara A, Quintana F (2012) Fully nonparametric regression for bounded data using bernstein polynomials. Technical report, Department of Statistics, Pontificia Universidad Católica de Chile

Caron F, Davy M, Doucet A, Duflos E, Vanheeghe P (2006) Bayesian inference for dynamic models with Dirichlet process mixtures. In: International conference on information fusion, Florence, 10–13 July 2006

De Iorio M, Müller P, Rosner GL, MacEachern SN (2004) An ANOVA model for dependent random measures. J Am Stat Assoc 99:205–215

De Iorio M, Johnson WO, Müller P, Rosner GL (2009) Bayesian nonparametric non-proportional hazards survival modelling. Biometrics 65:762–771

De la Cruz R, Quintana FA, Müller P (2007) Semiparametric Bayesian classification with longitudinal markers. Appl Stat 56(2):119–137

Dey D, Mueller P, Sinha D (1998) Practical nonparametric and semiparametric Bayesian statistics. New York: Springer

Dorans N, Pommerich M, Holland P (2007) Linking and aligning scores and scales. New York: Springer.

Dunson DB, Herring AH (2006) Semiparametric Bayesian latent trajectory models. Technical report, ISDS Discussion Paper 16, Duke University

Dunson DB, Park JH (2008) Kernel stick-breaking processes. Biometrika 95:307–323

Ferguson T (1973) A bayesian analysis of some nonparametric problems. Ann Stat 1:209–230

Ferguson TS (1974) Prior distribution on the spaces of probability measures. Ann Stat 2:615–629

Ferguson TS (1983) Bayesian density estimation by mixtures of normal distributions. In: Siegmund D, Rustage J, Rizvi GG (eds) Recent advances in statistics: papers in honor of Herman Chernoff on his sixtieth birthday, Bibliohound, Carlsbad, pp 287–302

Gelfand AE, Kottas A, MacEachern SN (2005) Bayesian nonparametric spatial modeling with Dirichlet process mixing. J Am Stat Assoc 100:1021–1035

Gelman A, Carlin J, Stern H, Rubin D (2003) Bayesian data analysis, 2nd edn. Chapman and Hall, London

Ghosh J, Ramamoorthi R (2003) Bayesian nonparametrics. New York: Springer

Ghosal S, Van der Vaart AW (2007) Posterior convergence rates of Dirichlet mixtures at smooth densities. Ann Stat 35:697–723

Ghosal S, Ghosh JK, Ramamoorthi RV (1999) Posterior consistency of Dirichlet mixtures in density estimation. Ann Stat 27:143–158

González J (2014) SNSequate: Standard and Nonstandard Statistical Models and Methods for Test Equating. J Stat Softw 59(7):1–30

González J, von Davier M (2013) Statistical models and inference for the true equating transformation in the context of local equating. J Educ Meas 50(3):315–320

Griffin JE, Steel MFJ (2006) Order-based dependent Dirichlet processes. J Am Stat Assoc 101:179–194

Hanson T, Johnson W (2002) Modeling regression error with a mixture of Polya trees. J Am Stat Assoc 97(460):1020–1033

Hjort NL, Holmes C, Müller P, Walker S (2010) Bayesian nonparametrics. Cambridge University Press, Cambridge

Holland P, Rubin D (1982) Test equating. Academic, New York

Jara A, Hanson T (2011) A class of mixtures of dependent tail-free processes. Biometrika 98: 553–566

Jara A, Lesaffre E, De Iorio M, Quintana FA (2010) Bayesian semiparametric inference for multivariate doubly-interval-censored data. Ann Appl Stat 4:2126–2149

Jara A, Hanson T, Quintana F, Müller P, Rosner G (2011) DPpackage: Bayesian non-and semi-parametric modelling in R. J Stat Softw 40:1–30

Kolen M, Brennan R (2004) Test equating, scaling, and linking: methods and practices. Springer, New York
Lavine M (1992) Some aspects of polya tree distributions for statistical modelling. Ann Stat 20:1222–1235
Lavine M (1994) More aspects of polya tree distributions for statistical modelling. Ann Stat 22:1161–1176
Lijoi A, Prünster I, Walker S (2005) On consistency of non-parametric normal mixtures for Bayesian density estimation. J Am Stat Assoc 100:1292–1296
Lo AY (1984) On a class of Bayesian nonparametric estimates I: Density estimates. Ann Stat 12:351–357
Lorentz G (1986) Bernstein polynomials. Chelsea, New York
MacEachern S (1999) Dependent nonparametric processes. In: ASA proceedings of the section on Bayesian statistical science, pp 50–55
MacEachern SN (2000) Dependent Dirichlet processes. Technical report, Department of Statistics, The Ohio State University
Mauldin R, Sudderth W, Williams S (1992) Polya trees and random distributions. Ann Stat 20(3):1203–1221
Müller P, Mitra R (2013) Bayesian nonparametric inference–why and how. Bayesian Anal 8(2):269–302
Müller P, Quintana F (2004) Nonparametric bayesian data analysis. Stat Sci 19:95–110
Müller P, Erkanli A, West M (1996) Bayesian curve fitting using multivariate normal mixtures. Biometrika 83:67–79
Müller P, Quintana FA, Rosner G (2004) A method for combining inference across related nonparametric Bayesian models. J R Stat Soc Ser B 66:735–749
Müller P, Rosner GL, De Iorio M, MacEachern S (2005) A nonparametric Bayesian model for inference in related longitudinal studies. J R Stat Soc Ser C 54:611–626
Petrone S (1999) Random bernstein polynomials. Scand J Stat 26(3):373–393
R Development Core Team (2013). R: a language and environment for statistical computing. R Foundation for Statistical Computing, Vienna. ISBN:3-900051-07-0
Rodriguez A, Dunson DB, Gelfand A (2008) The nested Dirichlet process. J Am Stat Assoc 103:1131–1154
Sethuraman J (1994) A constructive definition of dirichlet priors. Stat Sin 4:639–650
Smith BJ (2007) Boa: An r package for mcmc output convergence assessment and posterior inference. J Stat Softw 21:1–37
Teh YW, Jordan MI, Beal MJ, Blei DM (2006) Hierarchical Dirichlet processes. J Am Stat Assoc 101:1566–1581
Tokdar ST, Zhu YM, Ghosh JK (2010) Bayesian density regression with logistic Gaussian process and subspace projection. Bayesian Anal 5:1–26
von Davier A (2011) Statistical models for test equating, scaling, and linking. Springer, New York
von Davier A, Holland P, Thayer D (2004) The kernel method of test equating. Springer, New York

Chapter 14
Using a Modified Multidimensional Priority Index for Item Selection Under Within-Item Multidimensional Computerized Adaptive Testing

Ya-Hui Su and Yen-Lin Huang

Abstract Computerized adaptive testing (CAT) not only enables efficient and precise ability estimation but also increases the security of testing materials since examinees are given different sets of items from a large item bank. The construction of assessments usually involves fulfilling a large number of non-statistical constraints, such as item exposure control and content balancing. To improve measurement precision, test security, and test validity, the priority index (PI) and multidimensional priority index (MPI) were proposed to monitor many constraints simultaneously for unidimensional and multidimensional CATs, respectively. Many educational and psychological tests are constructed under a multidimensional framework. Some of the items (multidimensional items) in a test are often intended to assess multiple latent traits. However, Yao's MPI method was developed for a between-item multidimensional framework. When a within-item multidimensional test is assembled, a modified MPI algorithm is necessary. Therefore, the purposes of the study were to derive an algorithm for the modified MPI method for the within-item multidimensional CATs and to investigate the efficiency of the modified MPI method through simulations.

Keywords CAT • Priority index • Multidimensional • Item selection • IRT

14.1 Introduction

Computerized adaptive testing (CAT) not only enables efficient and precise ability estimation but also increases the security of testing materials since examinees are given different sets of items from a large item bank. CAT may also provide diagnostics information to parents, teachers, and students, which can be used

---

Y.-H. Su (✉) • Y.-L. Huang
Department of Psychology, National Chung Cheng University, Chiayi County, Taiwan
e-mail: psyyhs@ccu.edu.tw

R.E. Millsap et al. (eds.), *Quantitative Psychology Research*, Springer Proceedings in Mathematics & Statistics 89, DOI 10.1007/978-3-319-07503-7_14

to direct additional instruction to the areas needed most by individual students. Therefore, CAT may greatly improve the efficiency, security, and usefulness of educational and psychological assessments.

The construction of assessments usually involves fulfilling various non-statistical constraints in addition to statistical optimization. Examples include content balancing (selecting proportionate numbers of items from different content areas), key balancing (distributing correct answers evenly between options A, B, C, etc.), limiting specific types of items (such as those with negative stems), and so on. It is challenging to meet many non-statistical constraints simultaneously in CATs because items are selected sequentially. Several methods (Chang and van der Linden 2003; Stocking and Swanson 1993; van der Linden and Chang 2003) have been proposed to monitor content balancing flexibly; however, these methods require rather complex linear programming techniques. To improve measurement precision, test security, and test validity, the maximum priority index (PI) method can be used to handle several non-statistical constraints simultaneously (Cheng and Chang 2009; Cheng et al. 2009) under unidimensional CATs, and it was found that the PI method leads to fewer constraint violations and better exposure control while maintaining the same level of measurement precision.

Many educational and psychological tests are constructed within a multidimensional framework. One primary benefit of the multidimensional CAT is that information provided by items of correlated dimensions can lead to greater measurement efficiency, manifested by either greater precision or reduced test lengths (Segall 1996; Wang and Chen 2004). In practice, multidimensional CAT rather than unidimensional CAT is feasible. The multidimensional priority index (MPI; Yao 2011, 2012, 2013) method can be used to monitor item exposure control and content constraints under the framework of multidimensional CATs. However, Yao's MPI method was developed for a between-item multidimensional test. The item pool used in Yao's studies was the CAT Armed Services Vocational Aptitude Battery (CAT ASVAB), which is a between-item multidimensional test because each test in the battery is assumed to measure only one distinct latent trait, and the overall assessment is assumed to measure four latent traits. By contrast, some tests might have a within-item multidimensional structure such that individual items are intended to assess multiple latent traits. For instance, a science performance-based item can be used to assess both scientific declarative and procedural knowledge, a composition task can be used to assess both content understanding and language skills; or an arithmetic item can be used to assess both symbolic representation and calculation. As it might be inappropriate to use Yao's MPI method when a within-item multidimensional test is assembled, it is necessary to extend Yao's MPI method to within-item multidimensional CATs.

The objectives of this study were to derive an algorithm for a modified MPI method under within-item multidimensional CATs and to investigate its efficiency through simulations.

14.1.1 The Priority Index (PI) Method and its Development

To improve measurement precision, test security, and test validity, the maximum priority index (PI) method was proposed to monitor several non-statistical constraints simultaneously (Cheng and Chang 2009). Denote the constraint relevancy matrix $\mathbf{C}_{I \times K}$, where I is the number of items in the pool and K is the total number of constraints. Let $c_{ik} = 1$ represent constraint k being relevant to item i and $c_{ik} = 0$ otherwise. The $\mathbf{C}$ matrix is identified before item selection by content experts and psychometricians. Each constraint k is associated with a weight w_k. Usually, major constraints such as content balancing are given larger weights than others. The priority index of item i can be computed as

$$\mathrm{PI}_i = I_i \prod_{k=1}^{K} (w_k f_k)^{c_{ik}}, \tag{1}$$

where I_i represents the Fisher information of item i being defined as a function of the current $\widehat{\theta}$. The term f_k measures the scaled 'quota left' of constraint k. For a content constraint k, the PI can be considered in a certain content area. After x_k items have been selected, the resulting scaled 'quota left' is

$$f_k = \frac{(X_k - x_k)}{X_k}. \tag{2}$$

Note that when $c_{ik} = 0$, meaning item i is not restricted by constraint k, the term $w_k f_k$ will not contribute to the final product PI_i. For every available item in the pool, the PI can be computed according to Eq. (1). Instead of selecting the item with the largest Fisher information, the item with the largest PI value will be chosen in the CAT algorithm. When more than one item has the same highest PI value, the item with the largest Fisher information will be selected.

Item exposure control can be implemented as follows. Assume constraint k requires the item exposure rates of all items to be less than or equal to $r_{\max}$. Among the N examinees who have taken the CAT, n examinees have seen item i. Then, the term f_k can be calculated as

$$f_k = \frac{1}{r_{\max}} \left(r_{\max} - \frac{n}{N} \right), \tag{3}$$

where n/N is the provisional exposure rate of item j after N examinees have taken the CATs.

When flexible content balancing constraints are required, Cheng and Chang (2009) suggested that the PI method be used jointly with the two-phase item selection strategy (Cheng et al. 2007). Each flexible content balancing constraint involves a lower bound l_k and an upper bound u_k. Denote the number of items to be selected from content area k as μ_k. Then,

$$l_k \leq \mu_k \leq u_k, \tag{4}$$

and

$$\sum_{k=1}^{K} \mu_k = L, \tag{5}$$

where K ($k = 1, 2, \ldots, K$) and L are the total number of content areas and test length, respectively. In the first phase, l_k items are selected from each content area to meet the lower bound constraints such that $L_1 = \sum_{k=1}^{K} l_k$. After x_k items have been selected, the resulting scaled 'quota left' is

$$f_k = \frac{1}{l_k}\left(l_k - x_k\right). \tag{6}$$

Then, in the second phase, the remaining $L_2 = L - L_1$ items are selected within the upper bounds of each content area. The f_k can be computed as

$$f_k = \frac{1}{u_k}\left(u_k - x_k\right). \tag{7}$$

It was found that the PI method leads to fewer constraint violations and better exposure control while maintaining the same level of measurement precision. However, the PI method leaves almost half of the items in the pool unused. According to the study of Chang and Ying (1999), item selection methods based on the maximum information criterion (Thissen and Mislevy 2000), which selects the item with the largest Fisher information evaluated at the provisional ability, provide the most efficient ability estimation but tend to overexpose items with high discrimination.

To increase pool usage, Cheng et al. (2009) proposed constraint-weighted a-stratification for CAT with non-statistical constraints, which implemented the PI method with the a-stratified design. When flexible content balancing constraints are considered, a one-phase item selection strategy can be used by incorporating both upper bounds and lower bounds. The PI becomes

$$\mathrm{PI}_i = I_i \prod_{k=1}^{K} \left(f_{1k} f_{2k}\right)^{c_{ik}}, \tag{8}$$

where

$$f_{1k} = \frac{1}{u_k}\left(u_k - x_k - 1\right), \tag{9}$$

and

$$f_{2k} = \frac{(L - l_k) - (t - x_k)}{L - l_k}, \tag{10}$$

where t is the number of items that have already been administered and $t = \sum_{k=1}^{K} x_k$. The term f_{1k} in Eq. (9) measures the closeness to the upper bound. The $L - l_k$ in Eq. (10) is the maximum of the sum of items that can be selected from other content areas. When the term f_{2k} equals to 0, this implies that the sum of administered items from other content areas has reached its maximum. Cheng et al. (2009) indicated that item selection with a-stratification should be considered on the basis of matching the item difficulty parameter b to the current $\widehat{\theta}$, rather than matching the Fisher information to the current $\widehat{\theta}$. They modified the PI for one-phase and two-phase item selection as

$$\mathrm{PI}_i = \frac{1}{\left| b_i - \widehat{\theta} \right|} \prod_{k=1}^{K} (f_{1k} f_{2k})^{c_{ik}}, \tag{11}$$

and

$$\mathrm{PI}_i = \frac{1}{\left| b_i - \widehat{\theta} \right|} \prod_{k=1}^{K} (f_k)^{c_{ik}}, \tag{12}$$

respectively. This version of a-stratification allows for inclusion of many constraints on item type and format as well as constraints to ensure balanced item exposure. It was found the weighted mechanism successfully addresses the constraints. This method not only helps to a great extent in balancing item exposure rates but also improves measurement precision.

14.1.2 Yao's Multidimensional Priority Index (MPI) Method

Yao (2011) defined the multidimensional priority index (MPI) for each item i as

$$\mathrm{MPI}_i = \prod_{d=1}^{D} {f_{id}}^{c_{id}}, \tag{13}$$

where the constraint matrix $\mathbf{C}_{I \times D}$ has row dimension I equal to the number of items in the pool and column dimension D equal to the total number of domains, and c_{id} is the loading information for item i on domain d such that $c_{id} = 1$ if item i is from domain d and $c_{id} = 0$ otherwise. Including the item exposure rate, content constraints with upper and lower limits for each domain, and the estimated domain score precision, Yao (2013) defined the term f_{id} in Eq. (13) with the standard error stopping rule as

$$f_{id} = \left[\max\left\{\left[1-\left(\frac{p_d}{\widehat{p}_d}\right)^a+\varepsilon_1\right],0\right\}\right]\left[\max\left\{\left(\frac{r_i-n_i/N}{r_i}\right),0\right\}\right]$$
$$\left[1_{x_d\le l_d}\left(\frac{l_d-x_d}{l_d}+\varepsilon_2/x_d\right)+1_{x_d>l_d}\max\left\{1-\left(\frac{x_d}{u_d}\right)^b,0\right\}\right], \tag{14}$$

where p_d and $\widehat{p}_d$ represent the required standard error of measurement (SEM) and the SEM estimates based on the administered items for the domain d ability estimates, respectively. The smaller the SEM, the larger the precision. If the required precision of domain d has been achieved, then the items loading in domain d will not be selected further [the first term in Eq. (14)]. If an item has been selected so as to reach the required exposure rate, then it will not be selected further [the second term in Eq. (14)]. Each domain will have the minimum required number of items (the first part of the third term in Eq. (14)), and no further items will be selected from a domain if the number of selected items from that domain has reached its maximum limit [the second part of the third term in Eq. (14)]. Here, the smaller the values of a and b, the larger the weight given to the precision. The term ε_1 is a small number that can be adjusted so that the precision of the estimates can be slightly above the required precision, whereas the term ε_2 is a small number that can be adjusted so that the minimum required number of items for each domain can be administered first.

14.1.3 Statement of the Problems

Yao' MPI method (2011, 2012, 2013) in Eqs. (13) and (14) can be used for assembling between-item multidimensional tests, such as CAT ASVAB, in which each test in the battery is assumed to measure only one distinct latent trait, and the overall assessment is assumed to measure four latent traits. There are three potential problems when Yao's MPI (2013) method is used under within-item multidimensional CATs. Because every item measures only one latent trait in CAT ASVAB, the loading information for item i is only on one domain d. However, it is common for educational and psychological tests to have within-item multidimensional structure such that items are intended to assess multiple latent traits. A multidimensional item has loading information on more than one domain. For instance, as mentioned earlier, an arithmetic item can be used to assess both symbolic representation and calculation. This item i has loading information on two domains in Eq. (13). Applying Yao's MPI in Eqs. (13) and (14), the MPI for item i becomes

$$
\begin{aligned}
\mathrm{MPI_i} &= \left(f_{iSymbolicRepresentation}\right)^1 \left(f_{id}\right)^0 \cdots \left(f_{iCalculation}\right)^1 \left(f_{id}\right)^0 \\
&= \Big(\left[\mathrm{DomainPrecision}_{SymbolicRepresentation}\right] \left[\mathrm{ItemExposureControl}_i\right] \\
&\qquad \left[\mathrm{ContentConstraints}_{SymbolicRepresentation}\right] \Big)^1 \\
&\quad \Big(\left[\mathrm{DomainPrecision}_{Calculation}\right] \left[\mathrm{ItemExposureControl}_i\right] \\
&\qquad \left[\mathrm{ContentConstraints}_{Calculation}\right] \Big)^1
\end{aligned}
\tag{15}
$$

First, the domain precision term measures the distance between the required SEM and the SEM estimates based on the administered items, and its value is smaller than 1 [the first terms of decomposed f_{id} for symbolic representation and calculation in Eq. (15)]. The larger the domain precision term, the higher the priority for selecting the item. The MPI of the arithmetic item measuring symbolic representation and calculation is smaller than that of an item measuring only symbolic representation or calculation. Hence, the arithmetic item is much less likely to be administered. Second, the item exposure control term measures the distance between the required exposure rate for item i and the frequency with which the item i has been exposed, and its value is smaller than 1 [the second terms of decomposed f_{id} for symbolic representation and calculation in Eq. (15)]. The larger the item exposure control term, the higher the priority for selecting the item. The item exposure control term is calculated twice in Yao's MPI method for the arithmetic item. For this reason also, the item's MPI would generally have a smaller value than an item measuring only symbolic representation or calculation. Again, this arithmetic item is much less likely to be administered. In practice, a multidimensional item usually has much higher information than a unidimensional item. However, this arithmetic item is less likely selected than an item measuring only symbolic representation or calculation when Yao's MPI algorithm is applied. Third, the content constraints in MPI are domain constraints [the last terms of decomposed f_{id} for symbolic representation and calculation in Eq. (15)]. If one considers content constraints under some domain, Yao's MPI is not available.

In addition, Yao (2013) found high-quality items tend to be administered to examinees who take the test earlier. Although the first few items were randomly chosen, Yao still found the order affected the performances of some item selection procedures, especially for the first 200 examinees. In practice, those items that are most informative and useful in CATs are not needed in the early stages when ability estimation is very uncertain. Hence, a-stratification (Chang et al. 2001; Chang and Ying 1999) should be implemented in within-item multidimensional CATs to save informative items for the later stages and achieve better item usage in the study.

There are two additional problems noticed by author in the one-phase item selection strategy of the PI method (Cheng et al. 2009). For flexible content balancing constraints, both upper bounds and lower bounds are incorporated for the one-phase item selection strategy in Eqs. (8), (9), and (10). First, the f_{1k} in Eq. (9) measures closeness to the upper bound of constraint k. When only one more item is needed to reach the upper bound, f_{1k} in Eq. (9) is equal to 0. If item i is related to constraint k ($c_{ik} = 1$), the PI is equal to 0 and item i is impossible to select for administration; if item i is not related to constraint k ($c_{ik} = 0$), the PI is not certain to be 0 and item i can potentially select for administration. Therefore, it is impossible to have one more item for constraint k such that the upper bound of constraint k in Eq. (4) can be reached. Hence, it is suggested by the author that the last term of the numerator in Eq. (9), -1, be removed from the equation. The modified f_{1k} is defined as

$$f_{1k} = \frac{1}{u_k}\left(u_k - x_k\right). \tag{16}$$

Second, when the f_{2k} in Eq. (10) is equal to 0, it indicates that the sum of items from other domains has reached its maximum. However, a similar situation as for the f_{1k} happens here. If item i is related to constraint k ($c_{ik} = 1$), the PI is equal to 0 and item i is impossible to select for administration; if item i is not related to constraint k ($c_{ik} = 0$), the PI is not certain to be 0 and item i can potentially select for administration. All contents but constraint k have reached their maxima; however, items related to constraint k cannot be selected for administration. Hence, it is suggested by the author that the $f_{1k}f_{2k}$ for constraint k in Eq. (8) be defined as 1 when f_{2k} is equal to 0. Then, the PI will not always be 0 and item i can be selected for administration if this item is related to constraint k.

14.1.4 Purpose of the Study

It is of great value to develop a multidimensional CAT item selection procedure that facilitates efficient control over non-psychometric constraints, item exposure, and content balance simultaneously. It is also important to develop quality control procedures for integration in the item selection algorithm to identify potential problems in the item pool structure design. Therefore, the purpose of the study is threefold. First, to derive an algorithm of the modified MPI method for the within-item multidimensional CATs. Second, to develop a procedure of integrating the a-stratified design with the MPI method under the multidimensional CATs. Third, to evaluate the efficiency of the modified MPI methods in terms of constraint management, measurement precision, exposure control, and test length through simulations.

14.2 Method

14.2.1 The Modified MPI Method

The main framework of the PI method in Eq. (1) is included in the modified MPI method. For a fixed-length content constraint k, the term f_k defined in Eq. (2) can be included in the modified MPI method. For item exposure control, the term f_k defined in Eq. (3) can be included in the modified MPI method. Since item exposure control is one of the constraints in Eq. (1), the modified MPI method will not include it twice. For flexible content balancing constraints in Eqs. (4) and (5), the term f_k in Eq. (1) can be replaced with Eqs. (6) and (7) for a two-phase item selection strategy; Or, the term f_k in Eq. (1) can be replaced with $f_{1k}f_{2k}$ defined in Eqs. (16) and (10) for a one-phase item selection strategy by incorporating both upper bounds and lower bounds, and $f_{1k}f_{2k}$ is defined as 1 when f_{2k} in Eq. (10) is equal to 0.

14.2.2 Integrating a-Stratification with the Modified MPI Method

Chang and Ying (1996, 1999, 2007) and Hua and Chang (2001) suggested that a parameters should be selected in an ascending order. This means item selection begins with low discriminating items and high discriminating items are saved to later stages of testing. The rationale is that less discriminating items at the initial stage of testing are more appropriate when the latent trait estimation is not reliable and high discriminating items are more appropriate at the later stages of testing when the latent trait estimation is of greater certainty. In this way, measurement efficiency and accuracy can be improved.

The item pool is stratified into several strata, usually three or more, in such a way that the distributions of difficulty parameters in these strata remain roughly constant and discrimination parameters have ordered distributions across these strata. This is achieved by rank ordering all of the items by their difficulty parameters and by taking an adjacent K (*number of strata*) items and separating them into K different bins according to the size of their corresponding discrimination parameters. This results in K strata that have ordered distributions of discrimination parameters and roughly balanced difficulty parameters. The above considers an a-stratification design under a unidimensional framework. The a-stratification needs be modified to fit into the multidimensional framework when more than one dimension is considered. The item pool is stratified into K^D strata for a D-dimensional CAT if K strata are used for a unidimensional framework. The discrimination parameters have ordered distributions from the stratum with the lowest a parameters to the stratum with the highest a parameters for all dimensions.

The item pool is firstly divided into strata. Item selection in a-stratification involves moving upward through these K^D strata as the test proceeds and matching the current ability estimate with the closest difficulty parameter within each stratum. In this way, item exposure balance is achieved simultaneously during the test. Under the multidimensional framework, one-phase and two-phase item selection in a-stratification with the modified MPI method in Eq. (1) are achieved by

$$\text{modified MPI}_i = \frac{1}{\sqrt{(\theta_1 - b_i)^2 + (\theta_2 - b_i)^2 + \ldots (\theta_D - b_i)^2}} \prod_{k=1}^{K} (w_k f_{1k} f_{2k})^{c_{ik}}, \quad (17)$$

and

$$\text{modified MPI}_i = \frac{1}{\sqrt{(\theta_1 - b_i)^2 + (\theta_2 - b_i)^2 + \ldots (\theta_D - b_i)^2}} \prod_{k=1}^{K} (w_k f_k)^{c_{ik}}, \quad (18)$$

respectively. For flexible content balancing constraints, all of the simulations in this study are based on the one-phase approach in Eq. (17). For fixed-length constraints, the MPI in Eq. (18) is used.

14.2.3 Simulation Study

14.2.3.1 Data Generation

A popular multidimensional model used in this study is the multidimensional three-parameter logistic (M3PL; Hattie 1981; Reckase 1985) model, which is defined as

$$p_{ni1} = c_i + (1\text{-}c_i) \frac{\exp\left[\mathbf{a}_i'(\theta_n - b_i\mathbf{1})\right]}{1 + \exp\left[\mathbf{a}_i'(\theta_n - b_i\mathbf{1})\right]}, \quad (19)$$

where p_{ni1} is the probability of a correct response; $\theta_n' = (\theta_1, \theta_2, \ldots, \theta_p)$ represents the p-dimensional latent traits; $\mathbf{a}_i$ is a $p \times 1$ vector of the discrimination parameter; b_i and c_i are the difficulty and the guessing parameters of item i, respectively; and $\mathbf{1}$ is a $p \times 1$ vector of 1 s. When there is only one latent trait, Eq. (19) reduces to the three-parameter logistic model (Birnbaum 1968).

Our study considers one thousand M3PL items from a two-dimensional pool, in which 40 % of the items measure the first dimension, 30 % of the items measure the second dimension, and the remaining 30 % of the items measure both dimensions. Therefore, some items are unidimensional whereas others are two-dimensional. The items are randomly assigned to two dimensions according to the percentage of each dimension. The discrimination parameters are drawn from a uniform distribution on the interval of real numbers (0.5, 1.5) for each dimension, difficulty parameters are drawn from a standard normal distribution, and guessing parameters are drawn from a uniform distribution on (0, 0.4). All item responses are generated according to Eq. (19). The number of content areas used for these two dimensions are 3 and 2, and items are randomly assigned to these areas with equal probability. The lower and upper bounds of items needed by each content area for the first dimension are 3–5, 5–7, and 4–6, respectively. The lower and upper bounds of items needed by each content area for the second dimension are 5–8 and 6–9, respectively. In addition, the lower and upper bounds of the answer keys for each of four choices are 5–10. All 3,000 simulated examinees are drawn from a multivariate standard normal distribution with correlation 0.8, indicating high correlation. The total test length is $L = 30$. The MAP method with a multivariate standard normal distribution (correlation is set at 0.8) prior is used to estimate $\widehat{\theta}$ until the response pattern contains both a 0 and 1. After that the MLE method is used.

14.2.3.2 Simulation Design

Six conditions are simulated in this study: four experimental conditions with the MPI method and two control conditions. The two control conditions, treated as baseline, are the maximum determinant of the Fisher information matrix (MDFIM) method and the randomized (R) item selection method. The four experimental conditions implemented with MPI method are (1) a method without a-stratification (NonStr), (2) a method without a-stratification but with item exposure (NonStr-Expo), (3) a method with a-stratification (Str), and (4) a method with a-stratification and item exposure (StrExpo). For the conditions without a-stratification, Eq. (8) is used for item selection. For the conditions with a-stratification, Eq. (17) is used as the item selection criterion after the item pool is stratified.

14.2.3.3 Evaluation Criteria

The results of the simulation study were analyzed and discussed based on the following criteria: (a) constraint management, (b) measurement precision, and (c) exposure control.

Constraint management is to check whether the test sequentially assembled for each student meets all the specified test-construction constraints. The number of constraints that are violated in each test is recorded, and then the proportion of tests violating a certain number of constraints is calculated. Finally, the effectiveness of constraint management is the averaged number of violated constraints ($\overline{V}$):

$$\overline{V} = \frac{\sum_{n=1}^{N} V_n}{N}, \tag{20}$$

where V_i represents the number of constraint violations in the nth examinees' test.

Measurement precision is evaluated by latent trait recovery through the bias (bias), mean squared error of estimation (MSE), and a measure of relative efficiency, which is the square root of MSE, for each method compared to that of the MDFIM. The formulas for bias and MSE are given as follows:

$$\text{bias} = \frac{1}{N}\sum_{n=1}^{N}\left(\widehat{\theta}_n - \theta_n\right), \tag{21}$$

and

$$\text{MSE} = \frac{1}{N}\sum_{n=1}^{N}\left(\widehat{\theta}_n - \theta_n\right)^2, \tag{22}$$

where $\widehat{\theta}_n$ and θ_n are the estimated and true abilities, respectively.

With respect to exposure control, the maximum item exposure rate, the number of overexposed items (i.e., items with exposure rates that are higher than 0.20), and the number of items that are never exposed will be reported. In addition, the χ^2 statistic can be used to measure the skewness of item exposure rate distribution (Chang and Ying 1999)

$$\chi^2 = \frac{1}{L/I}\sum_{i=1}^{I}\left(r_i - L/I\right)^2, \tag{23}$$

where r_i is the exposure rate of item i and L is the test length. The χ^2 statistic is a good index of the efficiency of item pool usage as it qualifies the discrepancy between the observed and the expected under a uniform distribution. The smaller the χ^2 statistic, the better the item exposure control.

14.3 Results

The results of the simulation study were summarized according to measurement precision, exposure control, and constraint management criteria in Tables 14.1, 14.2, and 14.3, respectively. With respect to measurement precision, the bias, RMSE, and relative efficiency for the six different item selection methods list in Table 14.1. The MDFIM and R item selection methods, treated as control conditions, were baselines in this study. Since the MDFIM item selection method was one of the baselines in this study, the relative efficiency was defined as the ratio of RMSE for each item selection method to that for the MDFIM method. Among the six item selection methods, the MDFIM item selection method obtained the best measurement precision with the smallest bias and RMSE; the R item selection method obtained the worse measurement precision with the largest bias and RMSE and it also had the smallest relative efficiency compared to the MDFIM item

Table 14.1 Measurement precision of the six item selection methods

	Bias		RMSE		Relative efficiency	
Methods	Dim1	Dim2	Dim1	Dim2	Dim1	Dim2
Non modified MPI						
R	0.014	0.024	0.428	0.444	0.545	0.549
MDFIM	0.002	0.009	0.233	0.244	1.000	1.000
Modified MPI						
NonStr	0.002	0.010	0.311	0.317	0.750	0.770
NonStrExpo	0.011	0.011	0.313	0.291	0.744	0.840
Str	0.016	0.020	0.308	0.303	0.756	0.805
StrExpo	0.020	0.028	0.309	0.311	0.753	0.786

Note: Six item selection methods in this study are (1) the maximum determinant of the Fisher information matrix (MDFIM) method, (2) the randomized (R) item selection method, (3) a method without a-stratification (NonStr), (4) a method without a-stratification but with item exposure (NonStrExpo), (5) a method with a-stratification (Str), and (6) a method with a-stratification and item exposure (StrExpo)

Table 14.2 Exposure control results for the six item selection methods

Methods	min	25 %	50 %	75 %	max	Chi-square	Unused items	Test overlap
Nonmodified MPI								
R	0.022	0.028	0.030	0.032	0.038	0.179	0	0.030
MDFIM	0.000	0.000	0.000	0.000	0.527	206.456	743	0.236
Modified MPI								
NonStr	0.000	0.000	0.000	0.000	0.586	202.646	755	0.233
NonStrExpo	0.000	0.011	0.021	0.059	0.106	23.613	135	0.053
Str	0.000	0.005	0.017	0.047	0.194	36.316	85	0.066
StrExpo	0.000	0.012	0.026	0.046	0.134	16.505	53	0.046

selection method. The other four item selection methods with the modified MPI methods performed very similar in terms of RMSE and relative efficiency, but the NonStr and NonStrExpo item selection methods performed slightly better with smaller bias than the other two methods.

With respect to exposure control, the item exposure rates of each item were calculated for the six item selection methods. The minimum, the 25th percentile, the 50th percentile, the 75th percentile, and the maximum of the item exposure rate distribution list in the first five columns of Table 14.2. In addition, the χ^2 statistic, the number of unused items, and test overlap rates list in the last three columns of Table 14.2. Among the six item selection methods, the MDFIM and NonStr item selection methods obtained the worse exposure control with the maximum item exposure rate 0.52 and 0.58, respectively. The MDFIM and NonStr item selection methods also yielded the largest values in χ^2 statistic, the number of unused items, and test overlap rates. Among the six item selection methods, the R item selection

Table 14.3 Constraint management results for the six item selection methods

Methods	0	1	2	3	4	5	6	7	8	9	Averaged violation
Nonmodified MPI											
R	10.18	27.64	27.98	19.94	9.86	3.54	0.66	0.16	0.02	0.02	2.06
MDFIM	14.94	21.60	30.64	21.32	9.14	1.84	0.32	0.16	0.02	0.02	1.96
Modified MPI											
NonStr	100	0	0	0	0	0	0	0	0	0	0
NonStrExpo	99.80	0.06	0.08	0.06	0	0	0	0	0	0	<0.01
Str	90.52	9.18	0.30	0	0	0	0	0	0	0	0.10
StrExpo	89.74	9.52	0.74	0	0	0	0	0	0	0	0.11

method obtained the best exposure control with the maximum item exposure rate 0.03, and yielded the smallest in χ^2 statistic, the number of unused items, and test overlap rates. The NonStrExpo, Str, and StrExpo item selection methods obtained the maximum item exposure rate less than 0.19, and the χ^2 statistic, the number of unused items, and test overlap rates much smaller than those of the MDFIM and NonStr item selection methods. In general, the StrExpo item selection method performed the best exposure control with the smallest values in the χ^2 statistic, unused items, and test overlap rates among the NonStrExpo, Str, and StrExpo methods.

With respect to constraint management, the proportions of assembled tests violating a certain number of constraints were calculated for the six item selection methods, which list in the first ten columns of Table 14.3. The average number of violated constraints was also calculated, which list in the last columns of Table 14.3. The R item selection method yielded the severest violation when assembling tests, followed by the MDFIM item selection method. The other four item selection methods with the modified MPI performed better. Among the other four item selection methods with the modified MPI method, those without *a*-stratification (NonStr and NonStrExpo) performed better than those with *a*-stratification (Str and StrExpo) in terms of averaged constraint violations. It was also found that the NonStr item selection method could meet all the specified test-construction constraints when the test sequentially assembled for each student.

Conclusions

It is not only of great value to develop a multidimensional CAT item selection procedure but also important to develop quality control procedures for integration in the item selection algorithm to identify potential problems in the item pool structure design. The purposes of this study were to develop an algorithm of the modified MPI method for within-item multidimensional CATs, to integrate the modified MPI method with constraint-weighted *a*-stratification,

(continued)

and to investigate its efficiency through simulations. These methods were evaluated according to the constraint management, item exposure control, and measurement precision criteria. It was found that the item selection with *a*-stratification and exposure control (that is StrExpo item selection method in the study) under the framework of the modified MPI method would obtain better pool usage and lower test overlap rates; however, it also yields some loss in measurement precision and constraint management.

Today one of the main challenges in educational and psychological measurement is to develop theories and methods for the new mode of large-scale implementation of computerized assessment, especially in developing item selection methods for CATs. The modified MPI method has great potential in operational CATs. Therefore, research findings from this study will advance our knowledge for item selection in multidimensional CAT.

This study has some limitations that can be addressed in future work. First, the algorithms of the modified MPI method derived for M3PL, which is for multidimensional dichotomous items, might not be appropriate for the polytomous items. In psychological inventories, it is common to have Likert-type items in which subjects specify their level of agreement or disagreement on a symmetric agree–disagree scale for a series of statements. Since the polytomous items provide more information than dichotomous items do, it is important to extend the MPI approach to polytomous items. In addition, a fixed test length of 30 items was used in this study as stopping rule. However, when a fixed precision is considered among all subjects, subjects might receive tests with variable test length. It is also important to investigate the efficiency of the modified MPI method when the fixed precision is used as stopping rule under multidimensional CATs in the future as well.

References

Birnbaum A (1968) Some latent trait models and their use in inferring an examinee's ability. In: Lord FM, Novick MR (eds) Statistical theories of mental test scores. Addison-Wesley, Reading, pp 397–479

Chang H-H, van der Linden WJ (2003) Optimal stratification of item pools in alpha-stratified computerized adaptive testing. Appl Psychol Meas 27:262–274

Chang H-H, Ying Z (1996) A global information approach to computerized adaptive testing. Appl Psychol Meas 20:213–229

Chang H-H, Ying Z (1999) *a*-stratified multistage computerized adaptive testing. Appl Psychol Meas 23:211–222

Chang H-H, Ying Z (2007) To weight or not to weight? Balancing influence of initial items in adaptive testing. Psychometrika. Prepublished online on December 8, 2007. doi:10.1007/s11336-007-9047-7

Chang H-H, Qian J, Ying Z (2001) *a*-stratified multistage CAT with *b*-blocking. Appl Psychol Meas 25:333–341

Cheng Y, Chang H-H (2009) The maximum priority index method for severely constrained item selection in computerized adaptive testing. Br J Math Stat Psychol 62:369–383

Cheng Y, Chang H-H, Yi Q (2007) Two-phase item selection procedure for flexible content balancing in CAT. Appl Psychol Meas 31:467–482

Cheng Y, Chang H-H, Douglas J, Guo F (2009) Constraint-weighted a-stratification for computerized adaptive testing with nonstatistical constraints: balancing measurement efficiency and exposure control. Educ Psychol Meas 69:35–49

Hattie J (1981) Decision criteria for determining unidimensionality. Unpublished doctoral dissertation, University of Toronto, Canada

Hua K, Chang H-H (2001) Item selection in computerized adaptive testing: should more discriminating items be used first? J Educ Meas 38:249–266

Reckase MR (1985) The difficulty of test items that measure more than one dimension. Appl Psychol Meas 9:401–412

Segall DO (1996) Multidimensional adaptive testing. Psychometrika 61:331–354

Stocking ML, Swanson L (1993) A method for severely constrained item selection in adaptive testing. Appl Psychol Meas 17:277–292

Thissen D, Mislevy RJ (2000) Testing algorithms. In: Wainer H (ed) Computerized adaptive testing: a primer, 2nd edn. Erlbaum, Mahwah, pp 101–133

van der Linden WJ, Chang H-H (2003) Implementing content constraints in alpha-stratified adaptive testing using a shadow test approach. Appl Psychol Meas 27:107–120

Wang W-C, Chen P-H (2004) Implementation and measurement efficiency of multidimensional computerized adaptive testing. Appl Psychol Meas 28:295–316

Yao L (2011) Multidimensional CAT item selection procedures with item exposure control and content constraints. Paper presented at the (2011) International Association of Computer Adaptive Testing (IACAT) conference, Pacific Grove, CA, October

Yao L (2012) Multidimensional CAT item selection methods for domain scores and composite scores: theory and applications. Psychometrika 77:495–523

Yao L (2013) Comparing the performance of five multidimensional CAT selection procedures with different stopping rules. Appl Psychol Meas 37:3–23

Chapter 15
Assessing Differential Item Functioning in Multiple Grouping Variables with Factorial Logistic Regression

Kuan-Yu Jin, Hui-Fang Chen, and Wen-Chung Wang

Abstract Differential item functioning (DIF) can occur among multiple grouping variables (e.g., gender and ethnicity). For such cases, one can either examine DIF one grouping variable at a time or combine all the grouping variables into a single grouping variable in a test without a substantial meaning. These two approaches, analogous to one-way analysis of variance (ANOVA), are less efficient than an approach that considers all the grouping variables simultaneously and decomposes the DIF effect into main effects of individual grouping variables and their interactions, which is analogous to factorial ANOVA. In this study, the idea of factorial ANOVA was applied to the logistic regression method for the assessment of uniform and nonuniform DIF, and the performance of this approach was evaluated with simulations. The results indicated that the proposed factorial approach outperformed conventional approaches when there was interaction between grouping variables; the larger the DIF effect size, the higher the power of detection; the more DIF items in the anchored test, the worse the DIF assessment. Given the promising results, the factorial logistic regression method is recommended for the assessment of uniform and nonuniform DIF when there are multiple grouping variables.

Keywords Differential item functioning • Logistic regression • Uniform differential item functioning • Nonuniform differential item functioning

Many tests and inventories have been developed to measure latent traits in the human sciences and to compare inter-individual differences. A major concern

K.-Y. Jin • W.-C. Wang
Assessment Research Centre, Hong Kong Institute of Education, 10 Lo Ping Road, Tai Po, New Territories, Hong Kong SAR
e-mail: kyjin@ied.edu.hk; wcwang@ied.edu.hk

H.-F. Chen (✉)
Department of Applied Social Sciences, City University of Hong Kong, Tat Chee Avenue, Kowloon, Hong Kong SAR
e-mail: hfchen@cityu.edu.hk

R.E. Millsap et al. (eds.), *Quantitative Psychology Research*, Springer Proceedings in Mathematics & Statistics 89, DOI 10.1007/978-3-319-07503-7_15

that arises under such group comparisons is whether or not test items reflect the same latent dimensions across all groups of examinees, termed measurement equivalence or measurement invariance (Candell and Hulin 1986; Drasgow 1987). A lack of measurement invariance leads to a problematic situation where examinees having the same underlying ability but belonging to different groups have different probabilities of success on an item. Thus, the test favors one or more groups of examinees but disadvantages others. Measures are not comparable across groups, and test fairness is threatened.

Assessment of differential item functioning (DIF) is a routine practice to investigate measurement invariance at the item level, especially for large-scale assessment programs such as the Program for International Student Assessment and the Trends in International Mathematics and Science Study. DIF refers to examinees with the same ability level from different groups having different probabilities of pass or endorsing an item. In the framework of item response theory (IRT), an item shows DIF if its response functions are not identical across groups. The psychometric properties differ across groups, and the differences in the measures across groups do not reflect true differences.

Most DIF studies focus on the difference between a reference group (e.g., majority) and a focal group (e.g., minority). Latent traits of the two groups of examinees are placed on the same metric based on an anchored test, and then the responses to a studied item are examined for DIF. Sometimes, more than two groups of examinees may be involved, such as in cross-cultural and cross-ethnic research (Iwata et al. 2002). In such cases, a group (e.g., white Americans) is selected to serve as the reference group, so the other focal groups can be compared against the reference group, one focal group at a time. This procedure is analogous to the independent-samples t-test. Just as the one-way ANOVA is statistically superior to multiple independent-samples t-tests, simultaneous DIF analysis across multiple groups has been found to be statistically more efficient than multiple two-group DIF analyses (Güler and Penfield 2009; Kim et al. 1995; Penfield 2001).

Specifically, Kim et al. (1995) developed the Q_j statistic using the vectors of item parameter estimates. If the vectors differ significantly across groups, then the item characteristic functions differ across groups, and the item is deemed to exhibit DIF. Being an IRT-based method, the Q_j statistic requires large sample sizes for stable item parameter estimation. To resolve this problem, Penfield (2001) proposed a non-IRT-based method: the generalized Mantel–Haenszel (MH) statistic (Somes 1986; Zwick et al. 1993). Simulation results confirmed that both methods yielded well-controlled Type I error rates and high power rates, but they differed in computation time and sample size requirements.

When DIF analysis is to be conducted on multiple grouping variables (factors), such as gender (two levels) and ethnicity (three levels), two approaches are often adopted: The first approach is to consecutively conduct DIF analysis, one grouping factor at a time. For example, one can conduct a gender DIF analysis, followed by an ethnicity DIF analysis. The second approach is to combine these two grouping factors into a pseudo-grouping factor with six levels and to implement the procedures proposed by Kim et al. (1995) or Penfield (2001). The first approach, analogous to conducting one-way ANOVA procedures consecutively, aims to evaluate whether there is a gender DIF or an ethnicity DIF. The second approach, also analogous to one-way ANOVA, creates a pseudo-grouping factor that often lacks substantial meaning. Both approaches are less statistically efficient than factorial ANOVA, where all grouping factors are simultaneously considered and the "total" DIF effect is partitioned into main effects of individual grouping factors and their interaction effects, such as a main effect of gender, a main effect of ethnicity, and an interaction effect between gender and ethnicity.

Factorial DIF analysis procedures in the framework of Rasch models have been proposed and proven to be effective in DIF assessment (Wang 2000a, b) and outperform conventional consecutive DIF analyses when an interaction exists between grouping factors (Chen et al. 2012). Embedded in the framework of Rasch models, such factorial procedures are parametric and not applicable to the assessment of nonuniform DIF. In this study, we adopt the logic of factorial DIF analysis and apply it to a nonparametric approach—the logistic regression (LR) method (Swaminathan and Rogers 1990)—which is applicable to both uniform and nonuniform DIF.

The LR method is one of the most widely used nonparametric approaches in DIF assessment (Kim and Oshima 2013; Li et al. 2012). It is simple, easy to implement, and does not require a large sample size or a specific form of item response functions. It can be easily implemented in common computer packages such as SPSS, SAS, or Matlab, or free software such as R. The LR method works equally as well as the MH method in uniform DIF assessment, and outperforms the MH method in nonuniform DIF assessment (Narayanan and Swaminathan 1994, 1996; Swaminathan and Rogers 1990). Often, a raw test score is treated as a matching variable to place examinees from different groups on the same metric, so studied items can be assessed for uniform or nonuniform DIF. Compared to IRT-based DIF assessment methods, disadvantages of the LR method include inflated Type I error rates when different groups of examinees have very different mean ability levels (Güler and Penfield 2009; Narayanan and Swaminathan 1996) and its poor performance when the underlying IRT model is a multiparameter logistic model (Bolt and Gierl 2006; DeMars 2010).

Given the importance of factorial DIF analysis and the simplicity and popularity of the LR method in uniform and nonuniform DIF assessment, this study develops the factorial logistic regression (FLR) method to assess DIF effects when there are multiple grouping factors. Its performance in DIF assessment is evaluated and compared to other LR methods via two simulation studies. In the following sections, we introduce the key ideas of the FLR method, present the results of the simulation studies, draw conclusions, and give suggestions for future studies.

15.1 The FLR Method

Let T_n denote the raw test score for person n. Let X_n be an indicator of group membership for person n; for example, $X_n = 1$ if person n belongs to the reference group, and $X_n = -1$ if person n belongs to the focal group. Let P_n be the probability of success on the studied item for person n. When the studied item is to be assessed for DIF, one can formulate the log-odds (or logit) of a correct answer over an incorrect answer as:

$$\log\left(\frac{P_n}{1-P_n}\right) = \tau_0 + \tau_1 T_n + \tau_2 X_n + \tau_3 X_n T_n, \tag{1}$$

where τ_0 - τ_3 are the regression coefficients for the studied item. If τ_2 or τ_3 is not zero, then the item is deemed to exhibit DIF. Normally, if τ_3 is not zero, then the item is deemed to exhibit nonuniform DIF; if τ_3 is zero but τ_2 is not, then the item is deemed to exhibit uniform DIF (Narayanan and Swaminathan 1994).

When there is one grouping factor and it has more than two groups ($g = 1, \ldots, G$), one can create a set of G - 1 dummy variables to represent the group membership: $\mathbf{X}_n{}' = (X_{n1}, \ldots, X_{n(G-1)})$. For example, if there are three groups, two dummy variables, X_1 and X_2, can be created. If examinee n is in group 1, then $X_{n1} = 1$, $X_{n2} = 0$; in group 2, $X_{n1} = 0$, $X_{n2} = 1$; in group 3, $X_{n1} = -1$, $X_{n2} = -1$. That is,

$$\mathbf{X}_n{}' = \begin{bmatrix} 1 & 0 \\ 0 & 1 \\ -1 & -1 \end{bmatrix}, \tag{2}$$

where the two columns stand for X_1 and X_2, and the three rows stand for the three groups. Equation (1) can then be extended as follows:

$$\log\left(\frac{P_n}{1-P_n}\right) = \tau_0 + \tau_1 T_n + \boldsymbol{\tau}_2{}'\mathbf{X}_n + \boldsymbol{\tau}_3{}'\mathbf{X}_n T_n, \tag{3}$$

where τ_0, τ_1, $\boldsymbol{\tau}_2$, and $\boldsymbol{\tau}_3$ are the regression coefficients for the studied item. For the three groups, Eq. (3) becomes

$$\log\left(\frac{P_n}{1-P_n}\right) = \tau_0 + \tau_1 T_n + \tau_{21} X_{n1} + \tau_{22} X_{n2} + \tau_{31} X_{n1} T_n + \tau_{32} X_{n2} T_n, \tag{4}$$

where $\boldsymbol{\tau}_2{}' = (\tau_{21}, \tau_{22})$, $\boldsymbol{\tau}_3{}' = (\tau_{31}, \tau_{32})$, and $\mathbf{X}_n{}' = (X_{n1}, X_{n2})$. If $\boldsymbol{\tau}_3$ is not a zero vector, then the item is deemed to exhibit nonuniform DIF; if $\boldsymbol{\tau}_3$ is a zero vector but $\boldsymbol{\tau}_2$ is not, then the item is deemed to exhibit uniform DIF.

The interpretation of $\boldsymbol{\tau}_2$ and $\boldsymbol{\tau}_3$ is analogous to that in standard logistic regression. Take the design matrix in Eq. (3) as an example. When there is no nonuniform DIF (i.e., $\boldsymbol{\tau}_3 = \mathbf{0}$), then Eq. (4) becomes

$$\text{Group 1 } (X_1 = 1,\ X_2 = 0):\ \log\left(\frac{P_n}{1-P_n}\right) = \tau_0 + \tau_1 T_n + \tau_{21}, \tag{5}$$

$$\text{Group 2 } (X_1 = 0,\ X_2 = 1):\ \log\left(\frac{P_n}{1-P_n}\right) = \tau_0 + \tau_1 T_n + \tau_{22}, \tag{6}$$

$$\text{Group 3 } (X_1 = -1,\ X_2 = -1):\ \log\left(\frac{P_n}{1-P_n}\right) = \tau_0 + \tau_1 T_n - \tau_{21} - \tau_{22}. \tag{7}$$

If $\boldsymbol{\tau}_2{}' = (\tau_{21}, \tau_{22}) = (0.4, -0.3)$, then for examinees with an equal ability level, the log-odds (logit) of group 1 examinees will be 0.8 higher than that of group 3 examinees, and the log-odds (logit) of group 2 examinees will be 0.6 lower than that of group 3 examinees.

Next, suppose there is more than one grouping factor. For illustrative simplicity, let there be two grouping factors, A (e.g., gender) and B (e.g., ethnicity), and let each factor have two levels (e.g., male and female; white and black), so that in total there are four groups of examinees (e.g., white male, white female, black male, and black female). Let X_1 be the dummy variable for factor A, and X_2 be the dummy variable for factor B. To account for the interactions between factors A and B, one additional dummy variable is needed: X_1X_2. Thus, a 4 by 3 matrix can be created:

$$\mathbf{X}_n{}' = \begin{bmatrix} 1 & 1 & 1 \\ -1 & 1 & -1 \\ 1 & -1 & -1 \\ -1 & -1 & 1 \end{bmatrix}, \tag{8}$$

where the three columns stand for X_1, X_2, and X_1X_2, and the four rows stand for the four groups. That is, $X_{n1} = 1$, $X_{n2} = 1$, $X_{n1}X_{n2} = 1$ if examinee n is in group 1 (white male); $X_{n1} = \text{-}1$, $X_{n2} = 1$, $X_{n1}X_{n2} = \text{-}1$ if in group 2 (white female); $X_{n1} = 1$, $X_{n2} = \text{-}1$, $X_{n1}X_{n2} = \text{-}1$ if in group 3 (black male); $X_{n1} = \text{-}1$, $X_{n2} = \text{-}1$, $X_{n1}X_{n2} = 1$ if in group 4 (black female). When the general form of Eq. (3) is applied, one has:

$$\log\left(\frac{P_n}{1-P_n}\right) = \tau_0 + \tau_1 T_n + \tau_{21}X_{n1} + \tau_{22}X_{n2} + \tau_{23}X_{n1}X_{n2} + \tau_{31}X_{n1}T_n + \tau_{32}X_{n2}T_n + \tau_{33}X_{n1}X_{n2}T_n, \tag{9}$$

in which $\boldsymbol{\tau}_2{}' = (\tau_{21}, \tau_{22}, \tau_{23})$, $\boldsymbol{\tau}_3{}' = (\tau_{31}, \tau_{32}, \tau_{33})$, and $\mathbf{X}_n{}' = (X_{n1}, X_{n2}, X_{n1}X_{n2})$. With the design matrix in Eq. (8), τ_{21} depicts the main effect of factor A on uniform DIF, τ_{22} depicts the main effect of factor B on uniform DIF, τ_{23} depicts the interaction effect of factors A and B on uniform DIF, τ_{31} depicts the main effect of factor A on nonuniform DIF, τ_{32} depicts the main effect of factor B on nonuniform DIF, and τ_{33} depicts the interaction effect of factors A and B on nonuniform DIF. When there is no nonuniform DIF, Eq. (9) becomes

$$\text{White Male } (X_1{=}1,\ X_2{=}1,\ X_1X_2{=}1):\ \log\left(\frac{P_n}{1-P_n}\right) = \tau_0+\tau_1 T_n+\tau_{21}+\tau_{22}+\tau_{23}, \tag{10}$$

$$\text{White Female } (X_1{=}-1,\ X_2{=}1,\ X_1X_2{=}-1):\log\left(\frac{P_n}{1-P_n}\right) = \tau_0+\tau_1 T_n-\tau_{21}+\tau_{22}-\tau_{23}, \tag{11}$$

$$\text{Black Male } (X_1{=}1,X_2{=}-1,X_1X_2{=}-1):\ \log\left(\frac{P_n}{1-P_n}\right) = \tau_0+\tau_1 T_n+\tau_{21}-\tau_{22}-\tau_{23}, \tag{12}$$

$$\text{Black Female } (X_1{=}-1,X_2{=}-1,\ X_1X_2{=}1):\ \log\left(\frac{P_n}{1-P_n}\right) = \tau_0+\tau_1 T_n-\tau_{21}-\tau_{22}+\tau_{23}, \tag{13}$$

If $\boldsymbol{\tau}_2{}' = (\tau_{21},\ \tau_{22},\ \tau_{23}) = (0.4,\ -0.3,\ 0.2)$, then it can be shown that, on average, males have a logit 0.8 higher than that of females; white people have a logit 0.6 lower than that of black people; and white males and black females have a logit 0.4 higher than that of white females and black males. A similar interpretation applies to $\boldsymbol{\tau}_3$.

The use of design matrices like Eq. (8) enables users to decompose uniform DIF and nonuniform DIF into a main effect of factor A, a main effect of factor B, and an interaction effect between factors A and B. Furthermore, Eq. (9) can be easily generalized to cover more than two grouping factors, which can be categorical or continuous, as in factorial ANOVA or ANCOVA (analysis of covariance).

The likelihood ratio test can be adopted to statistically test whether the $\boldsymbol{\tau}_2$ and $\boldsymbol{\tau}_3$ vectors are zero. By comparing the likelihood ratio of Eqs. (14) and (3), one can test whether the studied item has DIF:

$$\log\left(\frac{P_n}{1-P_n}\right) = \tau_0 + \tau_1 T_n, \tag{14}$$

against a chi-square distribution with degrees of freedom of the length of $\boldsymbol{\tau}_2$ and $\boldsymbol{\tau}_3$. Likewise, one can compare the likelihood ratio of Eqs. (15) and (3) to test whether the studied item has nonuniform DIF:

$$\log\left(\frac{P_n}{1-P_n}\right) = \tau_0 + \tau_1 T_n + \boldsymbol{\tau}_2{}'\mathbf{X}_n, \tag{15}$$

against a chi-square distribution with degrees of freedom of the length of $\boldsymbol{\tau}_3$. When $\boldsymbol{\tau}_3$ is a zero vector, it is desirable to test whether this item has uniform DIF, which can be done by comparing the likelihood ratio of Eqs. (14) and (15) against a chi-square distribution with degrees of freedom of the length of $\boldsymbol{\tau}_2$. All these equations and likelihood ratio tests can be easily implemented on commercial programs such as SPSS and SAS, or free software such as R.

In the following simulation studies, we were particularly interested in two questions: (a) Could the FLR method detect uniform DIF effectively under different conditions, as compared to traditional LR methods? and (b) Could the FLR method detect nonuniform DIF effectively under different conditions, as compared to traditional LR methods? Each question was answered by a simulation study. In both simulation studies, there were two grouping variables and each had two levels.

15.2 Simulation Study 1: Uniform DIF

15.2.1 Design

Let the two grouping variables be denoted A and B. Let X_1 be the dummy variable for factor A, X_2 be the dummy variable for factor B, and X_1X_2 be the dummy variable for factors A and B. The design matrix was identical to that in Eq. (5). Each of the four groups of examinees had a sample size of 125, and their ability levels were generated from $N(0, 1)$. There were 21 items in the test, in which items 1–20 were treated as an anchored test to place all the examinees from different groups on the same scale, so that item 21 could be detected for DIF. The item responses followed the Rasch model. There were three independent variables: (a) percentage of DIF items in the anchored test, 0, 10, and 20 % DIF items in the 20-item anchored test; (b) DIF size in the studied item, 0, 0.2, 0.4, and 0.6 logits; and (c) DIF source, consisting of main effect of factor A, main effects of factors A and B, the interaction effect, main effect of factor A and the interaction effect, and main effects of factors A and B and the interaction effect. Let the difficulty parameter be b when an item did not have DIF. It became $b \pm 0.2$, $b \pm 0.4$, and $b \pm 0.6$ for the four groups, according to the design matrix in Eq. (5) when the DIF size was 0.2, 0.4, and 0.6, respectively. Although an anchored test should preferably include exclusively DIF-free items, in reality, DIF items may be included in an anchored test. Inclusion of DIF items often results in poorer DIF assessment (Narayanan and Swaminathan 1996; Rogers and Swaminathan 1993). Scale purification procedures for logistic regression methods have been developed (French and Maller 2007). However, this study did not consider scale purification because its major purpose was to evaluate the FLR method and others, even when the anchored test included DIF items.

A total of 76 conditions were examined with 1,000 replications under each condition. Each simulated dataset was analyzed with the following four methods:

1. The LR-A method in which DIF analysis was conducted to assess DIF of grouping variable A;
2. The LR-B method in which DIF analysis was conducted to assess DIF of grouping variable B;
3. The LR-AB method in which DIF analysis was conducted to assess DIF of grouping variables A and B consecutively; and
4. The proposed FLR method.

Although there were two grouping variables and DIF analysis should be conducted on both variables (meaning that the LR-A and LR-B methods were not applicable in practice), the LR-A and LR-B methods were adopted, by which the LR-AB and FLR methods can be compared. The nominal level of hypothesis testing was set at 0.05. Note that in the LR-AB method there were two hypothesis tests, so the Bonferroni adjustment was applied.

The outcome variables were the Type I error rate and the power rate. The empirical Type I error rate (false positive rate) was computed as how many times in the 1,000 replications a DIF-free studied item (DIF size = 0) was mistakenly declared as having DIF; and the empirical power rate (true positive rate) was computed as how many times in the 1,000 replications a DIF item was correctly detected as having DIF.

It was expected that (a) when the anchored tests did not contain any DIF items, all four methods would yield well-controlled Type I error rates; (b) when the anchored tests contained DIF items, the performance of these four methods would be degraded; (c) the FLR method would have higher power than the other methods when the DIF source contained the interaction of factors A and B; and (d) the larger the DIF size, the higher the power rate.

15.2.2 Results

15.2.2.1 Empirical Type I Error Rates

When the anchored test did not contain any DIF items, the empirical Type I error rates were 0.058, 0.058, 0.053, and 0.047 for the FLR, LR-AB, LR-A, and LR-B methods, respectively. All methods yielded well-controlled Type I error rates, as expected. When the anchored test contained 10 % DIF items, as shown in the upper panel of Table 15.1, the Type I error rates were inflated, especially when the DIF size was large. In addition, it was evident that the LR-AB and FLR methods were more adversely affected than the LR-A and LR-B methods by the inclusion of DIF items in the anchored test. When the anchored test contained 20 % DIF items, as shown in the lower panel of Table 15.1, the inflation in the Type I error rates was even worse than it was in the condition of 10 % DIF items. For example, when the DIF source contained the interaction between factors A and B and the DIF size was large, the FLR method yielded a Type I error rate of 0.077 when there were 10 % DIF items in the anchored test, and 0.235 when there were 20 % DIF items. Thus, the second expectation was supported, too.

15.2.2.2 Empirical Power Rates

First, consider the case where the anchored test did not contain any DIF items. As shown in the upper panel of Table 15.2, when the DIF source contained exclusively the interaction between factors A and B, only the FLR method yielded high power rates: 0.462, 0.971, and 1.000 when the DIF size was small (0.2 logits), medium (0.4 logits), and large (0.6 logits), respectively, whereas the other three methods yielded power rates between 0.033 and 0.050. A close inspection of the panel revealed that the FLR method substantially outperformed the other three methods as long as the DIF source contained the interaction. When the DIF source contained exclusively the main effect of factor A, the LR-A method had the highest power rates, and the LR-B had the lowest power rates. It was also very clear that the larger the DIF size, the higher the power rate.

Second, consider the case in which the anchored test contained 10 or 20 % (uniform) DIF items, as shown in the middle and lower panels. Take the power rates when the anchored tests did not contain any DIF items as a reference. Across the 15 conditions (5 DIF sources by 3 DIF sizes), the mean power rate was increased by 1, 2, 5, and 2 %, for the FLR, LR-AB, LR-A, and LR-B methods, respectively, when the anchored tests contained 10 % DIF items, and increased by 4, -5, -4, and 2 % for the four methods, respectively, when the anchored tests contained 20 % DIF items. It appears that the inclusion of 10 or 20 % (uniform) DIF items in the anchored test did not substantially affect the power rates of these four methods.

15.3 Simulation Study 2: Nonuniform DIF

15.3.1 Design

This simulation study focused on the assessment of nonuniform DIF. Item responses were simulated according to the three-parameter logistic model. The settings were identical to those in Simulation Study 1, except (a) the discrimination parameters were generated from a log-normal distribution with mean of 0 and variance of 0.1, and the guessing parameters were fixed as 0.2 for all items; (b) the DIF occurred only on the discrimination parameters across different groups of examinees, and the DIF size on a logarithm scale was set at 0, 0.13, 0.26, and 0.39, representing DIF-free, small, medium, and large DIF effects, respectively. Let the discrimination parameter be a when an item did not have DIF. It became

Table 15.1 Type I error rates ($^{0}/_{00}$) of the four methods in uniform DIF

	FLR			LR-AB			LR-A			LR-B		
DIF source	Small	Medium	Large	Small	Medium	Large	Small	Medium	Large	Small	Medium	Large
10 % DIF items												
Interaction	49	81	77	53	60	48	45	57	53	44	53	45
Main effect of A	61	65	88	59	66	94	69	73	103	48	57	60
Main effect of A and interaction	63	80	133	57	73	108	59	77	120	60	45	58
Main effects of A and B	61	67	122	58	74	143	43	66	126	59	65	136
Main effects of A and B and interaction	70	75	155	60	63	133	57	62	114	58	75	121
20 % DIF items												
Interaction	73	115	235	52	43	61	52	58	53	46	40	43
Main effect of A	69	128	155	74	141	180	89	182	216	54	42	54
Main effect of A and interaction	74	132	379	60	90	220	68	111	291	46	54	60
Main effects of A and B	62	192	411	78	219	418	83	173	327	66	168	338
Main effects of A and B and interaction	77	220	616	80	177	404	84	150	321	66	152	347

Note: Small, medium, and large refer to DIF effect size

Table 15.2 Power rates ($^{0}/_{00}$) of the four methods in uniform DIF

DIF source	FLR			LR-AB			LR-A			LR-B		
	Small	Medium	Large	Small	Medium	Large	Small	Medium	Large	Small	Medium	Large
0 % DIF items												
Interaction	462	971	1,000	45	33	49	47	49	50	46	43	44
Main effect of A	559	1,000	999	618	1,000	1,000	707	1,000	1,000	50	44	42
Main effect of A and interaction	929	1,000	1,000	700	998	1,000	782	999	1,000	63	60	122
Main effects of A and B	803	1,000	1,000	789	998	1,000	662	986	1,000	626	982	1,000
Main effects of A and B and interaction	642	1,000	1,000	429	993	1,000	352	904	1,000	319	919	1,000
10 % DIF items												
Interaction	499	948	1,000	43	43	41	42	40	47	45	36	44
Main effect of A	499	959	996	556	977	998	657	985	1,000	31	47	41
Main effect of A and interaction	836	1,000	1,000	593	994	1,000	691	999	1,000	57	84	417
Main effects of A and B	821	1,000	1,000	808	1,000	1,000	653	998	1,000	660	1,000	1,000
Main effects of A and B and interaction	958	1,000	1,000	836	1,000	1,000	724	977	1,000	713	980	1,000
20 % DIF items												
Interaction	364	949	999	41	58	51	42	62	54	47	47	43
Main effect of A	346	976	1,000	385	989	1,000	479	993	1,000	63	42	49
Main effect of A and interaction	766	991	1,000	510	858	994	607	921	999	48	141	547
Main effects of A and B	608	998	1,000	580	999	1,000	464	969	1,000	457	961	1,000
Main effects of A and B and interaction	749	999	1,000	482	969	1,000	392	884	1,000	403	873	1,000

Note: Small, medium, and large refer to DIF effect size

$\log(a) \pm 0.13$, $\log(a) \pm 0.26$, $\log(a) \pm 0.39$, for the last three groups according to the design matrix in Eq. (8) when the DIF size was 0.13, 0.26, and 0.39, respectively. Note that the difficulty parameter did not exhibit DIF.

15.3.2 *Results*

15.3.2.1 Empirical Type I Error Rates

The Type I error rates were 0.054, 0.048, 0.052, and 0.044 for the FLR, LR-AB, LR-A, and LR-B methods, respectively, suggesting a very good control. As shown in Table 15.3, when the anchored test contained 10 or 20 % DIF items, the Type I error rates for the four methods were still very close to their expected value of 0.05. A comparison of the Type I error rates in Tables 15.1 (uniform DIF) and 15.3 (nonuniform DIF) reveals that the inclusion of uniform DIF items (with difference in the difficulty parameters across groups) in the anchored test had a more adverse effect on the DIF assessment than the inclusion of nonuniform DIF items (with difference in the discrimination parameters across groups). This was mainly because the inclusion of uniform DIF items in the anchored test would deteriorate the correspondence between the raw test score used in the LR methods and the ability level simulated from IRT models, whereas the correspondence was not substantially affected by the inclusion of nonuniform DIF items. Note that including DIF items with difference in both the difficulty and discrimination parameters across groups (referred to as nonuniform DIF items in the literature) would also exhibit an adverse effect.

15.3.2.2 Empirical Power Rates

The upper panel of Table 15.4 shows the power rates of the four methods when the anchored test did not contain any DIF items. When the DIF source contained exclusively the interaction between factors A and B, only the FLR method yielded high power rates: 0.084, 0.186, and 0.538 when the DIF size on the discrimination parameter was small (0.13), medium (0.26), and large (0.39), respectively; whereas the other three methods yielded power rates between 0.036 and 0.055. The panel also shows that the FLR method substantially outperformed the other three methods as long as the DIF source contained the interaction. When the main effect of factor was the only DIF source, the LR-A method had the highest power rates, and the LR-B had the lowest power rates. Furthermore, the larger the DIF size, the higher the power rate.

The middle and lower panels of Table 15.4 show the power rates of the four methods where the anchored test contained 10 or 20 % (nonuniform) DIF items, respectively. Take the power rates when the anchored tests did not contain any DIF items as a reference. Across the 15 conditions (5 DIF sources by 3 DIF sizes), the

Table 15.3 Type I error rates ($^0/_{00}$) of the four methods in nonuniform DIF

	FLR			LR-AB			LR-A			LR-B		
DIF source	Small	Medium	Large	Small	Medium	Large	Small	Medium	Large	Small	Medium	Large
10 % DIF items												
Interaction	45	58	54	37	58	47	44	60	52	35	45	42
Main effect of A	44	54	48	48	46	39	45	51	46	47	49	40
Main effect of A and interaction	54	47	51	61	49	48	61	56	44	43	43	47
Main effects of A and B	64	40	46	65	42	49	61	44	45	58	41	44
Main effects of A and B and interaction	47	49	61	50	46	58	55	48	51	43	50	51
20 % DIF items												
Interaction	53	41	58	40	50	57	41	56	50	33	40	56
Main effect of A	54	45	56	52	49	53	60	37	72	54	55	44
Main effect of A and interaction	50	53	46	44	48	59	50	46	51	48	48	59
Main effects of A and B	50	53	55	39	60	56	53	59	45	46	52	51
Main effects of A and B and interaction	53	41	58	40	50	57	41	56	50	33	40	56

Note: Small, medium, and large refer to DIF effect size

Table 15.4 Power rates ($^{0}/_{00}$) of the four methods in nonuniform DIF

	FLR			LR-AB			LR-A			LR-B		
DIF source	Small	Medium	Large	Small	Medium	Large	Small	Medium	Large	Small	Medium	Large
0 % DIF items												
Interaction	84	186	538	44	43	54	47	43	55	43	36	49
Main effect of A	117	573	505	128	665	596	165	751	677	45	49	49
Main effect of A and interaction	200	244	859	138	148	621	194	192	709	46	65	46
Main effects of A and B	201	379	794	202	389	747	154	300	616	170	310	629
Main effects of A and B and interaction	183	699	1,000	125	443	901	110	351	719	112	321	709
10 % DIF items												
Interaction	87	319	465	45	46	49	60	36	45	46	51	50
Main effect of A	81	225	943	85	276	969	104	348	985	59	50	42
Main effect of A and interaction	132	473	620	97	274	274	127	345	347	49	55	40
Main effects of A and B	97	353	763	116	356	749	95	283	613	103	283	576
Main effects of A and B and interaction	151	750	853	115	442	592	104	336	456	102	334	484
20 % DIF items												
Interaction	287	688	768	54	66	52	50	64	53	50	50	52
Main effect of A	52	168	464	53	198	548	59	276	646	49	43	58
Main effect of A and interaction	114	312	524	69	180	325	103	247	397	38	43	67
Main effects of A and B	205	987	809	198	980	785	168	917	630	173	912	638
Main effects of A and B and interaction	145	514	749	101	354	523	82	267	406	100	282	404

Note: Small, medium, and large refer to DIF effect size

mean power rate was increased by -2, -5, -5, and -2 % for the FLR, LR-AB, LR-A, and LR-B methods, respectively, when the anchored tests contained 10 % DIF items, and increased by 1, -5, 2, and -5 % for the four methods, respectively, when the anchored tests contained 20 % DIF items. Thus it can be concluded that the inclusion of 10 or 20 % nonuniform DIF items in the anchored test did not substantially affect the Type I error rates or power rates of these four methods.

Conclusion and Discussion

DIF assessment may be conducted across several grouping factors. In addition to detecting whether an item has DIF, it is also informative to account for DIF source: whether the DIF came from a specific grouping factor or from their interactions. In this study, we incorporated a factorial procedure on the commonly used logistic regression method. The use of design matrices, like those commonly used in factorial ANOVA, enables the decomposition of DIF source into main effects of individual grouping factors and their interaction effects. The parameters in the FLR methods can be interpreted as they are in standard logistic regression. Furthermore, being a nonparametric method, the FLR method is simple to implement and fast to converge, and does not require specification of an item response model or a large sample.

Two simulation studies were conducted to evaluate the performance of the FLR in the detection of uniform and nonuniform DIF, as compared to three other LR methods. The simulation results demonstrate the superiority of the FLR method over the LR-A, LR-B, and LR-AB methods when there was an interaction effect between grouping factors. In reality, interactions among grouping factors can occur and their magnitude may be too large to neglect. In such cases, among the four methods investigated in this study, only the FLR method can yield a higher power of detection. We also investigated whether the FLR method would be adversely affected by including 10 or 20 % DIF items in the anchored test. The results showed a small deflation in the mean power rates, but a substantial inflation in Type I error rates when the anchored test had uniform DIF items with large DIF sizes. The adverse effect was less obvious when the DIF items in the anchored test had different discrimination parameters but the same difficulty parameters across groups.

In this study, all groups were simulated to have an equal mean ability (i.e., no impact). In reality, different groups may have different means (i.e., with impact). It has been shown that the LR method yields inflated Type I error rates and deflated power rates when there is a large impact (Bolt and Gierl 2006; Güler and Penfield 2009). The test raw scores do not match ability levels and thus, the approach fails to place different groups on the same scale for DIF assessment, when groups have very different means. Roussos and Stout (1996) suggest a longer anchored test for large impacts. Even so, the

(continued)

advantages of the FLR method over the LR method would remain unchanged even with large impacts.

This study has implications for DIF research methodology and enables practitioners to assess DIF sources for future item revision. The FLR method can be generalized to assess DIF in polytomous items. Future studies can evaluate the FLR method under different conditions of test lengths, sample sizes, and combinations of uniform and nonuniform DIF items. It is also important to evaluate the FLR method when there is an impact, or when tests consist of both dichotomous and polytomous items.

Acknowledgment The research was supported by the General Research Fund, Hong Kong Research Grants Council (No. 844110).

References

Bolt D, Gierl MJ (2006) Testing features of graphical DIF: application of a regression correction to three nonparametric statistical tests. J Educ Meas 43:313–333. doi:10.1111/j.1756-3984.2006.00019.x

Candell GL, Hulin CL (1986) Cross-language and cross-cultural comparisons in scale translations: independent sources of information about item nonequivalence. J Cross Cult Psychol 17:417–440. doi:10.1177/0022002186017004003

Chen H-F, Jin K-Y, Wang W-C (2012) Assessing differential item functioning when interactions among subgroups exist. Paper presented at the Taiwan education research association international conference on education, Kaohsiung, Taiwan

DeMars CE (2010) Type I error inflation for detecting DIF in the presence of impact. Educ Psychol Meas 70:961–972. doi:10.1177/0013164410366691

Drasgow F (1987) Study of the measurement bias of two standardized psychological tests. J Appl Psychol 72:19–29. doi:10.1037/0021-9010.72.1.19

French BF, Maller SJ (2007) Iterative purification and effect size use with logistic regression for differential item functioning detection. Educ Psychol Meas 67:373–393

Güler N, Penfield RD (2009) A comparison of the logistic regression and contingency table methods for simultaneous detection of uniform and nonuniform DIF. J Educ Meas 46:314–329. doi:10.1111/j.1745-3984.2009.00083.x

Iwata N, Turner RJ, Lloyd DA (2002) Race/ethnicity and depressive symptoms in community-dwelling young adults: a differential item functioning analysis. Psychiatry Res 110:281–289. doi:10.1016/S0165-1781(02)00102-6

Kim J, Oshima TC (2013) Effect of multiple testing adjustment in differential item functioning detection. Educ Psychol Meas 73:458–470. doi:10.1177/0013164412467033

Kim SH, Cohen AS, Park TH (1995) Detection of differential item functioning in multiple groups. J Educ Meas 32:261–276. doi:10.1111/j.1745-3984.1995.tb00466.x

Li YJ, Brooks GP, Johanson GA (2012) Item discrimination and Type I error in the detection of differential item functioning. Educ Psychol Meas 72:847–861. doi:10.1177/0013164411432333

Narayanan P, Swaminathan H (1994) Performance of the Mantel–Haenszel and simultaneous item bias procedures for detecting differential item functioning. Appl Psychol Meas 18:315–328. doi:10.1177/014662169401800403

Narayanan P, Swaminathan H (1996) Identification of items that show nonuniform DIF. Appl Psychol Meas 20:257–274. doi:10.1177/014662169602000306

Penfield RD (2001) Assessing differential item functioning among multiple groups: a comparison of three Mantel–Haenszel procedures. Appl Meas Educ 14:235–259. doi:10.1207/S15324818AME1403_3

Rogers HJ, Swaminathan H (1993) A comparison of logistic regression and Mantel–Haenszel procedures for detecting differential item functioning. Appl Psychol Meas 17:105–116. doi:10.1177/014662169301700201

Roussos L, Stout W (1996) A multidimensionality-based DIF analysis paradigm. Appl Psychol Meas 20:355–371

Somes GW (1986) The generalized Mantel–Haenszel statistics. Am Stat 40:106–108. doi:10.1080/00031305.1986.10475369

Swaminathan H, Rogers HJ (1990) Detecting differential item functioning using logistic regression procedures. J Educ Meas 27:361–370. doi:10.1111/j.1745-3984.1990.tb00754.x

Wang W-C (2000a) Modeling effects of differential item functioning in polytomous items. J Appl Meas 1:63–82

Wang W-C (2000b) The simultaneous factorial analysis of differential item functioning. Methods Psychol Res 5:56–76

Zwick R, Donoghue JR, Grima A (1993) Assessment of differential item functioning for performance tasks. J Educ Stat 15:185–187. doi:10.1111/j.1745-3984.1993.tb00425.x

Chapter 16
MTP2 and Partial Correlations in Monotone Higher-Order Factor Models

Jules L. Ellis

Abstract For binary variables, multivariate positivity of order 2 (MTP2) implies nonnegative partial correlations (NPC). This is so because for any triple of variables, MTP2 is equivalent with conditional association.

Under weak distribution assumptions of the noise variables, monotone higher-order one-factor models imply MTP2 of the manifest variables. This remains true after discretization of the manifest variables. Therefore, MTP2 and NPC cannot be used to discriminate unidimensional monotone latent variable models from multidimensional monotone higher-order one-factor models.

Keywords Conditional association • Multivariate positivity of order 2 • Nonlinear factor analysis • Partial correlation • Second-order factor • Supermodularity

16.1 Introduction

Many item response theory (IRT) models belong to the class of unidimensional monotone latent variable models, as defined by Holland and Rosenbaum (1986). An interesting question is how these models can be characterized by restrictions of the manifest variables. For this, Junker and Ellis (1997) used the property of conditional association (CA) (e.g., Holland and Rosenbaum 1986; De Gooijer and Yuan 2011). The present paper will study the related condition that the manifest variables are multivariate totally positive of order 2 (MTP2) (e.g., Rinott and Scarsini 2006). Bartolucci and Forcina (2005) discussed this condition in the context of IRT models. In other fields, MTP2 is also known as supermodularity of the log density, the FKG inequality, or affiliation (Denuit et al. 2005, pp. 276–278). It is related to the concept of monotone likelihood ratio and uniform conditional stochastic order (Whitt 1982).

J.L. Ellis (✉)
Radboud University Nijmegen, School of Psychology and Artificial Intelligence, Montessorilaan 3, Postbus 9104, 6500 HE Nijmegen, The Netherlands
e-mail: j.ellis@psych.ru.nl

R.E. Millsap et al. (eds.), *Quantitative Psychology Research*, Springer Proceedings in Mathematics & Statistics 89, DOI 10.1007/978-3-319-07503-7_16

The first part of this paper describes how MTP2 is related to the result of Ellis (2014, Theorem 1). Ellis showed that for binary variables, conditional association implies that each triple of variables has nonnegative partial correlations:

$$\text{CA} \Rightarrow \text{NPC}$$

Here, it will be investigated whether the requirement of conditional association can be replaced by the weaker condition of MTP2:

$$\text{MTP2} \Rightarrow \text{NPC?}$$

The relationship between CA and MTP2 is discussed by Holland and Rosenbaum (1986), to which the present paper adds only some details. Holland and Rosenbaum show that for binary variables, CA implies MTP2 (their Theorem 10), but not conversely (their counterexample 6.1):

$$\text{CA} \Rightarrow \text{MTP2}$$

Thus, for binary variables, MTP2 is strictly weaker than CA, and therefore the implication MTP2 $\Rightarrow$ NPC is not directly obvious.

It is not difficult to prove that this implication is indeed true, because MTP2 is preserved under various forms of conditioning. This will be done in the first part of this paper. But then the question becomes: Is there even a difference between CA and MTP2? What kind of models imply MTP2 but not CA? This will be considered in the second part of the paper. It will be considered how MTP2 is related to monotone (possibly nonlinear) factor models.

The plan of the paper is as follows. First, the definitions of the various concepts related to MTP2 will be stated. Next, it will be shown that MTP2 implies NPC for binary variables. Regarding the difference between MTP2 and CA, it will be shown that MTP2 and CA are equivalent for triples of variables. The second half of the paper studies the MTP2 property in monotone factor models. First, it is shown that, under fairly general conditions, monotone one-factor models imply MTP2. Next, this result is generalized to monotone higher-order one-factor models. Finally, in the Discussion, I will point out some implications of this for the practice of testing unidimensionality of psychological tests.

Throughout the paper, some propositions will be labeled as *elementary*. These are propositions of which I suspect that authors in the field of MTP2 find them trivial. I do not find them trivial, so I provide proofs. However, I will omit the proofs of propositions that follow easily from their preceding proposition.

16.2 Definition of MTP2 and Related Concepts

The concept of MTP2 generalizes the idea of a positive correlation, and is also known as the FKG condition or affiliation (Denuit et al. 2005). The definitions of Rinott and Scarsini (2006) will be used here to define MTP2 and related concepts.

Let $\chi := \times_{i=1}^{m} \chi_m$ be a product lattice in $\mathbb{R}^m$. Let the lattice operators be

$$\mathbf{x} \vee \mathbf{y} = (\max\{x_1, y_1\}, \ldots, \max\{x_m, y_m\})$$

$$\mathbf{x} \wedge \mathbf{y} = (\min\{x_1, y_1\}, \ldots, \min\{x_m, y_m\})$$

Definition 1 (TP Order, MTP2, Association). Let $\mathbf{X}$ and $\mathbf{Y}$ be χ-valued random vectors with densities f and g, respectively.

(a) $f \preceq_{\mathrm{TP}} g$ if $f(\mathbf{x})g(\mathbf{y}) \leq f(\mathbf{x} \wedge \mathbf{y})g(\mathbf{x} \vee \mathbf{y})$ for all $\mathbf{x}, \mathbf{y} \in \chi$
(b) f is *MTP2* if $f \preceq_{\mathrm{TP}} f$
(c) $\mathbf{X} \preceq_{\mathrm{TP}} \mathbf{Y}$ if $f \preceq_{\mathrm{TP}} f$
(d) $\mathbf{X}$ is *MTP2* if f is MTP2
(e) If $\mathbf{X}$ consists of two variables, then the term *TP2* is commonly used instead of MTP2.
(f) $\mathbf{X}$ is *associated* (A) if $\mathrm{Cov}(\phi(\mathbf{X}), \psi(\mathbf{X})) \geq 0$ for all nondecreasing functions ϕ and ψ.

Holland and Rosenbaum (1986) discuss the conditional forms of MTP2 and association, where every subset of variables is MTP2 or associated conditionally on any event of the remaining variables.

Definition 2 (Conditional Association, Conditional MTP2).

(a) $\mathbf{X}$ is *conditionally associated* (CA) if for every partition $\mathbf{X} = (\mathbf{Y}, \mathbf{Z})$ and every measurable function η, $\mathbf{Y}|\eta(\mathbf{Z})$ is associated almost surely.
(b) $\mathbf{X}$ is *conditionally MTP2* (CMTP2) if for every partition $\mathbf{X} = (\mathbf{Y}, \mathbf{Z})$ and every measurable function η, $\mathbf{Y}|\eta(\mathbf{Z})$ is MTP2 almost surely.

For the sake of readability, the phrases "measurable" and "almost surely" will be omitted henceforth.

Ellis (2014) discussed how conditional association implies a restriction upon the bivariate correlations. Denote the correlation between variables X and Y by ρ_{XY}.

Definition 3 (Nonnegative Partial Correlations). $\mathbf{X}$ has *nonnegative partial correlations* (NPC) if for every triple (X, Y, Z) of variables in $\mathbf{X}$, $\rho_{XY} \geq \rho_{XZ}\rho_{ZY}$.

16.3 Nonnegative Partial Correlations

In this section it will be considered whether Theorem 1 of Ellis (2014) (for binary variables, CA $\Rightarrow$ NPC) can be generalized to the conclusion that, for binary variables, MTP2 $\Rightarrow$ NPC.

If one considers the proof of Ellis (2014, Theorem 1), then it becomes clear that most of the proof does not require CA. The only exception is the phrase "$\mathrm{Cov}(X, Y|Z) \geq 0$ by conditional association". Below, it will be shown that, under some mild regularity conditions,

$$(X,Y,Z) \quad \text{is MTP2} \Rightarrow \text{Cov}(X,Y|Z) \geq 0.$$

After this, we can obtain a proof for the claim that "for binary variables, MTP2 ⇒ NPC" in the following way: Copy the proof of Theorem 1 of Ellis, but replace the phrase "Cov(X, $Y|Z$) ≥ 0 by conditional association" by the phrase "Cov(X, $Y|Z$) ≥ 0 by MTP2".

It is well known (e.g., Karlin and Rinott 1980; Rinott and Scarsini 2006) that

$$\text{MTP2} \Rightarrow \text{A}$$

The fact that MTP2 and CMTP2 are distinct, nonequivalent conditions, implies that MTP2 is not always preserved under conditioning. It is, however, preserved under many forms of conditioning. One of these forms is described in the following proposition.

Proposition 1 (Elementary). *If* $(\mathbf{X}, \mathbf{Y})$ *is MTP2 and* $\mathbf{Y}$ *has positive densities, then* $\mathbf{X}|\mathbf{Y}$ *is MTP2.*

Proof. Let the densities of $\mathbf{X}|\mathbf{Y}$ and $\mathbf{Y}$ be f and g, respectively. Write the joint density of $(\mathbf{X}, \mathbf{Y})$ as $h(\mathbf{x}, \mathbf{y}) = f(\mathbf{x}|\mathbf{y})g(\mathbf{y})$. It is MTP2 by premise, so for all $\mathbf{x}_1, \mathbf{x}_2, \mathbf{y} \in \chi$, $h(\mathbf{x}_1, \mathbf{y})h(\mathbf{x}_2, \mathbf{y}) \leq h(\mathbf{x}_1 \wedge \mathbf{x}_2, \mathbf{y} \wedge \mathbf{y})h(\mathbf{x}_1 \vee \mathbf{x}_2, \mathbf{y} \vee \mathbf{y})$. After rewriting this with f and g, the four factors $g(\mathbf{y})$ cancel out against each other, yielding $f(\mathbf{x}_1|\mathbf{y})f(\mathbf{x}_2|\mathbf{y}) \leq f(\mathbf{x}_1 \wedge \mathbf{x}_2|\mathbf{y})f(\mathbf{x}_1 \vee \mathbf{x}_2|\mathbf{y})$. This means that $[\mathbf{X}|\mathbf{Y} = \mathbf{y}]$ is MTP2. □

According to Proposition 1, if (X, Y, Z) is MTP2, then $(X, Y)|Z$ is MTP2, and therefore Cov(X, $Y|Z$) ≥ 0. This implies that Ellis' (2014) Theorem 1 can be generalized to MTP2 binary variables.

Corollary 1. *For any triple of binary variables with positive densities (and hence positive variances and correlations smaller than 1): MTP2 ⇒ NPC.*

This answers the initial question, posed in the Introduction. However, since MTP2 is preserved under so many forms of conditioning, one may wonder whether there is at all a difference between MTP2 and CA in the present situation. This will be considered in the next section.

16.4 MTP2 and CA for Three Variables

The difference between MTP2 and CA in case of three variables is discussed in this section. Holland and Rosenbaum give an example with four binary variables that satisfies MTP2 but not CA. But here we consider three variables. In general, one difference between MTP2 and CA is the kind of conditioning events on which they are preserved. MTP2 of $(\mathbf{X}, \mathbf{Y})$ is preserved with conditioning upon events of the form $\mathbf{Y} = \mathbf{y}$, and many more events (Rinott and Scarsini 2006). But unlike CA, MTP2 is not necessarily preserved with conditioning upon events of the form $\eta(\mathbf{Y}) = c$, particularly not when this induces orthant events of the form $[Y_1 < y_1, \ldots, Y_i < y_i, Y_{i+1} > y_i, \ldots, Y_n > y_n]$. Such events provide in a sense conflicting conditioning information, because both $<$ and $>$ are being used. However, such conflicting information is not possible if there is only one conditioning variable.

Proposition 2. *If the triple of random variables (X, Y, Z) is MTP2, and η is a function with $P([\eta(Z) = c]) > 0$, then $(X, Y)|[\eta(Z) = c]$ is MTP2.*

Proof. Denote the range of a variable V by χ_V, and write $\eta^{-1}(\{c\}) := \{x \in \chi_Z : \eta(x) = c\}$. Define $A = B = \chi_X \times \chi_Y \times \eta^{-1}(\{c\})$. Adopting the definitions of Rinott and Scarsini (2006, p. 1253), we have $A \vee B = B$ and $A \wedge B = A$. Write $\mathbf{X} = (X, Y, Z)$; so $[\mathbf{X} \in A] = [\eta(Z) = c]$. Since $\mathbf{X}$ is MTP2, we have $\mathbf{X} \preceq_{\mathrm{TP}} \mathbf{X}$. Now apply Rinott and Scarsini's Theorem 2.5 with $\mathbf{X} = \mathbf{Y}$ and A and B as defined. This yields $\mathbf{X}|[\mathbf{X} \in A] \preceq_{\mathrm{TP}} \mathbf{X}|[\mathbf{X} \in A]$, which means that $\mathbf{X}|[\mathbf{X} \in A]$ is MTP2. □

Corollary 2. *If a triple of variables is MTP2, then it is CMTP2 and hence CA.*

Theorem 1. *For any triple of binary variables, CA $\iff$ MTP2 $\iff$ CMTP2.*

Proof. Holland and Rosenbaum (1986, Theorems 4 and 10) showed that for binary variables, CMTP2 $\iff$ CA $\Rightarrow$ MTP2. By Corollary 1, we also have MTP2 $\Rightarrow$ CMTP2. □

Note that the variables are supposed to be binary in Theorem 1, but not in Proposition 2 and Corollary 2.

16.5 MTP2 in One-Factor Models

Corollary 1 states that *MTP2 $\Rightarrow$ NPC* for binary variables, and this is applicable in models that imply that X is MTP2. But Ellis (2014) already showed that NPC holds in models where X is binary and CA, thus including unidimensional monotone latent variable models for binary variables. For an illustration of the present results it would be nice to find an example where X is MTP2 but not necessarily CA. Obviously, that example cannot be a unidimensional monotone latent variable model. To benefit from a logical structure of propositions, however, this section will first consider unidimensional models. Multidimensional models will be considered in the next section.

Consider a vector of manifest variables $\mathbf{Y} = (Y_1, \ldots, Y_n)$, where the Y_i may be continuous variables. The manifest variables are now denoted by $\mathbf{Y}$ rather than $\mathbf{X}$ to resemble the notation in structural equation modelling. The following definition describes a nonlinear factor model (e.g., Yalcin and Amemiya 2001; Sardy and Victoria-Peser 2012).

Definition 4 (One-Factor Model, Linear, Monotone, Normal, Nonnegative, Noise). $(\mathbf{Y}, \eta)$ is called a *one-factor model* if $\mathbf{Y} = \psi(\Lambda\eta) + \varepsilon$, where η is a scalar random variable, Λ is a matrix of factor loadings, $\boldsymbol{\psi} = (\psi_1, \ldots, \psi_n)$ is a function, and the components of ε are independent of each other and of η. The model will be called *linear* if $\boldsymbol{\psi}$ is the identity. The model will be called *monotone* if each component of $\boldsymbol{\psi}$ is monotone nondecreasing and $\Lambda \geq 0$. The model will be called *nonnegative* if $\Lambda \geq 0$. The model will be called *normal* if each component of ε and η has a normal density. The term *noise* will be used to designate ε.

In a normal linear one-factor model with $\Lambda = \mathbf{1}$ and equal variances of the noise components, it is easy to see that **Y** is MTP2. This is so because the correlation matrix of such **Y** is an equicorrelation matrix, and the inverse Σ^{-1} of such matrices is readily obtained (e.g., Raveh 1985). Σ^{-1} is an M-matrix, that is: Σ is nonsingular, $\Sigma \geq 0$, and $\Sigma^{-1} \leq 0$. For normal variables, that is equivalent to being MTP2 (Karlin and Rinott 1983, p. 422).

However, the conclusion that **Y** is MTP2 can be drawn much more generally. This can be done by adapting the method that Karlin and Rinott (1980) use in the proof of their Propositions 3.7 and 3.8. They use the concept of Pólya frequency functions of order 2 (PF2) (e.g., Efron 1965).

Definition 5 (PF2). A univariate density $f(x)$, with $x \in \mathbb{R}$, is *PF2* if $x_1 \leq x_2, y_1 \leq y_2$ implies

$$\begin{vmatrix} f(x_1 - y_1) & f(x_1 - y_2) \\ f(x_2 - y_1) & f(x_2 - y_2) \end{vmatrix} \geq 0$$

The normal density is an example of a PF2 density. Every PF2 density is log-concave (e.g., Efron 1965, p. 272). The property PF2 is closely related to TP2, the bivariate version of MTP2. TP2 means that for the bivariate density $f(x, y)$, with $x, y \in \mathbb{R}$, $x_1 \leq x_2, y_1 \leq y_2$ implies

$$\begin{vmatrix} f(x_1, y_1) & f(x_1, y_2) \\ f(x_2, y_1) & f(x_2, y_2) \end{vmatrix} \geq 0$$

Now, if $\Lambda = \mathbf{1}$ and each ε_i has a PF2 density, then the linear one-factor model has the form described in Proposition 3.8 of Karlin and Rinott (1980), which entails the conclusion that **Y** is MTP2. Their proof can easily be generalized to the case that the factor loadings are different and the model is merely monotone instead of linear. We need the following elementary fact.

Proposition 3 (Elementary). *Let* $g(x, y) = f(x - \psi(y))$, $\forall x, y \in \mathbb{R}$, *where* ψ *is a monotone nondecreasing function. If f is PF2, then g is TP2.*

Proof. Let $x_1 \leq x_2, y_1 \leq y_2$. Put $z_1 = \psi(y_1)$ and $z_2 = \psi(y_2)$, then $z_1 \leq z_2$. So, applying PF2,

$$f(x_1 - z_1) f(x_2 - z_2) - f(x_1 - z_2) f(x_2 - z_1) \geq 0,$$

$$f(x_1 - \psi(y_1)) f(x_2 - \psi(y_2)) - f(x_1 - \psi(y_2)) f(x_2 - \psi(y_1)) \geq 0,$$

$$g(x_1, y_1) g(x_2, y_2) - g(x_1, y_2) g(x_2, y_1) \geq 0. \quad \square$$

This yields the following result. For binary variables, a similar result was obtained by Holland (1981) and Holland and Rosenbaum (1986), who showed that a unidimensional monotone latent variable model implies CA and CA implies MTP2. However, in such models the noise is generally not independent of the latent variable; so the next proposition pertains to a different class of models. Moreover, the variables are not required to be binary here.

Proposition 4. *If* $(\mathbf{Y}, \eta)$ *is a monotone one-factor model where each noise component* ε_i *has a PF2 density, then* $\mathbf{Y}$ *is MTP2.*

Proof. Denote the density function of any variable Z by f_Z. Then the joint density of $\mathbf{Y}$ is

$$f_{\mathbf{Y}}(y_1,\ldots,y_n) = \int \left(\prod_{i=1}^{n} f_{\varepsilon_i}(y_i - \psi_i(\lambda_i \eta)) \right) f_\eta(\eta)\, d(\varepsilon_1,\ldots,\varepsilon_n,\eta).$$

By Proposition 3, the function $g_i(y_i,\eta) := f_{\varepsilon_i}(y_i - \psi_i(\lambda_i\eta))$ is TP2, because f_{ε_i} is PF2 and ψ_i is nondecreasing and $\lambda_i \geq 0$. Now, the product of MTP2 functions is MTP2, and the integral of MTP2 functions is MTP2 too (Proposition 3.4 of Karlin and Rinott 1980), which shows that $f_{\mathbf{Y}}$ is MTP2. □

16.6 MTP2 in Second and Higher Order Factor Models

In this section we will generalize the result of the previous section (monotone one-factor model $\Rightarrow$ MTP2) to models with second-order factors, and subsequently to models with higher-order factors. Many psychological theories use a second-order factor model (e.g., Chen et al. 2005, and the references therein; Yung et al. 1999). The following definition describes a possibly nonlinear version of such models.

Definition 6 (Monotone Second-Order One-Factor Model). $\mathbf{Y}$ satisfies a *monotone second-order one-factor model with PF2 noise* if all of the following four conditions hold:

1. The variables are a priori clustered into different contents, say $\mathbf{Y} = (\mathbf{Y}_1, \ldots, \mathbf{Y}_k)$ with $\mathbf{Y}_i = (Y_{i1},\ldots,Y_{in_i})$.
2. Each content $\mathbf{Y}_i$ satisfies a monotone one-factor model $\mathbf{Y}_i = \boldsymbol{\psi}_i(\Lambda_i \eta_i) + \boldsymbol{\varepsilon}_i$.
3. The vector variable of factors $\boldsymbol{\eta} = (\eta_1, \ldots, \eta_k)$ in turn satisfies a monotone one-factor model $\boldsymbol{\eta} = \Xi(\Gamma\xi) + \zeta$. Here, ξ is called the *second-order factor.*
4. The vector variable $(\boldsymbol{\varepsilon}_1, \ldots, \boldsymbol{\varepsilon}_k, \zeta, \xi)$ has independent components and each component of $(\boldsymbol{\varepsilon}_1, \ldots, \boldsymbol{\varepsilon}_k, \zeta)$ has PF2 densities.

Proposition 5. *If* $\mathbf{Y}$ *satisfies a monotone second-order one-factor model with PF2 noise, then* $\mathbf{Y}$ *is MTP2.*

Proof. Write $\varepsilon_i = (\varepsilon_{i1}, \ldots, \varepsilon_{in_i})$, $\Lambda_i = (\lambda_{i1}, \ldots, \lambda_{in_i})$ and $\psi_i = (\psi_{i1}, \ldots, \psi_{in_i})$. The joint density of $\mathbf{Y}$ at $\mathbf{y} = (y_{11}, \ldots, y_{kn_k})$ is

$$\int \left(\prod_{i=1}^{k} \prod_{j=1}^{n_i} f_{\varepsilon_{ij}} (y_{ij} - \psi_{ij} (\lambda_{ij} \eta_i)) \right) f_{\boldsymbol{\eta}} (\eta_1, \ldots, \eta_k) d (\varepsilon_{11}, \ldots, \varepsilon_{kn_k}, \eta_1, \ldots, \eta_k)$$

By the Proposition 3, $f_{\varepsilon_{ij}} (y_{ij} - \psi_{ij} (\lambda_{ij} \eta_i))$ is TP2 as a function of (y_{ij}, η_i). By Proposition 4, $\boldsymbol{\eta}$ is MTP2, that is, $f_{\boldsymbol{\eta}}$ is MTP2. So the integrand is a product of MTP2 functions, which is MTP2; and the integral of MTP2 functions is MTP2 (Proposition 3.4 of Karlin and Rinott 1980). □

This proposition might seem to be a special case of Theorem 7 of Holland and Rosenbaum (1986), who use Proposition 3.4 of Karlin and Rinott (1980). However, I am not convinced that their theorem can be applied here, because it requires that the density of $\mathbf{Y}|\boldsymbol{\eta}$ is MTP2 as a function of $(\mathbf{y}, \boldsymbol{\eta})$.

By induction, we can generalize Proposition 5 to higher-order factor models.

Theorem 2. *If* $\mathbf{Y}$ *satisfies a monotone higher-order one-factor model with PF2 noise variables at each level, then* $\mathbf{Y}$ *is MTP2.*

Independent variables satisfy a monotone one-factor model, with all loadings equal to 0. So instead of the restriction that there is a single highest-order factor, we may allow many highest-order factors if these are independent and PF2.

Corollary 3. *If* $\mathbf{Y}$ *satisfies a monotone higher-order multi-factor model, with independent PF2 highest-order factors, and with PF2 noise variables at each level, then* $\mathbf{Y}$ *is MTP2.*

16.7 Discrete Manifest Variables

Many IRT models can be expressed in a form where the manifest variables are obtained by discretization of continuous latent variables. In this section it will be shown that if these latent variables are MTP2, then the discrete manifest variables are MTP2 too. As a background, the model is sketched in Fig. 16.1.

Proposition 6 (Elementary). *If two variables* (X, Y) *are TP2, and* ϕ *is a nondecreasing function, possibly with finite or countable range, then* $(\phi(X), Y)$ *is TP2.*

Proof. Denote the density of (X, Y) at (x, y) by p_{xy}, and the density of $(\phi(X), Y)$ at (n, y) by f_{ny}. These densities might be densities with respect to different probability measures (for example, if ϕ has finite range while X is continuous in the sense that it has a density with respect to the Lebesgue measure). Nonetheless, we can write the new density as

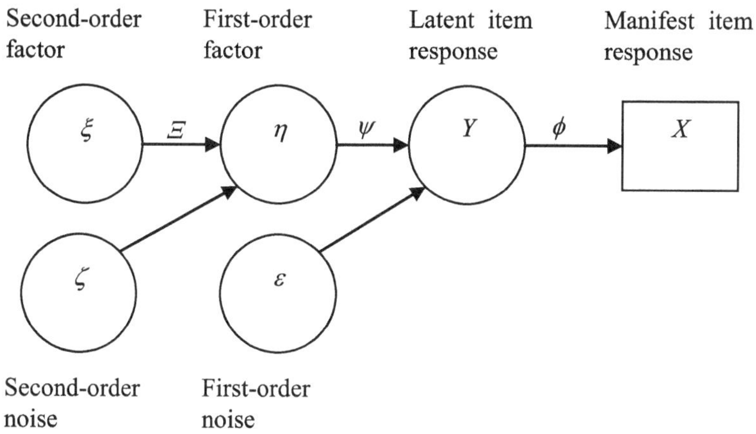

Fig. 16.1 Overview of transformations in a second-order factor model with discretization

$$f_{ny} = \int_{x \in \phi^{-1}(n)} p_{xy} = \int_{u \in \phi^{-1}(n)} p_{uy}.$$

Now, $(\phi(X), Y)$ is TP2 if, for all $m \leq n, y \leq z$,

$$f_{my} f_{nz} \geq f_{mz} f_{ny}.$$

This can be rewritten as

$$\int_{x \in \phi^{-1}(m)} p_{xy} \int_{u \in \phi^{-1}(n)} p_{uz} \geq \int_{x \in \phi^{-1}(m)} p_{xz} \int_{u \in \phi^{-1}(n)} p_{uy}$$

$$\int_{x \in \phi^{-1}(m)} \int_{u \in \phi^{-1}(n)} p_{xy} p_{uz} \geq \int_{x \in \phi^{-1}(m)} \int_{u \in \phi^{-1}(n)} p_{xz} p_{uy}$$

This is true if $p_{xy} p_{uz} \geq p_{xz} p_{uy}$ for all $x \in \phi^{-1}(m), u \in \phi^{-1}(n), y \leq z$, which is true because (X, Y) is TP2. □

For the next result, we need the support condition used in Proposition 2.15 of Rinott and Scarsini (2006). However, for ease of reading we will replace it by the more restrictive condition that all densities are positive. Recall that χ is the product lattice in which $(X_1, \ldots, X_n)$ assumes values.

Proposition 7 (Elementary). *Suppose the density of* $(X_1, \ldots, X_n)$ *is everywhere positive within* χ. *If* $(X_1, \ldots, X_n)$ *is MTP2, and* ϕ *is a nondecreasing function, then* $(\phi(X_1), X_2, \ldots, X_n)$ *is MTP2.*

Proof. Use the fact that $(X_1, \ldots, X_n)$ is MTP2 if and only if each pair of variables is TP2 given the other variables (Proposition 2.15 of Rinott and Scarsini 2006). For $A \subseteq \{1, \ldots, n\}$, denote the variables X_i with $i \notin A$ as $\mathbf{X}_{-A}$. The premise implies that each $(X_i, X_j)|\mathbf{X}_{-\{i,j\}}$ is MTP2, and then by Proposition 6 we have that $(\phi(X_1), X_j)|\mathbf{X}_{-\{1,j\}}$ is MTP2. It remains to be proven that for $i, j > 1$, $(X_i, X_j)|\phi(X_1), \mathbf{X}_{-\{1,i,j\}}$ is MTP2. This follows from Theorem 2.5 of Rinott and Scarsini (2006), with $(X_1, X_i, X_j)|\mathbf{X}_{-\{1,i,j\}}$ as their $\mathbf{X}$ and $\mathbf{Y}$, and $[\phi(X_1) = c]$ as their $\mathbf{A}$ and $\mathbf{B}$, using the fact that $(X_1, X_i, X_j)|\mathbf{X}_{-\{1,i,j\}}$ is MTP2. □

Proposition 8 (Elementary). *Suppose the density of $(X_1, \ldots, X_n)$ is everywhere positive within χ. If $(X_1, \ldots, X_n)$ is MTP2, and $\phi_1, \ldots, \phi_n$ are nondecreasing functions, then $(\phi_1(X_1), \ldots, \phi_n(X_n))$ is MTP2.*

Proof. Apply Proposition 7 repeatedly. □

Now suppose that $\mathbf{Y}$ satisfies a factor model of Theorem 2, and that $\mathbf{X}$ is obtained from $\mathbf{Y}$ by nondecreasing transformations $X_i = \phi_i(Y_i)$. An example of this would be if Y_i contains the latent response to the ith question of a psychological test, and the subjects determine their observable response X_i by discretizing Y_i. This is the model underlying polychoric correlations (e.g., Olsson 1979). So, even if the range of each Y_i is $\mathbb{R}$, the range of each X_i may be a subset of $\mathbb{N}$, such as $\{1, 2, 3, 4\}$.

Theorem 3. *If $\mathbf{Y}$ satisfies a monotone higher-order one-factor model with PF2 noise variables at each level, and has positive densities everywhere, and $\mathbf{X}$ is obtained from $\mathbf{Y}$ by monotone nondecreasing transformations (possibly discretization), then $\mathbf{X}$ is MTP2.*

In this way we have constructed a fairly large class of psychometric models that have manifest variables that are MTP2 but not necessarily CA.

16.8 Discussion

According to Corollary 1, Ellis' (2014) Theorem 1 can be extended from binary CA variables to binary MTP2 variables. The subsequent results show that this is so because, for triples of variables, MTP2 and CA are in fact equivalent. So we have the following implications for binary variables, shown in Fig. 16.2.

In a (possibly nonlinear) monotone one-factor model with noise components that have PF2 densities, the manifest variables are MTP2. So, in a monotone second-order factor model with similar restrictions, the first-order factors are MTP2. This can be used to show that the manifest variables are MTP2, too. By induction, it follows that in any monotone higher-order one-factor model with PF2 noise components, the manifest variables are MTP2. It was shown that this remains true after discretization of the manifest variables with nondecreasing functions.

The latter conclusion implies that testing of MTP2 cannot be used to distinguish between unidimensional monotone latent variable models or monotone one-

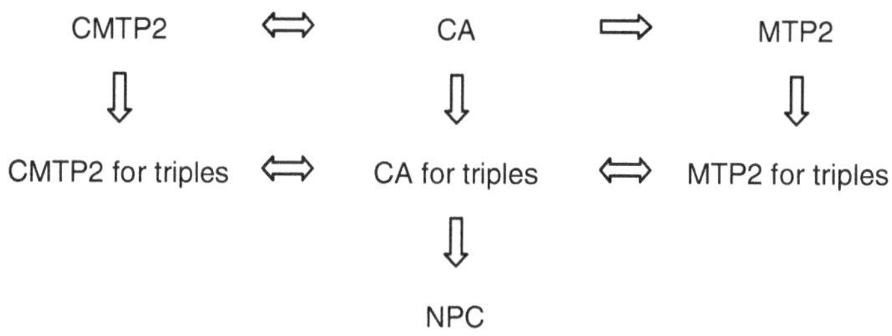

Fig. 16.2 Implications between types of association for binary variables

factor models, on the one hand, versus multidimensional monotone higher-order one-factor models with PF2 noise, on the other hand. This is important, because many psychological tests are constructed within a domain for which a second-order or third-order factor model holds according to the theory. All items belonging to the same higher-order factor would be MTP2, so testing of MTP2 cannot be used to assess whether they belong to the same first-order factor.

For example, suppose intelligence tests satisfy Cattell–Horn–Carroll (CHC) theory (Flanagan et al. 2010) with PF2 noise, and that the scores on items within each test can be modelled by discretization in this way. Then all intelligence items jointly should be MTP2. Then, within the domain of intelligence items, one would generally expect to find item sets that are MTP2, even if they are not unidimensional in the sense of a unidimensional monotone latent variable model or a monotone one-factor model. For example, combining items from crystallized and fluid intelligence would lead to a test that is multidimensional but MTP2. As far as one believes CHC-theory, therefore, MTP2 would not be very useful in the assessment of unidimensionality of intelligence tests. However, if a violation of MTP2 is found, this would be all the more important, because it suggests a violation of CHC-theory.

References

Bartolucci F, Forcina A (2005) Likelihood inference on the underlying structure of IRT models. Psychometrika 70:31–43

Chen FF, Sousa KH, West SG (2005) Testing measurement invariance of second-order factor models. Struct Equ Model 12:471–491

Denuit M, Dhaene J, Goovaerts M, Kaas R (2005) Actuarial theory for dependent risks. Wiley, Chichester

De Gooijer JG, Yuan A (2011) Some exact tests for manifest properties of latent trait models. Comput Stat Data Anal 55:34–44

Efron B (1965) Increasing properties of Pólya frequency functions. Ann Math Stat 36:272–279

Ellis JL (2014) An inequality for correlations in unidimensional monotone latent variable models for binary variables. Psychometrika 79:303–316. doi:10.1007/S11336-013-9341-5

Flanagan DP, Fiorello CA, Ortiz SO (2010) Enhancing practice through application of Cattell–Horn–Carroll theory and research: a "third method" approach to specific learning disability identification. Psychol Sch 47:739–760. doi:10.1002/pits

Holland PW (1981) When are item response models consistent with observed data? Psychometrika 46:79–92
Holland PW, Rosenbaum PR (1986) Conditional association and unidimensionality in monotone latent variable models. Ann Stat 14:1523–1543
Junker BW, Ellis JL (1997) A characterization of monotone unidimensional latent variable models. Ann Stat 25:1327–1343
Karlin S, Rinott Y (1980) Classes of orderings of measures and related correlation inequalities, I. Multivariate totally positive distributions. J Multivar Anal 10:467–498
Karlin S, Rinott Y (1983) M-matrices as covariance matrices of multinormal distributions. Linear Algebra Appl 52(53):419–438
Olsson U (1979) Maximum likelihood estimation of the polychoric correlation coefficient. Psychometrika 44:443–460
Raveh A (1985) On the use of the inverse of the correlation matrix in multivariate data analysis. Am Stat 39:39–42
Rinott Y, Scarsini M (2006) Total positivity order and the normal distribution. J Multivar Anal 97:1251–1261
Sardy S, Victoria-Peser M-P (2012) Isotone additive latent variable models. Stat Comput 22:647–659
Whitt W (1982) Multivariate monotone likelihood ratio and uniform conditional stochastic order. J Appl Probab 19:695–701
Yalcin I, Amemiya Y (2001) Nonlinear factor analysis as a statistical method. Stat Sci 16:275–294
Yung Y-F, Thissen D, McLeod LD (1999) On the relationship between the higher-order factor model and the hierarchical factor model. Psychometrika 64:113–128

Chapter 17
A Comparison of Confirmatory Factor Analysis of Binary Data on the Basis of Tetrachoric Correlations and of Probability-Based Covariances: A Simulation Study

Karl Schweizer, Xuezhu Ren, and Tengfei Wang

Abstract Although tetrachoric correlations provide a theoretically well-founded basis for the investigation of binary data by means of confirmatory factor analysis according to the congeneric model, the outcome does not always meet the expectations. As expected from analyzing the procedure of computing tetrachoric correlations, the data must show a high quality for achieving good results. In a simulations study it was demonstrated that such a quality could be established by a very large sample size. Robust maximum likelihood estimation improved model-data fit but not the appropriateness of factor loadings. In contrast, probability-based covariances and probability-based correlations as input to confirmatory factor analysis yielded a good model-data fit in all sample sizes. Probability-based covariances in combination with the weighted congeneric model additionally performed best concerning the absence of dependency on item marginals in factor loadings whereas probability-based correlations did not. The results demonstrated that it is possible to find a link function that enables the use of probability-based covariances for the investigation of binary data.

Keywords Confirmatory factor analysis • Binary data • Congeneric model • Weighted congeneric model • Tetrachoric correlation • Probability-based covariance • Link function

---

K. Schweizer (✉) • T. Wang
Department of Psychology, Goethe University Frankfurt, Grüneburgplatz 1, 60323 Frankfurt a. M., Germany
e-mail: K.Schweizer@psych.uni-frankfurt.de; wangtfpsy@gmail.com

X. Ren
Institute of Psychology, Huazhong University of Science and Technology, 1037 Luoyu Rd., Wuhan 430074, China
e-mail: renxz@hust.edu.cn

R.E. Millsap et al. (eds.), *Quantitative Psychology Research*, Springer Proceedings in Mathematics & Statistics 89, DOI 10.1007/978-3-319-07503-7_17

17.1 Introduction

The investigation of the structure of binary data by means of confirmatory factor analysis is especially demanding since binary data do not show the characteristics that qualify data for the investigation by this method directly. Binary data differ from what is expected concerning the scale level and the distribution. So it is necessary to modify either the data or the model of confirmatory factor analysis appropriately before conducting the investigation. In the past the modification of the data usually preceded confirmatory factor analysis of binary data. Tetrachoric correlations were computed for this purpose and used as input to confirmatory factor analysis (Muthén 1984, 1993). These correlations are expected to provide estimates of the correlations between the underlying variables that are assumed to be continuous. Unfortunately the results of confirmatory factor analysis achieved this way were not always as good as expected. Therefore, the use of the robust maximum likelihood estimation method (Bryant and Satorra 2012; Satorra and Bentler 1994) was suggested in combination with tetrachoric correlations. This estimation method is expected to compensate for deviations from the normal distribution. Such deviations were found to have a detrimental influence on the outcome of confirmatory factor analysis (Fan and Hancock 2012; West et al. 1995).

The research work presented in this paper is guided by the hypothesis that the unfavorable outcomes of investigating tetrachoric correlations by means of confirmatory factor analysis are the results of a low quality of the binary data that is mainly due to a low sample size. Since increasing the sample size is expected to improve the quality of data, in a simulation study the effect of the sample size on the outcome of confirmatory factor analysis is investigated. This investigation is restricted to confirmatory factor analysis according to versions of the congeneric model of measurement (Jöreskog 1971). Furthermore, an alternative method of investigating binary data is considered. This method requires probability-based covariances as input to confirmatory factor analysis (Schweizer 2013). In this point it is in agreement with the original purpose for which confirmatory factor analysis was proposed (Jöreskog 1970). Another characteristic is the integration of a link function into the model of measurement. It gives rise to a weighted version of the congeneric model.

17.1.1 The Tetrachoric Correlation and Its Threshold Problem

This section serves the presentation of the tetrachoric correlation and the argument that the computation of this correlation is impaired by the threshold problem. This problem denotes the special sensitivity of the estimation of thresholds as part of the computation of tetrachoric correlations to the influence of imprecision and error. It is a sensitivity that comes into play when the probabilities of the binary events are very small or very high. In the following paragraphs this sensitivity is traced back to the normal distribution function that plays a major role in the computation of tetrachoric correlations.

The idea of a correlation that estimates the relationship between two continuous variables on the basis of binary data, which are assumed to originate from these continuous variables, was presented by Pearson (1900). This correlation is denoted tetrachoric correlation. It is computed from binary data that follow a binomial distribution; but the outcome of the computation is expected to refer to the underlying variables that are continuous and follow the normal distribution. Therefore, the method of computing tetrachoric correlations must not only provide an estimate of the relationship between two variables but also accomplish the switch from the binomial to normal distributions.

There are several methods that have been proposed for estimating tetrachoric correlations (e.g., Divgi 1979; Owen 1956; Tallis 1962). The most influential method appears to be the maximum likelihood estimation method. A major characteristic of this method is the estimation of latent thresholds (Tallis 1962). The cumulative normal distribution function plays an important role in estimating latent thresholds. In order to arrive at a formal description, assume the continuous random variable V following the normal distribution, the binary random variable X with zero and one as values and the threshold τ. In the first step the relationship of the probability that X equals one $\Pr(X = 1)$ and the probability that V is larger than τ $\Pr(V > \tau)$ is specified:

$$\Pr(X = 1) = \Pr(V > \tau) \tag{17.1}$$

Next, the probability that V is larger than τ is described by means of the cumulative normal distribution function:

$$\Pr(V > \tau) = \int_{-\infty}^{\tau} \frac{e^{-v^2/2}}{\sqrt{2\pi}} dv \tag{17.2}$$

where τ limits the cumulative normal distribution function and v is a quantity varying between $-\infty$ and τ. The short term that is usually selected for representing this function is Φ:

$$\Phi(\tau) = \int_{-\infty}^{\tau} \frac{e^{-v^2/2}}{\sqrt{2\pi}} dv \tag{17.3}$$

Relating Eqs. (17.1)–(17.3) to each other establishes a relationship between parameters of the binomial and normal distributions.

In the case of the computation of the tetrachoric correlation it is necessary to estimate the threshold instead of the probability that X equals one. Therefore, the inverse of the cumulative normal distribution function Φ^{-1} needs to be considered:

$$\tau = \Phi^{-1}[\Pr(X = 1)] \tag{17.4}$$

Equation 17.4 is achieved in considering the Eqs. (17.1)–(17.3). It relates the threshold to the probability that X equals one. It is useful for the computation of tetrachoric correlations since probabilities serve as the input for the computation.

The threshold problem that denotes the proneness of estimates to distortions due to imprecision and error becomes especially obvious in the investigation of the properties of the normal distribution function ϕ:

$$\phi(v) = \frac{e^{-v^2/2}}{\sqrt{2\pi}} \tag{17.5}$$

From Eq. (17.5) it is obvious that for v larger than two and v smaller than minus two ϕ returns a rather small number. It is asymptotic. Furthermore, the slope of this function is nonlinear, as it is obvious from the first derivative:

$$\frac{d}{dv}\phi(v) = -v\frac{e^{-v^2/2}}{\sqrt{2\pi}} \tag{17.6}$$

and approaches zero for large positive and negative values of v. In the tail areas of the distribution, which in this paper are the areas of the normal distribution that are at least two standard deviations away from the mean, it returns a value larger than -0.11 (but smaller than 0), respectively, smaller than 0.11 (but larger than zero).

Because of the low slope and the asymptotic course of the function in the tail areas a major change of the threshold within these areas can be expected to have a very minor effect on the probability that X equals one only. In contrast, even a minor change of the probability can lead to a large effect on the threshold in these tail areas. So, if the probability that X equals one is rather low or high in a binary random variable, a *small* distortion due to imprecision or error can have a *large* effect on the estimate of the corresponding threshold and, consequently, on the estimation of the tetrachoric correlation. Especially in small sample sizes the probability computed as the number of selected events divided by all events may not precisely reflect the true probability and lead to an inappropriate estimate of the threshold because of imprecision.

However, since the high sensitivity to distortion due to imprecision or error is restricted to the tail areas, it can be expected that the tetrachoric correlation does well if the considered binary variables show probabilities that are neither very high nor very low. Furthermore, the quality of the data is of importance. If the quality is very high that is usually achieved by a very large sample size, this sensitivity is not at all disadvantageous. There were attempts to meet this quality demand by the transformation of the margins (Genest and Lévesque 2009) and an asymptotic expansion of the distribution (Ogasawara 2010).

17.1.2 *The Probability-Based Covariance Complemented by a Link Function*

This section concentrates on the probability-based covariance as basis for the investigation of binary data by means of confirmatory factor analysis. Although the probability-based covariance is especially well suited for confirmatory factor analysis that expects variances and covariances as input, it is not without problems. The problem is that it does not consider the switch from the distribution of the binary random variables, on the one hand, to the normal distribution, on the other hand. In the following paragraphs the probability-based covariance is presented and a link function for overcoming this problem is described.

The probability-based covariance is a covariance that is achieved on the basis of probabilities. It was proposed in order to overcome the difference between the scale levels characterizing binary random variables and continuous random variables (Schweizer 2013). The computation of the probability-based covariance is accomplished in two steps. At first probabilities are computed. Given two binary random variables X_i and X_j $(i, j = 1, \ldots, p)$ with zero and one as values it is necessary to compute the probabilities that X_i equals one $Pr(X_i = 1)$, that X_j equals one $Pr(X_j = 1)$, and that both at the same time equal one $Pr(X_i = 1 \wedge X_i = 1)$. Then the probability-based covariance of the binary random variables X_i and X_j $cov(X_i, X_j)$ is computed according to the following definition:

$$\mathrm{cov}(X_i, X_j) = \Pr(X_l = 1 \wedge X_j = 1) - \Pr(X_i = 1)\Pr(X_j = 1) \tag{17.7}$$

The right-hand part of this equation relates the probabilities to each other and retains the scale level of the probabilities that is continuous. Therefore, the probability-based covariance is well suited as input to confirmatory factor analysis concerning the scale level. The standard confirmatory factor model is the congeneric model that assumes continuous variables (Jöreskog 1971).

However, the probability-based covariance is not without a major problem. The problem is the difference between the distributions of the data and of the variables of the model of measurement. Binary data show a binomial distribution whereas the model of measurement includes continuous variables following the normal distribution. Because of this difference the completely standardized factor loadings computed even from probability-based covariances show dependency on item marginals (Kubinger 2003; Torgerson 1958) that characterizes factor loadings obtained from ordinary covariances and correlations. This dependency becomes obvious in comparing the completely standardized factor loadings associated with very low and very high probabilities of the binary events with the completely standardized factor loadings obtained from medium degrees of probability. Quite large differences can be observed this way.

Dependency on item marginals can be eliminated by means of a link function. The generalized linear model (McCullagh and Nelder 1985; Nelder and Wedderburn 1972) includes a link function for accomplishing the switch between different distributions. Various link functions have been proposed for this purpose, which mostly concentrate on means. The link function g relates the random variable η serving as latent predictor to the random variable μ serving as criterion such that

$$\eta = g(\mu) \tag{17.8}$$

(see McCullagh and Nelder 1985, p. 20). The link function for relating probability-based covariances to the model of the covariance matrix of confirmatory factor analysis (Jöreskog 1970) must apply to variances and covariances instead of to means. The function w has been proposed as link function for this purpose (Schweizer 2013). This function that is actually a weight function is defined with respect to the binary random variable X_i ($i = 1, \ldots, p$) with zero and one as values such that

$$\mathrm{w}(X_i) = \sqrt{\Pr(X_i = 1)\left[1 - \Pr(X_i = 1)\right]/0.25} \tag{17.9}$$

Because of the constant of 0.25 the weight function returns numbers between zero and one. This link function has done well when considered in combination with models including constrained factor loadings.

Furthermore, two ways of employing this weight function have been proposed: the criterion-focused and predictor-focused ways because these ways create different properties. The *predictor-focused way* demands the multiplication of weights with factor loadings. The various weights are inserted into the $p \times p$ diagonal matrix $\mathbf{W}$ as the diagonal elements and presented as part of the model of the covariance matrix

$$\Sigma = (\mathbf{W}\Lambda)\Phi(\mathbf{W}\Lambda)' + \Theta \tag{17.10}$$

where Σ is the $p \times p$ model-implied matrix of variances and covariances, Λ is the $p \times q$ matrix of factor loadings, $\mathbf{\Phi}$ the $q \times q$ matrix of the variances and covariances of latent variables, and Θ the $p \times p$ diagonal matrix of error variances.

In contrast, the *criterion-focused way* requires the division of the probability-based covariances by the corresponding weights, and in doing so the constant (0.25) is omitted. Again, for the formal representation the weights are included into a weight matrix. Since this time the weights have to serve as dividers, the weight matrix of the criterion-focused way is represented by the $p \times p$ diagonal matrix $\mathbf{W}^{-1}$. Finally the empirical $p \times p$ matrix $\mathbf{S}$ that is approximated in confirmatory factor analysis is achieved by weighting the $p \times p$ matrix of the probability-based covariances $\mathbf{C}_{\mathrm{PbC}}$ appropriately:

$$\mathbf{S} = \mathbf{W}^{-1}\mathbf{C}_{\mathrm{PbC}}\mathbf{W}^{-1} \tag{17.11}$$

This way of employing the weight function yields correlations that are addressed as probability-based correlations and should be similar to Phi correlations. Because of the omission of the constant of .25 the inverse weight matrix W-1 of Equation 11 is not the exact inverse of W of Eq. (17.10).

The two ways of employing the link function are not equivalent. Instead they show a fundamental difference. In the criterion-focused way the link function is applied to the true and error variances in the same way. Implicitly it is assumed that the distortion as part of the initial dichotomization leading to the binary nature of the data affected the true and error variances equally. The outcome of selecting this way is a correlation matrix. In contrast, in the predictor-focused way the link function is applied to the true component of measurement, and its influence is restricted to the true variance. In this case the assumption is that the deviation of the observed distribution from the symmetric binomial distribution is the result of a systematic modification of the originally continuous and normally distributed data. Systematic modification means that the true component of measurement is modified in a systematic way and that the true variance is affected by the modification but not the error variance. According to this position it would contradict the random nature of error to assume that the error component and error variance reflect the systematic modification of the data.

17.1.3 The Standard and Weighted Versions of the Congeneric Model of Measurement

The investigation of the binary data can be accomplished by means of the congeneric model of measurement (Jöreskog 1971) that is to be considered as the standard model of confirmatory factor analysis. This model is given by the following equation:

$$\mathbf{y} = \boldsymbol{\mu} + \boldsymbol{\Lambda}\boldsymbol{\eta} + \boldsymbol{\varepsilon} \tag{17.12}$$

where $\mathbf{y}$ is the $p \times 1$ vector of observations, $\boldsymbol{\mu}$ the vector of intercepts, $\boldsymbol{\Lambda}$ is the $p \times q$ matrix of factor loadings, $\boldsymbol{\eta}$ the $q \times 1$ vector of latent variables (= latent factors), and $\boldsymbol{\varepsilon}$ the $p \times 1$ vector of error components. The first part (a) of Fig. 17.1 gives a graphical representation of this model.

The ellipse represents the latent variable and the rectangles the manifest variables. Arrows with solid shafts represent parameters that need to be estimated whereas dashed shafts signify that the parameters are constrained. The variance of the latent variable is constrained. This model is suitable for the investigation of tetrachoric correlations and also probability-based correlations in the criterion-focused way.

Realizing the predictor-focused way as a congeneric model is a bit of a problem since the weight matrix must be integrated into the model of measurement in order to achieve the weighted congeneric model. Equation (17.12) needs to be changed accordingly:

$$\mathbf{y} = \boldsymbol{\mu} + (\mathbf{W}\boldsymbol{\Lambda})\boldsymbol{\eta} + \boldsymbol{\varepsilon} \tag{17.13}$$

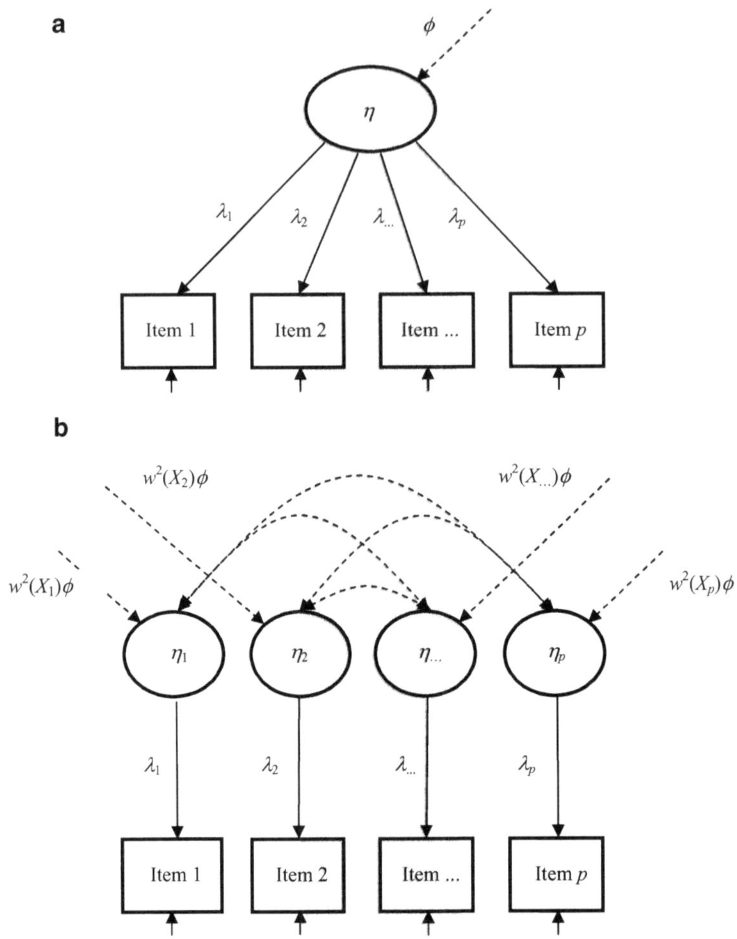

Fig. 17.1 Illustrations of the original (**a**) and weighted (**b**) congeneric models of measurement

where **W** is the $p \times p$ diagonal matrix including the weights. The problem with the right-hand part of Eq. (17.13) is that the weights are fixed whereas the factor loadings need to be estimated. In order to be able to estimate the parameters, it is necessary to separate the weights and factor loadings from each other.

Unfortunately, the separation demands a major modification of the standard congeneric model. The first step in doing so is concerning the number of latent variables. The latent variable of the original model that is normally expected to represent one construct is replaced by as many latent variables as there are manifest variables. These latent variables are assumed to represent the same construct and, therefore, to correlate perfectly with each other. Furthermore, since each latent variable has one factor loading from one manifest variable only, the weight can be merged with the variance of the corresponding latent variable, i. e. they are multiplied with each other. Because of the replacement of one by several latent variables the definitions of some components of Eq. (17.10) need to be changed: the original $q \times q$ matrix of the variances and covariances of latent variables $\mathbf{\Phi}$ is modified and subdivided into two $p \times p$ matrices $\mathbf{\Phi}_{\mathrm{V}}$ and $\mathbf{\Phi}_{\mathrm{C}}$ such that

$$\mathbf{\Phi} = \mathbf{\Phi}_{\mathrm{V}} + \mathbf{\Phi}_{\mathrm{C}} \tag{17.14}$$

where $\mathbf{\Phi}_{\mathrm{V}}$ is a diagonal matrix including the variances of the latent variables that are set equal to one and each element of $\mathbf{\Phi}_{\mathrm{C}}$ corresponds to the number one with the exception of the elements of the main diagonal since these elements are zero. Additionally, the original $p \times q$ matrix of factor loadings Λ becomes a $p \times p$ matrix. The elements of the main diagonal are estimated whereas the other elements are fixed to zero. The model of the covariance matrix that reflects the modification necessary for realizing the weighted congeneric model of measurement is given by

$$\Sigma = \Lambda\left(\mathbf{W}\mathbf{\Phi}_{\mathrm{V}}\mathbf{W}' + \mathbf{\Phi}_{\mathrm{C}}\right)\Lambda' + \Theta \tag{17.15}$$

The definitions of the other components of Eq. (17.15) correspond to the definitions provided for Eq. (17.10). Because of the in-built assumption that there is perfect correlation between the latent variables the factor loadings are estimated with respect to one latent variable only. However, this model is not without problems since varying sizes of the variances may influence the correlations among the latent variables. The second part (b) of Fig. 17.1 provides an illustration of this weighted congeneric model. As is obvious from the dashed lines, the modified variances of the latent variables and the relationships between the latent variables are constrained whereas the factor loadings are free for estimation.

17.2 The Present Study

The major objective of the study was to compare the two methods of investigating binary data by means of confirmatory factor analysis by contrasting their properties and by conducting a simulation study. Since the investigation of the properties already made obvious that the performance of the tetrachoric correlation would heavily depend on the characteristics and the quality of the data, four different sample sizes were considered: 200, 400, 1,000, and 2,000, in addition to a broad range of probabilities.

Table 17.1 Population pattern used for the generation of simulated data

1.00								
0.25	1.00							
0.25	0.25	1.00						
0.25	0.25	0.25	1.00					
0.25	0.25	0.25	0.25	1.00				
0.25	0.25	0.25	0.25	0.25	1.00			
0.25	0.25	0.25	0.25	0.25	0.25	1.00		
0.25	0.25	0.25	0.25	0.25	0.25	0.25	1.00	
0.25	0.25	0.25	0.25	0.25	0.25	0.25	0.25	1.00

17.2.1 Data Generation and Analysis

The generation of the random data was conducted according to a specific population pattern. This pattern was assumed to result from correlating nine continuous variables with each other where all correlations were 0.25. Table 17.1 shows the lower triangle of this population pattern.

The next step served the generation of four types of matrices of continuous and normally distributed random data: 200×9, 400×9, $1{,}000 \times 9$, and $2{,}000 \times 9$ matrices. In order to achieve the structure according to the population pattern, these matrices were re-computed in using weights achieved by means of a procedure proposed by Jöreskog and Sörbom (2001). The outcomes of the re-computation were the matrices of simulated data that provided the outset for the construction of binary data. Furthermore, these matrices served as continuous data for the standard case of confirmatory factor analysis since they could be assumed to follow the normal distribution.

Next, the numbers of the columns of the re-computed matrices were dichotomized by transforming them into zeros and ones. In order to create binary items that were very demanding to the methods of data analysis, splits of the continuous data giving rise to a broad range of probability levels were selected. There were splits according to the following nine proportions: 0.10, 0.20, 0.30, 0.40, 0.50, 0.60, 0.70, 0.80, and 0.90. So the 10 % smaller numbers of the first column were transformed into zeros and the remaining numbers into ones. In the second column zeros replaced the 20 % smaller numbers whereas the other numbers were changed into ones. The third to ninth columns were processed in the same way in considering the other splits of the list in corresponding order. The data matrices obtained this way provided the basis for computing matrices of tetrachoric correlations and of probability-based covariances, respectively, correlations.

It was the plan to compute 100 matrices of simulated data of each type of matrix. However, it turned out that the outcomes showed a very high degree of variability if tetrachoric correlations were investigated by means of the congeneric model of measurement and the sample sizes were 200, 400, and 1,000, as it is especially obvious from the chi-squares obtained for the sample size of 400 (see Fig. 17.2).

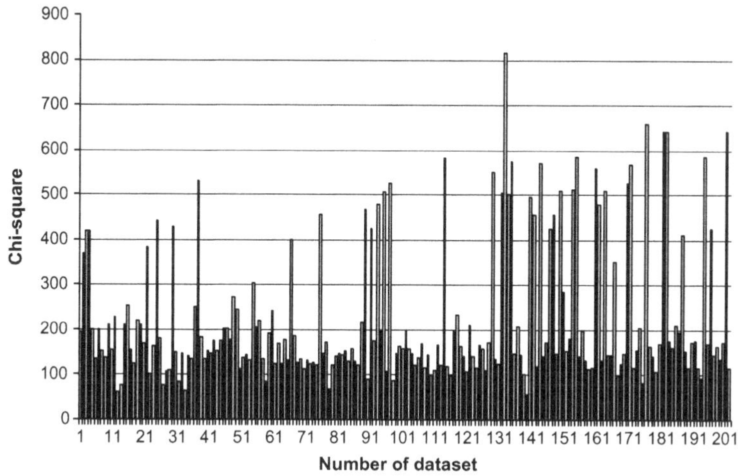

Fig. 17.2 Chi-squares observed in confirmatory factor analysis according to the congeneric model of measurement with tetrachoric correlations as input for $N = 400$

As is obvious from this figure, the chi-squares show an enormous variability. Therefore, it was decided to have 200 matrices for this kind of investigations in sample sizes of 200, 400, and 1,000. Furthermore, matrices leading to tetrachoric correlations larger than 0.80 or showing lack of convergence in the investigation of structure were eliminated and replaced by new matrices. As a consequence, 210 matrices of the 200×9 type, 260 matrices of the 400×9 type, and 206 matrices of the $1{,}000 \times 9$ type were generated for the combination of the congeneric model and tetrachoric correlations. In contrast, it was not necessary to have more than 100 matrices of the $2{,}000 \times 9$ type.

Confirmatory factor analysis according to the congeneric model (Jöreskog 1971) was conducted if tetrachoric correlations served as input or probability-based covariances that were additionally transformed by a link function, as it is described by Eq. (17.11), for obtaining probability-based correlations. Furthermore, confirmatory factor analysis according to the weighted congeneric model [see Eqs. (17.13) and (17.15)] was conducted. In the first case the model comprised one latent variable and nine manifest variables. In the second case there were nine latent and nine manifest variables, and the latent variables were constrained to correlate perfectly with each other. Because of the special demands of the weighted congeneric model the following link function that was actually a weight function leading to squared weights $w^2(X_i)$ was considered:

$$w^2(X_i) = \left\{ \sqrt{\frac{0.25}{\mathrm{var}(\mathrm{Pr}_i)\left[1 - \mathrm{var}(\mathrm{Pr}_i)\right]}} + \frac{0.25}{\mathrm{var}(\mathrm{Pr}_i)\left[1 - \mathrm{var}(\mathrm{Pr}_i)\right]} \right\} / 2$$

where X_i ($i = 1, \ldots, 9$) represented the binary random variable with zero and one as values and $\Pr_i$ the probability that X_i was equal to one. The numerators of the ratios that were 0.25 corresponded to the variance for $\Pr = 0.5$. This weight was the mean of two ratios that counterbalanced each other in order to achieve factor loadings of equal size for all columns. Its construction was only partly theory-driven. Since $w^2(X_i)$ for $\Pr_i = 0.5$ differed from one, all factor loadings had to be divided by this weight that was 1.244 in order to achieve the expected size. Furthermore, disattenuation of the factor loadings was necessary (Schweizer 2013).

The investigations of the various matrices were conducted by means of LISREL (Jöreskog and Sörbom 2006). The maximum likelihood estimation method was selected for most of the investigations. The robust maximum likelihood estimation method was additionally considered in combination with tetrachoric correlations. The results of the investigations were evaluated with respect to model-data fit and the sizes of the completely standardized factor loadings. The report of the results of investigating model fit includes the following fit indexes: chi-square, degree of freedom, normed chi-square, RMSEA, SRMR, CFI, TLI, and GFI. Cut-offs provided by Kline (2005) and Hu and Bentler (1999) served the evaluation of the results (RMSEA 0.06, SRMR 0.08, CFI 0.95, TLI 0.95, GFI 0.90). Furthermore, normed chi-squares below 2 ($N = 200$), 3 ($N = 400$), and 5 ($N = 1{,}000$ and larger) were taken as indications of a good model fit. Two perspectives were taken in investigating the sizes of the completely standardized factor loadings. First, the recovery of the completely standardized factor loadings that were expected to correspond to the factor loadings obtained for the population pattern and for the continuous data was checked. The size that characterized these factor loadings was 0.50. Second, the absence of the dependency on item marginals was checked. This check was conducted by means of Hartley's $F_{\max}$ test. Since the same size was expected for each completely standardized factor loadings, the variances of the factor loadings obtained in investigating binary data at the level of the means were compared with the variance of the factor loadings achieved in investigating continuous data at the level of the means. In this check the $F_{\max}$ statistic served in the first place as a kind of summary statistic.

17.2.2 *The Results Concerning Model Fit*

The following sections are organized in the following way: at first, the results of investigating the model fit are presented and subsequently the results of investigating the completely standardized factor loadings. In order to facilitate the reading of the tables including fit statistics, the superscript "M" was added to a mean statistic if the mean was favorable when compared with the corresponding cut-off. If the confidence interval meaning 95 % of the distribution of the observed results was in the favorable area, it was replaced by the superscript "CI." In contrast, no further information was added to the means of the completely standardized factor loadings. The outcomes of the $F_{\max}$ test are reported in the text.

Table 17.2 Means and standard deviations (printed in italics) of the fit results for the population pattern and simulated continuous data in different sample sizes (N = 200, 400, 1,000, 2,000)

Input	Sample size	χ^2	df	Normed χ^2	RMSEA	SRMR	CFI	TLI	GFI
Population pattern	–	0	27	0	–	–	–	–	–
Covariances	200	27.36	27	1.01[CI]	0.015[CI]	0.041[CI]	0.99[CI]	1.00[CI]	0.97[CI]
SD		*7.16*		*0.26*	*0.02*	*0.01*	*0.01*	*0.02*	*0.01*
Covariances	400	27.87	27	1.03[CI]	0.012[CI]	0.029[CI]	0.99[CI]	1.00[CI]	0.98[CI]
SD		*8.04*		*0.30*	*0.01*	*0.01*	*0.01*	*0.02*	*0.00*
Covariances	1,000	27.15	27	1.01[CI]	0.007[CI]	0.018[CI]	1.00[CI]	1.00[CI]	0.99[CI]
SD		*7.78*		*0.29*	*0.01*	*0.00*	*0.01*	*0.01*	*0.00*
Covariances	2,000	28.01	27	1.04[CI]	0.005[CI]	0.013[CI]	1.00[CI]	1.00[CI]	1.00[CI]
SD		*8.24*		*0.30*	*0.01*	*0.00*	*0.00*	*0.00*	*0.00*

[CI]The 95 % confidence interval is in the favorable area; M: the mean is in the favorable area
[M]The mean is in the favorable area

Table 17.2 provides the results for the population pattern (first row) and for the covariance matrices computed from continuous data (other rows). The numbers printed normal are means and the numbers printed in italics are standard deviations. The chi-squares obtained for the population pattern indicated a perfect model fit. As a consequence, the majority of statistics could not be estimated and, therefore, was not available. The fit statistics obtained in investigating the continuous data reveal that there was an overall good model-data fit. In all cases with one exception the results were according to the expectations. Furthermore, the sample size showed virtually no influence on model-data fit.

The results obtained for tetrachoric correlations computed from binary data contrasted the results reported in the previous paragraph. These results are included in the first quarter of Table 17.3.

The majority of results indicated a bad model-data fit. The chi-square results of the first column were rather large and showed a very special characteristic: there was a decrease in chi-square if the sample size was increased from 200 to 1,000. This observation was quite unusual since normally an increase in sample size was likely to be accompanied by an increase in chi-square. Only the means and confidence intervals of a few SRMR and GFI statistics were good. It was only in the sample size of 2,000 that there were four fit statistics that were good according to the confidence interval and another one that was good according to the mean. As it is obvious from the second quarter of Table 17.3, robust maximum likelihood estimation improved the chi-squares considerably. Without robust estimation the range of the chi-squares was from 151 to 186 whereas in combination with robust estimation there was variation between 28 and 46. As a consequence, the normed chi-squares and the RMSEAs indicated a good model-data fit for all sample sizes. However, in the smallest sample size there were still four fit statistics indicating a bad degree of model-data fit whereas in the largest and second to largest sample sizes virtually all results were good.

Table 17.3 Means and standard deviations (printed in italics) of the fit results for the congeneric model applied to binary data in different sample sizes (N = 200, 400, 1,000, 2,000)

Input	Sample size	χ^2	df	Normed χ^2	RMSEA	SRMR	CFI	TLI	GFI
ML estimation									
TetraCor[a]	200	186.5	27	6.9	0.163	0.113	0.68	0.57	0.85
SD		*101.2*		*3.7*	*0.06*	*0.05*	*0.13*	*0.20*	*0.08*
TetraCor[a]	400	161.7	27	5.9	0.109	0.070[CI]	0.78	0.71	0.92[M]
SD		*67.6*		*2.5*	*0.02*	*0.01*	*0.07*	*0.10*	*0.03*
TetraCor[a]	1,000	151.2	27	5.6	0.067	0.043[CI]	0.91	0.88	0.97[CI]
SD		*40.1*		*1.5*	*0.01*	*0.01*	*0.03*	*0.04*	*0.01*
TetraCor[b]	2,000	164.8	27	6.1	0.050[CI]	0.031[CI]	0.97[CI]	0.96[M]	0.98[CI]
SD		*54.9*		*2.0*	*0.01*	*0.00*	*0.01*	*0.02*	*0.01*
Robust ML estimation									
TetraCor[a]	200	46.2	27	1.71[M]	0.051[M]	0.130	0.94	0.93	0.85
SD		*30.3*		*1.12*	*0.04*	*0.06*	*0.07*	*0.10*	*0.08*
TetraCor[a]	400	42.3	27	1.53[CI]	0.026[M]	0.087	0.98[M]	0.98[M]	0.92[M]
SD		*49.2*		*0.35*	*0.05*	*0.04*	*0.03*	*0.04*	*0.03*
TetraCor[a]	1,000	30.4	27	1.09[CI]	0.008[CI]	0.048[M]	1.00[CI]	1.00[CI]	0.97[CI]
SD		*15.1*		*0.55*	*0.02*	*0.02*	*0.00*	*0.01*	*0.01*
TetraCor[b]	2,000	28.8	27	1.06[CI]	0.006[CI]	0.031[CI]	1.00[CI]	1.00[CI]	0.98[CI]
SD		*9.2*		*0.34*	*0.01*	*0.00*	*0.00*	*0.00*	*0.01*
ML estimation—criterion-focused way									
PbCor[b]	200	26.1	27	0.96[CI]	0.012[CI]	0.046[CI]	0.97[M]	1.03[M]	0.97[CI]
SD		*7.0*		*0.26*	*0.02*	*0.01*	*0.05*	*0.16*	*0.01*
PbCor[b]	400	26.7	27	0.99[CI]	0.010[CI]	0.033[CI]	0.98[M]	1.00[M]	0.99[CI]
SD		*7.2*		*0.27*	*0.01*	*0.01*	*0.03*	*0.06*	*0.01*
PbCor[b]	1,000	29.7	27	1.10[CI]	0.009[CI]	0.022[CI]	0.99[CI]	0.99[M]	0.99[CI]
SD		*8.2*		*0.31*	*0.01*	*0.00*	*0.01*	*0.03*	*0.01*
PbCor[b]	2,000	32.1	27	1.19[CI]	0.009[CI]	0.016[CI]	0.99[CI]	0.99[M]	1.00[CI]
SD		*9.8*		*0.36*	*0.01*	*0.00*	*0.01*	*0.02*	*0.00*
ML estimation—predictor-focused way									
PbCOV[b]	200	26.3	27	0.97[CI]	0.012[CI]	0.046[CI]	0.97[M]	1.02[M]	0.97[CI]
SD		*7.5*		*0.28*	*0.02*	*0.01*	*0.05*	*0.13*	*0.01*
PbCOV[b]	400	28.1	27	1.04[CI]	0.012[CI]	0.034[CI]	0.98[M]	0.99[M]	0.98[CI]
SD		*7.3*		*0.27*	*0.01*	*0.00*	*0.03*	*0.06*	*0.00*
PbCOV[b]	1,000	29.8	27	1.10[CI]	0.010[CI]	0.022[CI]	1.00[CI]	0.99[M]	0.99[CI]
SD		*8.2*		*0.30*	*0.01*	*0.00*	*0.01*	*0.03*	*0.01*
PbCOV[b]	2,000	32.6	27	1.19[CI]	0.009[CI]	0.016[CI]	0.99[CI]	0.99[M]	1.00[CI]
SD		*9.8*		*0.36*	*0.01*	*0.00*	*0.01*	*0.02*	*0.00*

TetraCor tetrachoric correlations, *PbCor* probability-based correlations, *PbCOV* probability-based covariances

[a]The number of datasets is 200

[b]The number of datasets is 100

[CI]The 95 % confidence interval is in the favorable area; M: the mean is in the favorable area

[M]The mean is in the favorable area

The investigation of probability-based covariances and the probability-based correlations obtained in realizing the two ways of applying the link function led to the results reported in the third and fourth quarters of Table 17.3. There were only minor differences between the results achieved in investigating probability-based correlations and covariances so that there was no need to discuss them separately. The chi-squares observed for the four sample sizes varied between 26 and 32. There was a small but continuous increase from the sample size of 200 to the sample size of 2,000. In all sample sizes the normed chi-squares, RMSEAs, SRMRs, and GFIs were good according to the confidence interval. The remaining fit statistics were at least good according to the mean.

In summary, the results for tetrachoric correlations confirmed the expected dependency on sample size. The increase of the sample size led to an overall increase in model-data fit. A sample size of 2,000 appeared to be necessary in order to achieve a good or acceptable degree of model-data fit. Combining the robust estimation method with tetrachoric correlations led to an improvement of fit. In contrast, the results obtained in the investigations of probability-based covariances and probability-based correlations were generally good, and there was virtually no dependency on the sample size.

17.2.3 The Results Concerning the Sizes of the Completely Standardized Factor Loadings

Table 17.4 provides the means and standard deviations of the completely standardized factor loadings achieved in investigating the population pattern (first row) and the covariance matrices computed from continuous data (other rows).

The numbers printed normal are means and the numbers printed in italics are standard deviations. All completely standardized factor loadings obtained for the

Table 17.4 Means and standard deviations (printed in italics) of the completely standardized factor loadings obtained for the population pattern and simulated continuous data in different sample sizes (N = 200, 400, 1,000, 2,000)

		Position of variable								
Input	Sample size	1	2	3	4	5	6	7	8	9
Population pattern	–	0.50	0.50	0.50	0.50	0.50	0.50	0.50	0.50	0.50
Covariances	200	0.49	0.51	0.49	0.50	0.50	0.49	0.51	0.51	0.51
SD		*0.07*	*0.07*	*0.06*	*0.06*	*0.07*	*0.07*	*0.06*	*0.06*	*0.07*
Covariances	400	0.50	0.51	0.50	0.50	0.50	0.50	0.51	0.52	0.50
SD		*0.05*	*0.05*	*0.05*	*0.05*	*0.05*	*0.05*	*0.04*	*0.10*	*0.06*
Covariances	1,000	0.50	0.50	0.50	0.50	0.50	0.50	0.50	0.49	0.50
SD		*0.04*	*0.04*	*0.04*	*0.03*	*0.04*	*0.04*	*0.04*	*0.04*	*0.03*
Covariances	2,000	0.50	0.50	0.50	0.50	0.50	0.50	0.50	0.50	0.50
SD		*0.02*	*0.02*	*0.02*	*0.02*	*0.02*	*0.02*	*0.02*	*0.02*	*0.02*

population pattern were 0.50. Since there was only one population pattern, there was no variability. The means for the continuous data varied between 0.49 and 0.52. Whereas in the sample sizes smaller or equal than 1,000 the means showed some variation, in the sample size of 2,000 all means of the completely standardized factor loadings were 0.50. Furthermore, the variability decreased when the sample size was increased.

The results obtained in investigating binary data are presented in Table 17.5.

Table 17.5 Means and standard deviations (printed in italics) of the completely standardized factor loadings for the congeneric model applied to binary data in different sample sizes (N = 200, 400, 1,000, 2,000)

		Position of variable								
Input	Sample size	1	2	3	4	5	6	7	8	9
ML estimation/robust ML estimation										
TetraCor[a]	200	0.60	0.48	0.43	0.45	0.44	0.44	0.46	0.50	0.62
SD		*0.26*	*0.18*	*0.14*	*0.14*	*0.15*	*0.14*	*0.14*	*0.20*	*0.24*
TetraCor[a]	400	0.52	0.49	0.48	0.47	0.49	0.47	0.47	0.47	0.56
SD		*0.16*	*0.12*	*0.11*	*0.11*	*0.11*	*0.10*	*0.11*	*0.13*	*0.17*
TetraCor[a]	1,000	0.51	0.51	0.50	0.49	0.50	0.49	0.50	0.50	0.53
SD		*0.10*	*0.06*	*0.07*	*0.06*	*0.06*	*0.06*	*0.06*	*0.08*	*0.09*
TetraCor[b]	2,000	0.51	0.50	0.50	0.50	0.50	0.50	0.50	0.50	0.51
SD		*0.05*	*0.04*	*0.04*	*0.03*	*0.04*	*0.04*	*0.03*	*0.04*	*0.06*
ML estimation—criterion-focused way										
PbCor[b]	200	0.38	0.48	0.54	0.56	0.59	0.56	0.54	0.48	0.41
SD		*0.12*	*0.12*	*0.16*	*0.15*	*0.13*	*0.13*	*0.12*	*0.15*	*0.13*
PbCor[b]	400	0.38	0.51	0.53	0.55	0.57	0.56	0.54	0.51	0.41
SD		*0.09*	*0.09*	*0.08*	*0.09*	*0.08*	*0.09*	*0.09*	*0.12*	*0.08*
PbCor[b]	1,000	0.40	0.49	0.54	0.57	0.58	0.56	0.55	0.49	0.41
SD		*0.05*	*0.05*	*0.06*	*0.05*	*0.06*	*0.06*	*0.06*	*0.05*	*0.05*
PbCor[b]	2,000	0.41	0.49	0.54	0.57	0.57	0.56	0.55	0.49	0.41
SD		*0.03*	*0.03*	*0.03*	*0.03*	*0.03*	*0.03*	*0.02*	*0.03*	*0.03*
ML estimation—predictor-focused way										
PbCOV[b]	200	0.49	0.50	0.49	0.51	0.52	0.50	0.51	0.52	0.51
SD		*0.14*	*0.11*	*0.10*	*0.10*	*0.09*	*0.10*	*0.10*	*0.14*	*0.13*
PbCOV[b]	400	0.50	0.50	0.50	0.51	0.52	0.50	0.52	0.51	0.51
SD		*0.09*	*0.07*	*0.07*	*0.07*	*0.07*	*0.08*	*0.08*	*0.09*	*0.10*
PbCOV[b]	1,000	0.49	0.50	0.51	0.51	0.52	0.51	0.51	0.50	0.51
SD		*0.06*	*0.05*	*0.05*	*0.04*	*0.04*	*0.04*	*0.05*	*0.05*	*0.06*
PbCOV[b]	2,000	0.51	0.50	0.51	0.51	0.51	0.51	0.51	0.50	0.51
SD		*0.04*	*0.04*	*0.03*	*0.03*	*0.3*	*0.03*	*0.04*	*0.04*	*0.04*

TetraCor tetrachoric correlations, *PbCor* probability-based correlations, *PbCOV* probability-based covariances

[a]The number of datasets is 200

[b]The number of datasets is 100

[CI]The 95 % confidence interval is in the favorable area; M: the mean is in the favorable area

[M]The mean is in the favorable area

The first part of this table includes the completely standardized factor loadings for the tetrachoric correlations. Since the two estimation methods are known to lead to the same completely standardized factor loadings, there are no separate results sections for these methods. The investigation of tetrachoric correlations revealed quite a bit of variability. In the sample size of 200 the mean factor loadings varied between 0.43 and 0.62, in 400 between 0.47 and 0.56, in 1,000 between 0.49 and 0.53 and in 2,000 between 0.50 and 0.51. Furthermore, the F_{max} test results indicated deviations from the expected equality of the completely standardized factor loadings with the exception of the largest sample size [$N = 200$: $F_{max}(2{,}200) = 140.06, p < 0.05$; $N = 400$: $F_{max}(2{,}400) = 29.30, p < 0.05$; $N = 1{,}000$: $F_{max}(2{,}1000) = 4.69$, $p < 0.05$; $N = 2{,}000$: $F_{max}(2{,}2000) = 0.61$, n.s.]. Note. The original F_{max} test does not allow for values smaller than one since the larger number always has to be assigned to the numerator. Since in the present investigation variances smaller than the comparison level are desirable, in such cases the F_{max} statistic is deliberately used in an unconventional way.

The investigation of the completely standardized factor loadings obtained on the basis of probability-based correlations by means of the congeneric model revealed a characteristic pattern (see second part of Table 17.5): the smallest factor loadings were observed for the first and last columns that were associated with the most extreme splits (first column: 0.38, 0.38, 0.40, 0.41 for $N = 200$, 400, 1,000, 2,000 and last column: 0.41, 0.41, 0.41, 0.41 for $N = 200$, 400, 1,000, 2,000) whereas the largest factor loadings were found for the fifth column that was based on the median split (0.59, 0.57, 0.58, 0.57 for $N = 200$, 400, 1,000, 2,000). Apparently, there were considerable degrees of dependency on item marginals. This dependency was also obvious from the F_{max} test results ($N = 200$: $F_{max}(2{,}200) = 160.23$, $p < 0.05$; $N = 400$: $F_{max}(2{,}400) = 140.06$, $p < 0.05$; $N = 1{,}000$: $F_{max}(2{,}1000) = 142.41$, $p < 0.05$: $F_{max}(2{,}2000) = 129.00$, $p < 0.05$).

Finally there were the results achieved in investigating probability-based covariances in considering the weighted congeneric model of measurement. These results are included in the third part of Table 17.5. The means showed a considerably lower degree of variability than the means reported in the other parts of this table: there was variation between 0.49 and 0.52 in the sample size of 200, between 0.50 and 0.52 in the sample size of 400, between 0.49 and 0.51 in the sample size of 1,000 and between 0.50 and 0.51 in the sample size of 2,000. Furthermore, the investigations of the equality of the factor loadings by means of the F_{max} test revealed substantial differences for the sample sizes up to 1,000 although the F_{max} values appeared to be small when compared with the values observed for tetrachoric correlations and probability-based correlations ($N = 200$: $F_{max}(2{,}200) = 4.69$, $p < 0.05$; $N = 400$: $F_{max}(2{,}400) = 2.17$, $p < 0.05$; $N = 1{,}000$: $F_{max}(2{,}1000) = 2.35$, $p < 0.05$). In contrast, in the sample size of 2,000 there was no indication of a deviation [$F_{max}(2{,}2000) = 0.60$, n.s.].

After focussing on the issue of the equality of the completely standardized factor loadings, the correspondence of the observed sizes and the expected size was considered. Investigating the tetrachoric correlations led to the mean factor loadings of 0.49, 0.49, 0.50, and 0.50 for the sample sizes of 200, 400, 1,000, and 2,000. In probability-based correlations and probability-based covariances all mean factor loadings were 0.51.

All in all, the investigation of the equality of the completely standardized factor loadings yielded agreeable results for the tetrachoric correlations and the probability-based covariances in the larger sample sizes. In contrast, the completely standardized factor loadings obtained for probability-based correlations showed the typical dependency on item marginals. The comparisons of the observed sizes with the expected size of factor loadings that were performed on the level of the means revealed a good degree of agreement for all types of input to confirmatory factor analysis.

Conclusions

The investigation of binary data by means of confirmatory factor analysis is especially demanding since the properties of these data and the requirements of the method do not fit to each other. The use of tetrachoric correlation has been proposed in order to improve the fit. The analysis of the properties of tetrachoric correlations reveals that this method of computing correlations is especially demanding to the quality of the data. If the quality of the data is high, it can be expected to do well although it must be mentioned that tetrachoric correlations do not completely meet the requirements since confirmatory factor analysis is a method for the investigation of covariances in the first place (Jöreskog 1970). In contrast, bad results can be expected in data showing a low quality. The results of the simulation study confirmed this expectation. In small sample sizes the outcomes of confirmatory factor analysis were not favorable, and the increase in sample size was associated with a sizable improvement.

Robust maximum likelihood estimation is expected to compensate for deviations from normality. Therefore, in the simulation study confirmatory factor analysis with tetrachoric correlations as input was conducted separately by means of the maximum likelihood estimation method and the robust maximum likelihood estimation method. The replacement of the estimation method led to a considerable improvement of the model-data fit. Only in the smallest sample size the majority of fit statistics did not indicate a good fit after the replacement. The comparison of the results obtained by the two estimation methods revealed that the majority of fit indexes showed an effect. Only the SRMRs and GFIs were not changed considerably, and the factor loadings stayed the same. So as a result of such a replacement, it can happen that the model-data fit changes from bad to good but the estimated factor loadings still deviate considerably from the expected factor loadings.

The use of probability-based covariances and correlations in the simulation study led to generally good results concerning model-data fit. This good

(continued)

degree of model-data fit even seems to be independent of the sample size and is obvious in all the considered fit indexes. This outcome is no surprise since the computation of probability-based covariances and correlations does not imply the estimation of parameters in considering an asymptotic function. The use of the asymptotic areas of such a function is risky since small deviations due to imprecision and error are considerably magnified. Furthermore, probability-based covariances and correlations turn out to be rather robust since in no case there were problems due to lack of convergence or factor loadings that were out of range.

The investigation thought to secure the absence of dependency on item marginals (Kubinger 2003; Torgerson 1958) has revealed problems when probability-based correlations served as input to confirmatory factor analysis. The sizes of the completely standardized factor loadings were considerably lower than expected for the extreme splits. The sizes increased if the split became more and more moderate. The largest sizes were found for the median split. This kind of change is characteristic of dependency on item marginals. In contrast, in probability-based covariances the sizes of the completely standardized factor loadings showed the highest degree of similarity among each other, as it becomes obvious in the comparisons with the factor loadings obtained for tetrachoric correlations and probability-based correlations. Although the F_{max} test yielded a substantial result in three sample sizes, the F_{max} values obtained for the probability-based covariances were in all conditions the smallest ones.

Apparently, the link function selected for the investigation of probability-based covariances was efficient in securing the absence of dependency on item marginals. It is a link function that was derived from the original link function by optimizing performance in considering the special characteristics of the weighted congeneric model of measurement. The avoidance of dependency on item marginals is a very important property because in this case there is no more a distortion of the relations between the factor loadings. This is an important prerequisite for the investigation of binary data by means of confirmatory factor analysis.

References

Bryant FB, Satorra A (2012) Principles and practice of scaled difference chi-square testing. Struct Equ Model 19:373–398

Divgi DR (1979) Calculation of the tetrachoric correlation coefficient. Psychometrika 44:169–172

Fan W, Hancock GR (2012) Robust means modeling: an alternative for hypothesis testing of independent means under variance heterogeneity and nonnormality. J Educ Behav Stat 37:137–156

Genest C, Lévesque J-M (2009) Estimating correlation from dichotomized normal variables. J Stat Plan Inference 139:3785–3794
Hu L, Bentler PM (1999) Cutoff criteria for fit indexes in covariance structure analysis: conventional criteria versus new alternatives. Struct Equ Model 6:1–55
Jöreskog KG (1970) A general method for analysis of covariance structure. Biometrika 57: 239–257
Jöreskog KG (1971) Statistical analysis of sets of congeneric tests. Psychometrika 36:109–133
Jöreskog KG, Sörbom D (2001) Interactive LISREL: user's guide. Scientific Software International Inc., Lincolnwood
Jöreskog KG, Sörbom D (2006) LISREL 8.80. Scientific Software International Inc., Lincolnwood
Kline RB (2005) Principles and practice of structural equation modeling, 2nd edn. Guliford, New York
Kubinger KD (2003) On artificial results due to using factor analysis for dichotomous variables. Psychol Sci 45:106–110
McCullagh P, Nelder JA (1985) Generalized linear models. Chapman and Hall, London
Muthén B (1984) A general structural equation model with dichotomous, ordered categorical, and continuous variable indicators. Psychometrika 49:115–132
Muthén B (1993) Goodness of fit with categorical and other nonnormal variables. In: Bollen KA, Long JS (eds) Testing structural equation models. Sage, Newbury Park, Thousand Oaks, pp 205–234
Nelder JA, Wedderburn RWM (1972) Generalized linear models. J R Stat Soc Ser A 135:370–384
Ogasawara H (2010) Accurate distribution and its asymptotic expansion for the tetrachoric correlation coefficient. J Multivar Anal 101:936–948
Owen DB (1956) Tables for computing bivariate normal probabilities. Ann Math Stat 27: 1075–1090
Pearson K (1900) Mathematical contributions to the theory of evolution. VII. On the correlation of characters not quantitatively measurable. Philos Trans R Soc Lond 195:1–47
Satorra A, Bentler PM (1994) Corrections to the test statistics and standard errors on covariance structure analysis. In: von Eye A, Glogg CC (eds) Latent variable analysis. Sage, Thousand Oaks, pp 399–419
Schweizer K (2013) A threshold-free approach to the study of the structure of binary data. Int J Stat Probab 2:67–75
Tallis GM (1962) The maximum likelihood estimation of correlation from contingency tables. Biometrics 18:342–353
Torgerson WS (1958) Theory and method of scaling. Wiley, New York
West SG, Finch JF, Curran PJ (1995) Structural equation models with nonnormal variables: problems and remedies. In: Hoyle RH (ed) Structural equation modeling: concepts, issues, and applications. Sage, Thousand Oaks, pp 56–75

Chapter 18
On Cronbach's Alpha as the Mean of All Split-Half Reliabilities

Matthijs J. Warrens

Abstract A famous description of Cronbach's alpha is that it is the mean of all (Flanagan–Rulon) split-half reliabilities. The result is exact if the test is split into two halves that are equal in size. This requires that the number of items is even, since odd numbers cannot be split into two groups of equal size. In this chapter it is shown that alpha is approximately identical to the mean of all split-half reliabilities, if a test consists of an odd number of items and has at least eleven items.

Keywords Split-half reliability • Spearman–Brown prophecy formula • Flanagan–Rulon split-half

18.1 Cronbach's Alpha

An important concept in psychometrics and measurement theory is the reliability of a test score. Reliability of a test score concerns the overall consistency of a participant's score. It can be conceptualized in different ways. In layman's terms a test score is said to be reliable if it produces similar outcomes for participants when administration conditions are consistent. In classical test theory reliability is defined as the ratio of the true score variance and the total score variance (McDonald 1999; Lord and Novick 1968; Revelle and Zinbarg 2009). Since the true score variance cannot be directly observed, the reliability of a test score needs to be estimated. Examples of reliability estimation methods are the test-retest method and the internal consistency method (Osburn 2000). The latter method can be used if there is only one test administration available. The most commonly used coefficient of internal consistency in psychology and other behavioral sciences is coefficient alpha (Cortina 1993; Cronbach 1951; Field 2009; Furr and Bacharach 2008; Osburn 2000; Sijtsma 2009).

Coefficient alpha was proposed by Guttman (1945) as lambda 3 and later popularized as alpha by Cronbach (1951). The coefficient has been applied in thousands of research studies and the number of citations of Cronbach's paper is

---

M.J. Warrens (✉)
Institute of Psychology, Leiden University, Leiden, The Netherlands
e-mail: warrens@fsw.leidenuniv.nl

R.E. Millsap et al. (eds.), *Quantitative Psychology Research*, Springer Proceedings in Mathematics & Statistics 89, DOI 10.1007/978-3-319-07503-7_18

impressive (Cortina 1993; Sijtsma 2009). Various authors have criticized the use of alpha. Examples have been presented that show that alpha is not a measure of the one-dimensionality of a test (Cronbach 1951; Grayson 2004; Sijtsma 2009). Furthermore, there are several coefficients that are higher lower bounds to the reliability of a test score than alpha (Revelle and Zinbarg 2009; Sijtsma 2009). However, most critics and reviewers of alpha agree that it is likely that the coefficient will continue to be a standard tool in reliability estimation in the near future (Cortina 1993; Sijtsma 2009). Moreover, many years after Cronbach's paper, alpha is still a hot topic in current research. For example, the derivation of alpha is based on several assumptions from classical test theory (Lord and Novick 1968; Thorndike 1971). Robustness of alpha to violations of essential tau-equivalence and uncorrelated errors have been documented in Grayson (2004), Green and Hershberger (2000), Green and Yang (2009), while robustness to non-normal data has been studied in Sheng and Sheng (2012).

A famous description of alpha is that it is the mean of all split-half reliabilities (Cortina 1993; Cronbach 1951). The split-half method is another approach to estimating the reliability of a test score when there is only one administration (Field 2009; Furr and Bacharach 2008; Revelle and Zinbarg 2009). In this method the test is randomly split into two halves, and the sum scores of the two halves are compared as if they were two separate administrations of the same test score. The correlation between the sum scores of the two halves is an estimate of the reliability of the half test. This estimate must then be corrected for the fact that the tests were half tests rather than full tests (Field 2009; Revelle and Zinbarg 2009). Different split-half formulas have been proposed in the literature (Brown 1910; Flanagan 1937; Rulon 1939; Spearman 1910). The problem with the split-half approach is that there are multiple ways to divide the items of the test into two halves. The estimate therefore depends on the way the split is made (Field 2009). Cronbach (1951) showed that if the test is split into two subtests of equal size, then alpha for the full test is the mean of all possible split-half reliabilities. Using alpha instead of the split-half estimate removes in a way the arbitrariness of how to split a test.

There are two limitations to "the average of all possible split-half estimates" description of alpha. As noted by Cortina (1993) the result holds for the split-half reliability proposed in Flanagan (1937) and Rulon (1939), not for the more famous split-half formula proposed in Spearman (1910) and Brown (1910). There is no simple relationship between alpha and the mean of all Spearman–Brown split-half reliabilities. The second limitation is that Cronbach (1951) showed that alpha is the mean of all (Flanagan–Rulon) split-half reliabilities if the test is split into two halves that are equal in size. This requires that the number of items is even, since odd numbers cannot be split into two groups of equal size.

In this chapter we study how alpha is related to the mean of all (Flanagan–Rulon) split-half reliabilities when the number of items is odd. We present conditions under which the difference between the two quantities is negligible for most practical purposes. A formula of the mean of the split-half reliabilities is first derived in Sect. 18.2. Raju (1977) showed that alpha always exceeds the mean if the halves have unequal sizes. Furthermore, he argued that the two quantities can be quite different when the number of items is odd. In Sect. 18.3 it is shown that if the test consists of at least eleven items and one half of the split contains one more item than the other half, then the difference between alpha and the mean of all possible split-half reliabilities is less than 0.01. Section 18.4 contains a conclusion. We conclude that given a moderate number of items, alpha is approximately identical to the mean of all (Flanagan–Rulon) split-half reliabilities.

18.2 The Mean of All Split-Half Reliabilities

Suppose we have a test that consists of $k \geq 2$ items. Let σ_{ij} denote the covariance between items i and j with $1 \leq i, j \leq k$, and let σ_T^2 denote the variance of the test (sum) score. Guttman's lambda 3 or Cronbach's alpha is defined as

$$\alpha = \frac{k}{k-1} \cdot \frac{\sum_{i \neq j} \sigma_{ij}}{\sigma_T^2}. \tag{18.1}$$

Suppose we split the test into two halves of sizes k_1 and k_2 with $1 \leq k_1, k_2 < k$ and $k_1 + k_2 = k$. Furthermore, let $p_1 = k_1/k$ and $p_2 = k_2/k$ denote the proportions of items in the two halves, and let σ_{12} denote the covariance between the sum scores of the two halves. Flanagan (1937) and Rulon (1939) proposed the split-half formula

$$\alpha_2 = \frac{4\sigma_{12}}{\sigma_T^2}. \tag{18.2}$$

The formula in (18.2) is denoted by α_2 because it is a special case of alpha in (18.1) (Cronbach 1951; Raju 1977). Cronbach (1951) showed that if $k_1 = k_2$, then $\alpha = E(\alpha_2)$, that is, the overall alpha is the mean of all possible split-half reliabilities defined in (18.2). A proof can also be found in Lord and Novick (1968) and Raju (1977). Raju (1977) showed that $\alpha > E(\alpha_2)$ if $k_1 \neq k_2$.

In this paper we are interested in how much α is bigger than $E(\alpha_2)$. To investigate this question we will use the non-negative difference $\alpha - E(\alpha_2)$. An expression for the expected value $E(\alpha_2)$ is presented in the following theorem.

Theorem 1. $E(\alpha_2) = \alpha \cdot 4p_1p_2$.

Proof Since σ_T^2 is the same for each split we have

$$E(\alpha_2) = \frac{4}{\sigma_T^2} \cdot E(\sigma_{12}). \tag{18.3}$$

The total number of possible splits in groups of sizes k_1 and k_2 is given by Abramowitz and Stegun (1970, p. 823)

$$T = \frac{k!}{k_1!k_2!}. \tag{18.4}$$

Furthermore, since the covariance is a bilinear form, the covariance of two sums of two random variables is given by

$$\sigma(A+B,C+D) = \sigma(A,C) + \sigma(A,D) + \sigma(B,C) + \sigma(B,D).$$

Hence, to determine $E(\sigma_{12})$ in (18.3) we must find how often two items i and j are not in the same half if we sum over all possible splits T. The number of times two items are together in the first half is, using (18.4),

$$\binom{k-2}{k_1-2} = \frac{(k-2)!}{(k_1-2)!(k-k_1)!} = \frac{k_1(k_1-1)}{k(k-1)} \cdot T.$$

We have a similar expression for how often two items i and j are in the second half. The number of times two items are in the same half is thus given by

$$\frac{k_1(k_1-1)+k_2(k_2-1)}{k(k-1)} \cdot T.$$

The number of times two items are not in the same half is then given by

$$S = \left(1 - \frac{k_1(k_1-1)+k_2(k_2-1)}{k(k-1)}\right) T = \frac{2k_1k_2}{k(k-1)} \cdot T = \frac{k}{k-1} \cdot 2T p_1 p_2. \tag{18.5}$$

Using (18.4) and (18.5) we can write $E(\sigma_{12})$ as

$$E(\sigma_{12}) = \frac{2S}{T} \sum_{i \neq j} \sigma_{ij} = p_1 p_2 \cdot \frac{k}{k-1} \sum_{i \neq j} \sigma_{ij} = \alpha \cdot \sigma_T^2 \cdot p_1 p_2. \tag{18.6}$$

Finally, using (18.6) in (18.3) we obtain $E(\alpha_2) = \alpha \cdot 4p_1p_2$. □

It follows from Theorem 1 that if the two halves have the same size, that is, $p_1 = p_2 = \frac{1}{2}$, then we have $E(\alpha_2) = \alpha$. This case was originally proved in Cronbach (1951). Theorem 1 presents an alternative proof of the identity $\alpha = E(\alpha_2)$ if $k_1 = k_2$. The difference $\alpha - E(\alpha_2)$ is further studied in the next section.

18.3 Difference Between Alpha and the Split-Half Mean

Using Theorem 1 we have

$$\alpha - E(\alpha_2) = \alpha(1 - 4p_1p_2). \tag{18.7}$$

Identity (18.7) shows that the difference depends on α and $p_1 = 1 - p_2$. Since $0 \leq \alpha \leq 1$ we have the inequality

$$\alpha - E(\alpha_2) \leq 1 - 4p_1p_2. \tag{18.8}$$

Since the right-hand side of (18.8) only depends on $p_1 = 1 - p_2$, this inequality allows us to study difference (18.7) independent of the value of α. We will say that α is approximately equal to $E(\alpha_2)$ if the difference is less than 0.01. A difference of 0.01 is negligible for most practical purposes. Using (18.8) the requirement is satisfied if $1 - 4p_1p_2 \leq 0.01$ or

$$4p_1p_2 \geq 0.99. \tag{18.9}$$

In the remainder of this chapter we study several ways of splitting a test in half. First of all, suppose the number of items k is odd. If we want the sizes of the halves to be as similar as possible, one half must contain one more item, and we have

$$p_1 = \frac{k-1}{2k} \quad \text{and} \quad p_2 = \frac{k+1}{2k}. \tag{18.10}$$

Using the proportions in (18.10) we have

$$4p_1p_2 = \frac{(k-1)(k+1)}{k^2} = \frac{k^2-1}{k^2}. \tag{18.11}$$

Since the right-hand side of (18.11) is increasing in k, inequality (18.9) holds for sufficiently large k. For $k = 9$ items we have

$$4p_1p_2 = \frac{80}{81} < \frac{99}{100},$$

but for $k = 11$ items we have

$$4p_1p_2 = \frac{120}{121} > \frac{99}{100}.$$

Hence, if we put one more item in one half, then alpha is approximately identical to the mean of all possible split-half reliabilities if the test consists of at least eleven items.

Next, suppose that the number of items k is even. Instead of a perfect split we may put 2 more items in one half. In this case we have

$$p_1 = \frac{k-2}{2k} \quad \text{and} \quad p_2 = \frac{k+2}{2k}. \tag{18.12}$$

Using the proportions in (18.12) we have

$$4p_1p_2 = \frac{k^2-4}{k^2}. \tag{18.13}$$

The right-hand side of (18.13) is increasing in k. For $k = 20$ items we have

$$4p_1p_2 = \frac{396}{400} = \frac{99}{100}.$$

Hence, for this split, alpha is the mean of all the split-half reliabilities if we have at least twenty items.

If a difference of 0.01 is not small enough, we may also study difference (18.7) with respect to other numbers. For example, suppose we want difference (18.7) to be equal or less than 0.001. Using (18.8) this requirement is satisfied if

$$4p_1p_2 \geq 0.999. \tag{18.14}$$

Using $k = 31$ items in (18.11) we have

$$4p_1p_2 = \frac{960}{961} < \frac{999}{1000},$$

but for $k = 33$ items we have

$$4p_1p_2 = \frac{1088}{1089} > \frac{990}{1000}.$$

Hence, if we put one more item in one half, then alpha is very close to the mean of all possible split-half reliabilities if the test consists of at least 33 items.

For the functions in (18.11) and (18.13) we have the limits

$$\lim_{k\to\infty} \frac{k^2-1}{k^2} = \lim_{k\to\infty} \frac{k^2-4}{k^2} = 1.$$

These limits suggest that for any split-half inequality (18.9) may hold for sufficiently large k. This is however not the case. For example, consider the split

$$p_1 = \frac{1}{k} \quad \text{and} \quad p_2 = \frac{k-1}{k}. \tag{18.15}$$

If we want the halves to have approximately equal sizes, this is the worst possible split. Using the proportions in (18.15) we have

$$4p_1p_2 = \frac{4(k-1)}{k^2}.$$

Due to the k^2 term in the denominator we have $4p_1p_2 \to 0$ as $k \to \infty$.

18.4 Conclusion

Coefficient alpha is the most commonly used statistic for estimating reliability of a test score if there is only one test administration (Cortina 1993; Cronbach 1951; Field 2009; Furr and Bacharach 2008; Osburn 2000; Sijtsma 2009). A famous description of alpha is that it is the mean of all (Flanagan–Rulon) split-half reliabilities. This is an important result because it provides a proper interpretation of alpha. The result is exact if the test is split into two halves that are equal in size. In this chapter we studied how alpha is related to the mean of all (Flanagan–Rulon) split-half reliabilities when the number of items is odd. The split was made so that the group sizes were as similar as possible, that is, one half contained one more item. It was shown in Sect. 18.3 that the difference between alpha and the mean of all split-half reliabilities is less than 0.01 if the test consists of at least 11 items. We conclude that given a moderate number of items alpha is approximately identical to the mean of all (Flanagan–Rulon) split-half reliabilities.

Acknowledgements This research was done while the author was funded by the Netherlands Organisation for Scientific Research, Veni project 451-11-026.

References

Abramowitz M, Stegun IA (1970) Handbook of mathematical functions (with formulas, graphs and mathematical tables). Dover, New York
Brown W (1910) Some experimental results in the correlation of mental abilities. Br J Psychol 3:296–322
Cortina JM (1993) What is coefficient alpha? An examination of theory and applications. J Appl Psychol 78:98–104
Cronbach LJ (1951) Coefficient alpha and the internal structure of tests. Psychometrika 16:297–334
Field A (2009) Discovering statistics using SPSS, 3rd edn. Sage, Los Angeles
Flanagan JC (1937) A proposed procedure for increasing the efficiency of objective tests. J Educ Psychol 28:17–21
Furr RM, Bacharach VR (2008) Psychometrics. an introduction. Sage, Los Angeles
Graham JM (2006) Congeneric and (essential) tau-equivalent estimates of score reliability. Educ Psychol Meas 66:930–944
Grayson D (2004) Some myths and legends in quantitative psychology. Underst Stat 3:101–134
Green SB, Hershberger SL (2000) Correlated errors in true score models and their effect on coefficient alpha. Struct Equ Model 7:251–270 (2000)
Green SB, Yang Y (2009) Commentary on coefficient alpha: a cautionary tale. Psychometrika 74:121–135
Guttman L (1945) A basis for analyzing test-retest reliability. Psychometrika 10:255–282
Lord FM, Novick MR (1968) Statistical theories of mental test scores (with contributions by A. Birnbaum). Addison-Wesley, Reading
McDonald RP (1999) Test theory: a unified treatment. Erlbaum, Mahwah
Osburn HG (2000) Coefficient alpha and related internal consistency reliability coefficients. Psychol Methods 5:343–355
Raju NS (1977) A generalization of coefficient alpha. Psychometrika 42:549–565

Revelle W, Zinbarg RE (2009) Coefficients alpha, beta, omega, and the GLB: comments on Sijtsma. Psychometrika 74:145–154
Rulon PJ (1939) A simplified procedure for determining the reliability of a test by split-halves. Harvard Educ Rev 9:99–103
Sheng Y, Sheng Z (2012) Is coefficient alpha robust to non-normal data? Front Psychol 3:1–13
Sijtsma K (2009) On the use, the misuse, and the very limited usefulness of Cronbach's alpha. Psychometrika 74:107–120
Spearman C (1910) Correlation calculated from faulty data. Br J Psychol 3:271–295
Thorndike RL (1971) Educational measurement. American Council on Education, Washington

Chapter 19
An Empirical Assessment of Guttman's Lambda 4 Reliability Coefficient

Tom Benton

Abstract Numerous alternative indices for test reliability have been proposed as being superior to Cronbach's alpha. One such alternative is Guttman's L4. This is calculated by dividing the items in a test into two halves such that the covariance between scores on the two halves is as high as possible. However, although simple to understand and intuitively appealing, the method can potentially be severely positively biased if the sample size is small or the number of items in the test is large.

To begin with this paper compares a number of available algorithms for calculating L4. We then empirically evaluate the bias of L4 for 51 separate upper secondary school examinations taken in the UK in June 2012. For each of these tests we have evaluated the likely bias of L4 for a range of different sample sizes. The results show that the positive bias of L4 is likely to be small if the estimated reliability is larger than 0.85, if there are less than 25 items and if a sample size of more than 3,000 is available. A sample size of 1,000 may be sufficient if the estimate of L4 is above 0.9.

Keywords Assessment • Reliability • Split-half • Lambda 4 • Bias • Sample size

19.1 Introduction

The reliability of a test score is defined as the extent to which the result achieved by any pupil would be repeated if the entire exercise were replicated (Brennan 2001). In particular we are often interested in the extent to which pupils' results would change had a different (but equally valid) set of items been used in the test rather than those that were actually included. Conceptually, the aim is to try to calculate the likely correlation between scores on the test actually sat by pupils and another (theoretical) test designed to the same specification.

T. Benton (✉)
Cambridge Assessment, 1 Hills Rd, Cambridge CB1 2EU, UK
e-mail: Benton.T@cambridgeassessment.org.uk

R.E. Millsap et al. (eds.), *Quantitative Psychology Research*, Springer Proceedings in Mathematics & Statistics 89, DOI 10.1007/978-3-319-07503-7_19

Answering the above question has become a fairly routine task within psychometrics. Whilst the most commonly applied metric used to quantify reliability is Cronbach's alpha (Cronbach 1951), research suggests that in many cases this may not be the most appropriate technique and will underestimate the true reliability of a test (Sijtsma 2009; Revelle and Zinbarg 2009).

An alternative method to calculate reliability is Guttman's[1] L4 (Guttman 1945). The concept behind the method is quite simple. Reliability is calculated by first splitting a test into two halves. For example, this might be all the odd numbered versus all the even numbered questions, or all the questions in the first half of a test versus all the questions in the second half. Now the covariance between the scores pupils achieve on each half is calculated. The variance of the total test score (that is, including both halves) is also calculated. The overall test reliability coefficient can now be calculated by the formula below.

$$\text{Reliability Coefficient} = \frac{4\text{Covariance}(\text{Half 1 scores}, \text{Half 2 scores})}{\text{Variance}(\text{Total score on test})}$$

Although the above formula can be applied to any split half, L4 is generally taken to mean the reliability from the split that maximises this coefficient.

Although L4 is an appealing reliability coefficient in terms of being easy to understand and being less likely to underestimate reliability than Cronbach's alpha, it has two notable drawbacks. Firstly, routines to calculate L4 are not included in most standard statistical packages. Secondly, as has been noted by Ten Berge and Socan (2004) there is the danger that L4 may *overestimate* reliability if there are a large number of items or if the sample size is small.

This paper intends to address both of these drawbacks. The first issue will be addressed by evaluating the performance of two recently published R packages in terms of their ability to accurately identify L4. Furthermore, R code for two further methods to calculate L4 is provided in the appendix of this paper. To address the second issue we shall empirically evaluate the bias of L4 for a number of real assessments and examine how this varies dependent upon the sample size and the number of items in the test.

19.2 Algorithms to Find L4

There are a number of possible algorithms that could be used to find the optimal split of the items into two halves.

[1]Although most subsequent literature refers to this reliability index as "Guttman's", this same coefficient was presented in an earlier work by Rulon (1939). As such it is also sometimes referred to as the "Flanagan-Rulon" coefficient.

1. An exhaustive search of all possible splits to identify the split leading to the highest reliability, although such a method will be computationally demanding if our test has a large number of items.
2. A reduced exhaustive search, where, to begin with, pairs of items that are highly correlated are deemed to be in opposite halves. This method is applied in the R package *Lambda4* written by Tyler Hunt and published in 2012.[2]
3. A cluster analysis based method drawing on the item correlation matrix. This method is applied in the R package *psych*[3] by William Revelle and first published in 2007.[4]
4. The method of Callender and Osburn (1977) based on sequentially adding one item to each half so as to maximise the reliability coefficient at each step.
5. A method based on beginning with an initial split of the items into two groups and then iteratively improving the reliability by swapping items until no further improvements are possible. This procedure is relatively straightforward and only requires the item covariance matrix as an input. It works from the fact that if X is the total current score on half 1, Y is the total current score on half 2, and we wish to switch items Xi and Yj to opposite sides then the improvement in the covariance between the two halves that will be yielded by the switch is

$$\begin{aligned}\mathrm{Cov}\left(X - Xi + Yj, Y + Xi - Yj\right) - \mathrm{Cov}\left(X, Y\right) \\ = 2\mathrm{Cov}\left(Xi, Yj\right) + \mathrm{Cov}\left(X, Xi\right) + \mathrm{Cov}\left(Y, Yj\right) \\ - \mathrm{Cov}\left(X, Yj\right) - \mathrm{Cov}\left(Y, Xi\right) - V\left(Xi\right) - V\left(Yj\right).\end{aligned}$$

All of these terms can be quickly calculated from the item covariance matrix. This allows us to identify the best possible swap and then recalculate possible improvements for subsequent swaps.

For this last method there are clearly a number of options for how to split items into two groups to start with. For many assessments, because items dealing with similar subjects are often placed consecutively in a test, a split into odd and even items may provide a sensible starting point. However, in order to increase our chances of identifying the best possible split, we may prefer to try several different starting splits and see which leads to the largest reliability coefficient overall. Hadamard matrices provide a possible effective method for trying numerous different starting splits as they can ensure that each new starting split is as different as possible from starting splits that have been tried before.

---

[2]Hunt (2013).

[3]Revelle (2013).

[4]Although the functions for finding L4 were not introduced until 2009.

R code for methods 1 and 5 is provided in the appendix[5] along with code showing how method 5 can be applied from multiple different starting values derived from a Hadamard matrix.[6]

19.3 Evaluation of Alternative Algorithms

Each of the methods described in the previous section was evaluated against data from 51 separate upper secondary school examinations taken in the UK in June 2012. These tests each contains between 10 and 37 questions[7] and were each taken by a minimum of 5,000 candidates. The number of available marks per question ranged between 1 and 22 with both the mean and the median number of available marks per question equal to 5. For each of these assessments, L4 was calculated using each of the algorithms described in the previous section. Because the *psych* package works from the correlation matrix rather than the covariance matrix, all item scores were standardised before applying any of the methods.[8]

Table 19.1 shows the results of analysis in terms of how often each algorithm identifies the best possible split of those that were identified. The table also shows the mean and median L4s from each algorithm as well as the largest amount by which the algorithm underestimated the best L4. As can be seen, the algorithm used in the *psych* package failed to find the best possible split in any of the 51 assessments. In general the reliabilities estimated by this method were not too far below the optimum (0.02 on average) but could be as high as 0.05 below the actual maximum L4. The Callender–Osburn algorithm performed a little better, identifying the optimal split in 4 out of 51 cases. More importantly, the estimated reliability from this algorithm was never more than 0.02 below the maximum L4. The algorithm in the *Lambda4* package also failed to find the optimal split for the majority of assessments. Having said this, the differences between the L4 estimated by this algorithm and the maximum L4 tended to be extremely small; roughly 0.002 on average and never more than 0.01. The start-then-improve algorithm based on starting with odd and even question numbers identified the best split for over half the assessments (28 out of 51). Once again, where this algorithm failed to find the optimum split, the difference from the largest L4 tended to be very small. The start-then-improve algorithms tended to identify the best possible split for almost

[5]The code in the appendix also applies to adjustments proposed by Raju (1977) and Feldt (1975) for cases where the split halves may be of unequal length.

[6]Hadamard matrices are generated using the *survey* package published by Thomas Lumley and available from http://cran.r-project.org/web/packages/survey/index.html (Lumley 2004).

[7]Whole question scores were analysed for the purposes of calculating reliability rather than items from the same question stem. This was to avoid the possibility of irrelevant associations between item scores within the same question spuriously inflating the reliability estimate.

[8]The same analysis was also run with unstandardized item scores. The results were very similar.

Table 19.1 Relative performance of different methods of optimising L4

Algorithm used to maximise L4	Number of times largest L4 identified (out of 51)	Mean L4	Median L4	Furthest distance below largest L4
R package *psych*	0	0.846	0.856	0.050
Callender–Osburn algorithm	4	0.861	0.867	0.020
R package *Lambda4*	13	0.863	0.868	0.010
Start-then-improve (odd/even start)	28	0.864	0.868	0.008
Start-then-improve (odd/even and 5 other random starts)	46	0.865	0.869	0.002
Start-then-improve (odd/even and 12 further starts from Hadamard matrix)	51	0.865	0.869	0.000

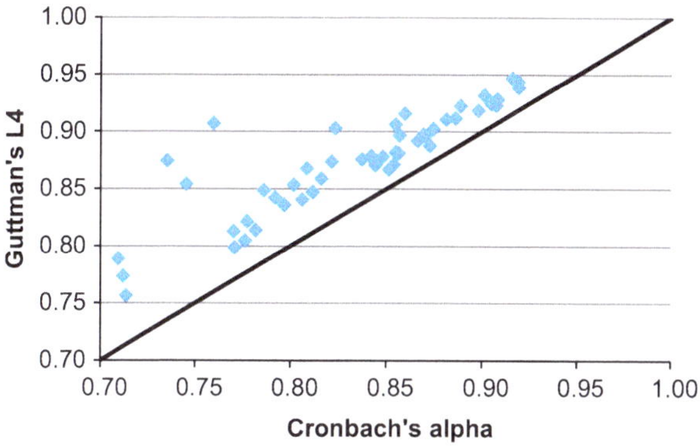

Fig. 19.1 The relationship between estimated Cronbach's alpha and L4

all assessments if an additional five random starting splits were used (46 out of 51), and for all assessments if a Hadamard matrix was used to provide additional starting splits.

Thirty-nine of the 51 assessments contained 15 questions or fewer. For these assessments the algorithm based upon exhaustive search was also applied. In every case, the best split identified by exhaustive search matched the split identified by the start-then-improve algorithm using a Hadamard matrix.

A plot of Cronbach's alpha for each of these assessments against the maximised value of L4 is shown in Fig. 19.1. As can be seen the value of L4 is universally larger than the value of alpha (as we would expect). On average there was a difference of 0.04 between the two reliability indices, although, as can be seen, for some assessments the difference was somewhat larger than this.

19.4 Examining the Level of Positive Bias in L4

Having identified an efficient algorithm to calculate L4, we now turn our attention to the issue of how the likely positive bias of L4 changes dependent upon the sample size and the number of items.

For each of the 51 assessments, ten samples at each of sizes 100, 200, 400, 800, 1,500, 3,000, and 5,000 were drawn from the available data. L4 was calculated[9] for each of the samples and the average reliability coefficient was computed for each sample size for each assessment. The results of this analysis are shown in Fig. 19.2. As can be seen, for each of the assessments, there is a tendency for the estimated value of L4 to decrease as the sample size increases. The rate of decrease is particularly evident for smaller sample sizes, indicating that in such cases L4 is likely to be severely positively biased.

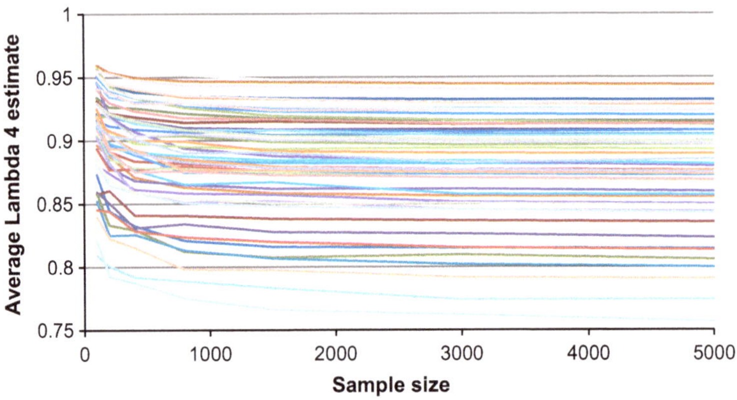

Fig. 19.2 Average values of L4 for different sample sizes for each of 51 assessments

Using the results in Fig. 19.2, it is possible to estimate a bias corrected version of L4 based upon the method suggested by Verhelst (2000, pp. 31–32). This method involves a regression analysis of estimated L4 values on the reciprocal of the square root of the sample size. The intercept[10] of this regression analysis (that is, the predicted value of L4 for an infinite sample size) is then a bias corrected estimated of L4. This procedure was applied for each of the 51 assessments allowing us to identify the estimated bias of L4 for each sample size. Of particular interest was identifying the sample size where the bias of L4 was likely to fall below 0.01 meaning that for most practical purposes the estimate could be treated as unbiased. These required sample sizes were termed the *critical sample size*.

[9]This time without standardising item scores before beginning.

[10]The intercept is referred to as the "additive coefficient" in the report by Verhelst.

The critical sample size required is plotted against the number of items for all 51 assessments in Fig. 19.3. Different coloured points are used to identify assessments with different levels of L4. For assessments with high levels of L4 (above 0.85) it can be seen that there is a fairly clear relationship between the number of items on the test and the critical sample size. On a practical note we can see that if we have less than 25 items then a sample size of 3,000 appears to be always sufficient in these cases. Furthermore, if the estimated L4 is greater than 0.9 a sample size of 1,000 appears to be usually sufficient. However, where the size of L4 is below 0.85, the relationship between the number of items and the required sample size is less clear-cut. For the small number of such assessments included in this analysis, sample sizes between 1,000 and 5,000 were required with little evidence of the required sample size being closely determined by the number of items. This indicates that, for assessments with lower estimated reliabilities, it is probably necessary to make an assessment of the likely positive bias of L4 on a case-by-case basis. This may prove particularly difficult for small sample sizes as it will require greater amount of extrapolation from the regression method used to generate bias corrected estimates.

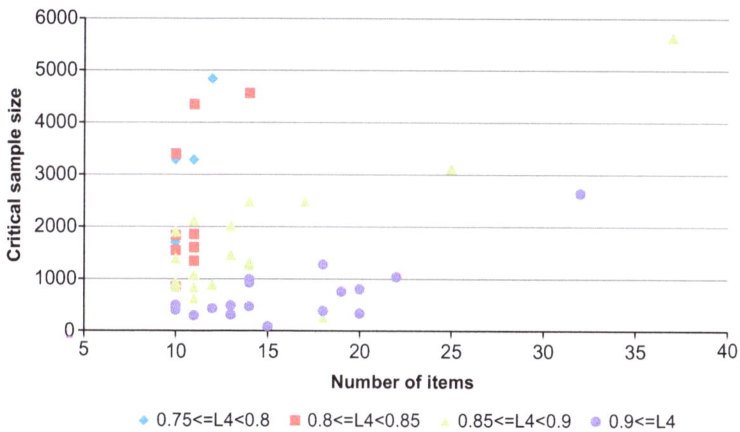

Fig. 19.3 The relationship between estimated L4, number of items and critical sample size

Conclusion

Guttman's L4 provides a reliability coefficient that is relatively simple to understand and can be easily computed using code written in R. In addition to the code provided in the appendix of this paper, the *Lambda4* package by Tyler Hunt also appears to provide a robust estimation method.

(continued)

Our analysis has confirmed that L4 can suffer from positive bias for small sample sizes. Positive bias is less likely to be an issue if the estimated value of L4 is above 0.85, if the number of items is below 25, and if the sample size is bigger than 3,000. Potentially, a sample size of 1,000 may be sufficient if the estimated value of L4 is greater than 0.9. However, our analysis shows that if the estimated value of L4 is below 0.85 it is difficult to identify the necessary sample size dependent upon the number of items. In such cases the likely bias of the method should be evaluated on a case-by-case basis.

A.1 Appendix: R Code to Find Best Split Using the "Start-Then-Improve" Algorithm

#Function to find best split half from a given starting split

```
MaxSplitHalf = function(data,xal){
#data - matrix of items scores (row=candidates,column=items)
#xal - vector of 0s and 1s specifying initial split
nite = ncol(data)
cov1 = cov(data)
v = diag(cov1)
yal = 1-xal
ones = rep(1,nite)
covxy = t(xal)%*%cov1%*%yal

#Code to examine all possible swaps
maxchg1=9;
while(maxchg1>0){
#Calculate change for swapping items in X and Y;
#This is equal to 2covxiyj+covxix+covyyj-vx-vy-covxiy-covxyj;
covxiyj = cov1
covxix = (cov1%*%xal)%*%t(ones)
covyyj = ones%*%(yal%*%cov1)
vx = v%*%t(ones)
vy = t(vx)
covxiy = (cov1%*%yal)%*%t(ones)
covxyj = ones%*%(xal%*%cov1)
result = 2*covxiyj+covxix+covyyj-vx-vy-covxiy-covxyj
for (i in 1:nite){for (j in 1:nite){if (xal[i]==xal[j])
  {result[i,j]=0}}}
#Add bits for swapping with no other item
result = cbind(result,as.vector(cov1%*%xal-cov1%*%yal-v)*xal)
result = rbind(result,c(as.vector(cov1%*%yal-cov1%*%xal-v)*yal,0))
#find indices of maximum change;
maxchg=0
maxchgx=0
maxchgy=0
which1=which(result==max(result),arr.ind=TRUE)[1,]
if (result[which1[1],which1[2]]>0){maxchgx=which1[1]
```

```
maxchgy=which1[2]
maxchg=result[which1[1],which1[2]]}
maxchg1 = maxchg
if (maxchgx>0 & maxchgx<(nite+1)) {xal[maxchgx]=0}
if (maxchgy>0 & maxchgy<(nite+1)) {xal[maxchgy]=1}
if (maxchgx>0 & maxchgx<(nite+1)) {yal[maxchgx]=1}
if (maxchgy>0 & maxchgy<(nite+1)) {yal[maxchgy]=0}
covxy = t(xal)%*%cov1%*%yal}

guttman = 4*covxy/sum(cov1)
pites = sum(xal)/nite
raju = covxy/(sum(cov1)*pites*(1-pites))

v1 = t(xal)%*%cov1%*%xal
v2 = t(yal)%*%cov1%*%yal
feldt = 4*covxy/(sum(cov1)-((v1-v2)/sqrt(sum(cov1)))**2);

res = list(guttman=as.vector(guttman),
raju=as.vector(raju),
feldt=as.vector(feldt),
xal=xal)
return(res)}
```

#Maximise L4 starting from odd/even and 12 splits from 12x12 Hadamard matrix

```
library(survey)
MaxSplitHalfHad12 = function(data){
#data - matrix of items scores (row=candidates,column=items)
#start with odd vs even
nite = ncol(data)
sequence = 1:nite
xal = (sequence%%2)
res1 = MaxSplitHalf(data,xal)
#now try 12 further splits based on 12*12 Hadamard matrix
had = hadamard(11)
for (iz in 1:12){
nextra = max(nite-12,0)
resrand = MaxSplitHalf(data,c(had[,iz],rep(0,nextra))[1:nite])
if (resrand$guttman>res1$guttman){res1 = resrand}}
return(res1)}
```

#Maximise using exhaustive search

```
library(Lambda4)
MaxSplitExhaustive = function(data){
#data - matrix of items scores (row=candidates,column=items)
cov1 = cov(data)
nite = dim(data)[2]
mat1 = (bin.combs(nite)+1)/2
res1 = list(guttman=0,xal=rep(-99,nite))
for (jjz in 1:length(mat1[,1])){
xal = mat1[jjz,]
gutt1 = 4*(t(xal)%*%cov1%*%(1-xal))/sum(cov1)
resrand = list(guttman=gutt1,xal=xal)
if (resrand$guttman>res1$guttman){res1 = resrand}}
return(res1)}
```

#Examples of use (using data from the Lambda4 package)

```
data(Rosenberg)
MaxSplitHalf(Rosenberg,c(0,1,0,1,0,1,0,1,0,1))
MaxSplitHalfHad12(Rosenberg)
MaxSplitExhaustive(Rosenberg)
```

References

Brennan R (2001) An essay on the history and future of reliability from the perspective of replications. J Educ Meas 38:295–317
Callender J, Osburn H (1977) A method for maximizing and cross-validating split-half reliability coefficients. Educ Psychol Meas 37:819–826
Cronbach L (1951) Coefficient alpha and the internal structure of tests. Psychometrika 16:297–334
Feldt L (1975) Estimation of the reliability of a test divided into two parts of unequal length. Psychometrika 40:557–561
Guttman L (1945) A basis for analysing test-retest reliability. Psychometrika 10:255–282
Hunt T (2013) Lambda4: collection of internal consistency reliability coefficients. R package version 3.0. http://CRAN.R-project.org/package=Lambda4
Lumley T (2004) Analysis of complex survey samples. J Statist Softw 9:1–19
Raju N (1977) A generalization of coefficient alpha. Psychometrika 42:549–565
Revelle W (2013) Psych: procedures for personality and psychological research. Northwestern University, Evanston. http://CRAN.R-project.org/package=psych
Revelle W, Zinbarg R (2009) Coefficients alpha, beta, omega, and the glb: comments on Sijtsma. Psychometrika 74:145–154
Rulon P (1939) A simplified procedure for determining the reliability of a test by split-halves. Harv Educ Rev 9:99–103
Sijtsma K (2009) On the use, the misuse and the very limited usefulness of Cronbach's alpha. Psychometrika 74:107–120
Ten Berge J, Socan G (2004) The greatest lower bound to the reliability of a test and the hypothesis of unidimensionality. Psychometrika 69:613–625
Verhelst N (2000) Estimating the reliability of a test from a single test administration. CITO, Arnhem. http://www.cito.com/en/research_and_development/psychometrics/~/media/cito_com/research_and_development/publications/cito_report98_2.ashx

Chapter 20
A Test for Ordinal Measurement Invariance

Rudy Ligtvoet

Abstract One problem with the analysis of measurement invariance is the reliance of the analysis on having a parametric model that accurately describes the data. In this paper an ordinal version of the property of measurement invariance is proposed, which relies only on nonparametric restrictions. This property of ordinal measurement invariance provides a coarse (initial) indication of measurement invariance, based on the sum scores. A small example is given to illustrate the procedure for testing the property of ordinal measurement invariance.

20.1 Introduction

Many of the questions asked in psychological research are of the type "Does group A score lower on X than group B?", where the groups A and B may differ, for example, according to their demographics or with respect to the treatment the members of the group received, and X is an observable measure of some psychological attribute on which the groups are to be compared. Because most psychological attributes do not render themselves for direct observations, psychological test usually comprises of multiple test items, which are assumed to elicit responses thought to be typical for the attribute that the test is suppose to measure. These responses are assigned item scores, and these multiple item scores need to be aggregated to obtain X. Let Y_i denote the item score variable of item i, with scores $y_i \in \{1, 2, \ldots, m_i\}$ assigned to it, and also let $Y = (Y_1, \ldots, Y_k)$ denote the vector with the k item score variables. Before comparing two groups, two questions need to be addressed. The first of these questions is: What scoring rule should be used to obtain X? In item response theory, a latent variable Θ is assumed to account for the associations that exist between the item scores, and if an IRT model is found to accurately describe Y, then the scoring rule could simply consist of the estimation of Θ based on, say, maximum likelihood or Bayesian methods. In practice, however, we find that the simple sum score $\sum_{i=1}^{k} Y_i$ is the most popular scoring rule (and is used often without any empirical support). But beside the choices of a scoring rule, there is also the question concerning the

R. Ligtvoet (✉)
University of Amsterdam, Nieuwe Achtergracht 127, 1018 WS Amsterdam, The Netherlands
e-mail: r.ligtvoet@uva.nl

R.E. Millsap et al. (eds.), *Quantitative Psychology Research*, Springer Proceedings in Mathematics & Statistics 89, DOI 10.1007/978-3-319-07503-7_20

comparability of the scores to consider: Are the measures X for the different groups commensurable? Does the attribute as expressed by X bare the same meaning for the different groups, or are we comparing apples with oranges? For example, asking men questions about women's rights might reflect their attitude towards a liberal society, whereas for women, the same questions might be a measure of their personal freedom. Ignoring the question of commensurable measures might lead to the conclusion that men are more positive towards a liberal society than women feel free. But this would be a meaningless comparison.

In IRT, the question of commensurable measures is addressed by the analysis of measurement invariance (Mellenbergh 1989; Meredith and Millsap 1992; Millsap and Everson 1993). To define measurement invariance, Meredith and Millsap (1992) considered a selection rule that operates on the demographics of the members of a parent group (here $A \cup B$) for which measurements from the IRT model are deemed appropriate. This selection rule creates the subgroups (A and B) by selecting only the members of a particular group, and measurement invariance corresponds to the case for which the distribution of Y given $\Theta = \theta$ is the same irrespective of the selection rule (i.e., the same for A and B). The implication of this definition is that (1) the same IRT model should hold for both groups A and B, as well as their parent, and (2) to guarantee that the distribution of Y given $\Theta = \theta$ is the same for both groups, all item parameters should be the same. For the practical analysis of measurement invariance this amounts to testing the IRT model for both groups and imposing equality restrictions across the item parameters of the two groups. But what if we cannot find an appropriate IRT model?

The problem with the analysis of measurement invariance as outlined above is that it relies heavily on having an adequate IRT model for the item scores. Failure of an IRT model to accurately describe the item scores may lead to incorrect conclusions with regard to the property of measurement invariance. To alleviate the burden of finding an adequate parametric IRT model, a more general type of model may be considered (Mokken 1971; Molenaar 1997). Such general ordinal models are characterized by inequality restrictions, like monotonicity, where the item score functions relating Θ to Y_i (for $i = 1, \ldots, k$) are not subjected to a particular parametric shape. Instead, these ordinal models provide information on whether some scores of Y may be more or less likely for some values of θ. Having an adequate ordinal model does, however, not guarantee that the distribution of Y is exactly equal across groups for a given value θ. So the problem with the analysis of measurement invariance is that the burden on the IRT model is of the all-or-nothing type with respect to the parametric requirements it imposes on Y; but see also Shealy and Stout (1993). In this paper, an ordinal version of measurement invariance is introduced to provide a middle ground for the analysis of measurement invariance. For this ordinal version of measurement invariance only the first implication of finding an adequate model for A and B is tested. So, we say that for the two groups A and B ordinal measurement invariance holds, if it is found that: (a) (a falsifiable) model holds for group A, and the same model also holds for (b) group B, and (c) the combination of the groups A and B (i.e., $A \cup B$). Here, the adjective "falsifiable" is added to the definition to exclude most trivial cases. As a model for Y, the isotonic partial credit model is here considered (Ligtvoet 2012). The reason for considering this model is (1) it is general in the sense that it does not impose any parametric restriction onto the item score distribution, and may thus be applicable to a wider range of test scores, (2) it implies a stochastic ordering of Θ by the sum scores $\sum_{i=1}^{k} Y_i$, thus providing a scoring rule for obtaining ordinal measures, and (3) it imposes restrictions on the distribution of Y that allow the model to be tested empirically (Ligtvoet in press).

20.2 Model and Procedure

Like most IRT models, the assumptions of conditional independence and monotonicity are at the heart of the isotonic partial credit model. Conditional independence states that the item scores are independent given $\Theta = \theta$. The monotonicity assumption pertains to the local odds of a score $Y_i = y_i$ over $Y_i = y_i - 1$, which corresponds to a class of models (Hemker et al. 1997; Thissen and Steinberg 1986) to which, for example, the partial credit model belongs (Masters 1982). Monotonicity means that the local odds are non-decreasing in θ. In addition to the conditional independence and monotonicity assumptions, the isotonic partial credit model assumes that these local odds are decreasing for higher values of y_i given $\Theta = \theta$ (Ligtvoet 2012). In case the item i is assigned binary scores (i.e., $y_i \in \{1,2\}$), only a single local odds exist for the item, and the third assumption becomes superfluous. Hence, for binary item scores (i.e., $m_i = m = 2$), the isotonic partial credit model is equivalent to the monotone homogeneity model (Mokken 1971). For the case of binary item scores this means that the analysis proposed below for ordinal measurement invariance may also be viewed as an initial test for measurement invariance before subjecting the item scores to the parametric requirements of, say, the Rasch model (Rasch 1960) or the 2-parameter logistic model (Birnbaum 1968). For the present purpose, the two important properties of the isotonic partial credit model are that it provides a direct method for testing the model based on the observable Y, and that it allows for the sum score $\sum_{i=1}^{k} Y_i$ to be used for the ordinal comparison of the groups on Θ.

Consider a partition of Y into three non-empty sets of item scores, whereby we compute the sum score of each of the three sets. Ligtvoet (in press) showed that the isotonic partial credit model implies that the three-variate distribution of the three sum scores is totally positive (Karlin and Rinott 1980). This means that the isotonic partial credit model implies that each of the bivariate 2×2 sub-tables of the joint distribution of two of the sum scores has a non-negative determinant conditional on any value of the third sum score. To test whether this ordinal restriction on the distribution of the three sum scores holds for any of these sub-tables, Ligtvoet (in press) proposed a test, which basically looks at all the implied inequalities, selects the largest (if any) standardized violation of the restrictions, and tests whether this violation is significant. A significant result would discredit the hypothesis that the isotonic partial credit model provides an adequate description of the item scores. One problem to take into consideration is that the three-variate distribution of the three sum scores may contain many empty or sparse numbers of observations, which would produce unreliable test results. This problem of sparse numbers of observations was tackled by joining adjacent sum scores to obtain a more coarse but better supported distribution of the observed scores, and subsequently test the largest violation at $\alpha = 0.01$; see Ligtvoet (in press) for details of the testing procedure.

20.3 Example

To illustrate the test procedure, a hypothetical example is considered, consisting of the scores on six items, with $m_i = 3$ if i is an even number, and with binary scores for the odd numbered items. Consider also a sample of size 500 from group A, whereby the item scores are partitioned into the three sets containing the first two, the middle two, and the last two items, respectively; i.e., $Y = ((Y_1, Y_2), (Y_3, Y_4), (Y_5, Y_6))$. Table 20.1 shows the observed three-variate distribution of the sum scores on the three sets of item score variables. Table 20.2 shows the distribution after joining the sum scores 3–5 of the first set and 4–5 of the third set to account for the sparse data, where observations were considered sparse in case of fewer than three observations. In boldface it also shows a 2×2 sub-table for which the determinant is negative. These boldface observations correspond to the largest standardized violation: $z = -2.136, p = 0.016$, which is not significant according to the criterion of $\alpha = 0.01$. Hence, on the basis of these observations, the isotonic partial credit model is not rejected for group A.

Next, consider also group B with a sample size of 500 responding to the same items. Table 20.3 shows the observed three-variate distribution of the sum scores on the three sets of item score variables after joining the sum scores 2–4 of the second set and 1–2 of the third set to account for the sparse data. Again, the observations

Table 20.1 Observed three-variate sum-score distribution of group A

	2				3				4				5			
	2	3	4	5	2	3	4	5	2	3	4	5	2	3	4	5
2	14	31	28	5	14	27	24	5	7	16	11	8	2	4	1	1
3	7	28	21	6	7	17	24	12	1	10	14	9	2	5	7	5
4	1	6	8	6	4	13	17	11	0	1	11	14	0	1	2	4
5	0	0	2	2	0	1	4	4	0	0	0	6	0	1	0	8

Table 20.2 Observed three-variate sum-score distribution after joining adjacent sum scores

	2				3				4–5			
	2	3	4	5	2	3	4	5	2	3	4	5
2	14	31	28	5	**14**	27	24	5	**9**	20	12	9
3–5	8	34	31	14	**11**	31	45	27	**3**	18	34	46

Table 20.3 Distribution after joining sum scores for group *B*

	2–3		4		5	
	2-4	5	2-4	5	2-4	5
2	18	5	6	4	3	7
3	30	19	20	23	11	30
4	18	**23**	15	**46**	26	60
5	8	**22**	10	**30**	18	48

Table 20.4 Counter example

A		*B*		$A \cup B$	
1	1	2	4	3	5
2	2	1	2	3	4

Table 20.5 Observed distribution, after joining adjacent sum scores, for $A \cup B$

	2			3			4			5		
	2-3	4	5	2-3	4	5	2-3	4	5	2-3	4	5
2	49	31	8	**44**	32	7	**28**	12	12	7	3	8
3	37	28	9	**31**	38	28	**14**	31	32	10	15	35
4–5	9	12	16	22	39	52	4	33	96	4	44	120

that corresponding to the largest standardized violation are indicated in boldface: $z = -0.519, p = 0.302$. For group *B*, the isotonic partial credit model is also not rejected.

For testing ordinal measurement invariance, it is not sufficient to test the isotonic partial credit model for groups *A* and *B* separately, because the model for both groups separately does not guarantee that the model also holds for the two groups together (i.e., the parent $A \cup B$). To illustrate this consider the values in Table 20.4, for the 2×2 tables of observations of groups *A* and *B*. For both groups, the determinant is non negative, but combining the frequencies by joining the groups results in a negative determinant. Hence, a third test is performed for the isotonic partial credit model on the combined observations of the two groups.

Table 20.5 shows the observed distribution of the sum scores on the three sets of item score variables after joining the sum scores 4–5 of the first set and 2–3 of the third set to account for the sparse data. Again, in boldface the observations are indicated corresponding to the largest standardized violation: $z = -1.984, p = 0.024$, which is again not significant at $\alpha = 0.01$. On the basis of the above three tests, it is thus concluded that *the hypothesis of ordinal measurement invariance could not be rejected for this example.*

Finally, to assess whether group *A* score lower on $\sum_{i=1}^{k} Y_i$ than group *B*, Table 20.6 shows the cumulative proportions of the sum scores of both groups. For group *B*, the cumulative proportions in Table 20.6 are smaller than the proportions of group *A* for each sum score, so it may be inferred that *the distribution of the sum scores of group A stochastically dominates the distribution of group B*. A significance test for this type of ordering of distributions was proposed by Darnanoni and Forcina (1998).

Table 20.6 Cumulative proportions of the sum scores for group *A* and group *B*

$\sum Y_i$	6	7	8	9	10	11	12	13	14	15
A	0.028	0.132	0.328	0.520	0.686	0.820	0.912	0.964	0.984	1.000
B	0.002	0.008	0.028	0.090	0.146	0.268	0.430	0.690	0.904	1.000

For this example, such a statistical test is redundant as the unrestricted proportions all satisfy the ordinal restrictions, a situation which always favours the hypothesis that the distribution of the sum score of group *A* dominates the distribution of group *B*. (The same conclusion holds when testing the difference of medians or performing a statistical test on the rank numbers.)

20.4 Discussion

The hypothesis of ordinal measurement invariance based on the isotonic partial credit model implies that the ordering by the sum scores reflects an ordering on Θ, irrespective of the group membership. It should be stressed, however, that the analysis of ordinal measurement invariance does not undermine the importance or replace the need for measurement invariance analysis based on adequate parametric models. It seems, for example, necessary to impose equality restrictions onto the item score distribution to be able to make inferences about the fairness of any comparison on the individual level (Shealy and Stout 1993). Ordinal measurement invariance only provides a coarse comparison of groups that differ with respect to the sum-score distribution. However, if the application at hand only requires such a coarse comparison, without the need to compare individual group members, then the proposed procedure does offer an extension to measurement invariance research that reaches beyond the realm of parametric IRT models.

References

Birnbaum A (1968) Some latent trait models and their use in inferring an examinee's ability. In: Lord FM, Novick MR (eds) Statistical theories of mental test scores. Addison-Wesley, Reading, pp 397–479

Darnanoni V, Forcina A (1998) A unified approach to likelihood inference on stochastic orderings in a nonparametric context. J Am Stat Assoc 93:1112–1123

Hemker BT, Sijtsma K, Molenaar IW, Junker BW (1997) Stochastic ordering using the latent trait and the sum score in polytomous IRT models. Psychometrika 62:331–347

Karlin S, Rinott Y (1980) Classes of orderings of measures and related correlation inequalities. I. Multivariate totally positive distributions. J Multivar Anal 10:467–498

Ligtvoet R (2012) An isotonic partial credit model for ordering subjects on the basis of their sum scores. Psychometrika 77:479–494

Ligtvoet R (in press) A test for using the sum score to obtain a stochastic ordering of subjects. J Multivariate Anal

Masters G (1982) A Rasch model for partial credit scoring. Psychometrika 47:149–174

Mellenbergh GJ (1989) Item bias and item response theory. Int J Educ Res 13:127–142

Meredith W, Millsap RE (1992) On the misuse of manifest variables in the detection of measurement bias. Psychometrika 57:289–311

Millsap RE, Everson HT (1993) Methodology review: statistical approaches for assessing measurement bias. Appl Psychol Meas 17:297–334

Mokken RJ (1971) A theory and procedure for scale analysis. Mouton, The Hague

Molenaar IW (1997) Nonparametric models for polytomous responses. In: van der Linden WJ, Hambleton RK (eds) Handbook of modern item response theory. Springer, New York, pp 369–380

Rasch G (1960) Probabilistic models for some intelligence and attainment tests. Nielsen & Lydiche, Copenhagen

Shealy R, Stout W (1993) A model-based standardization approach that separates true bias/DIF from group ability differences and detects test bias/DTF as well as item bias/DIF. Psychometrika 58:159–194

Thissen D, Steinberg L (1986) A taxonomy of item response models. Psychometrika 51:567–577

Chapter 21
Model Selection Criteria for Latent Growth Models Using Bayesian Methods

Zhenqiu (Laura) Lu, Zhiyong Zhang, and Allan Cohen

Abstract Research in applied areas, such as statistical, psychological, behavioral, and educational areas, often involves the selection of the best available model from among a large set of candidate models. Considering that there is no well-defined model selection criterion in a Bayesian context and that latent growth mixture models are becoming popular in many areas, the goal of this study is to investigate the performance of a series of model selection criteria in the framework of latent growth mixture models with missing data and outliers in a Bayesian context. This study conducted five simulation studies to cover different cases, including latent growth curve models with missing data, latent growth curve models with missing data and outliers, growth mixture models with missing data and outliers, extended growth mixture models with missing data and outliers, and latent growth models with different classes. Simulation results show that almost all the proposed criteria can effectively identify the true models. This study also illustrated the application of these model selection criteria in real data analysis. The results will help inform the selection of growth models by researchers seeking to provide states with accurate estimates of the growth of their students.

21.1 Introduction

Traditional criteria are available for researchers to select the best-fit model from among a large set of candidate models. Akaike (1974) proposed the Akaike's information criterion (AIC), which offers a relative measure of the information lost. For Bayesian models the Bayes factor, which is the ratio of posterior odds to prior odds, can work for both hypothesis testing and model comparison. But the Bayes factor is often difficult or impossible to calculate, especially for models that involve random effects, large numbers of unknowns or improper priors. To approximate

Z. Lu (✉) • A. Cohen
University of Georgia, Athens, GA 30602, USA
e-mail: zlu@uga.edu; acohen@uga.edu

Z. Zhang
University of Notre Dame, Notre Dame, IN 46556, USA
e-mail: zhangzhiyong@nd.edu

R.E. Millsap et al. (eds.), *Quantitative Psychology Research*, Springer Proceedings in Mathematics & Statistics 89, DOI 10.1007/978-3-319-07503-7_21

the Bayes factor, Schwarz (1978) developed the Bayesian information criterion (BIC, sometimes called the Schwarz criterion). To obtain more precise criteria, Bozdogan (1987) proposed the consistent Akaike information criterion (CAIC), and Sclove (1987) proposed the sample-size adjusted Bayesian information criterion (ssBIC). The deviance information criterion (DIC, Spiegelhalter et al. 2002) is a recently developed criterion designed for hierarchical models. It is based on the posterior distribution of the log-likelihood and is useful in Bayesian model selection problems where the posterior distributions have been obtained by Markov chain Monte Carlo (MCMC) simulation. DIC is usually regarded as a generalization of AIC and BIC. It is defined analogously to AIC or BIC with a penalty term of the number equal to effective model parameters in Bayesian models. In practice, rough DIC (RDIC or DICV in some literature, e.g., Oldmeadow and Keith 2011) is an approximation of DIC. The mathematical forms of AIC, BIC, CAIC, ssBIC, and DIC are closely related to each other. They all try to find a balance between accuracy and complexity of the fitting model. The accuracy of a model can be shown by a deviance $D(\theta) = -2log(f(y|\theta)) + C$ for some constant C where θ is a vector of model parameters. For all the criteria above, the model with a smaller criterion value is better supported by data.

Bayesian approach is becoming increasingly important in estimating models as it provides many advantages in dealing with complex statistical models with complicated data structure (e.g., Dunson 2000). However, there is no well-defined model selection criterion in a Bayesian context (e.g., Celeux et al. 2006). There are at least three problems. First, in a Bayesian context there are two versions of deviance because the Bayesian procedure generates Monte Carlo Markov chains for each parameter. One version is the posterior estimate which can be expressed as $D(\hat{\theta}) = -2log(p(y|E_{\theta|y}[\theta])) + C$, which is analogous to a frequentist estimate. It can be estimated by adopting a point parameter estimate of θ. Another version is the Monte Carlo estimate of the expected deviance, which can be calculated as $\overline{D(\theta)} = E_{\theta|y}[-2log(p(y|\theta))] + C$, which is based on Bayesian iterations. It can be estimated as the posterior mean across a converged Markov chain. Conceptually, $\overline{D(\theta)}$ is the average of all deviances, and $D(\hat{\theta})$ is the deviance of the average of all estimates. The second problem is related to the complexity of the raw data. The data often come from heterogeneous populations which almost unavoidable contain outliers and attrition. The estimates from mis-specified models may result in severely misleading conclusions. The third problem relates to the likelihood function. When latent variables are considered in statistical models, the likelihood function can be an observed-data likelihood function, a complete-data likelihood function, or a conditional likelihood function (Celeux et al. 2006). Furthermore, if data come from heterogeneous populations, the class membership indicator may have different versions, for example, a posterior mode or a posterior mean. Also, with missing data, the likelihood functions have different ways to construct.

To address these problems, new criteria are expected. As latent growth modeling is becoming increasingly popular in applied research, such as in statistical, psychological, behavioral, and educational areas, in this study we consider to use latent growth models to test the performance of proposed model selection criteria.

Specifically, the goal of this paper is to examine the performance of the Bayesian model selection criteria with more general growth models, such as non-normally distributed growth models, robust growth mixture models, and robust extended growth mixture models. Lu et al. (2013b) proposed a series of Bayesian criteria, based on the traditional model selection criteria. However, in Lu et al. (2013b) the performances of these criteria were investigated when data are non-mixture, normally distributed, and with simple non-ignorable missingness. And only latent growth models were used. In this study, data are more complex. We conduct five simulation studies. The results will help inform the selection of growth models by researchers seeking to provide people with accurate estimates of growth across a variety of possible contexts.

21.2 Robust Growth Models with Non-ignorable Missingness

Our investigation of the performance of the Bayesian selection criteria involves fitting growth models to complex data. In this section, different types of growth models are briefly introduced. Given the fact that the data used in growth models are almost inevitably contain attrition (e.g., Little and Rubin 2002; Yuan and Lu 2008; Lu et al. 2011) and outliers (e.g., Maronna et al. 2006), different types of growth models are developed, which include traditional latent growth curve models with missing data (Lu et al. 2013b), robust growth curve models (Zhang et al. 2013) with missing data (Lu et al. 2013a), growth mixture models (e.g., Bartholomew and Knott 1999) with missing data (Lu and Zhang 2014), extended growth mixture models (EGMMs, Muthén and Shedden 1999) with missing data (Lu and Zhang 2014), and robust growth mixture models with missing data (Lu and Zhang 2014).

In the following, we discuss three types of models: traditional growth models (including growth curve models, growth mixture models, and extended growth mixture models), robust growth models (including three types of robust models), and models that account for missingness (we mainly focus on non-ignorable missingness). By combining different elements of these models, it becomes possible to consider a series of growth models with a variety of missing data mechanisms and contaminated data.

21.2.1 Traditional Growth Models

The density for a latent growth curve model is

$$\begin{cases} y_i = \Lambda \eta_i + \mathbf{e}_i, \\ \eta_i = \boldsymbol{\beta} + \boldsymbol{\xi}_i, \end{cases} \tag{21.1}$$

where y_i is a $T \times 1$ vector of outcomes for participant $i\,(i = 1,\ldots,N)$, η_i is a $q \times 1$ vector of latent effects, Λ is a $T \times q$ matrix of factor loadings for η_i, $\mathbf{e}_i$ is a $T \times 1$ vector of residual or measurement errors, $\boldsymbol{\beta}$ is a $q \times 1$ vector of fixed-effects, and $\boldsymbol{\xi}_i$ captures the variation of η_i. We have to note that $\mathbf{e}_i$ and $\boldsymbol{\xi}_i$ are usually assumed normally distributed but not necessary. When data have outliers and are heavy-tailed, this assumption might cause estimate biases. To reduce the effects of outliers, we adopt robust models in this study.

The density function of a growth mixture model is

$$f(y_i) = \sum_{k=1}^{K} \pi_k f_k(y_i), \tag{21.2}$$

where π_k is the invariant class probability (or weight) for class k satisfying $0 \le \pi_k \le 1$ and $\sum_{k=1}^{K} \pi_k = 1$ (e.g., McLachlan and Peel 2000), and $f_k(y_i)(k = 1,\ldots,K)$ is the density of a latent growth model for class k.

For extended growth mixture models (EGMMs, Muthén and Shedden 1999), π_k is not invariant across individuals. It is allowed to vary individually depending on covariates, so it is expressed as $\pi_{ik}(\mathbf{x}_i)$. If a probit link function is used, then

$$\begin{cases} \pi_{i1}(\mathbf{x}_i) = \Phi(X_i'\,\varphi_1), \\ \pi_{ik}(\mathbf{x}_i) = \Phi(X_i'\,\varphi_k) - \Phi(X_i'\,\varphi_{k-1}),\ (k = 2,3,\ldots,K-1) \\ \pi_{iK}(\mathbf{x}_i) = 1 - \Phi(X_i'\,\varphi_{K-1}), \end{cases} \tag{21.3}$$

where $\Phi(\cdot)$ is the cumulative distribution function (CDF) of the standard normal distribution, and $X_i = (1, \mathbf{x}_i')'$ with an $r \times 1$ vector of observed covariates $\mathbf{x}_i$. Note that $\Phi(X_i'\varphi_k) = \sum_{j=1}^{k} \pi_{ij}(\mathbf{x}_i)$ and $\Phi(X_i'\varphi_K) \equiv 1$.

A dummy variable $\mathbf{z}_i = (z_{i1}, z_{i2}, \cdots, z_{iK})'$ is used to indicate the class membership. If individual i comes from group k, $z_{ik} = 1$ and $z_{ij} = 0$ $(\forall j \neq k)$. $\mathbf{z}_i$ is multinomially distributed (McLachlan and Peel 2000, p. 7), that is, $\mathbf{z}_i \sim MultiNomial(\pi_{i1}, \pi_{i2}, \ldots, \pi_{iK})$.

21.2.2 Robust Growth Models

When data have outliers and are heavy-tailed, robust methods are used to reduce the effects of outliers. As t-distributions are more robust than normal distributions, the following are robust growth models (Lu et al. 2013a; Zhang et al. 2013).

(1) t-Normal (TN) model in which the measurement errors are t-distributed and the latent random effects are normally distributed,

$$\begin{cases} \mathbf{e}_i \sim Mt_T(\mathbf{0}, \boldsymbol{\Theta}, \nu), \\ \boldsymbol{\xi}_i \sim MN_q(\mathbf{0}, \boldsymbol{\Psi}), \end{cases} \tag{21.4}$$

where $Mt_T(\mathbf{0}, \boldsymbol{\Theta}, \nu)$ is a T-dimensional multivariate t-distribution with a scale matrix $\boldsymbol{\Theta}$ and degrees of freedom ν, and $MN_q(\mathbf{0}, \boldsymbol{\Psi})$ is a q-dimensional multivariate Normal distribution with a covariance matrix $\boldsymbol{\Psi}$.

(2) Normal-t (NT) model in which the measurement errors are normally distributed but the latent random effects are t-distributed,

$$\begin{cases} \mathbf{e}_i \sim MN_T(\mathbf{0}, \boldsymbol{\Theta}), \\ \boldsymbol{\xi}_i \sim Mt_q(\mathbf{0}, \boldsymbol{\Psi}, u). \end{cases} \tag{21.5}$$

(3) t-t (TT) model in which both the measurement errors and the latent random effects are t-distributed,

$$\begin{cases} \mathbf{e}_i \sim Mt_T(\mathbf{0}, \boldsymbol{\Theta}, \nu), \\ \boldsymbol{\xi}_i \sim Mt_q(\mathbf{0}, \boldsymbol{\Psi}, u). \end{cases} \tag{21.6}$$

21.2.3 Non-ignorable Missingness

To build models with non-ignorable missingness, selection models (Glynn et al. 1986; Little 1993, 1995) are used. For individual i, let $\mathbf{m}_i = (m_{i1}, m_{i2}, \ldots, m_{iT})'$ be a missing data indicator for y_i, with $m_{it} = 1$ when y_{it} is missing and 0 when observed. Let $\tau_{it} = p(m_{it} = 1)$ be the probability that y_{it} is missing. Then $m_{it} \sim \text{Bernoulli}(\tau_{it})$, so its density function is $f(m_{it}) = \tau_{it}^{m_{it}}(1-\tau_{it})^{(1-m_{it})}$. The missingness probability τ_{it} can have different forms. Lu and Zhang (2014) proposed the following non-ignorable missingness mechanisms for mixture models.

(1) Latent-Class-Intercept-Dependent (LCID) missingness in which τ_{it} is a function of latent class, covariates, and latent individual initial levels. For example, students are more likely to miss a test if their starting levels of that course are low. We model it as follows.

$$\tau_{it} = \Phi(\mathbf{z}_i'\boldsymbol{\gamma}_{zt} + I_i\gamma_{It} + \mathbf{x}_i'\boldsymbol{\gamma}_{xt}), \tag{21.7}$$

where I_i is the latent initial levels for individual i, γ_{It} is the coefficient for I_i, $\boldsymbol{\gamma}_{zt}$ is the coefficient for class membership, and $\boldsymbol{\gamma}_{xt}$ are coefficients for covariates. For non-mixture homogenous growth models, LCID can be simplified to Latent-Intercept-Dependent (LID) without the class membership indicator $\mathbf{z}_i$ and expressed as $\tau_{it} = \Phi(\gamma_{0t} + I_i\gamma_{It} + \mathbf{x}_i'\boldsymbol{\gamma}_{xt})$, where γ_{0t} is the intercept.

(2) Latent-Class-Slope-Dependent (LCSD) missingness in which τ_{it} is a function of latent class, covariates, and latent individual slopes of growth. For example, students are more likely to miss a test if they have slow growth of the course. In this case, τ_{it} can be modelled as

$$\tau_{it} = \Phi(\mathbf{z}_i'\boldsymbol{\gamma}_{zt} + S_i\gamma_{St} + \mathbf{x}_i'\boldsymbol{\gamma}_{xt}), \tag{21.8}$$

where S_i is the latent slope for individual i, and γ_{St} is the coefficient for S_i. Similarly, for non-mixture homogenous growth models, LCSD is simplified to Latent-Slope-Dependent (LSD) case as $\tau_{it} = \Phi(\gamma_{0t} + S_i\gamma_{St} + \mathbf{x}_i'\boldsymbol{\gamma}_{xt})$.

(3) Latent-Class-Outcome-Dependent (LCOD) missingness in which τ_{it} is a function of latent class, covariates, and potential outcomes that may be missing. For example, a student who feels he/she is not doing well on the test may be more likely to give up taking the rest of the test. We express τ_{it} as

$$\tau_{it} = \Phi(\mathbf{z}_i'\boldsymbol{\gamma}_{zt} + y_{it}\gamma_{yt} + \mathbf{x}_i'\boldsymbol{\gamma}_{xt}), \tag{21.9}$$

where y_{it} is the potential outcomes for individual i at time t, and γ_{yt} is the coefficient for y_{it}. And LCOD can be simplified to Latent-Outcome-Dependent (LOD) for non-mixture homogeneous growth models with a probability of missingness $\tau_{it} = \Phi(\gamma_{0t} + y_{it}\gamma_{yt} + \mathbf{x}_i'\boldsymbol{\gamma}_{xt})$.

In a more general framework, LCID and LCSD can be further encompassed into Latent-Class-Random Effect-Dependent missingness as intercept and slope are different random effects according to different situations under consideration. And for non-mixture structure, LID and LSD are encompassed into Latent-Random Effect-Dependent missingness.

21.3 Bayesian Selection Criteria

Based on Lu et al. (2013a), model selection criteria are proposed in the framework of Bayesian growth models with missing data. The definitions of selection criteria are listed in Table 21.1. The model selection criteria in the table are based on two versions of deviance in the Bayesian context, $E_{D|y}[D(\theta)]$ and $D(E_{\theta|y}[\theta])$. As we have discussed in the introduction section, $E_{\theta|y}[D]$ is the expected value of all the deviances, and $D(E_{\theta|y}[\theta])$ is the deviance score based on the expected parameters. For different models, the detailed mathematical form of these two deviances is different. In this paper, we focus on both homogeneous and heterogenous latent growth models with non-ignorable missing data.

(1) We first look at the homogeneous growth curve models with non-ignorable missing data. One version of deviance, $E_{D|y}[D(\theta)]$, is approximated by

$$\begin{aligned} E_{D|y}[D(\theta)] \approx \overline{D(\theta)} &= -\frac{2}{S}\sum_{s=1}^{S}\sum_{i=1}^{N}\sum_{1=t}^{T} l_{it}^{(s)}(\theta|y,m) \\ &= -\frac{2}{S}\sum_{s=1}^{S}\sum_{i=1}^{N}\sum_{1=t}^{T}\left[(1-m_{it}^{(s)})l_{it}^{(s)}(y) + l_{it}^{(s)}(m)\right], \end{aligned} \tag{21.10}$$

Table 21.1 Model selection criteria

Criterion(Index) =	Deviance +	Penalty
Dbar.AIC[a]	$\overline{D(\theta)}$[b]	2 p
Dbar.BIC[c]	$\overline{D(\theta)}$	log(N) p
Dbar.CAIC	$\overline{D(\theta)}$	(log(N)+1) p
Dbar.ssBIC	$\overline{D(\theta)}$	log((N+2)/24) p
RDIC	$\overline{D(\theta)}$	var(Dbar)/2
Dhat.AIC	$D(\hat{\theta})$[d]	2 p
Dhat.BIC	$D(\hat{\theta})$	log(N) p
Dhat.CAIC	$D(\hat{\theta})$	(log(N)+1) p
Dhat.ssBIC	$D(\hat{\theta})$	log((N+2)/24) p
DIC[e]	$D(\hat{\theta})$	2 pD

[a] p is the number of parameters, which are on the same level as the likelihood value is.
[b] $\overline{D(\theta)}$ is shown as in Eq. (21.10) for growth curve models and as in Eq. (21.13) for growth mixture models. It is one type of the approximations of the deviance score.
[c] N is the sample size.
[d] $D(\hat{\theta})$ is shown as in Eq. (21.12) for growth curve models and as in Eq. (21.14) for growth mixture models
[e] $pD = \overline{D(\theta)} - D(\hat{\theta})$

where S is the number of iterations for converged Markov chains, $l_{it}^{(s)}(\theta|y,m) = log(L_{it}^{(s)}(\theta|y,m))$ is a conditional joint loglikelihood function (see, Celeux et al. 2006) of y and m, m_{it} is the missing data indicator for individual i at time t with a likelihood function $l_{ikt}(m) = m_{it}log(\tau_{it}) + (1-m_{it})log(1-\tau_{it})$, where τ_{it} is the missing data rate for individual i at time t and is defined differently for different missingness models as in the previous section. When y_{it} is missing, the corresponding likelihood is excluded. So combining y and m, the conditional likelihood function of a selection model with non-ignorable missing data can be expressed as

$$L_{it}(\theta|y,m) = [f(y_{it}|\eta_i)(1-\tau_{it})]^{(1-m_{it})}\,\tau_{it}^{m_{it}}, \tag{21.11}$$

And the other version of deviance, $D(E_{\theta|y}[\theta])$, is approximated by

$$D(E_{\theta|y}[\theta]) \approx D(\hat{\theta}) = -2\sum_{i=1}^{N}\sum_{t=1}^{T}\left[(1-m_{it})l_{it}(y|\hat{\theta}) + l_{it}(m|\hat{\theta})\right], \tag{21.12}$$

where $\hat{\theta}$ is the posterior mean of parameter estimates across S iterations.

(2) For growth mixture models with missing data, $E_{\theta|y}[D]$ is expressed as

$$E_{D|y}[D(\theta)] \approx \overline{D(\theta)} = -\frac{2}{S}\sum_{s=1}^{S}\sum_{i=1}^{N}\sum_{k=1}^{K} z_{ik}^{(s)} \sum_{1=t}^{T} \left[(1-m_{it})l_{ikt}^{(s)}(y) + l_{ikt}^{(s)}(m)\right], \quad (21.13)$$

where $\mathbf{z}_i = (z_{i1}, z_{i2}, \ldots, z_{iK})$ is the class membership indicator which follows a multinomial distribution, $\mathbf{z}_i \sim MultiNomial(\pi_{i1}, \pi_{i2}, \ldots, \pi_{iK})$, and $z_{ik}^{(s)}$ is the class membership estimated at iteration s. And

$$D(E_{\theta|y}[\theta]) \approx D(\hat{\theta}) = -2\sum_{i=1}^{N}\sum_{k=1}^{K} \hat{z}_{ik} \sum_{t=1}^{T} \left[(1-m_{it})l_{ikt}(y|\hat{\theta}) + l_{ikt}(m|\hat{\theta})\right], \quad (21.14)$$

where $\hat{z}_{ik}$ is the posterior mode of class membership, $\hat{\theta}$ is the posterior mean of parameter estimates across all S iterations. In both the $\overline{D(\theta)}$ and $D(\hat{\theta})$ definitions of deviance, $l_{ikt}(y)$ and $l_{ikt}(m)$ are the conditional loglikelihood functions for y_{it} and m_{it}, respectively, for individual i in class k at time t.

If people calculate deviance scores using $D(\hat{\theta})$, then $\overline{D(\theta)}$ is the sum of an approximation of the deviance score ($D(\hat{\theta})$) and some penalties. The difference between $\overline{D(\theta)}$ and $D(\hat{\theta})$ can be quantified by a statistic called pD (Spiegelhalter et al. 2002),

$$pD = \overline{D(\theta)} - D(\hat{\theta}). \quad (21.15)$$

Based on the Jensen's inequality (Casella and George 1992), when $D(\theta)$ is convex, then $\overline{D(\theta)} \geq D(\hat{\theta})$ and as a result pD is positive. When $D(\theta)$ is concave, then $\overline{D(\theta)} \leq D(\hat{\theta})$ and pD is negative.

21.4 Simulation Studies

In this section, five simulation studies are conducted to evaluate the performance of the Bayesian criteria. For each study, four waves of complete data were generated first and then missing data were created on each occasion according to pre-designed missing data rates. After data are generated, full Bayesian methods are used by adopting uninformative priors, obtaining conditional posterior distributions through application of a data augmentation algorithm, generating Markov chains through a Gibbs sampling procedure, conducting convergence testing, and making statistical inference for model parameters. For all simulations, the software OpenBUGS is used for the implementation of Gibbs sampling, and R codes are written for data-generation, convergence testing, and parameter estimation.

The five studies are designed such that the data complexity increases from study 1 to study 5. Studies 1–2 focus on non-mixture growth data and thus, latent growth curve models with missing data are used. Studies 3–5 focus on mixture growth data and thus, growth mixture models with missing data are used. Simulation factors include measurement error distributions, random effect distributions, missingness patterns, sample size, and class separation (Anderson and Bahadur 1962). Under each condition, 100 converged replications are used to calculate the model selection proportion. Table 21.2 lists the design details.

Study 1 investigated the performance of the Bayesian criteria when data were non-mixture homogenous, normally distributed with non-ignorable missingness. The true model was NN-XS, which was the model with normally distributed measurement errors ($\mathbf{e}_i$) at level 1 and random effects ($\boldsymbol{\xi}_i$) at level 2, with missingness depending on covariate x and latent slope S. Specifically, $\mathbf{e}_i \sim MN(\mathbf{0}, \mathrm{I})$, $\eta_i \sim MN_q(\boldsymbol{\beta}, \Psi)$ where $\boldsymbol{\beta} = (\text{Intercept}, \text{Slope}) = (1,3)$ and Ψ was a 2 by 2 symmetric matrix with $Var(I) = 1$, $Cov(I,S) = 0$, and $Var(S) = 4$. For missingness, the bigger the latent slope was, the higher the missing data rate would be. The missingness probit coefficients were set as $\gamma_0 = (-1,-1,-1,-1)$, $\gamma_x = (-1.5,-1.5,-1.5,-1.5)$, and $\gamma_S = (0.5,0.5,0.5,0.5)$. For example, if a participant had a latent growth slope 3, with a covariate value 1, then his or her missing probability at each wave was $\tau \approx 16\%$; if the slope was 5, with the same covariate value, the missing probability increased to $\tau = 50\%$; but if the slope was 1, then the missing probability decreased to $\tau = 2.3\%$. The covariate x was also generated from a normal distribution, $x \sim N(1, sd = 0.2)$. In study 1, totally there were 16 conditions with 4 missingness mechanisms (XS non-ignorable, XY non-ignorable, XI non-ignorable, and ignorable) combined with 4 levels of sample size (1,000, 500, 300, and 200). Table 21.3 lists the model selection proportions across 100 replications for each of these criteria across all conditions in study 1. The largest proportion across four missingness models is indicated in the shaded cell for each criterion. When sample size is relatively large, 1,000 or 500, all of the model selection criteria, except for the rough DIC (RDIC), correctly identify the true model with 100 %. When sample size becomes smaller, 300 or 200, except for the RDIC, all of the model selection criteria choose the true model with certainty above 93 %. Comparing the criteria defined based on Dbar with those defined based on Dhat, one can see that the former performs a little bit better.

Study 2 investigated the performance of these criteria when data were non-mixture homogeneous with outliers and non-ignorable missingness. The main difference between study 2 and 1 was that the data for study 2 contain outliers such that they are not normally distributed. So robust growth curve models were used. The true model was TN-XS, which means measurement errors ($\mathbf{e}_i$) at level 1 followed a t-distribution. Specifically, $\mathbf{e}_i$ were generated from a t distribution with 5 degrees of freedom and a scale matrix I, i.e., $\mathbf{e}_i \sim Mt(\mathbf{0}, \mathrm{I}, 5)$. Other settings were kept the same as those in study 1. In this study, totally 32 conditions were considered with 4 data distributions (NN, TN, NT, and TT), 4 missingness patterns (XS non-ignorable, XY non-ignorable, XI non-ignorable, and ignorable), and 2 levels of sample size (1,000 and 500). Table 21.4 lists the model selection proportions. The largest proportion across 16 missingness models is indicated in the shaded cell for each criterion. Except for the RDIC, all of the model selection criteria correctly identify the true model. TT-XS is a competing model, which also gains high selection probabilities. This is because the normal distribution is almost identical

Table 21.2 Simulation study design

		Data distribution				Missingness depends on					Sample size	Class separation[c]	
		$\mathbf{e}_i^a$		η_i^b									
Study	Model	N[d]	t^e	N	t	C[f]	X[g]	I[h]	S[i]	Y[j]	Different	M	S
Study 1	Normal LGCMs: use relative small sample sizes due to single-class data												
	NN-ignorable	✓		✓			✓						
	NN-XI	✓		✓			✓	✓					
	NN-XS[k]	✓		✓			✓		✓				
	NN-XY	✓		✓			✓			✓			
Study 2	Robust LGCMs: use relative small sample sizes due to single-class data												
	TN-ignorable		✓	✓			✓						
	TN-XI		✓	✓			✓	✓					
	TN-XS		✓	✓			✓		✓				
	TN-XY		✓	✓			✓			✓			
	TT-ignorable		✓		✓		✓						
	TT-XI		✓		✓		✓	✓					
	TT-XS		✓	✓			✓		✓				
	TT-XY		✓	✓			✓			✓			
	NT-ignorable	✓			✓		✓						
	NT-XI	✓			✓		✓	✓					
	NT-XS	✓			✓		✓		✓				
	NT-XY	✓			✓		✓			✓			
	NN-ignorable	✓		✓			✓						
	NN-XI	✓		✓			✓	✓					
	NN-XS	✓		✓			✓		✓				
	NN-XY	✓		✓			✓			✓			

(continued)

Table 21.2 (continued)

Study	Model	Data distribution $\mathbf{e}_i$[a] N[d]	Data distribution $\mathbf{e}_i$[a] t[e]	Data distribution η_i[b] N	Data distribution η_i[b] t	Missingness depends on C[f]	Missingness depends on X[g]	Missingness depends on I[h]	Missingness depends on S[i]	Missingness depends on Y[j]	Sample size Different	Class separation[c] M	Class separation[c] S
Study 3	Robust GMMs (RGMMs): use relative large sample sizes due to multiple classes data, and use small class separation due to fixed class probabilities												
	TN-ignorable		✓	✓			✓					✓	
	TN-XI		✓	✓			✓	✓				✓	
	TN-XS		✓	✓			✓		✓			✓	
	TN-XY		✓	✓			✓			✓		✓	
	TT-ignorable		✓		✓		✓					✓	
	TT-XI		✓		✓		✓	✓				✓	
	TT-XS		✓		✓		✓		✓			✓	
	TT-XY		✓		✓		✓			✓		✓	
	NT-ignorable	✓			✓		✓					✓	
	NT-XI	✓			✓		✓	✓				✓	
	NT-XS	✓			✓		✓		✓			✓	
	NT-XY	✓			✓		✓			✓		✓	
	NN-ignorable	✓		✓			✓					✓	
	NN-XI	✓		✓			✓	✓				✓	
	NN-XS	✓		✓			✓		✓			✓	
	NN-XY	✓		✓			✓			✓		✓	
Study 4	Robust Extended GMMs (REGMMs): select 5 competing models based on the performance in Study 3 use relative large sample sizes due to multiple-class data and varied class probabilities												
	TN-CXS		✓	✓		✓	✓		✓			✓	✓
	TN-CX		✓	✓		✓	✓					✓	✓

	TT-CXS		✓			✓		✓	✓		✓							✓	✓
	NN-CXS	✓			✓			✓	✓		✓							✓	✓
	NN-CX	✓			✓			✓	✓									✓	✓
Study 5	Single-Class LGCMs vs. Multiple-Class RGMMs																		
	1 Class LGCMs																		
	TN-XS		✓		✓				✓		✓								
	TT-XS		✓			✓			✓		✓								
	NN-XS	✓			✓				✓		✓								
	2 Classes RGMMs																		
	TN-XS		✓		✓				✓		✓							✓	
	TT-XS		✓			✓			✓		✓							✓	
	NN-XS	✓			✓				✓		✓							✓	
	3 Classes RGMMs																		
	TN-XS		✓		✓				✓		✓								
	TT-XS		✓			✓			✓		✓								
	NN-XS	✓			✓				✓		✓								
	4 Classes RGMMs																		
	TN-XS		✓		✓				✓		✓								
	TT-XS		✓			✓			✓		✓								
	NN-XS	✓			✓				✓		✓								

[a]Measurement errors
[b]Random effects
[c]Class separation (Anderson and Bahadur 1962) when generating data (S: small = 1.7, M: medium = 2.7)
[d]Normal distribution
[e]t distribution
[f]Latent class dependent (non-ignorable)
[g]Observed covariates
[h]Latent intercept dependent (non-ignorable)
[i]Latent slope dependent (non-ignorable)
[j]Potential outcome *y* dependent (non-ignorable)
[k]The shaded model is the true model

Table 21.3 Model selection proportion in study 1

	N = 1,000				N = 500			
	Non-ignorable			Ignorable	Non-ignorable			Ignorable
Criteron[a]	**NN-XS**[b]	NN-XY[c]	NN-XI[d]	NN[e]	**NN-XS**	NN-XY	NN-XI	NN
Dbar.AIC	1[f]	0.000	0.000	0.000	1	0.000	0.000	0.000
Dbar.BIC	1	0.000	0.000	0.000	1	0.000	0.000	0.000
Dbar.CAIC	1	0.000	0.000	0.000	1	0.000	0.000	0.000
Dbar.ssBIC	1	0.000	0.000	0.000	1	0.000	0.000	0.000
RDIC	0.013	0.000	**0.987**	0.000	0.038	0.000	**0.962**	0.000
Dhat.AIC	1	0.000	0.000	0.000	1	0.000	0.000	0.000
Dhat.BIC	1	0.000	0.000	0.000	1	0.000	0.000	0.000
Dhat.CAIC	1	0.000	0.000	0.000	1	0.000	0.000	0.000
Dhat.ssBIC	1	0.000	0.000	0.000	1	0.000	0.000	0.000
DIC	1	0.000	0.000	0.000	1	0.000	0.000	0.000
	N = 300				N = 200			
Dbar.AIC	**0.98125**	0.01875	0.000	0.000	**0.975**	0.025	0.000	0.000
Dbar.BIC	**0.98125**	0.01875	0.000	0.000	**0.975**	0.025	0.000	0.000
Dbar.CAIC	**0.98125**	0.01875	0.000	0.000	**0.975**	0.025	0.000	0.000
Dbar.ssBIC	**0.98125**	0.01875	0.000	0.000	**0.975**	0.025	0.000	0.000
Rough DIC	0.1125	0.000	**0.8875**	0.000	0.2	0.03125	**0.76875**	0.000
Dhat.AIC	**0.95**	0.05	0.000	0.000	**0.9375**	0.06875	0.000	0.000
Dhat.BIC	**0.95**	0.05	0.000	0.000	**0.9375**	0.06875	0.000	0.000
Dhat.CAIC	**0.95**	0.05	0.000	0.000	**0.9375**	0.06875	0.000	0.000
Dhat.ssBIC	**0.95**	0.05	0.000	0.000	**0.9375**	0.06875	0.000	0.000
DIC	1	0.000	0.000	0.000	**0.98125**	0.0125	0.00625	0.000

[a]The definition of each criterion is given in Table 21.1
[b]The shaded model is the true model. The model is normal-distribution-based with latent-slope-dependent missingness
[c]The model is normal-distribution-based with potential-outcome-dependent missingness
[d]The model is normal-distribution-based with latent-intercept-dependent missingness
[e]The model is normal-distribution-based with ignorable missingness
[f]The shaded cell has the largest proportion

to a t-distribution with large degrees of freedom. The degrees of freedom of t is also estimated by the model. Also, the Dbar-based criteria perform a little bit better than the Dhat-based criteria. Among them, Dbar-based BIC and CAIC perform best.

Study 3 was designed for mixture data with outliers and non-ignorable missing data. As data were mixture, growth mixture models were used. In this study, the true model was 2-class mixture TN-XS RGMM. Only intercepts of these 2 classes were different, with 5 for class 1 and 1 for class 2. Other settings for each class were the same as in study 2. Both classes have t_5 distributed measurement errors. Based on Anderson and Bahadur (1962), the class separation is around 2.7. In this study, we assumed they are traditional mixture models, i.e., class probabilities were fixed. We were fixed as (50 %, 50 %) in this study. Similar as in study 2, there were 32 conditions considered with 4 data distributions (NN, TN, NT, and TT), 4 missingness patterns (XS non-ignorable, XY non-ignorable, XI non-ignorable, and ignorable), and 2 levels of sample size (1,000 and 1,500). As mixture data require more data to obtain estimates, we increased the sample size. Table 21.5 shows the results for study 3. The shaded cell indicates the largest proportion across 16 missingness models for each criterion. Again, almost all of the model selection criteria correctly identify the true model. And the Dbar-based criteria perform a little bit better than the Dhat-based criteria. Specifically, Dbar-based BIC and CAIC perform best among these criteria, and then Dbar-based ssBIC also performs well.

Study 4 extended study 3 such that the class probabilities were not fixed. Instead, they depended on values of covariates. Also, the non-ignorable missingness in this study was allowed to depend on the corresponding observations' latent class membership. The true model in this study was 2-class mixture TN-CXS robust extended growth mixture models (REGMM). The differences between this study and study 3 were (1) the class proportions in this study were predicted by the value of covariate x; (2) the missing data rates were predicted by the latent class membership; (3) both medium size, 2.7, and small size, 1.7, class separations were used. Specifically, for small class separation, the intercept for class 1 was 3.5 and the intercept for class 2 was 1. To simplify the simulation, based on the findings in study 3, 5 competing mixture models (TN-CXS, TT-CXS, TN-CX, NN-CXS, and NN-CX) were chosen to fit the data. Totally, we considered 20 conditions with 5 mixture models, 2 levels of sample size (1,500 and 1,000), and 2 levels of class separation (2.7 and 1.7). Table 21.6 shows the model selection proportions in study 4. Again, almost all of the model selection criteria correctly identify the true model. Specifically, Dbar-based BIC and CAIC perform best among these criteria.

Study 5 focused on the number of classes. In this study, different growth curve models with different numbers of classes were fitted and compared. In total, 9 conditions were considered, including 3 models (TN-XS, TT-XS, NN-XS) and 3 numbers of classes (1, 2, and 3). The true model was the 2-class mixture TN-XS model. The simulation results for study 5 were presented in Table 21.7. Among these criteria, Dhat-based criteria perform better than Dhbar-based criteria. Specifically, Dhat-based BIC and CAIC perform best, and ssBIC and AIC also provide high certainty.

Table 21.4 Model selection proportion in study 2

Criterion		N = 1,000				N = 500			
		Non-ignorable				Non-ignorable			
		XS[a]	XY	XI	Ignorable	XS	XY	XI	Ignorable
Dbar.AIC	TN[b]	**0.519**	0.000	0.000	0.000	**0.597**	0.013	0.000	0.000
	TT[c]	0.469	0.000	0.000	0.012	0.377	0.000	0.000	0.000
	NT[d]	0.000	0.000	0.000	0.000	0.006	0.000	0.000	0.000
	NN[e]	0.000	0.000	0.000	0.000	0.006	0.000	0.000	0.000
Dbar.BIC	TN	**0.781**	0.000	0.000	0.000	**0.855**	0.013	0.000	0.000
	TT	0.200	0.000	0.000	0.019	0.113	0.000	0.000	0.000
	NT	0.000	0.000	0.000	0.000	0.006	0.000	0.000	0.000
	NN	0.000	0.000	0.000	0.000	0.013	0.000	0.000	0.000
Dbar.CAIC	TN	**0.819**	0.000	0.000	0.000	**0.888**	0.012	0.000	0.000
	TT	0.162	0.000	0.000	0.019	0.075	0.000	0.000	0.000
	NT	0.000	0.000	0.000	0.000	0.000	0.000	0.000	0.000
	NN	0.000	0.000	0.000	0.000	0.019	0.000	0.000	0.000
Dbar.ssBIC	TN	**0.625**	0.000	0.000	0.000	**0.631**	0.012	0.000	0.000
	TT	0.362	0.000	0.000	0.012	0.338	0.000	0.000	0.000
	NT	0.000	0.000	0.000	0.000	0.006	0.000	0.000	0.000
	NN	0.000	0.000	0.000	0.000	0.006	0.000	0.000	0.000
RDIC	TN	0.000	0.000	0.106	0.000	0.000	0.000	0.094	0.000
	TT	0.000	0.000	0.100	0.000	0.000	0.000	0.113	0.000
	NT	0.000	0.000	0.394	0.000	0.000	0.000	0.390	0.000
	NN	0.000	0.000	**0.400**	0.000	0.000	0.000	**0.403**	0.000
Dhat.AIC	TN	**0.544**	0.000	0.000	0.000	**0.547**	0.025	0.000	0.000
	TT	0.506	0.006	0.000	0.000	0.447	0.019	0.000	0.000
	NT	0.000	0.000	0.000	0.000	0.000	0.000	0.000	0.000
	NN	0.000	0.000	0.000	0.000	0.000	0.000	0.000	0.000
Dhat.BIC	TN	**0.675**	0.006	0.000	0.000	**0.717**	0.025	0.000	0.000
	TT	0.319	0.000	0.000	0.000	0.245	0.013	0.000	0.000
	NT	0.000	0.000	0.000	0.000	0.000	0.000	0.000	0.000
	NN	0.000	0.000	0.000	0.000	0.000	0.000	0.000	0.000
Dhat.CAIC	TN	**0.700**	0.006	0.000	0.000	**0.788**	0.025	0.000	0.000
	TT	0.294	0.006	0.000	0.000	0.169	0.012	0.000	0.000
	NT	0.000	0.000	0.000	0.000	0.000	0.000	0.000	0.000
	NN	0.000	0.000	0.000	0.000	0.000	0.000	0.000	0.000
Dhat.ssBIC	TN	**0.575**	0.006	0.000	0.000	**0.588**	0.025	0.000	0.000
	TT	0.419	0.006	0.000	0.000	0.369	0.012	0.000	0.000
	NT	0.000	0.000	0.000	0.000	0.000	0.000	0.000	0.000
	NN	0.000	0.000	0.000	0.000	0.000	0.000	0.000	0.000
DIC	TN	0.325	0.000	0.000	0.000	**0.415**	0.006	0.000	0.000
	TT	**0.462**	0.000	0.000	0.194	0.409	0.000	0.000	0.000
	NT	0.012	0.000	0.000	0.000	0.088	0.000	0.000	0.000
	NN	0.006	0.000	0.000	0.000	0.082	0.000	0.000	0.000

[a]Other abbreviations are as given in Table 21.3
[b]Growth model with t-distributed measurement errors and normally distributed random effects
[c]Growth model with t-distributed measurement errors and t-distributed random effects
[d]Growth model with normally distributed measurement errors and t-distributed random effects
[e]Growth model with normally distributed measurement errors and random effects

Table 21.5 Model selection proportion in study 3

		N = 1,500					N = 1,000			
		Non-ignorable					Non-ignorable			
Criterion		XS	XY	XI	Ignorable		XS	XY	XI	Ignorable
Dbar.AIC	TN	0.621	0.000	0.000	0.000		0.593	0.000	0.000	0.000
	TT	0.357	0.000	0.000	0.000		0.314	0.000	0.000	0.000
	NT	0.000	0.000	0.000	0.000		0.021	0.000	0.000	0.000
	NN	0.021	0.000	0.000	0.000		0.071	0.000	0.000	0.000
Dbar.BIC	TN	0.864	0.000	0.000	0.000		0.843	0.000	0.000	0.000
	TT	0.114	0.000	0.000	0.000		0.064	0.000	0.000	0.000
	NT	0.000	0.000	0.000	0.000		0.014	0.000	0.000	0.000
	NN	0.021	0.007	0.000	0.000		0.079	0.000	0.000	0.000
Dbar.CAIC	TN	0.893	0.000	0.000	0.000		0.857	0.000	0.000	0.000
	TT	0.079	0.000	0.000	0.000		0.043	0.000	0.000	0.000
	NT	0.000	0.000	0.000	0.000		0.007	0.007	0.000	0.000
	NN	0.021	0.007	0.000	0.000		0.086	0.000	0.000	0.000
Dbar.ssBIC	TN	0.729	0.000	0.000	0.000		0.750	0.000	0.000	0.000
	TT	0.250	0.000	0.000	0.000		0.157	0.000	0.000	0.000
	NT	0.000	0.000	0.000	0.000		0.014	0.000	0.000	0.000
	NN	0.021	0.007	0.000	0.000		0.079	0.000	0.000	0.000
RDIC	TN	0.071	0.000	0.000	0.000		0.143	0.000	0.000	0.000
	TT	0.086	0.000	0.000	0.000		0.071	0.000	0.000	0.000
	NT	0.450	0.000	0.000	0.000		0.393	0.007	0.000	0.000
	NN	0.393	0.000	0.000	0.000		0.379	0.007	0.000	0.000
Dhat.AIC	TN	0.586	0.000	0.000	0.000		0.621	0.000	0.000	0.000
	TT	0.379	0.000	0.000	0.000		0.329	0.000	0.000	0.000
	NT	0.014	0.000	0.000	0.000		0.014	0.007	0.000	0.000
	NN	0.014	0.007	0.000	0.000		0.057	0.000	0.000	0.000
Dhat.BIC	TN	0.757	0.000	0.000	0.000		0.793	0.000	0.000	0.000
	TT	0.207	0.000	0.000	0.000		0.121	0.000	0.000	0.000
	NT	0.007	0.000	0.000	0.000		0.007	0.007	0.000	0.000
	NN	0.021	0.007	0.000	0.000		0.071	0.000	0.000	0.000
Dhat.CAIC	TN	0.757	0.000	0.000	0.000		0.814	0.000	0.000	0.000
	TT	0.207	0.000	0.000	0.000		0.100	0.000	0.000	0.000
	NT	0.007	0.000	0.000	0.000		0.007	0.007	0.000	0.000
	NN	0.021	0.007	0.000	0.000		0.071	0.000	0.000	0.000
Dhat.ssBIC	TN	0.586	0.000	0.000	0.000		0.664	0.000	0.000	0.000
	TT	0.379	0.000	0.000	0.000		0.250	0.000	0.000	0.000
	NT	0.014	0.000	0.000	0.000		0.014	0.007	0.000	0.000
	NN	0.014	0.007	0.000	0.000		0.064	0.000	0.000	0.000
DIC	TN	0.507	0.000	0.000	0.000		0.364	0.007	0.000	0.000
	TT	0.371	0.000	0.000	0.000		0.286	0.000	0.000	0.000
	NT	0.043	0.036	0.000	0.000		0.129	0.029	0.007	0.000
	NN	0.043	0.000	0.000	0.000		0.150	0.029	0.000	0.000

Abbreviations are as given in Table 21.3

Table 21.6 Model selection proportion in study 4

Criterion	**TN-CXS**	TT-CXS	NN-CXS	TN-CX	NN-CX		**TN-CXS**	TT-CXS	NN-CXS	TN-CX	NN-CX
Class separation = 2.7, N = 1,500							Class separation = 2.7, N = 1,000				
Dbar.AIC	**0.567**	0.425	0.000	0.008	0.000		**0.558**	0.375	0.000	0.067	0.000
Dbar.BIC	**0.808**	0.158	0.000	0.033	0.000		**0.750**	0.125	0.000	0.125	0.000
Dbar.CAIC	**0.850**	0.108	0.000	0.0042	0.000		**0.767**	0.100	0.008	0.125	0.000
Dbar.ssBIC	**0.667**	0.300	0.000	0.033	0.000		**0.633**	0.292	0.000	0.075	0.000
RDIC	0.042	0.042	**0.908**	0.000	0.008		0.092	0.075	**0.808**	0.000	0.025
Dhat.AIC	**0.475**	0.392	0.000	0.133	0.000		0.350	**0.358**	0.000	0.292	0.000
Dhat.BIC	**0.550**	0.233	0.000	0.217	0.000		**0.450**	0.175	0.000	0.375	0.000
Dhat.CAIC	**0.525**	0.233	0.000	0.242	0.000		**0.442**	0.150	0.000	0.4	0.008
Dhat.ssBIC	**0.467**	0.367	0.000	0.167	0.000		**0.392**	0.300	0.000	0.308	0.000
DIC	0.467	**0.500**	0.033	0.000	0.000		0.417	**0.450**	0.108	0.008	0.017
Class separation = 1.7, N = 1,500							Class separation = 1.7, N = 1,000				
Dbar.AIC	**0.512**	0.444	0.044	0.000	0.00		**0.550**	0.400	0.050	0.000	0.000
Dbar.BIC	**0.744**	0.212	0.044	0.000	0.00		**0.719**	0.194	0.081	0.006	0.000
Dbar.CAIC	**0.781**	0.175	0.044	0.000	0.00		**0.750**	0.162	0.081	0.006	0.000
Dbar.ssBIC	**0.612**	0.344	0.044	0.000	0.00		**0.638**	0.300	0.062	0.000	0.000
RDIC	0.306	0.238	**0.350**	0.006	0.10		0.244	0.256	**0.362**	0.000	0.138
Dhat.AIC	**0.475**	**0.475**	0.031	0.019	0.00		**0.694**	0.231	0.012	0.062	0.000
Dhat.BIC	**0.712**	0.238	0.031	0.019	0.00		**0.644**	0.294	0.012	0.050	0.000
Dhat.CAIC	**0.712**	0.238	0.031	0.019	0.00		**0.694**	0.231	0.012	0.062	0.000
Dhat.ssBIC	**0.475**	**0.475**	0.031	0.019	0.00		**0.575**	0.388	0.012	0.025	0.000
DIC	0.381	**0.450**	0.169	0.000	0.00		**0.344**	0.331	0.319	0.000	0.006

Abbreviations are as given in Table 21.3

Table 21.7 Model selection proportion in study 5

	2 CLASSES			1 CLASS			3 CLASSES		
Criterion	TN-XS	TT-XS	NN-XS	TN-XS	TT-XS	NN-XS	TN-XS	TT-XS	NN-XS
Dbar.AIC	0.000	0.000	0.057	0.393	0.129	0.000	0.021	0.007	0.393
Dbar.BIC	0.000	0.000	0.036	0.821	0.064	0.000	0.000	0.000	0.079
Dbar.CAIC	0.000	0.000	0.036	0.864	0.043	0.000	0.000	0.000	0.057
Dbar.ssBIC	0.000	0.000	0.057	0.593	0.100	0.000	0.000	0.000	0.25
RDIC	0.036	0.014	0.2	0.014	0.014	0.679	0.014	0.014	0.014
Dhat.AIC	0.621	0.343	0.064	0.000	0.000	0.000	0.000	0.000	0.000
Dhat.BIC	0.793	0.136	0.071	0.000	0.000	0.000	0.000	0.000	0.000
Dhat.CAIC	0.814	0.114	0.071	0.000	0.000	0.000	0.000	0.000	0.000
Dhat.ssBIC	0.664	0.264	0.071	0.000	0.000	0.000	0.000	0.000	0.000
DIC	0.000	0.000	0.000	0.164	0.193	0.121	0.000	0.000	0.521

Abbreviations are as given in Table 21.3

21.5 Application

In this section, a real data set on mathematical growth is analyzed to demonstrate the application of the criteria. The same sample that has been analyzed in Lu et al. (2011) is used here. It is a mathematical ability growth sample from the NLSY97 survey (Bureau of Labor Statistics, U.S. Department of Labor 1997), which were collected from $N = 1{,}510$ adolescents yearly from 1997 to 2001 when each adolescent was administered the Peabody Individual Achievement Test (PIAT) Mathematics Assessment to measure their mathematical ability. There are some outliers at all five grades. Lu et al. (2011) conducted a power transformation to normalize the sample and assumed the data are normally distributed without outliers. In this study, however, we use the original non-transformed data with outliers, so robust methods are used. Also, different non-ignorable missingness mechanisms are considered. Overall, the means of mathematical ability increased over time with a roughly linear trend. The missing data rates range from 4.57 to 9.47 %, and the raw data show the missing pattern is intermittent. About half of the sample is female.

The analysis is conducted following the steps in Table 21.8. In step 1, a tentative model (the TT-ignorable model) is fitted to the data. Gender is a covariate. The estimates of degrees of freedom of t for both classes are 2.342 and 3.263 for measurement errors and 75.65 and 50.96 for random effects, which indicates that measurement errors are t distributed while random effects are approximately normally distributed (i.e., a TN model). And then in step 2, to compare models with different non-ignorable missingness and numbers of classes, 10 models are fitted to the data. During estimation we use uninformative priors which carry little information for model parameters. A burn-in period is run first to ensure estimates are based on the Markov chains that have converged. For testing convergence, the history plot is examined and the Geweke's z statistic (Geweke 1992) is checked for each parameter. The Geweke's z statistics for all the parameters are smaller than

Table 21.8 Steps and fitting models in real data analysis

Step 1:	Fit a tentative 2 classes model, and check the estimated df of t									
		$\mathbf{e}_i$		η_i		missingness				
	Model	N	T	N	T	C	X	I	S	Y
	TT-ignorable		✓		✓					
Step 2:	Try models with different missingness and number of classes									
	2 Classes RGMMs									
	TN-X		✓	✓			✓			
	TN-XI		✓	✓			✓	✓		
	TN-XS		✓	✓			✓		✓	
	TN-XY		✓	✓			✓			✓
	2 Classes REGMMs									
	TN-CX		✓	✓		✓	✓			
	TN-CXI		✓	✓		✓	✓	✓		
	TN-CXS		✓	✓		✓	✓		✓	
	TN-CXY		✓	✓		✓	✓			✓
	3 Classes GMMs									
	NN-X	✓		✓			✓			
	4 Classes GMMs									
	NN-X	✓		✓			✓			
Step 3:	Compare selection criteria									
Step 4:	Interpret results obtained from the selected model									

Abbreviations are as given in Table 21.2

1.96, which indicates converged Markov chains. To make sure all the parameters are estimated accurately, the next 50,000 iterations are then saved for data analysis. The ratio of Monte Carlo error (MCerror) to standard deviation (S.D.) for each parameter is smaller than or close to 0.05, which indicates parameter estimates are accurate (Spiegelhalter et al. 2003). In step 3, model selection criterion is used to compare the ten models. The indices are listed in Table 21.9. And in step 4, the results obtained from the final selected model are interpreted.

As suggested by Dhat.CAIC, Dhat.ssBIC, Dhat.BIC, and Dhat.AIC, without further substantive information, the TN-CXY model would appear to be a good candidate for best-fitting model. Table 21.10 provides the results of the TN-CXY REGMM model. It can be seen that (1) class 1 has a higher average initial level but a smaller average slope; (2) class 2 has larger variations for initial levels and slope; (3) the residual variance of class 2 is much larger than that of class 1; (4) in class 1 the initial level and the slope are significantly negatively correlated at the confidence level of 95 %; (5) the missingness is not related to gender because none of the coefficients of gender are significant at the α level of 0.05; (6) at grade 11, adolescents in class 2 are more likely to miss tests than those in class 1 because the probit coefficient of class membership for grade 11 is significantly positive; and (7)

Table 21.9 Model selection in real data analysis

	2 CLASSES								3 CLASSES	4 CLASSES
Criterion[a]	TN-CXS	TN-CXY	TN-CXI	TN-CX	TN-XS	TN-XY	TN-XI	TN-X	NN-X	NN-X
Dbar.AIC	17,392	17,472	17,502	17,502	17,392	17,482	17,502	17,512	17,372	17,126
Dbar.BIC	17,583.52	17,663.52	17,693.52	17,666.92	17,556.92	17,646.92	17,666.92	17,650.32	17,536.92	17,328.15
Dbar.CAIC	17,619.52	17,699.52	17,729.52	17,697.92	17,587.92	17,677.92	17,697.92	17,676.32	17,567.92	17,366.15
Dbar.ssBIC	17,469.15	17,549.15	17,579.15	17,568.44	17,458.44	17,548.44	17,568.44	17,567.72	17,438.44	17,207.44
RDIC	22,759.24	22,704.5	22,378.14	22,601.28	22,562.65	22,755.44	22,973.52	22,520.18	22,843.52	23,333.2
Dhat.AIC	15,192	14,942	17,482	19,822	21,922	23,622	25,722	27,352	15,872	15,716
Dhat.BIC	15,383.52	15,133.52	17,673.52	19,986.92	22,086.92	23,786.92	25,886.92	27,490.32	16,036.92	15,918.15
Dhat.CAIC	15,419.52	15,169.52	17,709.52	20,017.92	22,117.92	23,817.92	25,917.92	27,516.32	16,067.92	15,956.15
Dhat.ssBIC	15,269.15	15,019.15	17,559.15	19,888.44	21,988.44	23,688.44	25,788.44	27,407.72	15,938.44	15,797.44
DIC	19,520	19,930	17,450	15,120	12,800	11,280	9,220	7,620	18,810	18,460

The shaded cell has the smallest value
[a]The definition of each criterion is given in Table 21.1

Table 21.10 Estimates of TN-CXY REGMM in real data analysis

		Parameter	Mean	S.D.	MC.e./S.D.[a]	Lower[b]	Upper[c]	Geweke t[d]
Growth curve parameters	Class 1	Intercept	8.647	0.037	0.026	8.572	8.717	0.007
		Slope	0.229	0.009	0.023	0.211	0.247	0.014
		Var(I)	0.234	0.028	0.024	0.183	0.293	−0.009
		Var(S)	0.014	0.002	0.018	0.011	0.017	0.004
		Cov(I,S)	−0.036	0.006	0.022	−0.049	−0.026	−0.005
		Var(e)	0.044	0.004	0.031	0.037	0.053	0.024
		df_y[e]	2.386	0.205	0.043	2.118	2.900	0.050
	Class 2	Intercept	6.196	0.047	0.020	6.103	6.287	0.054
		Slope	0.315	0.011	0.022	0.295	0.336	0.036
		Var(I)	1.326	0.084	0.017	1.167	1.497	0.020
		Var(S)	0.034	0.004	0.022	0.027	0.042	0.010
		Cov(I,S)	0.010	0.014	0.021	−0.018	0.037	−0.023
		Var(e)	0.372	0.020	0.033	0.336	0.412	−0.061
		df_y	3.200	0.195	0.040	2.850	3.600	−0.042
Probit parameters	Class	φ_{10}[f]	−0.214	0.119	0.051	−0.438	0.018	−0.039
		φ_{11}	−0.223	0.077	0.051	−0.372	−0.076	0.026
	Grade 7	γ^*_{01}[g]	−0.711	0.532	0.066	−1.843	0.204	−0.255
		γ^*_{11}[h]	−0.132	0.216	0.058	−0.527	0.310	0.231
		γ_{x1}[i]	−0.154	0.108	0.046	−0.368	0.058	0.008
		γ_{Y1}[j]	−0.087	0.059	0.065	−0.190	0.038	0.251
	Grade 8	γ^*_{02}	−1.157	0.446	0.064	−2.097	−0.447	−0.373
		γ^*_{12}	0.046	0.217	0.055	−0.345	0.489	0.347
		γ_{x2}	0.113	0.114	0.046	−0.109	0.334	0.032
		γ_{Y2}	−0.108	0.045	0.062	−0.188	−0.021	0.330
	Grade 9	γ^*_{03}	−0.613	0.454	0.065	−1.519	0.163	−0.462
		γ^*_{13}	−0.057	0.181	0.056	−0.403	0.292	0.381
		γ_{x3}	−0.147	0.094	0.046	−0.332	0.038	0.045
		γ_{Y3}	−0.074	0.045	0.064	−0.155	0.022	0.459
	Grade 10	γ^*_{04}	−0.032	0.512	0.066	−0.861	0.985	−0.426
		γ^*_{14}	−0.324	0.204	0.059	−0.732	0.029	0.362
		γ_{x4}	0.059	0.101	0.047	−0.142	0.251	0.128
		γ_{Y4}	−0.166	0.050	0.065	−0.266	−0.084	0.378
	Grade 11	γ^*_{05}	−1.298	0.421	0.065	−2.130	−0.442	−0.192
		γ^*_{15}	0.341	0.176	0.055	0.015	0.708	0.159
		γ_{x5}	−0.087	0.091	0.045	−0.263	0.083	0.001
		γ_{Y5}	−0.019	0.040	0.064	−0.092	0.062	0.189

[a]Ratio of MC error to standard deviation. A value around or less than 0.05 indicates that the corresponding estimate is accurate (Spiegelhalter et al. 2003)

[b,c]The lower 2.5 percentile and upper 97.5 percentile

[d]Geweke test t value. An absolute value less than 1.96 indicates that the corresponding chain has passed the convergence test

[e]The degrees of freedom of the multivariate-t

[f]The probit coefficient of the class probability for class 1, defined in Eq. (21.3)

[g]The probit coefficient of the class membership 1 at Grade 7, defined in Eq. (21.9)

[h]The probit coefficient of the class membership 2 at Grade 7, defined in Eq. (21.9)

[i]The probit coefficient of the covariate at Grade 7, defined in Eq. (21.9)

[j]The probit coefficient of the potential output Y at Grade 7, defined in Eq. (21.9)

at grades 8 and 10, students with higher potential scores are more likely to miss tests than the students having lower scores because the probit coefficients of the potential outcomes y at the two grades are significantly negative.

21.6 Conclusions and Future Research

Based on the results from the five simulation studies, one can conclude that (1) almost all of the model selection criteria, except for the rough DIC (RDIC), can correctly choose the true model with high certainty; (2) if the number of classes is correctly identified, then the Dbar-based criteria perform better than the Dhat-based criteria; if candidate models have different numbers of classes, then the Dhat-based criteria might be used to select the best-fit model; (3) across five studies, CAIC and BIC provide higher probabilities than those ssBIC, AIC, or DIC does. The results will help inform the selection of growth models by researchers seeking to provide people with accurate estimates of growth across a variety of possible contexts. The real data analysis demonstrated the application of the criteria to typical longitudinal growth studies such as educational, psychological, and social research. Future research of this study includes proposing more effective model selection criteria, such as Bayes factors, and testing their performance with more practice statistical models, such as survival models.

Acknowledgments The authors thank the reviewer Dr. Daniel Bolt for his very helpful comments and suggestions, which greatly improved the quality of this article.

References

Akaike H (1974) A new look at the statistical model identification. IEEE Trans Automat Contr 1919(6):716–723

Anderson TW, Bahadur RR (1962) Classification into two multivariate normal distributions with different covariance matrices. Ann Math Stat 33:420–431

Bartholomew DJ, Knott M (1999) Latent variable models and factor analysis: Kendall's library of statistics, vol 7, 2nd edn. Edward Arnold, New York

Bozdogan H (1987) Model selection and Akaike's information criterion (AIC): the general theory and its analytical extensions. Psychometrika 52:345–370

Bureau of Labor Statistics, U.S. Department of Labor (1997) National longitudinal survey of youth 1997 cohort, 1997–2003 (rounds 1–7). [computer file]. Produced by the National Opinion Research Center, the University of Chicago and distributed by the Center for Human Resource Research, The Ohio State University. Columbus, OH: 2005. Retrieved from http://www.bls.gov/nls/nlsy97.htm

Casella G, George EI (1992) Explaining the Gibbs sampler. Am Stat 46(3):167–174

Celeux G, Forbes F, Robert C, Titterington D (2006). Deviance information criteria for missing data models. Bayesian Anal 4:651–674

Dunson DB (2000) Bayesian latent variable models for clustered mixed outcomes. J R Stat Soc B 62:355–366

Geweke J (1992) Evaluating the accuracy of sampling-based approaches to calculating posterior moments. In: Bernado JM, Berger JO, Dawid AP, Smith AFM (eds) Bayesian statistics, vol 4. Clarendon Press, Oxford, pp 169–193

Glynn RJ, Laird NM, Rubin DB (1986) In: Wainer H (ed) Drawing inferences from self-selected samples. Springer, New York, pp 115–142

Little RJA (1993) Pattern-mixture models for multivariate incomplete data. J Am Stat Assoc 88:125–134

Little RJA (1995) Modelling the drop-out mechanism in repeated-measures studies. J Am Stat Assoc 90:1112–1121

Little RJA, Rubin DB (2002) Statistical analysis with missing data, 2nd edn. Wiley-Interscience, New York

Lu Z, Zhang Z (2014) Robust growth mixture models with non-ignorable missingness data: models, estimation, selection, and application. Comput Stat Data Anal 71:220–240

Lu Z, Zhang Z, Lubke G (2011) Bayesian inference for growth mixture models with latent-class-dependent missing data. Multivariate Behav Res 46:567–597

Lu Z, Zhang Z, Cohen A (2013a) Bayesian inference for latent growth curve models with non-ignorable missing data. Struct Equ Modeling (manuscript submitted for publication)

Lu ZL, Zhang Z, Cohen A (2013b) In: Millsap RE, van der Ark LA, Bolt DM, Woods CM (eds) New developments in quantitative psychology, vol 66. Springer, New York, pp 275–304

Maronna RA, Martin RD, Yohai VJ (2006) Robust statistics: theory and methods. Wiley, New York

McLachlan GJ, Peel D (2000) Finite mixture models. Wiley, New York

Muthén B, Shedden K (1999) Finite mixture modeling with mixture outcomes using the EM algorithm. Biometrics 55(2):463–469

Oldmeadow C, Keith JM (2011) Model selection in Bayesian segmentation of multiple DNA alignments. Bioinformatics 27:604–610

Schwarz GE (1978) Estimating the dimension of a model. Ann Stat 6(2):461–464

Sclove LS (1987) Application of mode-selection criteria to some problems in multivariate analysis. Psychometrics 52:333–343

Spiegelhalter DJ, Best NG, Carlin BP, van der Linde A (2002) Bayesian measures of model complexity and fit. J R Stat Soc Series B Stat Methodol 64(4):583–639

Spiegelhalter DJ, Thomas A, Best N, Lunn D (2003) WinBUGS manual Version 1.4 (MRC Biostatistics Unit, Institute of Public Health, Robinson Way, Cambridge CB2 2SR, UK, http://www.mrc-bsu.cam.ac.uk/bugs)

Yuan K-H, Lu Z (2008) SEM with missing data and unknown population using two-stage ML: theory and its application. Multivariate Behav Res 43:621–652

Zhang Z, Lai K, Lu Z, Tong X (2013) Bayesian inference and application of robust growth curve models using student's t distribution. Struct Equ Modeling 20(1):47–78

Chapter 22
A Comparison of the Hierarchical Generalized Linear Model, Multiple-Indicators Multiple-Causes, and the Item Response Theory-Likelihood Ratio Test for Detecting Differential Item Functioning

Mei Ling Ong, Laura Lu, Sunbok Lee, and Allan Cohen

Abstract The purpose of this study was to compare the DIF detection performance of the hierarchical generalized linear model (HGLM), the multiple-indicators multiple-causes (MIMIC) method, and the IRT likelihood ratio (IRT-LR) test in simulated hierarchical data. Conditions in the simulation study included the number of clusters, cluster sizes, and the intraclass correlation coefficient (ICC). Those methods are compared in terms of Type I error rates. These rates should be close to 0.05 when the level of significance is set at 0.05. Results show that the HGLM maintained the marginal Type I error rate. The MIMIC model maintained a Type I error control rate better than the other two methods when cluster sizes were small. When cluster size and intraclass correlation ρ increased, however, the Type I error rates increased as well. The IRT-LR test maintained a marginal Type I error control for small sample cluster sizes but failed to do so for larger cluster sizes.

M.L. Ong (✉)
Quantitative Methods, Department of Education Psychology, University of Georgia, 126H Aderhold Hall, Athens, GA 30602, USA
e-mail: tmlong@uga.edu

L. Lu
Department of Education Psychology, University of Georgia, 325V Aderhold Hall, Athens, GA 30602, USA
e-mail: zlu@uga.edu

S. Lee
Center for Family Research, 1095 College Station Rd., Athens, GA 30602, USA
e-mail: sunboklee@gmail.com

A. Cohen
Department of Education Psychology, University of Georgia, 125 Aderhold Hall, Athens, GA 30602, USA
e-mail: acohen@uga.edu

R.E. Millsap et al. (eds.), *Quantitative Psychology Research*, Springer Proceedings in Mathematics & Statistics 89, DOI 10.1007/978-3-319-07503-7_22

Keywords DIF • MIMIC • HGLM • IRT-LR test • Rasch model • Type I error rates

A well-constructed test is the best way to evaluate students' mastery in a particular field after they have been taught the material. To this end, all items and the complete assessment as well should be reviewed in order to make sure that they are as free as possible from irrelevant variables, which could interfere with students' abilities to demonstrate their knowledge and skills (NAEP 2009). Detecting differential item functioning (DIF) involves testing examinees from different groups that share the same abilities but differ in their probabilities of giving correct responses on test items (Holland and Thayer 1988) and can be seen as a critical step in detecting biased items and assessing test score validity. To detect DIF, we usually consider two groups, a reference group and a focal group, with the majority typically treated as the reference group. There are two types of DIF, uniform and non-uniform. The former occurs when the difference in the item difficulty parameters between a reference and a focal group is the same at all ability levels. That is, uniform DIF shows no interaction between the ability levels of the two groups (Camilli and Shepard 1994). This type of DIF occurs when other item parameters are the same in reference- and focal- groups. The latter, also called crossing DIF, refers to the case in which the item discriminates differently across ability levels in the reference and focal groups. In this type of DIF, there is an interaction between ability level and group. In other words, non-uniform DIF examines the difference in the item discrimination parameters (Cohen et al. 1996).

The presence of DIF is a potential threat to validity (Thissen et al. 1993), as it may result in providing misleading ability estimates for one or more groups of examinees. Thus, DIF items need to be revised or removed, because the existence of DIF items may seriously affect the fairness of a test (Kim and Cohen 1998). Detecting DIF can be done for dichotomous or polytomous items by checking the probability of the responses modeled using any of the different item response functions. In the present study, without loss of generality, we focus on uniform DIF detection and dichotomous items, specifically in the context of the Rasch model (Rasch 1960), which is appropriate for dichotomous responses. With the Rasch model, the discriminations of all items are set to be equal to one. The model assumes the probability of a correct answer is solely a function of the difference between the student's ability, θ, and the difficulty of the item, b. The difficulty of the item is defined for the Rasch model as that point on the ability scale at which the probability of a correct response to the item is 0.5 (Baker and Kim 2004). The Rasch model is given as (Baker and Kim 2004)

$$P_i(\theta_j) = \frac{\exp(\theta_j - b_i)}{1 + \exp(\theta_j - b_i)}, \tag{22.1}$$

where θ_j is students' ability, and b_i is item difficulty.

Traditionally, there are two popular methods for detecting DIF, non-IRT (or observed-score) methods and IRT based methods. Non-IRT methods include methods such as the Mantel–Haenszel (Holland and Thayer 1988) and the standardization method (Dorans and Kulick 1986). IRT based methods include Lord's chi-square (Lord 1980), Raju's area measures (Raju 1988, 1990), and the likelihood ratio test for DIF (Thissen et al. 1993). In this paper, we focus on IRT based methods.

Note that standard IRT methods such as these do not consider the possible nested structure of the data. However, in educational research, data often include a nested structure, for example repeated observations are nested within individuals who are, in turn, nested within schools (Raudenbush and Bryk 2002). Raudenbush and Bryk (2002) note that ignoring this nesting structure can result in biased estimates of students' abilities. This kind of nesting structure is quite common, for example, in state-level achievement test data (French and Finch 2013). Another example is that teachers may teach more than one level of a course within a subject area (e.g., elementary algebra, geometry, and trigonometry). Also, teachers may teach the same subject in more than one school in a district. In such contexts as these, if traditional IRT methods are used for the detection of DIF, there is a risk of ignoring hierarchical structure (Kamata and Vaughn 2011), with results that bias point estimates, standard errors, and corresponding conference intervals. Incorrect DIF detection in such a context would result in inflated Type I error rates in DIF detection. Recently, hierarchical liner models (HLM) in the context of IRT have been reported in a number of studies (e.g., Acar 2012; French and Finch 2010). Likewise, structural equation models (SEM) have been discussed in the context of IRT (French and Finch 2010; Woods 2009).

With respect to HLM and IRT, French and Finch (2010) compared logistic regression and hierarchical logistic regression based on a two-parameter logistic (2PL) model. Type I error rates for hierarchical logistic regression were at or below the nominal level of 0.05 under several combinations of intraclass correlation, ρ, and cluster size, N, in the between-cluster condition. Finch and French concluded that ignoring the multilevel structure may result in failure to correctly identify DIF items. Further, accounting for the multilevel structure clearly demonstrated control of a Type I error in the detection of DIF.

Regarding SEM and IRT, Finch (2005), for example, compared the multiple-indicators, multiple-causes (MIMIC) method with the Mantel–Haenszel, SIBTEST, and IRT-LR for 2PL and 3PL models. The results suggested that the MIMIC model for detecting DIF has an inflated Type I error rate for shorter tests (20-items) in the 3PL model but a viable option for longer tests (50-items) in the 2PL models. In addition, the MIMIC model performed well when the proportion of DIF items was large. Woods (2009) also compared the MIMIC model with the IRT-LR test for 2PL models and indicated that "With small focal-group samples, tests of uniform DIF with binary or five-category ordinal responses were more accurate with MIMIC models than IRT-LR-DIF. At all values of N_F, the Type I error was well below the nominal α level [0.05] and power was greater for the MIMIC approach than for IRT-LR-DIF" (p. 23). In sum, the HLM was found to be more accurate when using multilevel structures of data, and the MIMIC was recommended for detecting DIF in small sample sizes, when compared to other IRT methods.

However, so far no study has compared these three methods under the same conditions. As the hierarchical generalized linear model (HGLM) is increasingly becoming popular in the IRT area, the purpose of the current study is to compare the performance of three models for detecting DIF, the IRT-LR test, the HGLM, and the MIMIC. In the following, the first section reviews these three methods, the IRT-LR, the HGLM, and the MIMIC, for detecting DIF. The second section describes simulation studies. The third section discusses the results. The fourth section presents a discussion of the findings.

22.1 Three Methods for DIF Detection

22.1.1 IRT-LR Test

The IRT-LR was proposed by Thissen, Steinberg, and Gerrard (1986) and Thissen et al. (1993) to assess the significance of differences in item parameter estimates between reference and focal groups (Kim and Cohen 1998). Thissen et al. (1988) noted that the IRT-LR test method is preferable for theoretical reasons, because the comparison of item parameters and an area measure require accurate estimates of variances and covariances of the item parameters. In the IRT-LR, some items are used to establish a common metric between the reference and focal groups. These are referred to as the *anchor* items and are assumed to be DIF-free. The anchor item parameters are constrained to be equal between these groups. The studied items are then evaluated for DIF by releasing them to be freely estimated. This can be done one item at a time (e.g., Cohen et al. 1996) or in groups (e.g., Thissen et al. 1993; Woods 2008).

The IRT-LR test procedure can be used to detect both uniform and non-uniform DIF. This method compares an augmented model, which is the model with the studied item response that is to be tested, and a constrained model in which the items are all constrained to be equal across the two groups (Thissen et al. 1993). The metric of the compact model and the augmented model is established on a common scale by the anchor items (Cohen et al. 1996). The null hypothesis for this test assumes that the parameters of the studied items in the reference and focal groups are equal. Item parameters for all items except those for the studied items are constrained to be equal (Cohen et al. 1996). These items form the anchor set in an augmented model. Because the augmented model includes all parameters of the compact model and additional parameters of the studied items, the compact model is hierarchically nested within the augmented model (Cohen et al. 1996). The test statistic for the IRT-LR test is the difference between the values of −2log likelihood for the compact model (L_C) and that for the augmented model (L_A). The IRT-LR test is defined as (Thissen 2001):

$$G^2(d.f.) = -2\log L_C - (-2\log L_A), \qquad (22.2)$$

where $G^2(d.f.)$ is distributed as chi-square. The degrees of freedom for this statistic are the difference between the number of parameters in the augmented and the compact models. The number of items considered determines the degrees of freedom. If a single item is the studied item under the Rasch model, then the degrees of freedom is 1. If more than one item is studied at a time, then the degrees of freedom will be usually more than 1. For instance, if three items are studied in the same augmented model, then the degrees of freedom would be 3, that is, one degree of freedom for each of the studied items. If this statistic is significant at the nominal level selected for this test, then DIF is defined as existing in the studied item.

22.1.2 HGLM

In addition to the traditional IRT methods for detecting DIF, several recent findings use alternative methods for detecting DIF. The HGLM models hierarchical data when the outcome is categorical data, such as nominal or ordinal-scaled data (Raudenbush and Bryk 2002). This model is an extension of the generalized linear model (GLM) to multilevel data (McCullagh and Nelder 1989; Kamata 1998). The level-1 model in the two-level HGLM consists of a sampling model, a link function, and a structural model. According to Raudenbush and Bryk (2002), a binomial sampling and a logit link are used when the outcome is binary. Based on the binomial distribution, the expected value and variance of Y_{ij} for the level-1 sampling model for the two-level model can be written as

$$E\left(Y_{ij}\middle|\varphi_{ij}\right) = \varphi_{ij}, \quad \text{and} \quad \text{Var}\left(Y_{ij}\middle|\varphi_{ij}\right) = \varphi_{ij}\left(1-\varphi_{ij}\right), \tag{22.3}$$

where φ_{ij} is the probability of examinee j giving a correct response to item i. The level-1 logit link function in the HGLM can be written as

$$\eta_{ij} = \log\left(\frac{\varphi_{ij}}{1-\varphi_{ij}}\right), \tag{22.4}$$

where η_{ij} represents the log of the odds of examinee j giving a correct response to item i. It can take any real value. φ_{ij} is constrained to the values between 0 and 1, since it is a probability. If φ_{ij} is equal to 0.5, the odds of a correct response is equal to 1, i.e., $0.5/0.5 = 1$, and the logit is 0, $\log(1) = 0$. If φ_{ij} is smaller than 0.5, then the logit is negative; if φ_{ij} is larger than 0.5, then the logit is positive. The level-1 structural question, which defines the relationship between the item indicators and the transformed predicted value, can be written as

$$\eta_{ij} = \beta_{0j} + \beta_{1j}X_{1ij} + \beta_{2j}X_{2ij} + \ldots. + \beta_{kj}X_{kij} = \beta_{0j} + \sum_{h=1}^{k} \beta_{hj}X_{hij}, \tag{22.5}$$

where X_{hij} is the h-th item-indicator dummy variable for examinee j, with value 1 when $h = i$ and 0 when $h \neq i$, for item i related to a coefficient β_{hj}, where $h = 1, \ldots, k$. β_{0j} is the intercept of the structural equation.

For the two-level HGLM model, which is algebraically the same as the Rasch model, the frameworks of the GLM and the HLM can produce the Rasch model (Kamata 2001, 2002). A link function and a linear predictor model can be specified as the lowest level or item-level model. In fact, the two-level HGLM can be easily expanded to a three-level latent regression model, which provides estimated group- and person-level abilities, allows the analysis of a variation of examinees' performances across groups, such as in schools, and exhibits the variation of the interactive effect of person- and group-characteristic variables (Kamata 2001).

In this study, we employ three-level hierarchical models, with item responses as Level 1 variables, students as Level 2 variables, and schools as Level 3 variables. The outcome variables to be considered are dichotomous and are assumed to be following a binomial distribution (Raudenbush and Bryk 1986). The logit link function for the three-level Rasch model is given as (Kamata 2002):

$$\eta_{ijm} = \log\left[\frac{\varphi_{ijm}}{1-\varphi_{ijm}}\right], \tag{22.6}$$

where φ_{ijm} is the probability that the i-th response is correct for student j in school m. η_{ijm} is the log-odds of probability that the i-th response is correct for student j in school m. When the Rasch model is fit into the two-level HGLM framework, the equation without any predictors of Level 1 is given as

$$\log\left(\frac{\varphi_{ij}}{1-\varphi_{ij}}\right) = \eta_{ij} = \theta_j - b_i = \theta_j + \beta_i, \tag{22.7}$$

where $\beta_i = -b_i$. By adding predictors or covariates, the conditional three-level HGLM models of Level 1 can be written as

$$\begin{aligned}\log\left(\frac{\varphi_{ijm}}{1-\varphi_{ijm}}\right) &= \eta_{ijm} = \beta_{0jm} + \beta_{1jm}X_{1ijm} + \ldots. + \beta_{kjm}X_{kijm} \\ &= \beta_{0jm} + \sum_{h=1}^{k} \beta_{hjm}X_{hijm},\end{aligned} \tag{22.8}$$

where the outcome variable is connected to a predictor with a logistic link function. X_{hijm}, which is used to identify the items in the linear predictor model, is the h-th item-indicator dummy variable ($h = 1, \ldots k$), with values of either 1 or 0, for student j for item i in school m. The coefficient β_{0jm} is an intercept term, and it is the only item that has an effect when every X_{hijm} has a value of zero. The coefficient β_{hjm} is related to X_{hijm}. The Level 1 model predicts the probability of student j in school m answering item i correctly. The Level 2 model is the student-level model for student j in school m.

22.1.2.1 Level 2 Model

$$\begin{cases} \beta_{ojm} = \gamma_{00m} + u_{0jm}, \quad \text{with} \quad u_{0jm} \sim N(0, \tau_\gamma) \\ \beta_{1jm} = \gamma_{10m} + \gamma_{11m}(\text{group})_{jm} \\ \vdots \\ \beta_{kjm} = \gamma_{k0\text{m}} + \gamma_{k1\text{m}}(\text{group})_{jm}, \end{cases} \tag{22.9}$$

where $(group)_{jm}$ is an indicator variable for binary group membership, with value 0 = focal group and value 1 = reference group. γ_{00m} is a random intercept representing the average ability of a specific group m . If the magnitude of γ_{k1m} is statistically significantly different from zero, item l is a DIF item. u_{0jm} is the ability of student j in school m, specifying how much the student's ability originates in the average ability of that student in school m. If DIF is detected in an item, the interest is in whether the DIF differs across schools. Thus, in order to test for such a difference, the model is extended to a level-3 model, and the DIF parameters, γ_{11m} through γ_{k1m}, are treated as random effects (Chu 2002). In a level-3 model, which is a school-level model, $\gamma_{00m,}$ the intercept, is the only term that varies across schools.

22.1.2.2 Level 3 Model

$$\begin{cases} \gamma 00m = r00m, \quad \text{with} \quad r00m \sim N(0, \omega) \\ \gamma 10m = \pi 100 \\ \gamma 11m = \pi 110 + r11m \\ \vdots \\ \gamma k0m = \pi k00 \\ \gamma k1m = \pi k10 + rk1m, \end{cases} \tag{22.10}$$

where r_{oom} is a random component of γ_{00m}, and it is the random effect related to school m. r_{oom} is the average ability of students in school m; r_{11m} through r_{k1m} indicate the variance of DIF at the school level. This study is interested in the magnitudes of variance (r_{k1m}). The DIF magnitude differs across school units if the var(r_{k1m}) is large (Binici 2007). The procedure for analyzing the HGLM model is to examine and evaluate which items contain DIF. Note that in order to achieve "full rank" for the design matrix of the model, one of the dummy variable items must be dropped or no-intercept model can be fitted (Kamata and Cheong 2007; Kamata and Vaughn 2011). This study does not include the intercept term π_{000}, and it retains all dummy variable items in a level-3 model. Hence, there are no grand means in level-3, and ability is a random effect, r_{oom}.

22.1.3 *MIMIC*

Other than the HGLM, many studies employ the SEM method to detect DIF. The link between the IRT model and SEM, such as the multiple-group analysis and the MIMIC models, for detection of DIF has been discussed in recent research (e.g., Finch 2005; Finch and French 2010; Shih and Wang 2009; Willse and Goodman 2008; Woods 2009) The multiple-group analysis allows a great deal of flexibility in observing group differences and can be used to investigate both uniform and non-uniform DIF. When a sample size is large, the multiple-group analysis can examine more types of hypotheses than the MIMIC model (Woods 2009). The MIMIC model is popular with estimation methods appropriate for dichotomous data because of its flexibility in multiple applications and efficiency under different practical testing conditions (Woods et al. 2009). It is also simple and effective to extend this to the multilevel context, and it is based on a single covariance matrix. In addition, the analysis of the MIMIC model is based on the regression of latent variables onto group variables (Willse and Goodman 2008). The MIMIC model has several advantages. One of the most important features of the MIMIC model is that a latent variable can be predicted by at least one observed variable (Woods 2009). It can also be estimated using ordinal or continuous data, data with different numbers of groups and with multiple independent continuous or categorical variables (Woods 2009). Further, it supplies information for the structural and measurement models (Muthén 1989) and does not require large sample sizes. It is also based on matching with a latent variable, which may be more accurate than an observed score (Woods et al. 2009). In addition, establishing a common metric does not seem to be necessary (Jones 2006). The disadvantages of the MIMIC model include that: (1) it is sensitive to uniform DIF only; (2) it cannot justify the lower asymptote, c, in the three-parameter model; (3) it has been discovered to have an inflated Type I error rate for shorter tests; and (4) it does not provide any effect size estimates when DIF exists (Finch and French 2010). Even though the MIMIC model does not provide an effect size, the detection of DIF is dependent solely on the results of the hypothesis test (Finch and French 2010). The MIMIC model is used in this study, because the focus is only on uniform DIF. Figure 22.1 illustrates a MIMIC model for detecting uniform DIF. A unidimensional IRT model with ability, a latent variable, η, is regressed on an observed grouping variable for testing DIF (Woods 2009). In this figure, the dotted line is used to indicate the case in which group membership is found to predict item response directly. This is evidence that DIF is present in the item. In other words, when the group variable and an item in question have a direct significant relationship, DIF is determined to exist in the item. If the discrimination parameters are invariant, this means the discrimination parameter is equal to 1.

22.2 Comparison

Table 22.1 shows the comparison of three models for detecting DIF.

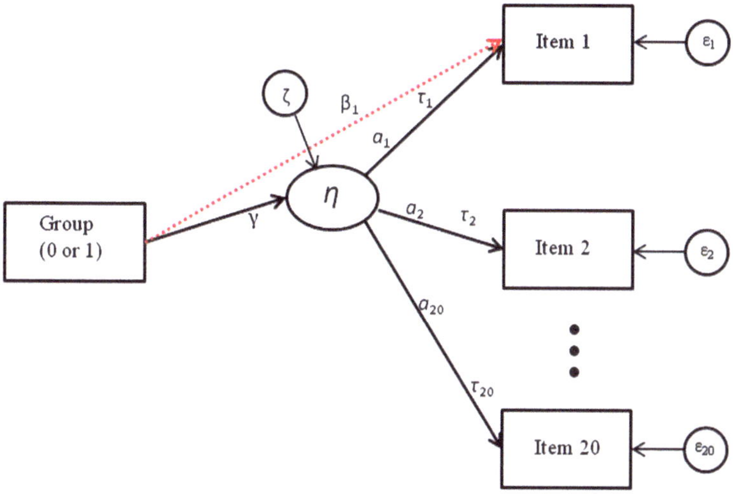

Fig. 22.1 A MIMIC model is shown here as used for the detection of DIF in this study. Rectangles are observed variables; circles are latent variables; γ = the regression coefficient displaying the mean difference on the latent variable; β_i = the group difference in the threshold for item i and the grouping variables, $i = 1, 2, \ldots, k$; a_k = discrimination parameter (all $a_k = 1$); τ_k = threshold parameter (τ_k depends on the group if DIF exists in an item); ε_i = the measurement error for item i; ζ = a residual for η

22.3 Simulation Studies

A simulation study was conducted where the performance of the HGLM wascompared to the MIMIC and the standard IRT-LR methods on the outcome variable of the Type I error rate for uniform DIF detection. The Type I error rate was determined by the ratio of the number of times DIF was incorrectly identified by each method across replications. Item responses were generated to have multilevel data structures based on Eqs. (22.8), (22.9), and (22.10) for the multilevel Rasch model in the previous section. A test length of 20 dichotomous items was simulated. The value of the difficulty parameters of the 20 items were arbitrarily fixed to −1, −0.5, 0, 0.5, and 1 (Cheong and Kamata 2013) with four repetitions. The variance of level 1 was to be $\pi^2/3$ based on Snijder and Bosker (2012). The variance, $\tau_{y,}$ of level 2 was to be 1. Based on the previous research (Snijder and Bosker 2012), the variance, ω, of level 3 was proposed to be ICC*[$\sigma^2 + (1 + ((0.5)\hat{}2)^* \ \tau_y)$ / (1−ICC)]. In other words, to assess the type I errors of the DIF tests for Item 1, item responses for Item 1 were generated without any DIF across the hypothetical group variable. Specifically, the coefficient of the group covariate for Item 1 in Eq. 22.9, which is γ_{11m}, was fixed to zero. Item responses for all of the other 19 items were generated to have DIF across the group variable. Various conditions were manipulated to aid in the comparison of the HGLM, the MIMIC, and the IRT-LR

Table 22.1 The comparison of three DIF test methods (focus on the methods used in this study only)

Comparison	Method	Similarities and differences	
Anchor items?	IRT-LR	Yes. Items 2–20 in this study	
	MIMIC	Yes. Items 2–20 in this study	
	HGLM	Yes. Items 2–20 in this study	
Test each non-anchor studied item individually?	IRT-LR	Yes	
	MIMIC	Yes	
	HGLM	Yes	
Technique	IRT-LR	Test if the IRT based LR test statistic between two models is statistically significantly different from zero	Full model (without latent variables): all parameters for the studied item *i* permitted to vary between groups
		(In both models, parameters for all anchors are constrained equal between groups)	Restrict model (without latent variables): all parameters for the studied item *i* constrained equal between groups
	MIMIC	Test if the LR test statistic between two models is statistically significantly different from zero	Full model (with latent variables): presumes DIF in all studied items
		(In both models, parameters for all anchors are constrained equal between groups)	Restrict model (with latent variables): with the DIF path removed for studied item *i*
	HGLM	Test if the magnitude of the coefficient of a group variable is statistically significantly different from zero	

methods, including one grouping variable, two number of clusters, three number of examinees per cluster, and three intraclass correlation coefficients (ICC), ρ.

1. Group variable for DIF: A within-group variable referred to level 2, which, for instance, could be gender or ethnicity, and this variable was simulated to be dichotomous.
2. ICC: The ICC was set up at .1, .2, and .3 for the target item based on Maas and Hox (2005).
3. Number of clusters: The numbers of clusters simulated were 30 and 50 clusters. Previous researchers (Hox and Maas 2001; Maas and Hox 2005) have used similar values.
4. Number of examinees within cluster: The cluster sizes were simulated balanced sizes with 5, 30, and 50. These values matched prior research (Maas and Hox 2005) investigating hierarchical data.

There are $2 \times 3 \times 3$ factorial designs for a total of 18 conditions. We generated 1,000 simulated data sets for each of the 18 conditions. Data were generated using a program written in *R* Program. Analyses were conducted with lme4 (Bates et al. 2013) in *R* for the HGLM. M*plus* 7.1 (Muthén and Muthén 1998–2012) was used to estimate the MIMIC model with a robust weighted least squares estimator for categorical outcomes, and the discrimination parameters of the items were set to 1. BILOG-MG 3 (Zimowski et al 2003) was used for the IRT-LR test. Each simulated data set for each condition was analyzed three times, including the HGLM, the MIMIC, and the IRT-LR test, respectively. Item2–Item20 are specified the anchor item in testing DIF using those three methods since they are constrained to be equal across groups in both constrained and augmented model.

22.4 Results

Table 22.2 shows the Type I error rates for the HGLM, MIMIC, and IRT-LR methods across the number of clusters, cluster sizes, and for different ICCs. As noted earlier, the nominal Type I error rate for this study was 0.05. The Type I error rates for the HGLM indicate marginal control was maintained for specific conditions. The Type I error rates for the MIMIC model were higher than the HGLM. When the cluster size was small, such as in the 30-cluster, 5-examinee or 50-cluster, 5-examinee conditions, the performance of the MIMIC model appeared to maintain better Type I error control. However, when the level 3 cluster size and ρ increased, the Type I error rates also increased, such that no control was maintained at the nominal level. The IRT-LR test showed no control of the Type I error in any of the conditions simulated.

Figure 22.2 shows the tendency of the Type I error rates for HGLM to remain at the nominal 0.05 level for most of the conditions in this study. When the level 3 cluster sizes were small, the Type I error rates for the MIMIC model remained close to the nominal 0.05 level. When cluster sizes and ρ increased, Type I error

Table 22.2 The mean of type I error rates with a theoretical value of 0.05 for the three methods for number of groups, the group sizes, and ICC value

Number of groups	Group size	ICC	Methods HGLM	MIMIC	IRT-LR
30	5	0.10	0.066	0.051	0.080
		0.20	0.065	0.057	0.076
		0.30	0.068	0.054	0.065
	30	0.10	0.055	0.117	0.473
		0.20	0.068	0.121	0.380
		0.30	0.055	0.130	0.473
	50	0.10	0.046	0.145	0.686
		0.20	0.059	0.182	0.565
		0.30	0.067	0.172	0.496
50	5	0.10	0.070	0.054	0.147
		0.20	0.054	0.046	0.107
		0.30	0.054	0.068	0.076
	30	0.10	0.050	0.108	0.720
		0.20	0.066	0.146	0.594
		0.30	0.054	0.158	0.594
	50	0.10	0.064	0.169	0.894
		0.20	0.058	0.209	0.812
		0.30	0.070	0.228	0.741

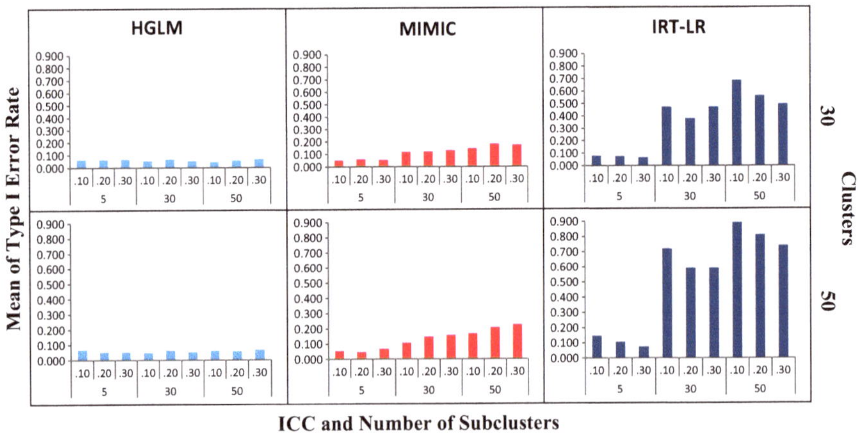

Fig. 22.2 The tendency of the type I error rates

control for the MIMIC model failed to be maintained. The results for the IRT-LR test indicate the complete lack of control for the conditions studied here. These results appear to suggest that ignoring the multilevel structure in the data leads to inflated Type I errors.

In sum, the Type I error rates for the HGLM model were not as seriously affected by the number of clusters, cluster sizes, and ρ as were the MIMIC and IRT-LR tests. When the number of clusters, cluster sizes, and ρ increased, they appeared to influence the outcomes for the MIMIC model. For the largest cluster sizes and ρ sizes considered, the Type I error rate was inflated for the MIMIC. Results of this study suggest that standard IRT methods which ignore the multilevel structure in the data are not appropriate for the detection of DIF when the data have a multilevel structure. Overall, the results support previous research (e.g., French and Finch 2010; Woods 2009) which suggests that multilevel modeling is more appropriate for detecting DIF when a multilevel structure is present in the data.

22.5 Discussion

A great deal of educational data is hierarchical data. However, using standard methods, such as a non-IRT based methods or IRT based methods which do not account for this kind of structure, could result in biased results. Previous research has examined the HLM, SEM, and IRT- LR methods. Thus far, however, no study directly compares these methods on the same data. In this research, we compared the Type I error rates of these approaches to determine whether they yielded similar or different results for the detection of uniform DIF in multilevel data.

Results of this study supported previous findings that HLM was more accurate for controlling the Type I error rate when the data structure is multilevel. In order to simulate the real-world situations, anchor items are assumed to have DIF in this study. Consistent with the results from the previous study (Finch 2005), the Type I error rate of the IRT-LR test was more sensitive to the item contamination of the anchor items than the Type I error rate of the MIMIC model. It would be useful for future research to investigate the effect of multilevel data on DIF detection with no anchor items and to consider the effect sizes of DIF tests with multilevel data. A single test length was used in this study. It is possible that other test lengths might differentially affect detection of DIF in multilevel data. Other conditions which might be considered include the percentage of DIF items present and the power and detection of DIF using other dichotomous and polytomous IRT models.

References

Acar T (2012) Determination of a differential item functioning procedure using the hierarchical generalized linear model: a comparison study with logistic regression and likelihood ratio procedure. SAGE Open. Advance online publication. doi:10.1177/2158244012436760

Baker FB, Kim S-H (2004) Item response theory: parameter estimation techniques. Taylor & Francis, Boca Raton

Bates D, Marchler M, Bolker B (2013) Linear mixed-effects models using S4 classes (R package). http://cran.rproject.org/web/packages/lme4/lme4.pdf

Binici S (2007) Random-effect differential item functioning via hierarchical generalized linear model and generalized linear latent mixed model: a comparison of estimation methods. Unpublished doctoral dissertation. Florida State University
Camilli G, Shepard LA (1994) Methods for identifying biased test items. Sage, Thousand Oaks
Cheong YF, Kamata A (2013) Centering, scale indeterminacy, and differential item functioning detection in hierarchical generalized linear and generalized linear mixed models. Appl Meas Educ 26(4):233–252
Chu K (2002) Equivalent group test equating with the presence of differential item functioning. Unpublished doctoral dissertation. Florida State University
Cohen AS, Kim S-H, Wollack JA (1996) An investigation of the likelihood ratio test for detection of differential item functioning. Appl Psychol Meas 20(1):15–26
Dorans NJ, Kulick E (1986) Demonstrating the utility of the standardization approach to assessing unexpected differential item performance on the scholastic aptitude test. J Educ Meas 23(4):355–368
Finch WH (2005) The MIMIC model as a method for detecting DIF: comparison with Mantel-Haenszel, SIBTEST, and the IRT likelihood ratio. Appl Psychol Meas 29(4):278–295
Finch WH, French BF (2010) Detecting differential item functioning of a course satisfaction instrument in the presence of multilevel data. J First Year Exp Stud Transit 22(1):27–47
French BF, Finch WH (2010) Hierarchical logistic regression: accounting for multilevel data in DIF detection. J Educ Meas 47(3):299–317
French BF, Finch WH (2013) Extensions of Mantel-Haenszel for multilevel DIF detection. Educ Psychol Meas. doi:10.1177/0013164412472341, Advance online publication
Holland PW, Thayer DT (1988) Differential item functioning and the Mantel-Haenszel procedure. In: Wainer H, Braun HI (eds) Test validity. Lawrence Erlbaum Associates, Hillsdale, pp 129–145
Hox JJ, Maas CJM (2001) The accuracy of multilevel structural equation modeling with pseudobalanced groups and small samples. Struct Equ Model 8:157–174
Jones RN (2006) Identification of measurement differences between English and Spanish language versions of the mini-mental state examination: detecting differential item functioning using MIMIC modeling. Med Care 44(11):124–133
Kamata A (1998) One-parameter hierarchical generalized linear logistic model: an application of HGLM to IRT. Paper presented at the annual meeting of the American Educational Research Association, April, California
Kamata A (2001) Item analysis by the hierarchical generalized linear model. J Educ Meas 38(1):79–93
Kamata A (2002) Procedure to perform item response analysis by hierarchical generalized linear model. Paper presented at the annual meeting of the American Educational Research Association, April, New Orleans
Kamata A, Cheong YF (2007) Multilevel Rasch models. In: von Davier M, Carstensen CH (eds) Multivariate and mixture distribution Rasch models: extensions and applications. Springer Science + Business Media, New York, pp 217–232
Kamata A, Vaughn BK (2011) Multilevel IRT modeling. In: Hox JJ, Roberts JK (eds) Handbook of advanced multilevel analysis. Taylor and Francis Group, New York, pp 41–57
Kim S-K, Cohen AS (1998) Detection of differential item functioning under the graded response model with the likelihood ratio test. Appl Psychol Meas 22(4):345–355
Lord FM (1980) Applications of item response theory to practical testing problems. Lawrence Erlbaum Associates, Hillsdale
Maas CJM, Hox JJ (2005) Sufficient sample sizes for multilevel modeling. Methodology 1(3): 86–92
McCullagh P, Nelder JA (1989) Generalized linear models, 2nd edn. Chapman and Hill, London
Muthén BO (1989) Latent variable modeling in heterogeneous populations. Psychometrika 54(4):557–585
Muthén LK, Muthén BO (1998–2012) Mplus user's guide, 7th edn. Muthén & Muthén, Los Angeles

National Assessment of Educational Progress (2009). Reading assessment and item specifications. Retrieved March 14, 2014 from http://www.state.nj.us/education/assessment/naep/results/temspecs09.pdf
Raju NS (1988) The area between two item characteristic curves. Psychometrika 53(4):495–502
Raju NS (1990) Determining the significance of estimated signed and unsigned areas between two item response functions. Appl Psychol Meas 14(2):197–207
Rasch G (1960) Probabilistic models for some intelligence and attainment tests. The Danish Institute for Educational Research, Copenhagen
Raudenbush S, Bryk AS (1986) A hierarchical model for studying school effects. Sociol Educ 59(1):1–17
Raudenbush SW, Bryk AS (2002) Hierarchical linear models: applications and data analysis methods, 2nd edn. Sage, Newbury
Shih C-L, Wang W-C (2009) Differential item functioning detection using the multiple indicators, multiple causes method with a pure short anchor. Appl Psychol Meas 33(3):184–199
Snijder TAB, Bosker RJ (2012) Multilevel analysis: an introduction to basic and advanced multilevel modeling, 2nd edn. Sage, Thousand Oaks
Thissen D (2001) IRTLRDIF v2.0b: Software for the computation of the statistics involved in item response theory likelihood-ratio tests for differential item functioning [Computer software documentation]. L. L. Thurstone Psychometric Laboratory, University of North Carolina, Chapel Hill
Thissen D, Steinberg L, Gerrard M (1986) Beyond group mean differences: the concept of item bias. Psychol Bull 99(1):118–128
Thissen D, Steinberg L, Wainer H (1988) Use of item response theory in the study of group differences in trace lines. In: Wainer H, Braun HI (eds) Test validity. Erlbaum, Hillsdale, pp 147–169
Thissen D, Steinberg L, Wainer H (1993) Detection of differential item functioning using the parameters of item response model. In: Holland PW, Wainer H (eds) Differential item functioning. Lawrence Erlbaum Associates, Hillsdale, pp 67–114
Willse JT, Goodman JT (2008) Comparison of multiple-indicators, multiple-causes- and item response theory-based analyses of subgroup differences. Educ Psychol Meas 68(4):587–602
Woods CM (2008) Likelihood-ratio DIF testing: Effects of nonnormality. Appl Psychol Meas 32(7):511–526
Woods CM (2009) Evaluation of MIMIC-model methods for DIF testing with comparison to two-groups analysis. Multivar Behav Res 44(1):1–27
Woods CM, Oltmanns TF, Turkheimer E (2009) Illustration of MIMIC-Model DIF testing with the schedule for nonadaptive and adaptive personality. J Psychopathol Behav Asses 31(4):320–330
Zimowski MF, Muraki E, Mislevy RJ, Bock RD (2003) BILOG-MG 3 [Computer software]. Scientific Software International, Lincolnwood

Chapter 23
Comparing Estimation Methods for Categorical Marginal Models

Renske E. Kuijpers, Wicher P. Bergsma, L. Andries van der Ark, and Marcel A. Croon

Abstract Categorical marginal models are flexible models for modelling dependent or clustered categorical data which do not involve any specific assumptions about the nature of the dependencies. Categorical marginal models are used for different purposes, including hypothesis testing, assessing model fit, and regression problems. Two different estimation methods are used to estimate marginal models: maximum likelihood (ML) and generalized estimating equations (GEE). We explored three different cases to find out to what extent the two types of estimation methods are appropriate for investigating different types of research questions. The results suggest that ML may be preferred for assessing model fit because GEE has limited fit indices, whereas both methods can be used to assess the effect of independent factors in regression. Moreover, ML is asymptotically efficient, while GEE loses efficiency when the working correlation matrix is not correctly specified. However, for parameter estimation in regression GEE is easier to apply from a computational perspective.

23.1 Introduction

In the social and behavioral sciences, researchers frequently collect data that are correlated or dependent, such as longitudinal data, dyadic data, and data obtained from psychological or educational testing in which each respondent answers several

R.E. Kuijpers (✉)
Department of Methodology and Statistics, Tilburg University, P.O. Box 90153, 5000 LE Tilburg, The Netherlands
e-mail: r.e.kuijpers@tilburguniversity.edu

W.P. Bergsma
London School of Economics, London, UK

L.A. van der Ark
University of Amsterdam, Amsterdam, The Netherlands

M.A. Croon
Tilburg University, Tilburg, The Netherlands

R.E. Millsap et al. (eds.), *Quantitative Psychology Research*, Springer Proceedings in Mathematics & Statistics 89, DOI 10.1007/978-3-319-07503-7_23

items. Although the dependencies are not always of main interest for the research, they cannot be ignored. Ignoring the dependencies in the analysis may produce incorrect standard errors and p-values. Categorical marginal models (Bergsma et al. 2009) are flexible models for categorical data that take these dependencies into account without making assumptions about their nature. These models are useful when researchers investigate research questions concerning the marginal distributions of a set of variables instead of testing hypotheses with respect to the joint distribution for all variables in a certain data set.

Categorical marginal models are used to answer various types of research questions. Two types of research questions we encountered in the literature are research questions that involve hypothesis testing and research questions that involve parameter estimation. An example of a research question that involves hypothesis testing is provided by Kuijpers et al. (2013a). They proposed fitting categorical marginal models to test the hypothesis that Cronbach's alpha is equal for two or more subgroups. Other examples include testing marginal models for scalability coefficients (Van der Ark et al. 2008; Kuijpers et al. 2013b), marginal homogeneity (Bergsma et al. 2009), and ordinal association measures (e.g., Lang 2004).

For the second type of research question, the main interest lies in the values of the estimated regression parameters. For example, Molenberghs and Verbeke (2005) used marginal models to investigate the effect of two types of vaccinations from two different companies on the presence/absence of headaches and respiratory problems in two trial periods. Other examples include (1) modelling the effect of different demographic variables on the relation between smoking and drinking behavior in different subgroups of the Belgian Interuniversity Research on Nutrition and Health study (Kesteloot et al. 1989) and (2) investigating whether different (combinations of) variables such as gender, age, education, and religiosity have a significant effect on the attitude towards women's roles (Bergsma et al. 2009, pp. 168–171).

Both likelihood methods and quasi-likelihood methods have been used to estimate marginal models. For likelihood methods, which include maximum likelihood (ML) estimation (Bergsma 1997), maximum empirical likelihood (MEL) estimation, and maximum augmented empirical likelihood (MAEL) estimation (Van der Ark et al. 2013), the full likelihood is optimized under the marginal model of interest and under the assumption that the data follow a multinomial distribution. ML, MEL, and MAEL estimation differ with respect to whether or not they use all possible item-score patterns of a set of items for the estimation of a model. For research questions that concern hypothesis testing, the authors have used ML (e.g., Kuijpers et al. 2013a,b; Van der Ark et al. 2008). For this paper, we only consider ML estimation. The most popular quasi-likelihood method is generalized estimating equations (GEE; Liang and Zeger 1986). GEE is not based on a specific probability model for the data. The estimation method assumes only a mean-variance relationship for the dependent variable. GEE is mainly used for estimating regression models (e.g., Agresti 2013; Molenberghs and Verbeke 2005; Pawitan 2001). Skrondal and Rabe-Hesketh (2004, p. 200) noted that GEE has some limitations with respect to hypothesis testing and assessing model adequacy.

In this study, we explored to what extent ML estimation and GEE are appropriate for investigating the three types of research questions. We considered three different research questions, referred to as Case 1, Case 2, and Case 3. Let θ denote a particular coefficient, and let c denote a fixed value. In this study θ can refer to either the mean (μ) or the reliability coefficient Cronbach's alpha (α). In Case 1, we investigated whether θ is equal to a fixed value c (i.e., $\theta = c$); in Case 2, we investigated whether θ is equal for two groups (i.e., $\theta_1 = \theta_2$); and in Case 3, we investigated whether θ is a linear function of independent variable X (i.e., $\theta = \beta_0 + \beta_1 X$). In each case, we investigated the two coefficients μ and α, and we compared the results obtained with ML estimation and GEE. We illustrated each case with a real-data example.

The remainder of this paper is organized as follows. First, we briefly explain categorical marginal models. Second, we discuss the two groups of estimation methods. Third, we discuss how to express μ and α in an appropriate notation for ML estimation. Fourth, using a real-data set, we compare the estimation methods for the three cases. Finally, we discuss the outcomes and provide recommendations for future research.

23.2 Categorical Marginal Models

In order to use categorical marginal models for testing hypotheses for a coefficient or for estimating parameters in a regression model, the first step is to write the coefficient or the regression model as a function of the frequencies of the item-score patterns that are observed in the data. Consider a set of J items, each item having $z+1$ ordered answer categories $(0, 1, \ldots, z)$; this produces $L = (z+1)^J$ possible item-score patterns. Let $\mathbf{n}$ be an $L \times 1$ vector containing the observed frequencies of the L possible item-score patterns. For example, a dichotomously scored test consisting of $J = 3$ items (denoted by a, b, and c) has $L = 2^3 = 8$ possible item-score patterns; hence, vector $\mathbf{n}$ equals

$$\mathbf{n} = \begin{pmatrix} n_{abc}^{000} \\ n_{abc}^{001} \\ n_{abc}^{010} \\ n_{abc}^{011} \\ n_{abc}^{100} \\ n_{abc}^{101} \\ n_{abc}^{110} \\ n_{abc}^{111} \end{pmatrix}, \tag{23.1}$$

where the subscripts denote the items and the superscripts the item scores. The observed frequencies of the item-score patterns in vector $\mathbf{n}$ are given in lexicographic order, running from $00\ldots0$ to $zz\ldots z$ with the last digit changing fastest and the digit in the first column changing slowest.

The expected frequencies under a categorical marginal model are collected in an $L \times 1$ vector $\mathbf{m}$. Because there may be more than one set of expected frequencies that satisfy a marginal model, $\mathbf{m}$ is as close as possible to $\mathbf{n}$. Let matrix $\mathbf{C}$ be a *marginal matrix* consisting of zeros and ones, such that $\mathbf{C}'\mathbf{m}$ produces the relevant marginals from the contingency table. Vector $\boldsymbol{\beta}$ contains the K model parameters β_k ($k = 0, 1, \ldots, K-1$). Then, let $\mathbf{Z}$ be the design matrix of the marginal model that uses effect coding in order to select the right parameters from vector $\boldsymbol{\beta}$. In a categorical marginal model, a function of the relevant marginals is then written as

$$\mathbf{f}(\mathbf{C}'\mathbf{m}) = \mathbf{Z}\boldsymbol{\beta}, \tag{23.2}$$

where $\mathbf{f}$ is an appropriate vector function. Alternatively, the model can be written without parameter vector $\boldsymbol{\beta}$ (Agresti 2013, pp. 460–461; Aitchison and Silvey 1958; Bergsma et al. 2013). Let $\mathbf{B}$ be the orthogonal complement of $\mathbf{Z}$, then $\mathbf{B}'\mathbf{Z} = 0$. By premultiplying both sides of Eq. (23.2) by $\mathbf{B}'$, the categorical marginal model can be written as a set of constraints

$$\mathbf{B}'\mathbf{f}(\mathbf{C}'\mathbf{m}) = \mathbf{B}'\mathbf{Z}\boldsymbol{\beta} = \mathbf{0}.$$

Because $\mathbf{B}$ and $\mathbf{C}$ are known design matrices, we can write $\mathbf{g}(\mathbf{m}) = \mathbf{B}'\mathbf{f}(\mathbf{C}'\mathbf{m})$. Then, a concise notation for a categorical marginal model, as is used throughout the literature (e.g., Bergsma 1997; Kuijpers et al. 2013a; Van der Ark et al. 2008), is

$$\mathbf{g}(\mathbf{m}) = \mathbf{0}. \tag{23.3}$$

Let D be the number of constraints on the expected frequencies $\mathbf{m}$. Each constraint is a scalar function, so, for example, $g_1(\mathbf{m}) = d_1$, and can be collected in the vector $\mathbf{g}(\mathbf{m})$. So $\mathbf{g}(\mathbf{m})$ contains all constraints that are placed on a vector $\mathbf{m}$. The constraints in Eq. (23.3) constitute the categorical marginal model. Some examples of constraints are $\alpha = 0.80$ and $\mu_1 = \mu_2$.

23.3 Estimation Methods

23.3.1 Likelihood Methods

Likelihood methods use the constraint notation in Eq. (23.3) in combination with ML estimation. The unconstrained log-likelihood function (for more details see Bergsma 1997) is

$$\ell(\mathbf{m}|\mathbf{n}) = \mathbf{n}' \log \mathbf{m}.$$

The maximum likelihood estimate $\widehat{\mathbf{m}}$ maximizes $\ell(\mathbf{m}|\mathbf{n})$ subject to the constraints implied by the categorical marginal model, $\mathbf{g}(\mathbf{m}) = \mathbf{0}$ [Eq. (23.3)], and to the constraint that $\sum_i m_i = \sum_i n_i = N$, where N denotes the total sample size.

Let $\boldsymbol{\lambda}$ be a $D \times 1$ vector of Lagrange multipliers and let ν be a single Lagrange multiplier, then under some regularity conditions, the ML estimates under Eq. (23.3) are a saddle point of the Lagrangian log-likelihood

$$\ell(\mathbf{m}|\mathbf{n}, \boldsymbol{\lambda}, \nu) = \mathbf{n}' \log \mathbf{m} - \nu(\mathbf{1}'\mathbf{m} - N) - \boldsymbol{\lambda}'\mathbf{g}(\mathbf{m}). \tag{23.4}$$

Bergsma (1997) proposed a Fisher scoring algorithm to find the vector $\mathbf{m}$ in Eq. (23.4). The fit of the categorical marginal model can be assessed by means of a likelihood ratio test $G^2 = 2\mathbf{n}' \log(\mathbf{n}/\widehat{\mathbf{m}})$ or a Pearsons' chi-square test $X^2 = (\widehat{\mathbf{m}} - \mathbf{n})'\mathbf{D}_{\widehat{\mathbf{m}}}^{-1}(\widehat{\mathbf{m}} - \mathbf{n})$ with D degrees of freedom. Here, $\mathbf{D}_{\widehat{\mathbf{m}}}$ is a diagonal matrix with the elements of vector $\widehat{\mathbf{m}}$ on the diagonal. Because ML estimation is based on the likelihood function, models can be compared and statistical inferences about parameters can be made.

23.3.2 Generalized Estimating Equations

GEE specifies a link function for the mean, and specifies the dependence of the variance on the mean. Furthermore, GEE replaces the often complex dependence structure by a so-called *working correlation* structure that is more straightforward to define. GEE can be used to fit any categorical marginal model expressed in terms of Eq. (23.2), but traditionally GEE is used for regression models for longitudinal data. In the case of longitudinal data, Y_{it} is the response for person i (with $i = 1, 2, \ldots, N$) on time point t (with $t = 1, 2, \ldots, T$). For GEE, for person i, the model of interest is equal to

$$h(\boldsymbol{\mu}_i) = \mathbf{Z}_i \boldsymbol{\beta}, \tag{23.5}$$

In Eq. (23.5), $h(\cdot)$ is a link function that applies element by element to vector $\boldsymbol{\mu}_i$. Vector $\boldsymbol{\mu}_i$ contains the expected responses (i.e., for person i, $\boldsymbol{\mu}_i = (\mu_{i1}, \ldots, \mu_{iT})'$).

GEE links the mean μ to a linear predictor and in addition specifies a variance function that describes how the variance of Y_{it} depends on μ_{it} (Agresti 2013, p. 462). This model applies to the marginal distribution for each Y_{it}. The estimating equation used in GEE is

$$\sum_{i=1}^{N} \frac{\partial \boldsymbol{\mu}_i}{\partial} \boldsymbol{\beta} \mathbf{V}_i^{-1} (\mathbf{y}_i - \boldsymbol{\mu}_i) = \mathbf{0} \tag{23.6}$$

where $\mathbf{y}_i$ is a vector with t observed responses (i.e., $\mathbf{y}_i = (y_{i1}, \ldots, y_{iT})'$), and $\mathbf{V}_i$ is an appropriately chosen working correlation matrix. The estimates of the parameters β_i in vector $\boldsymbol{\beta}$ are a solution of Eq. (23.6). For an exponential family $\mu_{it} = E(Y_{it})$.

For GEE, the particular working correlation structure needs to be specified for the relation between the t different responses of person i collected in $\mathbf{y}_i$. Different correlation structures can be chosen, depending on the nature of the dependencies between the different responses (Pawitan 2001, p. 396). Choosing a working correlation structure that approximates the true correlation structure between the dependent responses enhances the efficiency of the parameter estimates (Agresti 2013, p. 463). Commonly used specifications of the working correlation matrix are: (1) the independence structure, which treats the different responses as independent; thus, no dependency exists; (2) the exchangeable structure, which assumes constant dependency; thus, the correlations between the different responses are assumed to be equal for each observed response; (3) the autoregressive structure, which is often used for measurement over time, and treats the correlations as an exponential function of the time lag; thus, this structure assumes that observations farther apart in time have weaker correlations; and (4) the unstructured structure, which assumes a free specification of the working correlation matrix, implying a separate correlation for each pair of observations (see Agresti 2013, p. 462, and Pawitan 2001, pp. 396–397, for more details).

The choice of the working correlation structure determines the GEE estimates of the model parameters and the accompanying standard errors (Agresti 2013, pp. 462–463). However, even if the working correlation matrix is misspecified, the estimates of the parameters are consistent. In contrast, the estimates of the standard errors of the parameters are not accurate, and need to be adjusted for misspecification of the working correlation matrix by using the so-called sandwich estimator (e.g., Agresti 2013, p. 467). Liang and Zeger (1986) proposed estimating the GEE parameter estimates and the standard errors by means of a Fisher scoring algorithm.

GEE can also be used for fitting categorical marginal models that are defined by more complex functions than the link function $h()$, and by functions that have $\mathbf{n}$ rather than $\mathbf{y}$ as an argument. Here, $\mathbf{f}(\mathbf{C}'\mathbf{n})$ is a function of the observed responses and $\mathbf{Z}\boldsymbol{\beta} = \mathbf{f}(\mathbf{C}'\mathbf{m})$ is a function of the expected responses, so Eq. 23.6 becomes

$$\mathbf{Z}'\mathbf{V}^{-1}(\mathbf{f}(\mathbf{C}'\mathbf{n}) - \mathbf{Z}\boldsymbol{\beta}) = \mathbf{0}. \tag{23.7}$$

A marginal model $\mathbf{Z}\boldsymbol{\beta}$ can represent a wide range of parameters or coefficients, with $\mathbf{f}(\mathbf{C}'\mathbf{n})$ being the corresponding sample value (Bergsma et al. 2013). Equation (23.7) can easily be solved by using

$$\boldsymbol{\beta} = (\mathbf{Z}'\mathbf{V}^{-1}\mathbf{Z})^{-1}\mathbf{Z}'\mathbf{V}^{-1}\mathbf{f}(\mathbf{C}'\mathbf{n}), \tag{23.8}$$

which is equivalent to weighted least squares, with $\mathbf{V}^{-1}$ being a weight matrix. By means of Eq. (23.8), estimates for the parameters in $\boldsymbol{\beta}$ can be obtained.

23.4 Expressing Item Means and Cronbach's Alpha in Terms of the Generalized Exp-Log Notation

Maximizing the Lagrangian likelihood in Eq. (23.4) requires the matrix of first partial derivatives of $\mathbf{g}(\mathbf{m})$ with respect to $\mathbf{m}$. This matrix, also known as the Jacobian, is usually difficult to obtain. However, if $\mathbf{g}(\mathbf{m})$ is written in the so-called exp-log notation (Bergsma 1997; Kritzer 1977), the derivation of the Jacobian is straightforward, and an automated recursive algorithm can be used to compute the Jacobian for a particular categorical marginal model (Bergsma 1997, p. 68).

23.4.1 Item Means in Exp-Log Notation

For testing hypotheses about the means in vector $\boldsymbol{\mu}$, the coefficient should first be rewritten in the generalized exp-log notation. In this recursive exp-log notation let $\mathbf{A}_1$ and $\mathbf{A}_2$ be appropriate design matrices. Then $\boldsymbol{\mu}$ is equal to

$$\boldsymbol{\mu} = \exp(\mathbf{A}_2 \log(\mathbf{A}_1 \mathbf{m})). \tag{23.9}$$

Let $\mathbf{R}$ be a $J \times L$ matrix that contains all L possible item-score patterns. The rows of $\mathbf{R}$ correspond to the J different items. The item-score patterns in $\mathbf{R}$ are from left to right in lexicographic order, running from $00\ldots0$ to $zz\ldots z$ with the digit in the last row changing fastest and the digit in the first row changing slowest, just as is the case in vectors $\mathbf{m}$ and $\mathbf{n}$. Furthermore, let $\mathbf{u}'_L$ be a $1 \times L$ unit row vector. The $[J+1] \times L$ design matrix $\mathbf{A}_1$ is a concatenation of matrix $\mathbf{R}$ and vector $\mathbf{u}'_L$; that is,

$$\mathbf{A}_1 = \begin{pmatrix} \mathbf{R} \\ \mathbf{u}'_L \end{pmatrix}.$$

For a dichotomously scored test consisting of $J = 3$ items [Eq. (23.1)] this produces

$$\mathbf{A}_1\mathbf{n} = \begin{pmatrix} 0\,0\,0\,0\,1\,1\,1\,1 \\ 0\,0\,1\,1\,0\,0\,1\,1 \\ 0\,1\,0\,1\,0\,1\,0\,1 \\ 1\,1\,1\,1\,1\,1\,1\,1 \end{pmatrix} \begin{pmatrix} n_{abc}^{000} \\ n_{abc}^{001} \\ n_{abc}^{010} \\ n_{abc}^{011} \\ n_{abc}^{100} \\ n_{abc}^{101} \\ n_{abc}^{110} \\ n_{abc}^{111} \end{pmatrix} = \begin{pmatrix} \Sigma X_a \\ \Sigma X_b \\ \Sigma X_c \\ N \end{pmatrix}. \tag{23.10}$$

As the first three elements of the right-hand side of Eq. (23.10) show, $\mathbf{Rn}$ produces a vector containing the sum of the scores on items a, b, and c across respondents, and $\mathbf{u}_L'\mathbf{n}$ produces the sample size N.

Let $\mathbf{I}_J$ be an identity matrix of order J. Then, the $J \times [J+1]$ design matrix $\mathbf{A}_2$ is a concatenation of matrix $\mathbf{I}_J$ and unit vector $-\mathbf{u}_J$

$$\mathbf{A}_2 = \begin{pmatrix} \mathbf{I}_J & -\mathbf{u}_J \end{pmatrix}.$$

For the three items a, b, and c, substituting the right-hand side of Eq. (23.10) for $\mathbf{A}_1\mathbf{n}$, $\exp(\mathbf{A}_2 \log(\mathbf{A}_1\mathbf{n}))$ yields

$$\exp\left[\begin{pmatrix} 1 & 0 & 0 & -1 \\ 0 & 1 & 0 & -1 \\ 0 & 0 & 1 & -1 \end{pmatrix} \log \begin{pmatrix} \Sigma X_a \\ \Sigma X_b \\ \Sigma X_c \\ N \end{pmatrix}\right] = \begin{pmatrix} \overline{X}_a \\ \overline{X}_b \\ \overline{X}_c \end{pmatrix}. \tag{23.11}$$

Equation (23.11) shows that $\exp(\mathbf{A}_2 \log(\mathbf{A}_1\mathbf{n}))$ produces the mean score for each item in a data set.

23.4.2 *Coefficient α in Exp-Log Notation*

Kuijpers et al. (2013a) used categorical marginal models for testing different hypotheses about Cronbach's alpha (Cronbach 1951). They showed that Cronbach's alpha, denoted by α, can be written as a function of $\mathbf{m}$ in the generalized exp-log notation:

$$\alpha = \mathbf{A}_5 \exp(\mathbf{A}_4 \log(\mathbf{A}_3 \exp(\mathbf{A}_2 \log(\mathbf{A}_1\mathbf{m})))), \tag{23.12}$$

where matrices $\mathbf{A}_1$ to $\mathbf{A}_5$ are appropriate design matrices. For the exact specification of the design matrices and more details about the procedure, see Kuijpers et al. (2013a).

23.5 Three Cases

23.5.1 *Data*

The use of the two different estimation methods to test three different cases is illustrated by means of a data set obtained by administering a questionnaire to $N = 496$ Dutch union members (Van der Veen 1992). The questionnaire measures the attitudes and opinions on general militancy, and consists of four subscales—

Table 23.1 Item means and Cronbach's alpha for each subscale

	Subscales			
Items	General attitude	Permissibility	Effectiveness	Intention
Strike	1.383	1.208	1.698	1.151
Work-to-rule	2.278	1.556	1.788	1.536
D. walkout	2.266	1.573	1.702	1.442
C. walkout	2.161	1.546	1.560	1.450
Protest meeting	2.653	2.258	1.835	1.589
Street protest	2.214	1.810	1.625	1.351
Cronbach's alpha	0.744	0.840	0.738	0.877

D. walkout demonstrative walkout, *C. walkout* collective walkout

General Attitude, Permissibility, Effectiveness, and Intention—which each contains six items. Each of the six items in a subscale refers to different actions union members can engage in, such as a strike, a protest meeting, or a street protest. For the subscales Permissibility and Intention, the answer categories range from 0 to 3, and for the subscales General Attitude and Effectiveness the answer categories range from 0 to 4. Table 23.1 shows the item means, and the values for Cronbach's alpha for each subscale.

Coefficient θ is used to express the different hypotheses. In what follows, θ will be replaced by either the mean (μ) or Cronbach's alpha (α). For ML estimation, we used the R package `cmm` (Bergsma and Van der Ark 2013), and for GEE, we used the R package `geepack` (Yan et al. 2012).

23.5.2 *Case 1:* $\theta = c$

First, we tested whether the mean value of General Attitude towards a Strike was significantly greater than 1 (sample value 1.383, Table 23.1). Second, we tested whether Cronbach's alpha of the subscale Permissibility was significantly greater than 0.80 (sample value 0.84, Table 23.1). Nunnally (1978, pp. 245–246) argued that tests used for making decisions about groups should have at least a reliability of 0.80. The research question is of the form $\theta > c$, and the associated null hypothesis is $\theta = c$.

For investigating $\theta = c$ by means of ML estimation, $\theta = c$ should be written in the constraint notation, $g(\mathbf{m}) = \theta - c = 0$. In the generalized exp-log notation, $g(\mathbf{m}) = \theta - c$ equals

$$g(\mathbf{m}) = \begin{bmatrix} 1 & -c \end{bmatrix} \exp\left(\begin{bmatrix} 1 & 0 \\ 1 & -1 \end{bmatrix} \log\left(\begin{bmatrix} 1 \\ 1 \end{bmatrix} \theta \right) \right). \tag{23.13}$$

The categorical marginal model estimates vector $\mathbf{m}$ under the constraint $\theta = c$.

Replacing θ in Eq. (23.13) by μ [Eq. (23.9)] and letting $c = 1$ yields the hypothesis $\mu = 1$. In general, G^2 pertains to a two-sided test. Here, the hypothesis is one-sided, so for a significance level of 0.05 the value of G^2 at the 2×0.05 significance level is used. Comparing the observed and expected frequencies allowed us to reject the hypothesis ($G^2 = 77.662$, $df = 1$, $p \leq 0.000$), and conclude that $\mu > 1$. Replacing θ in Eq. (23.13) by α [Eq. (23.12)], and letting $c = 0.80$ yields the hypothesis $\alpha = 0.80$. Comparing the observed and expected frequencies allowed us to reject the hypothesis ($G^2 = 9.489$, $df = 1$, $p = 0.002$), and conclude that $\alpha > 0.8$. This example illustrates that likelihood methods can be used to investigate research questions of the type $\theta = c$.

For testing whether $\theta = c$ by means of GEE, $\theta = c$ should be written as $\theta = \mathbf{Z}\boldsymbol{\beta}$. It trivially follows that $\mathbf{Z}$ equals the scalar 1, and $\boldsymbol{\beta} = c$, so $\hat{\theta}$ is trivially fixed to c, and the standard error is zero. The software did not provide goodness of fit statistics. Because $\hat{\theta}$ is fixed to c and no model fit statistics are available, we could not use GEE to meaningfully answer research questions that can be cast into $\theta = c$. This is in accordance with Skrondal and Rabe-Hesketh (2004, p. 200), who stated that GEE has limitations with respect to hypothesis testing and assessing model fit.

23.5.3 *Case 2:* $\theta_1 = \theta_2$

In this example, we considered whether the population means of the two items General Attitude towards a Demonstrative Walkout and General Attitude towards a Collective Walkout were equal. The sample means for the items were 2.266 and 2.161, respectively (see Table 23.1). Furthermore, we investigated whether the alphas of the two subscales Permissibility and Intention were equal. For the subscale Permissibility $\widehat{\alpha} = 0.840$, for subscale Intention $\widehat{\alpha} = 0.877$ (see Table 23.1). This categorical marginal model can be useful when one wants to compare the alphas of two subscales or tests, or for assessing change in reliability over time. Differences between the reliabilities of two alternate test forms can indicate that the two forms differ in content and measure slightly different traits (Nunnally 1978, p. 231).

For investigating this model by means of ML estimation, $\theta_1 = \theta_2$ has to be rewritten in the constraint notation, $g(\mathbf{m}) = \theta_1 - \theta_2 = 0$. Because the two coefficients we compared are dependent, vector $\mathbf{n}$ first should be premultiplied by $\mathbf{A}_0$, a marginal matrix (Bergsma et al. 2009, pp. 52–56). Multiplication by matrix $\mathbf{A}_0$ yields the marginal frequencies of the item-score patterns for both sets of items separately. Let L_1 and L_2 be the number of possible item-score patterns for which coefficients θ_1 and θ_2 are computed, respectively. Let $\otimes$ denote the Kronecker product. The general form of the $(L_1 + L_2) \times (L_1 L_2)$ matrix $\mathbf{A}_0$ is

$$\mathbf{A}_0 = \begin{pmatrix} \mathbf{I}_{L_1} \otimes \mathbf{u}'_{L_2} \\ \mathbf{u}'_{L_1} \otimes \mathbf{I}_{L_2} \end{pmatrix}.$$

After premultiplying vector $\mathbf{n}$ by $\mathbf{A}_0$, the two coefficients for the two sets of items are computed using design matrices that are constructed as follows. Let design matrix $\mathbf{A}_q$, with $q = 1,\ldots,q$, be the particular qth design matrix constructed for the particular coefficient. For testing the equality of two coefficients, design matrices $\mathbf{A}_1$ to $\mathbf{A}_q$ are the direct sum of $\mathbf{A}_q$ and $\mathbf{A}_q$. Since for each design matrix $\mathbf{A}_q$ the procedure is the same, it can be expressed in a general form

$$\mathbf{A}_q^* = \mathbf{A}_q \oplus \mathbf{A}_q = \begin{pmatrix} \mathbf{A}_q & 0 \\ 0 & \mathbf{A}_q \end{pmatrix}.$$

For more details, see Kuijpers et al. (2013a).

In the generalized exp-log notation, $g(\mathbf{m}) = \theta_1 - \theta_2$ equals

$$g(\mathbf{m}) = \begin{bmatrix} 1 & -1 \end{bmatrix} \begin{bmatrix} \theta_1 \\ \theta_2 \end{bmatrix}. \tag{23.14}$$

The categorical marginal model estimates vector $\mathbf{m}$ under the constraint $\theta_1 - \theta_2 = 0$. Then, vectors $\mathbf{m}$ and $\mathbf{n}$ are compared by means of G^2 in order to assess whether the two coefficients are equal.

If the coefficient of interest is the mean μ, the population means for the two items are denoted by μ_1 and μ_2, and calculated by using Eq. (23.9). For testing Case 2, θ_1 and θ_2 in Eq. (23.14) should be replaced by μ_1 and μ_2, respectively. Comparing the observed and expected frequencies allowed us to reject the null hypothesis ($G^2 = 5.429$, $df = 1$, $p = 0.020$), and conclude that the means are significantly different from each other.

If the coefficient of interest is Cronbach's alpha, the population alphas for the two subscales are denoted by α_1 and α_2, and calculated using Eq. (23.12). For testing Case 2, θ_1 and θ_2 in Eq. (23.14) should be replaced by α_1 and α_2, respectively. Comparing the observed and expected frequencies allowed us to reject the null hypothesis ($G^2 = 8.939$, $df = 1$, $p = 0.003$), and conclude that the alphas are not equal.

For GEE estimation, constraint $\theta_1 = \theta_2$ must be cast into Eq. (23.2). One possibility is defining a regression model with only an intercept β_0, which can be interpreted as the value of the coefficient under the constraint that $\theta_1 = \theta_2$. Let $\mathbf{Z} = \mathbf{u}_2$, then $\theta_1 = \theta_2$ is equivalent to

$$\mathbf{f}(\mathbf{C}'\mathbf{m}) = \begin{pmatrix} \theta_1 \\ \theta_2 \end{pmatrix} = \mathbf{u}_2\beta_0.$$

If the vector of sample estimates of θ_1 and θ_2 is represented by $(\hat{\theta}_1, \hat{\theta}_2)'$, then the estimating equation [Eq. (23.7)] reduces to

$$\mathbf{u}_2'\mathbf{V}^{-1}\left(\begin{bmatrix} \hat{\theta}_1 \\ \hat{\theta}_2 \end{bmatrix} - \mathbf{u}_2\beta_0\right) = \mathbf{0}. \tag{23.15}$$

For an arbitrary correlation matrix **V**, Eq. (23.15) reduces to

$$\begin{bmatrix} \hat{\theta}_1 \\ \hat{\theta}_2 \end{bmatrix} - \mathbf{u}_2\beta_0 = \mathbf{0},$$

which is minimized for $\hat{\beta}_0 = \frac{\hat{\theta}_1+\hat{\theta}_2}{2}$. So the estimated values for θ_1 and θ_2 are then both equal to the mean of the two values. The hypothesis $\theta_1 - \theta_2 = 0$ can be tested by computing the standard errors by means of the sandwich estimator, computing the confidence interval, and then checking whether 0 is included in the interval.

Using GEE for testing the equality of the means of the two items General Attitude towards a Demonstrative Walkout and General Attitude towards a Collective Walkout, the analysis only estimates a mean value for both values and a standard error, model fit statistics are not available. The estimated mean value for the two means is equal to 2.214, which is obtained independent of the correlation structure. The standard error equals 0.037. To test whether the hypothesis of equal means could be rejected, a 95 % Wald confidence interval for the difference between the two means (denoted by $\Delta\mu$) was constructed using $\widehat{\Delta\mu} \pm 1{,}96 * se(\widehat{\Delta\mu})$. Zero was not included in the interval, so the means are significantly different. GEE was also used for testing the equality of the two alphas of the subscales Permissibility and Intention. The mean value for the two alphas equaled 0.859. The standard error equaled 0.013. A 95 % confidence interval for the difference between the two alphas was constructed in a way similar to the computation for the means. Zero was not included in the confidence interval, so the alphas are significantly different.

23.5.4 *Case 3:* $\theta = \beta_0 + \beta_1 X$

Here, the question was whether the Effectiveness of an action can explain the General Attitude towards that action. We used Effectiveness measured for a Strike (denoted by X_1) and a Work-to-rule (X_2) as the explanatory variables, and General Attitude measured for a Strike (Y_1) and a Work-to-rule (Y_2) as the outcome variables. Hence, we had $T = 2$ actions and $z + 1 = 5$ levels of the exploratory variable. In longitudinal research, one would consider T time points rather than actions. Estimating a regression model in which Cronbach's alpha is the dependent variable seemed artificial from a substantive point of view. Hence, we only investigated Case 3 for μ. However, there are other situations in which testing the effects of one or more (continuous) variables on the value of a particular coefficient is interesting. For instance, using the log-odds ratio as a measure of association, Bergsma et al. (2013) tested whether the association between two categorical variables remained stable over time.

The regression model is $\mathbf{f}(\mathbf{C}'\mathbf{m}) = \mathbf{Z}\boldsymbol{\beta}$ [Eq. (23.2)], where $\mathbf{f}(\mathbf{C}'\mathbf{m})$ is the $T(z+1) \times 1$ vector of conditional means:

$$\begin{pmatrix} E(Y_1|X_1=0) \\ E(Y_2|X_2=0) \\ E(Y_1|X_1=1) \\ E(Y_2|X_2=1) \\ E(Y_1|X_1=2) \\ E(Y_2|X_2=2) \\ E(Y_1|X_1=3) \\ E(Y_2|X_2=3) \\ E(Y_1|X_1=4) \\ E(Y_2|X_2=4) \end{pmatrix}.$$

Matrix $\mathbf{Z}$ is a $T(z+1) \times 2$ design matrix:

$$\begin{pmatrix} 1 & 0 \\ 1 & 0 \\ 1 & 1 \\ 1 & 1 \\ 1 & 2 \\ 1 & 2 \\ 1 & 3 \\ 1 & 3 \\ 1 & 4 \\ 1 & 4 \end{pmatrix}.$$

The first column is a column of ones, and the second column contains the levels of X_1 and X_2. Vector $\boldsymbol{\beta} = (\beta_0, \beta_1)'$ contains the intercept and the regression parameter. Vector $\mathbf{m}$ refers to the joint distribution of (X_1, X_2, Y_1, Y_2).

For ML estimation, first $\mathbf{C}'$ and $\mathbf{f}$ should be determined. In our example, premultiplying $\mathbf{n}$ by the $(T(z+1)^2 \times L)$ marginal matrix

$$\mathbf{C}' = \begin{pmatrix} \mathbf{I}_{z+1} \otimes \mathbf{u}'_{z+1} \otimes \mathbf{I}_{z+1} \otimes \mathbf{u}'_{z+1} \\ \mathbf{u}'_{z+1} \otimes \mathbf{I}_{z+1} \otimes \mathbf{u}'_{z+1} \otimes \mathbf{I}_{z+1} \end{pmatrix}$$

produces the bivariate marginal frequencies of (X_1, Y_1) and (X_2, Y_2). Function $\mathbf{f}$ consists of two design matrices: $\mathbf{A}_1$ and $\mathbf{A}_2$. Let $\mathbf{r}_{z+1}$ be a $(z+1) \times 1$ vector containing scores $0, 1, \ldots, z$; then $\mathbf{A}_1$ is a $2T(z+1) \times T(z+1)^2$ matrix

$$\mathbf{A}_1 = \mathbf{I}_T \otimes \begin{pmatrix} \mathbf{I}_{z+1} \otimes \mathbf{r}'_{z+1} \\ \mathbf{I}_{z+1} \otimes \mathbf{u}'_{z+1} \end{pmatrix}$$

and

$$\mathbf{A}_2 = \mathbf{I}_T \otimes \left(\mathbf{I}_{(z+1)} \ -\mathbf{I}_{(z+1)\cdot} \right)$$

Hence,

$$\mathbf{f}(\mathbf{C}'\mathbf{m}) = \exp\left(\mathbf{A}_2 \log\left(\mathbf{A}_1\mathbf{C}'\mathbf{m}\right)\right).$$

Second, $\mathbf{B}$, the orthogonal complement of $\mathbf{Z}$, should be determined such that $\mathbf{B}'\mathbf{Z} = \mathbf{0}$. Third, the expected categorical marginal model $\mathbf{B}'\mathbf{f}(\mathbf{C}'\mathbf{m}) = \mathbf{0}$ is estimated, producing estimates for vector $\mathbf{m}$. Using this method for maximizing the likelihood includes the constraints, such that the expected frequencies in vector $\widehat{\mathbf{m}}$ sum to N (Agresti 2013, p. 460). Fourth, the estimates $\widehat{\mathbf{m}}$ are plugged into model $\mathbf{f}(\mathbf{C}'\mathbf{m}) = \mathbf{Z}\boldsymbol{\beta}$, producing $\mathbf{f}(\mathbf{C}'\widehat{\mathbf{m}})$. Fifth, parameters $\boldsymbol{\beta}$ are obtained by solving

$$\hat{\boldsymbol{\beta}} = (\mathbf{Z}'\mathbf{Z})^{-1}\mathbf{Z}'\mathbf{f}(\mathbf{C}'\widehat{\mathbf{m}}).$$

Finally, the standard errors of $\hat{\boldsymbol{\beta}}$ are computed using the delta method (for more details, see, for instance, Bergsma et al. 2009, pp. 71–73), so that each individual parameter in $\boldsymbol{\beta}$ can be tested for significance.

The regression model describes the linear relation between the means that are calculated for each dependent variable given the response to the corresponding independent variable (i.e, the means for Y_1 given the different scores on X_1, and the means for Y_2 given the different scores on X_2). Table 23.2 provides the estimates for the parameters in the regression model.

The categorical marginal model also tests whether the regression model that assumes a linear relation between the means fits the data. The results of the analysis showed that the linear regression model does not fit the data, with $G^2 = 173.071$, $df = 8$ and $p < 0.000$, which implies that the means cannot be fitted onto a single straight line; thus, there is not a strictly common linear relation between the conditional means of Y_1 and Y_2 given the scores on X_1 and X_2. However, the regression coefficient is significant, meaning that the scores on X_1 and X_2 have a significant effect on the mean scores of Y_1 and Y_2.

Also, GEE was used to test whether the items Effectiveness of a Strike and Effectiveness of a Work-to-Rule predicted the mean response to General Attitude towards a Strike and General Attitude towards a Work-to-Rule. Table 23.3 shows the

Table 23.2 Parameter estimates using ML estimation

Parameter	Estimate	Standard error
β_0	1.003	0.063
β_1	0.471	0.032

Table 23.3 Parameter estimates using GEE estimation

Parameter	Estimate	Standard error
β_0	0.921	0.056
β_1	0.522	0.027

GEE estimates of the parameters in the regression model, as defined by Eq. (23.2). The regression coefficient is significantly different from zero, which indicates that the scores on X_1 and X_2 have a significant effect on the mean scores of Y_1 and Y_2. For the regression problems, alternative model fit statistics exist for GEE (e.g., Lipsitz and Fitzmaurice 2009, pp. 62–64; Molenberghs and Verbeke 2005, pp. 160–161) but these statistics were unavailable in the R package `geepack`, so the model fit could not be investigated.

23.6 Discussion

For this study, we explored to what extent the two estimation methods are appropriate for investigating and testing three types of research questions. The two estimation methods, ML and GEE, both have advantages and disadvantages. ML estimation is based on the likelihood function, so that model fit statistics can be obtained, models can be compared, and inferences about individual parameters can be made. In contrast to ML estimation, GEE does not assume a specific probability model for the data, but only assumes a mean-variance relationship for the response variable, making it impossible to obtain likelihood based model fit statistics. Furthermore, GEE replaces the often complex dependence structure by a simpler working correlation matrix. Therefore, GEE is more straightforward to compute than ML methods. For a large number of items, in contrast to GEE, using ML estimation becomes problematic, since it uses each cell of the contingency table for computation of the estimates (Bergsma et al. 2013; Van der Ark et al. 2013). However, ML estimation is asymptotically efficient (e.g., Agresti 2013), whereas GEE is not when the working correlation structure is not correctly specified.

By means of the three cases, we showed that ML estimation has to be preferred when one is more interested in testing hypotheses and assessing the fit of the marginal model. Both methods are appropriate when one investigates the effect of the independent factors in regression models. For Case 1, GEE could not be used. This is in line with Skrondal and Rabe-Hesketh (2004, p. 200) who stated that GEE has limitations with respect to hypothesis testing and assessing model adequacy. An alternative to solve some of the limitations would be to estimate the standard error of the saturated model, and then use a Wald-based confidence interval to assess whether the value c is included in the confidence interval (Lipsitz and Fitzmaurice 2009, p. 55). Furthermore, since standard goodness of fit statistics are unavailable for GEE, Lipsitz and Fitzmaurice (2009, pp. 62–64) suggested some alternative model fit diagnostics. For Case 2, ML was easier to apply than GEE, and for ML model fit statistics could be obtained right away. For Case 3, we found that GEE was easier to apply than ML from a computational perspective.

ML estimation uses all item-score patterns that are possible for a set of items, so all elements in vector **n** are used. ML estimation becomes problematic for large numbers of items (e.g., Agresti 2013, p. 462) because the number of elements in vector **n** and the size of the design matrices increase rapidly (Bergsma et al. 2013;

Van der Ark et al. 2013). For instance, for a set of ten items ($J = 10$) each with five answer categories ($z+1=5$), the number of elements in vector $\mathbf{n}$ is equal to $(z+1)^J = 5^{10} = 9{,}765{,}625$. An alternative is using MEL estimation (Owen 2001). MEL uses only the observed item-score patterns, so that the zero-frequencies in vector $\mathbf{n}$ can be ignored. MEL uses much less memory space than ML estimation, and as a result it also is computationally less complex. Therefore, computation time is much shorter, and MEL can be used for large numbers of variables. However, for large sparse contingency tables the empty set problem and the zero likelihood problem can occur when using MEL estimation (for details, see Van der Ark et al. 2013; also see Bergsma et al. 2012), which causes MEL to break down. Van der Ark et al. (2013) proposed MAEL estimation as a solution for the problems with MEL. MAEL uses all observed item-score patterns, plus a few well-chosen unobserved item-score patterns, the choice of which depends on different factors; see Van der Ark et al. (2013) for more details.

For marginal models, GEE and the likelihood methods require further research. We only illustrated the use of both estimation methods by means of three simple cases for two different coefficients. Many more cases and situations can be investigated. The research can be extended to more complex models and to other coefficients. Furthermore, the cases also can be investigated for MEL and MAEL estimation, which can be compared to GEE estimation in order to investigate which method yields more efficient estimates.

Acknowledgements The authors would like to thank Klaas Sijtsma for commenting on earlier versions of the manuscript.

References

Agresti A (2013) Categorical data analysis. Wiley, Hoboken

Aitchison J, Silvey SD (1958) Maximum likelihood estimation of parameters subject to restraints. Ann Math Stat 29:813–828

Bergsma WP (1997) Marginal models for categorical data. Tilburg University Press, Tilburg

Bergsma WP, Van der Ark LA (2013) cmm: An R-package for categorical marginal models (Version 0.7) [computer software]. http://cran.r-project.org/web/packages/cmm/index.html. Accessed 24 Feb 2013

Bergsma WP, Croon MA, Hagenaars JA (2009) Marginal models: for dependent, clustered, and longitudinal categorical data. Springer, New York

Bergsma WP, Croon MA, Van der Ark LA (2012) The empty set and zero likelihood problems in maximum empirical likelihood estimation. Electron J Stat 6:2356–2361

Bergsma WP, Croon MA, Hagenaars JA (2013) Advancements in marginal modelling for categorical data. Sociol Methodol 43:1–41

Cronbach LJ (1951) Coefficient alpha and the internal structure of tests. Psychometrika 16: 297–334

Kesteloot H, Geboers J, Joossens JV (1989) On the within-population relationship between nutrition and serum lipids, the birnh study. Eur Heart J 10:196–202

Kritzer HM (1977) Analyzing measures of association derived from contingency tables. Sociol Methods Res 5:35–50

Kuijpers RE, Van der Ark LA, Croon MA (2013a) Testing hypotheses involving Cronbach's alpha using marginal models. Br J Math Stat Psychol 66:503–520. doi: 10.1111/bmsp.12010

Kuijpers RE, Van der Ark LA, Croon MA (2013b) Standard errors and confidence intervals for scalability coefficients in Mokken scale analysis using marginal models. Sociol Methodol 43:42–69

Lang JB (2004) Multinomial-Poisson homogeneous models for contingency tables. Annals of Statistics, 32:340–383.

Liang K-Y, Zeger SL (1986) Longitudinal data analysis using generalized linear models. Biometrika 73:13–22

Lipsitz S, Fitzmaurice G (2009) Generalized estimating equations for longitudinal data analysis. In: Fitzmaurice G, Davidian M, Verbeke G, Molenberghs G (eds) Longitudinal data analysis. Chapman & Hall/CRC, Boca Raton, pp 43–78

Molenberghs G, Verbeke G (2005) Models for discrete longitudinal data. Springer, New York

Nunnally JC (1978) Psychometric theory. McGraw-Hill, New York

Owen AB (2001) Empirical likelihood. Chapman & Hall/CRC, London

Pawitan Y (2001) In all likelihood: statistical modelling and inference using likelihood. Clarendon Press, Oxford

Skrondal A, Rabe-Hesketh S (2004) Generalized latent variable modeling: multilevel, longitudinal, and structural equation models. Chapman & Hall/CRC, Boca Raton

Van der Ark LA, Croon MA, Sijtsma K (2008) Mokken scale analysis for dichotomous items using marginal models. Psychometrika 73:183–208

Van der Ark LA, Bergsma WP, Croon MA (2013) Augmented empirical likelihood estimation of categorical marginal models for large sparse contingency tables (under review)

Van der Veen G (1992) Principes in praktijk: CNV-leden over collectieve acties [Principles into practice. Labour union members on means of political pressure]. J.H. Kok, Kampen

Yan J, Højsgaard S, Halekoh U (2012) geepack: Generalized Estimating Equation package. (Version 1.1-6) [computer software]. http://cran.r-project.org/web/packages/geepack/index.html. Accessed 13 Dec 2013

Chapter 24
Evaluating Simplicial Mixtures of Markov Chains for Modeling Student Metacognitive Strategies

April Galyardt and Ilya Goldin

Abstract Modeling and discovery of the strategies that students use, both cognitive and metacognitive, is important for building accurate models of student knowledge and learning. We present a simulation study to examine whether simplicial mixtures of Markov chains (SM-MC) can be used to model student metacognitive strategies. We find that SM-MC models cannot be estimated on the moderately sized data sets common in education, and must be adapted to be useful for strategy modeling.

24.1 Introduction

An increasingly popular instructional practice involves learners using educational technologies such as homework practice systems or intelligent tutoring systems (ITS) (VanLehn 2008). For example, in secondary-school geometry courses, students may work problems on a computer, rather than on paper. Depending on the user interface of the system, the computer may be able to capture not only a student's final answer to the problem but also the solution process and the use of various learning aids and resources.

We aim to build a psychometric model of problem solving. Such a model could help us describe student activity, and diagnose student weaknesses for formative feedback and assessment. A student's solution process may reveal the student's problem-solving strategy, such as when a problem may be solved in multiple ways. The use of learning resources may reveal the student's metacognitive strategy, i.e., the ways in which the student goes about choosing a problem-solving strategy or

A. Galyardt (✉)
University of Georgia, Athens, GA, USA
e-mail: galyardt@uga.edu

I. Goldin
Center for Digital Data, Analytics & Adaptive Learning, Pearson, USA
e-mail: ilya.goldin@pearson.com

R.E. Millsap et al. (eds.), *Quantitative Psychology Research*, Springer Proceedings in Mathematics & Statistics 89, DOI 10.1007/978-3-319-07503-7_24

acquires missing knowledge to carry out the problem-solving. Thus, weaknesses may lie either in domain knowledge or in learning skills, such as in knowing how to study an example.

Students will differ in the strategies they choose. For example, a tutoring system may allow a student to request hints, which may be arranged in a sequence from most general to most specific. Some students may never seek hints, even when they should (possibly a case of hint avoidance), and some may seek hints too often, even when they should solve a problem on their own (Aleven et al. 2006).

Even within a student, choice of problem-solving and metacognitive strategies is not static. A student may try a novice strategy when first learning how to solve a kind of problem, and may use an expert strategy for the same kind of problem after acquiring sufficient skill. Similar strategy-switching may happen at the level of steps within a problem, some of which may be new and others familiar. Even while attempting a single step of a single problem, the student may switch between novice and expert strategies. Moreover, a student may switch metacognitive strategies, such as from attempting to solve the problem to trying to guess the answer, and then to requesting a hint.

Thus, a psychometric model of problem-solving needs to represent not merely the final correct/incorrect scores, as in traditional Item Response Theory models, and not only whether students follow some prescribed textbook like solution path, but also the variety of problem-solving and metacognitive strategies that students may use. Further, the model needs to allow for individual differences among students.

At the same time, it is not sensible to treat the space of strategies as infinite. Suppose we identify a new way to solve a problem; that adds just one strategy to the set of possible strategies. Similarly, at the metacognitive level, there may be no fundamental difference between making one versus two unsuccessful problem-solving attempts prior to requesting a hint. Thus, a psychometric model should constrain the space of possible strategies.

Ultimately, an effective model will characterize learning and problem-solving processes, differences among students, the domain of study, and the learning resources or instructional supports available to the students. For instance, we hope to learn whether students benefit by using hints, whether different types of hints differ in effectiveness, and what actions students take on a problem that they do not know how to solve.

24.2 Target Problem

We use data that reflect student problem-solving in an intelligent tutoring system (ITS). An ITS is first and foremost a learning environment; students solve problems within the system and receive immediate feedback and hints designed to assist with the learning process. They are implemented as part of the curriculum and are used regularly by students over an entire unit, semester, or school year. The log data from students interacting with these systems provides us with a large amount of fine-grained data for examining student knowledge, learning, and strategies.

The modeling challenge here is very different than in the "standard assessment paradigm" (Mislevy et al. 2012). In a setting such as a high-stakes test that is a typical context for psychometric modeling, we can often plausibly assume that there is no learning over the brief duration of the test. Further, modeling for summative assessment often aims to reduce performance on a variety of questions to placement along a unidimensional latent trait. Instead, given that an ITS is meant to stimulate learning and that ITS use takes place over a long time period, our data-generation context is very different. In this context, we aim to identify and measure which strategies a student is using to learn from the available resources.

While working in an ITS, when students encounter a problem step, they can (1) enter a correct response, (2) enter an incorrect response, or (3) request a hint. A student can attempt each step multiple times, and must correctly complete all problem steps before moving on to the next problem. For the study in this paper, we simulated data consistent with this pattern of behavior.

A similar real assessment data set has previously been studied using IRT-style and multinomial models, including observed covariates on each student's history of skill practice with the system, random effects accounting for the effectiveness of hints of different types for each student, and covariates for textual predictors of difficulty with hint comprehension (Goldin et al. 2012; Goldin and Carlson 2013; Goldin et al. 2013). The prior models did not represent strategies or strategy-switching, which is our goal in this paper.

The sequence of actions that a student takes on each item are indicators of the student's metacognitive strategy. If a student enters an incorrect answer, pauses, enters another incorrect answer, pauses and enters a correct answer, then this would indicate one strategy. On the other hand, if a student asks for 3 hints in a row without pausing, then that sequence of actions indicates a different strategy, namely a hint abuse strategy.

We wish to identify the common strategies over the entire population of students, as well as estimate how much each student uses each strategy. Mixed membership models are designed to model exactly this sort of structure where latent profiles are common across the population, and observational units have membership in multiple profiles (Blei and Lafferty 2009; Galyardt 2014). Girolami and Kaban (2005) introduced the simplicial mixtures of Markov chains (SM-MC) model to describe sequences of actions that users take in different software environments, including sequences of editing commands in word processing programs and sequences of clicks on a website. In this paper, we test whether this same model can be used to model sequences of student actions in an intelligent tutoring system.

24.3 Simplicial Mixtures of Markov Chains

We assume that there is a single set of metacognitive strategies over the whole population of students, indexed $k = 1,\dots,K$. Second, we assume that each student, $i = 1,\dots,N$, may use these strategies in different proportions. For example, some students may be more likely to guess when they don't know an answer, while other students may be more likely to ask for a hint. How much each student uses each strategy is parameterized by the vector $\theta_i = (\theta_{i1},\dots,\theta_{iK})$. θ_i must be non-negative and sum to 1, so that θ_{ik} is the proportion of problems on which student i uses strategy k. These assumptions form the basis of the mixed membership class of models (Erosheva et al. 2004).

For each student, we record a series of actions $X_i = (X_{i0}, X_{i1},\dots,X_{it},\dots,X_{iT_i})$. This is one sequence of actions over the entire set of items that student i sees. If a student gets two items in a row correct, then $\{X_{i,t}, X_{i,t+1}\}$ ={correct, correct}. On the other hand, if a student answers one item correctly, then makes an incorrect attempt at the next problem before answering it correctly, then $\{X_{i,t}, X_{i,t+1}, X_{i,t+2}\}$ ={correct, incorrect, correct}. Note that the length of the sequence will be different for each student; some students may have seen more problems, and some students may have had many more hints or incorrect tries before successfully solving a problem.

The mixed membership model structure allows for students to switch between strategies (Galyardt 2014). The exchangeability assumptions in SM-MC allow for this strategy-switching to occur between every action. As we shall see, this may allow for too much flexibility in the model, and in future work, we may need to alter this assumption. For each action a student takes, they will choose (consciously or not) a strategy $Z_{it} \in \{1,\dots,K\}$for their next action:

$$P(Z_{it} = k|\theta_i) = \theta_{ik}, \tag{24.1}$$

or equivalently,

$$Z_{it}|\theta_i \sim Multinomial(\theta_i). \tag{24.2}$$

Each strategy is defined by a discrete time Markov process. The state-space for the Markov chain is the set of observable student actions such as answering correctly, answering incorrectly, or asking for a hint. Each Markov process $k = 1,\dots,K$ is parameterized by a transition probability matrix P_k, where the entry $\{r,s\}$ in the matrix gives the probability of moving from state r to state s.

$$P_{[krs]} \;=\; P(X_t = s \mid \{X_{t-1},\dots X_{t-m}\} = r,\ Z_t = k). \tag{24.3}$$

Note that for an mth order Markov process with S states, P will have dimensions $S^m \times S$. An individual will choose strategy k with probability θ_{ik}, so the probability of student i's t^{th} action is:

$$Pr(X_{it} = x_t \mid \theta_i, \{X_{t-1}, \ldots X_{t-m}\} = r_t) = \sum_{k=1}^{K} \theta_{ik} P_{k r_t x_t}. \quad (24.4)$$

The likelihood of an individual's sequence is then given by:

$$Pr(X_i = x | \theta_i) = \sum_{k=1}^{K} \theta_{ik} \left[\pi_{k x_0} \prod_{t=1}^{T_i} P_{k r_t x_t} \right], \quad (24.5)$$

where π_k is the initial state probability.

It is worth noting that SM-MC is one of the special cases when the blending interpretation of mixed membership is also available (Galyardt 2014). We can interpret individuals as switching between strategies according to the membership vector θ. Additionally, if we notice that Eq. (24.5) defines an individual Markov transition matrix P_i that will be "between" the profile matrices P_k, this allows us to interpret an individual as using a strategy that is a blend of the profile strategies.

24.4 Simulations and Results

The size of the simulations was chosen to correspond to the size of the data analyzed in Girolami and Kaban (2005), which are larger than our data from the Geometry Cognitive Tutor. The word processor command usage data set from Girolami and Kaban contained $S = 23$ states, and $N = 1460$ chains each at least of length three, $T_i \geq 3$. The model was fit with $K = 10, \ldots, 80$ profiles, and Markov processes of 0th to 3rd order were considered. To make the model easier to estimate, we increased the number of actions per student (the length of each chain), decreased the number of profiles, decreased the number of states, and focused on 2nd order Markov processes. The smaller number of profiles and states are consistent with the number of strategies and states that we would observe in data from an ITS system.

Each row of the transition matrices, P_{ks}, was randomly generated from Dirichlet(α), with $\alpha = (0.05, \ldots, 0.05)$. This created sparse and distinct matrices for each profile. Details for each simulation are listed in Table 24.1.

We used Markov Chain Monte Carlo (MCMC) for estimation in all 3 simulations. In addition, the variational approximation method from Girolami and Kaban (2005) produced identical results to the MCMC estimation for Simulation 1.

24.4.1 Simulation 1

The first simulation represents a "simplest possible case," with only three profiles, and very distinct profile transition matrices (Fig. 24.1). The estimated posterior distribution collapsed to a single global average distribution. The estimated profile

Table 24.1 Summary of simulation parameters

	Simulation 1	Simulation 2	Simulation 3
N	1,500	1,500	1,500
T	200	200	200
K simulated	3	4	5
K estimated	3	4	15
$\theta \sim$ Dirichlet(α)	$\alpha = (0.1, 0.1, 0.1)$	$\alpha = (1, 0.1, 0.1, 0.05)$	$\alpha = (0.1, 0.1, 0.1, 0.1, 0.1)$
Number of states	6	6	6
Order of Markov Process	2	2	2
$P_{ks\cdot} \sim$ Dirichlet(α)	$\alpha = (0.05, \ldots, 0.05)$	$\alpha = (0.05, \ldots, 0.05)$	$\alpha = (0.05, \ldots, 0.05)$

transition matrices are essentially identical (Fig. 24.2), and the distribution of the membership parameter is a point-mass at $\left(\frac{1}{K}, \frac{1}{K}, \frac{1}{K}\right)$, as shown in Fig. 24.3. We were unable to recover the original transition matrices.

24.4.2 *Simulation 2*

In the ITS setting, we expect to find that one strategy is much more common than the others. Namely, most students get items correct most of the time. Simulation 2 reflects this situation with a distribution of the membership parameter θ that is highly asymmetric. As in Simulation 1, the estimated posterior distribution collapsed to a single global average distribution, and we were unable to recover the transition matrices (Figs. 24.4, 24.5, and 24.6).

24.4.3 *Simulation 3*

The third simulation considers the possibility that SM-MC overfit the word processor data in Girolami and Kaban (2005). These simulations use N and T similar that data set, but Girolami and Kaban fit an SM-MC model with a much larger K and S, and thus many more model parameters. To explore the possibility of overfitting the data, we simulated data with $K = 5$, and estimated the model with $K = 15$. Yet again, SM-MC was unable to recover the transition matrices, the distribution of θ collapsed to a point-mass, and all 15 transition matrices represent a single global transition matrix (Figs. 24.7 and 24.8).

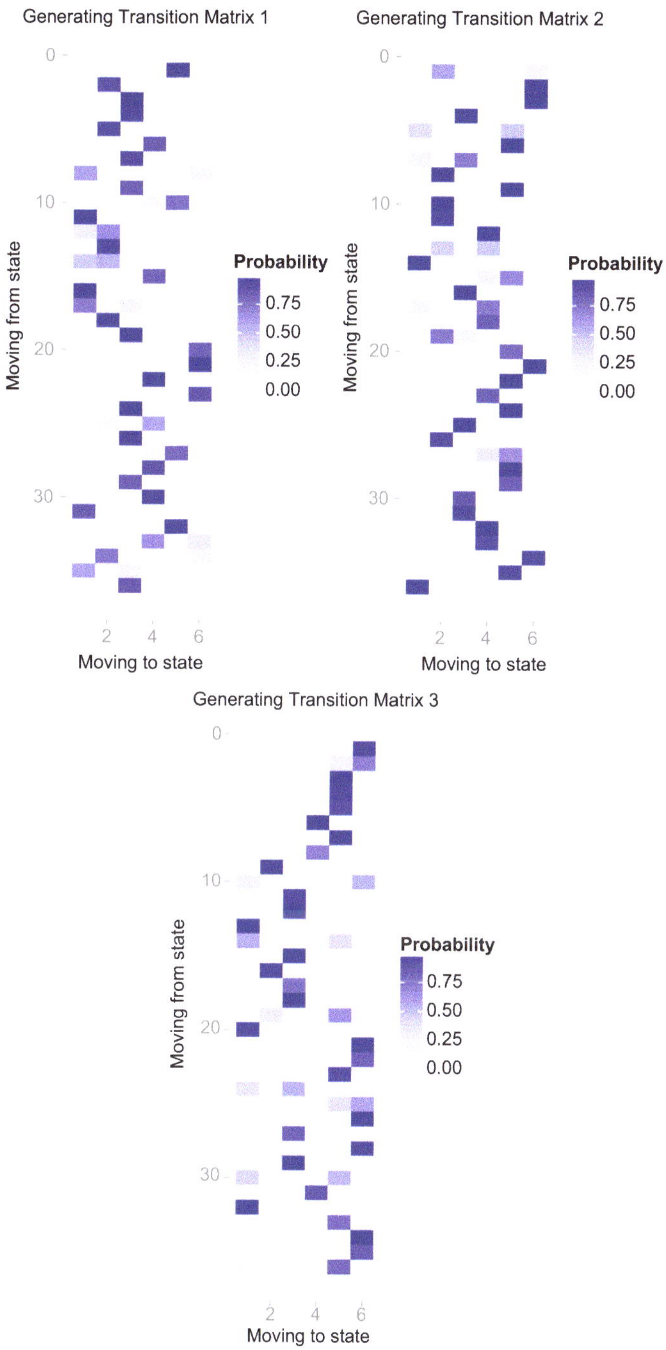

Fig. 24.1 Transition matrices used to generate data for Simulation 1, represented as heat maps. (Three strategy profiles, six states, second order Markov process.) Row 2 is the probability of moving into each of the six states when the last two states are {1,2}, whereas row 7 is when the previous two states are {2,1}

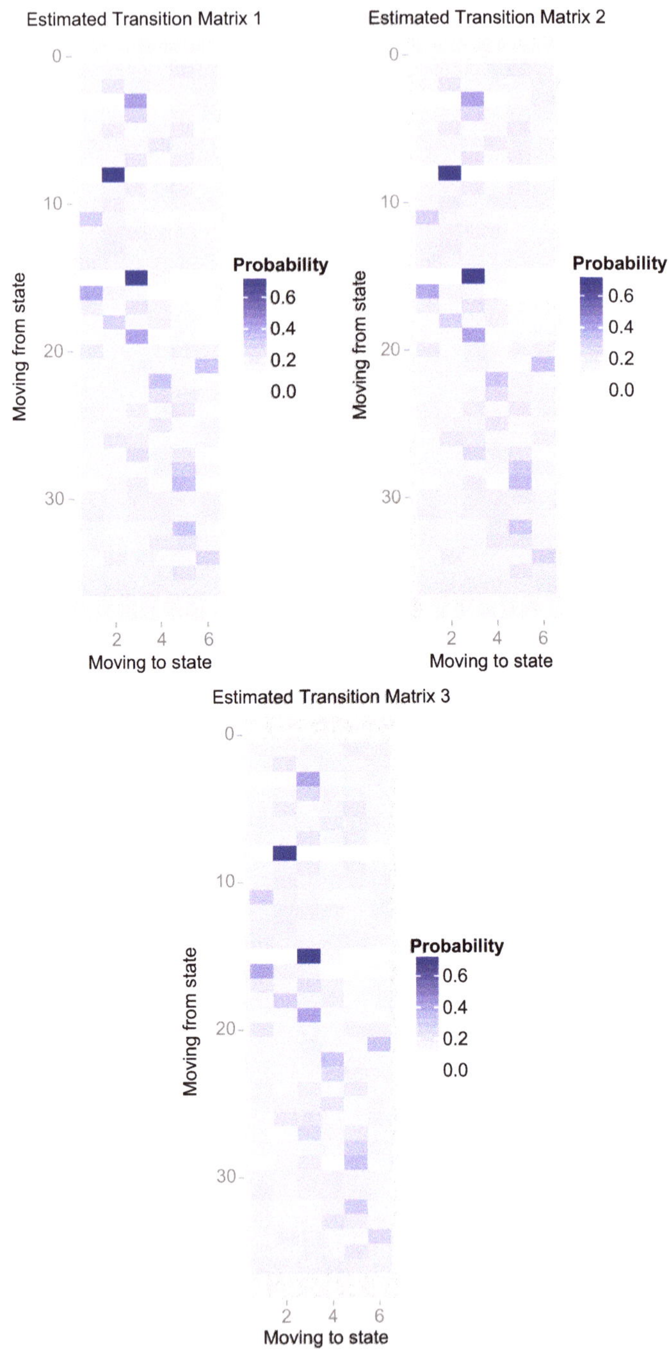

Fig. 24.2 Posterior mean transition matrices for Simulation 1, represented as heat maps. (Three strategy profiles, six states, second order Markov process.) Row 2 is the probability of moving into each of the six states when the last two states are {1,2}, whereas row 7 is when the previous two states are {2,1}

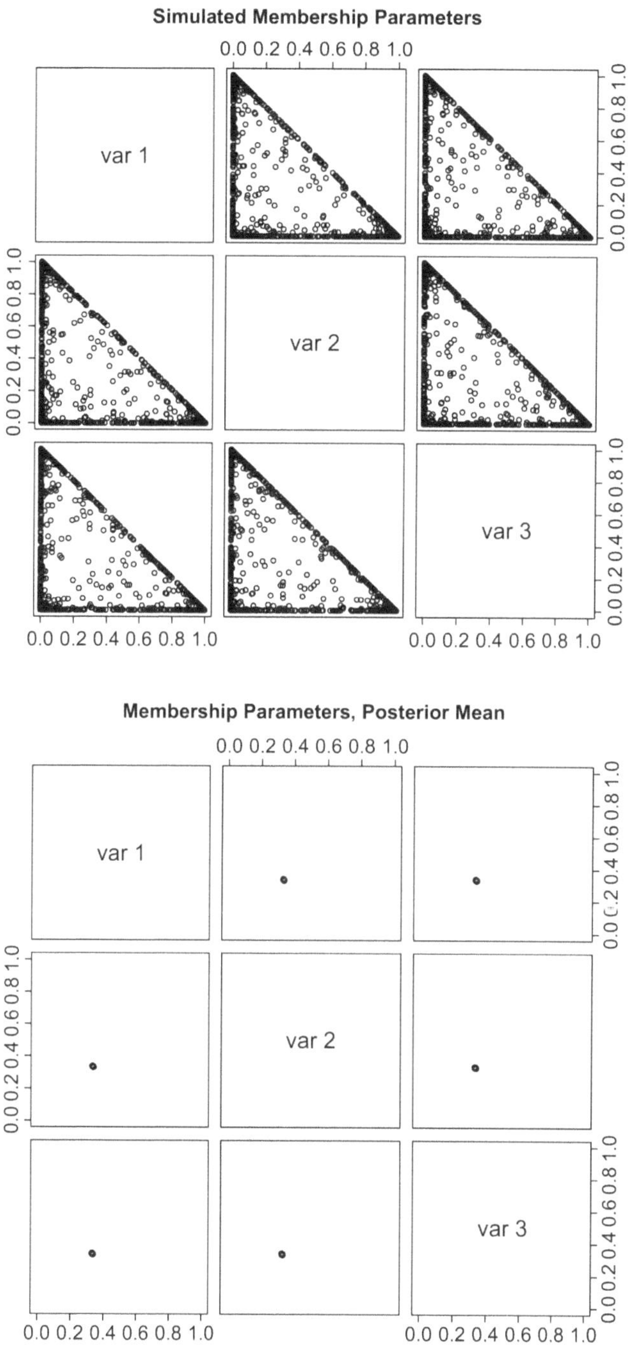

Fig. 24.3 On the *top* are the simulated values of the membership parameters θ_i for Simulation 1. On the *bottom* are the posterior means for θ_i. Notice that the posterior distribution has collapsed to a single point $\theta = (\frac{1}{3}, \frac{1}{3}, \frac{1}{3})$

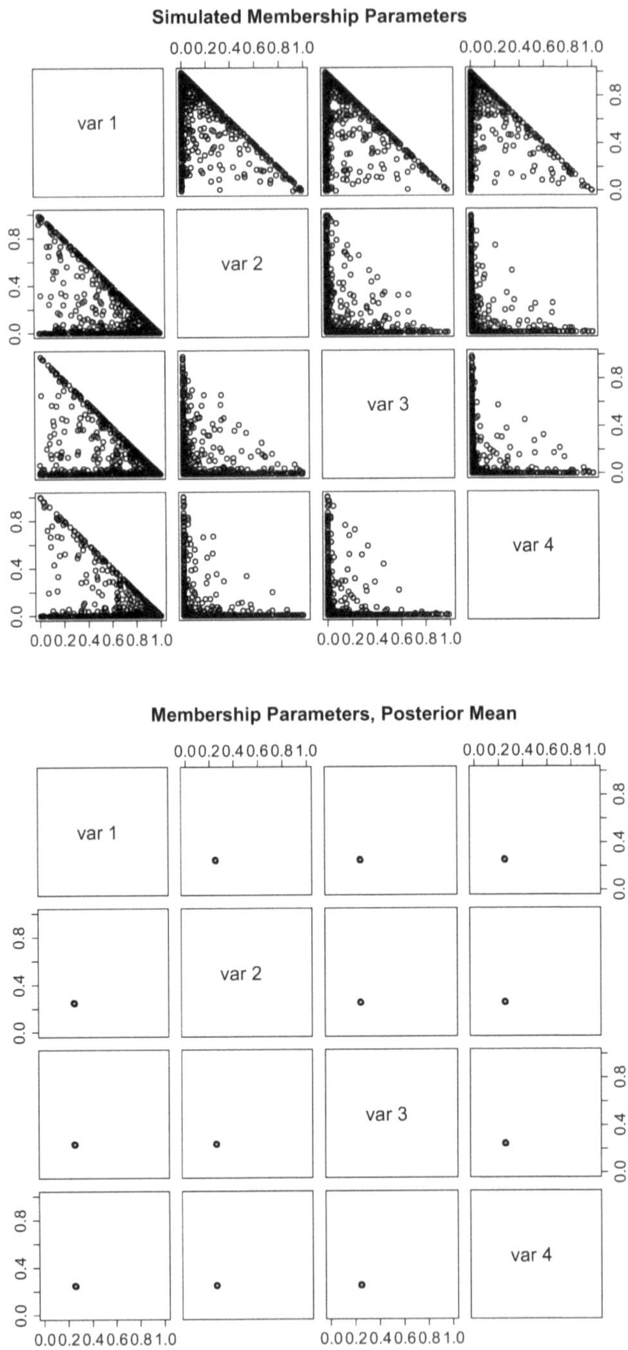

Fig. 24.4 On the *top* are the simulated values of the membership parameters θ_i for Simulation 2. On the *bottom* are the posterior means for θ_i. Notice that the posterior distribution has collapsed to a single point, $\theta_{ik} = \frac{1}{4}$

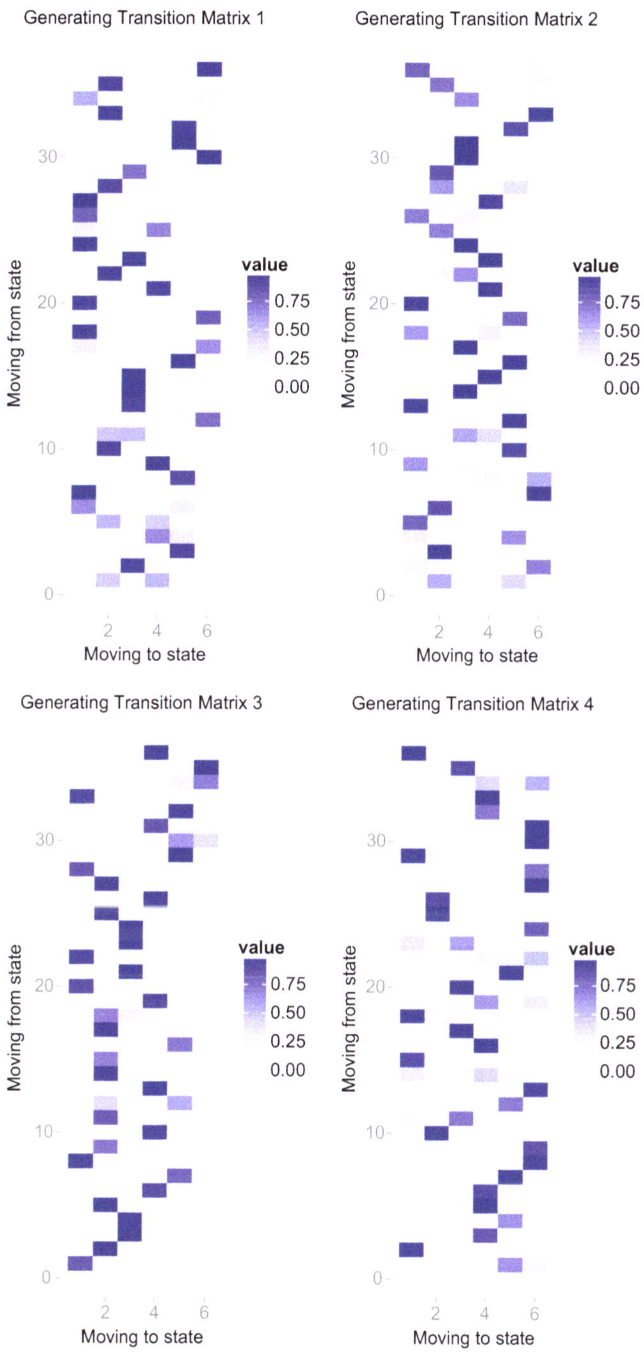

Fig. 24.5 Transition matrices used to generate data for Simulation 2, represented as heat maps. (Four strategy profiles, six states, second order Markov process.) Row 2 is the probability of moving into each of the six states when the last two states are {1,2}, whereas row 7 is when the previous two states are {2,1}

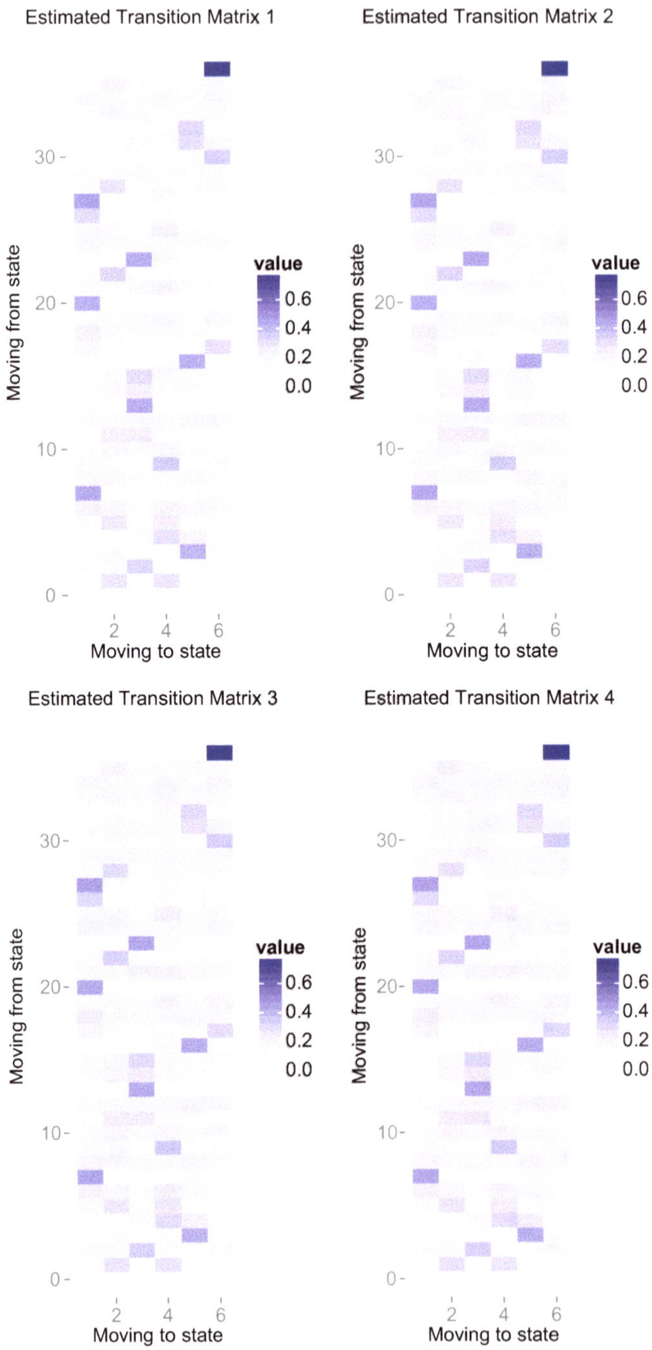

Fig. 24.6 Posterior mean transition matrices for Simulation 2, represented as heat maps. (Four strategy profiles, six states, second order Markov process.) Row 2 is the probability of moving into each of the six states when the last two states are {1,2}, whereas row 7 is when the previous two states are {2,1}

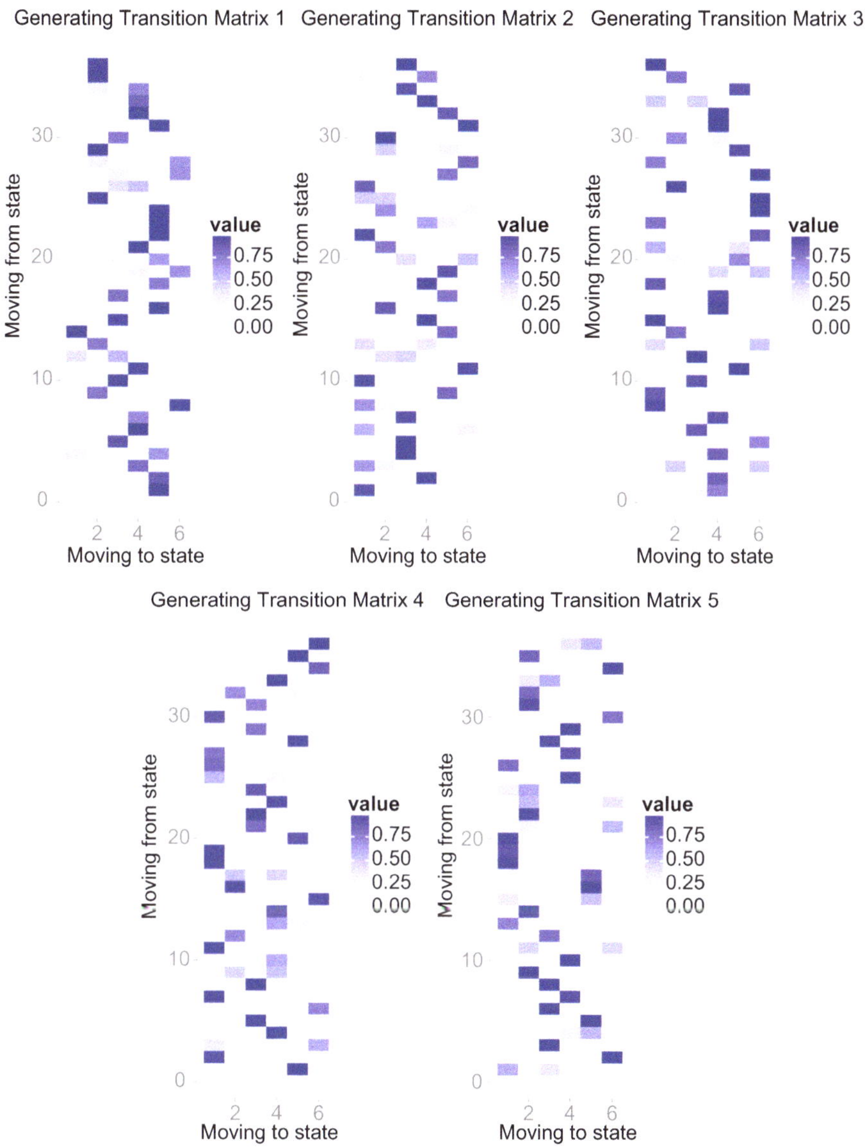

Fig. 24.7 Transition matrices used to generate data for Simulation 3, represented as heat maps. (Simulated with five strategy profiles, six states, second order Markov process.) Row 2 is the probability of moving into each of the six states when the last two states are {1,2}, whereas row 7 is when the previous two states are {2,1}

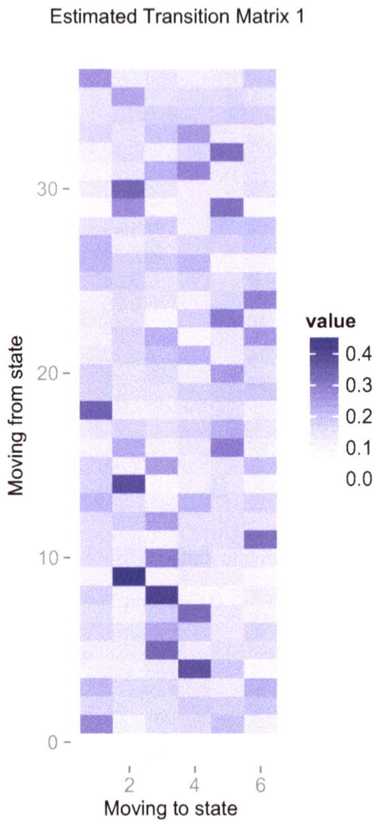

Fig. 24.8 Posterior mean transition matrices for profiles $k = 1, \ldots, 5$ in Simulation 3, represented as heat maps. (Simulated with five strategy profiles, six states, second order Markov process, estimated with 15 strategy profiles.) All 15 estimated strategy profiles are identical. Row 2 is the probability of moving into each of the six states when the last two states are {1,2}, whereas row 7 is when the previous two states are {2,1}

24.5 Discussion

In all three simulations, SM-MC was unable to recover profiles and membership parameters. Instead, the posterior distribution converged to a global mean transition matrix and a point-mass distribution of membership parameters. This phenomenon has been observed in other mixed membership applications when either the number of individuals or the number of observations per individual is not large enough (Galyardt 2012). Further simulations that consider larger sample sizes, or longer chains for each individual may reveal under what conditions the SM-MC model becomes useful.

However, it is desirable to find a solution that is also useful for the "medium-sized" data sets common in education. In future work, we will consider a model with fewer opportunities for "switching" strategies. Rather than assuming students may switch strategies between each action, we will assume that every action taken to solve a particular problem stem (a single psychometric item) came from the same strategy. The resulting model, mixed membership-Markov chains (MM-MC), is described fully in section "Description of the Mixed Membership: Markov Chain Model" in Appendix. This change in the exchangeability assumptions should mean that it is easier to estimate the transition matrices in MM-MC than in SM-MC.

At the same time, these models do not represent important aspects of the domain, e.g., properties of students, items, and skills. For example, we may wish to account for differential difficulty of items, and student expertise in skills relevant to each item. Moreover, these models do not account for change over time. For instance, we may wish to describe strategy-switching behavior after accounting for student experience or training with strategies.

Automatic discovery of cognitive or metacognitive strategies that students use while engaged with computerized learning systems is a difficult problem. This work represents only a first step towards this goal by testing out an existing model for the purpose.

Appendix

Description of the Mixed Membership: Markov Chain Model

First, we assume that there is a single set of metacognitive strategies that is common across all students, indexed $k = 1,\ldots,K$. Second, we assume that each student, $i = 1,\ldots,N$, may use these strategies in different proportions. Some students may be more likely to guess when they don't know an answer, while other students may be more likely to ask for a hint. How much each student uses each strategy is parameterized by the vector $\theta_i = (\theta_{i1},\ldots,\theta_{iK})$, so that θ_{ik} is the proportion of problems that student i uses strategy k.

For each item (or problem step), $r = 1,\ldots,R$, that student i encounters, they will take a sequence of actions $X_{ir} = (X_{ir1},\ldots,X_{irt},\ldots,X_{irT_{ir}})$. Note that the length of the sequence T_{ir} differs from student to student and item to item. In this application, the last action in every sequence is that a student correctly answers the item, $X_{irT_{ir}} = Correct$. When a student begins a problem, they will choose (*consciously or unconsciously*) a strategy $Z_{ir} \in \{1,\ldots,K\}$ which will determine the likely sequence of actions.

$$Pr(Z_{ir} = k|\theta_i) = \theta_{ik} \tag{26.6}$$

or, equivalently,

$$Z_{ir}|\theta_i \sim Multinomial(\theta_i). \tag{26.7}$$

In this formulation of the model, the strategy Z_{ir} depends only on the person i, not the item r. This is an oversimplification which seems highly unlikely to be true; students may be more willing to guess on items they perceive to be easy and more ready to ask for a hint on items they perceive to be difficult. Future work will explore the interaction between students and items in generating the strategy choice Z.

Each strategy is defined by a discrete time Markov process. The state-space for the Markov chain is the set of observable student actions such as answering correctly, answering incorrectly, or asking for a hint. Each Markov chain $k = 1,\ldots,K$ is parameterized by the initial probability vector π_k, and the transition probability matrix P_k. Thus, the probability of a student's sequence of actions X_{ir} given their strategy choice Z_{ir} is modeled as:

$$Pr(X_{ir}=x|Z_{ir}=k) = Pr(X_{ir1}=x_1|Z_{ir}=k)\prod_{t=2}^{T_{ir}} Pr(X_{irt}=x_1|Z_{ir}=k, X_{ir(t-1)}=x_{t-1}) \quad (26.8)$$

$$= \pi_{k,x_1}\prod_{t=2}^{T_{ir}} P_{kx_{t-1}x_t} \quad . \quad (26.9)$$

Thus,

$$Pr(X_{ir}=x|\theta_i) = \sum_{k=1}^{K} Pr(Z_{ir}=k|\theta_i)Pr(X_{ir}=x|Z_{ir}=k) \quad (26.10)$$

$$= \sum_{k=1}^{K} \theta_{ik}\left[\pi_{k,x_1}\prod_{t=2}^{T_{ir}} P_{kx_{t-1}x_t}\right], \quad (26.11)$$

and finally, if we denote $X_i = (X_{i1},\ldots,X_{ir},\ldots,X_{iR})$, we have,

$$Pr(X_i=x|\theta_i) = \prod_{r=1}^{R}\left[\sum_{k=1}^{K}\theta_{ik}\left[\pi_{k,x_{r1}}\prod_{t=2}^{T_{ir}} P_{kx_{r(t-1)}x_{rt}}\right]\right]. \quad (26.12)$$

Note that these equations are written using a first-order Markov process, but they are easily extensible to higher order processes.

The primary difference between SM-MC and MM-MC is in when students are modeled as switching strategies. In SM-MC, the model allows students to switch strategies between each and every action. In MM-MC, students are modeled as having the opportunity to switch strategies only between items.

Acknowledgements This research has been supported in part by a postdoctoral award from the US Department of Education, Office of Education, Institute of Education Sciences to Ilya Goldin, award #R305B110003.

References

Aleven V, Mclaren B, Roll I, Koedinger K (2006) Toward meta-cognitive tutoring: a model of help seeking with a cognitive tutor. Int J Artif Intell Educ 16:101–128

Blei D, Lafferty J (2009) Topic models. In: Srivastava A, Sahami M (eds) Text mining: classification, clustering, and applications. Data mining and knowledge discovery series. Chapman & Hall/CRC, Boca Raton

Erosheva E, Fienberg SE, Lafferty J (2004) Mixed-membership models of scientific publications. Proc Natl Acad Sci 101(Suppl 1):5220–5227

Galyardt A (2012) Mixed membership distributions with applications to modeling multiple strategy usage. Ph.D. thesis, Carnegie Mellon University. http://www.stat.cmu.edu/~galyardt/Galyardt-Dissertation-Final-7-19.pdf

Galyardt A (2014) Interpreting mixed membership models: Implications of Erosheva's representation theorem. In: Airoldi EM, Blei D, Erosheva E, Fienberg SE (eds) Handbook of mixed membership models. Chapman and Hall, Boca Raton

Girolami M, Kaban A (2005) Sequential activity profiling: latent dirichlet allocation of markov chains. Data Min Knowl Discov 10:175–196

Goldin IM, Carlson R (2013) Learner differences and hint content. In: Proceedings of 16th international conference on artificial intelligence in education, Memphis, 2013

Goldin IM, Koedinger KR, Aleven VAWMM (2012) Learner differences in hint processing. In: Yacef K, Zaïane O, Hershkovitz A, Yudelson M, Stamper J (eds) Proceedings of 5th international conference on educational data mining, Chania, 2012, pp 73–80

Goldin IM, Koedinger KR, Aleven VAWMM Hints: You can't have just one. In: D'Mello SK, Calvo RA, Olney A (eds) Proceedings of 6th international conference on educational data mining, 2013

Mislevy RJ, Behrens JT, DiCerbo KE, Levy R (2012) Design and discovery in educational assessment: evidence-centered design, psychometrics, and educational data mining. J Educ Data Min 4(1):11–48

VanLehn K (2008) Intelligent tutoring systems for continuous, embedded assessment. In: Dwyer C (ed) The future of assessment: shaping teaching and learning, Erbaum, pp 113–138

Chapter 25
Partitioning Variance Into Constituents in Multiple Regression Models: Commonality Analysis

Burhanettin Ozdemir

Abstract Commonality analysis is a method of partitioning the explained variance in a multiple regression analysis into variance constituents associated with each independent variable uniquely and variance associated with common effects of one or more independent variables in various combinations. By partitioning variance, commonality analysis helps to determine accurately the degree of multicollinearity between the independent variables, suppressor variable and related importance of independent variables. In addition, commonality analysis provides regression effects (R^2) of all possible simple and multiple regression models that can be constructed by the independent variables and thus helps researchers choose the most appropriate regression model. The purposes of this study are to (a) provide a general overview of multiple regression analysis and its application, (b) explain how to conduct commonality analysis in a regression model, and (c) determine the degree of multicollinearity between independent variables and suppressor variable in the model by means of commonality analysis results. For these purposes, OBBS data set which was collected during a project in Turkey was used to provide a heuristic example. In this example, three independent variables that are assumed to predict students' academic performance were selected to create model and then multiple regression analysis and commonality analysis were conducted.

Keywords Variance analysis • Commonality analysis • Multiple regression models

25.1 Introduction

Some studies require investigating phenomena associated with educational and social sciences, as the nature of these phenomena, the researcher must employ multivariate statistical techniques. Thus, researchers have access to a more

B. Ozdemir (✉)
Hacettepe University, Ankara, Turkey
e-mail: b.ozdemir@hacettepe.edu.tr

R.E. Millsap et al. (eds.), *Quantitative Psychology Research*, Springer Proceedings in Mathematics & Statistics 89, DOI 10.1007/978-3-319-07503-7_25

comprehensive and realistic results which increases both the reliability and the validity of the research results. One of the most commonly used multivariate statistical techniques is multiple linear regression model.

Multiple regression analysis is a statistical tool used to predict a dependent variable (DV) from multiple independent variables (IVs) (Harlow 2005; Stevens 2009). The focus of multiple regression is to investigate which, if any, of these predictor variables can significantly predict the dependent variable. The multiple linear regression equation is as follows:

$$y = b_0 + b_1x_1 + b_2x_2 + \ldots.. + b_nx_n + \varepsilon$$

where y is the predicted or expected value of the dependent variable, X_1 through X_n are n independent or predictor variables, b_0 is the value of Y when all of the independent variables (X_1 through X_n) are equal to zero, and b_1 through b_n are the estimated regression coefficients.

Multiple regression holds increase utility within the social sciences as it allows for more comprehensive analysis of constructs related to human behavior. However, it is critical to recognize that multiple regression is inherently a correlation technique and cannot explain the causalities that may underlie the relationship between the variables being observed (Stevens 2009). Apart from the advantages of using multiple regression analysis methods, researchers must be careful when it comes to interpreting regression results.

Courville and Thompson (2001) found in their review of all the articles published in multiple volumes of one journal that the authors of all articles using regression analyses interpreted only beta weights. The relative importance of the predictor variables cannot correctly be evaluated solely on the basis of interpreting the regression beta weights (i.e., standardized regression weights; Thompson 2006). When predictor variables are correlated, structure coefficients (denoted by r_s), which are the Pearson correlation coefficients between the given predictors and the predicted Y outcome scores (i.e., 9), must also be consulted (Thompson and Borrello 1985).

Some researchers use stepwise methods when they have a large pool of predictors, either to evaluate (erroneously) the relative importance of the predictors or to select a subset of predictors that has almost as large an R^2 effect size as the full set of predictors (Zientek and Thomspon 2006). Unfortunately, as Thompson (1995) explained the best team might not include the best players. Similarly, the best set of predictors, with the highest R^2, might not include any of the five predictors picked by stepwise.

Regression analysis is a poor method to determine the degree of multicollinearity and to detect a suppressor effect. Multicollinearity occurs when the independent variables are highly correlated and as the nature of social and behavioral science, it is common to have correlated IVs. As Zientek and Thomspon (2006) stated "collinearity is not problematic with respect to data analysis, but does complicate result interpretation" (p. 299).

Another problem with multiple regression which obscures interpreting regression results is having a suppressor variable in the model. Suppressor variables are IVs that by themselves have very little impact on the DV. However, when combined with other IVs, suppressors can improve the predictive power of other IVs in the regression equation (Smith et al. 1992).

Especially in the presence of multicollinearity and suppressor variables, interpretation of regression results becomes much more complex and may lead to misinterpretation. In order to increase accuracy of interpretation, regression analysis should be reinforced by other techniques. A useful solution would be to conduct supplemental analyses to help uncover the complex interrelationships that make up a regression effect (Seibold and McPhee 1979). In this research, commonality analysis was conducted alongside with regression analysis in order to uncover complex relationship between the variables in the model.

25.1.1 Commonality Analysis

Commonality analysis has been applied across disciplines in social science research, including education (e.g., Zientek and Thomspon 2006), counseling (e.g., Gill et al. 2010), human resource development (e.g., Nimon et al. 2010), behavioral science (e.g., Sorice and Conner 2010), and information science (e.g., Nimon and Gavrilova 2010). Across these disciplines and others, commonality analysis allows rich interpretation of the regression effect that advances theory and the application of research findings (Nimon and Gavrilova 2010).

Commonality analysis is a method of partitioning the explained variance (R^2) into the variance constituents associated with each independent variable **uniquely** and the variance associated with the one or more independent variables **commonly in** various combinations. In a multiple regression analysis by partitioning variance, commonality analysis helps to determine accurately;

- The degree of multicollinearity between IVs,
- The relative importance of IVs in a model (regardless of predictors order),
- Suppressor effect (if any).

In addition, commonality analysis provides regression effects (R^2) of all possible simple and multiple regression sub-models that can be constructed by given independent variables and thus it helps researchers decide the most appropriate regression model. Considering the advantages of commonality analysis mentioned above, it overcomes shortcomings of multiple regression such as multicollinearity, suppressor effects and determining relative importance of IVs without conducting hierarchical regression analysis.

Commonality analysis has the advantage of producing the same results for a given set of predictors—regardless of the order in which the predictors are entered into the model (Amado 2003). Therefore, commonality analysis overcomes some of the shortcomings inherent in multiple regression (Thompson 1995)

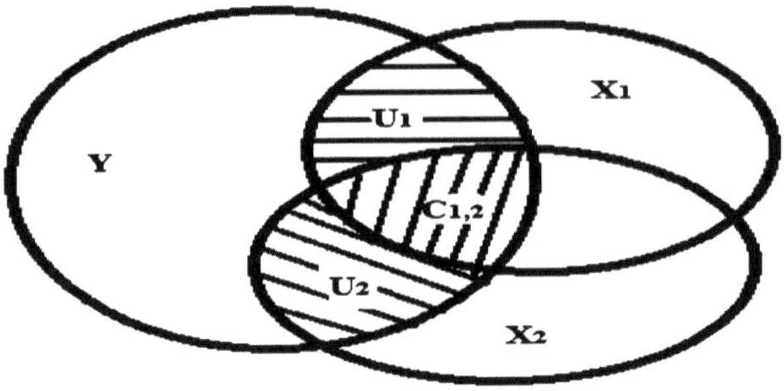

Fig. 25.1 Venn diagram of hypothetical commonality variance partitions of two predictors

The process of conducting commonality analysis includes four steps. The first step is to perform an all possible subsets (APS) regression. The second step is to derive a formula for each unique and common effect. The third step is to populate (substitute) the resulting formulas with the appropriate R^2 values from the APS regression. The fourth step is to verify results and interpret the unique and common variance for each predictor in the model.

Not only should the sum of all unique and common effects equal the multiple R^2 value for the full regression model, the sum of unique and common effects associated with each predictor should equal the r^2 between the predictor and criterion variable (Nimon and Reio 2011).

Figure 25.1 shows a Venn diagram for a hypothetical case involving two predictor variables (X_1 and X_2) and a criterion variable (Y). The hatched area represents the total explained variance. The variance in Y that is explained by X_1 and X_2 ($R^2{}_{y\cdot 12}$) can be partitioned into three components:

U_1 = unique effect of X_1 to $R^2{}_{y\cdot 12}$
U_2 = unique effect of X_2 to $R^2{}_{y\cdot 12}$
C_{12} = common effect of X_1 and X_2 to $R^2{}_{y\cdot 12}$.

Formulas for computing variance components:

$U_1 = R^2{}_{y\cdot 12} - R^2{}_{y\cdot 2}$
$U_2 = R^2{}_{y\cdot 12} - R^2{}_{y\cdot 1}$
$U_{12} = R^2{}_{y\cdot 1} + R^2{}_{y\cdot 2} - R^2{}_{y\cdot 12}$

At that point it is important to understand difference between common variance associated with two or more IVs and interaction effects of IVs in ANOVA. Common variance accounts for overlapping variance between IVs and determines the degree of multicollinearity in a regression model, whereas in ANOVA the interaction effect is perfectly uncorrelated with the main effects (Zientek and Thomspon 2006).

It is quite easy to compute unique and common variance when there are only two predictors in a regression model. However, as the number of predictor variables increases, the process becomes more complicated. This is due to the fact that the number of commonality coefficients is exponentially related to the number of predictor variables (2^n-1). For example, the number of commonality coefficients for three, four or five predictor variables is $2^3-1=7$, $2^4-1=15$ and $2^5-1=31$, respectively. In addition, the formulas to compute commonality coefficients differ according to the number of predictors in the model (Nimon and Gavrilova 2010).

Without the aid of software, this process can be laborious and even almost impossible, depending on the number of predictor variables. But with the development of software, researchers have the opportunity to conduct commonality analysis using traditional software packages such as SPSS, SAS, SYSTAT and R.

25.2 Method

In this study, a data set from OBBS 2005 which was administered by Ministry of National Education was used to provide a heuristic example. OBBS stands for "The Student Achievement Test" and it is a national large-scale examination which aims to assess primary and secondary school students' academic achievement routinely in Turkey. It was first performed in 1994 and then repeated every three-year circle (EARGED 2010). Totally, 93.806 secondary school students (6th, 7th and 8th grade students) participated in OBBS 2005. Since large sample size may lead to the rejection of a null hypothesis even if the actual effect is so small, thus a random sample of 937 (1% of total sample) was drawn from the secondary school data set.

In this example, three independent variables that were *interest* (students' interest to Turkish class), *perception* (students' perception of passing the Turkish exam) and *social science* (students' score on social science) were selected as IVs, and *Turkish* (students' Turkish score) was selected as the DV in a multiple regression analysis and a commonality analysis. The analysis was conducted in SPSS. Moreover, an SPSS scriptfile (Nimon et al. 2008, available from http://profnimon.com/commonality.sbs), was used to conduct commonality analysis.

25.3 Results

Before conducting regression commonality analysis, it is better to examine correlation between variables in the model which gives insight into relationship between the variables and existence of multicollinearity.

Table 25.1 shows the Pearson's correlation matrix of the four variables. The first two IVs are correlated modestly with the DV ($r=0.150$ and 0.426) and with each other ($r=0.394$). *Social science* was correlated higher with Turkish (DV) ($r=0.689$), indicating a clear relationship between *social science* and *Turkish*.

The multiple regression results are displayed in Table 25.2. In a multiple regression equation, *social science* and perception were found to be statistically significant predictors of the DV ($p<0.001$), while interest variable was not ($p=0.370$). Given the magnitude of the correlation between students' social science and Turkish, it

Table 25.1 Correlation matrix of variables in the model ($N = 937$)

	Turkish	Interest	Perception	Social science
Turkish	1.00			
Interest	0.150	1.00		
Perception	0.426	0.394	1.00	
Social science	0.689	0.140	0.384	1.00

Note. All correlations are statistically significant ($p < 0.001$)

Table 25.2 The multiple regression results

Model-1	B	Standardized beta(β)	p	R	R^2	ANOVAp
Intercept	1.189		0.032	0.712[a]	0.507	0.000
Social science	0.794	0.622	0.000			
Interest	−0.140	−0.023	0.370			
Perception	1.290	0.190	0.000			

is not surprising that *social science* was found to be the most powerful predictor of *Turkish* (DV) in the model ($\beta = 0.794$). Nevertheless, the students perception of success provided a useful contribution to predicting Turkish ($p = 0.00$). In total, the three IVs had an R^2 value of 50.7 %.

Using the information supplied, the script generates three SPSS data files (*CommonalityMatrix.sav, CCByVariable.sav* and *ModelAps.sav)* providing the commonality analysis results. Tables 25.3, 25.4, and 25.5 show the results from these SPSS files.

Table 25.3 contains the unique and common commonality coefficients as well as the percent of variance in the regression effect that each coefficient contributes. The individual entries in the table can be used to determine how much variance is explained by each effect as well as which coefficients contribute most to the regression effect.

Table 25.3 Commonality matrix

	Predictors	Commonality coefficients (R^2)	Percentile (% R^2)
Unique effect (U_n)	Social science	0.330	65.100
	Interest	0.001	0.122
	Perception	0.027	5.249
Common effect (C_n)	Social science—interest	0.001	0.244
	Social science—perception	0.131	25.856
	Interest—perception	0.001	0.189
	Social science—interest-perception	0.016	3.240
	Total	0.507	100.000

According to commonality coefficients in Table 25.3, the major contributor to the regression effect was the unique variance associated with *social science*. Excluding its relationship with *interest* and *perception*, it uniquely contributed 65.1 % of the regression effect.

The other major contributor to the regression effect was common variance associated with *social science* and *perception*, which accounted for 25.81 % of the regression effect. This indicates the amount of multicollinearity between *social science* and *perception* variables. Although regression analysis results showed no sign of multicollinearity, according to commonality analysis results, a month of common variance associated with *social science* and *perception* indicated multicollinearity between *social science* and *perception* variables. Thus, in the presence of *social science*, perception could be excluded from the regression model.

In commonality analysis negative commonality coefficients are possible. As Pedhazur stated "negative commonalities may be obtained in situations where some of the variables act as suppressors, or when some of the correlations among the independent variables are positive and others are negative" (Pedhazur 1997, p. 271). In Table 25.3, all commonality coefficients are positive which means there is no suppressor variable which obscures regression results and complicates regression results interpretation.

Table 25.4 provides another view of the commonality effects. The unique effect for each of the predictors was displayed, as well as the total of all common effects for which the predictor was involved. In order to calculate the common variance of a predictor variable in the model, all common variance components associated with that predictor variable, shown in Table 25.3, have to be added up. For example, total common variance associated with *social science*, shown in Table 25.4, is equal to the sum of all common effect that *social science* variable is involved ($0.148 = 0.001 + 0.131 + 0.016$). The last column is the sum of the unique and common effect and is equivalent to the squared correlation (r_s^2) between the predictor and dependent variable.

Table 25.4 Commonality coefficients

Predictors	Unique variance (R_u^2)	Common variance (R_c^2)	Total variance (R_i^2)
Social Science	0.330	0.149	0.479
Interest	0.001	0.019	0.019
Perception	0.027	0.148	0.175

One might observe the role that *interest* plays in the regression effect. Not only does it have a small beta weight and small structure coefficient, its unique effect indicates that it could be excluded from the regression model with only a small reduction in R^2 ($0.507 - 0.0006 = 0.5064$). The discrepancy between the significance of the *interest*'s beta weight and its contribution to the regression effect could easily be explained as most of its effect was due to variance that it shared common with other predictor.

Perception itself explains 17.5 % of variance in criterion variable. At first it seems that perception makes an important contribution to the model. However, small unique variance of perception alongside with large common variance with social science variable indicates that there is multicollinearity between *social science* and *perception*.

Thus, at first the multiple linear regression model appeared to consist of three IVs, but in fact *interest* and *perception* variables could be excluded from the model because of their small contribution in the presence of *social science* variable and our regression model turned out to be a simple regression model with a dependent variable. In addition, all commonality coefficients found to be positive which means there is no suppressor variable in the model.

Table 25.5 provides R^2 effect size of all possible simple and multiple regression models (All Possible Sub-Models -APS) that can be constructed by the given independent variables and thus it helps researcher decide the most appropriate regression model.

Table 25.5 R^2 of all possible sub-models

Independent variables	K	R^2
Social science	1	0.478
Interest	1	0.019
Perception	1	0.175
Social science—interest	2	0.480
Social science—perception	2	0.506
Interest—perception	2	0.177
Social science—interest-perception	3	0.507

The first column in Table 25.5 represents which of the three predictor variables are involved in predicting criterion variable. Dividing the variance sum by the regression effect yields the percent variance explained by each variable, equivalent to a squared correlation coefficient ($U_1 + C_1/R^2 = r_s{}^2$). One can observe from Table 25.5 that *social science* explained 47.8 % of variance in *Turkish*. However, adding *interest* and *perception* variables to the model caused an increase of 2.8 % in R^2 effect size which was very small compared to contribution of *social science* itself.

Table 25.6 presents an example of how the commonality effects by variables can be displayed alongside with traditional multiple regression output to add another layer of consideration when evaluating the importance of predictors. Such a table allows researchers to simultaneously consider beta weights, structure coefficients, unique effects, and common effects when interpreting regression effects and predictor importance.

The last column in Table 25.6 presents sum of the squared structure coefficients ($r_s{}^2$) associated with each independent variables. One can observe from Table 25.6 that *social science* explained 94.44 % of the total variance explained by the model. The sum of the squared structure coefficients of IVs

Table 25.6 Regression commonality analysis results

Model-1	B	Beta	p	R	R^2	Unique variance ($R_u{}^2$)	Common variance ($R_c{}^2$)	Total variance ($R_i{}^2$)	% R^2
Intercept	1.189		0.032	0.712[a]	0.507				
Social science	0.794	0.622	0.000			0.330	0.149	0.479	94.44 %
Interest	−0.140	−0.023	0.370			0.001	0.019	0.019	3.79 %
Perception	1.290	0.190	0.000			0.027	0.148	0.175	34.34 %

(94.44 % + 3.79 % + 34.34 % = 132.57 %) in the regression model is higher than 100 %, which indicates that there is multicollinearity between predictors.

To conclude, at first the regression model appeared to consist of three IVs, but in fact *interest* and *perception* variables could be excluded from the model because of their small contribution in the presence of *social science* variable. Our multiple regression model turned out to be a simple regression model with an independent variable. In addition, all commonality coefficients found to be positive which means there is no suppressor variable in the model.

25.4 Discussion

In this article, we tried to demonstrate commonality analysis which can provide important information about the variables in the regression model that may not be revealed by only examining beta weights and structure coefficients.

Considering the advantages of commonality analysis mentioned above, it overcomes shortcomings of multiple regression such as multicollinearity, suppressor effect and determining relative importance of IVs without conducting hierarchical regression analysis. In addition, commonality analysis provides regression effects (R^2) of all possible simple and multiple regression sub-models that can be constructed by the given independent variables and thus it helps researcher decide the most appropriate regression model.

Although there are a lot of advantages of commonality analysis, Warne (2011) identified a few caveats associated with the method. The first one, common variance components between variables should not be interpreted as the presence of an interaction effect (Thompson and Borrello 1985) in ANOVA. Because, interaction effects between variables are unique relationships with the DV that develop as differing levels of the IVs interact with one another. Another difference between common variance and interaction effects is that the latter can be subjected to hypothesis testing, while the former cannot (Warne 2011; Mood 1971). Another caveat with commonality analysis is that it can quickly become a complex method as the number of independent variables increases. However, development of software which enables conducting commonality analysis for any number of IVs has solved this problem.

Recently, a lot of work has done on the development of software which enables conducting regression commonality analysis such as Nimon et al. (2008) and Nimon and Gavrilova (2010). Researchers now have the opportunity to conduct commonality analysis using traditional software packages such as SPSS, SAS, SYSTAT, and R with the development of software.

We suggest researchers and practitioners to conduct commonality analysis alongside with other multivariate statistical methods such as canonical correlations and ANOVA which of them aims to examine undetected relationship between the variables in social and educational science. Conducting Supplementary analyses such as commonality analysis helps researchers have access to a more comprehensive and realistic results which increases both the reliability and the validity of the research results.

References

Amado AJ (2003) Partitioning predicted variance into constituent parts: a primer on regression commonality analysis. Res Schools 10(1):91–97

Courville T, Thompson B (2001) Use of structure coefficients in published multiple regression articles: B is not enough. Educ Psychol Meas 61:229–248. doi:10.1177/0013164401612006

Eğitim, Araştırma ve Geliştirmesi Daire Başkanlığı (EARGED) (2010) *İlköğretim ÖBBS raporu 2005*. Ankara, Milli Eğitim Bakanlığı. http://yegitek.meb.gov.tr/dosyalar/obbs/2005/matematik.pdf

Gill CS, Barrio Minton CA, Myers JE (2010) Spirituality and religiosity: factors affecting wellness among low-income, rural women. J Couns Dev 77:293–303

Harlow LL (2005) What is multivariate thinking? The essence of multivariate thinking. Lawrence Erlbaums, Mahwah, pp 3–27

Mood AM (1971) Partitioning variance in multiple regression analyses as a tool for developing learning models. Am Educ Res J 8:191–202

Nimon K, Gavrilova M (2010, February) Commonality analysis: Demonstration of an SPSS solution for regression analysis. Poster presented at the 2010 Conference, University of Illinois at Urbana-Champaign

Nimon K, Reio TG Jr (2011) Regression commonality analysis: a technique for quantitative theory. Hum Resource Dev Rev 10:329. doi:10.1177/1534484311411077

Nimon K, Lewis M, Kane R, Haynes RM (2008) An R package to compute commonality coefficients in the multiple regression case: an introduction to the package and a practical example. Behav Res Methods 40:457–466. doi: 10.3758/BKM204020220457

Nimon K, Gavrilova M, Roberts JK (2010) Regression results in human resource development research: Are we reporting enough? In: Graham C, Dirani K (eds) Proceedings of the human resource development 2010 international conference, AHRD, Knoxville, TN, pp. 803–812

Pedhazur EJ (1997) Multiple regression in behavioral research: explanation and prediction, 3rd edn. Harcourt Brace, Ft Worth

Seibold DR, McPhee RD (1979) Commonality analysis: a method for decomposing explained variance in multiple regression analysis. Hum Commun Res 5:355–363

Smith RL, Ager JW Jr, Williams DL (1992) Suppressor variables in multiple regression/correlation. Educ Psychol Meas 52:17–29. doi:10.1177/001316449205200102

Sorice MG, Conner JR (2010) Predicting private landowner intentions to enroll in an incentive program to protect endangered species. Hum Dimens Wildl 15(2):77–89

Stevens JP (2009) Applied multivariate statistics for the social sciences, 5th edn. Routledge, New York

Thompson B (1995) Stepwise regression and stepwise discriminant analysis need not apply here: a guidelines editorial. Educ Psychol Meas 55(4):525–534

Thompson B (2006) Foundations of behavioral statistics: an insight-based approach. The Guilford Press, New York

Thompson B, Borrello GM (1985) The importance of structure coefficients in regression research. Educ Psychol Meas 45:203–209

Warne RT (2011) Beyond multiple regression: using commonality analysis to better understand R^2 results. Gift Child Q 55:313–318. doi:10.1177/0016986211422217

Zientek LR, Thomspon B (2006) Commonality analysis: partitioning variance to facilitate better understanding of data. J Early Interv 28(4):299–307

Chapter 26
Multilevel Random Mediation Analysis: A Comparison of Analytical Alternatives

Fang Luo and Hongyun Liu

Abstract The present article focuses on the multilevel random mediation effects model (1-1-1) and examines its various analytical procedures. The performances of these procedures under a variety of conditions were compared using Monte Carlo simulations. We compared the multilevel random mediation model with two compact models: the multilevel fixed mediation model and the single-level traditional mediation model. The results showed better performance for the multilevel random mediation model. The results also indicated that we can obtain unbiased estimation of the mediation effect, the correct standard error, and proper hypothesis testing results from the multilevel random mediation model. Moreover, the differences between the multilevel fixed mediation model and the single-level traditional mediation model are minimal. Several implications and recommendations for this application are discussed.

Keywords Multilevel random mediation model • Multilevel fixed mediation model • Single-level mediation model • Restricted maximum likelihood

26.1 Introduction

The analysis of mediation effects is important in the research of education, psychology, and other social sciences. In the context of traditional regression and path analysis, the methods for estimating and testing mediation are widely known and relatively standard (e.g., Imai et al. 2010; Baron and Kenny 1986; MacKinnon et al. 2002; Shrout and Bolger 2002). Such methods, however, are inappropriate when the data are hierarchical in nature, primarily because the assumption of independence of observations is violated and the standard errors are biased (Bryk and Raudenbush 2002). For this reason, the multilevel model, also known as the hierarchical linear or mixed model, has been proposed, and subsequently, methods

F. Luo (✉) • H. Liu
National Innovation Center for Assessment of Basic Education Quality, School of Psychology, Beijing Normal University, Beijing, China
e-mail: luof@bnu.edu.cn

R.E. Millsap et al. (eds.), *Quantitative Psychology Research*, Springer Proceedings in Mathematics & Statistics 89, DOI 10.1007/978-3-319-07503-7_26

for the analyses of mediation effects within the model have also been developed (Krull and MacKinnon 1999, 2001; Kenny et al. 2003; Bauer et al. 2006; Zhang et al. 2009).

In brief, a mediator is a variable that falls into the casual ordering and at least partially explains the effects of X (the independent variable) on Y (the dependent variable). In the field of organization psychology, for example, Vandenabeele (2009) examined how public service motivation raises job satisfaction and organizational commitment, which subsequently improves job performance. Similarly, Liu et al. (2011) found that individual's psychological empowerment mediates the effect of autonomy orientation on a team member's voluntary turnover.

Several procedures have been recommended and implemented in existing commercial software for the testing of mediation effects in multilevel models, such as SAS PROC MIXED, HLM, and Mplus. An important feature of multilevel mediation models is that predictors, mediators, and outcome variables can reside at different levels of the data. Adopting the notation proposed by Krull and MacKinnon (2001), we can differentiate several forms of multilevel mediation models, as summarized by Preacher et al. (2010). Because level 2 dependent variables are not permitted in the framework of multilevel modeling, the outcome variable is always restricted to being measured at level 1 (L1). The mediation in a two-level model may take three forms (Bauer et al. 2006). Specifically in the $2 \rightarrow 2 \rightarrow 1$ model, both predictor and mediator are at the group level (L2) while the dependent variable is at L1. In the $2 \rightarrow 1 \rightarrow 1$ model, only the predictor X is at L2 while in the $1 \rightarrow 1 \rightarrow 1$ model, the predictor, mediator, and outcome are all at L1.

The multilevel mediation model has attracted an increasing amount of attention, Krull and MacKinnon (2001), and Pituch et al. (2006) examined the 2-2-1 mediation model, and MacKinnon (2008), Pituch and Stapleton (2008), and Raudenbush and Sampson (1999) examined the 2-1-1 mediation model, and Krull and MacKinnon (1999, 2001) offered an alternative method to all three types of multilevel mediation, which is similar to the causal steps approach proposed by Baron and Kenny (1986).

These above methods assumed that the mediation effects are fixed. However, in the 2-1-1 and 1-1-1 models, the casual effects can be random because the predictors and/or the mediators may reside at L1. Particularly for the 1-1-1 model, the mediation effect can be random across L2 units and consists of two parts: the fixed part and the random part. This finding was first noted by Kenny et al. (2003) who proposed a two-step method for estimating and testing 1-1-1 models when the causal effects and the indirect effect are all random. They estimated each 1-1 model separately and then computed the covariance to obtain the overall mediation effect using L2 residuals. This two-step approach has the drawback that it cannot directly estimate the covariance of the random effects in the different L1 models, and this ad hoc approach is not an optimal strategy (Bauer et al. 2006). In contrast, the newer method implemented in SAS MIXED (Bauer et al. 2006) can estimate the mediation for models with L1 random effects. The method formulates and models a single L1 equation through the use of indicator variables.

The performance (e.g., efficiency, precision) of these multilevel mediation analysis approaches and the influential factors have been examined. Krull and

MacKinnon (2001) compared several types of multilevel mediation models (e.g., 2-2-1, 2-1-1, and 1-1-1) with the traditional single-level mediation approach and showed that an underestimation of the standard error of the mediated effect exists in single-level models with cluster data. Similarly, Pituch et al. (2005) conducted Monte Carlo studies to assess the power and Type I error rates of four methods using the joint significance test and the asymmetric confidence limits recommended by MacKinnon (2008), Baron and Kenny (1986), and Sobel (1982). The conditions simulated were actual multi-site experiments in which the number of sites, the number of participants within the sites, and effect sizes were all relatively small. However, because the mediated effects in these studies were fixed to be identical across the groups, they are not real random mediated models.

Subsequently, Bauer et al. (2006) proposed new procedures for evaluating random indirect effects in multilevel models and examined the difficulties in estimation, estimation bias, Type I errors, CI coverage rates, and power. They found that the estimates using the new procedures are unbiased under most conditions, and the confidence intervals based on a normal approximation or a simulated sampling distribution perform well.

Although Preacher et al. (2011) and Preacher et al. (2010) suggested that a multilevel structural equation modeling (MSEM) approach for assessing mediation in two-level data is more inclusive and flexible, their findings didn't generalize to the 1-1-1 model with random slopes. Therefore, at the present Bauer's procedure is more suitable for lower level random mediation model.

26.1.1 Lower Level Random Mediation Model and Bauer's Procedure

Following the notation of Kenny et al. (2003) and Bauer et al. (2006), the lower level (L1) equations for M (mediator) and Y (dependent variable) are:

$$M_{ij} = d_{Mj} + a_j X_{ij} + e_{Mij}$$

$$Y_{ij} = d_{Yj} + c'_j X_{ij} + b_j M_{ij} + e_{Yij}$$

where e_{Mij} and e_{Yij} are L1 residuals for M and Y, d_{Mj} and d_{Yj} are the intercepts for M and Y, b_j is the effect of M on Y controlling for X, c'_j is the direct effect of X on Y controlling for M, and a_j is the effect of X on M. Because all of these coefficients may vary across the upper level units, each of them has the subscript j. The respective L2 equations for the random L1 coefficients when there are no L2 predictors are:

$$d_{Mj} = d_M + u_{M0j}$$

$$a_j = a + u_{M1j}$$

$$d_{Yj} = d_Y + u_{Y0j}$$

$$c'_j = c' + u_{Y1j}$$

$$b_j = b + u_{Y2j}$$

The un-subscripted parameters are the average estimation values, while u_{M0j}, u_{M1j}, u_{Y1j} and u_{Y2j} are the L2 residuals for the L1 random parameters.

Several assumptions are made for this multilevel random mediation model. First, the predictors are uncorrelated with the random effects (intercepts and slopes) and the residuals both within and across equations (e.g., X_{ij} must be uncorrelated with d_{Mj}, a_j, and e_{Mij}, and M_{ij} should be uncorrelated with d_{Yj}, b_j, c'_j, and e_{Yij}). Second, the residuals e_{Mij} and e_{Yij} are both normally distributed with an expected value of zero, and they are uncorrelated with each other. Typically, the residuals for each outcome are assumed to be independent and homoscedastic across i within j, but these restrictions can be relaxed under certain circumstances (e.g., when residuals are expected to be auto-correlated with repeated measures). An additional assumption, which states that the residuals are uncorrelated across the outcomes, is required to identify the effect of M on Y. Third, the random effects are normally distributed with their means equal to the average effects in the population. Fourth, the L1 residuals are uncorrelated with the random effects both within and across equations (e.g., e_{Mij} is uncorrelated with d_{Mj}, a_j, d_{Yj}, b_j and c'_j. From assumptions 2 and 3, we can conclude that the distribution of M is normal, conditional on X, and the distribution of Y is normal, conditional on M and X.

Bauer et al. (2006) proposed a procedure to reformulate the model with a single L1 equation using indicator variables. In general, a new outcome variable Z is formed by stacking Y and M for each unit i within j. Two indicator variables, S_M and S_Y are then created to distinguish the two variables stacked in Z. The variable S_M is set to be equal to 1 and e_{Zij} equal to e_{Mij} when Z refers to M and is equal to 0 otherwise. Similarly, the variable S_Y is set to be equal to 1 and e_{Zij} equal to e_{Yij} when Z refers to Y and is equal to 0 otherwise. The L1 mediation model can be represented by a single equation:

$$Z_{ij} = S_{Mij}\left(d_{Mj} + a_j X_{ij}\right) + S_{Yij}\left(d_{Yj} + b_j M_{ij} + c'_j X_{ij}\right) + e_{Zij} \tag{26.1}$$

The two outcomes Y and M are distinguished in the model by the indicator variables. Using the indicator variable approach, we can estimate the complete lower level mediation model simultaneously.

26.1.2 Indirect Effect in Lower Level Random Mediation Model

The L1 equations reflect the heterogeneity in the causal effects through the L2 units. The indirect effects for a given unit j are represented by a_jb_j. Because a_j and b_j are not necessarily independent, the expected value of a_jb_j is (Goodman 1960)

$$E\left(a_jb_j\right) = ab + \sigma_{a_j,b_j}, \tag{26.2}$$

meaning the average indirect effect in the population is a function of the average effect of X on M (i.e., a), the average effect of M on Y (i.e., b), and the covariance between the two random effects (i.e., σ_{a_j,b_j}).

Assuming that a_j and b_j are normally distributed, Kenny et al. (2003) showed that the variance of a_jb_j is

$$Var\left(a_jb_j\right) = b^2\sigma^2_{aj} + a^2\sigma^2_{bj} + \sigma^2_{aj}\sigma^2_{bj} + 2ab\sigma_{aj,bj} + \sigma^2_{aj,bj} \tag{26.3}$$

The sampling variance of the estimated average indirect effect $\widehat{ab} + \widehat{\sigma}_{aj,bj}$ is

$$\begin{aligned} &Var\left(\widehat{ab} + \widehat{\sigma}_{aj,bj}\right) = \widehat{b}^2 Var\left(\widehat{a}\right) + \widehat{a}^2 Var\left(\widehat{b}\right) + Var\left(\widehat{a}\right) Var\left(\widehat{b}\right) \\ &+ 2\widehat{a}\widehat{b}Cov\left(\widehat{a},\widehat{b}\right) + Cov\left(\widehat{a},\widehat{b}\right)^2 + Var\left(\widehat{\sigma}_{aj,bj}\right) \end{aligned} \tag{26.4}$$

The variances and covariances in the equation (designated as Var and Cov) represent the asymptotic sampling variances and covariances of the fixed effect estimates $\widehat{a}$ and $\widehat{b}$ and the covariance estimate $\widehat{\sigma}_{a_j,b_j}$.

To develop inferences on the average indirect effect, we can form CIs for the estimates. One method to construct CIs assumes normality for the sampling distributions of the estimates. Under this assumption, a 95 % CI for the average indirect effect is obtained as

$$\left(\widehat{ab} + \widehat{\sigma}_{aj,bj}\right) \pm 1.96\left(Var\left(\widehat{ab} + \widehat{\sigma}_{aj,bj}\right)\right)^{1/2} \tag{26.5}$$

where ± 1.96 is the critical value of the z distribution and *Var* is used to indicate the estimated sampling variance obtained when the respective values in Eq. (26.4) are substituted by their sample-based estimates.

A promising alternative for the construction of CIs is the Monte Carlo (MC) method which was first applied to the mediation context by MacKinnon et al. (2004). The MC method has several distinct advantages over rival methods (e.g., the bootstrapping and distribution of the product method) (Preacher and Selig 2012). In this approach, the sampling distribution for the effect of interest is not assumed to be normally distributed, and instead, the CIs are simulated from the model estimates along with their respective asymptotic variances and covariances.

Following Bauer et al. (2006) study, the purpose of this work focuses on the 1-1-1 model and examines the improvement in performance using the multilevel random mediation model (MRMM) compared with two simple models, the multilevel fixed mediation model (MFMM) and the single-level mediation model (SLMM). The performances of these analytical models were compared using Monte Carlo simulations with respect to several factors, including the size of the true mediational relationship, the sample size, and the characteristics of the multilevel data.

26.2 The Simulation Study

26.2.1 Main Simulation Design

A simulation study was conducted to compare the performances of MRMM, MFMM, and SLMM analyses in estimating and testing indirect effects in multilevel data. The SAS programming language was used to generate simulated data sets to represent mediational chains in which an initial variable X affected a mediator M, which affected an outcome variable Y.

Utilizing the parameter simulation designs by Krull and MacKinnon (1999, 2001), Kenny et al. (2003), Bauer et al. (2006), Zhang et al. (2009), and Pituch et al. (2005), four factors were systematically varied in the simulations. The number of groups and the group size were manipulated so that the simulated data sets had a fixed total sample size of 800, and the number of groups was 32, 50, 100, and 160, with group sample sizes of 25, 16, 8, and 5, respectively. The ICCs for M_{ij} and Y_{ij} were identical, and were set to $\mathrm{ICC_M} = \mathrm{ICC_Y} = 0.05, 0.15$, and 0.30. The true values of parameters a_j and b_j, which referred to the averages of the random effects a_j and b_j also systematically varied. In the simulation model, we set $a = b = 0.1$, $a = b = 0.3$, and $a = b = 0.6$, and the random effects a_j and b_j were both normally distributed with variances of $\sigma^2_{a_j} = \sigma^2_{b_j} = 0.16$, and c'_j was normally distributed with a mean of $c'_j = 0.2$ and a variance of $\sigma^2_{c'_j} = 0.04$ The covariance between a_j and b_j ($\sigma_{aj,bj}$) was -0.113, 0, 0.0565, and 0.113. In addition, the predictor X was simulated from the equation $\mathrm{x_{ij}} = \overline{\mathrm{x}}_\mathrm{j} + \mathrm{e_{xij}}$, where $\overline{\mathrm{x}}_\mathrm{j} \sim N(0,1)$ and $\mathrm{e_{xij}} \sim N(0,1)$. For simplicity, the means of d_{Mj} and d_{Yj} were set to zero. These four factors combined to yield $4 \times 4 \times 3 \times 3 = 144$ conditions.

26.2.2 Supplemental Design for Examining Type I Error

To investigate the Type I error, we added a supplemental design to set the average indirect effect at $ab + \sigma_{aj,bj} = 0$. Similar to the method used by Bauer et al. (2006), we fixed the covariance between a_j and b_j to zero ($\sigma_{aj,bj} = 0$) and (1) set $a = b = 0$; (2) $a = 0$ and $b = 0.3$; and (3) $a = 0.3$, $b = 0$ to ensure $ab + \sigma_{aj,bj} = 0$ at each sample size and residual variance for M and Y. These situations combined to generate 36 conditions.

In addition, we also considered that the covariances between a_j and b_j were not zero, but varied at (1) $\sigma_{aj,bj} = -0.113$, $a = b = 0.336155$ (or -0.336155); (2) $\sigma_{aj,bj} = -0.0565$, $a = b = 0.237697$ (or -0.237697); (3) $\sigma_{aj,bj} = 0.0565$, $a = 0.237697$, $b = -0.237697$ (or $a = -0.237697$, $b = 0.237697$); and (4) $\sigma_{aj,bj} = 0.113$, $a = 0.33615$, $b = -0.33615$ (or $a = -0.33615$, $b = 0.33615$) to ensure $ab + \sigma_{aj,bj} = 0$. For simplicity, we fixed the residual variances to be 0.3 for M and Y in each situation. These situations combined to generate 32 conditions.

For each cell of the design, we simulated 500 sets of data, which were then used in SAS PROC to fit three models. The models were a traditional single-level mediation model (SAS PROC REG), a multilevel fixed mediation model (SAS PROC MIXED REML), and a multilevel random mediation model (SAS PROC MIXED REML). The performance of each model was evaluated according to six criteria, namely, (1) the convergence rates, (2) the bias and precision of the mediation effects estimates, (3) the coverage rates of the CIs constructed with the normal approximation and MC methods, (4) the estimated sampling variance of the indirect effect, (5) the statistical power in testing the indirect effect, and (6) the Type I error rates for the null hypothesis test on the average indirect effect. In addition, we examined the influences of four design factors on the indirect effect estimators.

26.3 Result

26.3.1 Convergence Behavior

The solutions for replicate were categorized as either non-converged or converged. All of the $144 \times 500 = 72{,}000$ replicates for both the MFMM and the SLMM converged. For the MRMM using the REML estimation method, only 0.7 % of the solutions did not converge. Non-convergence likely occurred because the MRMM is more complex than the fixed multilevel and single-level mediation models as there are more parameters to be estimated. In addition to these results, small effects from other factors were also identified. Generally, the MRMM was more likely to produce non-convergence, and it requires more iterations if a, b, or the absolute covariance of a_j and b_j were large.

26.3.2 Bias and Precision of Estimation

Bias was measured as the difference between the mean estimate and the corresponding population value, and the absolute bias was computed as the mean of absolute difference between the estimate and the corresponding population value. The bias and absolute bias were used to evaluate the precision of the parameter estimations. The estimate biases and the absolute biases of indirect effects for the three different models are presented in Table 26.1.

Table 26.1 Bias and absolute bias of indirect effect in different models

	MRMM		MFMM		SLMM	
Condition	BIAS	ABS(BIAS)	BIAS	ABS(BIAS)	BIAS	ABS(BIAS)
$\sigma_{aj,bj}$						
−0.113	−0.0015	0.0318	0.0849	0.0865	0.0883	0.0894
0	−0.0001	0.0345	0.0002	0.0253	0.0003	0.0255
0.057	0.0011	0.0368	−0.0426	0.0550	−0.0441	0.0555
0.113	0.0018	0.0399	−0.0848	0.0944	−0.0881	0.0961
Sample size						
(32,25)	0.0009	0.0445	−0.0102	0.0700	−0.0103	0.0714
(50,16)	0.0006	0.0377	−0.0101	0.0662	−0.0103	0.0677
(100,8)	0.0000	0.0313	−0.0106	0.0630	−0.0111	0.0644
(160,5)	−0.0002	0.0294	−0.0114	0.0621	−0.0118	0.0632
Parameters of a and b						
0.1	0.0007	0.0255	−0.0136	0.0700	−0.0136	0.0701
0.3	0.0001	0.0325	−0.0122	0.0664	−0.0124	0.0676
0.6	0.0002	0.0493	−0.0060	0.0595	−0.0067	0.0622
$ICC_M and\ ICC_Y$						
0.05	0.0002	0.0358	−0.0107	0.0653	−0.0109	0.0655
0.15	0.0005	0.0358	−0.0104	0.0653	−0.0107	0.0664
0.30	0.0002	0.0356	−0.0106	0.0652	−0.0111	0.0681
All replications	0.0003	0.0357	−0.0106	0.0653	−0.0109	0.0667

Note: *MRMM* Multilevel Random Mediation model, *MFMM* Multilevel Fixed Mediation model, *SLMM* Single-level Fixed Mediation model

The results indicated that across all 144 conditions, the mean bias and the mean absolute bias of the average indirect effect estimate were 0.0003 and 0.0357 for MRMM, -0.0106 and 0.0653 for MFMM, and -0.0109 and 0.0667 for SLMM. It is not surprising that the bias is the smallest for the MRMM model under all conditions because it is more complex and the random indirect effects are properly considered. The bias and the absolute bias of the MFMM were slightly smaller than those of the SLMM, although the differences between them were trivial.

Furthermore, when the covariance $\sigma_{aj,bj}$ between a_j and b_j is zero, the estimates of the average indirect effects were essentially unbiased for all three types of models. However, as the covariance between a_j and b_j increased, the bias also increased; for MRMM, $F(3,\ 140) = 17.21$, $p < 0.0001$, *partial* $\eta^2 = 0.269$; *for MFMM*, $F(3,\ 140) = 525.63$, $p < 0.0001$, *partial* $\eta^2 = 0.918$; *for SLMM*, $F(3,\ 140) = 728.51$, $p < 0.0001$, *partial* $\eta^2 = 0.940$, for SLMM; similarly for the absolute bias, for MRMM, $F(3, 140) = 2.829$, $p = 0.041$, *partial* $\eta^2 = 0.057$; *for MFMM*, $F(3, 140) = 134.88$, $p < 0.0001$, *partial* $\eta^2 = 0.743$; *for SLMM*, $F(3, 140) = 162.01$, $p < 0.0001$, *partial* $\eta^2 = 0.776$. It can be concluded that the estimates of the average indirect effects are nearly unbiased for MRMM, but the estimates of the other two models are imprecise when $\sigma_{aj,bj}$ was significantly different than zero.

For a fixed number of overall observations, the estimates of the average indirect effect became more precise (using absolute bias as index) when there was a larger number of L2 units for the MRMM; $F(3, 140) = 13.45$, $p < 0.0001$, *partial* $\eta^2 = 0.224$. The L2 sample size, however, had no effect on the precision of estimates for the other two simple methods. The absolute bias of the average indirect effect for MRMM increased as the average values of a and b increased; $F(2, 141) = 120.872$, $p < 0.0001$, *partial* $\eta^2 = 0.632$. However, the effects of the values of a and b on the bias and absolute biases for the other two simple models were not significant. Furthermore, the effects of the residual intraclass correlations ICC_M and ICC_Y on the precision of the average indirect effect estimates were not significant for all three models.

26.3.3 Coverage Rate

The 95 % confidence interval (CIs) were constructed with the normal approximation and Monte Carlo methods (Mackinnon et al. 2004). The precision of the average indirect effect estimates was examined, and the closer the coverage rates were to the 95 %, the more precise the estimates would be. The coverage rates for the CIs are presented in Table 26.2 for different design factors and models.

Across all 144 conditions in the factorial design, the mean coverage rates for MRMM were 94.51 and 94.44 % for the normal approximation and Monte Carlo methods, respectively, producing close to a 95 % coverage of the true population parameter values. For the MFMM, however, the mean coverage rates were 32.61 and 32.90 % for the normal approximation and Monte Carlo methods, respectively. Similarly, for the SLMM, the mean coverage rates were 32.18 and 32.46 % for the normal approximation and Monte Carlo methods, respectively. In each of the conditions in the simulation study, the CI coverage rates of MRMM were much higher than those of MFMM and SLMM and were close to 95 %.

For the MFMM and SLMM models, the CI coverage rates reached a maximum of approximately 69 % when the covariance $\sigma_{aj,bj}$ between a_j and b_j was zero. However, when the covariance $\sigma_{aj,bj}$ between a_j and b_j was different from zero, the CI coverage rates rapidly dropped below 30 %. For example, when the covariance $\sigma_{aj,bj}$ between a_j and b_j was 0.113, the coverage rates were not more than 18 %. The results indicated that the magnitude of the covariance $\sigma_{aj,bj}$ between a_j and b_j had significant effects on the CI coverage rates for the MFMM and SLMM. The CI coverage rates, however, were much smaller than the expected 95 % regardless of whether the covariance $\sigma_{aj,bj}$ between a_j and b_j was zero. Moreover, we can conclude that the effect of the covariance $\sigma_{aj,bj}$ between a_j and b_j on the CI coverage rates is not significant for MRMM.

For a fixed number of overall observations, we can conclude from Table 26.2 that (1) the number of group level units and values of a and b have significant effects on the CI coverage rates for the MFMM and SLMM, (2) the coverage rates increase as

Table 26.2 Confidence interval rates of indirect effect for three different models

Conditions	MRMM Normal approximation (%)	MRMM Monte Carlo (%)	MFMM Normal approximation (%)	MFMM Monte Carlo (%)	SLMM Normal approximation (%)	SLMM Monte Carlo (%)
Covariance						
−0.113	94.62	94.47	16.69	16.25	14.63	14.17
0	94.76	94.46	68.16	61.81	61.87	69.43
0.0565	94.53	94.54	28.21	28.83	28.49	29.16
0.113	94.11	94.27	17.37	17.69	16.71	17.06
Sample size						
(32, 25)	94.81	94.76	28.46	28.73	28.32	28.49
(50, 16)	94.70	94.73	31.53	31.77	31.27	31.46
(100, 8)	94.40	94.25	34.73	34.95	34.09	34.46
(160, 5)	94.11	94.00	35.72	36.13	35.02	35.42
Parameters of a and b						
$a = b = 0.1$	95.13	94.90	17.38	17.79	17.56	17.94
$a = b = 0.3$	94.38	94.35	25.65	26.07	25.92	26.38
$a = b = 0.6$	94.01	94.06	54.80	54.82	53.05	53.05
ICC_M *and* ICC_Y						
0.05	94.59	94.55	32.39	32.66	32.37	32.67
0.15	94.34	94.22	32.58	32.82	32.17	32.44
0.30	94.59	94.54	32.86	33.21	31.99	32.26
All replications	94.51	94.44	32.61	32.90	32.18	32.46

the L2 sample size increases, (3) the CI coverage rates increase as the values of a and b *increase*, and (4) for the MRMM, the magnitudes of the residual intracorrelations ICC_M and ICC_Y have no effect on the CI coverage rates.

26.3.4 Estimated Sampling Variance of Indirect Effect

With the assumption of normality for the random effects, the sampling variances of the indirect effect for the MRMM can be estimated using Eq. (26.4), while those for the MFMM an SLMM can be computed using the Sobel (1982) method as follows:

$$Var\left(\widehat{ab}\right) = \widehat{a}^2\sigma_{\widehat{b}}^2 + \widehat{b}^2\sigma_{\widehat{a}}^2 \tag{26.6}$$

The sampling errors under different design factors and models are presented in Table 26.3. Across all of the conditions, the sampling errors (standard errors) of the indirect effects were 0.002248 (0.0474), 0.000357 (0.0189), and 0.00037 (0.0192) for the MRMM, MFMM, and SLMM, respectively. The results indicated that for the MFMM and SLMM, the sampling errors of the indirect effects were largely underestimated. Although the sampling errors using the MFMM were slightly larger than those of the SLMM, the differences between them were small relative to the differences between the random effect model and the fixed effect models.

For the MRMM, the estimated sampling error of the indirect effect was a function of the covariance between the random effects a_j and b_j, i.e., the sampling error decreased as the covariance decreased: $F(3,\ 140) = 3.225$, $p = 0.025$, *partial* $\eta^2 = 0.065$. For a finite number of observations, the estimated sampling error of the indirect effect became smaller with the increase in the number of L2 units: $F(3,\ 140) = 16.263$, $p < 0.0001$, *partial* $\eta^2 = 0.258$. The sampling error also decreased as the values of the average effects a and b became smaller: $F(2,\ 141) = 68.695$, $p < 0.0001$, *partial* $\eta^2 = 0.494$. An interaction between the values of the average effects and the covariance of the random effects affected the sampling error estimates: $F(6,\ 132) = 3.41$, $p = 0.0037$, *partial* $\eta^2 = 0.134$, indicating that the difference in the estimated sampling error between different levels of covariance increased as the magnitude of the average effects a and b increased. Interactions between the values of the average effects and the group size also affected the sampling error estimates: $F(6,\ 132) = 11.009$, $p < 0.0001$, *partial* $\eta^2 = 0.334$, indicating that the difference in the sampling errors between the different group sample sizes was smaller for low average effects (a and b) than for those with high average effects.

The relative bias in the sampling error estimation was examined to detect the conditions under which the advantages of a multilevel random mediational analysis were most apparent. Because the true sampling error was not known, the estimated sampling error of 500 replicates for the MRMM was used as the comparison

Table 26.3 Average estimated variance of indirect effect

Conditions							
Indirect effect	Covariance	$a = b$	MRMM	MFMM	SLMM	R Bias of MFMM to MRMM	R Bias of SLMM to MRMM
−0.103	−0.113	0.1	0.0012	0.0000	0.0000	0.9713	0.9698
−0.023	−0.113	0.3	0.0015	0.0002	0.0002	0.8557	0.8484
0.247	−0.113	0.6	0.0025	0.0007	0.0008	0.6743	0.6621
Mean conditionals			0.0017	0.0003	0.0003	0.8337	0.8268
0.01	0	0.1	0.0010	0.0000	0.0000	0.9659	0.9638
0.09	0	0.3	0.0016	0.0002	0.0002	0.8531	0.8467
0.36	0	0.6	0.0036	0.0008	0.008	0.7352	0.7264
Mean conditionals			0.0020	0.0003	0.0004	0.8514	0.8456
0.067	0.057	0.1	0.0010	0.0000	0.0000	0.9669	0.9652
0.147	0.057	0.3	0.00118	0.0002	0.0002	0.8603	0.8549
0.417	0.057	0.6	0.0044	0.0009	0.0009	0.7594	0.7523
Mean conditionals			0.0024	0.0004	0.0004	0.8622	0.8574
0.123	0.113	0.1	0.0013	0.0000	0.0000	0.9688	0.9673
0.203	0.113	0.3	0.0022	0.0002	0.0002	0.8685	0.8647
0.473	0.113	0.6	0.0052	0.0009	0.0010	0.7764	0.7706
Mean conditionals			0.0029	0.0004	0.0004	0.8712	0.8676
Sample size							
(32, 25)			0.0036	0.0004	0.0004	0.9138	0.9090
(50, 16)			0.0025	0.0004	0.0004	0.8825	0.8769
(100, 8)			0.0016	0.0004	0.0004	0.8274	0.8215
(160, 5)			0.0013	0.0004	0.0004	0.7948	0.7900
ILL_M*and* ICC_Y							
0.05			0.0022	0.0004	0.0004	0.8556	0.8564
0.15			0.0022	0.0004	0.0004	0.8546	0.8514
0.30			0.0023	0.0004	0.0004	0.8538	0.8402
All replications			0.0022	0.0004	0.0004	0.8546	0.8494

standard. The relative bias (RB) of the estimated variance of the indirect effect of the MFMM compared to MRMM was calculated using the equation:

$$RB_{MFMM-MRMM} = \frac{Var(Indirect)_{MRMM} - Var(Indirect)_{MFMM}}{Var(Indirect)_{MRMM}} \tag{26.7}$$

and the relative bias of SLMM to MRMM was calculated using the equation:

$$RB_{SFMM-MRMM} = \frac{Var(Indirect)_{MRMM} - Var(Indirect)_{SLMM}}{Var(Indirect)_{MRMM}} \tag{26.8}$$

The results of the relative biases are shown in the last two columns in Table 26.3. Across all conditions in the simulation study, the relative biases of the MFMM to the MRMM and the SLMM to the MRMM were 0.855 and 0.850, respectively. For the MFMM model, the relative bias decreased as the number of group level units increased: $F(3, 140) = 9.450$, $p < .0001$, *partial* $\eta^2 = .168$. When the values of the average effects values a and b became smaller, the relative bias became larger: $F(2, 141) = 166.358$, $p < .0001$, *partial* $\eta^2 = .702$. In addition, the interaction between the number of units at L2 and the average effects values a and b was significant: $F(6, 132) = 46.275$, $p < .0001$, *partial* $\eta^2 = .678$. When the average effects values a and b were small (e.g., 0.1), the difference in the relative bias of the sampling errors among the different numbers of units was small. As the average effects values a and b became large, however, the differences in the relative bias of the sampling errors among the different numbers of units became large. Similar results were obtained for the SLMM model.

26.3.5 Type I Error

We examined the Type I error rates in testing the average indirect effect using a supplementary simulation design in which the population value of the average indirect effect was set to zero. There were 36 conditions in which the covariance $\sigma_{a_j b_j}$ between the random effects a_j and b_j was set to zero and 24 conditions in which the covariance $\sigma_{a_j b_j}$ between the random effects a_j and b_j was not set to zero. As is customary practice, we set the nominal error rate at 5 %. Type I error rates for different design factors and models were estimated (see Table 26.4).

When the covariance between the random effects was set to 0, a and b were also set to zero and the Type I error generated by both the normal approximation and the Monte Carlo methods varied with the models being examined. When the MRMM was used, the Type I errors were 0.0389 and 0.0440 for the normal approximation method and the Monte Carlo method, respectively. However, when MFMM was used, the Type I errors were 0.0612 and 0.0997 for the normal approximation method and the Monte Carlo method, respectively, and when the SLMM was used, they reached 0.0575 and 0.0949 for the normal approximation method and the

Table 26.4 Type I error rates of three type models

Conditions		MRMM		MFMM		SLMM	
Covariance	Average effects	Normal approximation	Monte Carlo	Normal approximation	Monte Carlo	Normal approximation	Monte Carlo
0.000	$a = b = 0$	0.039	0.044	0.061	0.100	0.058	0.095
0.000	$a = b$ (or $b = 0$)	0.043	0.052	0.297	0.309	0.290	0.302
−0.113	$a = b = 0.336$ (or −0.336)	0.046	0.050	0.994	0.994	0.994	0.994
−0.0565	$a = b = 0.238$ (or −0.238)	0.042	0.047	0.972	0.973	0.969	0.972
0.0565	$a = b = 0.238$ (or −0.238)	0.048	0.053	0.973	0.975	0.969	0.972
0.113	$a = b = 0.336$ (or −0.336)	0.052	0.055	0.994	0.995	0.994	0.994
Sample size							
Zero	(32, 25)	0.033	0.046	0.330	0.359	0.328	0.356
	(50, 16)	0.037	0.043	0242	0.268	0.242	0.263
	(100, 8)	0.051	0.057	0.177	0.193	0.168	0.184
	(160, 5)	0.047	0.052	0.124	0.138	0.112	0.128
No zero	(32, 25)	0.038	0.044	0.960	0.962	0.953	0.956
	(50, 16)	0.042	0.048	0.981	0.983	0.979	0.981
	(100, 8)	0.052	0.054	0.995	0.995	0.995	0.996
	(160, 5)	0.056	0.059	0.997	0.997	0.998	0.998

Monte Carlo method, respectively. Therefore, the MRMM with the Monte Carlo method was more likely to reach a 5 % Type I error. However, the Type I errors produced by the MFMM and SLMM models with either the normal approximation or Monte Carlo methods could also be controlled adequately. Under the condition that either a or b was 0, the Type I errors of the normal approximation and the Monte Carlo methods reached 0.0434 and 0.0518, respectively, for MRMM; 0.2968 and 0.3092, respectively, for the MFMM; and 0.2897 and 0.3016, respectively, for SLMM. Under this condition, the MRMM with the MC method was more likely to reach a 5 % Type I error level. In comparison, the MFMM and SLMM produced higher Type I error rates. Under the condition that the covariance between two random effects was 0 and the total sample size was set at 800, the smaller the sample size at L2, the more likely it was that the Type I error generated by the MFMM and SLMM was above 5 %. For the MRMM, if the sample size is very small, the MC method is superior to the normal approximation method.

When the covariance of the random effects was not 0, under the condition that $\sigma_{a_jb_j} + ab = 0$, the overall Type I error rates produced by the normal approximation and MC methods reached 0.0471 and 0.0513, respectively, for the MRMM; 0.9831 and 0.9843, respectively, for the MFMM; and 0.9813 and 0.9828, respectively, for the SLMM. Because the covariance was not considered in either the MFMM or the SLMM, the Type I error rate tended to be extremely large.

When the MRMM was used, a large sample size at L2 led to a large Type I error rate. The MC method was superior to the normal approximation method with a small sample size.

26.3.6 Power

To evaluate power, we calculated the proportion of replications with CIs for the average indirect effect excluding zero for each of the 144 cells in the factorial design. Similar to the CI coverage rates, both the normal approximation and the Monte Carlo methods were examined. The results are presented in Table 26.5. Across all conditions for the normal approximation method, the power estimates of the indirect effects were 0.7727, 0.8155, and 0.8089 for the MRMM, MFMM, and SLMM, respectively. For the MC method, the powers were 0.7784, 0.8416, and 0.8377 for the MRMM, MFMM, and SLMM, respectively. In general, the simple fixed indirect effect models (the MFMM and SLMM) resulted in power estimates superior to that of the MRMM, but the results were not completely consistent across the different conditions (see Table 26.4). Furthermore, high power was not an indicator of the strength of the model because it was based on an incorrectly underestimated standard error.

Because the power is affected by the magnitude of the indirect effects, we calculated the indirect effects by combining the average effects and the covariance of the random effects, i.e., $\sigma_{a_jb_j} + ab$. In the simulation study, there are 12 types of indirect effects with a mean of 0.188, a minimum of 0.01, and a maximum of 0.473.

Table 26.5 Power of test on indirect effect for different models

			MRMM		MFMM		SLMM	
Conditions indirect effect	Covariance	$a = b$	Normal approximation	Monte Carlo	Normal approximation	Monte Carlo	Normal approximation	Monte Carlo
0.01	0	0.1	0.056	0.061	0.455	0.535	0.434	0.522
−0.023	−0.113	0.3	0.080	0.086	0.987	0.987	0.988	0.988
0.0665	0.0565	0.1	0.603	0.624	0.498	0.576	0.477	0.561
0.09	0	0.3	0.660	0.680	0.998	0.998	0.998	0.998
−0.103	−0.113	0.1	0.936	0.944	0.309	0.396	0.297	0.389
0.123	0.113	0.1	0.987	0.991	0.541	0.609	0.515	0.597
0.1465	0.0565	0.3	0.963	0.969	0.999	0.999	0.999	0.999
0.203	0.113	0.3	1.000	1.000	0.999	0.999	0.998	0.999
0.247	−0.113	0.6	0.989	0.988	1.000	1.000	1.000	1.000
0.36	0	0.6	1.000	1.000	1.000	1.000	1.000	1.000
0.4165	0.0565	0.6	1.000	1.000	1.000	1.000	1.000	1.000
0.473	0.113	0.6	1.000	1.000	1.000	1.000	1.000	1.000
Sample size								
(32, 25)			0.716	0.730	0.810	0.830	0.805	0.825
(50, 16)			0.763	0.769	0.811	0.832	0.803	0.827
(100, 8)			0.801	0.803	0.819	0.849	0.814	0.844
(160, 5)			0.810	0.812	0.822	0.855	0.814	0.855
ICC_M *and* ICC_Y								
0.05			0.773	0.778	0.817	0.843	0.817	0.844
0.15			0.771	0.777	0.817	0.843	0.812	0.841
0.30			0.774	0.780	0.812	0.839	0.798	0.828
All replications			0.773	0.778	0.816	0.842	0.809	0.838

From Table 26.5, we can conclude that: (1) when the indirect effects were 0.15 or above, the power was high for both of the different methods and different models; (2) when the covariance σ_{a_j,b_j} between a_j and b_j was large (0.113 or -0.113) and average effects a and b were small ($a = b = 0.1$), the MRMM had greater power than the other two simple models; (3) power was increased with the size of the indirect effect for the MRMM but not for the MFMM and SLMM; and (4) similar to the MC method, which produced consistently narrower CIs than the normal approximation method, the MC method resulted in superior power in 140 of the 144 conditions in the simulation study. The differences in power were, however, quite small and never greater than 0.054.

In general, the power increased as the indirect effect increased when the indirect effects were between 0.123 and 0.247: $F(11, 132) = 376.60$, $p < 0.0001$, *partial* $\eta^2 = 0.969$ for the approximation normal method; and $F(11, 132) = 461.35$, $p < 0.0001$, *partial* $\eta^2 = 0.975$ for the MC method. Under the total 800-sample size, a larger number of group level units produced greater power, especially for the MRMM model. It was also observed that the magnitude of the residual intracorrelation ICC_M and ICC_Y had no effect on the power.

Discussion and Conclusion

Summary

This research aimed to investigate the conditions for proper MRMM analyses. We examined the indirect effects when the data are hierarchical under the condition that the three variables *X*, *M*, and *Y* are all from the lower level. If the effects of *X* on *M* and *M* on *Y* vary at the group level, the MRMM model, rather than the MFMM or SLMM models, should be used to obtain unbiased estimation of the indirect effect and the standard error. When the MFMM and SLMM methods are used and the covariance between a_j and b_j is different from 0, the mean indirect effect coefficient a (or b) will decrease, the point estimation bias of the indirect effect will increase, and the CI coverage rate for the true parameter will be smaller than 95 %. Even when the covariance is fixed at 0, which is an ideal situation for these two methods, the CI coverage rate will be less than 70 %. Therefore, the mean mediation effect is deleteriously affected when failing to account for its variability across grouping units, because the standard error of the mean mediation effect is being underestimated when it is treated as fixed, the Type I error rate tends to be too large, especially when the covariance is not zero.

Despite several possible desirable characteristics, the MRMM must be used with caution. First, if the indicator method developed by Bauer et al. (2006) is used to estimate the random mediation effect, the estimation preci-

(continued)

sion is influenced by the covariance between the random effects. However, the present study has not yet provided an explanation for this result, and further exploration is needed. Extra care is necessary when the covariance is positive (or negative), which results in an overestimated (or underestimated) mediation effect. Fortunately, this problem could be addressed by increasing the number of the groups.

Second, when the mediation effect is fixed to be larger than 0.103 and the sample size is similar to that used in this study, the power of the MRMM is greater than 90 %. Controlling for the total sample size, an increase in the sample size of the number of groups will help to improve the power of the MC method.

Third, when the sample size is at an intermediate level, such as a sample size of 50 at the group level and 16 at the individual level, or 100 at the group level and 8 at the individual level, the Type I error rate reaches 5 %. However, if the sample size of the group level is small, the Type I error rate produced by the MC method is more likely to reach 5 % than the normal approximation method.

Fourth, the MRMM model can lead to increased frequency of non-convergence. In empirical applications, when the normality assumptions are violated, the chance of non-convergence is great; this, however, can be addressed by increasing the sample size.

Fifth, the distribution of e_{Yij} has no effect on the mediation effect. The deviation from the normal distribution of b or "a_j *and* b_j" will affect the mediation effect, especially when the magnitude of the deviation and the covariance between these two effects are large.

Implications

First, there are situations when the MRMM outperforms other methods. Shrout and Fleiss (1979) suggested that the ICC obtained from a null model could be used to evaluate whether the data structure is clustered.

$$ICC = \frac{\sigma_b^2}{\sigma_b^2 + \sigma_w^2}$$

where σ_b^2 represents the variance at the group level, σ_w^2 represents the variance at the individual level, and the ICC represents the percentage of the total variance that occurs at the group level. A high ICC value indicates a high similarity among the individuals in each unit at the group level. Kreft (1996) recommended that the multilevel model should be used when the ICC is 0.1

(continued)

or higher. When the MRMM is used, the criteria could be even lower. In our studies, that the estimation of the indirect effect by the three different models was not affected by the values of the residuals, ICC_M and ICC_Y. This conclusion is consistent with the model containing the fixed mediation effect, as proposed by Krull and MacKinnon (1999) and Pituch et al. (2005). The conclusions of these studies indicate that, irrespective of the value of ICC, the MRMM is accurate provided that clustered data are involved and random effects are possible.

In addition, the variables at the individual level should be centered in the analyses of the random mediation effects in the multilevel model. Krull and MacKinnon (2001) suggested that for a multilevel mediation model without random slopes or for models with a random intercept only, the centering of the variable at the lower level will not have a significant impact on the results. However, for the model with random slopes (e.g., 2-1-1 and 1-1-1 random slope mediation models), it is critical and essential to center the predictors. Zhang et al. (2009) noted that it is difficult to differentiate the mediation effect at the group level from that at the individual level when the centering procedure is not used appropriately. The results have also been compared when centering was performed against those without centering using multilevel mediation models with fixed slopes, and a few conclusions were made: First, for the 2-2-1 model, the results of the two methods were almost the same, and the mediation effect at the two different levels (group level vs. individual level) could not be confounded. Second, for the 2-1-1 model, however, the results of the two methods were quite different. Under this condition, group centering was required in the analyses of the mediation effects at the group level. Third, for the 1-1-1 model, when the random mediation effect was not allowed, the results with centering were also different from those without centering. In this case, group centering was required to differentiate the mediation effect at the group level from that at the individual level.

On the basis of the findings in this study, a procedure with five steps is proposed as follows:

Step 1. Provide theoretical support and justification for the mediation effects model from the existing literature. A data-driven exploration for a mediation effect is not recommended.

Step 2. Identify the data structure and investigate whether the predictor, the mediating variable, and the outcome variable are all from the lower level in the model.

Step 3. Identify whether the effects of X on M and the effects of both X and M on Y have sufficiently large variances at the second level of the model.

(continued)

Step 4. If the multilevel random mediation model is used in investigating the mediation effect, the predictor variable X and M in the first level should be centered prior to the analysis to mitigate the multicollinearity, simplify the explanation of the intercept, enable the proper analysis of the interaction across the level, and differentiate the mediation effect at the individual and group levels. However, if the predictor variable at the first level is centered, the group mean of this variable should be used to predict the intercept at the second level so as to include the variance of this variable between the groups in the model. The multilevel random mediation model can be represented as follows:

$$\begin{cases} M_{ij} = \beta_{0j}^{m} + \beta_{1j}^{m}\left(X_{ij} - \overline{X}_{\bullet j}\right) + r_{ij}^{m} \\ \beta_{0j}^{m} = \gamma_{00}^{m} + \gamma_{01}^{m}\overline{X}_{\bullet j} + u_{0j}^{m} \\ \beta_{1j}^{m} = \gamma_{10}^{m} + u_{1j}^{m} \end{cases}$$
$$\begin{cases} Y_{ij} = \beta_{0j}^{y} + \beta_{1j}^{y}\left(X_{ij} - \overline{X}_{\bullet j}\right) + \beta_{2j}^{y}\left(M_{ij} - \overline{M}_{\bullet j}\right) + r_{ij}^{y} \\ \beta_{0j}^{y} = \gamma_{00}^{y} + \gamma_{01}^{y}\overline{X}_{\bullet j} + \gamma_{02}^{y}\overline{M}_{\bullet j} + u_{0j}^{y} \\ \beta_{1j}^{y} = \gamma_{10}^{y} + u_{1j}^{y} \\ \beta_{2j}^{y} = \gamma_{20}^{y} + u_{2j}^{y} \end{cases} \tag{26.9}$$

To use the method provided by Bauer et al. (2006), Eq. (26.9) can be rearranged as:

$$\begin{cases} M_{ij} = \gamma_{00}^{m} + \gamma_{01}^{m}\overline{X}_{\bullet j} + u_{0j}^{m} + \beta_{1j}^{m}\left(X_{ij} - \overline{X}_{\bullet j}\right) + r_{ij}^{m} \\ \quad = \gamma_{00}^{m} + \beta_{1j}^{m}\left(X_{ij} - \overline{X}_{\bullet j}\right) + \gamma_{01}^{m}\overline{X}_{\bullet j} + w_{ij}^{m} \\ Y_{ij} = \gamma_{00}^{y} + \gamma_{01}^{y}\overline{X}_{\bullet j} + \gamma_{02}^{y}\overline{M}_{\bullet j} + u_{0j}^{y} + \beta_{1j}^{y}\left(X_{ij} - \overline{X}_{\bullet j}\right) + \beta_{2j}^{y}\left(M_{ij} - \overline{M}_{\bullet j}\right) + r_{ij}^{y} \\ \quad = \gamma_{00}^{y} + \beta_{1j}^{y}\left(X_{ij} - \overline{X}_{\bullet j}\right) + \beta_{2j}^{y}\left(M_{ij} - \overline{M}_{\bullet j}\right) + \gamma_{01}^{y}\overline{X}_{\bullet j} + \gamma_{02}^{y}\overline{M}_{\bullet j} + w_{ij}^{y} \end{cases} \tag{26.10}$$

Equation (26.10) can be transformed into a form similar to that of Eq. (26.1):

$$\begin{aligned} Z_{ij} &= S_{Mij}\left[\gamma_{00}^{m} + \beta_{1j}^{m}\left(X_{ij} - \overline{X}_{\bullet j}\right) + \gamma_{01}^{m}\overline{X}_{\bullet j}\right] \\ &+ S_{Yij}\left[\gamma_{00}^{y} + \beta_{1j}^{y}\left(X_{ij} - \overline{X}_{\bullet j}\right) + \beta_{2j}^{y}\left(M_{ij} - \overline{M}_{\bullet j}\right) + \gamma_{01}^{y}\overline{X}_{\bullet j} + \gamma_{02}^{y}\overline{M}_{\bullet j}\right] + e_{Zij} \end{aligned} \tag{26.11}$$

(continued)

Step 5: The restricted maximum likelihood method of SAS PROC MIXED or other multilevel programs can be used to investigate the mediation effect in the model.

Limitations

This study investigated the use of the random mediation model in the hierarchical linear model. The influences of different simulation design factors on estimation bias and hypothesis testing were investigated in a series of simulation studies. Based on these findings, the general strategies and procedures to explore the mediating effects in multilevel data have been provided. Despite the potential contributions of this study, there are still limitations to be addressed. First, given that variables X and M are not centered, only the combined mediation relationship has been discussed in this study. Second, the mediating variable M and the outcome variable Y contain the group level variance component, whereas the group level variance of the predictor variable X has not been considered in the current model. One possible solution is to center X with the group mean and include $X-\overline{X}$ at the individual level and $\overline{X}$ in the group level. Third, the comparison of three approaches introduced by Bauer et al. (2006), Kenny et al. (2003), and Preacher et al. (2010) were not considered in this study. Further research to compare these methods is desirable. Fourth, the model discussed in this study is limited to a simple two-level model with one mediation effect. A two-level model consisting of multiple mediation effects or a three-level model with mediation effects have not been included in the present study. Although it is reasonable to generalize the estimation method to more complex models, caution should be taken in explaining the results. In addition, Preacher et al. (2010) have proposed to use a multilevel structural equation model to develop seven HLM models with mediation effects 2-2-1, 2-1-1, 1-1-1, 2-1-2, 1-2-1, 1-2-2, and 1-1-2. Only the first three models, however, have been examined here. Future research in this area is also highly recommended.

References

Baron RM, Kenny DA (1986) The moderator–mediator variable distinction in social psychological research: conceptual, strategic, and statistical considerations. J Pers Soc Psychol 51(6): 1173–1182

Bauer DJ, Preacher KJ, Gil KM (2006) Conceptualizing and testing random indirect effects and moderated mediation in multilevel models: new procedures and recommendations. Psychol Methods 11(2):142–163

Bryk AS, Raudenbush SW (2002) Hierarchical linear models: applications and data analysis methods, 2nd edn. Sage, Newbury Park

Goodman LA (1960) On the exact variance of products. J Am Stat Assoc 55:708–713

Imai K, Keele L, Tingley D (2010) A general approach to causal mediation analysis. Psychol Methods 15(4):309–334

Kenny DA, Korchmaros JD, Bolger N (2003) Lower level mediation in multilevel models. Psychol Methods 8(2):115–128

Kreft IGG (1996) Are multilevel techniques necessary? An overview, including simulation studies. California State University, Los Angeles

Krull JL, MacKinnon DP (1999) Multilevel mediation modeling in group-based intervention studies. Eval Rev 23:418–444

Krull JL, MacKinnon DP (2001) Multilevel modeling of individual and group level mediated effects. Multivar Behav Res 36:249–277

Liu D, Zhang S, Wang L, Lee TW (2011) The effects of autonomy and empowerment on employee turnover: test of a multilevel model in teams. J Appl Psychol 96(6):305–1316

MacKinnon DP (2008) Introduction to statistical mediation analysis. Erlbaum, New York

MacKinnon DP, Lockwood CM, Hoffman JM, West SG, Sheets V (2002) A comparison of methods to test mediation and other intervening variable effects. Psychol Methods 7(1):83–104

MacKinnon DP, Lockwood CM, Williams J (2004) Confidence limits for the indirect effect: distribution of the product and resampling methods. Multivar Behav Res 39:99–128

Pituch KA, Stapleton LM (2008) The performance of methods to test upper-level mediation in the presence of nonnormal data. Multivar Behav Res 43:237–267

Pituch KA, Whittaker TA, Stapleton LM (2005) A comparison of methods to test for mediation in multisite experiments. Multivar Behav Res 40:1–23

Pituch KA, Stapleton LM, Kang JY (2006) A comparison of single sample and bootstrap methods to assess mediation in cluster randomized trials. Multivar Behav Res 41:367–400

Preacher KJ, Selig JP (2012) Advantages of monte carlo confidence intervals for indirect effects. Commun Methods Meas 6:77–98

Preacher KJ, Zyphur MJ, Zhang Z (2010) A general multilevel SEM framework for assessing multilevel mediation. Psychol Methods 15(3):209–233

Preacher KJ, Zhang Z, Zyphur MJ (2011) Alternative methods for assessing mediation in multilevel data: the advantages of multilevel SEM. Struct Equ Model 18:161–182

Raudenbush SW, Sampson R (1999) Assessing direct and indirect effects in multilevel designs with latent variables. Sociol Methods Res 28:123–153

Shrout PE, Bolger N (2002) Mediation in experimental and nonexperimental studies: new procedures and recommendations. Psychol Methods 7(4):422–446

Shrout PE, Fleiss JL (1979) Intraclass correlations: uses in assessing rater reliability. Psychol Bull 86(2):420–428

Sobel M (1982) Some new results on indirect effects and their standard errors in covariance structure models. Sociol Methodol 16:159–186

Vandenabeele W (2009) The mediating effect of job satisfaction and organizational commitment on self-reported performance: more robust evidence of the PSM-performance relationship. Int Rev Adm Sci 75(1):11–34

Zhang Z, Zyphur MJ, Preacher KJ (2009) Testing multilevel mediation using hierarchical linear models: problems and solutions. Organ Res Methods 12:695–719

Chapter 27
Mediation Analysis for Ordinal Outcome Variables

Hongyun Liu, Yunyun Zhang, and Fang Luo

Abstract This study compared four methods with respect to three factors, namely sample size, size of mediating effects, and the number of categories of the outcome variable, as based on the work of MacKinnon, to analyze the mediation effects for ordinal outcome variables. Mplus 6.0 was used to generate the simulated datasets, and each condition was replicated 500 times. Each dataset was analyzed using all of the four methods. The results revealed that, first, for the mediating model with a binary or ordinal outcome variable, the approach using Product of Coefficient always performed better than the approach using the Difference in Coefficients irrespective of whether the logistic regression was used or not. Second, the general linear regression produced a lower precision of estimates, poorer performance in statistical tests, and an underestimation of SE, compared with the logistic regression. In conclusion, the approach using the Product of Coefficients with the logistic regression is the recommended method for mediation analyses of ordinal data.

Keywords Mediation analysis • Ordinal variable • Monte Carlo simulation

27.1 Introduction

Mediating effects play an important role in psychology research and application. In previous decades, the mediating effect, which refers to how the independent variable (X) affects the dependent variable (Y) by affecting the mediating variable (M), rather than by having a direct casual effect, has attracted a lot of interest. The relationships of the three elements of this model are shown in Fig. 27.1b.

In Fig. 27.1a, c refers to the effect of Y on X without considering the mediating variable; e_I refers to the corresponding error; b represents the effect of Y on M; c' is the direct effect of Y on X when considering the mediating variable M; and e_M and e_Y are the error of M and Y, respectively. Based on the model demonstrated

H. Liu • Y. Zhang • F. Luo (✉)
National Innovation Center for Assessment of Basic Education Quality,
School of Psychology, Beijing Normal University, No. 19 Xin Jie Kou Wai Street,
Hai Dian District, Beijing 100875, China
e-mail: luof@bnu.edu.cn

R.E. Millsap et al. (eds.), *Quantitative Psychology Research*, Springer Proceedings in Mathematics & Statistics 89, DOI 10.1007/978-3-319-07503-7_27

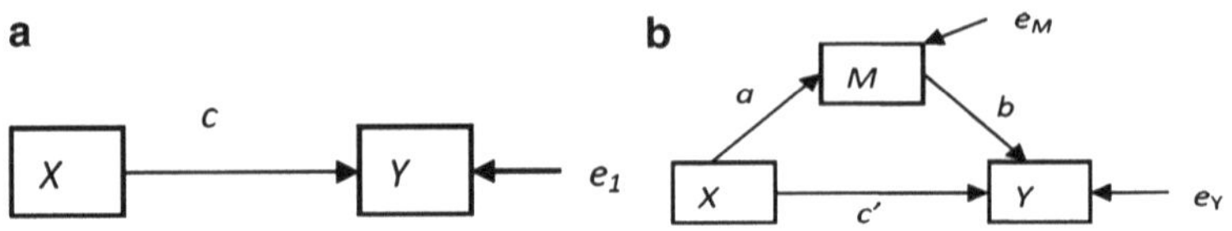

Fig. 27.1 Mediating effect model

in Fig. 27.1, the method and procedure for testing the mediating effect proposed by Baron and Kenny (1986) is still in use today. There are usually two methods to calibrate the mediating effect. One is Difference in Coefficient (or DC, for short), which computes $c - c'$ to represent the mediating effect and uses Freedman and Schatzkin's (1992) method to perform hypothesis testing. Another method is Product of Coefficient (or PC, for short), which regards the mediating effect as the product of two regression coefficients ($a*b$), the mediating variable on independent variable (a) and dependent variable on mediating variable (b). The Sobel test (Sobel 1982), Aroian test (Aroian 1994), and Goodman test (Goodman 1960) are widely used in testing the estimator $a*b$. For a dataset without missing values, general linear regression can be used to estimate the mediating effect for continuous variable, and in this condition, DC and PC have the same estimating value (MacKinnon et al. 1995). With the development of the structure equation model and new estimating methods, mediating effect analysis has been continually developed. MacKinnon et al. (1995) made a great contribution to the improvement of precision and accuracy of mediating effect estimation, and Baron and Kenny's method (1986) also has been improved in practical applications (Fang, Zhang and Qiu 2012; Wen et al. 2004; Zhao et al. 2010; Wen et al. 2012).

However, the former studies were restricted to the condition that the independent variables, mediating variables, and dependent variables are all continuous variables, and few studies focused on the condition that dependent variables are categorical or ordinal variables (Mackinnon et al. 2002). When the independent variable X is a categorical or ordinal variable, we can define a dummy variable to estimate the mediating effect, referring to the same procedure as used in the continuous variable condition. Nevertheless, if the dependent variable is categorical or ordinal and the independent variable is continuous, a logistic regression method should be used instead of general linear regression (Nelder and Wedderburn 1972; Pregibon 1981), and the scale of the regression coefficient should be converted to a Log scale. For the mediating effect analysis of binary data or the mix of binary and continuous data, researchers have come up with some solutions. Muthén (1984) proposed a computationally feasible three-stage estimator for any combination of observed variable types. This approach provides large-sample chi-square tests of fit and standard errors of estimates. Under the assumption of normal and binomial distribution, Winship and Mare (1983) built a probabilistic model for categorical observed variables using the threshold method and estimated the mediating effect with the general least squares method. Both methods have many theoretical assumptions and are not easy to apply to real data. Because of the different scaling of regression coefficients in different regression equations, MacKinnon and Dwyer (1993) proposed conducting a variance correction, i.e., standardization, to make the scaling of regression coefficients consistent with that of standardized predict variables. After that, MacKinnon et al. (2007) contrasted DC with PC, revealing different results and even large differences sometimes, and they also discussed the robustness of PC and made a recommendation. Iacobucci (2012) discussed the mediating effect for categorical outcome variables, emphasizing that researchers should focus on the character of the dependent variable and choose a proper estimation method for practical applications. In terms of application, Li et al. (2007) concluded that MacKinnon and Dwyer's Correction of PC is much more precise than DC when estimating the mediating effect of binary mediating variables.

Currently, almost all studies about the mediating effect concern continuous variables, although some researchers have extended this research to the context of non-continuous data, but such studies are relatively rare and the existing studies are mainly focused on binary outcome variables, while the mediating effects of outcome variables of ordinal variables with more than two categories require further study. In addition, whether the mediating effect analysis of ordinal data can be approximated as a continuous data procedure, as well as whether the number of categories of ordinal data will affect the results and some other relative issues, has not been discussed yet. Studies about other statistical methods, such as factor analysis, have revealed that if the number of categories of ordinal data is small (less than five), the estimated parameters, model fit indicators, and parameters' standard deviation will have a smaller bias with the increase in the number of categories when using maximum likelihood estimation, but when the number of categories is five or larger, the robust maximum likelihood estimation can obtain approximated unbiased parameters (Muthén and Kaplan 1985; Rhemtulla et al. 2012). Moreover, in the mediating effect analysis of ordinal outcome variables, there remains a question of whether the estimated parameters are more accurate with an increasing number of categories when using a continuous procedure.

This study will answer the following questions using a simulation method: (1) the nature of the contrast between logistic regression and general linear regression for the mediating effect model of ordinal outcome variables, (2) the nature of the contrast between DC and PC, and (3) whether the number of categories of the ordinal outcome variable will affect the mediating effect analysis results. In addition, the effect of sample size and the size of the mediating effect on the parameter estimation and statistics test will be explored. Finally, we will use a practical application example to illustrate the process of analyzing the ordinal outcome variable mediating effect model.

27.2 Mediating Effect Model with Ordinal Outcome Variable and Its Analysis Method

27.2.1 Mediating Effect Model with Binary Outcome Variable

For the mediating effect model shown in Fig. 27.1, several logistic regression equations can be established when the outcome variable is binary.

$$Y' = i_1 + cX + e_1 \tag{27.1}$$

$$Y'' = i_2 + c'X + bM + e_Y \tag{27.2}$$

$$M = i_3 + aX + e_M \tag{27.3}$$

The left terms of Eqs. (27.1) and (27.2) are not outcome variables but are the Logit odds of the two categories of the binary outcome variable (see Eqs. (27.4) and (27.5)).

$$Y' = LogitP\left(Y = 1\middle|X\right) = \ln\frac{P\left(Y = 1\middle|X\right)}{P\left(Y = 0\middle|X\right)} \tag{27.4}$$

$$Y'' = LogitP\left(Y = 1\middle|M,X\right) = \ln\frac{P\left(Y = 1\middle|M,X\right)}{P\left(Y = 0\middle|M,X\right)} \tag{27.5}$$

In mediating the effect model of a continuous outcome variable, the mediating effect is a*b or c - c'. However, in the Logistic regression model condition, b is the logit coefficient-unit and not on the same scale with a. Therefore, the mediating effect is not a*b. Similarly, in Eqs. (27.1) and (27.2), the conditional probabilities of the dependent variables are not affected by the same independent variables, and the regression coefficients c and c' are not on the same scale.

The regression coefficients of different equations are comparable, and the mediating effects are calculable when and only when the coefficients are on the same scale. According to the recommendation of MacKinnon and Dwyer (1993) and MacKinnon (2008), scale equalization of regression coefficients can be achieved through standardization of regression coefficients.

$$b^{std} = b \cdot \frac{SD(M)}{SD\left(Y''\right)} \tag{27.6}$$

$$c^{std} = c \cdot \frac{SD(X)}{SD(Y')} \tag{27.7}$$

$$c'^{std} = c' \cdot \frac{SD(X)}{SD(Y'')} \tag{27.8}$$

In the above equations, the left variables are marked with the superscript *std*, indicating the standardized regression coefficients converted from regression coefficients with logit units. $SD(X)$ and $SD(M)$ are available from the original data, and $SD(Y')$ and $SD(Y'')$ are available according to MacKinnon's method (2008).

$$\text{var}(Y') = c^2 \,\text{var}(X) + \frac{\pi^2}{3} \tag{27.9}$$

$$\text{var}(Y'') = c'^2 \,\text{var}(X) + b^2 \,\text{var}(M) + 2c'b\,\text{cov}(X, M) + \frac{\pi^2}{3} \tag{27.10}$$

In those equations, $\pi^2/3$ is the variance of the standard logistic distribution. According to Eqs. (27.6)–(27.9), we can calculate the standardized regression coefficients, and thus, the mediating effect and the proportions of the mediating effect can be obtained using either the DC or PC method.

27.2.2 *Mediating Effect Model of Ordinal Outcome Variable with Multi Categories*

In psychology studies, researchers often address ordinal data; typical examples are data obtained from Likert scales. A cumulative logistic regression can be applied to the analysis of those data when there are more than two categories for the ordinal outcome variable.

If the dependent variable Y has J categories, then there are J - 1 cumulative logistic regression models.

When $Y > j(0 \leq j < J - 1)$, then

$$Y' = LogitP(Y > j|X) = \ln \frac{P(Y > j|X)}{1\text{-}P(Y > j|X)} = i_{1j} + cX + e_1 \tag{27.11}$$

$$Y'' = Logit(Y > j|M, X) = \ln \frac{P(Y > j|M, X)}{1\text{-}P(Y > j|M, X)} = i_{2j} + c'X + bM + e_Y \tag{27.12}$$

$$M = i_3 + aX + e_M \tag{27.13}$$

X and M are continuous variables, and so Eqs. (27.13) and (27.3) are the same. In Eqs. (27.11) and (27.12), as c, b, and c' will not vary with different j values, the mediating effect will not be affected by the number of categories of ordinal outcome variables, and its standardized process is the same as with binary outcome variables.

27.2.3 Test of Mediating Effect of Ordinal Outcome Variable and Interval Estimation

The standard errors corresponding to standardized regression coefficients are as follows (MacKinnon 2008):

$$SE\left(b^{std}\right) = SE(b) \cdot \frac{SD(M)}{SD\left(Y''\right)} \tag{27.14}$$

$$SE\left(c^{std}\right) = SE(c) \cdot \frac{SD(X)}{SD\left(Y'\right)} \tag{27.15}$$

$$SE\left(c'^{std}\right) = SE\left(c'\right) \cdot \frac{SD(X)}{SD\left(Y''\right)} \tag{27.16}$$

For the PC method, ab^{std} is used to estimate the mediating effect, which is equal to that obtained by multiplying a^{std} by b^{std}, and Sobel's equation (1982) is used to obtain the standard error of ab^{std}, $SE\left(ab^{std}\right) = \sqrt{\left(a^{std}\right)^2\left[SE\left(b^{std}\right)\right]^2 + \left(b^{std}\right)^2\left[SE\left(a^{std}\right)\right]^2}$. A significant mediating effect can be decided by using the Sobel test, whose test statistic is $z = ab/SE(ab^{std})$, under the assumption of normality, and the confidence interval of the mediating effect is $[ab^{std} - z_{\alpha/2} \times SE(ab^{std}), ab^{std} + z_{\alpha/2} \times SE(ab^{std})]$.

For the DC method, we use the standardized regression coefficients c^{std} and c'^{std} to estimate the mediating effect, namely $c^{std} - c'^{std}$, and Freedman and Schatzkin's method (1992) to calculate the standard error of $c^{std} - c'^{std}$, with $SE\left(c^{std}\text{-}c'^{std}\right) = \sqrt{\left(SE\left(c^{std}\right)\right)^2 + \left[SE\left(c'^{std}\right)\right]^2 \text{-} 2SE\left(c^{std}\right)SE\left(c'^{std}\right)\sqrt{1\text{-}r_{XM}^2}}$. The test statistic is $t_{n\text{-}2} = \frac{c^{std}\text{-}c'^{std}}{SE\left(c^{std}\text{-}c'^{std}\right)}$. Under the assumption of normality, the confidence interval of the mediating effect is $[c^{std} - c'^{std} - t_{\alpha/2} \times SE(c^{std} - c'^{std}), c^{std} - c'^{std} + t_{\alpha/2} \times SE(c^{std} - c'^{std})]$.

27.3 Simulation Study

27.3.1 Simulation Design

In the simulation study, we mainly consider four factors: number of categories of ordinal outcome variable, sample size, mediating effect size, and analysis method.

(1) The number of categories (J) of the outcome variable has three levels: 2, 3, and 5. In the case of 2 categories, it follows a binomial distribution, and in the case of 3 and 5 categories, it follows a multinomial distribution. Independent variables and mediating variables are assumed to have standard normal distributions.
(2) The sample size has 5 levels: 50, 100, 200, 500, and 1,000.
(3) Mediating effect size has seven levels: 0, 0.0196, 0.0546, 0.0826, 0.1521, 0.2301, and 0.1521. Following MacKinnon, we investigated four values (0, 0.14, 0.39, and 0.59) for the three regression coefficients a, b, and c', which produces $4^3 = 64$ possible combinations. The combination $a = b = c' = 0.59$ produces an unfeasible mediating effect size. Each of the 63 other combinations produces a mediating effect size equal to one of the six levels. Thus, the 63 feasible combinations were aggregated to seven levels.
(4) The performances of PC and DC with the logistic regression (or LR, for short) and the general linear regression (or GR, for short) analyses are compared. Therefore, there are four analysis methods, which are DCLR, PCLR, DCGR, and PCGR.
(5) The simulation study generated $3 \times 5 \times 63 = 945$ groups of data and was repeated 500 times for each condition. For each group of data, we use four types of analysis methods to estimate the mediating effect. The simulation data's generation and analysis are both completed in Mplus 6.0, using SPSS to clean data and calculate relative indicators.

27.3.2 Indicators for Evaluation

The indicators for evaluating different methods mainly include the following: precision of estimation of mediating effect [including the bias of estimation and root mean square error (RMSE)], precision of estimation of mediating effect standard error, confidence interval recovery rate, statistical power and type I error rate.

27.4 Simulation Results

27.4.1 Model Convergences

The convergence rate was 100 % for PCGR and DCGR and between 96 and 100 % for the methods PCLR and DCLR. In some circumstances, for example, when the sample size is small (50) or the size of the mediating effect is large (b and c' both are 0.59), the simulation does not converge, but overall, the rate of non-convergence is very low. It is noteworthy that as the number of ordinal outcome variables category increases, the rate of non-convergence displays an increasing trend when the sample size is small.

27.4.2 Precision of Estimation of Mediating Effect

The precision of estimation of the mediating effect is mainly reflected by relative bias of estimation and RMSE. The relative bias is the result of a difference between the estimation value and true value divided by the true value. A positive relative bias indicates an overestimation of the true value, and a negative bias indicates an underestimation. The RMSE is mainly used to evaluate different models, the value of which reflects the ability of the method to estimate proper parameters, namely the ability to be close to the true values of this model. A smaller RMSE indicates a smaller difference between the estimation and true value and a smaller standard error. The relative bias and RMSE are defined by $Bias = \frac{1}{R}\sum_{r=1}^{R}\left(\frac{E-T}{T}\right)$ and $RMSE = \sqrt{\frac{1}{R}\sum_{r=1}^{R}(E-T)^2}$, respectively; R denotes the number of replications; E is the estimated mediating effect; and T is the true mediating effect.

For each group of data, four analysis methods were conducted. The biases of the different estimation methods are shown in Fig. 27.2a–c. Because PCGR and DCGR obtain the same results, the bias of PCGR is only shown here.

Figure 27.2a–c shows that the relative bias of the mediating effects is negative overall, and the mediating effects are underestimated to varying degrees for all methods. However, a smaller relative bias is yielded using the proper methods. For example, for binary outcome variables, three methods result in the largest difference. PCLR has the minimum relative bias (close to zero), followed by DCLR, and PCGR has the maximum bias. The difference between the three methods decreases with the increase in the number of categories of the outcome variable, and when the number is 5, the difference is nearly 0.

The relative bias increases with the increase in the mediating effect and is slightly affected by sample size. The RMSE indicates that for binary and 3 categories of outcome variables, PCLR will obtain the highest precision, whereas DCLR and PCGR are relatively low. Figure 27.2d–f shows how the RMSE of each method

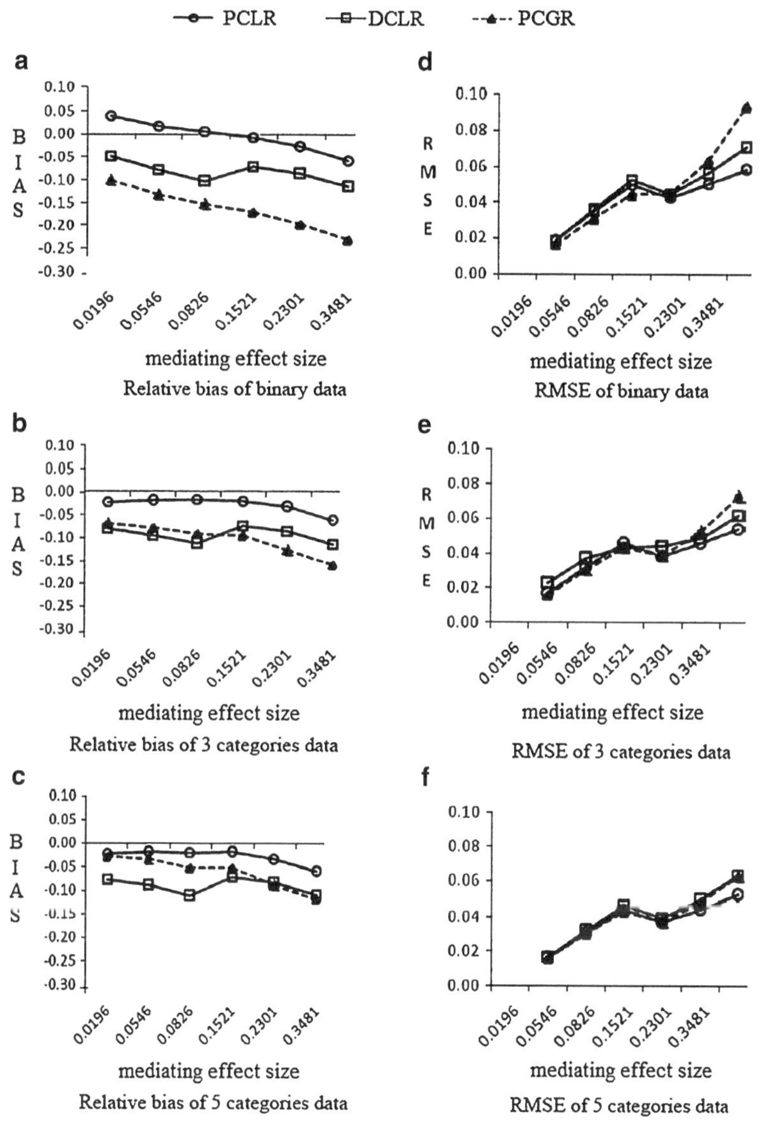

Fig. 27.2 Relative bias and RMSE of different methods

varies with the mediating effect size. Three methods all display the trend of RMSE increase with the increase in the mediating effect. For the binary outcome variables, the difference between *PCLR* and PCGR is small when the mediating effect is small. However, with the increasing mediating effect, the RMSE of *PCGR* gradually becomes greater than that of *PCLR*. Furthermore, the estimation of PC is slightly better than DC regardless of the condition.

Table 27.1 RMSE of estimated mediating effect

	Binary			Three categories			Five categories		
Sample size	PCLR	DCLR	PCGR	PCLR	DCLR	PCGR	PCLR	DCLR	PCGR
50	0.070	0.072	0.062	0.065	0.067	0.062	0.062	0.064	0.062
100	0.047	0.048	0.044	0.042	0.044	0.042	0.041	0.043	0.041
200	0.033	0.035	0.033	0.030	0.032	0.030	0.029	0.031	0.030
500	0.020	0.023	0.025	0.019	0.021	0.021	0.018	0.021	0.020
1,000	0.015	0.018	0.021	0.014	0.017	0.017	0.013	0.016	0.015

The RMSE shown in Fig. 27.2f is less than the values in Fig. 27.2d and e, which demonstrates that precision of the mediating effect estimation is affected by the number of categories of the outcome variable, such that the greater the number of categories, the better the parameter will be estimated. Finally, in Fig. 27.2f, when there are five categories, the RMSE of the GR analysis is nearly the same as the LR analysis.

The relative bias remains stable as the sample size varies, whereas the RMSE has a clearly decreasing trend with the increasing sample size (see Table 27.1). Even if we use PCLR, the RMSE is still very large when the sample size is small and is even larger than the RMSE of PCGR when the sample size is smaller than 200.

Therefore, for ordinal outcome data, the sample size should be larger if a more precise estimation is needed. Typically, when the sample size is larger than 200, the precision of LR analysis is superior to that of the GR analysis, especially for binary outcome data.

27.4.3 Precision of Estimation of Mediating Effect Standard Error

The standard error of the mediating effect is very important for the testing of the mediating effect and interval estimation. The relative bias is calculated to illustrate the precision of the estimation of the mediating effect standard error. For each condition, the standard deviation of 500 estimated mediating effect values (we regard this value as the true value of the standard error, denoted by T_{SE}) and the mean of the estimated standard error of the mediating effect (denoted by M_{SE}) were calculated under each condition. The relative bias of the standard error is $(M_{SE} - T_{SE})/T_{SE}$, which is concretely shown in Appendix 1. In each condition, regardless if LR or GR analysis was performed, the relative bias of PC is much lower than DC, and the relative bias of DC is below 0 for each condition, proving that DC underestimates the standard error of the mediating effect. Furthermore, the relative biases of two regression methods are very close in all conditions, which demonstrates that the bias of the standard error of the mediating effect is not large.

27.4.4 Confidence Interval Coverage Rate

We built a confidence interval by using an *estimated value* $\pm 1.96 \times$ *standard error*. The CI coverage rate is defined as the proportion of the confidence interval covered true value in 500 replications, which can reflect the precision of the estimation of the mediating effect to some extent. The CI coverage rates of the different methods are shown in Appendix 2. When using LR analysis, the CI coverage rate of the PC is nearly 95 % in most conditions. Moreover, the CI coverage rate is not affected by the mediating effect, sample size and categories of outcome variable, which indicates that PCLR is the best analysis method.

However, the CI coverage rate of DC is approximately 70 % and significantly lower than PC in all conditions. In association with the estimation precision discussed above, the results suggest that the low CI coverage rate is related to the underestimation of the standard error of DC. The CI coverage rate of PCGR is significantly smaller than that of PCLR; however, a smaller gap occurs as the categories increase.

Briefly, PCLR is the priority method based on CI coverage rate. Similar to the precision discussed above, the difference in the CI coverage rate of PCLR and PCGR decreases as the number of categories increases.

27.4.5 Statistical Power

When the true value of the mediating effect is not 0, the probability of the estimated mediating effect being non-zero reflects the statistical power. In the 500 repeat times of each condition, the proportion of significant test results (0.05) is called the power of this condition, which is described specifically in Appendix 3. As the mediating effect and sample size increase, the powers of both the LR and GR analyses increase. In addition, the difference in power of PCLR and PCGR is small. However, the power of DCGR is slightly higher than that of DCLR, especially in a small sample or small mediating effect condition. Compared with PC, the power of DC is slightly higher, which may be due to the underestimation of standard error. Moreover, the power has a slight increasing trend with an increasing category number change. The underestimations of both the standard error and mediating effect by GR analysis may result in a non-significant difference between the powers of PC and DC. Therefore, it cannot be rashly decided that the two estimation methods are the same.

27.4.6 Type I Error

When the true value of the mediating effect is 0 and the estimated mediating effect is significant, then a type I error occurs statistically. After 500 repeats for each condition, the proportion of results having a type I error is called the type I error rate.

In this study, there are three different conditions when the true value of the mediating effect is 0: (1) $a = b = 0$; (2) $a = 0$, $b \neq 0$; and (3) $a \neq 0$, $b = 0$. The type I error rates are shown in Appendix 4. Overall, the type I error rate of PCLR is 0.01270 and 0.01299 for PCGR, and the difference is less than 0.05 (level of significance). Comparatively, the type I error rate of DCLR is 0.11310 and 0.14530 for DCGR. They are slightly higher than for PC, which is consistent with the conclusion that DC underestimates the standard error. The type I error rate of PC is much lower than that of DC in each condition. In addition, for varying sample sizes, the type I error rates of PCLR and PCGR are very close, whereas the type I error rate of DCLR is less than that of DCGR. For the condition $a = b = 0$, the type I error rates of all methods are lower than for the $a = 0$, $b \neq 0$ or $a \neq 0$, $b = 0$ condition, and the type I error rate is maximum when $a = 0$, $b \neq 0$.

27.5 Practical Application and Concrete Procedures

We will use the following example of a practical application to illustrate the analysis steps of the mediating effect of ordinal outcome variables. Data for the example were drawn from Hair et al. (2006).

Research Question: In research examining the impact factors of customers' buying behavior in consumer psychology, the participants were asked to fill in rating scales for products' quality and satisfaction with the services of the company HBAT, and then the researchers recorded whether the participants bought the products, with the aim of studying the relation between customers' buying behaviors (Y), quality of products (X) and satisfaction of customers (M).

In this research, we assumed Y to be the dependent variable in which $y = 1$ stands for buying the product and $y = 0$ not buying; X is the independent variable and M is the mediating variable, both of which are continuous.

Step one: regression analysis

Three regressions need to be performed in this step:

1. To perform logistic regression of dependent variable Y on independent variable X, obtain the estimated value of c and standard error SEc. In this case, $c = 1.058$, and $SEc = 0.217$.
2. To perform a general linear regression of the dependent variable M on the independent variable X, obtain the estimated value of a and the accompanying standard error SEa. In this case, $a = 0.415$, and $SEa = 0.075$.
3. To perform logistic regression of the dependent variable Y on independent variables X and M, obtain the estimated value of b and c' and the accompanying standard errors SEb and SEc'. In this case, $b = 0.959$, $SEb = 0.283$, $c' = 0.755$, and $SEc' = 0.221$.

Step two: standardization

In this step, the regression coefficients obtained in step one are converted to a unified scale using a standardized method.

1. First, calculate the standard deviations, variances of X, M, Y' and Y'', and the covariance of X and M. In this case, $SD(X) = 1.396$, $SD(M) = 1.192$, $Var(X) = 1.950$, $Var(M) = 1.420$, and $Cov(X, M) = 0.809$. Using Eq. (27.9), calculate the variances of Y' and Y'', $Var(Y') = 5.473$, $Var(Y'') = 6.879$, $SD(Y') = 2.339$ and $SD(Y'') = 2.623$.
2. Next, standardize the regression coefficients through Eqs. (27.6)–(27.8). $b^{std} = 0.436$, $c^{std} = 0.631$, and $c'^{std} = 0.402$ in this case. For a, the standardized coefficient is calculated in a similar way, and it is equal to the standardized solution in SPSS.

$$a^{std} = a \cdot \frac{SD(X)}{SD(M)} = 0.415 \times \frac{1.396}{1.192} = 0.486$$

3. Calculate the standard errors of standardized regression coefficients using Eqs. (27.14)–(27.16). In this case, $SE(b^{std}) = 0.129$, $SE(c^{std}) = 0.130$, $SE(c'^{std}) = 0.118$, and $SE(a^{std}) = 0.088$.

Step three: calculation, testing, and interpretation of the mediating effect and standard error.

The standardized mediating effect is $ab^{std} = 0.486 \times 0.436 = 0.212$. In this study, PCLR was proved to be the optimal method and the standard error is $SE\left(ab^{std}\right) = \sqrt{(b^{std})^2 (SE\,(a^{std}))^2 + (a^{std})^2 (SE\,(b^{std}))^2} = 0.073$.

Using the Sobel test, $Z = 0.212/0.073 = 2.904$, the $2.904 > 1.96$ proves that the quality of products significantly affects customers' buying behaviors as mediated by product satisfaction. The 95 % confidence interval is (0.069, 0.355), and the proportion of the mediating effect in the total effect is $\frac{ab^{std}}{ab^{std} + c'^{std}} = 0.345$.

27.6 Discussion

In the mediation model, if the dependent variable is ordinal, then the logistic regression should be the best analysis method. If the general linear regression method is applied mistakenly, underestimations of the mediating effect and standard error and incorrect estimation of the confidence interval will occur. Thus, for the mediation model with an ordinal outcome variable, first, a logistic regression is chosen to obtain regression coefficients, and then a standardization procedure is performed to convert the coefficients to a unified scale to keep them comparable and computable.

Based on the results, we recommend PCLR as the optimal analysis method when dealing with a mediating effect model with an ordinal outcome variable.

This research examined the difference in two analysis methods: DC and PC. Regardless of whether LR or GR analysis was used, the result trends were consistent. That is, for all indicators, including the confidence interval coverage probability and type I error rate, PC was superior to DC, which is consistent with previous conclusions when the dependent variable is continuous (MacKinnon et al's. 2002). The reason for this finding is rooted in the two separate methods of representing the standard error of the mediating effect. Furthermore, the calculation method of the standard error of DC does not consider the effect of the mediating variable on the dependent variable sufficiently and directly, resulting in an underestimation of the standard error and a false higher statistical power than the PC method. On the contrary, PC's advantage lies in a more precise estimation and a lower type I error rate. Moreover, the confidence interval coverage rates of PCLR are approximately 95 %, consistent with MacKinnon (2008). These results indicate another significant advantage of PC.

In addition, in testing of the power and type I error rate with each condition, we find that the test of significance of the mediating effect of DC is more inclined to be reflected by the relation between the mediating variable and dependent variable, that is, for the fixed mediating effect ab, the larger b will more likely be significant, resulting in a higher statistical power and type I error rate, which is not the case with PC. For example, in a mediation model with a three-category outcome variable, if the mediating effect is 0.0826, then we have two alternative conditions, $a = 0.14$ and $b = 0.59$ or $a = 0.59$ and $b = 0.14$, and for a sample of 500, the statistical power is 0.93 and 0.50, respectively, which makes it easy to say that a higher b will lead to a higher power. Similar to MacKinnon et al.'s (2002) conclusion about continuous outcome variables, the type I error rate of the condition when $a = 0$ and $b \neq 0$ is always higher than when $b = 0$ and $a \neq 0$. The gap increases as the category number increases.

The differences between LR and GR analyses become increasingly smaller as the number of categories of the dependent variable increases. This indicates that the bias of GR analysis is too small to notice when the number of categories increases to a higher level. In this study, the confidence interval coverage rates of LR and GR analyses are 95 and 93 %, respectively, and the type I error rates are both approximately 0.014 when the number of categories is 5. Acceptable indicators can be expected with the increasing of categories. With the increasing number of categories, the ordinal data resemble continuous data more and thus better fit the assumption of ordinal linear regression. However, although this study proves that when the number of categories is 5 or larger, the GR analysis is appropriate, researchers still need to be careful to choose an appropriate method to obtain a suitable interpretation conveniently (Rucker et al. 2011). For instance, we can obtain the Logit odds of each category and intercept the difference in the categories by LR analysis. Therefore, if researchers are interested in the effect of the independent variable on Logit odds, cumulative logistic regression needs to be used.

In a small sample, the LR analysis results have difficult converging, especially when the mediating effect is large. LR analysis has obvious advantages with a larger sample, which implies that a larger sample is needed than for GR analysis if a more stable estimation is acquired. Based on this study, a sample size of at least 200 is suggested

Finally, when testing the mediating effect, the standardization of the standard error and mediation effect should be performed first. Complete standardization and partial standardization are two optional methods. In different software, the procedures have small differences. In SPSS or SAS, some calculations need to be performed manually or using Hayes syntax (see Appendix 5, from http://www.afhayes.com/). In Mplus, the STDYX procedure can obtain the standardized solutions directly using complete standardization, and it is more convenient and transplantable to a multivariable situation.

27.7 Limitations and Expectations

In this research, we compared several mediating effect analysis methods and explored the factors affecting them. The related tests and interval estimation method for each analysis method are not unique. With PC, for example, the method to estimate standard error can be based on a first-order method, $s_{First} = \sqrt{\widehat{a}^2 s_{\widehat{b}}^2 + \widehat{b}^2 s_{\widehat{a}}^2}$; second-order method, $s_{Second} = \sqrt{\widehat{a}^2 s_{\widehat{b}}^2 + \widehat{b}^2 s_{\widehat{a}}^2 + s_{\widehat{a}}^2 s_{\widehat{b}}^2}$; and unbiased method, $s_{Unbiased} = \sqrt{\widehat{a}^2 s_{\widehat{b}}^2 + \widehat{b}^2 s_{\widehat{a}}^2 - s_{\widehat{a}}^2 s_{\widehat{b}}^2}$. The method to estimate the interval can be based on a traditional normality assumption, the distribution of the product bootstrap and a Markov Chain Monte Carlo method. In addition, this study only used first-order standard error estimation methods and interval estimation methods with normality assumptions. Both methods are traditional, and thus, the other methods mentioned above need to be further investigated. In practical applications, researchers should be cautious when choosing methods to ensure superior interpretable results. Yuan and MacKinnon (2009) and Fang and Zhang (2012) make some suggestions in choosing interval estimation methods. Preacher and Kelley (2011) and Fang et al. (2012) both mention that a full report about the mediating effect should include the size of the mediating effect, in addition to hypothesis tests and parameter estimation.

In addition, only the ordinal dependent variable is considered, and the independent variable and mediating variable are ordinal is not included in this research. If the independent variable is ordinal, a dummy variable can be converted from the independent variable. As a result, ordinal linear regression can be applied to the analysis of the mediating effect. If the mediating variable is ordinal, a logistic regression of the mediating variable on the independent variable can be applied first, and the regression coefficient standardization procedure is the same as the method used in this article, with the conversion of the mediating variable to a dummy variable followed by finally applying general linear regression of the dependent variable to the mediating variable and using PC or DC to estimate the mediating effect and interval. Researchers should choose the appropriate analysis method, based first of all on the variable properties.

Conclusions
When using a mediating effect model, with an outcome variable that is binary or more categories, LR analysis should be used. If GR analysis is applied, biased results will be obtained, such as a lower precision for the estimated mediating effect, a lower confidence interval coverage rate and an underestimation of the standard error.

PC and DC provide different estimation results, and PC is more suitable for the mediating effect model with an ordinal outcome variable.

If the number of categories of the ordinal outcome variable is large (5 or more), the differences between the LR and GR analyses are small, and therefore, GR analysis can also be applied. Researchers should choose analysis methods considering sample size, size of the mediating effect and some other factors.

Appendix 1: Relative Bias and Standard Error of Estimated Mediating Effect

		Binary				3 categories				5 categories			
		LR		GR		LR		GR		LR		GR	
		PC	DC	FC	DC	PC	DC	PC	DC	PC	DC	PC	DC
Size of mediation effect	0.000	0.038	−0.385	0.038	−0.370	0.026	−0.390	0.029	−0.385	0.031	−0.388	0.034	−0.383
	0.0196	−0.014	−0.331	−0.010	−0.349	0.015	−0.339	0.010	−0.348	−0.003	−0.378	0.001	−0.377
	0.546	−0.024	−0.372	−0.018	−0.374	−0.007	−0.374	−0.006	−0.380	−0.007	−0.388	−0.006	−0.393
	0.0826	−0.018	−0.384	−0.012	−0.374	0.002	−0.367	0.006	−0.367	−0.003	−0.371	−0.001	−0.377
	0.1521	−0.019	−0.293	−0.003	−0.278	0.009	−0.326	0.011	−0.300	0.007	−0.359	0.010	−0.333
	0.2301	0.000	−0.306	0.019	−0.266	0.035	−0.324	0.033	−0.288	0.026	−0.354	0.027	−0.313
	0.3481	−0.002	−0.237	0.030	−0.181	0.022	−0.284	0.039	−0.219	0.014	−0.320	0.028	−0.258
Sample size	50	−0.004	−0.374	0.004	−0.352	0.007	−0.365	0.011	−0.353	0.001	−0.380	0.035	−0.368
	100	0.025	−0.342	0.030	−0.327	0.034	−0.357	0.037	−0.349	0.037	−0.368	0.039	−0.358
	200	0.008	−0.358	0.017	−0.343	0.026	−0.358	0.027	−0.350	0.023	−0.371	0.023	−0.363
	500	0.017	−0.355	0.022	−0.343	0.025	−0.360	0.027	−0.350	0.028	−0.367	0.032	−0.355
	1,000	0.001	−0.355	0.009	−0.343	−0.002	−0.381	0.000	−0.371	−0.003	−0.393	−0.002	−0.381
Overall		0.009	−0.357	0.016	−0.342	0.018	−0.364	0.021	−0.355	0.017	−0.376	0.020	−0.365

Appendix 2: Confidence Interval Recovery Rate (%)

		Binary				Three categories				Five categories			
		LR		GR		LR		GR		LR		GR	
		PC	DC	PC	DC	PC	DC	PC	DC	PC	DC	PC	DC
Size of mediation effect	0.000	97.32	67.00	97.28	71.23	97.09	66.72	97.07	70.39	97.12	66.85	97.11	70.15
	0.0196	92.26	75.37	88.76	71.95	92.45	74.36	91.36	73.39	92.25	72.36	92.23	72.84
	0.0546	94.06	70.74	90.37	68.94	94.38	69.55	93.55	70.52	94.35	68.72	94.25	70.23
	0.0826	94.68	66.85	90.85	66.68	95.14	66.82	94.24	69.38	94.96	66.80	94.72	69.29
	0.1521	93.25	76.43	75.44	59.46	93.85	74.27	88.42	72.19	93.85	72.35	91.86	75.74
	0.2301	93.71	71.71	64.13	48.03	94.42	69.29	80.60	62.34	94.17	67.98	86.05	68.02
	0.3481	89.96	64.12	42.47	32.89	89.83	60.52	62.01	47.41	89.69	58.34	73.13	56.95
Sample size	50	95.78	74.31	93.60	74.56	95.45	72.32	94.51	74.20	95.39	71.33	94.90	73.94
	100	95.73	72.48	92.01	71.06	95.10	70.64	93.55	72.21	94.97	70.11	94.39	72.56
	100	94.61	70.02	88.66	66.95	95.45	69.82	93.24	70.61	95.53	69.21	94.27	71.45
	500	95.29	66.59	83.53	59.40	91.56	66.29	90.23	64.79	95.48	66.00	92.57	66.63
	1,000	94.51	61.85	76.40	52.47	95.02	61.38	86.43	60.51	94.89	60.97	90.14	63.80
Overall		95.18	69.04	86.84	64.89	95.31	68.09	91.59	68.46	95.25	67.52	93.25	69.68

Appendix 3: Power of Statistics

		Binary				3 categories				5 categories			
		LR		GR		LR		GR		LR		GR	
		PC	DC	PC	DC	PC	DC	PC	DC	PC	DC	PC	DC
Size of mediation effect	0.0196	0.323	0.512	0.324	0.551	0.353	0.557	0.352	0.583	0.369	0.584	0.369	0.610
	0.0546	0.511	0.689	0.511	0.721	0.532	0.712	0.534	0.743	0.549	0.731	0.547	0.760
	0.0826	0.548	0.699	0.548	0.729	0.572	0.718	0.571	0.747	0.586	0.731	0.584	0.758
	0.1521	0.865	0.940	0.864	0.955	0.887	0.959	0.885	0.965	0.898	0.966	0.895	0.973
	0.2301	0.935	0.968	0.935	0.976	0.948	0.978	0.946	0.982	0.956	0.983	0.953	0.986
	0.3481	0.992	0.997	0.993	0.998	0.994	0.999	0.994	0.999	0.995	0.999	0.995	1.000
Sample size	50	0.339	0.544	0.342	0.586	0.369	0.568	0.367	0.598	0.383	0.583	0.383	0.619
	100	0.517	0.680	0.520	0.713	0.526	0.697	0.525	0.725	0.538	0.711	0.537	0.739
	200	0.648	0.789	0.648	0.818	0.679	0.822	0.680	0.845	0.694	0.842	0.694	0.860
	500	0.884	0.937	0.883	0.948	0.909	0.961	0.908	0.971	0.922	0.959	0.920	0.978
	1,000	0.989	0.996	0.989	0.997	0.996	0.998	0.996	0.999	0.997	0.999	0.997	0.999
Overall		0.676	0.789	0.677	0.812	0.696	0.809	0.695	0.827	0.707	0.821	0.706	0.839

Appendix 4: Type I Error Rate

		Binary				3 categories				5 categories			
		LR		GR		LR		GR		LR		GR	
		PC	DC	PC	DC	PC	DC	PC	DC	PC	DC	PC	DC
Situations	$a=b=0$	0.000	0.032	0.000	0.027	0.000	0.061	0.000	0.029	0.001	0.070	0.000	0.031
	$a=0, b\neq 0$	0.015	0.226	0.015	0.300	0.019	0.246	0.019	0.314	0.020	0.253	0.020	0.319
	$b=0, a\neq 0$	0.014	0.027	0.015	0.030	0.016	0.031	0.016	0.032	0.014	0.032	0.014	0.031
Sample size	50	0.008	0.102	0.009	0.106	0.009	0.060	0.009	0.111	0.009	0.120	0.009	0.115
	100	0.010	0.115	0.010	0.135	0.012	0.254	0.012	0.125	0.012	0.119	0.012	0.127
	200	0.016	0.115	0.017	0.142	0.016	0.242	0.016	0.155	0.015	0.142	0.015	0.155
	500	0.014	0.119	0.013	0.164	0.015	0.157	0.015	0.185	0.016	0.144	0.016	0.187
	1,000	0.016	0.115	0.016	0.179	0.022	0.104	0.022	0.187	0.022	0.136	0.021	0.187

Appendix 5: Syntax by Hayes (from http://www.afhayes.com/)

```
TITLE: this is an example of a Mediation in Categorical Data Analysis
DATA: FILE IS data.dat;
VARIABLE: NAMES ARE id x m y;
        CATEGORICAL ARE y;
ANALYSIS:
      ESTIMATOR = ML;
MODEL: y on x m;
        m on x;
OUTPUT: standardize
```

References

Aroian LA (1994) The probability function of the product of two normally distributed variables. Ann Math Stat 18:265–271

Baron RM, Kenny DA (1986) The moderator–mediator variable distinction in social psychological research: conceptual, strategic, and statistical considerations. J Pers Soc Psychol 51(6):1173–1182

Fang J, Zhang MQ (2012) Assessing point and interval estimation for the mediating effect: distribution of the product, nonparametric bootstrap and Markov Chain Monte Carlo methods. Acta Psychol Sin 44(10):1408–1420

Fang J, Zhang MQ, Qiu HZ (2012) Mediation analysis and effect size measurement: retrospect and prospect. Psychol Dev Educ 1:105–111

Freedman LS, Schatzkin A (1992) Sample size for studying intermediate endpoints within intervention trials of observational studies. Am J Epidemiol 136:1148–1159

Goodman LA (1960) On the exact variance of products. J Am Stat Assoc 55:708–713

Hair JF Jr, Black WC, Babin BJ, Tatham RL (2006) Multivariate data analysis, 6th edn. Pearson/Prentice-Hall, Upper Saddle River

Iacobucci D (2012) Mediation analysis and categorical variables: the final frontier. J Consum Psychol. doi:10.1016/j.jcps.2012.03.006

Li Y, Schneider JA, Bennett DA (2007) Estimation of the mediating effect with a binary mediator. Stat Med 26:3398–3414

MacKinnon DP (2008) Introduction to statistical mediation analysis. London Lawrence Erlbaum Associates, New York

MacKinnon DP, Dwyer JH (1993) Estimating mediated effects in prevention studies. Eval Rev 17:144–158

MacKinnon DP, Warsi G, Dwyer JH (1995) A simulation study of mediated effect measures. Multivariate Behav Res 30:41–62

MacKinnon DP, Lockwood CM, Hoffman JM, West SG, Sheets VA (2002) Comparison of methods to test mediation and other intervening variable effects. Psychol Methods 7(1):83–104

MacKinnon DP, Lockwood CM, Brown CH, Wang W, Hoffman JM (2007) The intermediate endpoint effect in logistic and probit regression. Clin Trials 4:499

Muthén B (1984) A general structural equation model with dichotomous, ordered categorical, and continuous latent variable indicators. Psychometrika 49:115–132

Muthén B, Kaplan D (1985) A comparison of some methodologies for the factor analysis of non-normal Likert variables. Br J Math Stat Psychol 38:171–189

Nelder JA, Wedderburn RWM (1972) Generalized linear models. J R Stat Soc A 135:370–384

Preacher KJ, Kelley K (2011) Effect size measures for mediation models: quantitative strategies for communicating indirect effects. Psychol Methods 16:93–115

Pregibon D (1981) Logistic regression diagnostics. Ann Stat 9:705–724

Rhemtulla M, Brosseau-Liard P, Savalei V (2012) How many categories is enough to treat data as continuous? A comparison of robust continuous and categorical SEM estimation methods under a range of non-ideal situations. Psychol Methods. Advance online publication. doi:10.1037/a0029315

Rucker DD, Preacher KJ, Tormala ZL, Petty RE (2011) Mediation analysis in social psychology: current practices and new recommendations. Soc Pers Psychol Compass 5(6):359–371

Sobel ME (1982) Asymptotic confidence intervals for indirect effects in structural equation models. In: Leinhardt S (ed) Sociological methodology 1982. American Sociological Association, Washington, pp 290–312

Wen ZL, Chang L, Hau KT, Liu HY (2004) Testing and application of the mediating effects. Acta Psychol Sin 36(5):614–620

Wen ZL, Liu HY, Hau KT (2012) Analysis of moderating and mediating effects. Educational Science Publishing House, Beijing

Winship C, Mare R (1983) Structural equations and path analysis for discrete data. Am J Sociol 89:54–110

Yuan Y, MacKinnon DP (2009) Bayesian mediation analysis. Psychol Methods 14(4):301–322

Zhao X, Lynch JG, Chen Q (2010) Reconsidering Baron and Kenny: myths and truths about mediation analysis. J Consum Res 37:197–206

Chapter 28
Comparison of Nested Models for Multiply Imputed Data

Yoonsun Jang, Zhenqiu (Laura) Lu, and Allan Cohen

Abstract The multiple imputation (MI) is one of the most popular and efficient methods to deal with missing data. For MI, the estimated parameters from imputed data sets are combined based on the Rubin's rule; however, there are no general suggestions on how to combine the log-likelihood functions. The log-likelihood is a key component for model fit statistics. This study compares different ways to combine likelihood functions when MI is used for hierarchically nested models. Specifically, three ways for pooling likelihoods and four weights for combined log-likelihood value suggested by Kientoff are compared. Simulation studies are conducted to investigate the performance of these methods under six conditions, such as different sample sizes, different missing rates, and different numbers of parameters. We imputed missing data using the multiple imputation by chained equations for MI.

28.1 Introduction

Missing data are almost inevitable in social science research, especially when data are collected through surveys, tests, or questionnaires (e.g., Little and Rubin 2002). Not considering missing data might lead to biased estimates as well as false conclusions. In general, there are three main types of missing data mechanisms

Y. Jang (✉)
The University of Georgia, 126H Aderhold Hall, The University of Georgia, Athens, GA 30602, USA
e-mail: corm@uga.edu

Z. (Larula) Lu
The University of Georgia, 325V Aderhold Hall, The University of Georgia, Athens, GA 30602, USA
e-mail: zlu@uga.edu

A. Cohen
The University of Georgia, 125 Aderhold Hall, The University of Georgia, Athens, GA 30602, USA
e-mail: acohen@uga.edu

R.E. Millsap et al. (eds.), *Quantitative Psychology Research*, Springer Proceedings in Mathematics & Statistics 89, DOI 10.1007/978-3-319-07503-7_28

missing at completely random (MCAR), missing at random (MAR), and missing not at random (MNAR) (e.g., Little and Rubin 2002). In the case of MCAR, the missing values occur completely randomly, so they are independent of any observed or latent variable in the estimation model. For MAR, the missing values are conditional on some observed variables in the estimation model. For MNAR, the missing values depend on some unobserved or latent variables. Generally, MCAR and MAR could be considered as an ignorable missing value because the model estimates won't be biased if the missingness mechanism is ignored, while MNAR is considered as a non-ignorable missing value and the missingness mechanism has to be modeled in order to get unbiased estimates.

Various methods have been proposed to deal with missing data. Among them, traditional methods include listwise deletion, pairwise deletion, and single imputation (SI). These traditional methods are very clear to understand and easy to apply; however, they introduce significantly biased results. First of all, we lose lots of information by deleting cases, and the results without enough information might not be valid. Also, we cannot guarantee that the new complete data after deletion represent the entire sample. In addition, the single imputation method reduces the variance of variables in data, and diminishes the relationship between variables. Modern methods include multiple imputation (MI) and maximum likelihood estimation (ML). These two methods to deal with missing data have a strong theoretical foundation, and a lot of empirical research supports their use. The most significant advantages of these approaches are that they require less stringent assumptions about the missing data mechanism. In addition, the results of these methods might be more accurate and powerful than traditional approaches such as listwise deletion or single imputation. In ML, the estimator uses a mathematical function called log-likelihood to quantify the standardized distance between the data points and the parameters for each case. Although the estimation process does not literally impute the missing values, it does borrow information from the observed responses when estimating parameters from incomplete data (Enders 2011). The ML commonly used for current statistical softwares, such as the full information maximum likelihood (FIML) option of SAS and *Mplus*. This option provides a very easy and statistically powerful method to deal with missing values, when missing occurs in a dependent variable. When missing occurs in independent variables, however, these softwares use listwise deletion. Unlike ML, the basic idea of multiple imputation is to substitute a set of reasonable guesses for each missing value and then proceed to do the analysis as if there were no missing values (Allison 2002). In MI, the natural variability of data could be maintained since the imputed values are determined based on variables which are correlated to the missing values. Not only that, the uncertainty could be solved by creating several sets of imputed data (Wayman 2003). There are three distinctive steps involved in MI. The first step is the imputation procedure. Multiple copies of data sets which contain different plausible values for missing are created during this step. A number of statistical approaches for this step have been proposed such as parametric regression methods, nonparametric methods, and Markov chain Monte Carlo (MCMC) methods (see, e.g., Enders 2010; Yuan 2000). The second step is the analysis procedure. Multiply imputed data sets are separately analyzed using the same statistical model. If there are m sets of imputed data, the analysis is repeated m times and we have m sets of estimated parameters. Thus, the last step of MI is a pooling of the results (i.e., several sets of estimated parameters) because the pooling results across multiple imputed data sets are more valid than the results relied on with any single data set. The many researches related to MI have been focused on the first step (i.e., imputation procedure); however, model comparison and selection after multiple imputation have not been fully developed (Lee and Chi 2012). For example, Davey (2005) evaluated several model fit indices like room mean squared error of approximation (RMSEA), normed fit index (NFI), and Tucker-Lewis Index (TLI) with missing data. Kientoff (2011) suggested different weights to adjust model fit indices for structural equation models using multiple imputation.

In general, there are two types of model comparison, nested models comparison and non-nested models comparison. Nested models are cases where a specific model (also called a reduced model) can be derived from a more general model (also called a full model) by putting some constraints on some model parameters. For example, in multilevel modeling, a reduced model with constant level 2 random effects is nested within a full model with varying random effects. Both models have the same fixed effects but different number of random effects. For comparing nested models, a deviance statistic, defined as $-2(log - likelihood)$, is commonly used. If the reduced model contains k restrictions on parameters of the full model, the difference of deviances for two nested models follows a chi-square distribution with k degree of freedom. This difference of deviance is also called a chi-square criterion, which measures the increase in discrepancy produced by changing from the full model to the reduced model (Busemeyer and Wang 2000). Thus, the lower deviance means the better model fit. For comparing non-nested models, many types of model fit indices have been developed, such as Akaike's Information Criterion (AIC), and Schwarz's Bayesian Information Criterion (BIC). The model that had the lowest value of AIC or BIC is considered to be the appropriate model. According to the equation of AIC and BIC (see, e.g., Hox 2002), AIC and BIC are calculated based on their deviance statistics which is based on likelihood functions. Therefore, for both types of model comparisons, the likelihood is a key component statistic. Regardless of the fact that the likelihood is the basic value for model comparison, there are a few studies about how to combine likelihood values of several sets of imputed data. So far, there is only one outline described by Meng and Rubin (1992) to compute the likelihood ratio test (LRT), and other research has been done based on the outline of Meng and Rubin (1992) (see, e.g., Asparouhov and Muthen 2010; Enders 2010).

As mentioned above, some statistical software provides a specific option like FIML for missing data, but they have some limitations in the implementation of ML. Also, other software still uses traditional methods such as pairwise deletion for multilevel models. For example, MLwiN and HLM, which are the popular statistical software for multilevel models delete all level-1 cases with missing values when missing occurs on any level-1 variables. And if missing occurs on higher level variables (e.g., level-2), all level-2 cases associated with missing, as well as all associated level-1 cases are deleted. The specific procedure for multilevel models of general purpose statistical software, such as SAS PROC MIXED, SPSS MIXED, and the R package nlme, also uses a similar way to deal with missing data (van Buuren 2011). In addition, MI is an intuitive and easy to understand method for especially less-advanced analysts. Moreover, any method or statistical software can be used with complete data sets. Therefore, MI is an attractive choice to deal with missing for multilevel models. The main goal of this paper is to investigate the performance of different methods to generate likelihood for multiple imputation. Specifically, three ways for pooling likelihoods and four weights for combined log-likelihood value suggested by Kientoff are compared. As hierarchical data are very common in social science research (Singer and Willett 2003), this study focuses on the hierarchically nested models with multiply imputed data. First, three different pooling ways for likelihoods are compared. In addition, four types of weights suggested by Kientoff (2011) for the LRT are compared. Simulation studies are conducted to compare nested models with multiply imputed data. The data sets are generated under two different sample sizes and three different missing rates. We only focus on MAR in this study since the multiple imputation fundamentally assumes that the missing mechanism of the data set is MAR.

28.2 Methods

28.2.1 Models

In this study, we focused on the basic two-level model with one continuous level-1 covariate. Two hierarchically nested models are compared. The following is the reduced model (i.e., Model 1), that is, the random intercept and fixed slopes model.

Level-1:

$$\widehat{Y}_{ij} = \beta_{0j} + \beta_{1j}(x_{ij}) + r_{ij} \tag{28.1}$$

where $r_{ij} \sim N(0, \sigma^2)$.

Level-2:

$$\begin{aligned} \beta_{0j} &= \gamma_{00} + u_{0j} \\ \beta_{1j} &= \gamma_{10} \end{aligned} \tag{28.2}$$

where $u_{0j} \sim N(0, \tau_0{}^2)$.

The full model (i.e., Model 2) is random intercept and random slopes model. The Model 1 is nested within Model 2. In the equation for Model 2, the level-1 is same with the Model 1; however, there are one more random parts (i.e., u_{1j}) in the level-2.

Level-1:

$$\widehat{Y}_{ij} = \beta_{0j} + \beta_{1j}(x_{ij}) + r_{ij} \tag{28.3}$$

where $r_{ij} \sim N(0, \sigma^2)$.

Level-2:

$$\begin{aligned} \beta_{0j} &= \gamma_{00} + u_{0j} \\ \beta_{1j} &= \gamma_{10} + u_{1j} \end{aligned} \tag{28.4}$$

where $\begin{pmatrix} u_{0j} \\ u_{1j} \end{pmatrix} = U_{ij} \sim MVN\left(\begin{pmatrix} 0 \\ 0 \end{pmatrix}, \begin{pmatrix} \tau_0{}^2 & \tau_{10} \\ \tau_{01} & \tau_1{}^2 \end{pmatrix}\right)$.

28.2.2 Data Generation

In the simulation, first, a complete data set is generated based on Model 1 (i.e., fixed slope model) and the parameters of this model are set as follows. For fixed effects, the average intercept is 30 and the average slope of level-1 covariate (i.e., x_{ij}) is 5. For random effects, the level-1 and level-2 variance are 80 and 20, respectively; the level-1 covariate follows a normal distribution with a mean of 0 and a standard deviation of 3. Second, missing values on the dependent variable (i.e., y_{ij}) are generated based on the complete data and pre-designed missingness probabilities. As mentioned in the previous section, we assumed the missing mechanism is MAR in this study, and the probability of missingness depends on the observed covariate (i.e., x_{ij}). The probability of missingness is set higher when x_{ij} has a larger value. In this simulation, we use three different missing data rates (10, 35, and 60 %) and two different sample sizes (500 and 1,000). In total, six conditions are generated with each condition having 1,000 replications. All data are generated by running the program R (R Development Core Team 2008).

28.2.3 Imputation Missing Values

To impute missing values, we use multiple imputation by chained equations (MICE). MICE is also called fully conditional specification and partially incompatible MCMC and a flexible approximate procedure. In MICE, an imputation model is used. Unlike the flat-file imputation methods that ignore hierarchical structures for nested data, the imputation model in MICE considers the multilevel structure (van Buuren 2011). The principle of the MICE is to treat in turn the imputation for each of the variables while considering the others as given, using these regression-type models, and cycle repeatedly through the variables (Snijders and Bosker 2012).

There are six steps using MICE (Azur et al. 2011). First, to do a simple imputation. For instance, mean imputations can be used in this step and these imputed means can be thought of as place holders. Second, the place holders for target variable are deleted to set back to missing. Third, to set a regression model, in which the target variable is treated as a dependent variable, and other variables are treated as predictors. Fourth, missing values of target variable are replaced with predictions from the regression model. Fifth, to repeat the fourth step from the second step by changing a target variable. At the end of this iteration, one imputed complete data set is created. Sixth, to repeat the whole iteration the number of imputation times.

In this study, generated data sets with missing values are imputed by using MICE method. The R package "mice" (van Buuren and Groothuis-Oudshoorn 2011) is used. The number of imputation for each condition is 10 as this number is generally advisable as a minimum value for multilevel data (Goldstein 2011).

28.2.4 Pooling Likelihood

When the imputation procedure is finished, there are m sets of estimated parameters, as well as likelihood values. And these several likelihood values have to be combined because we need one statistics for the model selection. We used three pooling ways to combine the likelihood value (i.e., deviance value) over m imputed data set.

(1) The first way is overall mean ($\overline{D}$) of likelihood values over m imputed data sets, and it defined like below:

$$\overline{D} = \frac{1}{m}\sum_{i=1}^{m} D_m. \tag{28.5}$$

(2) The second way is re-estimation of deviance value (D'), a likelihood value using posterior estimates of multiple imputations.

$$D' = D(posterior\ estimates). \tag{28.6}$$

(3) The third one is D_{imp}, a modification of D', and is defined as follows.

$$D_{imp} = \frac{D'}{(k_2 - k_1)(1 + r_3)}, \tag{28.7}$$

where (r_3) is a correction factor with k_1 is the number of parameters for the reduced model and k_2 is the number of parameters for the augmented model defined by Meng and Rubin (1992), and

$$r_3 = \frac{m+1}{(m-1)(k_2-k_1)}(\overline{D}-D^{'}). \tag{28.8}$$

With missing data, there are four types of weights to adjust the likelihood value. These four weights are suggested by Kientoff (2011), and are defined as follows.

$$w_1 = (1 - missing\ rate) \tag{28.9}$$

$$w_2 = min\left(1, (1 - missing\ rate) + \left(k+1+\frac{1}{m}\right)^{-1}\right) \tag{28.10}$$

$$w_3 = (1 - missing\ rate)\left(1 - \frac{1}{mk}\right) \tag{28.11}$$

$$w_4 = min\left(1, (1 - missing\ rate)\left(1+\frac{1}{k}\right)\right) \tag{28.12}$$

where k is the number of estimated parameters in the model, and m is the number of imputation. The w_1 is a correction based on the missing rate. This weight will decrease when the missing rate increases. Other weights are defined based on the w_1. The w_2 is modified the test statistics of Li et al. (1991). The number of estimated parameters and the number of imputed data sets are included in the w_3, and the $w_4$is considered only the number of estimated parameters. The range of these weights is zero to one. According to the Kientoff (2011), the results of w_3 are shown more reasonable output among other weights in the case of 20 and 40 % missing rate. However, the results of w_4 were better in the case of 50 % missing rate. Kientoff (2011) concluded that it is worth to consider the number of estimated parameters for all conditions. The calculated four kinds of weights for each condition are shown in Table 28.1 and Fig. 28.1. The number of imputation (m) is fixed as 10 and the numbers of estimated parameter (k) for the fixed slope model and random slope model are four and six, respectively.

As can be seen in Table 28.1, the w_1 for the fixed slope model and the random slope model are equal because it depends on the only missing rate. Thus, the w_1 are 0.900, 0.650, 0.400 in the case of missing rate is 10, 35, and 60 %, respectively. Since other weights are related to the missing rate, the number of estimated parameters, and the number of imputations, the w_1 differs according to conditions. For example, for the fixed slope model with 35 % missing rate, the w_2 is 0.846, the w_2 is 0.634, and the w_3 is 0.813. Each weight is multiplied to the pooled likelihood value to explore that which weight can make the most appropriate pooled likelihood value.

Table 28.1 Four kinds of weights

	Weight	Missing rate (%) 10	35	60
Fixed slope model	w_1	0.900	0.650	0.400
	w_2	1.000	0.846	0.596
	w_3	0.878	0.634	0.390
	w_4	1.000	0.813	0.500
Random slope model	w_1	0.900	0.650	0.400
	w_2	1.000	0.791	0.541
	w_3	0.885	0.639	0.393
	w_4	1.000	0.758	0.467

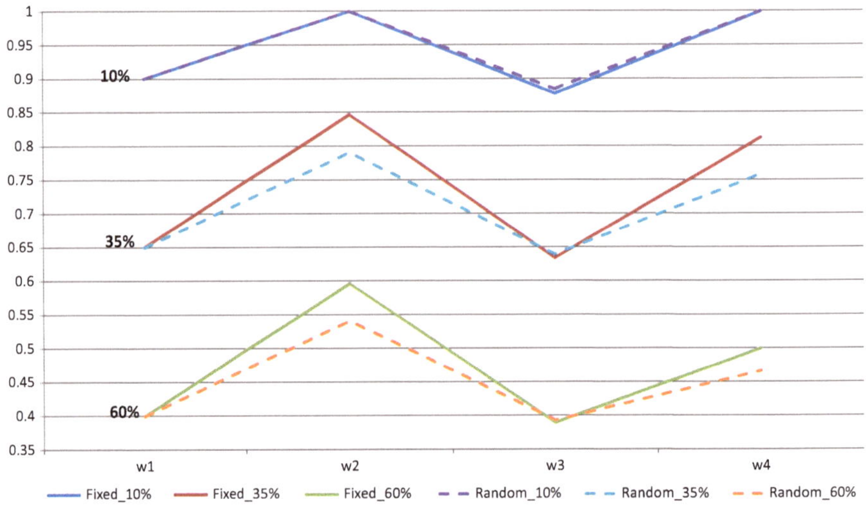

Fig. 28.1 Four kinds of weights

28.2.5 *Model Comparison*

We compared a fixed slope model (i.e., Model 1, the reduced model) and a random slope model (i.e., Model 2, the full model) in this study. Model 1 is nested in Model 2. The log-LRT is used for the comparison of nested models. However, the regular chi-square distribution in LRT has been approved not accurate when the difference in degrees of freedom of both models is one. In this case, the corrected likelihood ratio test (Corrected LRT) is suggested. For the corrected LRT, the 50–50 mixture chi-square distribution is used and it is also called chi-bar-square distribution. The corrected LRT is particularly suggested when the null hypothesis assumes the variance to be zero and the alternative hypothesis is nonnegative character of variance. The *p*-value for the difference of deviances between two nested models could be calculated as the average of the *p*-values from chi-square distribution with $df = p + 1$ and $df = p$, where $p + 1$ equals to a difference between the number of parameters for two nested models. Table 28.2 gives a part of critical values for 50–50 mixture chi-square distribution. Since our Model 1 has four number of parameters and Model 2 has six number of parameters (i.e., $p + 1 = 2$), the critical value is 5.14 with the significant level 0.05 (see, LaHuis and Ferguson 2009; Snijders and Bosker 2012).

Table 28.2 Critical values for 50–50 mixture chi-square distribution

	Significant level			
p	0.10	0.05	0.01	0.001
1	3.81	5.14	8.27	12.81
2	5.53	7.05	10.50	15.36
3	7.09	8.76	12.48	17.61

Source: Snijders and Bosker (2012), p. 99

Table 28.3 The false positive error rates

		Missing rate (%)								
		10			35			60		
Sample size	Weight	$\overline{D}$	D'	D_{imp}	$\overline{D}$	D'	D_{imp}	$\overline{D}$	D'	D_{imp}
500	No weight	0.052	0.034	0.084	0.054	0.033	0.094	0.028	0.024	0.089
	w_1	0.039	0.023	0.077	0.008	0.005	0.077	0.000	0.001	0.058
	w_2	0.052	0.034	0.084	1.000	1.000	0.069	1.000	1.000	0.073
	w_3	0.000	0.000	0.084	0.000	0.000	0.075	0.000	0.000	0.062
	w_4	0.052	0.034	0.084	1.000	1.000	0.068	1.000	1.000	0.068
1,000	No weight	0.067	0.033	0.016	0.117	0.033	0.024	0.090	0.034	0.034
	w_1	0.045	0.025	0.015	0.013	0.006	0.020	0.000	0.000	0.029
	w_2	0.067	0.033	0.016	1.000	1.000	0.015	1.000	1.000	0.031
	w_3	0.000	0.000	0.017	0.000	0.000	0.021	0.000	0.000	0.027
	w_4	0.067	0.033	0.016	1.000	1.000	0.015	1.000	1.000	0.026

Also, the null hypothesis for LRT is the variance of random slope equals zero. If the null hypothesis is rejected, that means the random slope model has better model-fit than the fixed slope model. Because our complete data sets are generated based on the fixed slope model, the rejection rate can be considered as the false positive error rate. We investigate the performance of pooling likelihood with missing data by checking false positive error rate.

28.3 Results

The false positive error rates for each condition are summarized in Table 28.3. Figures 28.2 and 28.3 visualized the false positive error rates of each condition for 500 sample size and 1,000 sample size, respectively.

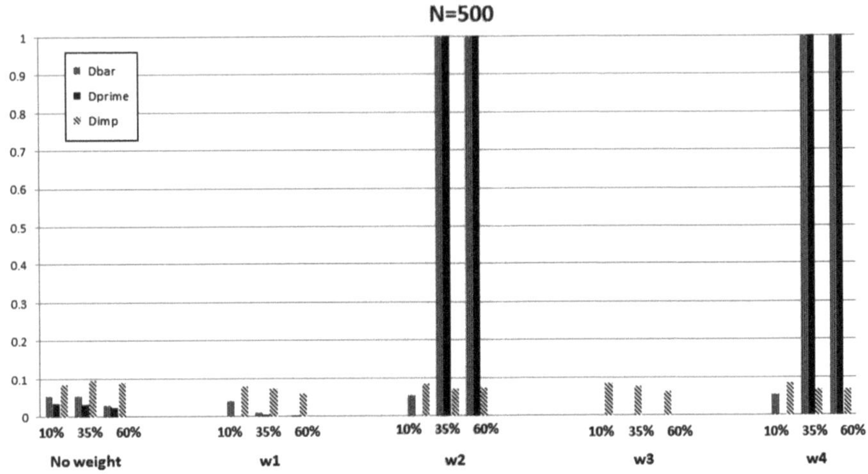

Fig. 28.2 The false positive error rates for 500 sample size

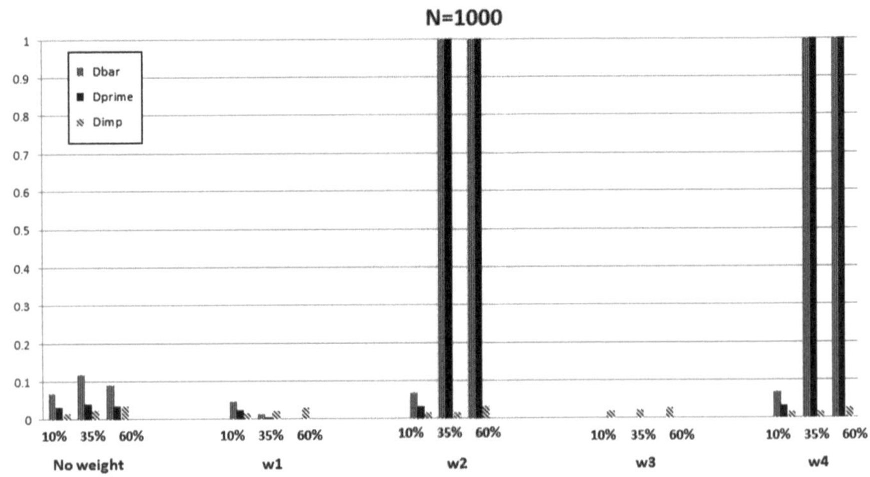

Fig. 28.3 The false positive error rates for 1,000 sample size

According to Bradley (1978), the test can be considered as robust if the false error rate is approximately equal to a significant level α. As can be seen in Table 28.3, for the 500 sample size, the false positive error rates of overall mean of likelihood ($\overline{D}$) and re-estimated likelihood values (D') without weight are closed to a significant level 0.05 when the missing rate are 10 and 35 %; however, these values are much smaller than 0.05 with large missing rate (i.e., 60 %). And all kinds of weights caused quite extreme false positive error rates for both $\overline{D}$ and D'. The false positive error rate of $\overline{D}$ (= 0.39) with w_1 and the false positive error rates of $\overline{D}$ (= 0.39) with w_2 and w_4 are reasonable for small missing rate (i.e., 10 % missing rate), but the false positive error rates for 35 and 60 % missing rates are almost zero. Similar to the results of $\overline{D}$, the false positive error rates of D' (= 0.34) with w_2 and w_4 are more reasonable than the other weighs. The false positive error rates of the modification of D' (D_{imp}) for all conditions are between 0.058 and 0.094. These false positive error rates are higher than a significant level 0.05, but these are more stable than other two pooling methods (i.e., $\overline{D}$ and D'). The results for 1,000 sample size were also pretty similar to the results for 500 sample size. These patterns of results also can be seen in Figs. 28.2 and 28.3. For the 1,000 sample size, the false positive error rates of $\overline{D}$ equal to 0.067 without weight, with w_2 and w_4. And the false positive error rate of $\overline{D}$ is 0.045 with w_1 at the 10 % missing rate. But the false positive error rates of $\overline{D}$ are not closed to 0.05 at 35 and 60 % missing rate. All false positive error rates of D' are not closed to the significant level 0.05. Unlike the 500 sample size, the false positive error rates of D_{imp} are smaller than 0.05 for all conditions.

The patterns of weights according to the number of parameters are shown in Fig. 28.4. The first weight, w_1, was excluded in Fig. 28.4 because w_1 depends on only missing rate by the definition, thus, these values would be same across different numbers of parameter. As can be seen in Fig. 28.4, the values of w_2 and w_4 are unstable at the small number of parameters for 35 and 60 % missing rate. But the values of w_2 and w_4 at between quite small number of parameters (i.e., between one and seven) are quite stable for 10 % missing rate. By the equations for w_2 and w_4, the number of estimated parameters has large influence on the weights, especially when a model has small number of estimated parameters. The values w_3 also relatively unstable at the small number of parameters compared at the large number of parameters. In this study, the number of estimated parameters was four for fixed slope model and six for random slope model. Thus, a big difference of weight according to these small numbers of parameters for our study models might be one reason of extreme false positive error rate.

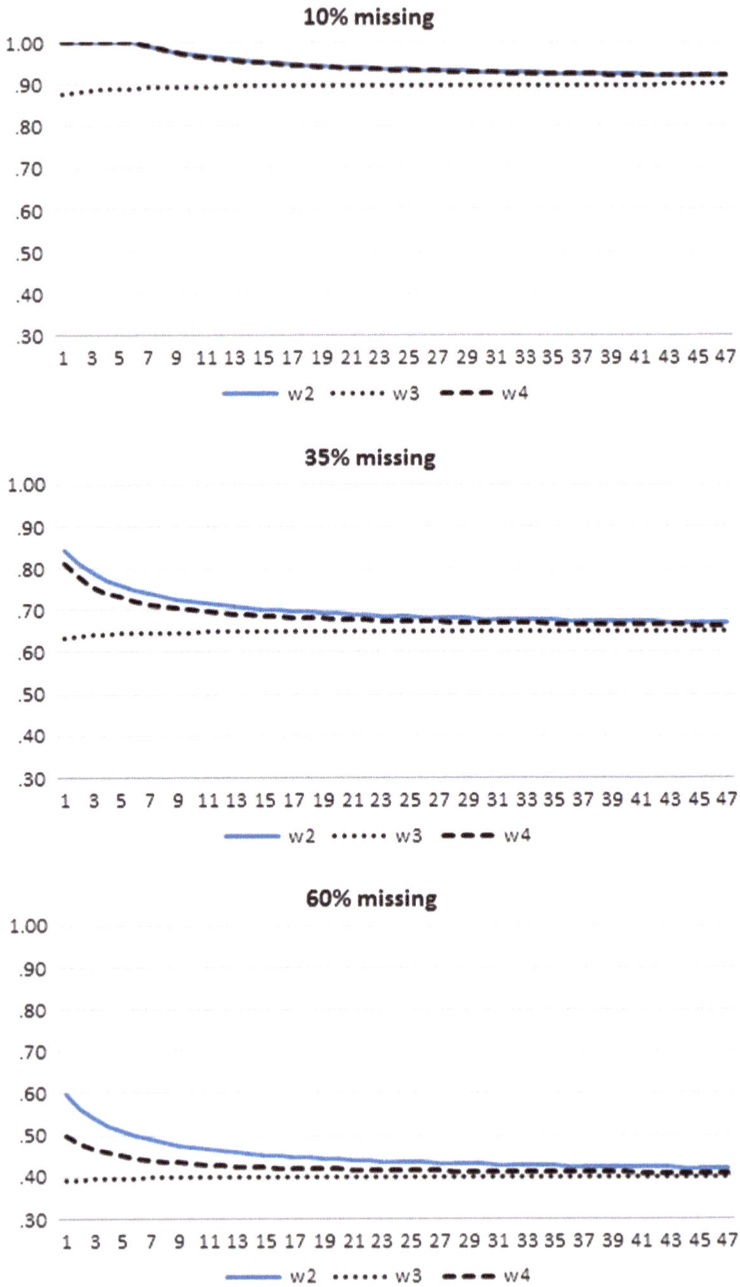

Fig. 28.4 Patterns of weights according to the number of parameters

Conclusion and Future Research

Based on our result, we could not find an appropriate weight to correct the combined likelihood value. Especially, w_2 and w_4 are led to very extreme false positive error rate (i.e., all rejections or all acceptances). As described in the results section, three weights except for the w_1 are related to the number of estimated parameters of models. In addition, the weights used in our study are originally suggested for the SEM model. Thus, these weights do not work to correct combined likelihood values of multiply imputed data for multilevel modeling.

For the small missing rate, using the overall mean of likelihood values ($\overline{D}$) without a weight is the most appropriate among three different ways to combine likelihood values over multiply imputed data sets. But the results of $\overline{D}$ are shown very extreme false positive error rate with weights. The modification of D' (i.e., D_{imp}) among three different pooling ways for likelihood value is the most stable across four different weights, although the false positive error rates are higher than 0.05 for the 500 sample size and smaller than 0.05 for the 1,000 sample size. This result differs with the results of previous studies (e.g., Meng and Rubin 1993; Asparouhov and Muthen 2010). In the Meng and Rubin (1992) and Asparouhov and Muthen (2010), D_{imp} was nicely worked, whereas our results showed inflated false positive error rates for the 500 sample size and deflated false positive error rates for the 1,000 sample size. According to the definition of correction factor r_3, the number of imputation, the number of estimated parameters for a reduced model, and an augmented model are involved in this factor. Therefore, the false positive error rates of D_{imp} might be affected by the difference of r_3. The number of estimated parameters and the number of imputation in our study differ from Meng and Rubin (1992) and Asparouhov and Muthen (2010). Our small difference of the number of parameters for two nested models might have an influence on the false positive error rate. Thus, we need to evaluate the effect of the correction factors on the D_{imp}. In addition, the LRT was used for the model comparison of the true model and the saturated model in the previous study. In our study, however, we compared two nested multilevel models. This different condition of model comparison might result in the different results between this study and previous studies.

For the future study, a specific pooling way of likelihood value for the hierarchically nested models is needed. In addition, a study to use more complex models with large number of estimated parameters is needed to test the weights as well as the correction factor. Another application is to use data set with missing values on covariate variables or on both dependent variable and covariate variables. Furthermore, we need to develop weights that can consider the characteristics of multilevel model such as a group size or an intra class correlation (ICC).

References

Allison PD (2002) Missing data. Sage, Los Angeles

Asparouhov T, Muthen B (2010) Chi-square statistics with multiple imputation. Technical Report. https://www.statmodel.com/download/MI7.pdf

Azur MJ, Stuart EA, Frangakis C, Leaf PJ (2011) Multiple imputation by chained equations: what is it and how does it work? Int J Methods Psychiatr Res 20(1):40–49

Bradley JV (1978) Robustness? Br J Math Stat Psychol 31:144–152

Busemeyer JR, Wang YM (2000) Model comparison and model selections based on generalization criterion methodology. J Math Psychol 44:171–189

Davey A (2005) Issues in evaluating model fit with missing data. Struct Equ Modeling 12(4): 578–597

Enders CK (2010) Applied missing data analysis. The Guilford Press, New York

Enders CK(2011) Analyzing longitudinal data with missing values. Rehabil Psychol 56(4): 264–288

Goldstein H (2011) Multilevel statistical models. Wiley, London

Hox JJ (2002) Multilevel analysis techniques and applications. Erlbaum, Mahwah

Kientoff CJ (2011) Development of weighted model fit indexes for structural equation models using multiple imputation. Doctoral dissertation. http://lib.dr.iastate.edu/etd/

LaHuis DM, Ferguson MW (2009) The accuracy of significant tests for slope variance components in multilevel random coefficient models. Organ Res Methods 12(3):418–435

Lee T, Chi L (2012) Alternative multiple imputation inference for mean and covariance structure modeling. J Educ Behav Stat 37(6):675–702

Li KH, Raghunathan TE, Rubin DB (1991) Large-sample significance levels from multiply imputed data using moment-based statistics and an *F* reference distribution. J Am Stat Assoc 86(416):1065–1073

Little RJA, Rubin DB (2002) Statistical analysis with missing data. Wiley-Interscience, New York

Meng XL, Rubin DB (1992) Performing likelihood ratio tests with multiply-imputed data sets. Biometrika 79(1):103–111

R Development Core Team (2008) R: a language and environment for statistical computing. R-Foundation for Statistical Computing. ISBN 3-900051-07-0. http://www.R-project.org

Singer JD, Willett JB (2003) Applied longitudinal data analysis: modeling change and event occurrence. Oxford University Press, New York

Snijders TAB, Bosker RJ (2012) Multilevel analysis: an introduction to basic and advanced multilevel modeling. Sage, Los Angeles

van Buuren S (2011) Multiple imputation of multilevel data. In: Hox JJ, Roberts JK (eds) The handbook of advanced multilevel analysis. Routledge, Milton park, pp 173–196

van Buuren S, Groothuis-Oudshoorn K (2011) Mice: multivariate imputation by chained equations in R. J Stat Softw 45(3):1–67

Wayman JC (2003) Multiple imputation for missing data: what is it and how can I use it? Paper presented at the 2003 annual meeting of the American Educational Research Association, Chicago

Yuan YC (2000) Multiple imputation for missing data: concepts and new development. SUGI Proceedings http://support.sas.com/rnd/app/stat/papers/multipleimputation.pdf

Chapter 29
A Paradox by Another Name Is Good Estimation

Mark D. Reckase and Xin Luo

Abstract This chapter describes the property of estimates of points in a multidimensional space that is labeled by some as paradoxical, shows when this property of the estimates is present, and also shows that the paradoxical result is not flaw in estimation because estimates improve with additional information even when the paradox occurs. The paradox is that when a correct response to a test item is added to the string of responses for an examinee to previous items, at least one of the coordinates of the new estimated θ-point decreases compared to the estimate based on the initial string of responses. The information presented in the chapter shows that this can occur whenever the likelihood function for the estimates has a particular form. This form is present in many cases when the item responses for a test can not be described by simple structure. Results are presented to show that the additional response improves the estimate of the θ-point even though the paradoxical result occurs.

Keywords Multidimensional item response theory • Estimation • Likelihood function • Compensatory model

29.1 Introduction

Recently, the term "paradoxical" has appeared in the research literature related to estimation of the location of persons in a multidimensional space using multidimensional item response theory (MIRT) (Hooker et al. 2009; Hooker 2010; Hooker

M.D. Reckase (✉)
CEPSE, Michigan State University, 461 Erickson Hall, 610 Farm Lane,
East Lansing, MI 48864, USA
e-mail: reckase@msu.edu

X. Luo
Department of Counseling Educational Psychology and Spec Ed, MQM, CEPSE,
College of Education, Michigan State University, 4th Floor, Erickson Hall,
East Lansing, MI 48823, USA
e-mail: luoxin1@msu.edu

R.E. Millsap et al. (eds.), *Quantitative Psychology Research*, Springer Proceedings
in Mathematics & Statistics 89, DOI 10.1007/978-3-319-07503-7_29

and Finkelman 2010; Finkelman et al. 2010; Jordan and Spiess 2012; van Rijn and Rijmen, 2012). There are two definitions of paradoxical that might be the intent of the use of the word in these articles. The first is "a statement or proposition that seems self-contradictory or absurd but in reality expresses a possible truth." The second definition is "a self-contradictory and false proposition" (Flexner and Hauck 1987). It seems that some of the authors think that estimation within MIRT follows the second definition while others believe that the first definition is more appropriate.

The phenomenon that is considered paradoxical is the observation that sometimes one of the estimated θ-coordinates in the θ-vector that indicates a person's location in the θ-space defined by a MIRT model decreases after a correct response to an item, or alternatively, increases after an incorrect response. More precisely, suppose a test has k items. After $k-1$ items are administered, the estimated location is $\widehat{\theta}_{k-1} = \left[\widehat{\theta}_{k-1,1}, \widehat{\theta}_{k-1,2}, \ldots, \widehat{\theta}_{k-1,m}\right]$. Then the kth item is administered and a correct response is observed. After the kth item is included in the estimation of the location in the space, the paradoxical result is that for at least one of the coordinates, $\widehat{\theta}_{k,i} < \widehat{\theta}_{k-1,i}$. This result is paradoxical because some authors expect that all coordinates should increase after a correct response and all coordinates should decrease after an incorrect response.

The purpose of this chapter is to provide explanations for why and when the paradoxical result occurs in the context of a commonly used MIRT model, the multidimensional extension of the two-parameter logistic model. There is a further discussion of whether the presence of paradoxical results constitutes a problem that needs to be addressed, or if it is a normal feature of the estimation of locations of a point in a multidimensional space.

The model that will be the focus of this study is given below as Eq. (29.1). This particular model is used because it is common in the MIRT literature and because its properties are well known (see Reckase 2009). It is expected that the results reported here will generalize to a wide variety of models that include linear combinations of the coordinates in the θ-space. The equation for the model used here is given by

$$P\left(u_{ij} = 1 \middle| \theta_i, a_j, d_j\right) = \frac{e^{a_j \theta_i' + d_j}}{1 + e^{a_j \theta_i' + d_j}} \tag{29.1}$$

where u_{ij} is the response by examinee i to item j, θ_i is the m-element row vector of coordinates representing the location of examinee i in the m-dimensional proficiency space, $\boldsymbol{a}_j$ is the m-element row vector of discrimination parameters for item j, and d_j is a scalar parameter for item j that is related to the difficulty of the item.

The paper that stimulated the current interest in paradoxical results for the estimation of location of persons in a multidimensional space was Hooker et al. (2009). However, the paradoxical result was evident in the MIRT literature before that paper, particularly in the literature on multidimensional adaptive testing. There is an example of the paradoxical result in Reckase (2009, p. 317) as part of an example of the functioning of a computerized adaptive test. In that example, the estimate of the location of an examinee in a three-dimensional MIRT space was

(−0.25, 2.55, 0.27) after six items, and (−0.30, 2.50, 1.23) after a correct response to the seventh item. In this example, two of the θ-coordinates decreased in magnitude while the third increased quite dramatically. This result was not highlighted in the discussion of that example because the estimates from the adaptive test converged on the true value as the number of items increased in this simulation. These slight decreases in the estimates of the coordinates for the first two dimensions were considered a normal part of the estimation process.

This chapter will first provide a simple example of the paradoxical results to set the stage for an explanation of the results related to the shape of the likelihood function for after $k-1$ items have been administered. Then a more complex example is provided. Next, a different criterion for the quality of estimates of location in a MIRT solution space is suggested as a way of dealing with the paradoxical result. Finally, a rotational solution is provided as a way of addressing the issue. All of these results are discussed in the final section with the intention of providing useful insights into what is considered as a paradoxical result in the research literature.

29.2 A MIRT Explanation of the Paradox Phenomenon

29.2.1 A Simple Example

To facilitate understanding of the paradoxical result, a two-dimension example is provided here. Suppose three items were administered to an examine and the item scores for the items are as listed in Table 29.1. The item parameters for the items for the multidimensional extension of the two-parameter logistic model are also presented in the table.

Table 29.1 Item parameters and responses for a three-item test

	a_1	a_2	d	Response
Item 1	0	1	0	Correct
Item 2	1	0	−1	Correct
Item 3	0.707	0.707	−1.5	Incorrect

After three items were administered, the maximum likelihood estimate (MLE) of the location in the MIRT space is $\widehat{\theta}_1 = 1.6$, $\widehat{\theta}_2 = 0.6$, and the distance of the estimated point from the origin of the θ-space (0, 0) is 1.71. Then a fourth item is administered and a correct response is observed. In order to determine when the paradoxical result occurs, a variety of items are considered as the fourth item. These items are specified as having their angle of best measurement with the θ_1-axis as ranging from 0° to 90° with an increment of 5° and the constraint that $a_1^2 + a_2^2 = 1$. The ability estimate $(\widehat{\theta}_{1\ \mathrm{new}}, \widehat{\theta}_{2\ \mathrm{new}})$ as well as the distance from the origin was determined after the administration of each of the possible fourth items. The estimates of location after the fourth item, and the differences between each coordinate estimate and the previous estimate are given in Table 29.2.

Table 29.2 Ability estimate and distance increase from the origin compared to the three-item solution

Angle	$\widehat{\theta}_{1\,\text{new}}$	$\widehat{\theta}_{2\,\text{new}}$	$\widehat{\theta}_{1\,\text{new}} - \widehat{\theta}_1$	$\widehat{\theta}_{2\,\text{new}} - \widehat{\theta}_2$	Distance increase
0	1.99	0.44	0.41	−0.14	0.35
5	1.97	0.48	0.39	−0.1	0.34
10	1.95	0.51	0.37	−0.07	0.33
15	1.93	0.55	0.35	−0.03	0.32
20	1.91	0.58	0.33	0	0.31
25	1.89	0.62	0.31	0.04	0.31
30	1.87	0.66	0.29	0.08	0.30
35	1.84	0.7	0.26	0.12	0.29
40	1.82	0.74	0.24	0.16	0.28
45	1.79	0.79	0.21	0.21	0.27
50	1.76	0.84	0.18	0.26	0.27
55	1.72	0.89	0.14	0.31	0.25
60	1.68	0.95	0.1	0.37	0.25
65	1.63	1.01	0.05	0.43	0.23
70	1.58	1.07	0	0.49	0.23
75	1.52	1.14	−0.06	0.56	0.22
80	1.46	1.2	−0.12	0.62	0.21
85	1.39	1.27	−0.19	0.69	0.20
90	1.33	1.33	−0.25	0.75	0.20

Table 29.2 shows an interesting pattern of results. After a correct response to the alternative fourth items, sometimes the θ_1-estimate increases and the θ_2-estimate decreases, sometimes the opposite pattern occurs, and sometimes both θ-coordinate estimates increase. The particular result that is observed is related to the direction of best measurement of the fourth item. If the fourth item has its direction of best measurement along Dimension 1 (0–15° from the θ_1-axis), the new θ_1-estimate increases, but the θ_2-estimate decreases; if the fourth item has its direction of best measurement along Dimension 2 (75–90° from the θ_1-axis), the opposite result is observed; if the fourth item has a direction of best measurement between the two coordinate axes (20–70° from the θ_1-axis), the estimates of the coordinates on both dimensions increase. The distance from the origin after a correct response is always greater than the three-item distance for all of the angles of best measurement. More illustrations of this phenomenon are given in Sect. 2.4.

29.2.2 *When Does the Paradox Occur?*

The example in Sect. 2.1 casts some light on when the paradoxical result occurs. However, before moving on to a further elaboration of when the paradoxical result occurs, the concept of an orbit in the statistical sense is needed. An orbit of a likelihood function is the set of points in the m-dimensional space that results in the same value of the likelihood. The orbits form closed curves when the likelihood function has a unique maximum (Reckase 2009). Figure 29.1 is a likelihood surface for a ten-item test and Fig. 29.2 shows a number of orbits for this likelihood function.

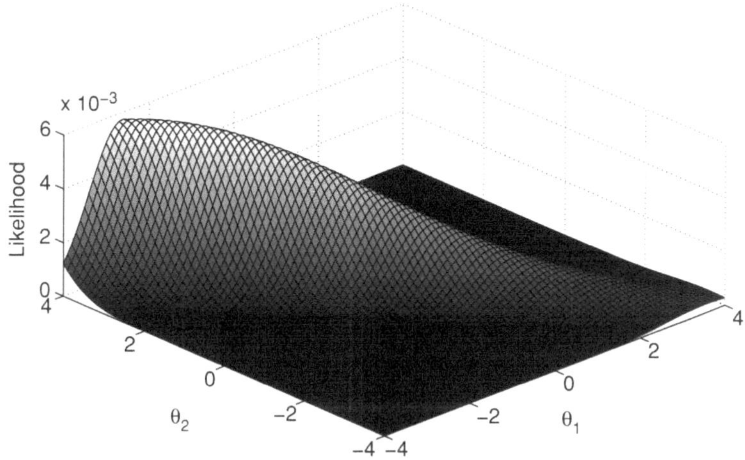

Fig. 29.1 Likelihood surface

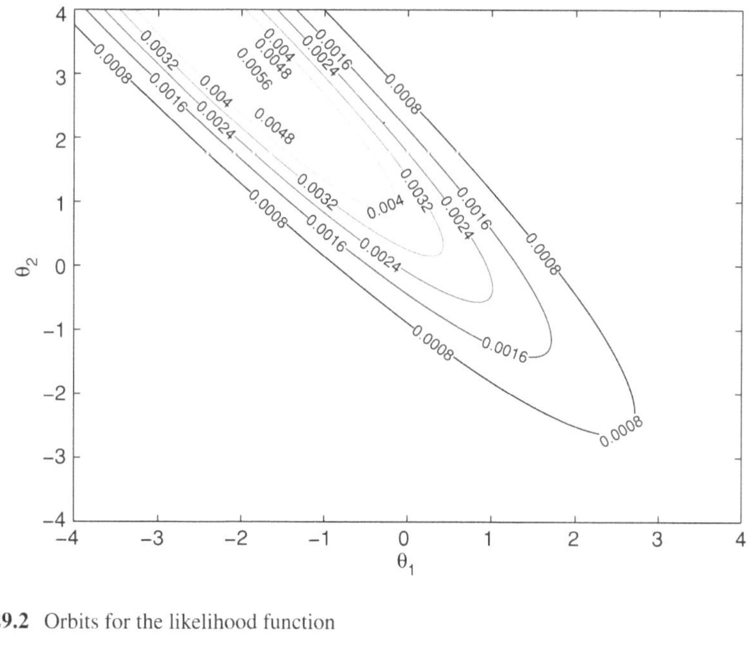

Fig. 29.2 Orbits for the likelihood function

The orbits shown in Fig. 29.2 are portions of approximately oval shaped curves. The full ovals could be seen if the range of values for the θ-axes were extended. The largest of the "ovals" shown in the figure is the 0.0008-orbit. That orbit is the set of points in the θ-space that yield a likelihood of 0.0008 for the item scores on the ten-item test. The smallest "oval" in the figure shows the 0.0056-orbit that surrounds the maximum of the likelihood function. The set of all possible orbits totally cover the θ-space.

A property of the "ovals" shown in Fig. 29.2 is that their major axis has a negative slope. The shape of the orbits and the slope of the major axis is a function of the characteristics of the items that were included in the ten-item test. A different set of items would result in orbits with different shapes and orientations.

Now suppose a new item measuring only along θ_1 is administered and the examinee responds correctly to the item. The vertical lines in Fig. 29.3 show the equal-probable contours for the item response surface from the MIRT model for the new item. Note that for every possible orbit of the likelihood function, there is also an equal-probability contour from the new item that is tangent to the curve for the orbit—actually for the cases where there is a unique MLE for the item scores for the ten-item test, there are two tangent equal-probability contours, one at either extreme of the orbit. The tangent points are shown as dots in Fig. 29.3 and an example for one orbit is given in Fig. 29.4. Figure 29.5 shows the likelihood along one of the equal-probability contours for the 11th item.

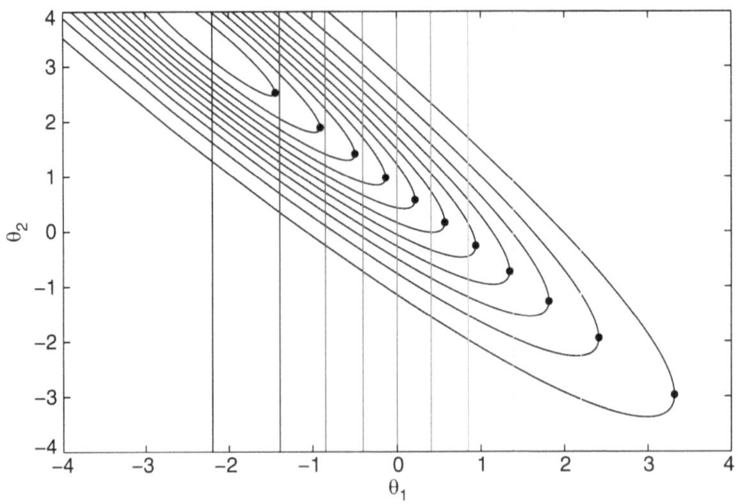

Fig. 29.3 Likelihood orbits and equal-probable contours

The likelihood function for the 11-item test, including the new item, is the product of the previous likelihood function and the probability of answering the new-added-item correctly. Because the probability of a correct response is the same along one of the equal-probability contours for the item, the likelihoods along the line after the addition of the item have the same shape and the maximum is at the

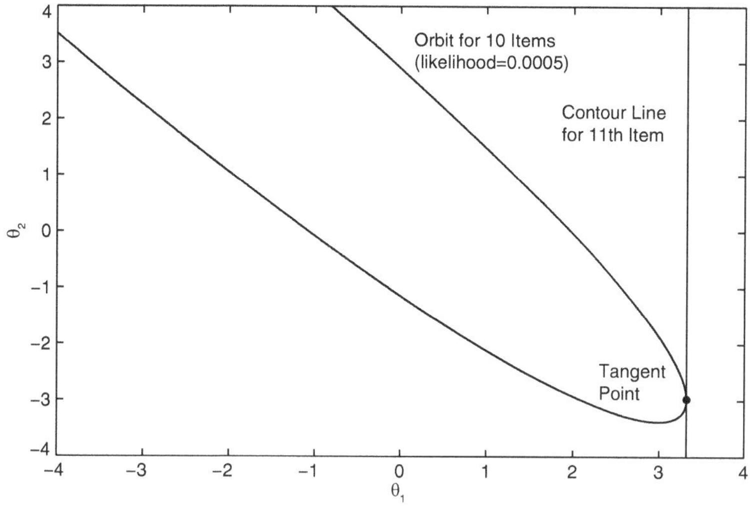

Fig. 29.4 Likelihood orbit and item equal-probable contour tangent line

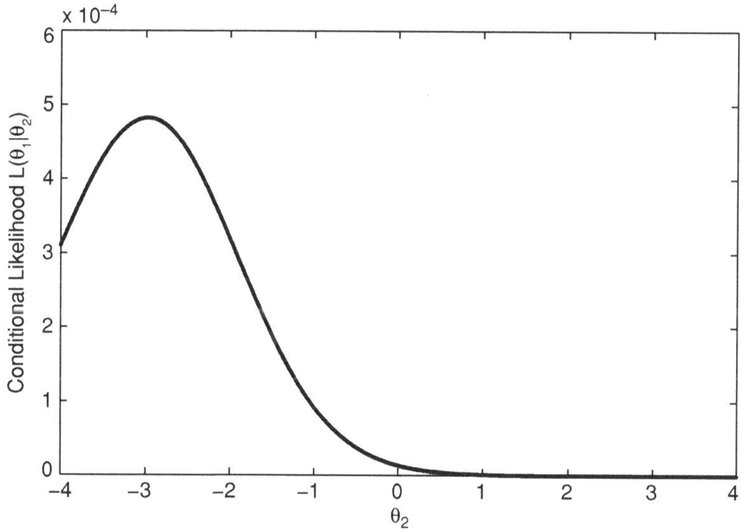

Fig. 29.5 Conditional likelihood along one equal-probability contour line

point of tangent with the original orbits. That is, the new MLE for the estimated location of the examinee in the θ-space must be on the line formed by all the points of tangent for the equal-probability contours and the orbits. If the line connecting the points for the conditional maxima has a negative slope, any change from the previous estimate must have a decrease in one of the coordinate axes.

Figure 29.6 is based on the ten-item test shown above. In Fig. 29.6, the round dot is the original MLE for the ten-item test. The black triangle is the new MLE after an item with direction of best measurement along the θ_1-axis is administered and a correct response is obtained. The black square is the true location of the examinee used to generate simulated responses to the test items. Because there is a negative slope for the major axis of the ovals for the orbits, the new estimate of location must be on the line connecting the points of tangent to the orbits. In this case, the maximum of the likelihoods at those tangent points is at the triangle which shows an increase in θ_1 and a decrease in θ_2. It indicates that a correct response to the new item will yield a decrease in θ_2, and in this sense the paradoxical result occurs. It also shows that, although the paradoxical result occurs, the new MLE is closer to the true location than the original estimate.

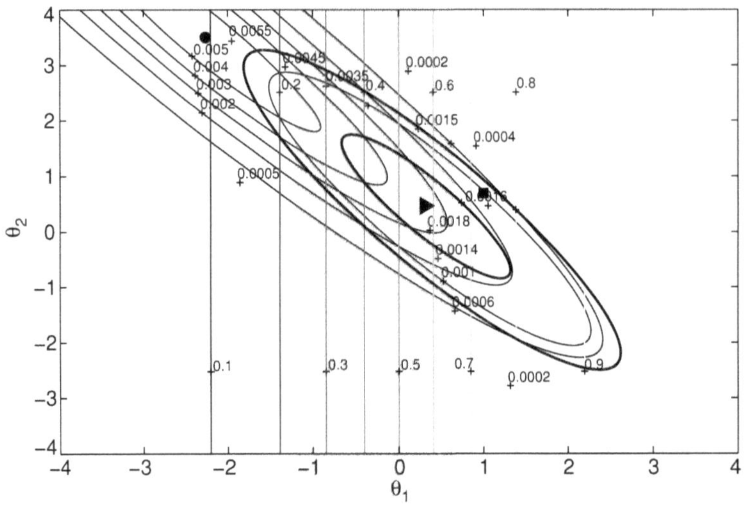

Fig. 29.6 Original and new orbits of the likelihood functions and the location estimates

The same relationship between likelihood orbits and equal-probability contours for the next item generalizes to the situation where the new item has a direction of best measurement that does not parallel one of the axes, i.e., the equal-probable lines are not vertical or horizontal. Figure 29.7 shows the result when the angle of best measurement for the new item and the θ_1-axis is 20°, and the new estimate for θ_2 is lower than the original one (the round dot is the original MLE and the black triangle is the new MLE).

An example of the administration of an additional item where the paradoxical result does not occur can be developed based on the results in Table 29.2. In Fig. 29.8, the round dot is the original MLE and the new MLE is the triangle. The angle of best measurement for the new item with the θ_1-axis is 30°. In this case, the line connecting the tangent points for the likelihood orbits and the equal-probable contours for the item does not have a negative slope. After answering the new item correctly, the coordinates for the new location increase for both dimensions.

The two-dimensional case has some special characteristics so it is important to determine if the pattern of results shown by the examples in two dimensions

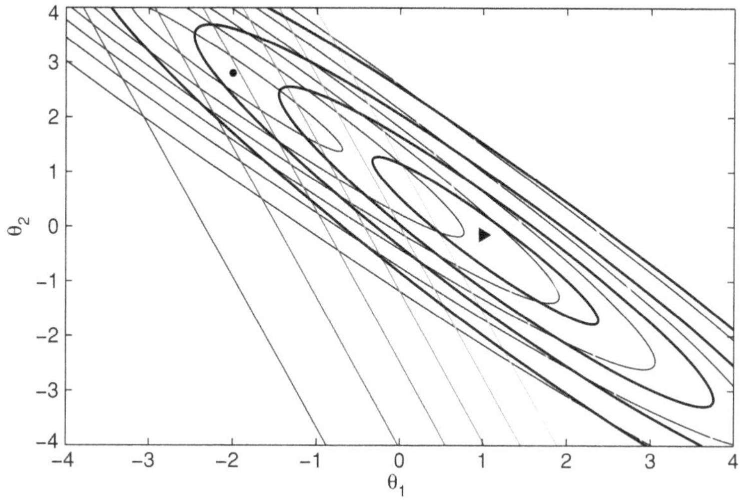

Fig. 29.7 The paradoxical result occurs when the new item measures both dimensions

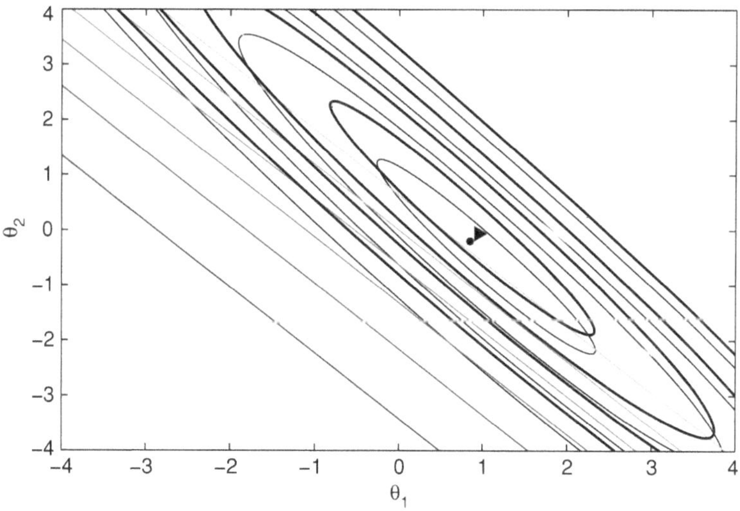

Fig. 29.8 An example that does not show the paradoxical result

generalizes to higher dimensional solutions. A three-dimensional case was investigated and the results are shown in Table 29.3. Table 29.3 presents the item parameters for a ten-item test measuring in a three-dimensional space along with simulated item scores. When items measure three dimensions, the orbits are approximately ellipsoidal surfaces rather than a two-dimensional ellipse. Figure 29.9 shows one of the orbits when likelihood is fixed at 0.00004. Figure 29.10 shows slices through the surface when each of the values of the coordinate axes is successively set to 0.

Table 29.3 Item parameters and item scores for a three-dimensional case

Item	a_1	a_2	a_3	d	Score	Item	a_1	a_2	a_3	d	Score
1	0.89	0.46	0.93	0.89	0	6	0.47	0.69	1.06	1.44	0
2	1.40	2.14	0.48	−1.15	0	7	0.64	0.71	0.95	0.33	0
3	0.34	0.95	0.95	−1.07	1	8	0.84	1.25	0.67	−0.75	1
4	1.00	0.72	1.31	−0.81	1	9	2.59	1.21	0.82	1.37	1
5	0.83	0.95	0.88	−2.94	0	10	1.95	1.22	0.56	−1.71	1

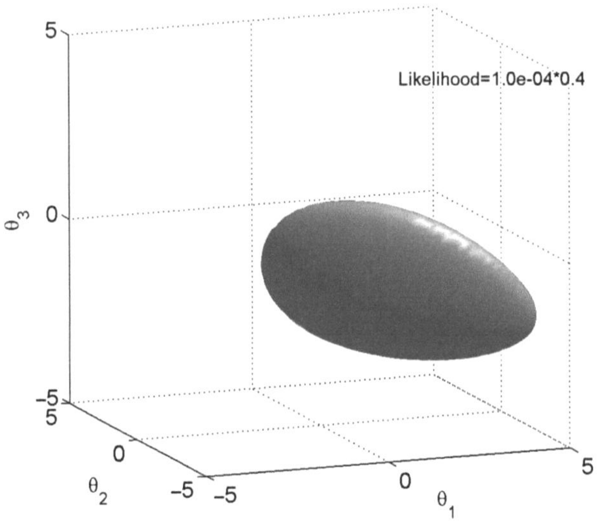

Fig. 29.9 Ellipsoidal orbit for a three-dimensional case

When the item response data are modeled in three dimensions, the equal-probable contours of a test item are planes rather than the straight lines shown for the two-dimensional cases given in Figs. 29.6 and 29.7. Figure 29.11 shows the 0.00004-orbit for the likelihood function with the tangent planes for an item that is measuring only along θ_1. As with the two-dimensional case, the conditional maxima for the likelihood function after the additional item is administered will be along the line that connects the tangents of the equal-probable planes with the likelihood surface for the previous set of items and responses. In this case, the coordinates of the tangent points are (−0.88, 1.60, −0.40) and (5.10, −2.40, −2.00). Because of the orientation of the likelihood surface in the three-dimensional space, the paradoxical result will also occur after administering an item measuring along θ_1 because the location of the tangent points result in reductions of θ_2 and θ_3 even though there is an increase in θ_1.

Figure 29.12 shows the likelihood orbits of the ten-item solution for likelihood values of 0.00009, 0.00006, and 0.00003. A slice has been cut into the end of the surface to show the nested structure of the successive likelihood orbits. The figure also has "dots" showing the tangent points for the equal-probable planes for an

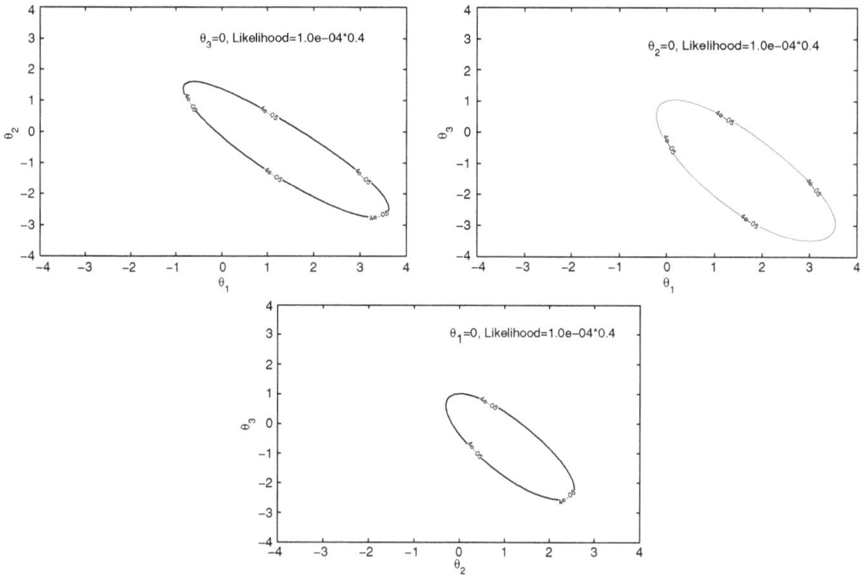

Fig. 29.10 Cross section of ellipsoidal orbit when θ_1, θ_2, and θ_3 are fixed to 0 (orbit value = 1.0e−04*0.4)

Fig. 29.11 Equal-probable item planes tangent to the likelihood surface from the first ten items

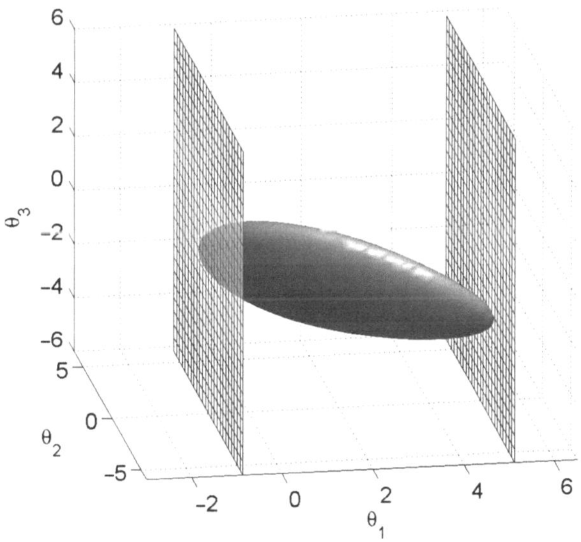

item measuring along θ_3. Figure 29.13 shows the pattern of the successive tangent points in the three-dimensional space. The MLE for the 11-item test with the 11th item measuring along θ_3 must fall on this line.

Fig. 29.12 Nested likelihood orbits for the ten-item test

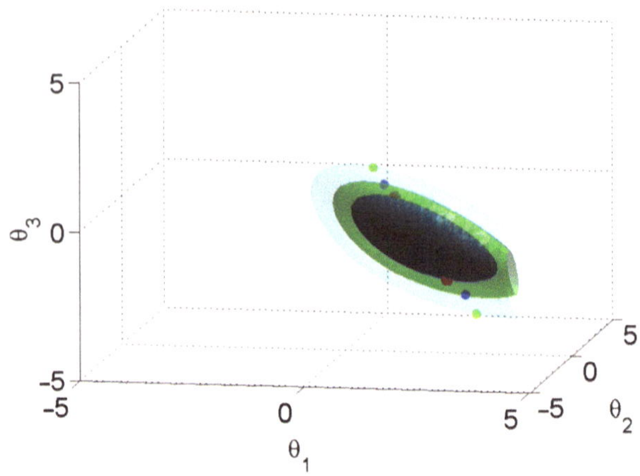

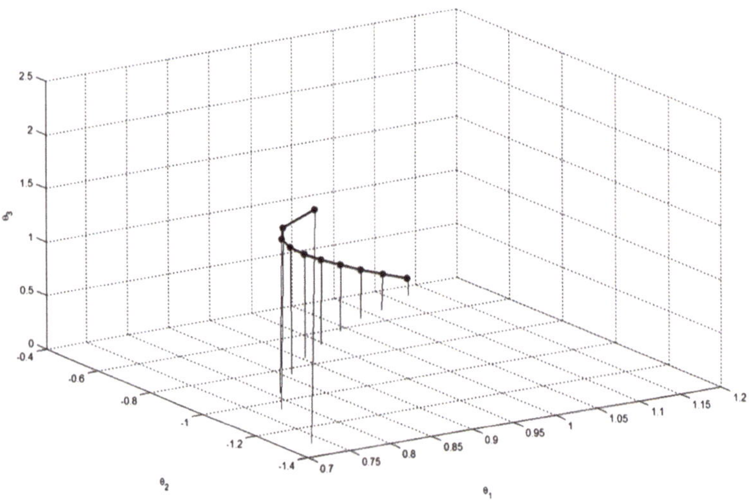

Fig. 29.13 Successive points of tangent with the likelihood orbits for an item measuring along θ_3

For the three-dimensional case, there is clear curvature in the line of tangent points. This indicates that the conditions under which the paradoxical result occurs are complex when the estimates of location are in a higher dimensional space.

29.2.3 The Shape of the Likelihood Function and Its Relationship to Test Information

The shape of the likelihood function (and its orbits) is dependent on the items that are selected for administration. The item parameters in the two-dimensional

Table 29.4 Item parameters for the two-dimensional example

Item	a_1	a_2	d	Item	a_1	a_2	d
1	1.11	0.90	−0.43	7	0.83	0.38	0.28
2	0.90	0.71	−1.75	8	0.72	1.01	−0.90
3	0.57	0.43	−0.44	9	0.89	0.46	0.49
4	1.12	0.68	0.16	10	0.50	0.48	−0.64
5	0.77	0.88	−0.27	11	1	0	0
6	1.05	0.69	0.92				

example are in Table 29.4 (the original test consisted of ten items, and the 11th item is the additional item). The original set of items measured best in a direction that is 30–40° from the θ_1-axis. The result is that the error of estimate of the location in the θ-space is smaller in that direction than along the coordinate axes.

The standard error pattern can be seen from the pattern of information in the two-dimensional space. Figure 29.14 shows the information provided by the ten-item test in directions in increments of 10° from the θ_1-axis. The length of the line from each point in the space indicates the information in that direction. The standard error in each direction is inversely proportional to the length of the line indicating the amount of information. The figure shows the same pattern of negative slope that indicates when paradoxical results can occur. That is, when the test information has this pattern, the major axis of the orbits of the likelihood function for the items will have a negative slope. The paradoxical results will occur when the next item is measuring along the axes of the solution.

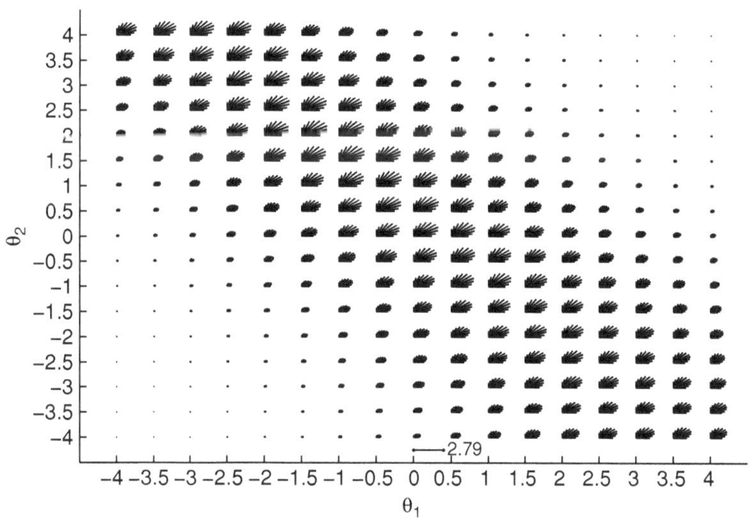

Fig. 29.14 Information for the ten items in Table 29.4 with directions in ten-degree increments

If the majority of the items exhibit simple structure (i.e., they only provide information along a single coordinate axis), the likelihood orbits will have a major axis that is parallel to one of the axes. For that case, the paradoxical result will not appear as long as the new item has non-negative discrimination parameter in each dimension. In fact, the only way to avoid the paradox is to have true simple structure or only administer items that yield a line connecting the tangent points that have positive slope. The latter case only occurs when the test items meet the requirements for essential unidimensionality. For the simple structure case, estimating the coordinates with separate tests would be equally good. However, no real achievement or licensure tests actually match simple structure. See more details about the simple structure case in Sect. 2.5.

29.2.4 Change the Evaluation Criteria

Whenever the item response data from a test do not meet the requirements for simple structure, the paradoxical result can occur. Most item response matrices do not meet the simple structure requirement. However, the presence of the paradox does not mean the new estimate is meaningless or that it is seriously flawed. In the simulated CAT example in Reckase (2009, Chap. 10), the paradoxical result occurred, but the CAT still converged to the true value.

Reckase proposes that one advantage of MIRT over IRT is it can estimate the ability on multiple dimensions simultaneously (Reckase 2009). And when evaluating the abilities and making decisions, these estimates should be considered all together, rather than make separate judgments about whether the examinee met the criterion along each dimension. For cases where the paradoxical result occurs, the estimates along at least one dimension decrease, but the new MLE is still closer to the true location than the old one. This can readily be shown with an example.

Assume 500 examinees were randomly selected from a bivariate normal distribution with mean vector **0** and the identity matrix for the variance/covariance matrix and each simulated person took the same ten-item test with items generated as follows: (a_1 log normal (−0.3, 0.35), a_2 log normal (−0.3, 0.35), and d normal (0, 1)). The item parameters and examinee parameters were then used to generate a 500*10 item score matrix using the multidimensional extension of the two-parameter logistic model. The ability estimates from the ten-item test were the old estimates. Then scores to an 11th item were simulated with the direction of best measurement for the item parallel to θ_1 and new estimates of location were computed. This process was replicated 30 times.

Table 29.5 presents the results from the simulation study. Each replication in the table gives the average of the distances between the estimates of location for the 500 simulated examinees after ten items and the true θ-vector used to generate the data, noted as *old distance,* and the average distance between the estimate of location after 11 items and the same true θ-vector, noted as *new distance*. For all 30 replications, the old distance is larger than the corresponding new distance with an average difference of the distances of 0.41. For all of the simulated examinees who answering the 11th item correctly θ_1 increased and θ_2 decreased. That, is the paradoxical result occurred. However, even when the paradoxical result did occur, the distance from the true point in the space to the estimated point decreases when the score from the additional item was added. This result shows that the paradoxical result is not an indicator of poor estimation. In this example, the maximum likelihood estimator is working. It should improve the estimate of the examinee's location even when there are paradoxical cases.

Table 29.5 Comparison of distance between old/new estimate and true ability

Replication	Old distance	New distance	Replication	Old distance	New distance
1	2.93	2.44	16	2.63	2.35
2	2.25	2.04	17	2.54	2.20
3	2.99	2.69	18	3.06	2.58
4	3.13	2.63	19	2.36	1.97
5	2.33	2.03	20	2.74	2.33
6	2.44	2.04	21	2.72	2.28
7	2.62	2.19	22	2.44	2.20
8	2.66	2.41	23	2.63	2.18
9	2.84	2.44	24	3.07	2.75
10	2.32	2.06	25	3.06	2.34
11	3.17	2.55	26	2.91	2.43
12	1.94	1.77	27	3.03	2.51
13	3.12	2.33	28	2.39	2.00
14	2.79	2.43	29	2.48	2.15
15	2.96	2.47	30	3.18	2.64

29.2.5 A Rotation Explanation for the Paradoxical Result

In MIRT, the selection of the orientation of the coordinate axes, the location of the origin and the units for each axis are arbitrary (Reckase 2009). The previous sections showed that the paradoxical result is a consequence of the shape of the likelihood surface and the characteristics of the test item added to the test. Some of these features of the causes of the paradoxical result are a consequence of the way that the coordinate system for the solution was selected. Considering how the coordinate system can be rotated may help in understanding of the paradoxical result. Figure 29.15 gives a representation of the measurement information provided by two sets of items: one set contains five items mainly measuring more in a direction along θ_1 than along θ_2 (the angle between the direction of best measurement and the θ_1-axis is 20°), and the other item set mainly measures more along the θ_2-axis than the θ_1 axis (the angle between the direction of best measurement and the θ_2-axis is 20°). Then an 11th item is administered, which has a direction of best measurement alongthe θ_1-axis.

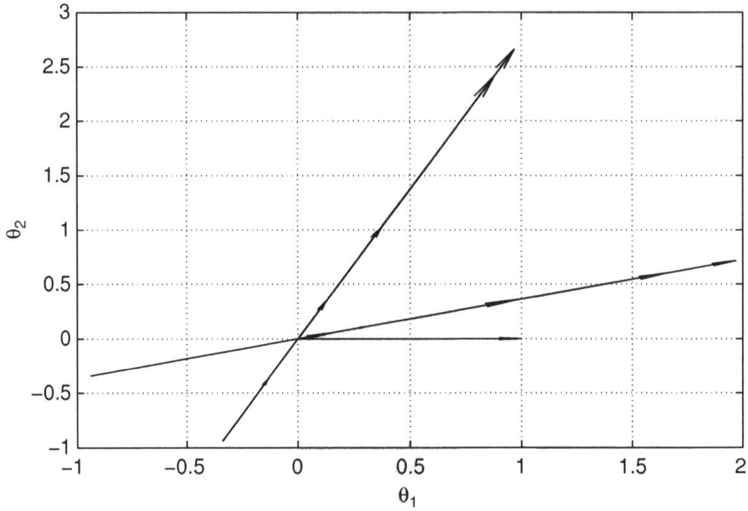

Fig. 29.15 Best measurement directions before rotation

Selected likelihood orbits for the estimate of location based on the responses to the ten-item test are shown in Fig. 29.16. These orbits have a negative slope for their major axis as in the previous examples. As a result, after adding a correct response to the 11th item, the paradoxical result occurs.

The information plot in Fig. 29.17 indicates that the items provide most information along a direction of approximately 45°.

But, the coordinate system that is shown in Figs. 29.15 and 29.16 is not uniquely determined by the MIRT model. It can be rotated and translated as long as the inverse transformation is applied to the item parameters. If done properly, the probability of correct response to the items will remain the same and the invariance property of the model holds. In this case, a non-orthogonal rotation (Reckase 2009) can be applied to the space to align the two coordinate axes with the directions of best measurement of the two item sets. The result is shown in Fig. 29.18. Note that the 11th item now has a negative discrimination along the new θ_2. Selected likelihood orbits for the rotated ten items are shown in Fig. 29.19 along with equal-probable contours for the 11th item.

If the new 11th item only measures the new θ_1 instead of the old θ_1 dimension, the best measurement direction after rotation is shown in Fig. 29.20. In this case, the paradoxical result does not occur because the tangents to the likelihood orbits fall along a horizontal line. The specifics of this particular case are shown in Fig. 29.21. The likelihood orbits for ten items have axes that are parallel to the θ_1 and θ_2 axes and the equal-probable contours for 11th item are vertical.

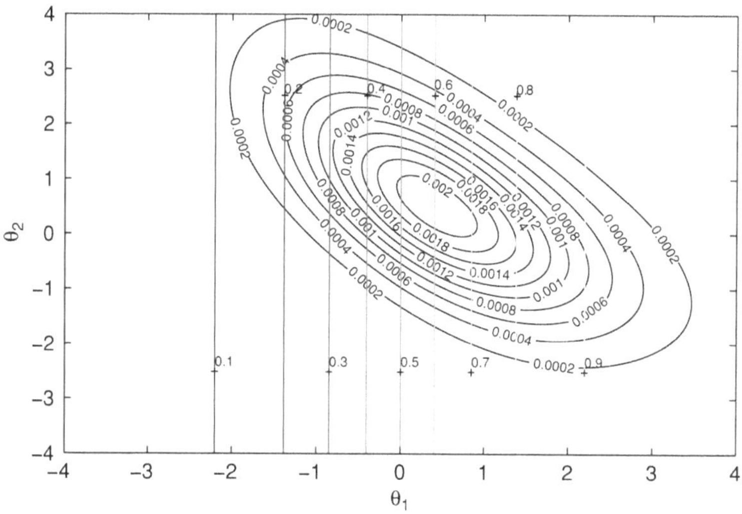

Fig. 29.16 Selected likelihood orbits and equal-probable contours

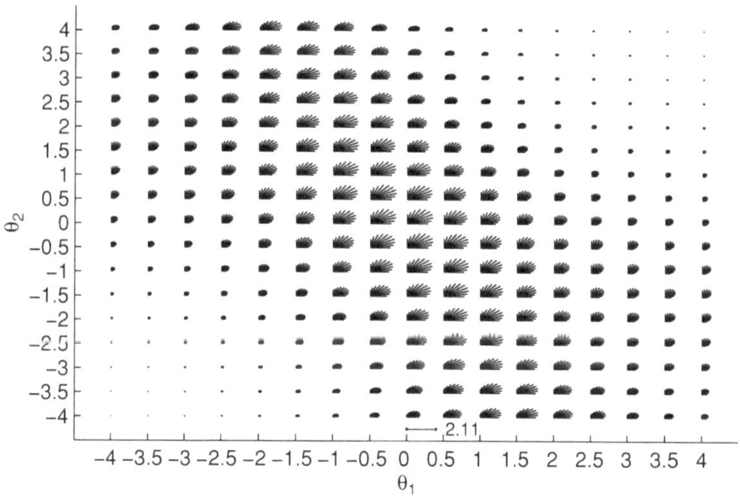

Fig. 29.17 Information plot for the ten-item test

The clamshell information plot for the ten-item test after rotation is shown in Fig. 29.22. It shows that the items provide almost equal information along each direction. This is the pattern of information that is present when the items exhibit simple structure. For this case, when the 11th item has non-negative discrimination power, the paradoxical result does not occur.

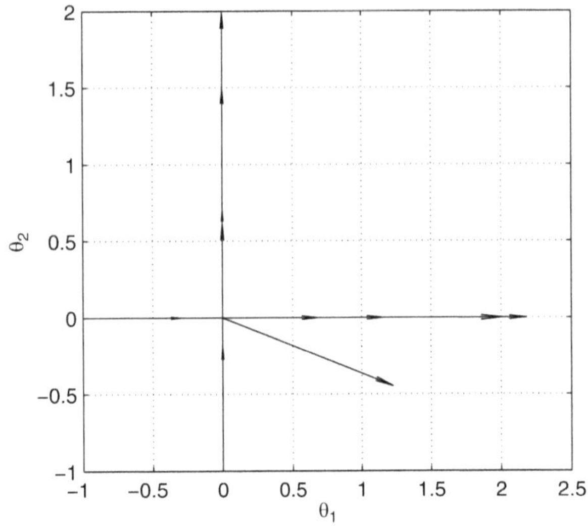

Fig. 29.18 Best measurement direction after rotation (the 11th item measures the old θ_1)

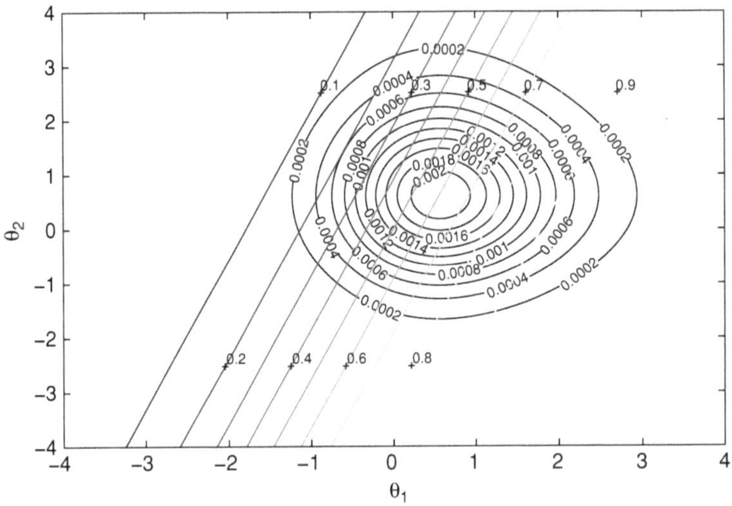

Fig. 29.19 Likelihood orbits and equal-probable contours after rotation (with 11th item only measures the old θ_1)

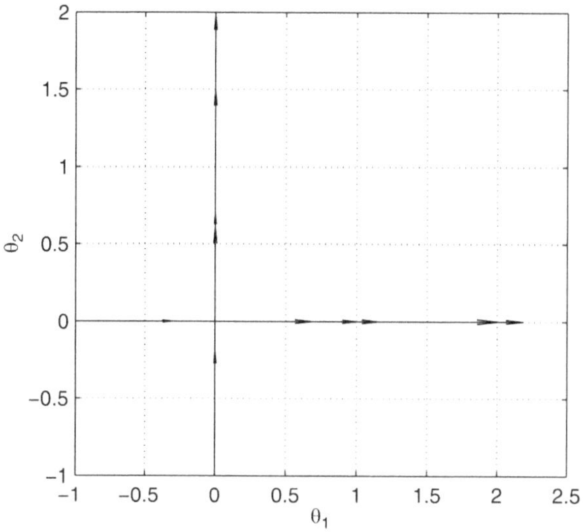

Fig. 29.20 Best measurement direction after rotation (with 11th item only measures the new θ_1)

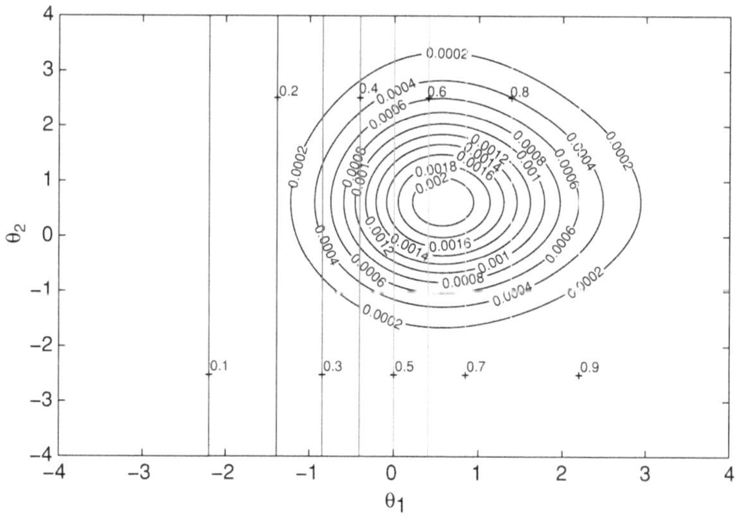

Fig. 29.21 Likelihood orbits and equal-probable contours after rotation (with 11th item only measures the new θ_1)

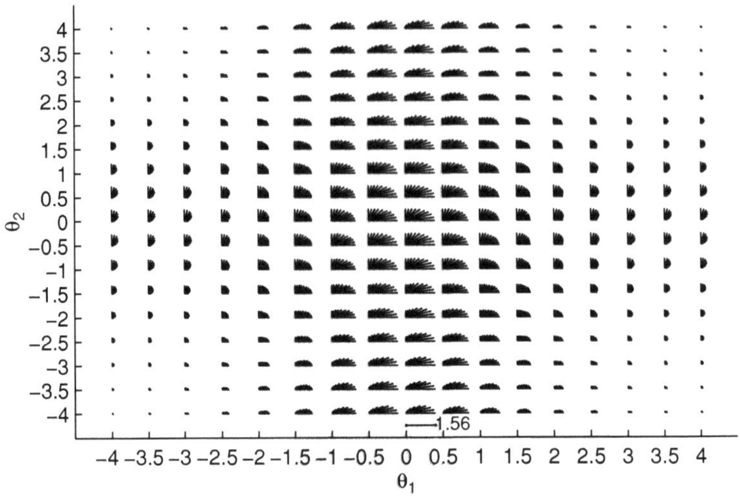

Fig. 29.22 Clamshell information plot for ten items after rotation

Discussion and Conclusions

At the beginning of this chapter, two interpretations were suggested for the paradoxical result that is sometimes observed when estimating the locations of individuals using MIRT models. One interpretation suggested that the paradoxical result indicates a flaw in the estimation process that gave poor estimates for the coordinates of the locations of the individuals. The other interpretation was that the paradoxical result is a natural result of the corrections that are made when additional information is used to improve the quality of the estimate of examinees locations. The information provided in this chapter shows that the second of the two interpretations is the correct one. The paradoxical result is a fairly frequent occurrence and thanks should be given to Hooker et al. for bringing it to our attention.

The analysis provided in this chapter shows that the paradoxical result is a result of the shape of the likelihood function for the prior set of items, and the direction of best measurement of the added item. If the likelihood function has a major axis that has a negative slope, the paradoxical result is possible when the next item is administered and it will occur when the item tends to measure along one of the coordinate axes. The likelihood function will have a negative slope for the major axis of the orbits for the function whenever a number of items have been administered that measure in a direction that does not parallel the coordinate axes—that is, the items measure a composite of skills and knowledge. This is often called complex structure. Most achievement and

(continued)

aptitude tests have this type of structure. The analysis presented here indicates that the paradoxical result will be present in almost all real test data analyses.

Because the paradoxical result is common, it is important to investigate whether it constitutes a problem that needs to be fixed. In this chapter, it is suggested that it is not a problem because the estimate including the additional item that shows the paradoxical result gives an estimate of location that is closer to the true location than was the case before the item was administered. The reason the paradoxical result is sometimes considered a flaw in the process is that the estimation process is thought to be considering each θ in the vector of locations independently rather than as being interrelated as indicators of a location in the space. Using a criterion such as the distance from the true location shows the interrelated nature of the θ coordinates and the improvement of the estimate with the increased information from the additional item.

The paradoxical result can be avoided in two ways. The first is to have a set of items that yields a likelihood function that does not have the property of a negative slope for the equal likelihood orbits. This can be achieved if the items have simple structure. A more complex way to achieve this is by rotating the solution so that the likelihood function has the desired form.

The second approach is to select items that have equal-probable contours that have tangents to the likelihood orbits that form a line with positive slope. This will require the items to be measuring composites of the dimensions and, if the test is long enough, will ultimately result in an item set that meets the requirements for essential unidimensionality. If that approach is taken to avoid the paradoxical result, it is probably not necessary to use a multidimensional model.

Several other researchers have presented analyses that address the paradoxical result in a much more elegant way than was presented in this paper. van der Linden (2012) and van Rijn and Rijmen (2012) present mathematical analyses that give theoretical explanations for the paradoxical result. Readers are urged to look at this work to gain other perspectives. The purpose of this chapter is to give a conceptual description of the paradoxical result that supplements the work done by these researchers.

References

Finkelman M, Hooker G, Wang J (2010) Prevalence and magnitude of paradoxical results in multidimensional item response theory. J Educ Behav Stat 35:744–761

Flexner SB, Hauck LC (eds) (1987) The Random House dictionary of the English language, 2, unabridgedth edn. Random House, New York

Hooker G (2010) On separable tests, correlated priors, and paradoxical results in multidimensional item response theory. Psychometrika 75:694–707

Hooker G, Finkelman M (2010) Paradoxical results and item bundles. Psychometrika 75:249–271
Hooker G, Finkelman M, Schwartzman A (2009) Paradoxical results in multidimensional item response theory. Psychometrika 74:419–442
Jordan P, Spiess M (2012) Generalizations of paradoxical results in multidimensional item response theory. Psychometrika 77:127–152
Reckase M (2009) Multidimensional item response theory. Springer, New York
Van der Linden WJ (2012) On compensation in multidimensional response modeling. Psychometrika 77:21–30
van Rijn PW, Rijmen F (2012) A note on explaining away and paradoxical results in multidimensional item response theory (Research Report RR-12-13). Educational Testing Service, Princeton, NJ

MIX
Papier aus verantwortungsvollen Quellen
Paper from responsible sources
FSC® C105338

If you have any concerns about our products,
you can contact us on
ProductSafety@springernature.com

In case Publisher is established outside the EU,
the EU authorized representative is:
Springer Nature Customer Service Center GmbH
Europaplatz 3, 69115 Heidelberg, Germany

Printed by Libri Plureos GmbH
in Hamburg, Germany